THE ASSASSINATION *of* JOHN F. KENNEDY

THE FINAL ANALYSIS

THE ASSASSINATION *of* JOHN F. KENNEDY

THE FINAL ANALYSIS

DAVID W. MANTIK, M.D., PH.D.
& JEROME R. CORSI, PH.D.

Introduction by DOUGLAS P. HORNE

A POST HILL PRESS BOOK
ISBN: 979-8-88845-716-0
ISBN (eBook): 979-8-88845-156-4

The Assassination of President John F. Kennedy: The Final Analysis:
Forensic Analysis of the JFK Autopsy X-Rays Proves Two Headshots from the Right Front and One from the Rear

Cover and interior design by Mark Karis

Post Hill Press
New York • Nashville
posthillpress.com

Published in the United States of America
1 2 3 4 5 6 7 8 9 10

FOR DOUGLAS P. HORNE

Whose diligent and painstakingly thorough investigation with the Assassination Records Review Board warrants a historically important role exposing the US government's coup d'état that assassinated President John F. Kennedy.

We are indebted to your devotion, your steadfastness, and your courage. You have served the nation and history well, above and beyond the call of duty.

CONTENTS

ACKNOWLEDGMENTS

BY DAVID W. MANTIK, M.D., PH.D.

DOUGLAS HORNE has gone beyond the call of duty, beyond popular expectations, and beyond all anticipation in his unparalleled attention to detail and to history.

I must publicly acknowledge my coauthor's indulgence with my occasional impatience and thank him for his unceasing courage and determination to complete this damnably daunting book.

The generous efforts of our predecessors—David Lifton, Harrison Livingstone, Gerald D. McKnight, Douglas Weldon, John Hunt, Harold Weisberg, Paul O'Connor, Dennis David, and Jerrol Custer—can no longer be repaid. We are merely their beneficiaries. The same is true for Parkland doctors Charles Crenshaw and Robert McClelland, but this is especially true for my long-ago good friends, Noel Twyman and Robert Livingston, MD.

William Matson Law's incomparable interviews—and patience—with the autopsy paraprofessionals have yielded incalculable dividends. I have met most of these heroic individuals and have visited Law at his home.

The research at the National Archives by Michael Chesser, MD, especially in corroborating my OD data, has been priceless. His incisive comments in the autobiography by James Jenkins add enormously to our understanding of the case. And the recollections of Jenkins have provided extraordinary insight into November 22, 1963.

The observations of Ed Reed and Tom Robinson (the two Rs) of illicit surgery in the morgue provided a major key to the injuries of the skull and brain. I do not know if they still live.

Cyril Wecht has been a steadfast friend from that first day of our visit together to the National Archives. Warren Commission critics can never fully repay him for his courage, persistence, and audacity.

Jim DiEugenio has persistently goaded me to write more, when otherwise I might have retired from this battlefield. His website remains a goldmine.

The contributions of Denise Hazelwood, Roy Schaeffer, and Doug Mizzer, all with amazingly keen eyesight, have yielded invaluable rewards.

Dr. Randy Robertson's persistence discovered the memo by Dr. James Young, which all by itself overturns the single-bullet theory.

Robert Groden's masterful photographic anthologies (and Zapruder film work) have enlightened this case for years. His stereo viewing at the National Archives has corroborated my own conclusions about the photographs of the back of the head. These stereo pairs yield only a 2D image, not a 3D one, which is a clear sign of photographic manipulation.

Quentin Schwinn viewed a (likely) original autopsy photograph that showed the right forehead entry site near the hairline—exposed before someone deliberately incised that wound.

Jeff Sundberg and Greg Burnham have comprised a persistent and stalwart emotional support team. Any author would pay a raft of gold for such valiant characters.

Jim Fetzer first roped me into this rodeo. Sometimes I am not sure whether I should thank him for this, but I can only wonder what path my life would have taken otherwise.

Finally, we should not neglect the unrivaled prowess of John Costella in unraveling the technical gyrations of the Zapruder film.

On the home front, I am blessed with two children and a wife who care. Without their unflagging support, I would have found myself in an alternate universe—one surely far less rewarding. What a wonderful set of gifts all of these amazing citizens have given me for my eighty-third birthday!

FOREWORD

ARCHBISHOP CARLO MARIA VIGANÒ,
FORMER APOSTOLIC NUNCIO TO THE UNITED STATES OF AMERICA

"Ask not what your country can do for you:
ask what you can do for your country."

—**JOHN FITZGERALD KENNEDY,** JANUARY 20, 1961

JOHN FITZGERALD KENNEDY was elected the 35th President of the United States of America at a time of great change that involved the whole world. A few years before the event that brought the first Catholic President in American history to the White House, Pope John XXIII had been elected, the Pontiff who convoked the Second Vatican Ecumenical Council and who believed he could open the doors of the Church to dialogue with the world. The early 1960s take us back to the Cold War, the Berlin Wall, the Cuban crisis, the threat of a looming nuclear conflict, and that perhaps forced and certainly simplistic *dualism* between right and left that has since begun to show signs of losing steam. Italy, along with the other NATO member countries, was in the midst of an economic boom in those years and 1968, the year of the great student and cultural revolution, the end of the old world, was still yet to come.

This work by David W. Mantik and Jerome R. Corsi touches on specialized topics of great interest not only to historians. It presents very credible evidence that Kennedy was killed on the orders of the CIA and leads us to ask a fundamental question: *Why did the Secret Service assassinate President Kennedy?* History will be able to answer this question when new documents will be declassified and it will be possible to reconstruct the troubled and complex events of those years. Nevertheless, I believe that each of us, observing the sequence of events from above, so to speak, is able to understand how correct is the intuition of the authors, who rightly identify in the murder of JFK the subversive action of a *coup d'état* at the hands of deviant components of the state apparatus. We could say that it was in those years that the *deep state* began to operate with greater incisiveness, which today shows itself in all its evidence, but which even then acted for the pursuit of purposes in contrast with the true interests of the Nation and against the good of the American people.

The term *deep state—derin devlet* in Turkish—was coined to indicate the network of power close to the Masonic Lodges that Mustafa Kemal Atatürk created, again in a subversive way, to flank the action of indoctrination to the so-called "democratic principles" of the Young Turks, just as in Italy, during the so-called Risorgimento, Giuseppe Mazzini created the *Giovine Italia* movement to bring down the pre-unification States and replace them with the Piedmontese Monarchy that was subservient to Freemasonry. The *deep state* is therefore a lobby entrenched in power, which controls and directs events through its emissaries. Its counterpart in the religious sphere is what I have called the *deep church*, which has the same goals and uses the same methods. Let us not forget that after the death of Pope Pius XII in 1958, the Conclave that led to the election of Angelo Roncalli was the scene of maneuvers and pressures aimed precisely at ensuring that the new Pope would represent a moment of novelty and rupture with the past. And it was no coincidence that John XXIII himself—too often dangerously close to the Masonic Lodges on the one hand and to exponents of Modernism on the other—wanted, so to speak, to defy Providence, by convoking an Ecumenical Council that the Roman Curia knew would bring into the ecclesial body the most extreme instances of modernization of the

Church in the doctrinal, moral, and liturgical fields.

In 1958, therefore, we had a progressive Pope, the so-called "*good pope*," the pope of dialogue and *renewal*, who was appreciated by circles hitherto hostile to the Roman Church. Then in 1960, Democrat John Fitzgerald Kennedy won the election against Republican Richard Nixon, apparently confirming the same trend. In 1962, the Second Vatican Council began. In 1963, the American President was assassinated in Dallas. These would all seem to be unrelated events to an inattentive observer; but if we understand what the aims of the *deep state* and the *deep church* were—that is, the two versions of an occult and subversive power—we cannot fail to find an incredible coherence in their respective actions. And perhaps we should ask ourselves if the fact that JFK was Catholic might have led the American *deep state* to want to eliminate from the international political scene a character who did not accept the role of being a *puppet* of the elite, unlike the current "president," the self-styled Catholic Joe Biden.

Church and State have today both been eclipsed by a power that has usurped them and now uses them for the opposite purpose to that which the two institutions ought to have, and we owe the fact that this is so evident today to decades—if not centuries—of subterranean action, of subversive powers which stop at nothing to achieve what they set out to do. The assassination of JFK by the CIA has been repeated with the fraudulent elimination of President Trump on the occasion of the 2020 election fraud; but even before that with the forced resignation in 2013 of Pope Benedict XVI, an event that was hoped for by the magic circle of the Clintons and John Podesta in their famous *Wikileaks* emails, and which was followed by the appointment—because to speak of election would be grotesque—of the Jesuit Jorge Mario Bergoglio by the Saint Gallen Mafia, with the key contribution of the serial predator and former cardinal Theodore McCarrick, who was a frequent visitor to the Obama White House.

In a famous speech at the Waldorf-Astoria Hotel on April 27, 1961, JFK said: "*For we are opposed around the world by a monolithic and ruthless conspiracy that relies primarily on covert means for expanding its sphere of influence: on infiltration instead of invasion, on subversion instead of elections, on intimidation instead of free choice, on guerrillas by night instead of armies by day."* Today we can understand his words in their disturbing truth: "*It is a system which has conscripted vast human and material resources into the building of a tightly knit, highly efficient machine that combines military, diplomatic, intelligence, economic, scientific, and political operations. Its preparations are concealed, not published; its mistakes are buried, not headlined; its dissenters are silenced, not praised. No expenditure is questioned; no rumor is printed; no secret is revealed.*" And so we understand why that system eliminated Kennedy, seeing him as a serious threat.

The Final Analysis has the merit of directly confronting the reality of the *coup d'état* that was perpetrated by the *deep state* through the assassination of President Kennedy, who was considered an obstacle to the achievement of objectives that today we understand were achieved in any case, with or without the approval of the "sovereign" people. A coup that has led the institutions of the United States of America—not unlike those of other nations and of the Catholic Church herself—to be the unique and totalitarian expression of a subversive power that dangerously combines the individualistic interests of capital with the tyrannical methods of communist collectivism. This *privatization* of the State is mirrored in the chronic and irreversible indebtedness of the citizens, who are called upon to pay the bankruptcy costs of the speculations of the very powerful international financial lobby. And it should not escape our notice that there is a parallel with the *privatization* of the Catholic Church, which has now been taken over by an elite no less subversive than that of the *deep state,* in which positions of power have been infiltrated by heretical and corrupt prelates who use the authority of Christ to guarantee obedience from the faithful.

It is clear to me—and this is the reason why, as Archbishop and former Apostolic Nuncio to the United States of America, I agreed to write this Preface—that this coup necessarily had to avail itself of the ideological support and moral authority of the Catholic Church, which otherwise would have represented an obstacle to the fulfillment of the project of the New World Order. This is why I believe that the events related to Kennedy's assassination should be read as part of one narrative together with those that led the Church of Rome to progressively become the spokesperson for the globalist plan, a plan on which the same lobbies were working that today are leading to the dissolution of the social, moral, religious, cultural, and economic fabric of Western countries.

"*Ask not what your country can do for you; ask what you can do for your country*"—these are the famous words pronounced by President Kennedy during his inaugural address on January 20, 1961. They are still valid today for every American citizen and must lead everyone to understand the need not to remain on the sidelines as inert spectators of political and social events, but on the contrary to take an active part in them with a courageous witness of faith, rectitude, and honesty. Knowing the enemy and understanding their intentions is crucial if you want to fight them effectively.

I hope that this book, written with passion and incorporating new evidence, can stimulate a re-reading of history in which the *coup d'état* of the globalist elite appears in all its evidence, so that those responsible are called to account for it, and above all so that future rulers have the *bonum commune* at heart, in the awareness that this will be the measure for how they will be judged by God.

—**CARLO MARIA VIGANÒ**, *Archbishop,*
former Apostolic Nuncio to the United States of America

April 21, 2024
Dominica III post Pascha

PROLOGUE

JFK ASSASSINATION COUP D'ÉTAT AND COVERUP: WHY THE GOVERNMENT OF THE UNITED STATES IS UNFIT TO RULE

BY JEROME R. CORSI, PH.D.

The Public must be satisfied that Oswald was the assassin; that he did not have confederates who are still at large; that the evidence was such that he would have been convicted at trial.
—**DEPUTY ATTORNEY GENERAL NICHOLAS KATZENBACH**, Monday, November 25, 1963 (the day of JFK's burial in Arlington National Cemetery, Virginia)[1]

FOR SIXTY YEARS NOW—since November 22, 1963—the federal government of the United States has lied to us about the assassination in Dallas of President John Fitzgerald Kennedy.

1 Memo from Deputy Attorney General Nicholas Katzenbach to Presidential Aide William Moyers, Monday, November 25, 1963. The Warren Commission. *Appendix to Hearings Before the Select Committee on Assassinations of the U.S. House of Representatives, Ninety-Fifth Congress, Second Session*, vol. 11, (Washington DC: U.S. Government Printing Office, 1979), p. 4, https://www.history-matters.com/archive/jfk/hsca/reportvols/vol11/html/HSCA_Vol11_0005b.htm.

When JFK's limousine arrived at Parkland Hospital, Secret Service agents destroyed evidence by wiping JFK's blood and brains from the limousine that carried him to his death. Still, today, US intelligence agencies continue to redact, classify, and conceal crucial documentary evidence.

We begin by acknowledging our debt to the scores of JFK assassination researchers who have devoted their time and effort to illuminate what happened on that dark day in Dallas sixty years ago.

After nine visits to the National Archives to examine the JFK autopsy X-rays, David Mantik, MD, PhD, acquired forensic proof that JFK was hit by three headshots, one from behind and two from the front. Headshots hitting nearly simultaneously from the back and the front prove that JFK died in a crossfire.

With a background both as a PhD physicist and a radiation oncologist with more than forty years of experience reading X-rays for patients, Mantik has forensically demonstrated that the remaining three JFK skull X-ray films in the National Archives cannot be originals. Via hundreds of measurements (directly from the extant films), he has proven that these are altered copies. He has also noted absurd anomalies in the autopsy photographs. He has produced his own fake X-ray films, just to show how it was done. The image of a fake bullet fragment was added to the AP (anterior posterior) skull X-ray film to incriminate Lee Harvey Oswald, thus intending to imply that all shots came from the rear. Furthermore, a mysterious T-shaped inscription on one film has been ignored by all prior investigations; it provides independent and corroborative proof that this particular film must be a copy. That the extant X-ray films are altered copies is proof that the Warren Report is disinformation. After all, why would anyone destroy original X-ray films in the most famous murder case in history? Therefore, merely because all the original skull X-ray films are missing is further evidence of a cover-up. Given the evidence accumulated in this book, the Warren Commission's conclusion that Oswald was the lone gunman can only be fiction.

Lyndon Johnson advanced the cover-up by appointing one of the chief co-conspirators, Allen Dulles, to the Warren Commission. JFK had Dulles fired from his position as head of the CIA. The job of the Warren Commission was to chisel into stone the government's lie that a lone assassin, Oswald, killed JFK by firing three shots from a sixth-floor window using an unreliable surplus Italian military rifle with an improperly adjusted scope.

The federal government simply could not allow the public to learn that JFK's assassination was a coup d'état originating at the federal government's highest levels. The government disinformation campaign began by destroying crime scene evidence as soon as the limousine arrived at Parkland. It continued by destroying evidence of a crossfire and culminated in manufacturing falsified evidence designed to frame Oswald as the lone gunman. With the overt and persistent assistance of the media, the disinformation campaign continues today via shaming anyone who dares to expose its lies. The CIA's relentless refusal to release critical documents is no surprise; their lawless intransigence, despite the President John F. Kennedy Assassination Records Collection Act of 1992, is likely to continue as long as this so-called republic lasts.

In addition to addressing the head wounds, we will examine the back and throat wounds. The back wound likely derived from shrapnel originating from a bullet that first struck Elm Street. But multiple bullets were reported—by John Connally, by Dr. James Young, and by more than one Secret Service agent. The throat wound derived from a frontal shot that did not transverse the body. The bullet came from the south side of the Triple Overpass (opposite the Grassy Knoll); after the bullet transited the windshield, a glass fragment entered JFK's throat. This bullet may have stayed inside the limousine. No bullet transited JFK's body, thus proving Arlen Specter's single-bullet theory to be a complete hoax.

The United States faces a unique moment in its history. After the federal government portrayed COVID-19 as a deadly pandemic that required a national lockdown, and the FDA approved a vaccine that did not prevent COVID-19, more and more Americans recognize that our leaders are careless with the truth. The forensic evidence in this case poses the uncomfortable realization that our government, for decades now, has been unfit to rule.

After nine visits to the National Archives, Mantik has spent far more time with these JFK artifacts than any other qualified expert. Furthermore, he has devoted thirty years of forensic thought to these issues. This book is written in the first person, thus allowing Dr. Mantik to use his own words to relate his personal odyssey.

We have dedicated this book to Douglas P. Horne, who was chief analyst for military records while serving on the Assassination Records Review Board (ARRB). He also introduced Mantik's work to the ARRB. He is a tireless researcher and the only former ARRB employee to record his encounter with darkness; his magnificent five-volume *Inside the Assassination Records Review Board* is the definitive treatment of the disinformation campaign regarding the medical evidence. Throughout this book, Mantik's accord with Horne will become obvious: a domestic conspiracy, paid for with tax dollars, killed JFK.

PREFACE

BY DAVID W. MANTIK, M.D., PH.D.

WHEN OLIVER STONE'S MOVIE, *JFK,* appeared in 1991, I became incensed that our historians (and the media, too) had failed to solve this greatest of American mysteries. I then had no strong conspiracy bias; as usual, I simply wanted to know the truth. If anything, I was biased toward one of my physics heroes, Nobel Laureate Luis Alvarez, whose pro-Warren Commission lecture I had attended in Los Alamos, New Mexico in 1975.

Soon I realized that it was time for me to do some serious detective work, so I applied to the Kennedy family attorney. After nearly one year, I finally received permission from Burke Marshall to view the JFK autopsy X-ray films and photographs, JFK's clothing, and the ballistic evidence. I thus became one of only a handful of fortunate non-government physicians to be granted access to these still-restricted materials. In 1993, I made the first of nine visits to these artifacts. No one else has made anywhere near that many visits to examine these materials or taken so many data points from the X-ray films and photographs. I first began visiting National Archives I in Washington, DC. Then later I visited these items in College Park, Maryland (my wife's parents' home was next door in Silver Spring), after these items were transferred to National Archives II. I have taken hundreds of measurements from the extant JFK X-ray films, examined the autopsy photographs in stereo on multiple occasions, viewed the Magic Bullet, bullet debris, JFK's clothing, copies of the Zapruder film, and the Secret Service re-enactment films.

My thick notebooks encompass three separate volumes. They contain precise locations for all metal debris on the extant skull X-ray films. I have interviewed many of the Bethesda Naval Hospital personnel, including the following: John Ebersole, the radiologist who supervised the X-ray films at the autopsy; Jerrol Custer, the X-ray technician who worked under Ebersole's supervision; James Curtis Jenkins, a student at the Medical Technology School at Bethesda, who assisted all night at the autopsy; Dennis David, Navy Administrative Technician at the hospital; and several Parkland treating physicians including Drs. Charles Crenshaw, Robert McClelland, and Ronald Jones. I also interviewed former FBI Special Agent James Sibert, one of the two FBI notetakers, who observed and recorded that "surgery" had been performed on JFK's head before the official Bethesda autopsy began.

On December 2, 1992, I interviewed Dr. John Ebersole, the autopsy radiologist on a telephone call. I questioned him about how the pathologists at Bethesda discovered that JFK's throat wound was a tracheotomy—performed over a bullet wound. I knew that Admiral George Burkley was the only doctor present at both Parkland Hospital and at the Bethesda autopsy, so he must have known about the throat wound. I could not understand why he did not tell Dr. James J. Humes (the chief pathologist) about it. Ebersole reported, "And it was, oh, ten thirty at night before we got the communication from Dallas," indicating telephone conversations had occurred between the Parkland and Bethesda physicians *during the autopsy*. This is consistent with what Ebersole had stated earlier. In particular, as soon as he heard about the throat wound (as an exit), he stopped taking X-rays—because he now had an explanation for the back wound (it was an entry, he assumed). So, if the projectile had transited, he no longer needed to look for metallic debris.[1]

What Ebersole clarified to me was that the origin of the single-bullet theory (SBT) had begun during the autopsy. In his testimony to the House Select Committee on Assassinations (HSCA), Ebersole affirmed that the Parkland and Bethesda doctors were in telephone communications during the autopsy.[2] Ebersole's X-ray films had found no bullets or fragments in Kennedy's back or throat. If Hume's mission was to convert the frontal shots into rear shots, he found his solution at Parkland. After Humes informed Malcolm Perry about the back wound, Perry told him about the throat wound. So, Humes concluded that he could transform the throat wound into an exit wound. But this depended critically on Perry's willingness to cooperate with this cover story. In turn, then Perry could claim that he had been mistaken at the Parkland news conference—because he did not know about the back wound. In other words, Humes had given Perry an easy escape route. But this scenario was all later to be upended—rather dramatically—as you shall discover as you read this adventure story.

---

1 David W. Mantik, trans. "Conversation with John Ebersole, MD, of 2 December 1992," in *Murder in Dealey Plaza: What We Know Now that We Didn't Know Then About the Death of JFK*, ed. James H. Fetzer (Chicago, IL: Catfeet Press, 2000), pp. 433–439, at p. 437.

2 The Warren Commission. "Testimony of John H. Ebersole, MD," in *Stenographic Transcript of Hearings Before the Medical Panel of the Select Committee on Assassinations of the U.S. House of Representatives, Medical Panel Meeting* (Washington DC: Alderson Reporting Company, Inc., 1979), pp. 1-68, at p. 64, https://www.history-matters.com/archive/jfk/arrb/master_med_set/md60/html/Image63.htm.

INTRODUCTION

BY DOUGLAS P. HORNE

THIS BOOK ADDRESSES THE TWO BASIC QUESTIONS: "Why doesn't the medical evidence in the assassination of President John F. Kennedy come together?" and "Why does the medical evidence in this case become more and more problematic, the more one studies it?"

The simple, honest, and extremely disturbing answer is that there is so much *fraud in the evidence*. This is what the mainstream media will not cover, and what the US government—including the National Archives—will not dare address, except to engage in unsupported, blanket denial that this is so.

Many first-generation JFK assassination researchers have run away from this conclusion of mine, despairing that *if there is fraud in the evidence*, then there is no hope of ever solving the mystery of what really happened. Foremost among those who have run away as fast as they can from the accumulating proof of massive fraud in the medical evidence is researcher and author Josiah Thompson, who expressed his dismay over the "fraud in the evidence" paradigm in a dinner speech at a 1992 JFK symposium in Chicago. Since then, a schism has developed within the JFK research community (and I use the term "community" loosely) over this very concept, with many old-line researchers and "institutionalists" resisting to the core of their being the very possibility that some, or even much, of the medical evidence exhibits fraud. (They prefer "incompetence" to be the explanation for most of the things wrong with the medical evidence.) I *do not* concur with them that if there is indeed fraud in the medical evidence that we cannot determine how JFK was really killed. The medical evidence fraud *can* be detected and understood; furthermore, what really happened to JFK in Dealey Plaza *can be explained*—following certain basic parameters—with a high degree of certainty today.

The JFK assassination has been likened to a 500-piece jigsaw puzzle, for which 250 pieces have been discarded (thrown away), and the 250 new pieces (substituted for the discarded pieces) are intentionally fraudulent, designed to create a picture of what happened that is very different from the reality on Elm Street in Dealey Plaza. The end result has been a puzzle that does not come together at all and will not allow the student of the assassination to create any coherent picture of what happened on November 22, 1963, unless the fraudulent puzzle pieces have first been identified and then thrown out. I submit that only after the fraudulent pieces of the puzzle are removed, can the missing pieces to the puzzle (i.e., the real evidence that was suppressed) be rediscovered, and the puzzle's true picture be reconstructed.

Throughout my adult lifetime of research into the JFK assassination, I have come to understand that the *fraud in the medical evidence* that I am discussing here includes the following:

There were *four sets* of official conclusions about how JFK was killed (i.e., about the wounds on his body) arrived at between November 22, 1963, and December 11, 1963—and all were demonstrably incorrect. The fact that there were four "official" sets of conclusions within about two-and-a-half weeks is the surest indicator that finding the truth was not the objective; rather, determining what tale could be sold to the American people—consistent with the straightjacketed, very limited evidence set acknowledged by the US government—was all that mattered. The US government has never acknowledged that this is the case, but the evolving JFK autopsy conclusions can be factually demonstrated, and

I have done so (in chapter 11 of *Inside the Assassination Records Review Board,*[1] and in a publicly delivered PowerPoint presentation titled "The Evolving JFK Autopsy Report"[2]). The official autopsy report in evidence today in the National Archives (CE 387, Appendix J) is the *fourth* set of official conclusions, and the *third written version* of the autopsy report.

- Two supplementary brain examinations were conducted following the autopsy on JFK's body: the first (on what remained of Kennedy's brain) was on November 25, 1963 (two-and-a-half days later), and a second brain exam (of a substitute, well-preserved medical school brain) was conducted sometime between November 29 and December 2, 1963. (Normally, of course, there can only be one "brain exam" following the autopsy on a decedent's body, since the brain is essentially destroyed by serial sectioning during the brain examination.) The photographs taken of the serial sections of JFK's actual brain on November 25 never made it into the official record (for they would have revealed two head shots from the front, as well as one from low and behind—all contrary to the official cover story and government narrative); and the dishonest photos subsequently placed into the official record were images taken of the *substitute brain* examined between November 29 and December 2 (photos which revealed a vastly different pattern of wounding than actually occurred in Dealey Plaza—a pattern of damage roughly corroborative of the official narrative, if not examined too closely). The evidence

---

1 Douglas P. Horne, *Inside the Assassinations Records Review Board: The U.S. Government's Final Attempt to Reconcile the Conflicting Medical Evidence in the Assassination of JFK* (Privately Printed, 2009), vol. 3, 11:845–882.

2 Douglas P. Horne, "The Evolving JFK Autopsy Report: Managing the Presentation of 'Facts' to Support the Myth of a Lone Assassin in Dallas," copy supplied to the authors electronically by Mr. Horne, n.d.

for the two different brain exams is set forth in great detail in chapter 10 of my ARRB memoir. It remains, in my view, the best evidence of a government conspiracy to suppress the true medical evidence, and to introduce fraudulent medical evidence into the record, for the two navy pathologists at JFK's autopsy—Drs. James J. Humes and J. Thornton Boswell—were present at *both* brain exams. They only invited the third JFK autopsy pathologist, poor Dr. Pierre Finck (whom they were attempting to use as a dupe), to the second brain examination, and he was kept unaware, and ignorant of, the first brain exam. *These facts forever make "incompetence" an inadequate excuse for the overall state of the medical evidence.* These actions by Humes and Boswell were *willful acts of commission, and proof of a conspiracy to cover up the true medical facts surrounding JFK's death.*

- As demonstrated by Dr. David Mantik (MD, PhD) during his nine visits to the National Archives to view the JFK autopsy materials, the three JFK skull X-rays that survive today are not originals but are *altered copy films.* In one of them (the anterior-posterior skull X-ray), a false image of an *apparent* "bullet fragment"—designed to match the caliber of the accused assassin's rifle and thereby incriminate him—has been photographically added to the copy film. (The three autopsy pathologists all testified to the ARRB in 1996 that no fragment of this size was removed from JFK's body during his autopsy, and two of the three pathologists testified to the ARRB that they *did not even recall seeing that "bullet fragment" on the A-P skull X-ray the night of the autopsy!*) In the two extant lateral skull X-rays, a large "white patch" has been photographically added to the two copy films in order to hide the massive tissue loss (of both bone and brain) in the right rear of the skull that was so consistently and vividly noted at Parkland Hospital. The altered copy films in the National Archives were discovered by a technique called *optical densitometry* used by Dr.

Mantik; this technique of study and discovery was unknown to the HSCA during the 1970s, so they failed to discover the fraud. (Dr. Michael Chesser has since replicated and confirmed Dr. Mantik's optical densitometry measurements and conclusions by studying and measuring himself the three extant skull X-rays in the National Archives at College Park, Maryland—as well as the one premortem JFK skull X-ray [taken in 1960] at the Kennedy Library in Boston-—using his own optical densitometer. The 1960 premortem JFK skull X-ray serves as the perfect "control" to prove how truly anomalous the White Patch is in the two lateral skull X-ray copy films emanating from the autopsy.)

- New information, pointing to more fraud: further examination of the three extant skull films by Dr. Chesser has revealed the specific entrance sites for two headshots originating from in front of the limousine. (Dr. Mantik concurs with Dr. Chesser's discoveries of the two frontal entrance wounds in JFK's skull X-rays at NARA [National Archives and Records Administration].) In other words, those who altered the skull X-rays photographically, after they were first developed as X-ray films, could not, or at least did not, eliminate the persuasive evidence of frontal entry from the new copy films. (The two entry sites for frontal shots found in the lateral skull films are high in the right forehead [well above the right eye], and just in front of the right ear, in the right temporal bone.) *The fraud, in this instance, involves the unwillingness (surely it was unwillingness, and not just "something they missed") of both the Clark Panel in 1968 and the HSCA staff leadership in 1978 and 1979 to report the evidence of these two frontal entry sites seen so clearly today (in person) on the extant skull films at the Archives II facility in College Park.* As Dr. Chesser has so eloquently explained in two different public, online PowerPoint presentations, *NEITHER VERSION* of what the HSCA calls JFK's right lateral skull X-ray published by the HSCA in 1979 (their photographic reproductions of both the unenhanced and enhanced lateral skull films) *ACCURATELY REFLECTS WHAT ONE SEES IN THE NATIONAL ARCHIVES DURING AN IN-PERSON VISIT. Please allow me to restate this for emphasis here: the HSCA published photographic images of both the unenhanced and enhanced right lateral JFK skull X-ray in its 1979 report that DO NOT accurately reflect what those images look like in person, when viewed at NARA in the Archives II facility.* The changes made to the lateral X-ray images published in volume 7 of the HSCA report contributed to hiding, from the public, the entry wound high in the forehead. This decision to knowingly suppress the full details of what the extant right lateral skull X-ray (both *unenhanced* and *enhanced* versions) actually looks like, when seen in person, had to have been made at the very highest levels of leadership within the HSCA staff hierarchy in 1978 and 1979. That decision will forever impugn the integrity of the HSCA. (The HSCA staff leadership got away with this subterfuge only because the restrictive provisions of the Kennedy family deed of gift prohibit all members of the public—except for a rare, select few admitted only on a case-by-case basis—from seeing the unenhanced and enhanced JFK skull films in person. It is high time that this cover-up be exposed.) The reader should be aware that Drs. Mantik and Chesser, once granted special access to the JFK autopsy materials for purposes of scientific study, are both now banned from further viewings. Apparently, it is not permissible to say: "The emperor is not wearing any clothes."

- Many of the autopsy photographs certainly appear to exhibit fraud for these reasons: (1) the location of the true entry wound low on the back of the head is not shown in *any* of the back-of-the-head photos; (2) the "red spot" high in the scalp on the back of the head—interpreted as an entry wound by both the Clark Panel and by the HSCA—was not recognized as an entry wound (or even seen) by anyone present at the autopsy; and (3) the intact appearance of the back of JFK's head (in all of the autopsy photos that show the rear of his cranium) is *in opposition* to what was seen by most autopsy witnesses (just about everyone other than Humes, Boswell, and Finck, who apparently perjured themselves in this regard), *and by the overwhelming majority of the Parkland doctors and nurses who treated JFK and tried to save his life.* When I wrote my ARRB book about the medical evidence, I was unsure whether to attribute the "intact back of the head" in the autopsy photos to the radical rearrangement of loose scalp (so as to fool the camera) or to photographic forgery. (At the time [in 2009] I leaned toward radically rearranged scalp, not altered photos, because the HSCA wrote in its 1979 report that it found no evidence of photographic forgery.) Today, many years later, I now favor photographic forgery as the *most likely* explanation. One of the reasons this mystery has not been resolved is because of the stranglehold the Kennedy family deed of gift has placed on the viewing and publication of the autopsy images at NARA's Archives II facility. But I do know one thing: regardless of how they were made, *the images of the apparently intact back of JFK's head are dishonest images.* The image of a large hole, or defect, in the right rear of JFK's head was prominent amongst the set of postmortem photos of JFK shown to US Information Agency (USIA) photographer Joe O'Donnell by White House photographer Robert Knudsen in late 1963; and this photo showed a large, apparent exit wound ("the size of a grapefruit") in the back of JFK's head that corroborated the consistent observations of an obvious exit wound in the posterior cranium by the overwhelming number of Parkland doctors and nurses who saw such a wound, and by most autopsy witnesses from Bethesda Naval Hospital.

- Furthermore, the images of the right front of JFK's head from the autopsy show a large, bright red, man-made incision, at the precise location where various witnesses (including Dennis David and Quentin Schwinn) saw a small, apparent entry wound (the size of a dime) high in the right forehead (above the right eye) *in autopsy photos that never made it into the official collection.* This blatant red incision is strong evidence of crude, brazen postmortem surgery, conducted at Bethesda Naval Hospital *before the autopsy began*, to obliterate any evidence of frontal shots. (The incision removed from the scalp the small, unmistakable entry wound high in the forehead above the right eye, the same entry wound seen today—high in the frontal bone above the right orbit—in the unenhanced right lateral skull X-ray when viewed in person at NARA.) Further evidence that there was postmortem surgery on JFK's skull prior to the autopsy comes from the realization that the skull X-rays were taken *only after* this postmortem surgery was conducted (to dramatically expand JFK's posterior cranial exit wound in order to obtain access to his brain and remove as much metal as possible from his cranium before the autopsy began). The condition of JFK's head seen in the autopsy photos (i.e., with the top of the head opened up and most of bone in the upper-right cranium missing) *does not* reflect the appearance of JFK's body when it arrived at Bethesda Naval Hospital, per Dr. Ebersole (the autopsy radiologist), Dr. Burkley (the president's military physician), and Captain Robert O. Canada (the navy doctor in charge of the treatment hospital). The top of JFK's head was (to all outward appearances) intact at both Parkland Hospital in Dallas, as well as when his body arrived at Bethesda Naval Hospital. *Only after the top of his cranium was opened up during postmortem surgery at Bethesda, to gain access to the brain (in an attempt to remove all large metal fragments from the brain), were the skull X-rays exposed and the first (major) round of autopsy photos (showing the metal head brace) taken. The fraud involved here is that of altering wounds on the president's body (altering a "crime scene"—obstruction of justice) before the commencement of the autopsy, and then strongly implying forever after that the photos and skull X-rays taken after the postmortem surgery "represent JFK's body the way it looked when it arrived at Bethesda."*

- While it is not a major topic of this book, I am absolutely convinced that the Zapruder film was altered at the Kodak headquarters R&D lab called "Hawkeyeworks"[3] during the weekend of the assassination, primarily for two reasons: (1) to remove exit debris traveling through the air (from JFK's head) toward the left rear and (2) to black out the large exit wound in the right rear of JFK's head. This large posterior exit wound (confirming what was seen by so many at Parkland Hospital) could *not* be allowed to remain in the film because it totally contradicted the US government's "lone nut firing from above and behind" narrative. (The exit wound in the right rear of the head was undeniable evidence of a fatal shot from the front, and therefore had to be suppressed.) Both items deleted from the Zapruder film (that is, the exit debris traveling to the left rear from JFK's head and the large posterior cranial exit wound) had to be taken out of the film if the public was to believe that Lee Harvey Oswald was the lone assassin. And so, they were. My friends Sydney Wilkinson and Thom Whitehead in Los Angeles discovered this "fraud in the evidence" in the third generation 35 mm dupe negative of the Zapruder film they purchased from the National Archives in 2008. The most egregious example of the blacked-out back of the head are their HD (2K), 4K, and state-the-art 6K digital scans of frame 317; frames 321 and 323 also show blatant signs

---

3 "Hawkeyeworks" refers to the Kodak "Hawkeye Plant" in Rochester, New York. See: Douglas Horne, *Inside the ARRB*, vol. 3, pp. 1363-1364.

> of crude alteration. The point here is that the coup plotters could not produce "autopsy photos" showing the back of JFK's head to apparently be intact, unless they *also* blacked out the exit wound in the right rear of JFK's head in the Zapruder film as well. The alteration of the Zapruder film went hand in hand with the alteration (and suppression) of JFK's wounds seen in the autopsy photographs and in the altered lateral skull X-rays. They all had to match.

It is time for me to draw this foreword to a close and let the authors address most of these issues in their book. They are writing for the future. Even if the mainstream media and the US government will not discuss these crucial issues of "fraud in the evidence," David Mantik and Jerome Corsi are courageously doing so.

Too many mainstream media producers and directors eschew any detailed discussion of the medical evidence, claiming: "You will lose the audience; they will get lost in the weeds." I have had this said to me, personally, by a documentary producer and director. To this I say "nonsense." It is a cop-out to adopt this attitude; and anyone who really believes this, and acts accordingly, is showing contempt for the average American citizen and the average member of the audience. People can understand anything if it is presented properly. The American people have grown up, for decades now, watching forensic crime shows and movies, and are fully capable of understanding the controversies involved when discussing the JFK medical evidence. Rather than getting "lost in the weeds," most people find these matters riveting and fully understand the importance of resolving the mysteries and conflicts surrounding the medical evidence.

Any discussion of the JFK assassination medical evidence that does not honestly and fairly deal with these issues of fraud is incomplete. That is generally what the public is subjected to every few years in November in these so-called documentaries on television: cherry-picked, incomplete, and therefore slanted presentations of the JFK assassination medical evidence. Another way of describing intentionally slanted and incomplete "documentaries" about the JFK assassination medical evidence would be to call them what they are: propaganda.

This book is the antidote.

1

THE FRAMING OF LEE HARVEY OSWALD

I don't think the people are going to believe this, this year, next year, or a hundred years from now. This thing will be challenged today, tomorrow, and forever.

—**ARLEN SPECTER**, 1964[1]

"Yes, I still believe Oswald was the lone gunman—despite everything," [Larry] Sabato told me in an email. "There has been too much magical thinking by theorists since the 1960s," Sabato said, pointing to the many, frequently outlandish theories you can easily find on the internet.

—**ANTHONY B. WOLF**, CNN, 2023[2]

---

1 Warren Gray, "History Lesson: Guns of the JFK Assassination," *Gunpowder Magazine*, July 27, 2020, https://gunpowdermagazine.com/history-lesson-guns-of-the-jfk-assassination/.

2 Anthony B. Wolf, "Why we're still learning new things about the JFK Assassination," MSN.com, originally from CNN, September 14, 2023, https://www.msn.com/en-us/news/us/why-we-re-still-learning-new-things-about-the-jfk-assassination/ar-AA1gG6GO?ocid=msedgdhp&pc=U531&cvid=e68972b93986486cb05efe4cadc62d10&ei=16.

Wolf was reporting on MSN.com about a broadcast that Jake Tapper had made on CNN, where he had interviewed Larry Sabato about former SS agent Paul Landis's recent book. See: Paul Landis, *The Final Witness: A Kennedy Secret Service Agent Breaks His Silence After Sixty Years* (Chicago, IL: *Chicago Review Press*, 2023). Of course, Sabato failed to note that my analysis has been based on hundreds of *experimental* pieces of data—taken at the Archives. In my view, his opinion is just another outlandish theory found on the internet. After all, what data has he taken

The most effective way to destroy people is to deny and obliterate their own understanding of their history.

—GEORGE ORWELL[3]

These three autopsy pathologists [Humes, Boswell, and Pierre Finck] were given a body, told here's the body, he was shot from behind. He fell forward, which they wrote in their autopsy report, figure out how the wounds fit the known circumstances of the shooting. But what this really speaks to is the fact that the autopsy was not in the control of the surgeons that were charged with doing it. It was in control of the people who were there, who were telling them what they could do and what they couldn't do.

—DR. GARY AGUILAR quoted in *JFK Revisited*, 2022[4]

---

at the Archives? Besides, my hardcover book cannot be read on the internet. All five-hundred-plus pages, with one-thousand-plus footnotes and countless color images, can be purchased and held in one's hand. Furthermore, if there has been any magical thinking in this case, defenders of the Warren Report have done more than their quota. Sadly, Larry Sabato is hopelessly mired in a primordial meme. I doubt that anyone can rescue him. For my hardcover book, see: David W. Mantik, Ph.D., M.D., *The JFK Assassination Decoded: Criminal Forgery in the Autopsy Photographs and X-rays* (Independently published, January 4, 2003). David Mantik originally published the hardcover book under the title *JFK's Assassination Paradoxes: Essays and Reviews & JFK's Head Wounds*. After the initial publication, Mantik changed the title to *The JFK Assassination Decoded*, as noted here.

See also: Larry J. Sabato, *The Kennedy Half Century: The Presidency, Assassination, and Lasting Legacy of John F. Kennedy* (New York: Bloomsbury USA, 2013).

3 "George Orwell Quotable Quotes," Goodreads, https://www.goodreads.com/quotes/7076-the-most-effective-way-to-destroy-people-is-to-deny.

4 James DiEugenio, *JFK Revisited: Through the Looking Glass* (New York: Skyhorse Publishing, Inc., 2022), p. 45.

ON FRIDAY, NOVEMBER 22, 1963, I had just finished my lunch in the biophysics laboratory at the University of Wisconsin-Madison when astonishing news arrived over our radio.[5] (We did not have a TV.) The stunning Dallas alert had come from nowhere. I was shocked and bewildered. Why would anyone shoot JFK? After all, his approval ratings were extremely high, as shown in Figure 1.1.[6]

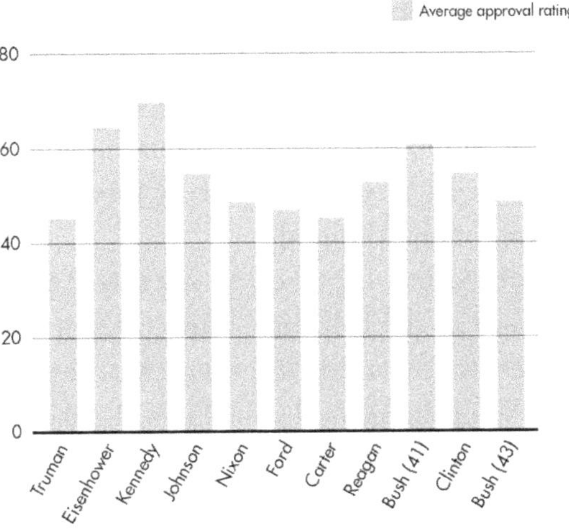

Figure 1.1
Approval Ratings of Presidents: Harry S. Truman through George W. Bush.

---

5 Only about 30 percent of Americans recall that event today. George Gao, "Where were you when JFK was shot? Only 28.9% of Americans can answer that," Pew Research Center, November 22, 2013, https://www.pewresearch.org/short-reads/2013/11/22/where-were-you-when-jfk-was-shot-only-28-9-of-americans-can-answer-that/.

6 Although this bar graph was excerpted from the internet while writing this book, we have been unable to trace its source. However, it is consistent with this summary: "Of the nine U.S. presidents who have served in the past 50 years, John F. Kennedy continues to earn the highest retrospective job approval rating from Americans, now at 85%. Ronald Reagan ranks second, with 74%." Lydia Saad, "Kennedy Still Highest-Rated Modern President, Nixon Lowest," Gallup, December 6, 2010, https://news.gallup.com/poll/145064/kennedy-highest-rated-modern-president-nixon-lowest.aspx.

See also: "Presidential Approval Ratings—Gallup Historical Statistics and Trends," Gallup, n.d., https://news.gallup.com/poll/116677/Presidential-Approval-Ratings-Gallup-Historical-Statistics-Trends.aspx.

I had just arrived in Madison that fall, after marinating my brain in biochemistry during the prior summer in Urbana, Illinois, where I had completed a master's degree in physics. I had left behind my gorgeous girlfriend Marilyn while I drove my olive green, 1953 Chevrolet to northern Wisconsin for a brief visit with my parents and siblings. Returning to Madison to pursue a PhD in physics, I promptly moved into a large bedroom overlooking W. Johnson St., a busy crosstown thoroughfare just off campus. I was insensible to its delphic name.

On Sunday, November 24, I returned from church. Since my residence had no TV, I strolled to the nearby Memorial Union on Lake Mendota to catch up on the news. To my utter amazement, I watched a TV replay as Jack Ruby shot Lee Harvey Oswald in the police basement. Now I was totally confused.

As the months passed, I focused on my career and paid little attention to politics—or to the JFK case. I do not even recall the arrival of the *Warren Report* in the fall of 1964, nor was I aware of the work of the early critics. While in medical school (1972–1976), I finally learned of Cyril Wecht's dissenting views. In late 1975, while at Los Alamos, NM (while touring the pion beam used for cancer patients), I heard one of my heroes (Luis Alvarez, Nobel Laureate in Physics) lecture on JFK's head snap in the Zapruder film. Luis was a dyed-in-the-wool Warren Commission (WC) supporter, so I still had no reason to doubt the *Warren Report*.[7]

---

7 Richard Whalen, an early WC critic, wrote that the report "tells us too much about too little." Richard Whalen, "The Kennedy Assassination," *Saturday Evening Post*, January 14, 1967, p. 20. Only about one tenth of its 912 pages deals with relevant facts. For example, there is no reference to the FBI laboratory's test (with a cotton swab) of the alleged weapon! This is the most basic possible test to determine if a weapon has recently been fired. Given the available data, it is even possible that the test was done, but was negative.

See also: WC: "Testimony of Ronald Simmons," *Hearings before the President's Commission on the Assassination of President Kennedy*, vol. 3 (Washington DC: U.S. Government Printing Office, 1964), pp. 441-451, at p. 443. Simmons testified: "They [the US Army marksmen] could not sight the weapon in using the telescope, and no attempt was made to sight it in using the iron sight. We did adjust the telescopic sight by the addition of two shims, one which tended to adjust the azimuth, and one which adjusted an elevation."

As a child, I had always loved magic. So, when we had our two children, we hired magicians for their birthday parties, and we would often take them to Las Vegas magic shows. I even had a professor in quantum mechanics at the University of Illinois[8] who performed his own magic shows. Little did I then know that the US government had used the magic of misdirection in JFK's murder. As Dariel Fitzroy (pen name Dariel Fitzkee) explained in his classic 1945 book, *Magic by Misdirection*,[9] successful magicians rely on distraction. Such deception allows a magician "*to influence the mind of the spectator, even in the face of that spectator's definite knowledge that the magician is absolutely*

Other glaring omissions from the report are JFK's death certificate and the testimonies of FBI agents Sibert and O'Neill. None of the thirty SS and FBI interviews with Dr. Malcolm Perry are present. Admiral George Burkley's interview is also missing. He was the only physician at both Parkland and Bethesda.

See William McHugh, "Oral History Interview with Admiral George G. Burkley," originally from John F. Kennedy Library, October 17, 1967, https://www.jfk-assassination.net/russ/testimony/burkley.htm. In that oral interview, in response to a question as to whether or not Burkley agreed with the WC on the number of bullets that entered JFK's body, Burkley responded, "I would not care to be quoted on that."

See also: Burkley's obituary. "George G. Burkley, 88, Dies," *Washington Post*, January 4, 1991, https://www.washingtonpost.com/archive/local/1991/01/04/george-g-burkley-88-dies/9473823e-44d2-4e1f-bf01-9547ecf3fd17/.

Also see Henry Hurt, *Reasonable Doubt: An Investigation into the Assassination of John F. Kennedy* (New York: Holt, Rinehart and Winston, 1985), p. 49. On that page, Hurt wrote: "In 1982 Dr. Burkley told the author in a telephone conversation that he believed that President Kennedy's assassination was the result of a conspiracy." It is also striking that the working outline for the WC *Report* was all ready to go by *three weeks before* its first witness (Marina) appeared! This is what we call justice in America.

8 H. J. Lipkin, *Quantum Mechanics: New Approaches to Select Topics* (Mineola, NY: Dover Publications, 2007).

9 Dariel Fitzkee, *Magic by Misdirection: A Discussion of the Psychology of Deception and the Application of Craft and Artifice for Accomplishing the Magician's Objectives* (San Rafael, CA: Saint Raphael House, 1945).

unable to do what the spectator ultimately must admit he does do."[10] Fitzkee emphasizes the psychology of deception (emphasis in original):

> *The true skill of the magician is in the skill he exhibits in influencing the spectator's mind. This is not a thing of mechanics. It is not a thing of digital dexterity. It is entirely a thing of psychological attack. It is completely a thing of controlling the spectator's thinking. Control of the perceptive facilities has nothing whatever to do with it. Convincingly interpreting, to the spectator, what the senses bring to him, in such a way that the magician's objectives are accomplished, is the true skill of the skilled magician.*[11]

If the performer's efforts have been successful, the audience sees magic. From the magician's viewpoint, though, it is all deception. While the spectators see miracles, the magician sees reality.[12]

Dariel Fitzkee would have promptly recognized the planted evidence in the JFK case as merely misdirection. For example, three shells in the Texas School Book Depository (TSBD) implied only three shots, but were the shells authentic, and why was one described as a live round? Was the shot from the TSBD a serious attempt—or was it merely a

---

10 Ibid., p. 33.

11 Ibid.

12 Ibid., p. 78. Here are two examples: A girl is loaded into a cannon. Then a rubber ball is shot from the cannon into the audience. As the audience watches the ball bounce from person to person, the girl escapes backstage. Another shot is suddenly heard at the *rear* of the audience. A female performer, an obvious doppelgänger, now runs down the aisle toward the stage. In another example, the magician has just made a ball disappear, but then quickly plucks it from behind his knee. All the while it was hidden in a pocket in the leg of his trousers.

This JFK case is bursting with duplicates (even doppelgängers, and sometimes even triplicates), which makes it ripe for magic. My hardcover book cites many examples: *The JFK Assassination Decoded: Criminal Forgery in the Autopsy Photographs and X-rays* (Independently Published, 2023), footnote 733, p. 359.

diversion?[13] The Magic Bullet suggested a single shot, but was this the actual bullet? The "Red Spot" (on the back of JFK's head) implied an entry wound, but was this JFK's hair?[14] See Figure 1.2A.

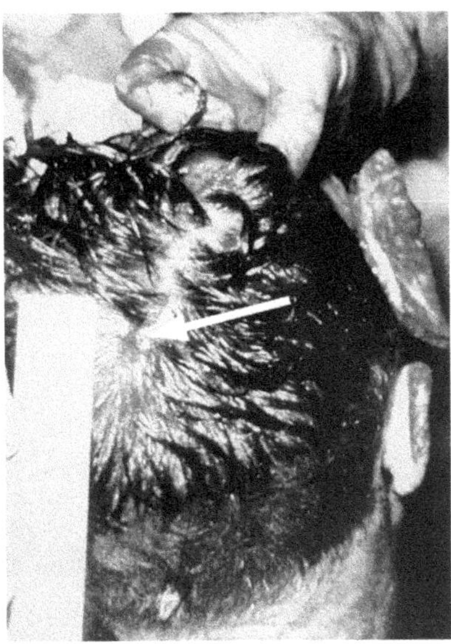

Figure 1.2A
The Red Spot (arrow) was chosen by the HSCA as the entry for the sole headshot, but no Parkland doctor recognized it.

---

13 Learn about the possible role of a diversionary shot by Loy Factor, a Chickasaw Indian, in *The Men on the Sixth Floor* (2011) by Glen Sample and Mark Collum. Although Factor claims to have seen Oswald with a weapon on the sixth floor, here is what remains unknown: Did Loy merely see an Oswald double? Although the authors are clearly aware of such doubles, somewhat astonishingly they do not consider this option for Loy's sixth floor Oswald. But George Schwimmer, PhD, does claim that two Lee Harvey Oswalds were at the TSBD that day; see *Doppelganger: The Legend of Lee Harvey Oswald* (2016).

14 You can do your own stereo viewing of the back of JFK's head—and decide for yourself. Just use the images in "JFK's Head Wounds," part 4 of my hardcover book, David W. Mantik, *The JFK Assassination Decoded*, op. cit., specifically *John F. Kennedy's Head Wounds: A Final Synthesis—and a New Analysis of the Harper Fragment* located at the back of my hardcover book, at p. 401, renumbered. In particular, see the page opposite the Preface for *John F. Kennedy's Head Wounds.* The complete book consists of five-hundred-plus pages, over one thousand footnotes, and innumerable full color images. My website also contains many pertinent essays. See "The Mantik View: Articles and Research on the JFK Assassination" at https://themantikview.org/.

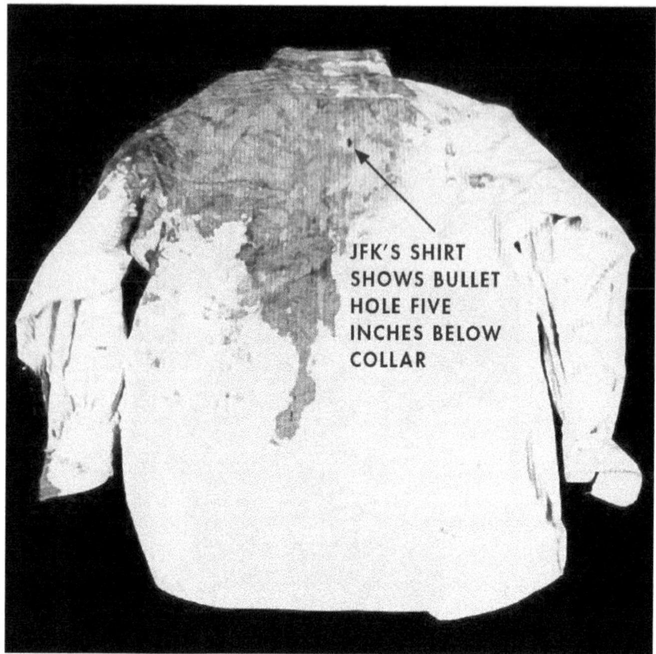

Figure 1.2B
Almost no blood is seen in the hair, but the shirt was soaked. So was the wrapping around his head, when his body arrived at the autopsy.

The 6.5 mm apparent bullet cross section on the frontal skull (AP) X-ray film matched the diameter of the 6.5 mm Mannlicher-Carcano bullet, but where was this bullet fragment during the autopsy? And where is it today at the National Archives? And what about that Black Spot on JFK's left back: Did a magician sneak into the autopsy room and change the color of this spot (and then draw a straight line through it) within just a few seconds?[15] That image is exactly what I observed at the Archives—during my *ninth* visit.

15 For the autopsy photograph of the small dark spot on JFK's left back, see Figure A.4.

DEALEY PLAZA

Figure 1.3
Bill and Gayle Newman on the Grassy Knoll, protecting their children. They stood about fifteen feet from JFK when he was executed. They thought a shot had come from behind them on the Knoll.

Multiple gunshots were heard, beginning just after the limousine passed the TSBD. No one clearly saw any shooters—and shooters were also absent[16] from the many still photographs and home movie films

16 One exceptional witness was a deaf mute, whose story has been chronicled in detail by two of my intrepid and relentless colleagues. See: Casey J. Quinlan and Brian K. Edwards, *Beyond the Fence Line: The Eyewitness Account of Ed Hoffman and the Murder of President Kennedy* (Southlake, TX: JFK Lancer Productions & Publications, Inc., 2008). Hoffman observed a gunman transfer his weapon to a collaborator. The likely purpose of this exchange was to allow the gunman to pass a paraffin test in case he was captured.

taken that day. The witnesses uniformly recalled that JFK had slumped forward.[17] The first sound seemed quite unusual to many. Bill Newman and his wife, Gayle, brought their two small sons to Dealey Plaza to see the president. "I thought someone had thrown a couple of firecrackers or something beside the President's car," Newman said. "I didn't even realize at that time it was gunfire."[18] I have suggested that this unusual first sound was due to a bullet traversing the windshield. Several witnesses thought that a bullet (or bullets) had struck Elm Street. Secret Service (SS) agent Glen Bennett saw JFK hit in the back "about four inches down from the right shoulder."[19] Clint Hill saw "an opening in the back, about six inches below the neckline."[20] Texas Governor John

---

17 Mary Moorman: "As I snapped the picture of President Kennedy, I heard a shot ring out. President Kennedy kind of slumped over."

I have summarized these highly consistent witnesses (to slumping forward) in "Special Effects in the Zapruder Film: How the Film of the Century was Edited," in James H. Fetzer, PhD, ed., *Assassination Science: Experts Speak Out on the Death of JFK* (Chicago, IL: Catfeet Press, 1998), pp. 263-344, at pp. 285-292.

Another excellent source is John P. Costella, "What Happened on Elm Street? The Eyewitnesses Speak," *Assassination Research*, 5:1 (2007), https://www.assassinationresearch.com/v5n1/v5n1costella.pdf. It is particularly striking that no promptly debriefed witness in Dealey Plaza reported the head snap that so dominates the extant Zapruder film. But no one seems to notice this—the Zapruder film has successfully performed another misdirection.

18 Larry A. Sneed, "Bill Newman: Eyewitness," in *No More Silence: An Oral History of the Assassination of President Kennedy* (Dallas, TX: Three Forks Press, 1998), pp. 94-101, at p. 95.

19 This is from the WC. "Letter dated May 14, 1964, from Secret Service to Commission, with copy of original notes of Special Agent Glen A. Bennett concerning his recollection of events surrounding assassination," *Hearings before the President's Commission on the Assassination of President Kennedy*, vol. 24 (Washington DC: U.S. Government Printing Office, 1964), pp. 541-542.

20 This is from the WC. "Testimony of Clinton J. Hill," *Hearings before the President's Commission on the Assassination of President Kennedy*, vol. 2 (Washington DC: U.S. Government Printing Office, 1964), pp. 132-144, at p. 143. The witnesses consistently referred to a wound in the shoulder or in the back—but never in the neck or the back of the neck. This is in radical disagreement with Boswell's fourteen-years-later elevation of the back wound into the neck. It is also in flagrant disagreement with Gerry Ford's attempt (with the WC) to play pathologist by elevating the back wound into the neck. Even Specter's memos to J. Lee Rankin referred to a back wound, but never to a neck wound.

Connally, sitting in the limousine jump seat immediately in front of JFK, swore that he was hit well after he heard the first sound.[21]

Roy Kellerman recalled: "...a flurry of shells come [sic] into the car."[22] Nick Prencipe, the US Park Police motorcycle officer, described a conversation he had with Bill Greer, the SS agent who drove the JFK limousine in Dealey Plaza. Greer told Prencipe that there were "shots coming from every direction," adding that "one of them came right through the windshield."[23] Bobby Hargis (the Dallas Police motorcycle officer riding inside on the left rear) stated: "...I thought at first I might have been hit."[24] Many witnesses recalled JFK's hair flying up and/or a bloody halo around his head. And many also recalled a shot near JFK's right ear.[25] At least one witness reported a

---

21 This is from the WC. "Testimony of Gov. John Bowden Connally, Jr.," *Hearings before the President's Commission on the Assassination of President Kennedy*, vol. 4 (Washington DC: U.S. Government Printing Office, 1964), pp. 129–146, at pp. 135–136.

22 This is from the WC. "Testimony of Roy H. Kellerman," *Hearings before the President's Commission on the Assassination of President Kennedy*, vol. 2 (Washington DC: U.S. Government Printing Office, 1964), pp. 61-112, at p. 74. It is quite striking that Roy, like many others, recalled a bullet entry near the right ear (ibid., p. 81). Also see Sylvia Meagher, *Accessories After the Fact* (Indianapolis, IN: Bobbs-Merrill, 1967), p. 162.

23 Read the first comment on this forum called "The White House Garage and a New Witness—Nick Prencipe": pjfk, reply to "Nick Prencipe in "SS-100-X" chapter of CAR CRASH CULTURE," Google Groups alt.assassination.jfk [forum], May 19, 2009, https://groups.google.com/g/alt.assassination.jfk/c/JinjQvhJKdM.

24 Quoted in the *Dallas Daily News*, November 24, 1963. See "Bobby Hargis," History-Matters.com, n.d., https://www.history-matters.com/analysis/witness/witnessMap/Hargis.htm.

25 Hurchel Jacks drove the VP car: "...the bullet had struck him above the right ear or near the temple" ("Statement of Hurchel Jacks, Texas Highway Patrolman, Made on November 28, 1963," *6*, vol. 18, CE 1024, op. cit., p. 801). SS Roy Kellerman (present at the autopsy) described an entry wound in the hairline just anterior to the right ear ("Testimony of Roy H. Kellerman," op. cit., p. 81). James Jenkins, who stood for hours at JFK's side during the autopsy, also saw this entry. He pointed it out to Finck, who seemed to concur. For Jenkins's comments, see William Matson Law with Allan Eaglesham, *In the Eye of History: Disclosures in the JFK Assassination Medical Evidence* (Southlake, TX: JFK Lancer Productions & Publications, Inc., 2005), pp. 72-74.

shot to JFK's forehead.[26] SS agent Clint Hill reached the limousine well after Zapruder Frame 313 (Z-313), but when he arrived, he heard another shot (and saw the large head wound)—*after* the supposed sole headshot at Z-313. Many witnesses (e.g., Mary Moorman) heard a shot (or shots) after the so-called sole headshot (supposedly at Z-313). Multiple witnesses saw smoke over the Grassy Knoll.

The motorcycle men recall Bobby Hargis dismounting and running *between* the two limousines, an event that is not seen in the extant Zapruder film. They watched as Douglas Jackson rode up the Grassy Knoll and another agent (besides Clint Hill) jumped into the presidential limousine. They saw a child (left of the limousine) pick up a piece of a skull, hand it to a SS agent, who then tossed it into the limousine.[27] These events are also missing from the extant Zapruder film.

As the limousine headed toward the Triple Overpass, Associated Press photographer James "Ike" Altgens (to the left front of the limousine) snapped a photograph. This famous "Altgens 6" photograph shows JFK through the limousine windshield. He is bending forward, apparently shot, with uplifted arms and elbows angled out; his fists are clutched before his throat.[28] The TSBD is in the background. At 2 p.m. CST, a poor copy of this photograph moved across the AP wire and was published in newspapers nationwide.[29]

---

26 Alan Smith: "The car was ten feet from me when a bullet hit the President in the forehead ..." from David W. Mantik, "Special Effects in the Zapruder Film: How the Film of the Century was Edited," in *Assassination Science*, op. cit., p. 275.

27 Larry Rivera, *The JFK Horsemen* (Crestview, FL: Moon Rock Books, 2018), pp. 556-557. These observations were based on audio interviews by Fred Newcomb with the motorcycle men. The (altered) extant Zapruder film, of course, does not record these events.

28 This windshield damage is displayed in high resolution in Figure 5.4. The color image in my hardcover book is especially dramatic.

29 Keith Moore, "JFK: The James 'Ike' Altgen's Photo Timeline by Larry Rivera and Roy Schaeffer," OpenGovTV.com April 2, 2015, opengovtv.com/index.php/sdvosb/item/4427-jfk-the-james-ike-altgens-photo-timeline

Oswald was promptly arrested. In less than two hours, the national media (mis)informed the entire country that the sole suspect was Oswald, an employee of the TSBD. Since Altgens 6 showed the TSBD behind the limousine, the public naturally concluded that all of the shots had come from the rear.

The Dallas police supposedly found three shells on the floor near the southeast corner window of the TSBD. Yet, Noel Twyman in his 1997 book *Bloody Treason,* reported a copy of an envelope with two negatives and four prints, all showing only two 6.5 mm bullets, plus one live 6.5 mm round. These were found on the sixth floor. The envelope was signed by FBI Special Agent J. Doyle Williams, dated November 22, 1963.[30] A rifle with a scope was hidden among hundreds of book boxes. But, again like magic, the bolt-action weapon was quickly switched

---

Another source is Larry Rivera, *The JFK Horseman* (2018), op. cit., pp. 3-30. Rivera and Schaeffer concluded that only severely degraded and cropped versions of Altgens 6 appeared by 2:00 p.m. CST that day. Walter Cronkite showed an extremely cropped version on television (for the first time) at 6:35 p.m. EST. Only a few West Coast newspapers and very late extra editions on the East Coast carried it. Schaeffer (then experienced at recognizing and transmitting such Thermofax images) received one at 7:15 a.m. EST on Saturday at the *Dayton Daily News.* He immediately recognized that it had been altered. The bottom line is simple: ample time existed on Friday afternoon to alter the original negative. Furthermore, on Friday afternoon, Altgens did not (contrary to his usual practice) develop his photograph—nor did he see it that day.

Richard Trask, in his 1994 book *Pictures of the Pain,* confirmed that Altgens took seven photographs of the motorcade, but he added that Altgens failed to take one when he heard "another report." Trask wrote: "A high velocity bullet punctured the rear of the President's head." How Trask (or even Altgens) could know that this was the sole headshot remains a mystery; Trask is totally insensible to this issue. He claimed that the original negatives were sent to Associated Press headquarters via a commercial flight to New York. Richard E. Sprague found negatives at AP in New York; Trask believed that these were the originals. However, writing twenty-four years after Trask, Schaeffer and Rivera would surely disagree with this. They claimed that the original Altgens 6 had long since disappeared. See Richard Trask, *Pictures of the Pain: Photography and the Assassination of President Kennedy* (Danvers, MA: Yeoman Press, 1994), ch.13, "The AP Man," pp. 307-324.

30 Noel Twyman, *Bloody Treason: The Assassination of John F. Kennedy On Solving History's Greatest Muder Mystery* (Rancho Santa Fe, CA: Laurel Publishing, 1997), pp. 90-91.

from a German-made 7.65 mm Mauser to an Italian-made 6.5 mm Mannlicher-Carcano.[31,32] Although spectators and police swarmed Dealey Plaza, no other physical evidence was (supposedly) found there.[33] The *Dallas Times Herald* original black and white photographs of the supposed sniper's nest showed only a *recreation*. That occurred because the Dallas police, while searching for evidence, had unsurprisingly moved the boxes from their original position, so another misdirection had occurred, this time unintentionally.[34] And no one saw a shooter fleeing the sixth floor. So, to a skeptic, this sixth-floor scenario could be viewed merely as a magic trick—i.e., misdirection designed merely to look like a sniper's nest.

The press enthusiastically followed the police into the TSBD. Within fifteen minutes, the police broadcasted a physical description of the suspect that miraculously matched Oswald. Their radio transcripts (at 12:45 p.m. CST) show that J. Herbert Sawyer broadcasted a radio alert: the "wanted person" was "a slender white male, about 30 [years],

---

31 Mark Lane: "I suggest it is very difficult for a police officer to pick up a weapon which has printed upon it clearly in English 'Made in Italy, Cal. 6.5' and then the next day draft an affidavit stating that it was in fact a German Mauser, 7.65 millimeters." "Testimony of Mark Lane Resumed," *Hearings before the President's Commission on the Assassination of President Kennedy*, vol. 5, pp. 546-561, at p. 561.

32 "...the Mannlicher-Carcano rifle was manufactured in Italy from 1891 until 1941; however, in the 1930s Mussolini ordered all arms factories to manufacture the Mannlicher-Carcano rifle. Since many concerns were manufacturing the same weapon, the same serial number appears on weapons manufactured by more than one concern. Some bear a letter prefix and some do not." This is found in a letter from J. Edgar Hoover, FBI, to J. Lee Rankin, general counsel, dated April 30, 1964, and accompanying documents detailing 6.5 mm Mannlicher-Carcano rifle shipments in the USA. See *Hearings before the President's Commission on the Assassination of President Kennedy*, vol. 25, CE-2562, p. 808.

33 During the ARRB, Noel Twyman discovered a receipt for a 7.65 mm Mauser shell from Dealey Plaza. This was recovered between November 22 and December 2, 1963. See *Reclaiming Parkland* (2013) by James DiEugenio, p. 92.

34 "The recreated sniper's perch at the Texas School Book Depository," The Portal to Texas History, last updated November 7, 2013, https://texashistory.unt.edu/ark:/67531/metapth184781/.

5'10", 165 [pounds]."[35]

L. Fletcher Prouty was an air force colonel who served as the chief of special operations for the Joint Chiefs of Staff during the JFK administration. He was in Christchurch, New Zealand at that moment. In Christchurch, the assassination occurred at 7:30 a.m. on Saturday, November 23, 1963. The *Christchurch Star* quickly published an extra edition. In his 1992 book *JFK: The CIA, Vietnam, and the Plot to Assassinate John F. Kennedy*, Prouty noted a complete newspaper report on Oswald, clearly identifying him as the assassin. Prouty inquired:

> Who were those sources, and how could so much intimate and detailed biographical information about Oswald have been obtained instantaneously? The answer is that it wasn't obtained "instantaneously." It had to have been prepared before the crime, and like everything else, prepackaged by the secret cabal."[36]

According to one estimate, Oswald was arrested at the Texas Theater at 1:45 p.m. CST.[37] Another report placed Oswald's arrest at 1:44 p.m., which was seventy-four minutes after the shooting.[38] Jim Marrs, an experienced Dallas news reporter, noted in his 1989 book *Crossfire*:

---

35 Dallas (Tex.) Police Department. "Radio Transcript for November 22, 1963," The Portal to Texas History, last updated January 4, 2021, p. 47, https://texashistory.unt.edu/ark:/67531/metapth339128/m1/47/?q=165.

See the WC: *Report of the President's Commission on the Assassination of President John F. Kennedy* (Washington, DC: U.S. Government Printing Office, 1964), pp. 63-64 and 143-146, at p. 144.

36 L. Fletcher Prouty, J.F.K.: *The CIA, Vietnam, and the Plot to Assassinate John F. Kennedy* (New York: Birch Lane Press, 1992), p. 306.

37 Alan Yuhas, "JFK assassination—timeline," *The Guardian,* November 22, 2013, https://www.theguardian.com/world/2013/nov/22/jfk-assassination-timeline.

38 Henry Machirella, "Lee Harvey Oswald is arrested, accused of killing JFK in 1963," originally published by the *New York Daily News,* November 23, 1963, https://www.nydailynews.com/news/national/lee-harvey-oswald-arrested-accused-killing-jfk-1963-article-1.2431162.

> ...rapid accumulation of evidence prompted Dallas County district attorney Henry Wade to proclaim to the media he had an open-and-shut case against Lee Harvey Oswald the day after the shooting.[39]

Of course, at that moment, Henry Wade knew nothing about Oswald's sojourn in Minsk. It would have been eye-opening to hear his response to Ernst Titovets, who was (according to Oswald's alleged diary) Oswald's "oldest existing acquaintance."[40] Ernst was born the year before me [Mantik]. Like me, he has both an MD and a PhD. Titovets is the author of *Oswald: Russian Episode* (2010)[41]; this is also available on Kindle. When Ernst visited the US in 2014, he autographed his book for Corsi. This biography is an enlightening portrayal of Oswald before he achieved infamy. It should be required reading of every serious student of the case.

PARKLAND HOSPITAL: TRAUMA ROOM ONE

In Trauma Room One, two wounds were readily visible. A small, round hole was seen in the midline of the throat. This became the site of Dr. Malcolm Perry's tracheotomy incision. In the occipital-parietal region (at the right rear of the head) was an avulsive wound nearly as large as a fist. Bone, scalp, and hair were missing, and brain tissue, including much of the cerebellum, was hanging from the opening.

---

39 Jim Marrs, *Crossfire: The Plot That Killed Kennedy* (New York: Carroll & Graf, 1989), p. 435.

40 Milicent Cranor, "Is US Effort to Block Oswald Friend and his "Revelations" Another Deception?" *WhoWhatWhy*, August 27, 2013, https://whowhatwhy.org/politics/government-integrity/is-us-effort-to-block-oswald-friend-and-his-revelations-itself-a-further-deception/. Also see Jeff Morley's recent (February 17, 2024) incisive comments on JFK Facts about Norman Mailer's 1992 encounter with Ernst Titovets: "Behind Norman Mailer's Sneaky Oswald Tale—A Portrait of the Great American novelist as an underhanded [US] government apologist." Justice Integrity Report - Book Launch Exclusive: Lee Harvey Oswald Friend Debunks Norman Mailer's Epic 'Oswald's Tale' (justice-integrity.org)

His website is here: Ernst Titovets (etitovets.com)

41 Ernst Titovets, *Oswald: Russian Episode* (Nezavisimosty Prospect, Belarus: 2010). A second edition was published by Custodian Books in 2014. The Kindle edition was published in 2013.

However, multiple witnesses (at Parkland and at Bethesda), including Dr. Charles Crenshaw, recalled one more wound—an entry high in JFK's right forehead, near the hairline (Figure 1.4A).[42]

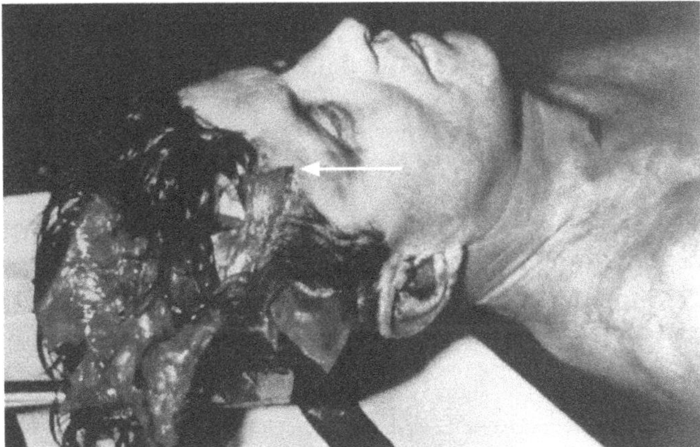

Figure 1.4A (Top), 1.4B (Bottom)

Top: Crenshaw points to his forehead (segment during Geraldo Rivera's television show, *Now It Can Be Told*, April 2, 1992). Bottom: Autopsy photograph. This incision was not seen at Parkland. Photographs were taken before any autopsy work began, so who made this incision?

---

42 Vince Palamara, "Now It Can Be Told – The Curse of JFK 5/6/92 with Dr. Charles Crenshaw," September 8, 2021, https://www.youtube.com/watch?v=AwbarV2PEWA. This image is also in my hardcover book, *The JFK Assassination Decoded,* op. cit., p. 143.

Most Parkland witnesses had missed this forehead entry wound because it was obscured by JFK's hair.[43] But Boswell[44] had noted an *incision* (presumably by a scalpel) precisely at that site (Figure 1.4B). This incision obscured the actual bullet wound. The autopsy photograph does show an incision, precisely at this site. If a bullet wound exists in this image, it is very difficult to see, as I ascertained at the National Archives.

Crenshaw recalled:

> I considered the throat wound to be an entrance wound and the large head wound to be an exit wound. Along with many of my Parkland colleagues, I believed at the time that President Kennedy had been hit twice from the front. I still believe this today.[45]

The Parkland medical personnel were remarkably consistent: JFK's head had a large hole at the right rear. In his 1993 book, *The Killing of a President,* Robert Groden displayed three pages of color photographs: each witness demonstrates (with their hand) exactly where the head

---

43 See the multiple witnesses to this wound in my hardcover book: *The JFK Assassination Decoded*, op. cit., p. 123. Also see specifically Photo 28 on the glossy page following p. 588 in David Lifton, *Best Evidence: Disguise and Deception in the Assassination of John F. Kennedy* (New York, London: MacMillan Publishing Co., 1980). In this photograph, Malcolm Kilduff, the White House acting press secretary, points to the same site that Crenshaw identified. Among others, the navy administrative technician at the Bethesda Naval Hospital (Dennis David) recalled seeing a wound to the right side of the forehead. See William Matson Law, "Interview with Dennis D. David" in *In the Eye of History: Disclosures in the JFK Assassination*, (Chicago, IL: Independent Publishers Group, 2015), expanded second edition, pp. 165-190, at p. 180.

44 During the Clay Shaw trial, as Pierre Finck's testimony was foundering, J. Thornton Boswell was asked to rescue Finck. Eventually, however, even though he was on site, Boswell did not take the stand. Boswell was also asked to perform the autopsy on Martin Luther King, Jr., but he also managed to escape responsibility for that. He seems to have been a "man for all seasons."

45 Charles Crenshaw, "Let's Set the Record Straight: Dr. Charles Crenshaw Replies," in *Assassination Science: Experts Speak Out on the Death of JFK,* ed. James H. Fetzer (Chicago: Catfeet Press, 1998), pp. 37-60, at p. 38.

wound lay—at the right rear of JFK's head.[46] They are amazingly consistent. In his more recent book, *JFK: Absolute Proof* (2013), Groden listed seventy-five witnesses, covering over eight pages, who saw the exit wound at the right rear.[47]

Gary Aguilar, MD, is still an ophthalmologist in private practice in San Francisco. For nearly fifty years, he has specialized in plastic and reconstructive surgery. He has been assistant clinical professor of ophthalmology at Stanford University and the University of California. Like me, Aguilar received permission to view the JFK artifacts at NARA and, on one occasion, we viewed the autopsy X-rays and photographs together. He is the leading specialist in eyewitness reports from Parkland and Bethesda.[48]

After the House Select Committee on Assassinations (HSCA) interviewed witnesses, Aguilar summarized their work. In his chapter, "The Converging Medical Case for Conspiracy in the Death of JFK," in Fetzer's *Murder in Dealey Plaza*, he created two witness lists: one from Parkland and another from Bethesda.[49] These two groups are in stunning agreement with one another. I have also noted the incredible *disagreement* of sixteen Parkland physicians with the autopsy photographs (more later on this):[50]

---

46 Robert J. Groden, *The Killing of a President: The Complete Photographic Record of the JFK Assassination, the Conspiracy, and the Cover-Up* (New York: Viking Studio Books, published by the Penguin Group, 1993), pp. 86-88.

47 Robert J. Groden, *JFK: Absolute Proof. New Evidence of Conspiracy in the Assassination of President John F. Kennedy* (Kansas City, MO: Conspiracy Publications, LLC, 2013), *The Killing of a President*, vol. 3, pp. 149-156.

48 John Simkin, "Gary L. Aguilar," in American History, The Assassination of JFK, Spartacus Educational, September 1997, updated January 2020, https://spartacus-educational.com/JFKaguilar.htm.

49 Gary Aguilar, MD, "The Converging Medical Case for Conspiracy in the Death of JFK," in *Murder in Dealey Plaza*, op. cit., pp. 175-218, at p. 199.

50 David Mantik, MD, PhD, "Paradoxes of the JFK Assassination: The Medical Evidence Decoded," *Murder in Dealey Plaza*, op. cit., pp. 219-298, at p. 240.

Kemp Clark	Marion Jenkins	Jackie Hunt	Malcolm Perry
Joe Goldstrich	Jim Carrico	Ronald Jones	Robert McClelland
Gene Akin	Paul Peters	Charles Baxter	Charles Crenshaw
Richard Dulaney	Fouad Bashour	Kenneth Salyer	Adolph Giesecke

That the gunshot patient was the president only heightened the everyday chaos of the emergency room—shock, grief, and panic prevailed. The first goal was to save his life, but only seconds existed to assess the wounds. The massive wound in the back of the head was obvious. This meant that JFK was technically dead on arrival (DOA). Yet, because this was the president, the medical team felt compelled to try all reasonable procedures, even though they knew the effort was useless. Universally, the Parkland medical team witnessed the massive head wound, but not everyone saw the small throat wound. And no one (except for a nurse) noticed the back wound—because their primary concern was the airway. Despite the prompt tracheotomy, JFK never resumed breathing, so there was no need to examine his body for irrelevant wounds. After JFK died, their job was done. Dr. Earl Rose, Dallas County medical examiner, was already there, waiting to perform the autopsy.

In his superb five-volume anthology, *Inside the Assassinations Records Review Board* (ARRB), Douglas Horne[51] cited a startling revelation made on March 20, 1997, by Nurse Audrey Bell during her ARRB interview (with him and Jeremy Gunn, the ARRB's chief counsel) at her Texas home. In 1963, she was Parkland Hospital's supervisor of operating and recovery rooms. After viewing JFK's wounds, she assisted with Connally's surgery. She told Horne and Gunn that when she got to work that Saturday morning (November 23, 1963) Perry complained to her

---

51 Douglas Horne worked on the ARRB staff for three years, from August 1995 through September 1998, finally becoming the chief analyst for military records. In that capacity, Horne played a crucial role in conducting unsworn interviews and formal depositions of witnesses and participants in the JFK autopsy. He also assisted in the authenticity study of the Zapruder film.

that "people from Bethesda" had been "bothering him on the phone all night long,[52] trying to get him to change his professional opinion about having seen an *entry* wound in the front of President Kennedy's neck, to one of having seen an *exit* wound instead."[53] Horne commented:

> I don't know what Dr. Perry told his tormentors on the evening of November 22-23, 1963, but I do know that he straddled the fence rather nicely during his March 1964 testimony before the Warren Commission, testifying to Arlen Specter that the wound in the front of the neck "*could have been either*" an entrance wound or an exit wound. By then, Perry was already compromising with the truth as he had first expressed it on the day the President died, when he stated unequivocally, 3 different times at the Parkland press conference while standing next to Dr. Clark, that the bullet that pierced the President's neck was coming *from the front*.[54]

And, regarding Nurse Bell's recollections, Horne stated:

> There it was—on the record with a US government agency—apparent attempts by members of the US government the night of the autopsy to change history by altering the recollections and testimony of a key assassination witness. Of course, it was hearsay, and would not have been admitted as evidence at a trial proceeding. But as Jeremy [Gunn] once pointed out to one of our own witnesses, hearsay *was*

---

52 Perry believed that his initial conversations with Humes occurred on Friday, November 22, *during* the autopsy. See "Testimony of Malcolm Perry," *Hearings before the President's Commission on the Assassination of President Kennedy,* vol. 3, op. cit., pp. 366-390, at p. 380. Also see "Testimony of Malcolm Perry," *Hearings before the President's Commission on the Assassination of President Kennedy,* vol. 6, op. cit., pp. 7-18, at p. 16.

53 Douglas Horne, *Inside the ARRB,* vol. 2, op. cit., p. 645. Emphasis in the original.

54 Ibid., p. 400.

allowed at depositions. And this wasn't even a deposition; it was an unsworn witness interview. It didn't matter to me that it was hearsay, because the source of the hearsay, Audrey Bell, was an unimpeachable witness of sterling character with tremendous credibility. After all, she had been the Supervisor of Operating and Recovery Rooms at Parkland Hospital.[55]

On an audio recording of her March 1997 testimony to the ARRB, Nurse Bell explained that she was in Trauma Room One for possibly only three minutes, but she stressed that she had focused carefully on Kennedy's wounds. In her role as supervisor, it was essential for her to identify Kennedy's wounds in case an operating room was required. She had entered the room just as Perry began the tracheotomy. She recalled:

> When I took the first look I could recognize the president, but I didn't see an injury because there was no injury around his face," she explained. I asked, 'Where's the injury?' And Dr. Perry was standing there, and he reached up on the president's head, and pulled it up a little bit, and turned his head to the left. There was a gaping hole. That's where the brain and fluids were dripping out. It [the wound in the back of JFK's head] could have been three or four inches [in diameter] that I saw.[56]

Retired Iowa cardiologist Joe Goldstrich, MD, was then a twenty-five-year-old fourth-year medical student on a neurosurgery rotation. In an interview on November 18, 2020 (fifty-seven years later at age eighty-two), Goldstrich noted that he was "the most junior person actively participating in the JFK resuscitation efforts." He called himself the "chief

---

55 Ibid., p. 645.

56 "ARRB Bell Interview Audio," History Matters, March 20, 1997, https://history-matters.com/archive/jfk/arrb/medical_interviews/audio/ARRB_Bell.htm.

gofer." He helped undress JFK, then ran to get the defibrillator, which "was about the size of a single-door refrigerator." Most significantly, he observed Dr. William Kemp Clark, head of neurosurgery at Parkland, entering Trauma Room One. Goldstrich watched as Clark observed Dr. Charlie Baxter performing closed-chest cardiac compressions. As Clark simultaneously noted the head wound, he stared at Dr. Baxter in amazement. Clark said to Baxter: "*My God, Charlie, what are you doing? His brains are on the floor.*"[57]

In his testimony, Dr. Robert McClelland gave the "most detailed description of the Kennedy head wound."[58] McClelland depicted the scene:

> As I took the position at the head of the table that I have already described, to help out with the tracheotomy, I was in such a position that I could very closely examine the head wound, and I noticed that the right posterior portion of the skull had been extremely blasted. It had been shattered, apparently, by the force of the shot so that the parietal bone was protruded up through the scalp and seemed to be fractured almost along its right posterior half, as well as some of the occipital bone being fractured in its lateral half, and this sprung open the bones that I mentioned in such a way that you could actually look down into the skull cavity itself and see that probably a third or so, at least, of the brain tissue, posterior cerebral tissue, and some of the cerebellar tissue had been blasted out. There was a large amount of bleeding which was occurring mainly from the large venous channels in the skull which had been blasted open.[59]

---

57 Randy Dotinga, "JFK in Trauma Room One: A Witness Remembers," MedPage Today, November 18, 2020, https://www.medpagetoday.com/emergencymedicine/emergencymedicine/89772. Emphasis added.

58 Josiah Thompson, *Six Seconds in Dallas: A Micro-Study of the Kennedy Assassination* (New York: Bernard Geis Associates, 1967), p. 107.

59 "Testimony of Dr. Robert M. McClelland," *Hearings before the President's Commission on the Assassination of President Kennedy*, op. cit., vol. 6, pp. 30-36, at p. 33.

While McClelland did not explicitly describe the head wound as an exit, his use of "blasted out" was even more dramatic. He also concluded that the throat wound was an entrance:

> At the moment [in the emergency room], of course, it was our impression before we had any other information from any other source at all, when we were just confronted with the acute emergency, the brief thoughts that ran through our minds were that this was one bullet, that perhaps entered through the front of the neck and then in some peculiar fashion which we really had, as I mentioned the other day, to strain to explain to ourselves, had coursed up from the front of the vertebra and into the base of the skull and out the rear of the skull.[60]

Charles Crenshaw vividly described his first impression of the wounds:

> Then I noticed that the entire right hemisphere of his brain was missing, beginning at his hairline and extending all the way behind his right ear. Pieces of skull that hadn't been blown away were hanging by blood-matted hair. Based on my experience with trauma to the head from gunshots, I knew that only a high-velocity bullet from a rifle could dissect a cranium that way. Part of his brain, the cerebellum, was dangling from the back of his head by a single strand of tissue, looking like a piece of dark gray, blood-soaked sponge that would easily fit in the palm of a hand.[61]

---

60 Ibid., p. 37.

61 Charles A. Crenshaw, MD, with Jens Hansen and J. Gary Shaw, *JFK: Conspiracy of Silence* (New York: Signet, paperback edition, 1992), pp. 78-79.

Crenshaw added:

> Blood was still seeping from the wound onto the gurney, dripping into the kick bucket on the floor. Seeing that, I became even more pessimistic. I also identified a small opening about the diameter of a pencil at the midline of his throat to be an entry bullet hole....I had seen dozens of them in the emergency room. At that point, I knew that he had been shot twice.[62]

After Perry had completed the tracheotomy and Crenshaw was sure that "the ABC's of trauma care had been completed,"[63] he focused on Kennedy's head wound:

> I walked to the President's head to get a closer look. His entire right cerebral hemisphere appeared to be gone. It looked like a crater—an empty cavity. All I could see there was mangled, bloody tissue. From the damage I saw, there was no doubt in my mind that the bullet had entered his head through the front, and as it surgically passed through his cranium, the missile obliterated part of the temporal and all the parietal and occipital lobes before it lacerated the cerebellum. The wound resembled a deep furrow in a freshly plowed field. Several years later when I viewed slow-motion films of the bullet striking the President, the physics of the head being thrown back provided final and complete confirmation of a frontal entry by the bullet to the cranium.[64]

Crenshaw dispensed with Bethesda's feeble excuse about the failure of the Parkland physicians to notice JFK's back wound:

---

62 Ibid., p. 79.

63 Ibid., p. 86.

64 Ibid.

> Usually, trauma victims are stripped of all clothing so that an injury will not be overlooked. But no one ever attempted to remove the President's briefs. I think it was out of respect for the man, the dignified position he held, and the principles for which he stood that we subconsciously didn't want to see him lying there naked. In addition, with the horrendous head wound he had sustained, we weren't concerned with the lower part of his body. If we could have stabilized him, there would have been plenty of time to check for additional injuries.[65]

Crenshaw noted President Kennedy was logged into Parkland as patient Number 24740 at 12:38 p.m. CST.[66] Dr. Kemp Clark had pronounced JFK dead at 1:00 p.m. CST. Crenshaw wrote:

> When I saw the severity of the head wound, I thought that everything we had done for him during those twenty minutes was a complete waste of time. It was a four-plus injury, which no one survives.[67]

He quoted Dr. Clark, "*My God, the whole right side of his head is shot off. We've got nothing to work with.*"[68]

PARKLAND HOSPITAL, 1:30 P.M. CST, NOVEMBER 22, 1963: THE SKIRMISH OVER JFK'S BODY

At Parkland Hospital, some ninety minutes after the shooting, a struggle arose over JFK's body. British journalist and author Anthony Summers related the incident in his 1980 book *Conspiracy*:

---

65 Ibid., p. 82.

66 Ibid., p. 74.

67 Ibid., pp. 86-87.

68 Ibid., p. 87.

> At the hospital, as the Secret Service team prepared to take the body to Washington, Dr. Earl Rose, the Dallas County Medical Examiner, backed by a Justice of the Peace, barred their way. The doctor said that, under Texas law, the body of a murder victim may not be removed until an autopsy ha[d] been performed. And the J.P., Judge Ward, declared, "It's just another homicide as far as I'm concerned."[69]

Unfortunately for history, Rose's argument did not prevail. Summers continued:

> The Secret Service agents put the doctor and the judge up against the wall at gunpoint and swept out of the hospital with the President's body. They were wrong in laws, and with hindsight they denied their President an efficient autopsy.[70]

From the moment the SS seized JFK's casket at gunpoint in the halls of Parkland Hospital until the moment of his burial in Arlington Cemetery on Monday, November 25, 1963, the US government had complete control over his body, which was the best evidence in the case.

PARKLAND HOSPITAL 1:31 P.M. CST, NOVEMBER 22, 1963: WHITE HOUSE ACTING PRESS SECRETARY ANNOUNCES JFK'S DEATH

At 1:31 p.m. CST, a deeply disturbed Malcolm Kilduff held a makeshift press conference in a Parkland classroom. He began with this: "President John F. Kennedy died at approximately one o'clock, Central Standard Time, today, here in Dallas. He died of a gunshot wound in the brain." In answering questions, Kilduff said, "Dr. Burkley told me it is a simple matter, Tom, of a bullet right through his head." Both a transcript and

---

69 Anthony Summers, *Conspiracy* (New York: McGraw-Hill Book Company, 1980), p. 42.

70 Ibid.

a film of Kilduff's press conference still exist. This was the first official announcement that JFK had died. Kilduff explained to the press that the shots that killed JFK "*came from the right side.*" (This clearly ruled out the TSBD.) Kilduff's source for his description apparently was Admiral George Burkley, MD, who was JFK's White House physician. Of particular note, Burkley was the only physician present in both in Trauma Room One and at the Bethesda autopsy. He was in an excellent position to see and precisely identify JFK's head wounds—at both Parkland and Bethesda.[71]

PARKLAND HOSPITAL 3:16 P.M. CST, NOVEMBER 22, 1963: THE PRESS CONFERENCE

At 3:16 p.m. CST, over two hours after JFK had died, Drs. Clark and Perry were the only two Parkland physicians at the press conference. They both made it clear that they had observed only two wounds in the emergency room: a "bullet hole"[72] puncture wound at the midline of the throat, just below the Adam's apple, and the large, gaping wound at the back of JFK's head. Three times, Dr. Perry affirmed that the throat wound was a frontal entrance wound. The first two times, Dr. Perry described the throat wound as an entrance wound:

> DR. PERRY: The neck wound, as visible on the patient, revealed a bullet hole almost in the midline.

---

71 Malcolm Kilduff, "Press Conference at the White House with Malcolm Kilduff at 1:31 p.m. CST," November 22, 1963, transcript found at the Lyndon B. Johnson Library, having been sent to the library by Malcolm Kilduff on July 20, 1971 (after Kilduff verified the transcript from a film of his press conference at Parkland Hospital on November 22, 1963), https://jfkassassinationfiles.files.wordpress.com/2019/08/parkland_press_1327btranscript.pdf. Emphasis added.

72 White House Transcript of Dallas Press Conference, 3:16 p.m. CST, History-Matters.com, p. 4. https://www.history-matters.com/archive/jfk/arrb/master_med_set/md41/html/Image0.htm.

Q. What was that?

DR. PERRY: Bullet hole almost in the midline.

Q. Would you demonstrate?

DR. PERRY: In the lower portion of the neck, in front.

Q. Can you demonstrate, doctor, on your own neck?

DR. PERRY: Approximately here (indicating).

Q. Below the Adam's apple?

DR. PERRY: Below the Adam's apple.

Q. Doctor, is it the assumption that it went through the head?

DR. PERRY: That would be conjecture on my part. There are two wounds, as Dr. Clark noted, one of the neck and one of the head. Whether they are directly related or two bullets, I cannot say.

Q. *Was that an entrance wound?*

DR. PERRY: *There was an entrance wound in the neck.* As regards the one on the head, I cannot say.

Q. Which way was the bullet coming on the neck wound? At him?

DR. PERRY: *It appeared to be coming at him.*[73]

---

73 Ibid., pp. 4-5. Emphasis added.

The third time occurred a few minutes later:

> Q. Doctor, describe the entrance wound. You think from the front in the throat?
>
> DR. PERRY: The wound appeared to be an entrance wound in the front of the throat; yes, that is correct.

At the Parkland press conference, Clark said the head wound "could have been either the exit wound from the neck or it could have been a tangent wound, as it was simply a large, gaping loss of tissue."[74] Clark speculated that the gaping posterior head wound could have resulted from a bullet that entered the throat or else from a separate bullet entry through the right side of the head. In either case, he clearly implied that the gaping wound at the right rear of JFK's head was an exit. He emphasized that he could not comment much on JFK's throat wound because he "was busy with his head wound."[75]

LBJ TELEPHONES PARKLAND

Crenshaw's book had one more bombshell. On Sunday, November 24, 1963, Oswald was taken to Parkland after Jack Ruby shot him. Crenshaw was one of the operating surgeons. He noticed a large man, a stranger to him, across the operating room. Crenshaw wrote:

> He resembled Oliver Hardy[76] in a scrub suit with no mask. Most alarming, there was a pistol hanging from his back pocket; if it had fallen to the floor, it could have discharged and killed someone.[77]

---

74 Ibid., p. 5.

75 Ibid., p. 4.

76 Hardy was an American comic actor, the stout member of the Laurel and Hardy team; the act had begun in the era of silent films and lasted from 1926 to 1957.

77 Charles A. Crenshaw, MD, with Jens Hansen and J. Gary Shaw, *JFK: Conspiracy of Silence*, op. cit., p. 184.

He handed the man a cap and mask. A nurse tapped him [Crenshaw] on the shoulder when he returned to the operation. "She had chosen me to take the call because I was the head of Surgical "B," the team that began the operation," he continued. So, he left the room to take the call. President Lyndon B. Johnson was on the line.

Crenshaw described the phone call:

> "This is Dr. Crenshaw, may I help you?"
>
> "This is President Lyndon B. Johnson," the voice thundered. "Dr. Crenshaw, how is the accused assassin?"
>
> I couldn't believe what I was hearing. The very first thought I had was, how did he know when to call?[78]

Here is how LBJ conveyed his request:

> "Dr. Crenshaw, I want a deathbed confession from the accused assassin. There's a man in the operating room who will take the statement. I will expect full cooperation in this matter," he said firmly.[79]

Since Oswald was obviously terminal, Crenshaw was mystified by the call. At that moment, Oswald's heart began to fail. Crenshaw walked over to "Hardy" and explained, "There won't be any deathbed confession today." The man disappeared (forever), and Oswald died without regaining consciousness.

---

78 Ibid., p. 186.

79 Ibid., p. 187.

THE BETHESDA AUTOPSY

In 1963, Commander James Joseph Humes was the director of laboratories at the Naval Medical School at the Naval Medical Center in Bethesda, Maryland. Humes was the senior pathologist "charged with the responsibility of conducting and supervising" the autopsy.[80] Humes's first assistant was Commander J. Thornton Boswell, chief of pathology at the Naval Medical School. The third pathologist was Lt. Col. Pierre Finck, on loan from the wound ballistics section of the Armed Forces Institute of Pathology.

Figure 1.5
The Three Bethesda Pathologists: Boswell, Humes, and Finck (1963).

80 "Testimony of Commander James J. Humes," *Hearings before the President's Commission on the Assassination of President Kennedy*, vol. 2, op. cit., pp. 347-376, at p. 348. Humes had joined the navy exactly twenty years earlier, so he was imminently due for full retirement benefits.

On the evening of November 22, 1963, FBI Special Agents Francis X. O'Neill and James W. Sibert witnessed JFK's autopsy at Bethesda Naval Hospital. In their official FBI 302 report (Appendix I), they noted that when JFK's body was removed from the casket, surgery was observed to have been previously performed to the top of his head. They wrote:

> The President's body was removed from the casket in which it had been transported and was placed on the autopsy table, at which time the complete body was wrapped in a sheet and the head area contained an additional wrapping which was saturated with blood. Following the removal of the wrapping, it was ascertained that the President's clothing had been removed and it was also apparent that a tracheotomy had been performed, as well as *surgery of the head area,* namely, in the top of the skull. All personnel with the exception of medical officers needed in the taking of photographs and X-Rays were requested to leave the autopsy room and remain in an adjacent room.[81]

Neither O'Neill nor Sibert were physicians; their job was merely to report what they had seen and heard. When JFK's body was removed from the casket, Humes (or Boswell) must have commented about the prior surgery to JFK's head.[82]

---

81 Emphasis added. Francis X. O'Neill, Jr. and James W. Sibert, "Autopsy of Body of President John Fitzgerald Kennedy," Gemberling Version, ARRB Master Set of Medical Exhibits, November 26, 1963, https://www.history-matters.com/archive/jfk/arrb/master_med_set/md44/html/Image0.htm.

Also see: James H. Fetzer, "Preface," in *John F. Kennedy's Head Wounds: A Final Synthesis and a New Analysis of the Harper Fragment* by David W. Mantik (Kindle edition, 2015). The Kindle edition is reprinted in my hardcover book, *The JFK Assassination Decoded,* op. cit., p. 401ff.

82 Of course, such comments might well have served Humes's furtive efforts. Such a statement would clearly divert attention from the possibility that he himself had (illegally) performed this surgery before the autopsy officially began—specifically to hide frontal shots.

The three pathologists described wounds that differed from the descriptions taken at Parkland. In particular, although most Bethesda observers recalled a huge hole, the official autopsy report (see Appendix J) does not describe a massive, gaping wound at the right rear of JFK's skull. Instead, it emphasizes an enormous exit wound at the top right and front of the head. The pathologists concluded that a bullet had entered the back of the head, furrowed through the brain, and exited from the right front top of the head (as it blew out a "head flap").

The discrepancy between Parkland and Bethesda may be understood from O'Neill and Sibert's report: surgery had been performed to the top of the head. If true, this had occurred before the official autopsy began. But only the US government had control of JFK's body. At this stage, the Russians and Cubans were quite out of the loop.

The real job of the three pathologists at Bethesda was defined by the requirements of the cover-up, not by the rules of forensic pathology. By 8:00 p.m. EST, when the Bethesda autopsy officially began, the national media, for hours, had identified Oswald as the suspected assassin who had shot JFK from the "sniper's nest" on the sixth floor of the TSBD.[83] As military men and government employees, Humes,

---

83 Paraffin tests of Oswald's cheeks were negative. However, the FBI later confirmed that every time the Mannlicher-Carcano was fired, paraffin tests were positive for barium, antimony, and gunpowder residues on the shooter's hands and right cheek. The WC heavily relied on one witness, Howard Brennan. Although the TSBD window was open only about fourteen inches, Howard claimed to have seen the gunman "from the belt up." But in a lineup later that day, Brennan could not (or would not) identify Oswald; he also denied seeing the weapon flash. The only person who saw Oswald actually enter the building that morning was Jack E. Dougherty, who did not recall Oswald carrying anything into the building. See: "Testimony of Jack Edwin Dougherty," *Hearings before the President's Commission on the Assassination of President Kennedy,* vol. 6, op. cit., pp. 373-382, at pp. 375-377. For the WC's version of the "curtain rod story," see: *Report of the President's Commission on the Assassination of President John F. Kennedy* (Washington, DC: U.S. Government Printing Office, 1964), pp. 129-130.

Even J. Edgar Hoover admitted that the evidence against Oswald was "not very, very strong." See: Michael R. Beschloss, *Taking Charge: The Johnson White House Tapes, 1963-1964* (New York: Simon and Schuster, 1997), p. 22.

Boswell, and Finck would have to risk their careers and retirements to defy the already-established narrative. So, instead, the three pathologists acquiesced quietly to what was required—namely all shots had been fired from the rear.

To the contrary, however, in his 1967 book *The Death of a President,* William Manchester explained that the Bethesda pathologists had received reports of the Parkland press conference before beginning the autopsy. Manchester wrote:

> They [the Bethesda pathologists] had heard reports of Mac Perry's medical briefing for the press, and to their dismay they had discovered that all evidence of what was being called an entrance wound in the throat had been removed by Perry's tracheostomy. Unlike the physicians at Parkland, they had turned the President over and seen the smaller hole in the back of his neck. They were positive that Perry had seen an exit wound. The deleterious effects of confusion were already apparent. Commander James J. Humes, Bethesda's chief of pathology, telephoned Perry in Dallas shortly after midnight, and clinical photographs were taken to satisfy all the Texas doctors who had been in Trauma Room No. 1.[84]

On December 2, 1992, I interviewed Dr. John Ebersole, the autopsy radiologist. He explained that his primary purpose at the autopsy was to look for bullets in the X-ray films.

> MANTIK: Your job was mainly to look for missing bullets, as I understand it, on the X-rays?

84 William Manchester, *The Death of a President: November 20–November 25, 1963* (New York: Harper & Row, Publishers, 1967), pp. 432-433.

EBERSOLE: Yes, because for a while everyone, investigating officers and so on, felt there was an entry wound, i.e., in the back, and no exit wound—[85]

In his testimony to the HSCA, Ebersole affirmed that the Parkland and Bethesda doctors were in telephone communications during the autopsy.[86]

Perry's testimony to the WC on March 25, 1964, strongly suggests that Perry and Humes first spoke on Friday night *during* the autopsy. Perry initially answered a Specter question by saying he remembered his first call from Humes on Friday, November 22, 1963. "I seem to remember it being Friday, for some reason,"[87] he explained to Specter. After Specter proposed that the record "would show" the first call from Humes was on Saturday morning, November 23, 1963, Perry relented. Humes testified to the WC that he first spoke with Perry on Saturday (after sunrise); Humes claimed that only then did he learn that the Parkland physicians had not discovered the back wound. Consider the following sequence in which Specter questioned Humes about when and how the pathologists learned the Parkland physicians had not turned JFK over to examine his back.

MR. SPECTER: In response to Mr. [Allen] Dulles' question a moment ago, Doctor Humes, you commented that they did not turn him over at Parkland. Will you state for the record what the source of your information is on that?

---

85 Ibid.

86 "Testimony of John H. Ebersole, MD," in Stenographic Transcript of Hearings before the Medical Panel of the Select Committee on Assassinations, U.S. House of Representatives: Medical Panel Meeting, op. cit., pp. 1-68, at p. 64, https://www.history-matters.com/archive/jfk/arrb/master_med_set/md60/html/Image63.htm.

87 "Testimony of Dr. Malcolm Oliver Perry," *Hearings before the President's Commission on the Assassination of President Kennedy*, vol. 6, at p. 16.

COMMANDER HUMES: Yes. This is a result of a personal telephone conversation between myself and Dr. Malcolm Perry early in the morning of Saturday, November 23.[88]

Humes also claimed that he had disclosed nothing about his autopsy observations to Perry during telephone conversations.[89] That may be technically correct, but what is more likely is this: Humes was still searching for a credible explanation for the throat wound.

Further evidence that government officials, including Humes, had pressured Perry throughout the night of the autopsy comes from an interview Nurse Bell gave to Harrison Edward Livingstone. In his 1992 book *High Treason 2*, Livingstone discussed his interview with Nurse Bell. She clarified that the point of Humes's discussions with Perry *during* the autopsy focused on coercing Perry to reverse, or otherwise qualify, his press conference pronouncement that JFK's throat wound was an entry:

> "Dr. Perry was up all night. He came into my office the next day and sat down and looked terrible, having not slept. I never saw anybody look so dejected! They called him from Bethesda two or three times in the middle of the night to try to get him to change the entrance wound in the throat to an exit wound," Audrey Bell told me.[90]

---

88 "Testimony of Commander James J. Humes," *Hearings before the President's Commission on the Assassination of President Kennedy,* vol. 2, pp. 347-376, at p. 371.

89 Ibid.

90 Harrison Edward Livingstone, *High Treason 2: The Great Cover-Up: The Assassination of President John F. Kennedy* (New York: Carroll & Graf, 1992), p. 121

Livingstone continued:

> "They really grilled Perry about it," Bell said. "They hounded him for a long time." Arlen Specter in fact went to great lengths to change what Perry had originally been quoted as saying. Specter's problem was that the entire staff at Parkland who had seen the wound insist today that it was an entrance wound.[91]

Livingstone clarified that Nurse Bell was offended by the way Washington treated the Parkland physicians.

> "He [Dr. Perry] was a senior man. He'd been doing trauma for years. He was really hounded by a lot of things," Bell told me.[92]

Livingstone also interviewed Perry. What Livingstone reports of that conversation may be a clue into how Washington pressured Perry.

> "My whole credibility as a trauma surgeon was at stake," Perry told me. "I *couldn't* have made a mistake like that. It destroys my integrity if I don't know an entrance wound from an exit wound!" he said.[93]

In volume 3 of *Inside the ARRB*, Horne also emphasized the importance of Humes's telephone discussions with Perry. Earlier in volume 3, he had documented that FBI agents O'Neill and Sibert had summarized the "autopsy conclusions" in a telex to the FBI's Baltimore office. They had dictated this on the telephone prior to 2:00 a.m. on November 23. The result was their written FD-302 report, dated November 26.

---

91 Ibid.

92 Ibid.

93 Ibid.

O'Neill and Sibert concluded that two shots hit JFK from behind. The fatal bullet "entered the back of the skull and exited from the top of the skull after fragmenting."[94] The other (non-fatal bullet) "entered the upper back 'just below the shoulders' and about 'two inches to the right of the middle line of the spinal column,' and had apparently worked its way out of the President's back at Parkland hospital while external cardiac massage was being administered during the attempt to save his life."

The ARRB concluded that O'Neill and Sibert left the autopsy at about midnight, or certainly no later than 12:30 a.m.[95] Horne emphasized that Humes changed his version of JFK's wounds to accommodate Perry's information (emphases in the original):

> Knowledge of a bullet wound in the throat, gained from Dr. Perry via the telephone in the morgue late Friday evening or early Saturday morning, necessitated the revision of the conclusions stated earlier that evening by the FBI agents [O'Neill and Sibert]. But the official story that *all* of the shots—and only *three* shots—had been fired *from behind*, from the sixth floor of the Texas School Book Depository, also necessitated that the bullet entry wound in the throat be *redescribed as an exit wound*, to fit the official legend of the shooting. Hence, the suggestion from 'civilians' [previously described by Horne only as "outsiders"] to Humes quoted above (that a bullet entered the rear of the skull and exited at the tracheotomy site), and the harassment of Dr. Perry throughout the night described in Chapter 7 by Nurse Audrey Bell. Another bullet wound in the body—in the anterior neck—required the shot total to change from 2 [i.e., the earlier autopsy conclusion as documented by O'Neill and Sibert] to 3, but those controlling the autopsy had to ensure this bullet wound was

94 Douglas Horne, *Inside the ARRB*, vol. 3, op. cit., p. 849.

95 Ibid., p. 850.

> redescribed as an exit; under no circumstances could it be characterized as an entry wound, since an entry would be evidence of a shot *from the front*, and would conflict with the cover story.[96]

Horne's clue to this changing story came from a 1978 HSCA interview with Richard Lipsey, the former military aide to the commanding general of the military district of Washington, General Philip C. Wehle. Horne emphasized that in 1978, Lipsey "was *very certain* of his recollections—his oral account is noteworthy for the conviction with which he recounted his memories."[97] He continued: "Mr. Lipsey relayed an account that is different from *both* the Sibert-O'Neill report, and from the autopsy now present in the Archives, CE 387."[98] He then stressed the following:

> It is a virtual certainty that the autopsy conclusions he [Richard Lipsey] was privy to were identical with the contents of the first draft of the autopsy which was reviewed by Drs. Humes, Boswell, and [Robert O.] Canada [the commanding officer of the naval medical hospital at Bethesda] on Saturday, November 23rd, and which was destroyed less than twenty four hours later in the fireplace of James J. Humes.[99]

According to Lipsey, sometime after midnight—and after the two FBI agents had disappeared—the pathologists declared that JFK had been hit by three shots from behind. That first autopsy draft had concluded that the *sole* headshot had "entered the back of the head and

96 Ibid., p. 862.

97 Ibid., pp. 856-857, at p. 857. Emphases in the original.

98 Ibid. Emphases in the original.

99 Ibid.

blew out part of the right side of the skull, creating one large defect that represented both the bullet's entrance and exit." It also concluded that a "*second bullet* entered very high up on the back of the neck, just inside the hairline, and exited from the throat"—and a "*third bullet* entered at the bottom of the neck, or high in the back, and did not exit."[100]

Horne asked a critical question: "Why didn't the autopsy conclusions, reported by Richard Lipsey, and committed to writing in the first draft of the autopsy report, become the official conclusions?"[101] He elucidated (emphases in the original):

> The answer to this question, I believe, is a simple one. By the time Drs. Humes, Boswell, and Canada met and reviewed the draft autopsy report on Saturday, November 23rd, the entire nation, and indeed the world, had become aware that <u>one shot had missed</u>, and had wounded bystander James Tague in the cheek, after striking a curb on Main Street in Dealey Plaza. This account was in the Dallas newspapers Saturday morning, and "hit the wire" the same day, thus becoming available to newspapers (and radio stations) all across the country. This meant that the autopsy conclusions witnessed by Richard Lipsey *could not stand*, for the central conclusion reached by the pathologists after midnight was that the President *had been hit by three shots*. It was for reason that the autopsy conclusions witnessed by Richard Lipsey, and likely memorialized in the first written draft of the autopsy protocol, did not last for even 24 hours. Because any report that postulated that President Kennedy had been hit by *three bullets* was now contradicted by 'the facts on the ground.' James J. Humes destroyed the first draft of the autopsy protocol, along with any notes

---

100 Ibid. Unfortunately for the pathologists, the hole in the shirt (Figure 1.2B) is too low to match their description of the back wound. Even worse, the hole in the shirt may not even match the back wound on the autopsy face sheet (Figure 1.7A). Also see Appendix A.

101 Ibid., p. 863. The original was in bold type.

indicating three shots hit the President, in his fireplace before dawn on Sunday November 24th, 1963. In response to the missed shot that hit James Tague, the autopsy conclusions now evolved back into a two-hit scenario, but one which now accounted for the bullet wound in the anterior neck.[102,103]

Horne concluded that "the 'stage props' used to frame the accused assassin" were the rifle and three shell casings found near the infamous sixth floor window of the TSBD.[104] He also noted that on November 22, 1963, the Dallas police and the national media established the mantra that "all shots came from above and behind the president," well before the autopsy had even begun.[105] So, "it was 'back to the drawing board' for James J. Humes following the review of his first draft at Bethesda between 10 a.m. and noon on Saturday, November 23rd."[106] In finalizing the autopsy report on Sunday, November 24, their only acceptable choice was that "the bullet which caused the entry wound in the upper back transited the body and caused the exit wound in the throat."[107]

---

102 Ibid.

103 Rear Admiral Calvin Galloway, the commanding officer of the National Naval Medical Center, personally ordered changes in the autopsy report after it was drafted.

See Harold Weisberg, *Post Mortem* (New York: Skyhorse Publishing, Inc., 2013), p. 236. Weisberg's source for concluding that Rear Admiral Calvin Galloway personally ordered changes in the autopsy report draft is from the second-day testimony of Pierre Finck at the Clay Shaw trial in New Orleans. See: "Clay Shaw Trial Transcript, 24 Feb 1969 (Testimony of Dr. Finck) part 2," MaryFerrell.org, https://www.maryferrell.org/showDoc.html?docId=1300#relPageId=6, pp. 4-5.

104 Douglas Horne, *Inside the ARRB*, op. cit., vol. 3, p. 863.

105 Ibid.

106 Ibid., p. 864.

107 For even more confusion, we have this report from the *New York Times* on December 17, 1963, p. 31, "Warren Inquiry to Fill All Gaps": "The FBI report said…Mr. Kennedy was hit by two bullets, one where the right shoulder joins the neck and the other in the right temple." This was one of the rare media reports to note the right temple entry, but there are several other media sources as well.

Thus, the single-bullet theory was conjured up directly after the autopsy in order to fit the official story that the media had established: Oswald was the sole assassin.

WARREN COMMISSION (WC) TESTIMONY

The JFK assassination is saturated with flagrant paradoxes. A major one is the discrepancy in the wounds between Parkland and Bethesda: (1) Parkland saw a fist-sized blowout at the back of JFK's head, whereas (2) the official autopsy report described a small "Red Spot" in the cowlick area (as depicted in the Ida Dox drawing, Figure 3.3).[108] No one at Parkland recalled the Red Spot. However, the Parkland witnesses were ignored and the HSCA accepted this Red Spot (visible in the autopsy photographs) as the entry for the (supposed) sole headshot. The HSCA concluded that this rear entry bullet had blown out the "head flap" at the right front of JFK's head, as seen in the Zapruder film (beginning at Z-313). On the other hand, although the official pathology report describes a defect in the frontal, parietal, and occipital areas (and Boswell's autopsy sketch is consistent with this),[109] the pathologists emphasized a massive skull defect primarily at the top of the head.

Perry's WC testimony (on March 25, 1964) strongly suggests that the pressure on Perry only intensified after the Bethesda autopsy. He enjoyed repeat visits from the SS (twenty-four agents) and from the FBI (six agents)[110]—all thirty wanted his opinion about the throat wound. Consider this exchange on March 25, 1964:

---

108 Douglas Horne, *Inside the ARRB*, vol. 3, op. cit., pp. 895-896.

109 See: Boswell's sketch from the autopsy, in Douglas Horne, *Inside the ARRB,* vol. 1, Figure 11. See also chapter 4, Figure 4.25 below.

110 "Testimony of Malcolm Perry," *Hearings before the President's Commission on the Assassination of President Kennedy*, vol. 6, op. cit., pp. 7-18.

SPECTER: Have you talked to any other representatives of the Federal Government besides the Secret Service men?

DR. PERRY: I talked to two gentlemen initially within—who identified themselves as being with the Federal Bureau of Investigation. I do not recall their names either.

MR. SPECTER: What did they ask you about?

DR. PERRY: Essentially the same questions in regard to what I might speculate as to the origin of the missiles and their trajectory, and I replied to them as I have to you that I could not ascertain this of my own knowledge, and described the wounds to the extent I saw them.[111]

THE PARKLAND DOCTORS REJECT SPECTER'S SINGLE-BULLET THEORY

Numerous WC medical witnesses scorned Specter's single-bullet theory (SBT), also known as the magic-bullet theory.[112] The WC interviewed

111 Ibid., p. 17.

112 Of course, they were not alone in their disbelief. In a telephone call, Senator Richard Russell told LBJ, "I don't believe it." And LBJ responded, "I don't either." See: Gerald D. McKnight, *Breach of Trust: How the Warren Commission Failed the Nation and Why* (Lawrence, KS: University Press of Kansas, 2005), p. 283.The FBI has never closed this murder case. In fact, J. Edgar Hoover wrote at the bottom of a memo, "We don't agree with the Commission as it says one shot missed entirely & we contend all 3 shots hit." To make his point, Hoover had underlined the word "it" twice! This is from Rosen to Belmont, 11/22/1966, FBI HQ JFK Assassination File, 62-109060-4267. Even today, it is still startling to realize that the FBI's five-volume report on the assassination is nowhere to be found in the twenty-six volumes of the WC Hearings. It is also stunning that, when the SS offered one, the FBI initially refused to accept a copy of the autopsy report before completing its own 833-page report! Incidentally, the SS agreed with the FBI's conclusion of precisely three successful shots. So, no Magic Bullet for either the FBI or the SS. How often does the media report this on every anniversary?

Sibert and O'Neill, the FBI notetakers at the autopsy, were also both adamant that the SBT was a fantasy. (See the chapters "James W. Sibert & Francis X. O'Neil, Parts One, Two, and Three"—especially pp. 317 and 354—in James W. Sibert and Francis O'Neill, *In the Eye of History: Disclosures in the Medical Evidence*, second edition, 2015, op. cit. Sibert also repeatedly stated that the back of JFK's head looked far too neat in the photographs.

Dr. Robert Shaw, a Parkland surgeon who operated on Connally. As he questioned Shaw, Specter added his own fantasy:

> Would it be possible for that bullet [i.e., the one that entered JFK's back and exited his throat] to have...struck Governor Connally in the back and have inflected the wound which you have described on the posterior aspect of his chest, and also on the anterior aspect of his chest?[113]

While Shaw accepted Specter's dubious premise, he strongly objected that CE 399 could not also have penetrated Connally's wrist:

> DR. SHAW: As far the wounds in the chest are concerned, I feel this bullet [CE 399] could have inflicted those wounds. But the examination of the wrist both by X-ray and at the time of surgery showed some fragments of metal that make it difficult to believe that the same missile could have caused these two wounds. There seems to be more than three grains of metal missing as far as the—I mean the wrist.[114]

Specter then gamed the discussion, asking Shaw whether a bullet "could have gone through the President in the way that I have described and proceed through the Governor causing all of his wounds without regard to whether or not it was bullet 399?"[115] But Shaw was steadfast:

---

113 "Testimony of Dr. Robert Roeder Shaw," *Hearings before the President's Commission on the Assassination of President Kennedy*, vol. 4, op. cit., pp. 101-117, at p. 113.

114 Ibid.

115 Ibid., p. 114.

DR. SHAW: I feel that there would be some difficulty in explaining all of the wounds as being inflicted by bullet Exhibit 399 without causing more in the way of loss of substance to the bullet or deformation of the bullet.[116]

Specter had the same challenge with Dr. Charles Francis Gregory, a Parkland surgeon, who assisted Shaw in Connally's surgery. Here is how Gregory answered Specter's imaginary SBT question:

DR. GREGORY: I believe one would have to concede the possibility, but I believe firmly that the probability is much diminished.

MR. SPECTER: Why do you say that, sir?

DR. GREGORY: I think that to pass through the soft tissues of the President would certainly have decelerated the missile to some extent. Having then struck the Governor and shattered a rib, it is further decelerated, yet it has presumably retained sufficient energy to smash a radius [an arm bone]. Moreover, it escaped the forearm to penetrate at least the skin and fascia of the thigh, and I am not persuaded that this is very probable. I would have to yield to possibility.[117]

GOVERNOR CONNALLY REJECTS SPECTER'S SBT

In his appearance before the WC, Governor Connally insisted that the first shot that hit JFK was not the same shot that hit him. Here is his critical exchange with Specter:

116 Ibid.

117 "Testimony of Dr. Charles Francis Gregory," *Hearings before the President's Commission on the Assassination of President Kennedy,* vol. 4, op. cit., pp. 117-129, at p. 127.

MR. SPECTER: In your view, which bullet caused the injury to your chest, Governor Connally?

GOVERNOR CONNALLY: The second one.

MR. SPECTER: And what is your reason for that conclusion, sir?

GOVERNOR CONNALLY: Well, in my judgment, it just couldn't conceivably have been the first one because I heard the sound of the shot. In the first place, I don't know anything about the velocity of this particular bullet, but any rifle has a velocity that exceeds the speed of sound, and when I heard the sound of that first shot, that bullet had already reached where I was, or it had reached that far, and after I heard that shot, I had time to turn to my right, and start to turn to my left before I felt anything. It is not conceivable to me that I could have been hit by the first bullet, and then I felt the blow from something that was obviously a bullet, which I assumed was a bullet, and I never heard the second shot, didn't hear it. I didn't hear but two shots. I think I heard the first shot and the third shot.[118]

Specter immediately grasped how devastating Connally's testimony would be for his SBT, which was required for any sole assassin. Connally, experienced with firearms, testified that he promptly recognized the first shot as a rifle shot and instantly guessed that it was an assassination. Specter asked a follow-up question that suggested he had no rebuttal to Connally's argument.

MR. SPECTER: Do you have any idea as to why you did not hear the second shot?

---

118 "Testimony of Gov. John Bowden Connally, Jr.," *Hearings before the President's Commission on the Assassination of President Kennedy,* vol. 4, op. cit., pp. 129-146, at pp. 135-136.

GOVERNOR CONNALLY: Well, first, again I assume the bullet was traveling faster than the sound. I was hit by the bullet prior to the time the sound reached me, and I was in either a state of shock or the impact was such that the sound didn't even register on me, but I was never conscious of hearing the second shot at all. Obviously, at least the major wound that I took in the shoulder through the chest couldn't have been anything but the second shot. Obviously, it couldn't have been the third, because when the third shot was fired, I was in a reclining position, and heard it, saw it and the effects of it, rather—I didn't see it, I saw the effects of it—so it obviously could not have been the third, and couldn't have been the first, in my judgment.[119]

EVEN HUMES AND FINCK DISPUTE SPECTER'S SBT

In retrospect, this is astonishing, but two of the pathologists initially *disagreed* with Specter's SBT. In his testimony to the WC on March 16, 1964, Arlen Specter showed CE 399 to Commander James Humes:[120]

MR. SPECTER: Now looking at that bullet, Exhibit 399, Doctor Humes, could that bullet have gone through or been any part of the fragment passing through President Kennedy's head in Exhibit No. 388 [i.e., the Rydberg drawing of a posterior headshot, soon to be discussed below].

COMMANDER HUMES: I do not believe so, sir.

MR. SPECTER: And could that missile have made the wound on Governor Connally's right wrist?

---

119 Ibid., p. 136.

120 "Testimony of Comdr. James J. Humes," *Hearings before the President's Commission on the Assassination of President Kennedy*, vol. 2, op. cit., pp. 348-376.

COMMANDER HUMES: I think that that is most unlikely. May I expand on those two answers?

MR. SPECTER: Yes, please do.

COMMANDER HUMES: The X-rays made of the wound in the head of the late President showed fragmentations of the missile. Some fragments we recovered and turned over, as has been previously noted. Also, we have X-rays of the fragment of skull which was in the region of, in our opinion, [the] exit wound showing these metallic fragments.[121]

Humes read aloud a sentence about CE 399. Parkland surgeons had removed several small bits of metal from Connally's wrist wound:

DR. HUMES: The reason I believe it most unlikely that this missile could have inflicted either of these wounds is that this missile is basically intact; its jacket appears to me to be intact, and I do not understand how it could possibly have left fragments in either of these locations.[122]

---

121 Ibid., pp. 374-375.

122 Ibid., p. 375. The most qualified ballistics expert was Dr. Joseph Dolce from the Edgewood Arsenal. In 1964, he was chairman of the army's Wound Ballistics Branch. He was emphatic that CE 399 was forensically *impossible*; he concluded that two bullets had hit Connally. However, Specter refused to call him as an official WC witness. In Dolce's experience, in "conferences you cannot disagree too often.... Especially when you're discussing bullets before three-and-four-star generals." So, instead, Specter interviewed Alfred G. Olivier and Frederick W. Light, but he was careful not to ask them any questions about the Dolce-Light ballistics experiments on human cadavers. When 6.5 mm bullets were fired through cadaver wrists, they all showed a "mushrooming" effect (from the Olivier-Dziemian report, filed as CRDLR 3264). See three long footnotes (numbers 18, 25, and 45) in Gerald McKnight, *Breach of Trust*, op. cit., pp. 185-189, 417, 418, and 420.

Realizing that if CE 399 was not the bullet that hit Connally's wrist, there had to be a second shooter, Specter persisted:

> MR. SPECTER: Dr. Humes, under your opinion in which you have just given us, what effect, if any, would that have on whether this bullet, 399, could have been the one to lodge in Governor Connally's thigh?
>
> DR. HUMES: I think that extremely unlikely. The reports, again Exhibit 392 from Parkland, tell of an entrance wound on the lower midthigh of the Governor, and X-rays taken there are described as showing metallic fragments in the bone, which apparently by this report were not removed and are still present in Governor Connally's thigh. I can't conceive of where they came from [in] this missile.[123]

Like Humes, Dr. Finck was equally unconvinced that CE 399 had struck JFK's head or had injured Connally's wrist. Finck appeared before the WC immediately after Dr. Humes:

> MR. SPECTER: And could that bullet [CE 399] have gone through Kennedy in [Exhibit] 388?
>
> DR. FINCK: Through President Kennedy's head? 388?
>
> MR. SPECTER: And remained intact in the way you see it now?
>
> DR. FINCK: Definitely not.
>
> MR. SPECTER: And could it have been the bullet which inflicted the wound on Governor Connally's right wrist?

---

123 Ibid., p. 376.

> DR. FINCK: No; for the reason that there are too many fragments described in that wrist.[124]

THE RYDBERG DRAWINGS

In her 1967 book *Accessories After the Fact*, Sylvia Meagher focused on the failure of the WC to examine the autopsy photographs and X-ray films. Aguilar characterized this failure as an "inexcusable omission."[125] Meagher noted that, according to Humes, "some 15 to 20 photographs were taken of [JFK's] body before and during the autopsy." He turned the photographs over to the SS "in their cassettes, unexposed, and Dr. Humes never saw them again."[126] Meagher noted that when Humes learned he was to appear before the WC, he "decided to have drawings made on the basis of his records."[127]

In his testimony to the WC, Humes explained why he asked Navy Corpsman Harold A. "Skip" Rydberg to produce drawings of JFK's head wounds—instead of using the autopsy photographs and X-rays for his WC testimony:

> When appraised of the necessity for our appearance before this Commission, we did not know whether or not the photographs which we had made would be available to the Commission. So to assist in making our testimony more understandable to the Commission members, we decided to have made [sic] drawings, schematic drawings, of the situation as we saw it, as we recorded it, and as we recall it.

---

124 "Testimony of Lt. Col. Pierre A. Finck, Physician, U.S. Army," *Hearings before the President's Commission on the Assassination of President Kennedy,* vol. 2, op. cit., pp. 377-384, at p. 382.

125 Gary L. Aguilar, MD, and Kathy Cunningham, "How Five Investigations into JFK's Medical/ Autopsy Evidence Got It Wrong," Part I-B, History Matters, op. cit., https://www.history-matters.com/essays/jfkmed/How5Investigations/How5InvestigationsGotItWrong.htm.

126 Sylvia Meagher, *Accessories After the Fact* (1967), op. cit., p. 143.

127 Ibid.

> These drawings were made under my supervision and that of Dr. Boswell by Mr. Rydberg, whose initials are H.A. He is a hospital corpsman, second class, and a medical illustrator in our command at Naval Medical School.[128]

Humes even had a second excuse: the photographs "were deemed too shocking, and out of deference to the Kennedy family, they had been sealed by the FBI and the Secret Service and were not available for testimony."[129] Aguilar dismissed this objection, emphasizing that the "problem could have been avoided by appointing a panel of experts to review the pictures, but this was not done. Instead, James Humes, MD, JFK's chief autopsist, commissioned drawings of JFK's wounds by an artist."[130]

In his WC testimony, Humes clarified that Rydberg worked strictly from his [Humes's] descriptions of Kennedy's wounds.

> MR. SPECTER: Did you provide him with the basic information from which these drawings were made?
>
> COMMANDER HUMES: Yes, sir.

---

128 "Testimony of Comdr. James J. Humes," *Hearings before the President's Commission on the Assassination of President Kennedy*, vol. 2, op. cit., pp. 349-350.

129 Barry Keane, "For the Sake of Historical Accuracy," Assassination of JFK, https://assassinationofjfk.net/for-the-sake-of-historical-accuracy/. This is an update to an article first published in the November 2002 edition of the journal *Dealey Plaza Echo*, from the British research group Dealey Plaza UK.

130 Gary L. Aguilar, MD, and Kathy Cunningham, "How Five Investigations into JFK's Medical/Autopsy Evidence Got It Wrong," part I-B, op. cit.

In his testimony to the ARRB, Humes commented that the Kennedy family objected to the autopsy photographs being made. See: Assassination Records Review Board. "Deposition of Dr. James Joseph Humes," corrected transcript, (College Park, Maryland: Miller Reporting Company, Inc., 1996), www.aarclibrary.org/publib/jfk/arrb/medical_testimony/pdf/Humes_2-13-96.pdf.

MR. SPECTER: Distances, that sort of thing?

COMMANDER HUMES: Yes, sir. We made certain physical measurements of the wounds, and of their position on the body of the late President, and we provided these and supervised directly Mr. Rydberg in making these drawings.[131]

The colloquy continued:

COMMANDER HUMES: I must state these drawings are in part schematic. The artist had but a brief period of some 2 days to prepare these. He had no photographs from which to work, and had to work under our description, verbal description, of what we had observed.[132]

In his testimony, Humes clarified that Rydberg had made the drawings under his and Boswell's supervision—without access to the body or to the autopsy X-rays and photographs! Rydberg later recanted his work and even published his own book.[133] In his five-volume anthology, Douglas Horne explained:

"Humes testified before the Warren Commission on Monday, March 16, 1964, at about 2 PM, so it is possible—indeed highly likely—that Rydberg worked on his illustrations from Friday, March 13th, through Sunday, March 15th."[134]

---

131 "Testimony of Comdr. James J. Humes," Hearings before the President's Commission on the Assassination of President Kennedy, vol. 2, op. cit., p. 350.

132 Ibid.

133 Harold A. Rydberg, *Head of the Dog* (Bloomington, IN: Authorhouse, 2001).

134 Douglas Horne, *Inside the ARRB*, vol. 4, op. cit., p. 1177.

Horne documented that Specter had met with Humes the week before, "so by this time Humes was well aware that Specter was not only relying on the 'transit' conclusion in the autopsy report (what became CE 387), but that Specter was insistent that the bullet which purportedly passed through JFK's body from back to front had also inflected all of the wounds on Governor Connally's body."[135]

The conclusion is simple: Humes was ordered to provide drawings that "proved" the SBT.

After meeting Rydberg at the JFK Lancer Conference in Dallas in November 2003, Barry Keane, then the vice-chairman of the British research group Dealey Plaza UK, described the conditions under which Rydberg worked:

> Over the weekend of 14th/15th March 1964, with a Marine guard just outside the door, Rydberg worked in a small empty ground floor office at Bethesda. There was no artist's table on which to work so he had to use a flat desk and had nothing but verbal descriptions from Humes and Boswell. He had to rely on his own memory of what Kennedy had looked like, and his expertise of anatomy.[136]

Keane continued:

> The drawings were life-size and in watercolor on separate 30" by 20" art boards. The two doctors were not present all the time Rydberg worked alone, he became increasingly skeptical of the methods and the accuracy and veracity of his own work. Despite this growing sense of unease, however, he completed his work.[137]

---

135 Ibid., p. 1178.

136 Barry Keane, "For the Sake of Historical Accuracy," op. cit.

137 Ibid.

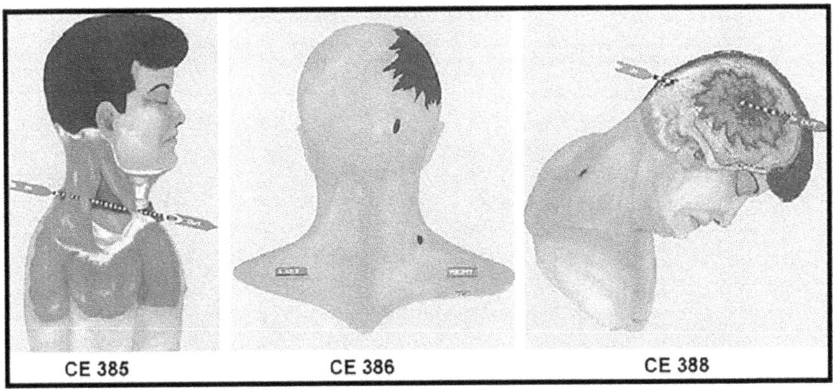

Figure 1.6
Warren Commission Exhibits 385 (left), 386 (center), and 388 (right). These drawings were produced by H.A. Rydberg, under the direction of Dr. James Humes. These drawings, not the autopsy photographs or X-ray films, were the only medical images that the WC reviewed. Source: *Hearings before the President's Commission on the Assassination of President Kennedy*, op. cit., vol. 16, pp. 977 and 984.

I wrote the preface to William Matson Law's 2005 book, *In the Eye of History: Disclosures in the JFK Assassination Medical Evidence.* (My preface was included in his second edition as well.) In Law's interview with Rydberg, the latter specified that Humes and Boswell instructed him to move JFK's back wound up to the lower neck so that the angle through the throat would be more credible. The result can be seen in the three sketches just above.

In 1977, during the HSCA, Boswell revised his own autopsy drawing—he noticeably elevated the back wound. It was now more consistent with the SBT (Figure 1.7A).

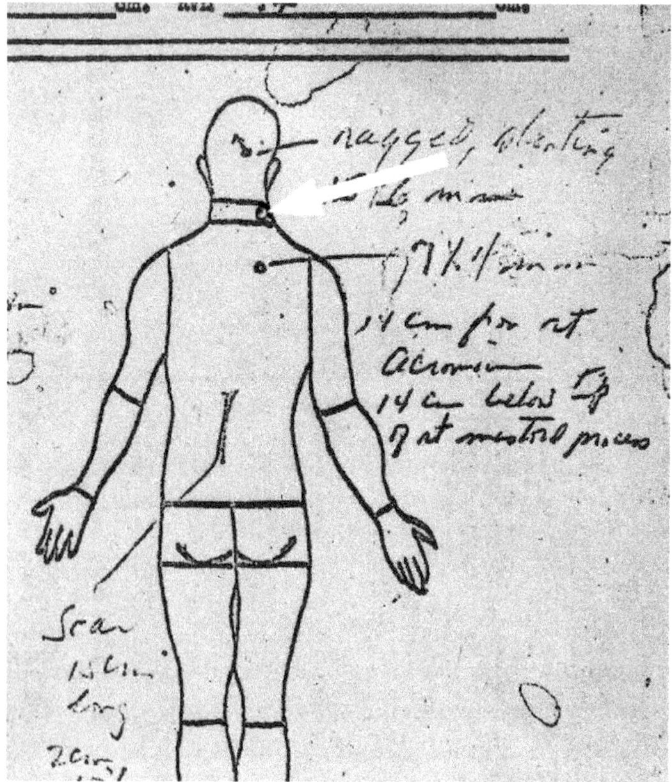

Figure 1.7A

In 1977, Boswell elevated the back wound, moving it to the large upper arrow—from its original site (labelled 7 x 4 mm). This supposedly reflected a major improvement in his memory during the preceding fourteen years.

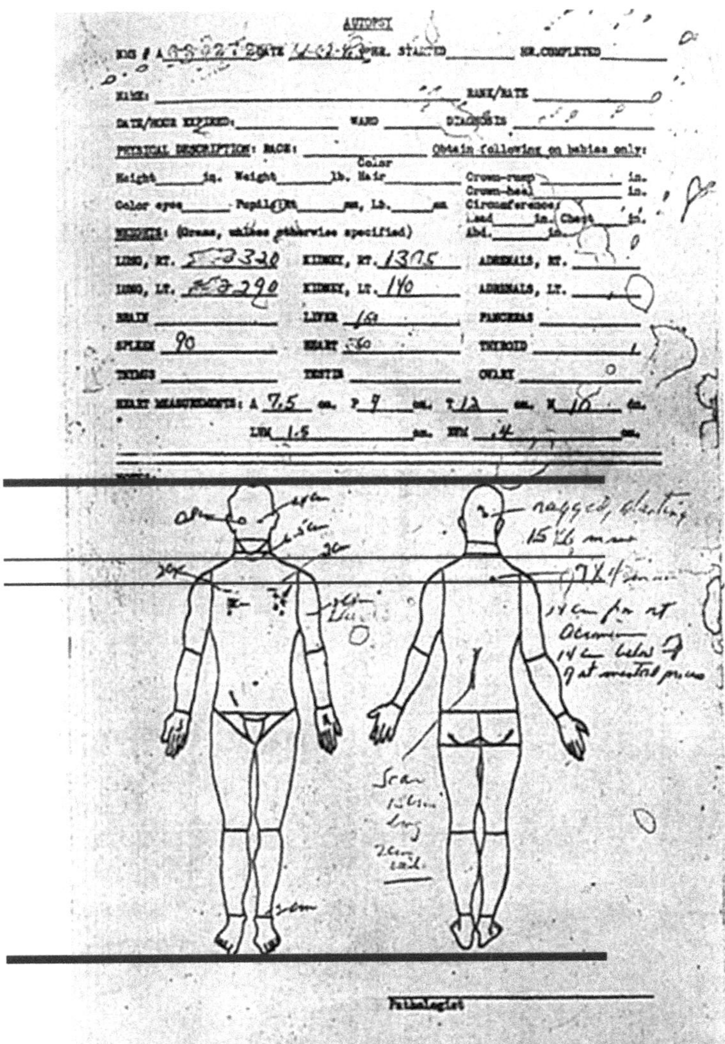

AUTOPSY

NAME: RANK/RATE

DATE/HOUR EXPIRED: WARD DIAGNOSIS

PHYSICAL DESCRIPTION: RACE: Obtain following on babies only:

Height in. Weight lb. Hair Color Crown-rump in. Crown-heel in.

Color eyes Pupils: Rt mm, Lt. mm Circumference: Head in. Chest in. Abd. in.

WEIGHTS: (Grams, unless otherwise specified)

LUNG, RT. 320 KIDNEY, RT. 1305 ADRENALS, RT.

LUNG, LT. 290 KIDNEY, LT. 140 ADRENALS, LT.

BRAIN LIVER PANCREAS

SPLEEN 90 HEART THYROID

THYMUS TESTIS OVARY

HEART MEASUREMENTS: A 7.5 cm. P 9 cm. T 12 cm. M 10 cm.

LVW 1.5 cm. RVW .4 cm.

NOTES:

Pathologist

Figure 1.7B

Notice that the lower horizontal line (of the middle two) identifies the back wound, while the upper horizontal line (of the middle two) identifies the throat wound. Next, compare the vertical level of this upper line in Figure 1.7B to Boswell's re-location of the back wound in Figure 1.7A—they are identical! The topmost and bottom most horizontal lines confirm that comparisons between the anterior and posterior anatomy are allowed.

The *Warren Report* (1964) had a similar epiphany. The initial draft stated: "A bullet had entered his back at a point slightly above the shoulder to the right of the spine." But WC member, then-Representative Gerald Ford (R-MI), slipped into the mantle of a pathologist: "A bullet had entered the back of his neck slightly to the right of the spine."[138] In his 2005 book *Breach of Trust: How the Warren Commission Failed the Nation and Why*, Professor Gerald D. McKnight commented: "Ford's revision brought the posterior wound in line with the Commission's no-conspiracy conclusion, repositioning it to make it consistent with what came to be called 'the single-bullet theory.' "[139]

Douglas Horne commented:

> Rydberg told Law that Humes orally described a wound low in the neck, at C-6 or C-7 (low in the neck), and Rydberg recalled that Humes told him it angled downward such that it would pass directly over the top of the right lung, bruising it, and exiting near the tie knot. This is precisely what Rydberg illustrated in what became known as CE 385.[140]

The verdict is clear. In their investigation, misdirection won the day for the WC—an innocent corpsman's drawings outstripped the autopsy photographs and X-ray films. But the WC was saved—these images did not become public until years later.

---

138 Gerald Ford's editing of the *Warren Report* draft (dated June 6, 1964) is archived in the J. Lee Rankin Papers, Box 26, Folder 385 at the Archives. For a brief story of how these documents were discovered, see William Matson Law, *In the Eye of History*, second edition, 2015, op. cit., p. 360. Rankin's son had a box of forty thousand documents that contained this incriminating one.

139 Gerald B. McKnight, *Breach of Trust: How the Warren Commission Failed the Nation and Why*, op. cit., pp. 174-175.

140 Douglas Horne, *Inside the ARRB*, vol. 4, p. 1178.

THE CLAY SHAW TRIAL

At Jim Garrison's 1969 trial of Clay Shaw in New Orleans, assistant district attorney Alvin Oser cross-examined Dr. Pierre Finck.[141] Finck was forced to admit that the autopsy team did not even attempt to track a bullet through the neck: "From what I recall, I looked at the trachea, there was a tracheotomy wound the best I can remember, but I didn't dissect or remove any of these organs." Consider the following exchange:

> MR. OSER: You are one of three autopsy specialists and pathologists at the time, and you saw what you described as an entrance wound in the neck area of the President of the United States who had just been assassinated, and you were only interested in the other wound [head] but not interested in the track through his neck, is that what you are telling me?
>
> COL. FINCK: I was interested in the track and I had observed the conditions of bruising between the point of entry in the back of the neck and the point of exit at the front of the neck, which is entirely compatible with the bullet path.
>
> MR. OSER: But you were told not to go into the area of the back of the neck, is that your testimony?

141 "Dr Pierre Finck: Dissecting JFK's Back and Throat Wounds," Official JFK Assassination Documents, 22 November 1963 [website], http://22november1963.org.uk/pierre-finck-jfk-back-throat-wounds.

The official transcript of the trial "State of Louisiana v. Clay L. Shaw," is catalogued as House Special Committee on Assassinations, Record Number: 180-10097-10183, with the three-part testimony of Dr. Pierre Finck archived at the Mary Ferrell Foundation website, http://www.maryferrell.org/mffweb/archive/docset/getList.do?docSetId=1016&page=2&sortBy=title.

COL. FINCK: From what I recall, yes, but I don't remember by whom.[142]

Finck had previously testified to the presence of admirals and generals in the morgue:

> It is a small autopsy room, and when you are called in circumstances like that to look at the wound of the President of the United States who is dead, you don't look around too much to ask people their names and take notes on who they are and how many there are.

He explained why he could not remember precisely who told him not to dissect JFK's neck:[143]

> The room was crowded with military and civilian personnel and federal agents, Secret Service agents, FBI agents, for part of the autopsy, but I cannot give you a precise breakdown as regards the attendance of people in that autopsy room at Bethesda Navy Hospital.[144]

He made it clear that military brass in uniform were giving orders to the pathologists during the autopsy:

> MR. OSER: Now, can you give me the name then of the General that was in charge of the autopsy, as you testified about?

---

142 "Clay Shaw Trial Transcript, 24 Feb 1969 (Testimony of Dr. Finck), Part 2," Mary Ferrell Foundation, transcript, p. 118, https://www.maryferrell.org/showDoc.html?docId=1300#relPageId=30.

143 Ibid.

144 "Clay Shaw Trial Transcript, 24 Feb 1969 (Testimony of Dr. Finck)," First Day Testimony, Mary Ferrell Foundation, transcript, p. 51, https://www.maryferrell.org/showDoc.html?docId=1299#relPageId=53.

DR. FINCK: Well, there was no General in charge of the autopsy. There were several people, as I have stated before, I heard Dr. Humes state who was in charge here, and he stated that the General answered "I am," it may have been pertaining to operations other than the autopsy. It does not mean the Army General was in charge of the autopsy, but when Dr. Humes asked who was in charge here, it may have been who was in charge of the operations, not of the autopsy, and by "operations," I mean the over-all supervision.[145]

Finck also testified that Admiral Edward Kenney placed a gag order on the Bethesda pathologists.

MR. OSER: There were Admirals?

DR. FINCK: Oh, yes, there were Admirals, and when you are a Lieutenant Colonel in the Army you just follow orders, and at the end of the autopsy we were specifically told—as I recall it, it was by Admiral Kenney, the Surgeon General of the Navy—this is subject to verification—we were specifically told not to discuss the case.[146]

So, we now know that senior military officers controlled the autopsy, telling the pathologists what they could or could not do. In his 1992 book (later updated) *Destiny Betrayed*, James DiEugenio commented on Dr. Finck's testimony (emphasis added):

---

145 "Clay Shaw Trial Transcript, 25 Feb 1969 (Testimony of Dr. Finck) Part 3," Mary Ferrell Foundation, transcript p. 6, https://www.maryferrell.org/showDoc.html?docId=1301#relPageId=9.

146 "Clay Shaw Trial Transcript, 24 Feb 1969 (Testimony of Dr. Finck) Part 1," op. cit., p. 52.

> When Oser asked if Humes was actually in charge, Finck made a disclosure which literally changed the face of the autopsy evidence forever. And it should have rocked the news media if [journalist James] Phelan had not been controlling it. Finck replied that Humes actually stopped and asked, "Who is in charge here?" Finck then said he heard an Army General say, "I am." Finck then added, "You must understand that in those circumstances, there were law enforcement officials, military people with various ranks, and *you have to coordinate the operations according to directions*."[147]

DiEugenio explained that Phelan's "assignment" was "to put a spin on each day's testimony [at the Clay Shaw trial] for the residing press corps." He explained that Phelan had rented a house during the trial. At the end of the day, Phelan invited all the reporters to the house, where he served refreshments and snacks. He would then "spell out the next day's story on a chalkboard."[148] DiEugenio concluded that Phelan's close relationship with J. Edgar Hoover explained Phelan's dismissive writing about Jim Garrison.[149]

---

147 James DiEugenio, *Destiny Betrayed: JFK, Cuba, and the Garrison Case* (New York: Skyhorse Publishing, second edition, 2012), p. 300. The first edition of his book was published in 1992.

148 Ibid., p. 290-291.

149 Ibid., p. 291. DiEugenio cited (as evidence of his claim that James Phelan was close to J. Edgar Hoover) an article that Pulitzer Prize-winning reporter David Chandler wrote in *Westword* magazine, November 25, 1992, vol. 16, no. 13, p. 21. In his footnote 18 to chapter 13, DiEugenio does not state the title of the article.

THE HOUSE SELECT COMMITTEE ON ASSASSINATIONS (1976–1978)[150]

In 1975, Senator Frank Church became the chairman of the Select Committee to Study Governmental Operations with Respect to Intelligence Activities. The Church Committee, as it was commonly referred to, shocked the nation by exposing the abuses of the CIA, the FBI, and the NSA (National Security Agency), including the involvement of the CIA in political assassinations and *of all three* agencies in domestic politics. This shocked the American public into awareness that all three agencies had engaged in illegal covert activities—in direct violation of their congressional charters. As two-time Pulitzer Prize-winner James Risen has noted in his 2023 bestselling book *The Last Honest Man*, "Frank Church and his committee took on the CIA, the FBI, and the NSA, and succeeded in bringing them under the rule of law for the first time."[151]

On March 6, 1975, JFK film expert Robert Groden, accompanied by Dick Gregory, appeared on ABC's *Good Night America,* hosted by Geraldo Rivera. They showed the Zapruder film to the American public for the first time. In 1976, the *Detroit News* reported that 87 percent of Americans did not believe the WC's conclusion that Oswald was the sole gunman. Coretta Scott King was also calling for an investigation of her husband's (Martin Luther King, Jr.) murder by a Senate

150 As this discussion shifts from JFK's body to the images of his body, James Sibert's quotation seems apt: "But I've said that when you perform an autopsy without the body, you're getting out of medicine into magic!" This is from William Matson Law, *In the Eye of History (*expanded second edition, 2015), op. cit., p. 328. Dariel Fitzkee would applaud Sibert's astute appraisal. Sibert was also quite cynical about Specter: "What a liar. I feel he got his orders from above—how far above I don't know." (See William Matson Law, *In the Eye of History*, op. cit., p. 317.)

151 James Risen with Thomas Risen, *The Last Honest Man: The CIA, the FBI, the Mafia, and the Kennedys—and One Senator's Fight to Save Democracy* (New York: Little, Brown and Company, 2023), p. 405.

select committee.[152] In the same year, the House Select Committee on Assassinations (HSCA) was created to investigate the assassinations of JFK and MLK, Jr.

On March 11, 1978, in his testimony before the HSCA Pathology Panel, Finck again affirmed that unidentified military officers at the autopsy had instructed the pathologists not to look for a trajectory in the neck. Cyril Wecht, MD, who has been strongly critical of the autopsy, raised the same issue with Finck:

> DR. WECHT: Pierre, in your subsequent testimony in the [Clay Shaw] trial I believe you were asked about the bullet wound in the back and in the neck and why it had not been dissected out and you stated that all of you had been ordered and that your recollection was that it was an Army General whose name you do not recall.
>
> DR. FINCK: And I still don't remember his name. I read my notes and I found in my notes an Army General and I don't know who it was.
>
> DR. WECHT: I was just saying with regard to what Charlie [Dr. Charles Petty, questioning Dr. Wecht on behalf of the HSCA medical panel] is asking you now, then you certainly remembered that somebody did give you orders not to do certain things.
>
> DR. FINCK: I cannot say that it was this Army General, I don't recall that precisely. I remember the prosecutors and Admiral [Calvin] Galloway. As far as saying now so and so told me that or didn't tell me that, it is extremely difficult. There was an Army General in that

152 John Simkin, "House Select Committee on Assassinations," in American History, The Assassination of JFK, Spartacus Educational, September 1997, updated January 2020, https://spartacus-educational.com/JFKassassinationsC.htm.

room and I cannot really pinpoint the origin of those instructions to comply with those family wishes. [153]

In his 2016 book *The JFK Assassination: The Evidence Today*, DiEugenio dismissed Finck's suggestion that the Kennedy family had ordered JFK's body not to be dissected:

> If RFK [Robert F. Kennedy] had told him [Dr. Finck] not to [trace the (supposed) trajectory of the neck and throat wounds]—or Kennedy's physician George Burkley had done so—wouldn't Finck have recalled it? And wouldn't he have readily answered the question since it would have gotten him off the hook for his negligence? The answer is obvious. And it renders silly the idea that it was the Kennedys and not the military that limited the autopsy. An autopsy so bad that fifty years later we still can't figure out what precisely happened to President Kennedy.[154]

So, Finck admitted that he had taken orders from admirals and generals; he even recalled that the surgeon general of the navy was present. Finck's characteristically cagy answers strongly suggest that high level government officials were transmitting orders to avoid the neck trajectory. On the other hand, if such a trajectory had been real, they would surely have insisted on a proper dissection. Given their position in the military pecking order, the (comparatively lowly) pathologists had no choice—they were required to misdirect in their description of the wounds.

---

153 "Testimony of Pierre A. Finck, MD," in Stenographic Transcript of Hearings before the Medical Panel of the Select Committee on Assassinations, U.S. House of Representatives: Medical Panel Meeting, op. cit., pp. 69-129, at pp. 75-76, https://www.maryferrell.org/showDoc.html?docId=611#relPageId=8.

154 James DiEugenio, *The JFK Assassination: The Evidence Today* (New York: Skyhorse Publishing, revised and expanded, 2018), p. 140. Skyhorse published the first edition of this book in 2016.

The HSCA completed its investigation in 1978 and issued its final report in 1979. They concluded that JFK was "probably" assassinated as a result of a conspiracy. But this conclusion was based solely on the acoustic evidence, which has been repeatedly discredited; see my website[155] and also the long discussion in my hardcover book. However, the HSCA still claimed that JFK had been struck by only one headshot, and that this had come from the rear. Disagreeing with the WC though, they elevated the skull entry site by 10 cm, which agreed with the Clark Panel report. This elevation was based solely on two bogus items: the (altered) autopsy photographs and the (fake) 6.5 mm object on the AP X-ray film. The pathologists did not agree with this change. They were right to disagree—after all, they had been duped by these two critically altered images.

The testimony of James Gochenaur confirms that Washington applied pressure to Perry. In his five volumes, Douglas Horne explained that in 1975, Gochenaur, a University of Washington graduate student, contacted the Church Committee. Gochenaur presented the committee with disturbing allegations regarding SS agent Elmer Moore.[156] Moore was assigned to the WC; he later transferred to the SS office in Seattle. Gochenaur alleged that Moore had pressured Perry in late 1963 "to change his opinion about the nature of President Kennedy's throat wound from entry to exit before Perry testified to the Warren Commission."[157] When the Church Committee staff contacted Moore, he admitted to meeting with Perry on November 29, 1963, but he denied that he had pressured Perry. Moore did admit to purchasing some photographs from Gochenaur (of demonstrators from a "riot" at a Seattle courthouse). Moore acknowledged that he had met with

---

155 "Articles and Research on the JFK Assassination by David W. Mantik M.D, PhD," The Mantik View, https://themantikview.org.

156 Douglas P. Horne, *Inside the ARRB*, vol. 2, op. cit., p. 651.

157 Ibid.

Gochenaur three or four times, "thus confirming that there was indeed a relationship between the two men."[158]

When the HSCA staff contacted Moore, "they received an angry stonewalling response."[159] Horne noted that on May 10, 1977, HSCA staff member Howard Gilbert interviewed Gochenaur by telephone. According to the HSCA transcript of the recorded phone call, Gochenaur explained that Moore felt JFK was "a traitor" for giving too much away in his dealings with Russia. He recalled that Moore had admitted to a five-hour meeting in Perry's office with Perry. Based on Moore's comments, Gochenaur concluded that Moore's purpose was to pressure Perry. In the recorded interview, he recalled meeting with Moore in a SS office on May 7, 1970, from around 4:30 p.m. to approximately 8:00 p.m. (emphasis in the original):

> GOCHENAUR: And, ah, then he [Moore] went on to say that ah, well, ah, one of the things that was pretty impressive to me was the fact that when I was talking with him [Moore], he said that, ah, *we had to do what we were told, in regards to, you know, the way they were investigating the assassination, or we get our heads cut off.*
>
> GILBERT: Did he say who told, who gave the orders?
>
> GOCHENAUR: No.[160]

The HSCA transcript continued:

> GOCHENAUR: OK, what he told me was this, he said *he had badgered doctor Perry into changing his testimony*, he did not feel good about that [emphasis in the original].

---

158 Ibid.

159 Ibid.

160 Ibid., p. 652.

GILBERT: He being Moore?

GOCHENAUR: Yes, Moore talked to Perry and, I guess, really laid it on the poor guy.

GILBERT: In what respect, what areas did he badger Perry with respect to?

GOCHENAUR: Ah, what Perry had seen as he was doing his emergency operation, apparently.

GILBERT: *Well, in what ways did he indicate to you that he had Perry distort the truth* [emphasis in the original]?

GOCHENAUR: In—I think that *what he was trying to say was [get] him to making a flat statement that there was no entry wound in the neck...*[emphasis in the original].[161]

Horne described the contretemps between Perry and Moore (emphases in the original):

> Let's sum up here: Dr. Perry was apparently pressured the night of President Kennedy's autopsy by telephone calls from Bethesda, and was apparently badgered again by Secret Service agent Moore about two weeks after the assassination (on or about December 11th), and by the time he testified before Warren Commission staff attorney Arlen Specter in March of 1964, he had changed his mind about what he was once sure was an *entrance wound* in the President's throat, and testified to Arlen Specter three times, under the onerous

161 Ibid., pp. 653-654.

influence of blatantly leading questioning, that the wound he had seen was consistent with an *exit wound.* And Perry has been "tap dancing" ever since.[162]

Horne continued:

I believe that Audrey Bell's recollections of Perry's troubled remarks the day after the assassination, and the excerpts above from the HSCA transcript of its interview of James Gochenaur, illustrate the mechanics of how a coverup is executed in this country. If you scare people a little bit, harass them, badger them, and possibly threaten them with ridicule (or worse), they will generally "go along to get along." And just to make sure, you confiscate the videotapes of what they said at the official press conference, and deny that a transcript exists, even though you have had one for four months. This is how the United States Secret Service and an ambitious and unscrupulous young staff attorney covered up evidence that President Kennedy was shot in the throat from the front.[163]

CRAIG ROBERTS (1987)

Why did the assassins wait until JFK's limousine had passed the TSBD? Craig Roberts reported in his 1994 book *Kill Zone* that professional snipers work in *teams.*[164] Once JFK's limousine turned left onto Elm Street, it continued toward the Triple Overpass over Elm Street. Jim

---

162 Ibid., p. 654.

163 Ibid.

164 Also read *Fry the Brain: The Art of Urban Sniping and its Role in Modern Guerrilla Warfare* (Kindle Direct Publishing, 2014) by John West. The author has been a professional sniper. He also comments in detail about the JFK case. I have never seen this book cited in the JFK assassination literature.

Marrs, in his 1989 book, *Crossfire: The Plot that Killed Kennedy*,[165] emphasized the critical role of a crossfire. After the limousine passed the TSBD, new firing sites appeared: behind the picket fence, buildings behind the limousine, and the south side of the Triple Overpass (opposite the Grassy Knoll). In his tour of Dealey Plaza, Roberts suddenly recognized, to his horror, what had happened that day. "A *coup d'état* had occurred, and then had successfully been covered up at the highest levels of government for over a quarter of a century," Roberts wrote. It was difficult for him to sleep that night. "The assassination of John F. Kennedy was not the issue," he explained. "It was the fact that the government, *my* government, had lied to me" [emphasis in the original].[166] Roberts argued that the only reason to fire from the TSBD was to create a diversion from the actual shooters. (Dariel Fitzkee would have loved this.) Once the Dallas police discovered the sniper's nest, Specter's job was to misdirect the shots to that site, even if—and especially if—the evidence pointed elsewhere.

MALCOM PERRY RECANTS

In his Vortex article, Aguilar wrote:

> Even though Dr. Perry swore [under oath in his 1964 testimony to the Warren Commission] that he believed the throat wound was an exit wound, he may not have actually believed what he said. On 2-14-92 an emergency room physician in Baltimore, Robert Artwohl, M.D., told an interesting tale in a "Prodigy" on-line post: Dr. Artwohl said that he had had a private conversation with Dr. Perry in 1986, and that Dr. Perry had said, *"one of the biggest regrets in his life was having to make the incision for the emergency tracheotomy through the bullet wound,*

165 Jim Marrs, *Crossfire: The Plot that Killed Kennedy* (New York: Carroll & Graf Publishers, Inc., 1989).

166 Craig Roberts, *Kill Zone*, op. cit., p. 14.

because he was certain that it was an entrance wound. He remembered making a very good mental note of the wound since he was cutting through it...speaking with Dr. Perry that night, one physician to another in [sic] *Dr. Perry stated he firmly believed the wound to be an entrance wound."*[167]

In 2017, at a mock trial of Lee Harvey Oswald held at the South Texas College of Law in Houston, Texas, Michael Chesser, MD, reported a conversation that Perry had with a medical colleague. Perry had privately advised this colleague that the throat wound had indeed been an entrance wound.[168]

We now have similar recollections from Dr. Donald Miller, Jr., a former University of Washington physician and professor.[169] In the 1970s, Miller worked with Perry at the University of Washington School of Medicine. Perry confided to Miller that he saw entry wounds on JFK—from both front and rear, thus contradicting his 1964 WC testimony. In particular, the throat wound was an entry. Perry recalled that he "was pressured by government officials and the Secret Service to back away from the entry wound claim since the official autopsy showed it to be an exit wound."[170] Miller wrote in a 2012 blog post that, after SS agent Elmer Moore and others pressured Perry to alter his story, "*This*

---

167 Gary L. Aguilar, MD, "Malcolm Perry, MD Falls into the Kennedy Vortex," ed. James DiEugenio, Kennedys and King, October 16, 2010, https://www.kennedysandking.com/obituaries/481. Emphasis added.

In the article, Aguilar cited his reference: "Prodigy interactive personal service, 2-14-92, 7:45 AM, in: 'Arts Club' bulletin board, books-nonfiction. In a posting to John Hensley (NXVX71A) from Robert Artwohl (BSMK63A)."

168 *State of Texas v. Lee Harvey Oswald*, a mock trial, was held November 16–17, 2017, at the South Texas College of Law in Houston, Texas. See: https://www.stcl.edu/home/state-of-texas-v-lee-harvey-oswald-nov-16-17-2017/.

169 Rick Anderson, "The JFK assassination files lead back to Seattle," Crosscut, November 19, 2017, https://crosscut.com/2017/11/john-f-kennedy-assassination-files-seattle-trump-release-shooters.

170 Ibid.

otherwise bold surgeon backed down and obligingly changed his testimony to suit the politically ordered truth that Oswald did it."[171]

But today we have even more. Author Rob Couteau recently discovered corroborative and contemporaneous evidence: Perry has always genuinely believed the throat wound to be an entry. Couteau found an online journal article by Martin Steadman, a reporter in Dallas at the time of the assassination. James DiEugenio confirmed that Steadman was indeed in Dallas "for several days after the assassination gathering information."[172] DiEugenio noted that some of Steadman's information got into print, but this newly discovered piece was not published. Steadman's article "50 Years from that Fateful Day in Dallas…" was, instead, published on a blog. *"I was in Dallas as a reporter for the* New York Herald Tribune, *there* [in Dallas] *to inquire into the unanswered questions surrounding the shocking events of November 22-24* [1963]."[173]

On the evening of December 2, 1963, Steadman, Stan Redding, a crime reporter for the *Houston Chronicle,* and Fred Ferretti, a colleague from the *New York Herald Tribune*, visited Perry at his home shortly after dinnertime. Steadman remembered "a little girl playing with her toys on the living room floor as the three reporters and her father talked about how he tried to save a President's life."[174] He commented that the controversy over Perry's Parkland press conference *"didn't erupt until government officials in Washington said all three shots at the President had been fired from a sixth-floor window of a building behind the President's limousine."* [Emphasis added.] He described the meeting:

---

171 Ibid. Emphasis added.

172 James DiEugenio, "The Ordeal of Malcolm Perry," ed. James DiEugenio, Kennedys and King, May 24, 2021, https://www.kennedysandking.com/john-f-kennedy-articles/the-ordeal-of-malcolm-perry.

173 Martin J. Steadman, "50 Years from that Fateful Day in Dallas," Eve's Magazine, ed. Eve Berliner, vol. 25, no. 55, Winter 2015, http://evesmag.com/jfkassassination.htm. Emphasis added.

174 Ibid.

Dr. Perry said he believed it was an entrance wound [in the throat] because the small circular hole was clean, with no [ragged] edges. In the course of the conversation, he was asked and answered that he had treated hundreds of gunshot victims in the Emergency Rooms at Parkland Memorial Hospital. At another point he said he was a hunter by hobby, and he was very familiar with guns and ammunition. He said he could tell at a glance the difference between an entrance wound and an exit wound with its ragged edges.[175]

Steadman continued:

But he [Perry] told us that throughout that night [November 22, 1963], he received a series of phone calls to his home from irate doctors at the Bethesda Naval Hospital, where an autopsy was being conducted, and the doctors there were becoming increasingly frustrated with his belief that it was an entrance wound. He said they asked him if the doctors in Dallas had turned the President over and examined the wounds to his back; he said they had not. They told him he could not be certain of his conclusion if he had not examined the wounds in the President's back. They said Bethesda had the President's body and Dallas did not. They told Dr. Perry he must not continue to say he cut across what he believed to be an entrance wound when there was no evidence of shots fired from the front. When he said again he could only say what he believed to be true, one or more of the autopsy doctors told him they would take him before a Medical Board if he continued to insist on what they were certain was otherwise. They threatened his license to practice medicine, Dr. Perry said.[176]

175 Ibid.

176 Ibid.

Perry had thus confirmed that the pathologists had literally threatened his livelihood. He realized that the pathologists had the body—and time to examine it—while he did not, so they would claim that he had been premature and irresponsible. Announcing his findings without autopsy evidence might even be used against him in a medical board inquiry.

After Perry finished this gripping tale, everyone was silent momentarily. Steadman then asked if he still thought the throat wound was an entry. The question "*hung there for a long moment.*" Then, Perry answered, "*Yes.*"[177]

DiEugenio made a final, important observation: *"What is so remarkable about this story is that it blows the cover off the idea that the autopsy doctors did not know about the anterior neck wound until the next day. Not only did they know about it that night, they were trying to cover it up that night."*[178]

DiEugenio also emphasized that McClelland, after viewing a documentary with the Parkland physicians, said that as Perry was walking out of the Parkland press conference, *"a man in a suit and tie grabbed him by the arm."* After the unidentified man got Perry's attention, "he forcefully said to Malcolm, '*Don't you ever say that again!*'"[179] After hearing McClelland say this, DiEugenio spoke to Robert Tanenbaum, the former deputy chief counsel for the HSCA, who was hosting the program. "I turned to Tanenbaum and said: '*This is about ninety minutes after Kennedy was pronounced dead.*' Tanenbaum said, '*Jim, they knew within the hour.*'"[180] The man who confronted Perry was never identified, according to DiEugenio. However, in *Accessories After the Fact*, Sylvia Meagher documented the extensive FBI and SS presence at Parkland (emphases in the original):

---

177 Ibid. Emphasis added.

178 James DiEugenio, "The Ordeal of Malcolm Perry," op. cit. Emphasis added.

179 Ibid. Emphasis added.

180 Ibid. Emphasis added.

> Subsequent to the first interview with Parkland Hospital doctors by two unnamed Secret Service agents sometime before November 29, 1963, additional interviews were conducted with the Parkland doctors, nurses, and orderlies by both the Secret Service and the FBI. There are known to be 24 Secret Service and 6 FBI interviews, or a total of 30 interviews. *Not one report on those 30 or more interviews has been included in the* [WC] *Hearings and Exhibits.*[181]

Steadman commented on Dr. Perry's testimony under oath to the WC:

> Ultimately Dr. Perry appeared as a witness before the Warren Commission. In substance he testified that he realized he had no proof the bullet hole in the President's neck was an entrance wound, and he conceded that the Bethesda doctors who autopsied the President would know better because they had all of the forensic evidence and he had but a fleeting recollection.[182]

Steadman concluded with these merciful comments:

> I can't fault Dr. Perry for his testimony before the Warren Commission. Surely it occurred to him that there was no point in holding out for a belief that couldn't be proved. And just as surely, this 34-year-old surgeon with an exemplary record and a brilliant future knew his life would be forever shadowed by conspiracy theories that relied heavily on a bullet fired from the front. He testified only as he most certainly had to testify. But I'll never forget what he said to three reporters that night in Dallas.[183]

---

181 Sylvia Meagher, *Accessories After the Fact: The Warren Commission, the Authorities, & the Report on the JFK Assassination* (Indianapolis: The Bobbs-Merrill Company, Inc., 1967), p. 155.

182 Martin J. Steadman, "50 Years from that Fateful Day in Dallas," op. cit.

183 Ibid.

On the other hand, if he had opted to tell the truth, Perry would have had to face down all of these opponents: the media, Arlen Specter, the SS, the FBI, the Department of Justice, the CIA, and the new American elite. But if he had told the truth, he might have received some support from the Parkland medical staff, i.e., JFK had been shot from the front (likely more than once).

CHARLES CRENSHAW BREAKS HIS SILENCE

We close this chapter with several incisive recollections from Dr. Charles Crenshaw. With his 1992 *New York Times* bestseller, *JFK: Conspiracy of Silence*, Dr. Charles A. Crenshaw, MD, reopened the debate about JFK's massive head wound.[184]

> From the time President Kennedy was wheeled into the emergency room, until the recent filming in Dallas of Oliver Stone's movie, *JFK*, the doctors who witnessed President Kennedy's death have always felt the necessity to continue what has evolved over the years as a conspiracy of silence....Had I been allowed to testify, I would have told them [the WC] that...the bullet that killed President Kennedy was shot from the grassy knoll area.[185]

But Crenshaw could not say this in 1963, so he was greatly relieved to escape the WC. In the immediate aftermath of the assassination, he had experienced firsthand the SS's arrogant intimidation tactics:

> I relived the tactics of intimidation practiced by the Secret Service agents. The "men in suits," as we referred to them, struck fear into Parkland's personnel as the agents went about providing more protection and concern for a dead President than they had shown for a

---

184 Charles A. Crenshaw, MD, with Jens Hansen and J. Gary Shaw, *JFK: Conspiracy of Silence* (New York: Signet, paperback edition, 1992), pp. 78-79.

185 Ibid., pp. 3 and 5.

> living President. I followed the heavily armed agents as their entourage surrounding the casket escorted President Kennedy's body out of Parkland Hospital, their arrogance almost palpable; Jacqueline Kennedy walked alongside, her hand resting on the coffin.[186]

Crenshaw acknowledged that government *"threats, intimidation, falsification and destruction of evidence, and even death, have played no small role in my silence of the past twenty-eight years."*[187] But having reached the age of fifty-nine, with his medical career now over, Crenshaw could write, *"I no longer fear the 'men in suits' nor the criticism of my peers."*[188] He was brutally honest in his contempt for the Bethesda pathologists:

> In my opinion, if Earl Rose, the pathologist at Parkland, had been allowed to perform the autopsy, and report the results to the Warren Commission, the outcome of that report would have been considerably different. And the photographs of President Kennedy would have reflected the true nature of his injuries. But of course, that is exactly why the 'men in suits' [the SS] took President Kennedy's body out of Parkland at gunpoint. They had their orders—orders from a high official in our government who was afraid of the truth.[189]

On Saturday, November 23, 1963, Crenshaw entered Parkland to find the hospital swarming with news crews. A CBS television reporter asked him if he believed Oswald had shot Kennedy in the back of the head from the TSBD. Crenshaw described his reaction:

---

186 Ibid., p. 8.

187 Ibid., p. 9. Emphasis added.

188 Ibid. Emphasis added.

189 Ibid., p. 152.

> The question shocked me. Instantly, a scenario began to form in my mind, and the thought was terrifying. If Lee Harvey Oswald was the lone assassin, they have a lunatic, a madman. But if I tell them the medical truth, that President Kennedy was shot from the front, then they have more than one gunman, they have a conspiracy, I thought to myself.[190]

He continued:

> Then I remembered Agent [Clint] Hill waving his pistol in Trauma Room 1, and how the men in suits had moved the President's body out of Parkland before an autopsy could be performed—how they would have shot Earl Rose and anyone else who had gotten in their way—how the President's limousine had been rushed out of view when the bullet hole in the windshield was noticed by the medical student. The people involved in this game played for keeps. For the first time, I sensed the presence of the pervasive influence of corruption, and it chilled me to the bone.[191]

When he refused to answer the question, Crenshaw entered the "conspiracy of silence."[192] He explained:

> I wasn't asked or told to do so, nor was any overt pressure placed on me. I was acting from an instinctive survival feeling, the one that had gotten me through medical school, through internship, and into one of the best surgical residency programs in the country. To do otherwise would have meant saying, *"Hell, no, Oswald didn't shoot*

---

190 Ibid.

191 Ibid.

192 Ibid.

> *him in the head because the President was shot from the front.*" None of us doctors were willing to do that. We all valued our medical careers too much.[193]

In a thoughtful paragraph, Crenshaw viewed the "conspiracy of silence" analytically:

> I believe there was a common denominator in our silence—a fearful perception that to come forward with what we believed to be the medical truth would be asking for trouble. Although we never admitted it to one another, we realized that the inertia of the established story was so powerful, so thoroughly presented, so adamantly accepted, that it would bury anyone who stood in its path. I had already witnessed that awesome, dictatorial force in the Earl Rose incident, the same fierceness that I would, for years to come, continue to recognize in the tragedies awaiting those people who sought the truth. I was as afraid of the men in suits as I was of the men who had assassinated the President. Whatever was happening was larger than any of us. I reasoned that anyone who would go so far as to eliminate the President of the United States would surely not hesitate to kill a doctor.[194]

Thirty years after he wrote *JFK: Conspiracy of Silence*, Crenshaw's book is still a chilling indictment—not just for its graphic depictions of JFK's head wounds, but also for the doctors' unanimous and Kafkaesque reluctance to speak the truth. Perry accurately perceived his personal risks had he used the second Parkland press conference to again describe the throat wound as an entry. (Precisely for that reason, he had declined to attend.) On the other hand, had Perry stayed true, his career might have been destroyed, and the authorities would thereby have ensured that no other Parkland physician would ever speak out. But such is the

---

193 Ibid., pp. 152-153. Emphasis added.

194 Ibid., pp. 153-154.

risk that freedom demands; every patriot going into battle accepts the risk of never going home. But as Crenshaw ultimately realized, those who bow in silence inevitably lose part of their own soul. On the other hand, some who refuse to genuflect (e.g., Giordano Bruno) risk losing their careers—or even their heads.[195]

The counterattack against Crenshaw's book was almost immediate. On May 27, 1992, the *Journal of the American Medical Association* (*JAMA*), the official journal of *my* American Medical Association (AMA), published two articles that attacked Crenshaw and his coauthor, J. Gary Shaw. The attack was personal. Then *JAMA* published a third article on October 7, 1992. Dennis L. Breo,[196] then *JAMA*'s national correspondent, had authored all three pieces, but the initial inspiration had come from *JAMA*'s then-editor, George Lundberg,[197] "a lifelong personal friend of Dr. Humes."[198] Self-serving Lundberg had utilized *his own journal* to rehabilitate the Bethesda autopsy.[199] It is almost beyond belief, but none of the three articles were peer reviewed.

On May 17, 1992, the AMA hosted a press conference in New York City to promote the upcoming May issue of *JAMA*. Lundberg dismissed Stone's film as "*skillful film fiction*" and Crenshaw's book as a "*sad fabrication*." Even four of Crenshaw's Parkland colleagues attacked him in these articles. Charles Baxter, MD, told *JAMA*, *"I've known him*

---

195 For examples (with photographs) of careers and lives lost for failure to genuflect, see my 2023 hardcover book, *The JFK Assassination Decoded*, pp. 375-377.

196 Breo won the Lisagor Award for these articles but, after our initial book (*Assassination Science* in 1998) appeared, doubt was cast on the award by Michael Miner, "Autopsy of a Lisagor," *Chicago Reader*, March 4, 1999, https://chicagoreader.com/news-politics/autopsy-of-a-lisagor/.

197 Lundberg was later ignominiously fired by *JAMA*. But *JAMA* does not learn. With no respect for science or common sense, they have just fired another editor: Nicole Chavez, "Top JAMA editor to step down after colleague questioned whether racism exists in health care," CNN, June 2, 2021, https://edition.cnn.com/2021/06/02/us/jama-editor-resigns-racism-comments/index.html.

198 Douglas Horne, *Inside the ARRB*, vol. 2, op. cit., p. 642.

199 Gary L. Aguilar, MD, "The Converging Medical Case for Conspiracy in the Death of JFK," *Murder in Dealey Plaza*, ed. James H. Fetzer, op. cit., pp. 175-177.

[Crenshaw] *since he was three years old. His claims are ridiculous....Most of those who know the facts express disgust at Crenshaw's claims and question if he was involved in the care of the President at all.*"[200]

On May 20, 1992, Lawrence K. Altman, MD, in the *New York Times*, described *JAMA*'s research as "*less than thorough*,"[201] noting that the WC had established that Crenshaw had indeed been in Trauma Room One, contributing to the medical efforts.[202] In 1993, Crenshaw and Shaw sued the AMA, among others, for libel, asking for damages of $35 million. Ultimately, the case settled, with Crenshaw and Shaw accepting the AMA insurer's offer of $213,000, but they were also given permission to publish their rebuttal in *JAMA*. On March 19, 1997, Douglas Horne and Jeremy Gunn interviewed Crenshaw at his home in Fort Worth. Horne summarized:

> The controversy garnered Crenshaw more attention and notoriety than he bargained for—he was even interviewed by the FBI regarding what he saw in Trauma Room One on November 22, 1963, following the publication of his book.[203]

---

200 Dennis L. Breo, "Dennis L. Breo's Reply," *Journal of the American Medical Association* (JAMA), vol. 273, no. 20, May 24/31, 1995, p. 1633, https://jamanetwork.com/journals/jama/article-abstract/388627. Emphasis added.

201 Lawrence K. Altman, MD, "28 Years After Dallas, A Doctor Tells His Story Amid Troubling Doubts," *New York Times*, May 26, 1992, https://www.nytimes.com/1992/05/26/health/doctor-s-world-28-years-after-dallas-doctor-tells-his-story-amid-troubling.html.

202 Lawrence K. Altman, MD, "Doctors Affirm Kennedy Autopsy Report," *New York Times*, May 20, 1992, https://timesmachine.nytimes.com/timesmachine/1992/05/20/653092.html?pageNumber=1.

Also see: D. Bradley Kizzia, "On the Trial of the Character Assassins," in Charles A. Crenshaw, MD, with J. Gary Shaw, D. Bradley Kizzia, JD, Gary Aguilar, MD, and Cyril Wecht, MD, JD, *Trauma Room One: The JFK Medical Coverup Exposed* (New York: Cosimo, 2001), chapter 7, pp. 156-169, at p. 157.

203 Douglas Horne, *Inside the ARRB*, vol. 2, op. cit., p. 642.

He also observed:

> I have reviewed his [Crenshaw's] FBI report and his statements therein are very consistent with his ARRB interview.[204]

Aguilar noted that the "exact nature, size, and position of the President's wounds...have been a source of controversy since Josiah Thompson first published a diagram"[205] supervised by McClelland (Figure 1.8). This showed the scalp and hair at the back being blown out and up, thus emphasizing the exit nature of the wound.[206]

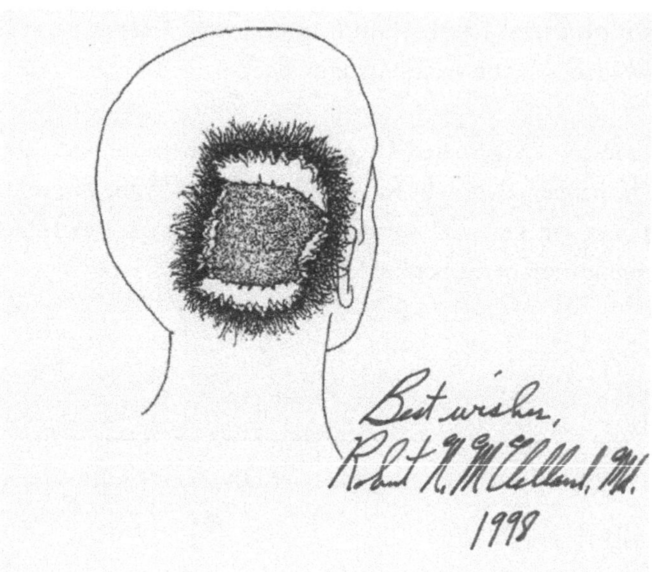

Figure 1.8
McClelland's Directed Sketch of the Head Wound. Source: Josiah Thompson (1967), *Six Seconds in Dallas*, op. cit., p. 107.

---

204 Ibid.

205 Gary L. Aguilar, MD, and Kathy Cunningham, "How Five Investigations into JFK's Medical/Autopsy Evidence Got It Wrong," Part I-B, op. cit.

206 "A pictorial representation of President Kennedy's head wound as described by Dr. Robert N. McClelland of Parkland Hospital," in Josiah Thompson, *Six Seconds in Dallas*, op. cit., p. 107.

In 1993, Crenshaw produced two sketches of JFK's skull wound for *Assassination Science* (Figure 1.9).[207] These agree closely with McClelland's sketch.

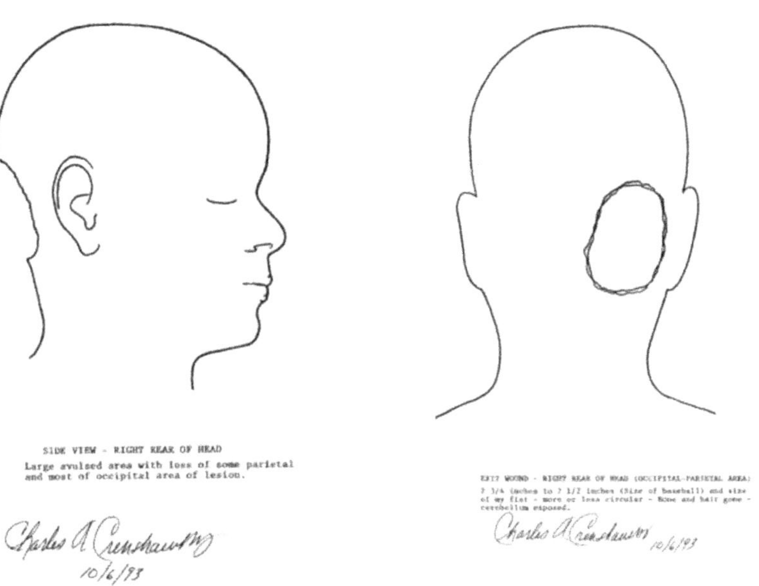

Charles Crenshaw, *Assassination Science* (1998)

Figure 1.9
Crenshaw's 1993 Sketches of the Head Wound. Source: Charles Crenshaw, MD, "Let's Set the Record Straight: Dr. Crenshaw Replies," in *Assassination Science*, op. cit.

Crenshaw's lateral view has the additional merit of showing another perspective of the blown-out site. In his *Assassination Science* article, Crenshaw addressed his *JAMA* critics:

---

207 Four drawings in "Observations of JFK Wounds in Trauma Room 1 by Charles Crenshaw, MD," in *Assassination Science*, appendix A, op. cit., p. 414. The McClelland and Crenshaw sketches are also shown in *JFK's Head Wounds* (included in my hardcover book), page v.

> There is no doubt in my mind that the attacks on me by a professional journal last summer were occasioned by my assertion that President Kennedy's wounds indicated to a doctor present on the scene that he had been shot from the front, which meant, of course, a conspiracy. The wound I saw in President Kennedy's throat was clearly a smooth and rounded entry wound. The wound in the right rear of the head, both in its location and its nature, must have been inflicted from the front. As I have stated, my conclusion in Trauma Room 1 was that these wounds were made by two shots striking President Kennedy from the front. That is still my firm conclusion today. And the official record—ignored by Breo and *JAMA*—will show that I was not alone in these conclusions.[208]

Occasionally, in history, one truth teller can drive out the darkness of the lie—providing only that this hero survives. According to his *New York Times* obituary, Crenshaw died young, at age sixty-eight, on November 15, 2001.[209] This was just before the thirty-eighth anniversary of the assassination, but Crenshaw had lived nine years after his book was published. I was fortunate to meet him.

In summary, Arlen Specter failed to convince the US Army's top ballistics experts that the SBT was real. In his 2005 book *Breach of Trust: How the Warren Commission Failed the Nation and Why*, Professor Gerald D. McKnight stressed that WC staff attorney Martin A. Eisenberg may have been "the most put-upon of the Commission lawyers" precisely because he had the impossible task of fitting Connally's wounds into the SBT. This was the sine qua non of the WC case for framing Oswald as the lone gunman.[210] In April 1964, Eisenberg held a ballistics conference

---

208 Charles Crenshaw, MD, "Let's Set the Record Straight: Dr. Crenshaw Replies," in *Assassination Science*, ed. James H. Fetzer, op. cit., pp. 37-60, at p. 42.

209 He died at his home in Fort Worth.

210 Gerald McKnight, *Breach of Trust*, op. cit., p. 185.

that included Dr. Joseph R. Dolce of the Biophysics Division at the Englewood Arsenal in Maryland and Governor Connally. Dolce, a US Army ballistics expert, was the conference's "most qualified" attendee because, during "World War II, he had spent a three-year tour of duty as a battlefield surgeon in the Pacific Theater; he had retired from the army as a full colonel. In 1964, he was chairman of the army's Wounds Ballistics Board."[211] As McKnight stressed, "When the Commission asked the army for its top ballistics man, it sent Dolce."[212] McKnight wrote: "According to Dolce, the Commission lawyers were up front about what they wanted from him. He was summoned to provide the answers that the Commission wanted, and when he failed, he was ignored."[213]

After viewing the Zapruder film and conferring with Connally, Dolce concluded that CE 399, Specter's "magic bullet," "could not have shattered the governor's wrist and still retain its virtually pristine condition," wrote McKnight. "All of Dulce's thirty-three years as a surgeon and his work in wound ballistics argued against it [the SBT]." He added, "The one who argued hardest, Dolce recalled, for CE 399 having produced all the nonfatal wounds in JFK and Connally was Arlen Specter."[214]

At the end of the April 1964 conference, the WC gave Oswald's Mannlicher-Carcano and one hundred 6.5 mm bullets to Dolce for testing. Dolce explained the results:

> And so they gave us the original rifle, the Mannlicher-Carcano, plus one hundred bullets, 6.5 millimeters. And we went, and we shot the cadaver wrists, and in every instance, the front, or the tip of the bullet was smashed. Under no circumstances, do I feel this bullet could hit the wrist [of Governor Connally], and still not be deformed.[215]

---

211 Ibid., p. 186.

212 Ibid.

213 Ibid., p. 187.

214 Ibid.

215 James DiEugenio, *JFK Revisited: Through the Looking Glass*, op. cit., p. 30.

By asserting that Specter's SBT explained Connally's wounds, the WC chose to embrace Specter's deviously crafted but ballistically impossible fantasy, thereby ignoring "the opinions and testimony of its own handpicked and most qualified expert medical and forensic witnesses."[216]

Before we focus on the extant JFK X-ray films in the next chapter, here is a fact for meditation: Charles de Gaulle was targeted by thirty-plus assassination attempts (some allegedly with CIA assistance),[217] most likely by *teams* of professional assassins. So, their record was zero hits in thirty plus tries = 0 percent. Given Oswald's vastly superior record of 100 percent (per the WC)—one can only wonder why Oswald was not simply hired for the de Gaulle hit. Perhaps Larry Sabato will soon deign to explain this paradox to us—after he completes his internet search for more "outlandish theories." Regrettably, there is no telling when he will read my hardcover book—or even this book.

And here is pertinent data from an unlikely source, i.e., Jared Diamond, the American geographer, historian, and ornithologist, who is best known for his popular science books. He summarized the success rate for attempted international assassinations in his 2019 book *Upheaval: Turning Points for Nations in Crisis*:[218]

> The database consisted of all 298 assassination attempts on national leaders from 1875 to 2005: 59 of them were successful, 239 unsuccessful.

---

216 Gerald McKnight, *Breach of Trust*, op. cit., p. 189.

217 Alex Ledsom, "How Charles de Gaulle Survived Over Thirty Assassination Attempts," Culture Trip, May 26, 2023, https://theculturetrip.com/europe/france/articles/how-charles-de-gaulle-survived-over-thirty-assassination-attempts.

218 Jared Diamond, *Upheaval: Turning Point for Nations in Crisis* (New York: Little, Brown and Company, 2019), p. 452.

This represents a global success rate *of only 20 percent.* We suspect that most of these international successes were team efforts, thus making Oswald's vaunted skill, especially as a lone gunman, undeniably astonishing. So, sometimes fiction (the WC) is indeed stranger than truth.

Per the WC, Oswald's success rate was one for one, i.e., 100 percent, even though no evidence exists of any target practice during the preceding four-plus years.[219] Marine Colonel Allison Folsom, while testifying before the WC, characterized Oswald (regarding a Marine weapons test zeroing a U.S. Rifle, Caliber .30, M-1 at a distance of two hundred yards) as "not a particularly outstanding shot."[220] Between May 8, 1959, and November 22, 1963, despite diligent efforts by the FBI, no evidence was ever unearthed to show that Oswald fired a weapon during those 1,600+ days. Oswald's highest rating in the Marines was 212, good enough for "sharpshooter."[221] Later, however (May 8, 1959) he scored just 191, thus *reducing* his rating to "marksman." Yet on November 22, 1963, using a far inferior weapon, he was supposedly peerless. Such are the priceless rewards of not practicing.

CHAPTER 1: SUMMARY

To explain seven wounds in two men, Arlen Specter, the hired gun for the WC, indulged his fantasy by creating the single-bullet theory (SBT).

---

219 For comparison, the US involvement in World War II lasted about 1340 days: "List of the lengths of United States participation in wars," Wikipedia, last updated October 20, 2023, https://en.wikipedia.org/wiki/List_of_the_lengths_of_United_States_participation_in_wars.

220 "Testimony of Allison G. Folsom, Lt. Col., USMC," *Hearings before the President's Commission on the Assassination of President Kennedy,* vol. 8, op. cit., pp. 303-11, at p. 311. https://www.aarclibrary.org/publib/jfk/wc/wcvols/wh8/pdf/WH8_Folsom.pdf.

221 My maternal grandfather won a "sharpshooter" medal while serving the czar (c. 1900). His color portrait, in a czarist uniform with his medal, appears in my hardcover book. Almost certainly, he would have been a better nominee than Oswald for the hit on JFK. Ironically, he was still alive and well in 1963. He was then eighty-seven years old and probably still could have matched Oswald on a real shooting range.

Unfortunately for him, his invention was scorned or ridiculed by almost everyone, including the FBI, the SS, J. Edgar Hoover, LBJ, Governor Connally, the autopsy pathologists, the government's top ballistics expert (Joseph Dolce), Connally's surgeons, and even half (three of six) of the WC commissioners themselves (Senator Richard B. Russell [D-GA.] Senator John Cooper [R-KY], and Congressman Hale Boggs [D-LA]).[222] In any case, J. Lee Rankin ensured that the three commissioners' dissent was scrubbed from the final report. Even today, especially every November, the American media still persistently cling to this myth, even though they are quite unable to defend it. Notice that they do not ask the FBI or the SS about the SBT.[223] And no one ever dares to ask them which bullet (of multiple possibilities) is the real Magic Bullet.

Virtually every Parkland physician recalled the large hole at the back of JFK's head, but none recalled the Red Spot in the autopsy photograph. Nor did the pathologists. Robert McClelland's recollection of a damaged cerebellum is particularly revealing. Furthermore, as many as nine Parkland doctors recalled this cerebellar damage even though the official brain photographs show only intact cerebellum.

Charles Crenshaw reported an entry wound in the high right forehead. This wound was also seen by others in Dealey Plaza and at Bethesda. The official autopsy photograph shows only an incision at this site, even though this incision was not seen in Dallas. Even J. Thornton Boswell described this site as an "incised wound," thereby implying that an incision had been made over a bullet entry site.

---

222 Gerald McKnight, *Breach of Trust,* op. cit., p. 283.

223 Even in November 2023, with ex-SS agent Landis in the news, they failed to take this opportunity to ask him why the SS has always denied the SBT.

2

THE MYSTERIOUS 6.5 MM OBJECT[1]

Who controls the past controls the future. Who controls the present controls the past.

—**GEORGE ORWELL**, *1984*[2]

Nothing tends so much to the advancement of knowledge as the application of a new instrument.

—**HUMPHRY DAVY**, president of the Royal Society (1820)[3]

---

1 Almost no JFK assassination articles are ever published in the peer-reviewed scientific literature, but my article was an exception. See: David W. Mantik, "The John F. Kennedy Autopsy X-Rays: The Saga of the Largest 'Metallic Fragment,'" Medical Research Archives, 2015, Issue 3, https://esmed.org/MRA/index.php/mra/article/view/177/78.

2 "1984 Quotes," Goodreads, https://www.goodreads.com/work/quotes/153313-nineteen-eighty-four.

3 Davy created the first incandescent light; discovered potassium (1807) and sodium; isolated barium, calcium, strontium, and magnesium; performed experiments on the photosensitivity of silver nitrate (which led to photography); and used laughing gas with wine to cure hangovers. But he claimed that his assistant, Michael Faraday, was his greatest discovery. Of course, his reference to a new instrument promptly reminded me of the optical densitometer, which had never before been used on the JFK X-ray films.

It is inconceivable that a secret arm of the government has to comply with all the overt orders of the government.

—JAMES JESUS ANGLETON[4]

The most dangerous and vicious of all forgeries are those committed in behalf of a cause—the cause of a nation, an institution, or a leader—and intended to bring about a permanent falsification of history.

—ALLAN NEVINS, *The Gateway to History*, 1938[5]

After securing permission from the Kennedy attorney, Burke Marshall, Dr. Mantik visited the National Archives on at least seven occasions [nine times, through 2001] to review and measure the autopsy photographs, the autopsy X-rays, JFK's clothing, and the ballistic evidence. Mantik's background as a radiation oncologist (certified by the American College of Radiology), together with his Ph.D. in physics (with a thesis on X-ray scattering) from the University of Wisconsin, make him uniquely qualified to address the conundrums of this exceptional case. No other individual with such strong credentials has ever reviewed this data. For the X-ray work, in particular, a background in medical physics (with an emphasis on X-rays) is essential. These skills would not be found in the ordinary radiologist, nor would a medical physicist, by himself, be competent to address the decisive medical issues that proliferate in this case. These talents—of physician and physicist—must be combined in a single individual, as fortuitously occurs with David W. Mantik. This case has long been waiting for such a synthesis.

—JAMES H. FETZER, PHD, *Murder in Dealey Plaza*, 2000[6]

---

4 Tim Weiner, *Legacy of Ashes: The History of the CIA* (New York: Doubleday, 2008), p. 336.

5 Allan Nevins, *The Gateway to History* (New York: D. Appleton-Century Company, 1938), p. 125. Nevins wrote the foreword to John F. Kennedy's *Profiles in Courage* (New York: Harper & Brothers, Publishers, 1956).

6 James H. Fetzer, PhD, "Editor's Note to Paradoxes of the JFK Assassination: The Medical Evidence Decoded," in *Murder in Dealey Plaza*, ed. James H. Fetzer, op. cit., p. 219.

Mantik's Book is the Final Word on JFK's Head Wounds: 2 shots from Right-Front, One from the Rear.... Dr. Mantik has provided medical evidence of a crossfire, and therefore of a conspiracy. So, all the old arguments of the Warren Commission supporters that "there were no shots from the front, because no frontal shots were mentioned in the autopsy report," can now be thrown into the dustbin of history. Equally as important, Dr. Mantik's conclusions about 3 head shots, and about the alteration of the extant skull X-rays, prove there was a massive government cover-up regarding how JFK was killed.

—**DOUGLAS HORNE**, book review, 2015[7]

ON OCTOBER 21, 1993, I arrived at the main entrance to the National Archives on Pennsylvania Avenue in Washington, DC. I was prepared to view the JFK assassination materials. "Archives I" is a monumental building that opened on the National Mall in 1927. It occupies an entire block, bordered on the north and south by Pennsylvania and Constitution Avenues and on the east and west by Seventh and Ninth Streets NW. Inside are our original founding documents—the Declaration of Independence, the Constitution, and the Bill of Rights.

Before entering the building, I stopped to admire Robert Aiken's statue of a youthful, classical woman sitting with a book open on her lap. Carved into the pedestal was the quotation from *The Tempest* by William Shakespeare: "What is past is prologue." I could only wonder if the JFK artifacts held any secrets about our nation's past.

7 Douglas Horne, book review of *John F. Kennedy's Head Wounds: A Final Synthesis—and a New Analysis of the Harper Fragment* by David W. Mantik, Amazon, August 9, 2015. Horne's comments were reprinted in my hardcover book, David W. Mantik, *The JFK Assassination Decoded: Criminal Forgery in the Autopsy Photographs and X-rays*, op. cit., in the first three unnumbered pages of the book.

Figure 2.1A (Left), 2.1B (Right)

Robert Aikens' Statues on Pennsylvania Avenue. 2.1A, Future Statue: "Study the Past." 2.1B, Past Statue: "What is Past is Prologue." National Archives I.

In 1994, "Archives II" opened in College Park,[8] Maryland to alleviate space restraints at Archives I on a parcel of land donated by the University of Maryland. After the JFK collection was transferred to Archives II, I visited the JFK materials there.

8 My wife attended high school and college near Silver Spring, so every fall for many years, we visited her parents to celebrate multiple birthdays, often in Williamsburg. Silver Spring is very close to College Park.

Figure 2.2
National Archives II. College Park, Maryland.

On that first visit, forensic pathologist Cyril Wecht, MD, JD, and I examined these materials. On subsequent visits, I carted an optical densitometer, a high-power microscope, and a stereo viewer. In 1993, I examined the JFK autopsy materials on four separate days (October 21–22 and 28–29); in 1994, I visited on two days (June 24 and October 7); and in 1995, I had two days (June 16[9] and October 20). These were all full days, from morning until late afternoon. The reviews included the autopsy photographs and X-ray films, JFK's clothing, the Magic Bullet (CE 399), and two tiny metal fragments removed from the skull. My ninth and last visit (another full day) was on April 12, 2001. By then, nearly six years had passed since my previous visit; during this long interval, the ARRB had come and gone. Based upon two new observations, that final visit turned out to be one of the most surprising of them all.[10]

---

9 While at the motel the day before this visit, I distinctly recall watching O. J. Simpson try on the gloves.

10 One new observation was a gross anomaly in an autopsy photograph. See the penultimate page of my hardcover book: *The JFK Assassination Decoded*, op. cit., "My Comment on the Autopsy Photo of JFK's Back."

During each visit, National Archives staff members directed us to an empty room with tables. After being seated, the staff carried the JFK materials into the room and placed them on a table before us. A National Archives employee, often Steven Tilley, then-director of the JFK collection, stayed with us while we viewed the materials. On some occasions, other Archives employees (e.g., Martha Murphy, Matt Fulgham, or David Painter) were present at the same time, often two at once. Employees always used cotton gloves while handling the JFK materials. The Archives personnel allowed me to handle the X-rays while making OD (optical density) measurements as long as I used gloves.

During my many hours at the Archives, the employees always paid full attention to me. Still, they were always careful to make no significant comments—even if I offered possible opportunities for them to contribute. We took a lunch break on full days, but usually took no other breaks. On several visits, colleagues examined these materials with me. On October 7, 1994, and October 20, 1995,[11] Gary Aguilar, MD, assisted in taking optical density data. Steve Majewski, PhD, now at the University of Virginia, joined me on October 7, 1994, and again on June 16, 1995. From his work on stars and galaxies, Steve is remarkably familiar with optical density measurements. The X-ray films are stored inside transparent plastic sheets. Typically, the Archives insist that visitors view them only inside these sheets. However, in 2001, when I needed to see the surface of the X-ray film directly, Steven Tilley was gracious enough to remove the X-ray films from their protective sleeves.[12]

---

11 A page from these notes appears in my hardcover book: *The JFK Assassination Decoded,* op. cit. See the last section of the reprinted e-book, *JFK's Head Wounds: A Final Synthesis—and a New Analysis of the Harper Fragment,* starting at p. 401, renumbered as pp. 1-92, at p. 40.

12 Note: X-rays are literally a form of electromagnetic radiation—they are not films coated with emulsion. Unfortunately, customary practice over decades has conflated the term "X-rays" to mean both electromagnetic radiation and the radiographs made from them. So also in this book, although the proper term ideally would be "X-ray films" (or even "radiographs"), we will sometimes use just "films," but at other times we might even use "X-rays." We are merely inheritors of our semantically muddled history.

In 1978, the HSCA obtained JFK's premortem skull X-ray film from the JFK Library in Waltham, Massachusetts. Anthropologists hired by the HSCA determined that the same person is in the premortem and postmortem X-ray films; they identified unique anatomical characteristics in the films that were identical. The HSCA also hired a forensic odontologist, Dr. Lowell Levine, who was experienced in the identification of persons killed in unnatural deaths. He determined that the dental characteristics of the JFK X-ray films at NARA matched the premortem dental X-ray films of JFK.[13] I agree with these conclusions.

THE JFK SKULL X-RAY FILMS: THE MAGICAL MATERIALIZATION OF THE LARGEST "METAL FRAGMENT"

My adventures in the JFK assassination began in earnest in 1992 shortly after Oliver Stone's movie, *JFK*, appeared. One morning, I sat down to breakfast with my seven-year-old son and my five-year-old daughter. (As usual, my wife, as director of the emergency department, was still in the hospital.) Over the preceding months, I had focused on JFK's X-ray films as published by David Lifton in his 1980 bestselling book *Best Evidence: Disguise and Deception in the Assassination of John F. Kennedy.*[14] Photo 32 in Lifton's book had captured my attention. Lifton identified this as HSCA Exhibit F-56, an anterior-posterior (AP) X-ray film of JFK's skull (digitally enhanced).

---

13 House Select Committee on Assassinations. "Section IV, Authenticity of the autopsy photographs and X-rays, Part II. Procedures in employed in examining the autopsy photographs and X-rays," in *Investigation of the Assassination of President John F. Kennedy, Appendix to Hearings Before the Select Committee on Assassinations of the U.S. House of Representatives*, vol. 7, (Washington, DC: U.S. Government Printing Office, March 1979), pp. 39-41.

14 David S. Lifton, *Best Evidence: Disguise and Deception in the Assassination of John F. Kennedy*, op. cit., photos 31 and 32, in the photo insert after p. 588.

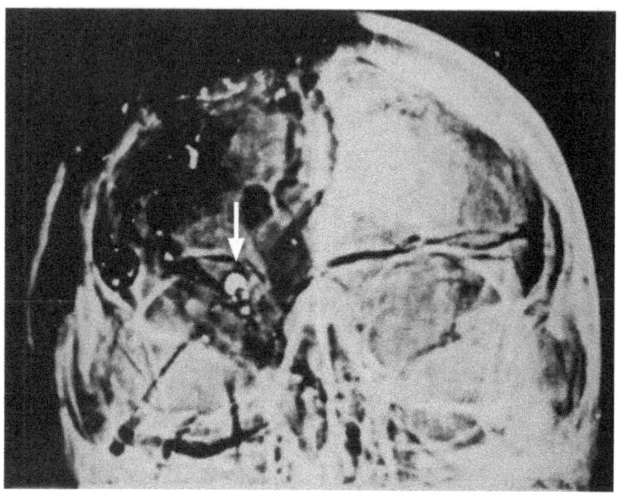

Figure 2.3

This is the anterior-posterior autopsy (AP) X-ray film, often abbreviated "AP." This view is also sometimes called a "frontal X-ray film." JFK was lying on his back. The film was placed directly behind his head, with the X-rays entering from the front. The arrow identifies the 6.5 mm object within JFK's right orbit.

As director of the radiation oncology department at Eisenhower Medical Center, my schedule permitted almost no free moments. So, I chose that brief interlude at the breakfast table to stare again at these puzzling images. I was particularly perplexed by the 6.5 mm object inside JFK's right orbit on the AP skull X-ray film. This (apparent) bullet cross-section was clearly the largest metal-like object in the X-ray films. But—under oath—none of the three autopsy pathologists could recall seeing it at the autopsy, nor did they remove it. Even more mysteriously (as I later discovered), that piece of "metal" is not in the National Archives.

Defenders of the pathologists have offered one absurd explanation after another for them. These excuses ranged from a suggestion that perhaps they actually had removed that bizarre 6.5 mm object from the back of the skull, even though they never described it in their autopsy report (Appendix J). On the contrary, they had only claimed to remove a much smaller metal fragment above the right frontal sinus (and an even tinier one adjacent to it), but not the large 6.5 mm object. Another defense is the inevitable psychological one—they felt so harassed that they couldn't see straight. Or perhaps, the large metal fragment had just fallen out of JFK's head before they could retrieve it. The problem was that the 6.5 mm object was preposterously obvious. Furthermore, the only reason to take these X-ray films was precisely to identify such metal fragments. Even worse though, of the dozens of eyewitnesses who observed these X-ray films on the view box that night, no one mentioned this object—nor did anyone recall any discussion of it. Because they were desperate to identify just such an object, the pathologists had even ordered *multiple sequences* of X-ray films! But the final embarrassing annihilation of their defense was this: the 6.5 mm object is absent from their autopsy report—and it has never been at the National Archives.

Humes confirmed to the HSCA that X-ray films had been taken prior to removal of any metal.[15] He also confirmed that the hair had not been washed before photographs were taken.[16]

At least one of the two radiology technicians (Edward Reed) confirmed that the lateral skull X-ray films had been taken *before* the AP X-ray film.[17] If so, and if the 6.5 mm object is truly metal, then someone sneaked a piece of metal onto JFK's skull between two successive X-ray film exposures!

The morticians washed JFK's hair in preparation for an open coffin. They confirmed that they did not locate any metal fragments during this process.

---

15 Humes: "Before the postmortem examination was begun, anterior, posterior, and lateral X-rays of the head, and of the torso were made..." See: "Testimony of Commander James J. Humes," *Hearings before the President's Commission on the Assassination of President Kennedy*, vol. 2, op. cit., pp. 347-376, at p. 349.

16 "Deposition of Dr. James Joseph Humes," corrected transcript, op. cit., at p. 156, www.aarclibrary.org/publib/jfk/arrb/medical_testimony/pdf/Humes_2-13-96.pdf.

17 Assassination Records Review Board. "Deposition of Edward Reed," in *In the Matter of Assassination Records Review Board in Re: President John F. Kennedy, Jr.*, (Washington, DC: Miller Reporting Company, Inc., 1997), pp. 31-42, https://history-matters.com/archive/jfk/arrb/medical_testimony/pdf/Reed_10-21-97.pdf. Reed also claimed to have seen the 6.5 mm fake object on the AP X-ray film that night. He is the sole autopsy attendant to make this claim (p. 85).

So, I decided it was time for a simple experiment. I began with Christopher, our seven-year-old.

"Christopher," I said, "Could you come here and find the bullet?" In a second, he was at my side. Without hesitation, he pointed straight at the 6.5 mm object. Now I wondered how far I could carry this, so I turned to our five-year-old, seated across the table; she had not seen Christopher point. "Meredith," I said, "Do you think you could find the bullet?" So, she marched around the table and looked at the image, momentarily puzzled. "Well, what's it supposed to look like?" she asked as she turned to look at me. When I told her that the bullet would look white in the film, there was only a momentary hesitation before she pointed directly at it and asked, "Is that it?" In summary, a five-year-old and a seven-year-old—neither trained in radiology—could easily spot this (supposed) bullet cross-section. But the WC would have us believe that three experienced pathologists, one radiologist, numerous ancillary medical personnel, and a crowd of onlookers had failed to spot this same object at the autopsy.[18] That such a prominent object in the X-ray film had gone unseen at the autopsy made no sense to me.

UNDERSTANDING OPTICAL DENSITY (OD)

Just as a stereo viewer can convert two-dimensional images into three-dimensional images, so also can optical density convert a 2D X-ray film image into a 3D data set.[19] In other words, the 3D information *latent*

---

18 This was clearly confirmed by Francis O'Neill, who saw "…every one of the X-rays." He clarified, "They didn't just show it [the AP skull film] to me, they took them and put them upon a dryer [sic] in that room, and they were all there and we were looking at them at the same time." Regarding the 6.5 mm object, O'Neill added that he did not recall it and "…it certainly wasn't pointed out to me." In addition, both O'Neill and Sibert adamantly rejected the SBT. See: William Matson Law, *In the Eye of History (*expanded second edition 2015), op. cit., pp. 305-306.

19 A hologram is also a 2D surface that can yield a 3D image. String theorists have even proposed that our universe can be understood as a hologram. See: Ethan Siegel, "Ask Ethan: Is our Universe a hologram?" Big Think, October 14, 2022, https://bigthink.com/starts-with-a-bang/universe-hologram/.

in any X-ray film can be extracted via optical density (OD) readings. Evidence of X-ray film forgery would be an OD value that is physically impossible, e.g., an area that is exceptionally transparent (white in prints) beyond reasonable expectations. For example, consider Figure 2.4, a 3D model of downtown Chicago, with an extremely tall building. This figure is an altered (i.e., forged) image of Chicago, with the bizarrely tall building (on the left side) created via a digital insert.

Figure 2.4
Altered 3D Image of Chicago with an Impossibly Tall Building.

This tall building mimics an anomalous OD value. Each Chicago building can be identified with a specific height. So also, each point on an X-ray film has a unique optical density number determined merely by measuring the transmission of light through that point on the X-ray film. Therefore, over the entire X-ray film, a highly detailed 3D bar graph could (in principle) be obtained for a single X-ray film. It would look a little like that 3D image of Chicago, but with greater detail. (No government investigation ever did this—even worse, they never even considered it.) Without scanning the entire film (likely disallowed by the Archives) a complete map is not possible, so instead I judiciously chose pertinent points on the skull X-ray films at the Archives.

Figure 2.4 is obviously altered—the building is impossibly tall. By analogy, if the optical density readings on the JFK X-ray films show impossibly deviant numbers, then we must suspect X-ray film alteration. After all, the physical world forces strict limits on possible images and so also on the corresponding OD values. This constraint will soon be discussed in detail, especially with respect to the 6.5 mm object inside JFK's right orbit. For details on how X-ray films were copied and could be altered in 1963, see Appendices C and D.

After sufficient data (actually hundreds of points), I eventually concluded that the three extant JFK skull X-ray films are copies, not originals. I also determined that all three skull X-ray films, although mostly authentic, have been altered at critical sites—most likely to suggest a single headshot from the rear. But before I explain how I arrived at these conclusions, a simple introduction to the science of optical density[20] will be useful. Understanding optical density is essential in order to grasp the undeniable evidence of JFK X-ray film forgery.

An X-ray film functions like a negative in print film photography. Air filled objects appear black on X-ray films because most of the X-rays pass through and strike the film. So, after development, the radiation-sensitive emulsion on the X-ray film (typically 95 percent silver bromide and 5 percent silver iodide) turns black—because during development the bromide (or iodide) has been converted to metallic silver, which remains on the

---

20 See appendix 10 in my review of John McAdams in my hardcover book: David W. Mantik, *The JFK Assassination Decoded*, op. cit., "How to Think Like John McAdams, pp. 159-184, at pp. 181-182. It contains a summary of the long history of optical density, including the noteworthy contributions of Arthur Haus, Kodak's (longtime) director of medical physics. I met Haus once in Los Angeles, and he read my article on the 6.5 mm object, which he found "very interesting."

film. Conversely, dense objects like bone (or metal) appear transparent on X-ray film (white in prints) because the bone blocks the X-rays from striking the X-ray film. When the X-ray film is developed, the silver salt is washed out, so the bone image looks transparent.

The mathematics and science of ODs may be complex for some readers. So too, the photographic techniques for forging X-ray films may appear complex. For those readers interested in a technical discussion of optical density, consult Appendix B.

For the purposes of this discussion, here are some simple rules:

A dense real-world object (like bone) blocks more X-rays. So, its image on the X-ray film appears transparent (white in print). A less dense real-world object (like an air cavity) blocks fewer X-rays, so its image on the X-ray film appears opaque (black in print).

In summary:

a transparent image on the X-ray film = an opaque real-word object (e.g., metal or bone);

a black image on the X-ray film = a transparent real-world object (e.g., air).

Let's use Figure 3.1 as an example.[21] The air around the skull is very black (e.g., I measured an optical density of about four). On the

---

21 This discussion is drawn from the following sources: (1) David W. Mantik, MD, PhD, "The JFK Assassination: Cause for Doubt," in *Assassination Science*, ed. James H. Fetzer, op. cit., pp. 93-139, at pp. 124-125 and (2) David W. Mantik, MD, PhD, "Were the John F. Kennedy Autopsy X-rays Altered?," in *Assassination Science*, op. cit., pp. 120-137. For a video demonstration of how optical density readings of X-rays are taken, see: X-Ray Education, "Optical Density April 2021," April 19, 2021, https://www.youtube.com/watch?v=3-E-_Am7Vfo.

other hand, the 6.5 mm object looks very white in print (transparent on the film at the Archives), which implies an exceptionally long piece of metal (from front to back). Its OD was a little over 0.5. On a lateral X-ray film, the area around the ear canal (the petrous bone) is white (in prints) because it is the densest bone in the body. Simply by glancing at a film, a radiologist quickly recognizes the tissues encountered by X-rays on their path. For example, a radiologist would promptly recognize the 6.5 mm object as a long piece of metal (from front to back). He would also realize that the very dark areas inside the skull represent a significant loss of brain, with its replacement by air.

Let's try a simple analogy: picture a road sign in a dense fog. For an X-ray, bone (or metal) acts like fog. So, a white area in an X-ray print means that the X-ray has transited a bone (or metal), thus obscuring other tissues on that same path. Vice versa, in the *absence* of bone, the intervening tissue becomes much easier to identify. So also, the road sign is easy to see in the *absence* of fog (analogous to mostly air in the X-ray scenario).

Now picture your twin in the same scenario, but he is standing alongside, in the sunshine well out of the fog, where he can see both you and the road sign. So, he can see how thick the fog is between you and the sign. Meanwhile, you can also see where the fog is thickest—because that's where the sign is obscured. You could even develop a scale (somewhat analogous to OD) for measuring how much fog existed in your line of sight—a scale simply based on how clear the sign was. Your twin in the sunshine, on the other hand, is like someone viewing the 6.5 mm object from the side (i.e., the lateral X-ray film)—because on that view he can see with his own eyes exactly how long the metal fragment is (from front to back). Now, on the AP X-ray film, you can measure the ODs and then calculate how *long* (front to back) this 6.5 mm (wide) object should be. But on the lateral film (like your twin), you can actually see how long it is; no calculation is needed. These two numbers should agree closely—unless, of course, the 6.5 mm object was a forgery and yielded impossible results.

The optical density at any point is simply calculated from the transmission of light through that point. Blacker objects in the film (e.g., air) represent transparent real-world objects, so they have higher optical density numbers (e.g., 2.0–4.0). Dense real-world objects (e.g., bone) have low ODs (0.5–1.5) because X-rays are blocked from the X-ray film. A satisfactory clinical range of ODs for an X-ray film is about 0.5–4.0. Objects whose ODs lie well outside this range (especially when compared to known objects in the film) are forgery suspects, like the ludicrous Chicago skyscraper (Figure 2.4).

One last point: in the JFK-era, X-ray film had emulsion on both sides. The 1941 book *Photographic Emulsion Technique*, explained why:

> The fact that only a low proportion of the incident rays is absorbed both by the intensifying screen [a sheet of celluloid coated with calcium tungstate that increases the emulsion's ability to absorb incident X-rays][22] *and* emulsion, led to the idea of coating film base with emulsion on both sides, when two intensifying screens could be used, one on either side of the double coated film.[23]

In other words, double emulsion films reduced the required X-ray exposure by one-half, which was a major safety feature for patients.

Let's summarize all of this:

> *A dense object (like a bone) blocks X-rays from striking the X-ray film. So, the silver salt emulsion is unaffected, and development removes the silver salt, leaving X-ray film transparent. The OD will then be low*

---

22 By themselves, X-rays make negligible impact on an X-ray film. It is only via the use of intensifying screens that images become feasible. These screens convert X-rays into light, to which the film is sensitive. Therefore, these screens decrease patient exposure times. Since shorter exposures are required, motion blur (from patients' movement) during exposure is also decreased.

23 T. Thorne Baker, *Photographic Emulsion Technique*, (Boston, MA: American Photographic Publishing Co., 1941) pp. 128-137, at p. 131. Emphasis in original.

(e.g., 0.5–1.5), and the radiologist will promptly suspect bone or metal. But he does not actually require an OD measurement; his eyes are trained to do this by visual inspection alone. Interpreting an X-ray requires thinking in reverse (bones are transparent; while air cavities are black), but radiologists subconsciously understand X-ray films as negatives.

In Table 2.1, we can now summarize how to interpret an X-ray film.

Real-World Object	Real-World Density	X-Ray Quality	Appearance on the film	OD Range
Bone or Metal	Dense Blocks X-Rays	Radio-opaque	White	0.5 to 1.5
Air Cavity	Not Dense Transparent to X-rays	Radiolucent	Black	2.0 to 4.0

Table 2.1
How Real-World Objects Translate into OD Ranges

There are "five basic radiographic densities: air, fat, water (soft tissue), bone, and metal. Air is the most radiolucent (blackest) and metal is the most radiopaque (whitest)."[24]

Optical density measurements are surprisingly simple to make. The densitometer is just a light source, aimed at a photoelectric cell.[25] After calibrating this small device (Figure 2.5), the film is placed on

---

24 Wendy Myer, "Radiography Review: Radiographic Density," *Veterinary Radiology & Ultrasound*, 18:5 (September 1977), pp. 138-140, https://onlinelibrary.wiley.com/doi/abs/10.1111/j.1740-8261.1977.tb01339.x#:~:text=The%20five%20basic%20radiographic%20densities,the%20most%20radiopaque%20(whitest).

25 While at the Archives, I noticed that they had their own densitometers. While viewing the extant JFK X-ray films, Dr. Mike Chesser used one of theirs for his OD data.

the surface. A light source shines through a tiny hole. (The size can be decreased a lot, as I did in these experiments.) The desired point on the film is placed directly over the light source; the arm is pushed down to make tight contact with the film (to exclude all outside light). The detector measures how much light gets through the film, and the device converts this to optical density units.

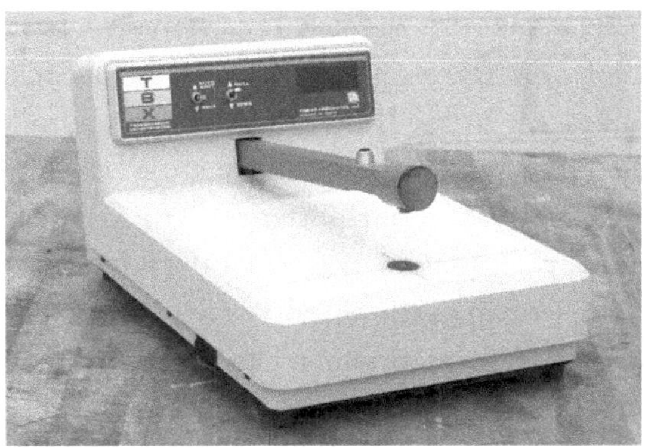

Figure 2.5
Tobias Optical Densitometer.

I used a model TBX optical densitometer from Tobias Associates of Ivyland, Pennsylvania; as delivered, it measures transmission through one-millimeter diameter circles. The device calculates the optical density directly from this transmission. No special effort is required by the experimenter. To assess reproducibility, I measured many sites repeatedly on successive days. This precision was within 1 or 2 percent, with the main uncertainty being due to manual positioning within the required one millimeter. I made nearly 400 individual measurements during October 1993 alone. Hundreds of additional data points were collected on subsequent visits, some with much smaller apertures. The work was tedious, especially across the 6.5 mm object, where more than *sixty-five* measurements were required for a complete graph, using intervals of only 0.1 mm.

A built-in control knob was employed at frequent intervals to zero (i.e., calibrate) the densitometer. Calibration against external reference film strips of known optical density was quickly and easily achieved across the observed OD range. The Small Systems Group, Inc. of Chico, California, supplied these reference strips. The densitometer was found to be both very stable during the measurements as well as consistent with respect to these external reference calibrations.

PROOF: THE MAGICAL LARGEST "METALLIC FRAGMENT" IS A FORGERY

In January 1969, the (Ramsey) Clark Panel finally released its long-awaited (1968) review of the JFK autopsy. That report described a 6.5 mm (nearly circular) cross section of an apparent bullet fragment inside JFK's right orbit on the anterior-posterior (AP) X-ray film (Figure 2.3 above).[26] Curiously, although it was by far the largest metal-like object, it had *not* been described in the autopsy report. In fact, this was its first appearance in history. Furthermore, it had not been removed during the autopsy—and it does not exist at the Archives today—even though the sole point of the X-ray films had been precisely to collect such objects for forensic purposes.

26 "1968 Panel Review of Photographs, X-Ray Films, Documents and Other Evidence Pertaining to the Fatal Wounding of President John E Kennedy on November 22, 1963 in Dallas, Texas," MD 59 – Clark Panel Report, ARRB Master Set of Medical Exhibits, Assassination Archives and Research Center, https://www.aarclibrary.org/publib/jfk/arrb/master_med_set/md59/html/Image00.htm.

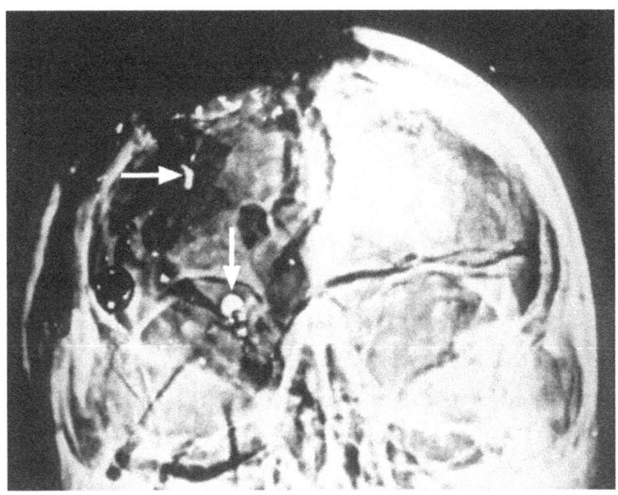

Figure 2.6
JFK's AP Skull X-ray Film.
The vertical arrow identifies the 6.5 mm object, which was not seen at the autopsy. The horizontal arrow identifies the 7 x 2 mm metal fragment, which was removed at the autopsy.

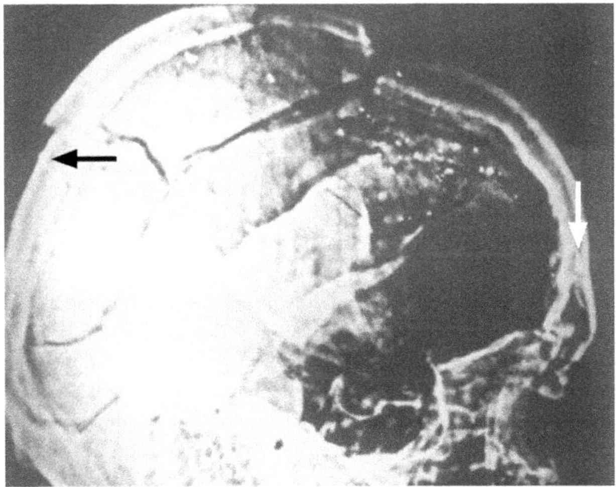

Figure 2.7
JFK's Lateral X-ray Film
The horizontal black arrow identifies the very faint (supposed) partner image of the 6.5 mm object. This authentic fragment was not removed at the autopsy. The vertical white arrow identifies the 7 x 2 mm metal fragment, which was removed at the autopsy. There is no evidence in this image for the 6.5 mm object (seen on the AP film).

The AP X-ray film (Figure 2.6) shows a nearly circular, 6.5 mm, very white object (in prints) within the upper right orbit. At the four to six o'clock sector, however, a portion is missing. On the AP film, this object is overwhelmingly the most impressive metal-like object. That was easily confirmed by my children. (They would have had more trouble with the lateral X-ray film.) On this AP film, there is another small piece of metal (7 x 2 mm); it lies directly above the right frontal sinus. The pathologists always refer to this one when asked about the largest metal fragment—they did remove it, and it was subjected to several scientific tests.[27] It is labeled at the Archives. Reference to this fragment is also found in the FBI 302 report by Sibert and O'Neill (see Appendix I):

> X-Rays of the brain area which were developed and returned to the autopsy room disclosed a path of a missile which appeared to enter the back of the skull and the path of disintegrated fragments could be observed along the right side of the skull. The largest section of this missile as portrayed by X-Ray appeared to be behind the right frontal sinus. The next largest fragment appeared to be at the rear of the skull at the juncture of the skull bone.[28]

---

27 From Michael Griffith: "CE 843 consists of three [metal] fragments that were supposedly removed from JFK's skull during the autopsy. However, these fragments look nothing like the fragments that Dr. James Humes said he removed from the skull and that appear on the autopsy skull x-rays. The 7x2 mm fragment is plainly visible on the AP x-ray, and it looks nothing like any of the fragments seen in CE 843. Moreover, Humes said he only removed two fragments, one 7x2 mm and the other 3x1 mm, not three." See: Michael Griffith, "CE 843: "Proof of Fraud in the JFK Autopsy Evidence," EducationForum.ipbhost.com, September 27, 2023, https://educationforum.ipbhost.com/topic/29690-ce-843-proof-of-fraud-in-the-jfk-autopsy-evidence/.

28 Francis X. O'Neill, Jr. and James W. Sibert, "Autopsy of Body of President John Fitzgerald Kennedy," Gemberling Version, ARRB Master Set of Medical Exhibits, November 26, 1963, op. cit., p. 4, https://www.history-matters.com/archive/jfk/arrb/master_med_set/md44/html/Image3.htm.

In the following discussion, for clarity—and simplicity—I shall label this authentic metal fragment at the back of the skull (on the lateral X-ray film, Figure 2.7) as SOF (Sibert-O'Neill Fragment). They described it as lying at the back of the skull (See Appendix I).

This small fragment (near the cowlick) is scarcely visible in prints, but it was much easier to see on the X-ray film at the National Archives. On this lateral view, it is about the same height as the 6.5 mm object on the AP film, but it is at most only 4 mm long (from front to back), as measured directly on the lateral X-ray film. It is thicker at the bottom than at the top.

THE PUZZLE OF THE LARGEST (6.5 MM) "METAL" FRAGMENT

In his five-volume masterpiece about the ARRB, Douglas Horne described the curious 6.5 mm object:

> In this anterior-posterior (front-to-rear) skull x-ray, there is an image of what appears to be an extremely radio-opaque, or dense (i.e., lucent) object seen on the x-ray which is purported to represent a metallic fragment—a cross section of the accused assassin's bullet as it entered the back of JFK's skull, and then lodged on the outside of his cranium, slightly below the purported entry wound in the bone. (This is the interpretation of both the Clark Panel and the HSCA's medical panel.) As seen on the AP skull x-ray, this purported bullet fragment is the brightest single object in the image, and therefore represents the densest object depicted in the anterior-posterior skull x-ray—it stands out "like a sore thumb." It is nearly circular and is about 6.5 mm in diameter.[29]

Horne implies that the 6.5 mm object is impossibly bright (transparent); its OD is far too low (way too much metal), which strongly

---

29 Douglas Horne, *Inside the ARRB*, op. cit., vol. 1, p. 49.

suggests a forgery. By analogy with our 3D Chicago example, this 6.5 mm object (if authentic) should appear impossibly long on a lateral X-ray film (Figure 2.8).

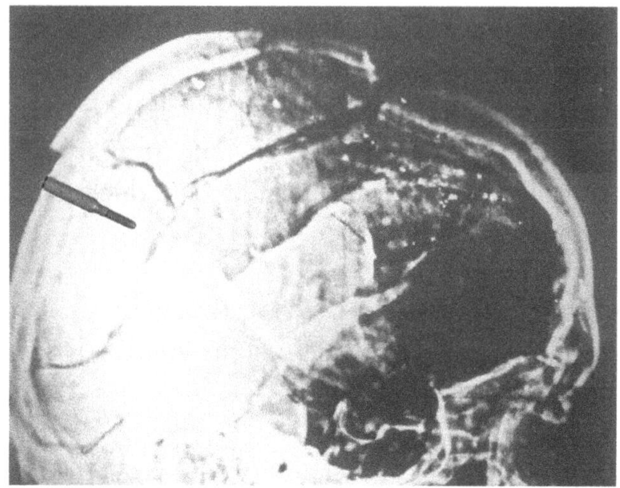

Figure 2.8
This is an analogy to the forged Chicago skyscraper. The predicted, but physically impossible, front-to-back length of the 6.5 mm object is superimposed on the lateral X-ray film. This prediction is strictly based on the ODs measured on the AP X-ray film. I prepared this digital insert purely for this analogy.

If this largest "metallic fragment" is so flagrantly obvious, how exactly did three competent pathologists overlook it during the autopsy? And why did John Ebersole, MD, the autopsy radiologist, abruptly stop discussing the autopsy with me when I asked him about this?

Horne continued, puzzling that no such object was ever recovered from President Kennedy's body at the autopsy (emphases are Horne's):

> The trouble is, no such fragment was ever recovered from the President's body at the autopsy; and yet the primary purpose for taking x-rays during the autopsy was to assist in recovering bullets and bullet fragments from the body! So, if the apparent bullet fragment on the A-P x-ray of the skull was so bright, *why was no such*

> *fragment recovered from the body*, and why was this obvious evidence of an apparent bullet fragment in the A-P x-ray *not mentioned in the autopsy report?* Were the prosecutors and the attending radiologist, Dr. Ebersole, simply incompetent—or could the apparent bullet fragment on the A-P x-ray be an *artifact* placed intentionally on the x-ray *subsequent to the autopsy?* That is, could the "fragment" be part of a *forgery* designed to incriminate Lee Harvey Oswald? (Oswald's [supposed] 6.5 mm carbine had been found on the sixth floor of the Texas School Book Depository building in Dealey Plaza, the site of the assassination.)[30]

Horne noted that a 6.5 mm carbine had (eventually) been found on the sixth floor of the TSBD.[31] His suspicion was that the 6.5 mm object was later inserted into the AP X-ray film by forgery, in order to create "evidence" that would tie metal in JFK's skull to Oswald's *supposed* 6.5 mm Mannlicher-Carcano weapon.

To further confound the mystery of the 6.5 mm object, during 1994–1998, each of JFK's three pathologists were asked (under oath) by the ARRB if they had seen this during the autopsy. Each one (independently) denied that they had. As an example, here is how Humes responded to Jeremy Gunn's questions in his deposition, as described by Horne (who was there), before the AARB on February 13, 1996:

---

30 Douglas Horne, *Inside the ARRB*, vol. 1, op. cit., p. 49.

31 Ibid., vol. 4, pp. 1102-1106.

The original TSBD rifle was reported as a 7.65 mm Mauser bolt-action with a scope, not a 6.5 mm Mannlicher-Carcano. Dallas County Deputy Constable Seymour Weitzman and Dallas Sheriff's Deputy Eugene Boone found it. For an early article on the substitution of the Mannlicher-Carcano for the initially found Mauser, see Walter F. Graf and Richard R. Bartholomew, "The Gun That Didn't Smoke, Part One," JFK Lancer Productions & Publications, *The Assassination Chronicles*, Spring 1997, pp. 20-38, jfk.hood.edu/Collection/Weisberg%20Subject%20Index%20Files/R%20Disk/Rifle%20Mauser%20Etc/Item%2001.pdf.

See also: Raymond Gallagher, "When Did Oswald order the Rifle?" *Probe Magazine*, September-October 1998, jfk.hood.edu/Collection/Weisberg%20Subject%20Index%20Files/S%20Disk/Shots%20Placement/Item%2006.pdf.

GUNN: [presents Humes with the AP skull X-ray] Dr. Humes … I'd like to ask you whether you have previously seen that x-ray. [See Figure 2.6 in this book.]

HUMES: I probably have. It's [the] anterior-posterior view of the skull and jaw.

GUNN: Did you notice what at least appears to be a radio-opaque fragment during the autopsy?

HUMES: Well, I told you we … retrieved one or two, and—of course, you get distortion in the x-ray as far as size goes. The ones we retrieved I don't think were of the same size as this would lead you to believe. [Humes is discussing the 6.5 mm, nearly circular, transparent image.]

GUNN: Did you think they were larger or smaller?

HUMES: Smaller. Smaller, considerably smaller … [Humes' curiosity was aroused. You could see it in his eyes.] … I don't remember retrieving anything of that size.

GUNN: Well, that was going to be a question, whether you had identified that as a possible fragment and then removed it.

HUMES: Truthfully, I don't remember anything that size when I looked at these films. They were more the size of those others. [By this time, Humes is perplexed.]

GUNN: What we're referring to is a fragment that appears to be semicircular.

HUMES: Yeah. I don't know.[32]

When the HSCA (in the 1970s) asked Humes about the largest metal fragment, he unhesitatingly referred to the fragment above the right frontal sinus. He never did discuss this 6.5 mm object on the AP X-ray film that is unequivocally at the back of the skull (as determined from the lateral view).[33] When Gary Aguilar, MD, more recently asked assistant pathologist J. Thornton Boswell about this fragment, Boswell also only described the fragment above the right frontal sinus. And he clearly added that all the other metal fragments were very small, distinctly smaller than the 7 x 2 mm fragment above the right frontal sinus. Boswell made no mention at all of the most obvious 6.5 mm metal-like object on the AP film.

There is wide agreement that the partner image (on the lateral X-ray film) of this mysterious 6.5 mm object must lie at the rear of the skull (near the cowlick area—Figure 2.7). However, when the forensic radiologist, Dr. John J. Fitzpatrick (as the premier expert for the ARRB—and actually the premier expert for every government investigation) reviewed the X-ray films, he remained forever puzzled by this 6.5 mm object. In fact, he was so perplexed that he returned for a second day to try to extract its secrets. Ultimately, he failed in this task, as he admitted:

> No object directly and clearly corresponding to the bright, 6.5 mm wide radio-opaque object in the A-P X-Ray could be identified by the consultant on the lateral skull X-Rays. Although there is a mere trace of some additional density near the fragment bilocation at the vertex of the skull, the consultant did not feel this object was anywhere

---

32 Douglas Horne, *Inside the ARRB*, op. cit., vol.1, pp. 52-53. The comments in brackets are by Douglas Horne.

33 From the WC: "Interview of Drs. James J. Humes and J. Thornton Boswell by the Forensic Pathology Panel, Subpanel of Doctors Had Not Reviewed the Autopsy Materials Previously," in *Appendix to Hearings Before the Select Committee on Assassination of the U.S. House of Representatives Ninety-Fifth Congress Second Session,* vol. 7, addendum I, op. cit., p. 251.

> near the density/brightness required for it to correspond to the bright, radio-opaque object on the A-P X-Ray. After briefly speculating that the small metallic density behind the right eye in the lateral X-rays Might correspond to the bright radio-opaque density in the AP X-Ray, this idea was abandoned because neither the locations nor the density/brightness of the 2 objects are consistent.[34]

For all practical purposes then, after this *failed* attempt (by the most appropriate specialist for the task) this 6.5 mm object became the most curious—and unsolved—mystery in the history of diagnostic radiology.

During the lifetime of the HSCA, Larry Sturdivan served as its ballistics consultant. In his subsequent 2005 book *JFK Myths,* he emphasized that he had never, in his entire career, seen a cross section of a bullet deposited in such an odd fashion on a skull.[35] So, totally contrary to all prior government investigations, he concluded that the 6.5 mm object could *not* be a metal fragment (emphasis in the original):

> I'm not sure what that 6.5 mm fragment is. One thing I'm sure it is NOT is a cross-section from the interior of a bullet. I have seen literally thousands of bullets, deformed and undeformed, after penetrating tissue and tissue simulants. Some were bent, some torn in two or more pieces, but to have a cross-section sheared out is physically impossible. That fragment has a lot of mystery associated with it. Some have said it was a piece of the jacket, sheared off by the bone and left on the outside of the skull. I've never seen a perfectly round piece of bullet jacket in any wound. Furthermore, the fragment seems to have great

---

34 Horne, "ARRB staff report of observations and opinions of forensic radiologist Dr. John J. Fitzpatrick, after viewing the JFK autopsy photos and X-rays, February 6-7, 1996," *Inside the ARRB*, Appendix 44, p. 225, https://www.maryferrell.org/showDoc.html?docId=145280#relPageId=224.

35 Larry Sturdivan, *JFK Myths: A Scientific Investigation of the Kennedy Assassination* (St. Paul, MN: Paragon House, 2005), pp. 192-194.

> optical density thin-face on [the AP X-ray] than it does edgewise [on the lateral X-ray].... The only thing I can think is that it is an artifact.[36]

This was a radical statement. After all, the HSCA, in particular, had relied on the metallic authenticity of this fragment in the most fundamental manner: the HSCA's scenario claimed that a bullet had deposited this 6.5 mm "metal fragment" at the back of the skull. So now, if this was merely an artifact, what was to become of the HSCA's conclusion?

Roy Kellerman of the SS (who sat in the right front seat of the limousine during the shooting) was interviewed by Jim Kelly and Andy Purdy of the HSCA at the Holiday Inn North in St. Petersburg, Florida on August 24-25, 1977. He said that the skull X-ray film showed a "... whole mass of stars, the *only large piece* (emphasis added) being behind the eye, which was given to the FBI agents when it was removed."[37] Since it was the 7 x 2 mm fragment that was removed, the implication is clear—Kellerman, like everyone else, knew nothing about the much larger 6.5 mm object. It is surely odd ("extraordinary" might be a more accurate adjective) that none of the government panels (prior to the ARRB) had ever asked the four autopsy physicians (three pathologists and one radiologist) whether they had seen this 6.5 mm object during the autopsy.

Shortly before his death some decades ago, I asked the radiologist, John H. Ebersole, MD, about that 6.5 mm object (during telephone conversations of November 2 and December 2, 1992). At the instant of that question, the entire interview came to an abrupt halt—so my question remained forever unanswered. My tape recording of that interview has now been donated to the National Archives. Anyone can play it for

36 The quotation is from an email that Larry Sturdivan sent to Stuart Wexler on March 9, 1998.

37 This is from the HSCA. "Memorandum: Interview with Roy Kellerman," MD 56: Kellerman-Purdy HSCA Interview, ARRB Master Set of Medical Exhibits, August 24-25, 1977, https://www.history-matters.com/archive/jfk/arrb/master_med_set/md56/html/Image0.htm.

themselves.[38] It has some other interesting moments concerning the JFK autopsy; unfortunately, Ebersole died shortly afterwards.

The 6.5 mm object is not cited in the 1964 *Warren Report* nor in its accompanying twenty-six volumes. Moreover, the X-ray films had not been introduced to the WC. The Commission, however, did conclude that both the nose and the tail of this (supposedly same) bullet had been found inside the presidential limousine (WC Exhibit Numbers 567 and 569—see Figure 5.17).[39] In other words, this 6.5 mm "metal fragment" supposedly represented an internal cross section from the *inside* of that *same* bullet, which was deposited onto the back of the skull (near the supposed entry site at the cowlick area—Figure 2.7). And then the nose and tail of that same bullet transited the entire skull and finally came to rest inside the limousine!

But how is it possible for a nearly complete cross section from inside a bullet to embed itself on the outside of the skull? In his forty years' experience with weapons of all types, firearms examiner and ballistics expert Howard Donahue never saw a nose fragment from a full metal-jacketed bullet embed itself in this manner, let alone a cross section from inside a bullet.[40] Furthermore, this (supposed) fragment is not at the HSCA's entry site—in fact, it lies one centimeter *inferior* to their chosen entry site! So, how does a metal fragment migrate one centimeter below its supposed entry site and then *embed* itself into the skull—while the nose and tail of this same bullet continue blissfully on through the brain? It seemed to me as if someone had invented clever

---

38 My transcript of this telephone conversation is in *Murder in Dealey Plaza* (2000). See: David W. Mantik, MD, PhD, ed., "Conversation with John Ebersole, MD, of 2 December 1992," in *Murder in Dealey Plaza,* ed. James Fetzer, Appendix E, op. cit., pp. 433-439.

39 "Commission Exhibit 567" and "Commission Exhibit 569," *Hearings before the President's Commission on the Assassination of President Kennedy*, vol. 17, op. cit., p. 256.

Also see: David Lifton, *Best Evidence*, op. cit., p. 92. Of course, if the two metal fragments derived from two different bullets, that would automatically mean conspiracy. The WC surely did not want to go there.

40 Bonar Menninger, *Mortal Error: The Shot That Killed JFK* (New York: St. Martin's Press, 1992), p. 68.

bullets before the smart bombs of the Gulf War. Needless to say, no one has ever explained this queer migration (and the odd termination of the nose and tail)—but that is the official story. How often do we hear that from the media every November?

The eyewitness testimony, therefore, is unanimous—this 6.5 mm object was not seen at the autopsy. It first appeared in the historical record with the release of the Clark Panel review in January 1969. But this is astonishing: the pathologists had become aware of it at least one year earlier—*before* the Clark Panel report! After all, they had seen this 6.5 mm object during their November 1966 DOJ review—but they never mentioned it! Even worse, they had rested their collective heads inside a guillotine—their signed document claimed that *no large metal fragment* existed on the X-ray films! Here is their official statement:

> *No other wounds.*—The X-ray films established that there were small metallic fragments in the head. However, careful examination at the autopsy, and the photographs and X-rays taken during the autopsy, revealed no evidence of a bullet or of a major portion of a bullet in the body of the President and revealed no evidence of any missile wounds other than those described above.[41]

We now know that the alteration of the three extant skull X-ray films was completed during 1963. Ebersole testified to the HSCA that "sometime within a month of the assassination," a member of the White House medical staff, Navy Captain James Young, telephoned him and asked him to review the JFK autopsy skull X-ray films to assist with measurements for a sculptor's bust of Kennedy. Ebersole testified that in taking the measurements, he drew some lines on the films.[42] At the

---

41 "Other autopsy considerations," Appendix to Hearings Before the Select Committee on Assassination of the U.S. House of Representatives Ninety-Fifth Congress Second Session, section 5, part 3, vol. 7, op. cit., p. 136.

42 Douglas Horne, *Inside the ARRB*, op. cit., vol. 2, pp. 556-561.

Archives, I observed the two pencil lines that Ebersole drew. They appear on only *one side* (emulsion is on both sides) of the lateral X-ray film. That is a critical observation—these pencil lines are not on the opposite side. Therefore, these must be the same films that Ebersole saw and penciled. If they had been copied since then, I would not have been able to see the distinct pencil lines on only one side, so we know that they have not changed since then. I believe the Ebersole episode was designed to appraise his reaction to the forgery—after all, the official excuse of needing Ebersole's help with a Kennedy bust was baloney. I have previously noted that Ebersole was either very tongue-in-cheek about this episode or else he was astonishingly naïve.[43] I favor the former.

Logically, it made more sense that this 6.5 mm object had later been superimposed onto the X-ray film. There is a particularly good reason why someone might want to do that. The weapon attributed to Lee Harvey Oswald was a 6.5 mm Mannlicher Carcano—exactly the same caliber as this fake object. Furthermore, Oswald had supposedly shot JFK from the TSBD, which was behind Kennedy. Therefore, since this bullet fragment was the right size and it was (apparently) located at the back of the skull, we were supposed to believe that Oswald did it.

AT THE NATIONAL ARCHIVES

At the Archives, I was ready to explore the 6.5 mm object (seen only on the AP film). On prints of the lateral X-ray film, the small metal fragment at the back of the skull, the supposed partner image (called SOF in the present discussion) of the 6.5 mm object, is scarcely visible. See the arrow in Figure 2.7. To my eye, SOF (on the lateral film) was about the same height as the 6.5 mm object, but it was visibly only 3-4 mm long (i.e., from front to back). The other lateral X-ray (not available to the public) excludes several centimeters of the posterior skull, so SOF cannot be seen there. On both the AP X-ray film and the two

43 David W. Mantik, MD, PhD, "The President John F. Kennedy Skull X-rays: Regarding the Magical Appearance of the Largest 'Metal' Fragment," in *Assassination Science*, ed. James H. Fetzer, postscript, op. cit., pp. 120-139, at p. 135.

lateral films, a second, much smaller, object (7 x 2 mm) lies directly above the right frontal sinus. I discuss this authentic fragment later. The pathologists removed it.

I first focused on the lateral X-ray film. Over its center, I scanned SOF from top to bottom, at 0.1 mm increments (Graph 2.1). What was quite surprising to me was how little the ODs changed from just outside this object (where bone was present) to inside the object. This meant that it must be quite thin (from left to right). This was unexpected; after all, on the AP X-ray film I could see with my eyes that it was supposedly 6.5 mm thick (from left to right). So immediately, I had encountered a serious paradox. More puzzles were soon to follow.

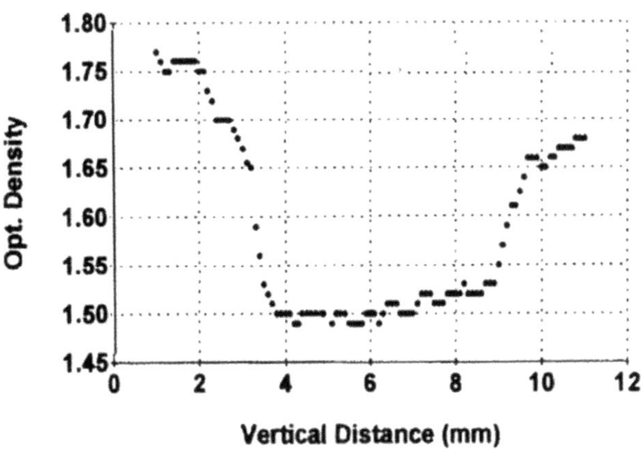

Graph 2.1

JFK Lateral Skull X-ray Film: SOF. This is the supposed partner image of the 6.5 mm object. Vertical scan: superior to inferior.

Next, on the lateral X-ray film, I took three more OD sequences over SOF. Instead of going vertically, this time I traversed horizontally. First, I focused on the center of SOF, again taking ODs at 0.1 mm intervals. As seen in Graph 2.2, the ODs progressively decreased from back to front, meaning that SOF was thicker at the front.

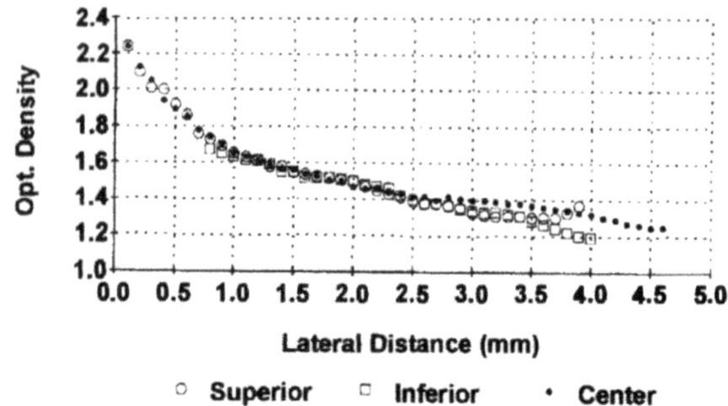

Graph 2.2

JFK Lateral X-ray Film: SOF—The Supposed Partner Image of the 6.5 mm Object. Three horizontal scans: posterior to anterior.

An almost identical result occurred with a similar scan across the top of SOF. But the bottom yielded a surprise. Here I expected less metal (i.e., higher ODs)—after all, I could see (on the AP X-ray film) that a bite had been removed at the four to six o'clock sector. But that is not what the ODs showed. Instead, all three scans were almost identical! The OD graph from the bottom (inferior) should lie well *above* the other two graphs, by at least one OD unit (and possibly more). The near identity of these three scans proclaims (quite loudly) that *no bite* has been removed from the four to six o'clock sector! But our eyes can obviously see that "metal" is missing on the AP X-ray film. Such an inconsistency is impossible in the world that we know. Objects cannot magically change their sizes and shapes merely because we view them from different perspectives. This is just one more proof that the 6.5 mm object (on the AP film) is a fake. (On the other hand, SOF is authentic—no one bothered to alter it.) And so, because the 6.5 mm object is a fake, *it is impossible for it to be consistent with its so-called partner image* (SOF) on the lateral film. But at the Archives, more radiographic and photographic surprises were still lurking for me.

I concluded that the metal fragment at the back of the head (in the lateral X-ray film) was genuine, but very thin. Since small fragments cannot travel far in tissue, SOF had probably resulted from a rear entry. Obviously, the forger did not alter the lateral view so that it would match the AP view—but he should have done this. He was merely careless.

I next turned to the AP view and scanned across the center of this 6.5 mm object, going from right to left (Figure 2.3). This scan tells us that there is more metal (quite a lot more) on the right side than on the left side. (By "right" and "left," I always refer to JFK's left and right sides.) That was a little odd, of course, because the object initially had looked round and uniform.

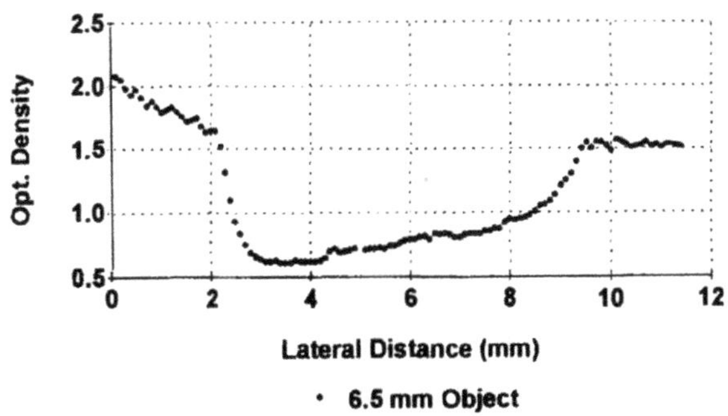

Graph 2.3
JFK AP X-ray Film: 6.5 mm Object. Horizontal scan: JFK's right to JFK's left.

Next, I removed my eyeglasses and just stared at the 6.5 mm object. I was then extremely nearsighted, so that without my eyeglasses I could easily see splinters in my children's fingers. (My son just reminded me of this—I was the designated splinter-remover, even though my wife was the director of the emergency department.) To my amazement, I could actually see that this 6.5 mm object was not merely a single image, but it was rather a composite. On the far right-side (JFK's right) of this object I could see a distinctly *separate* and smaller crescent-shaped metal fragment; its right border almost perfectly matched the right border of the 6.5 mm object. The width (left to right) of this separate (real world) fragment was only 2.5 millimeters maximum. Its medial borders were mostly irregular and ragged, as shrapnel often is. Additionally, I could even see at least one (additional) minuscule metal fragment *inside* the 6.5 mm object; this was separate from the crescent-shaped fragment. There were even tiny metal fragments just outside the 6.5 mm object. These latter pieces were so small, however, that I hadn't seen them in prints. And I could see (with my own eyes— via the phantom effect) that the bottom of this real-world, crescent-shaped fragment was definitely wider than the top. This is exactly what the ODs had also confirmed. I suddenly understood—I was seeing the original shrapnel (SOF) at the back of the skull *through* the superimposed 6.5 mm object. And what I saw was completely consistent with all of my measured ODs. In fact, this was the same fragment (SOF) that James Sibert and Francis O'Neill had described in their FBI 302 report. So, we had seen the same authentic fragment.

I was seeing a *phantom* effect—the result of a double exposure. This was only possible for me because I was then extremely myopic (-8.75 diopters). [44] It appeared that the forger had positioned the 6.5 mm image to precisely match the (anatomic) right border of the authentic metal fragment. In particular, by doing so, he had guaranteed that the 6.5 mm image would not be left without a partner image on the lateral

---

44 This observation (of a phantom effect) was confirmed on April 22, 2015 by Dr. Mike Chesser (a neurologist) during his own visit to the JFK X-rays at the National Archives (personal communication to author). Using an optical densitometer supplied by the Archives, he also measured the ODs of the 6.5 mm object, the petrous bone, and the posterior White Patch (more later about this patch). Results for these ODs are in excellent agreement with mine. That no one else has reported this phantom effect is not surprising—because "high" myopia is quite rare; only 4 percent of the general population is more myopic than -5.0 diopters. But at -8.75 diopters, my myopia was well beyond "high." Almost certainly, for this particular observation, Dame Fortune had not smiled on any government radiologist as generously as she had on me. And so, like Socrates, I owe a cock to Asclepius, the ancient god of health (for giving me such extreme myopia).

X-ray film. On the other hand, if he had not matched the 6.5 mm image to an authentic metal fragment, the 6.5 mm object would have risked no partner image on the lateral X-ray film, and the forgery would have been obvious to one and all.

Creating double-exposure images is a well-known Hollywood technique, often utilized to place an actor into a fictitious background. In his splendid 1965 book *The Technique of Special Effects Cinematography*, Raymond Fielding reports that a typical outcome of superposition special effects is the "phantom" effect, in which background detail can be seen through an actor. Fielding explained as follows:

> Mention has also been made of the "superimposition" of foreground action over background scenes through double exposure and double printing. Such techniques produce a "phantom" effect, however, in which background detail can be seen through the body of an actor.[45]

Likewise, if a photographic superposition process in the darkroom had produced this 6.5 mm object, that would explain the double images (of the authentic, crescent-shaped fragment and the inauthentic 6.5 mm object). As carefully as I could, I then sketched the real shrapnel; that sketch is still in my notebook (Figure 2.9). But on the AP film, the OD scan through the 6.5 mm object also tells us (Graph 2.3) how much shrapnel (relatively speaking) there was on the original X-ray film. The 6.5 mm object, since it was faked, is most likely uniform in OD, so any OD inhomogeneities across this object (on the AP film) are likely due to the overlapping original shrapnel. The OD graph shows just what I saw with my eyeglasses off—the authentic metal is almost completely on the right side (JFK's right) of the 6.5 mm object.

---

45 Raymond Fielding, *The Technique of Special Effects Cinematography* (Waltham, MA: Focal Press, 1985), fourth edition, p. 177.

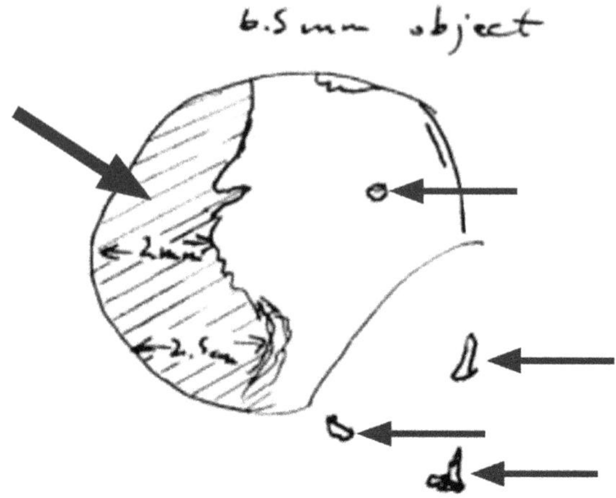

Figure 2.9

My magnified sketch of the 6.5 mm object, as drawn at the Archives. The crescent-shaped (cross-hatched) area represents the authentic fragment—the real one (SOF) that lay at the back of JFK's skull (*Assassination Science*, p. 127, Figure 4). Scattered tiny metal fragments are identified by horizontal arrows, including one (paradoxically) inside the 6.5 mm object.

EXPERIMENTING WITH A 6.5MM MANNLICHER-CARCANO BULLET

When I got home, I realized that I had to do an experiment: What would a real 6.5 mm metal fragment look like on an authentic human skull—and what would the OD scan look like? I already had a 6.5 mm Mannlicher-Carcano bullet—someone had given me one. It was time to sacrifice it. I sawed off about 3 mm of the base; lead was obvious in the bullet (Figure 2.10).

Figure 2.10
Sawed-off Mannlicher-Carcano Bullet.

From previous experiments, I already had several authentic human skulls. So, I taped this bullet fragment to the back of the skull, just like in the autopsy X-ray films (Figure 2.11). I adjusted the skull position under fluoroscopy until it precisely matched the autopsy X-ray films and then I took a lateral X-ray film (Figure 2.12). It looked remarkably similar to the autopsy film: the bullet cross section was in the right spot, and it overlapped the skull bone exactly right.

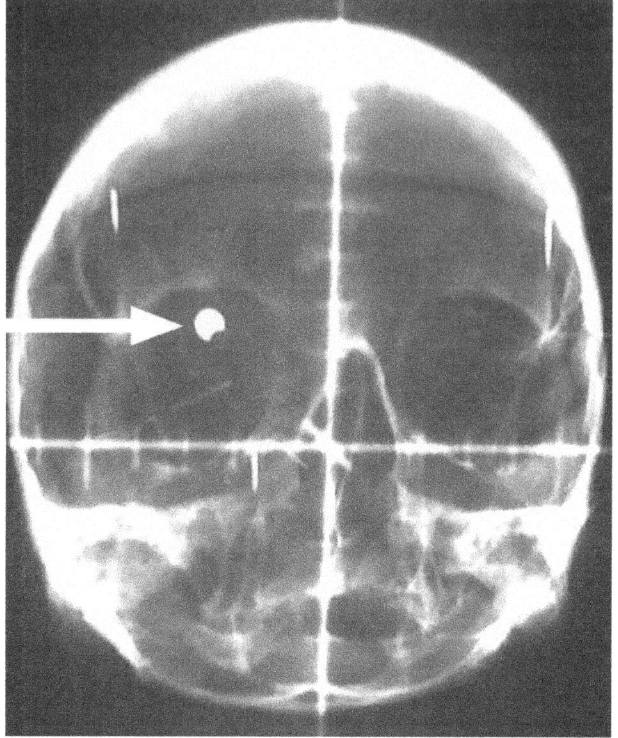

Figure 2.11

An AP X-ray film of an authentic (empty) human skull, showing the cross section (4 mm thick—from front to back) of an authentic 6.5 mm bullet. Its location is remarkably similar to Figure 2.3.

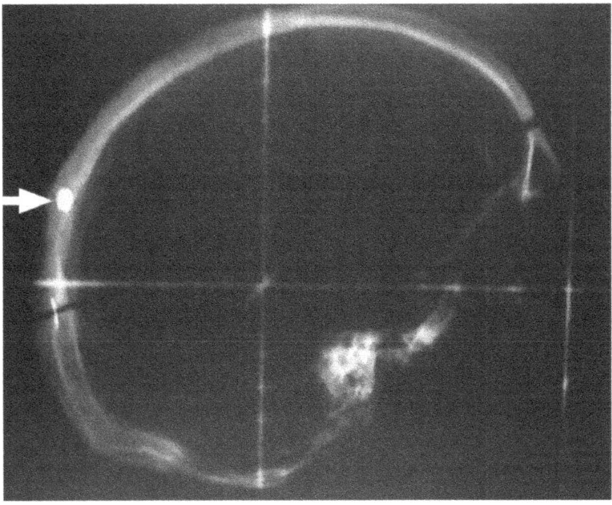

Figure 2.12
Lateral X-ray film of an authentic (empty) human skull, showing the cross section of an authentic 6.5 mm bullet. An authentic cross section should have been visibly obvious in JFK's lateral X-ray film (see Figure 2.7).

This comparison was quite striking. This comparison provides powerful, essentially conclusive, evidence that *the 6.5 mm object cannot be authentic.* In fact, the data are entirely consistent with its subsequent addition in the darkroom. On the lateral JFK X-ray film, whereas the OD of the tiny metal fragment at the back of the skull (SOF) was almost the same as the background bone (it was only about 0.2 OD units different), the OD of the real metal cross section (in my fluoroscopy suite) was almost 1.5 OD units different from the background (Graph 2.4).

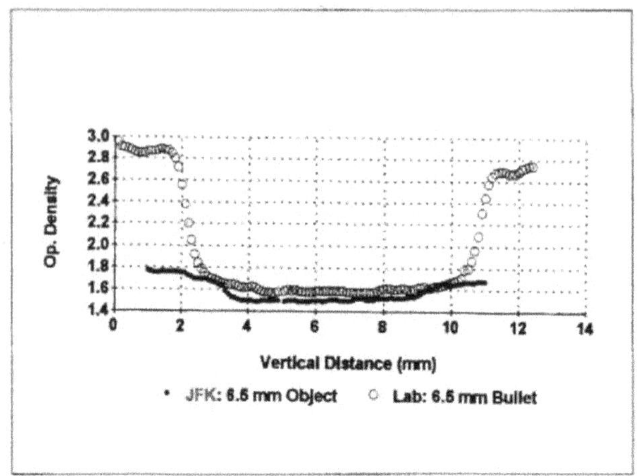

Graph 2.4

Lateral X-ray Films. JFK 6.5 mm object vs. authentic 6.5 mm bullet. Vertical Scans: superior to inferior.

This was an enormous difference: it meant that the image of the real metal transmitted over ten times as much light as the area right outside of it—but the autopsy image (SOF) did not even transmit twice as much light as the area just outside of its borders. That's why it was so hard to see in the prints. This experiment confirmed what I had already learned at the Archives. On the lateral X-ray film, a real 6.5 mm piece of metal should look much more transparent (or whiter in prints) than the object (SOF) on JFK's lateral X-ray film. On the autopsy film, it was real enough, all right, but it was very thin (left to right)—just as Sibert and O'Neill had reported, and just as I had seen (via the phantom effect) with my naked (and very myopic) eyes on the AP film.

The only viable explanation for the 6.5 mm object is this: it is indeed an artifact, one that was <u>deliberately</u> superimposed (in the dark room), directly over a pre-existing, authentic metal fragment (SOF) that lay at the back of the skull, and which is barely visible in Figure 2.7.

This explanation accounts for all of the mysteries of the 6.5 mm object. In particular, its diameter was deliberately chosen to match the caliber of a 6.5 mm bullet. It was intentionally placed directly over a preexisting (very small) metal fragment—so that it would be spatially consistent. An (inattentive) overexposure led to its remarkable transparency (and so also to its bizarre ODs). Furthermore, the timing of this superposition—shortly after the autopsy—explains why no one saw it that night. Finally, it certainly can explain why the radiologist, Dr. John Ebersole, refused to discuss this artifact with me. After all, he was the single individual most likely to possess the required expertise and creativity to perform X-ray alteration. In fact, we have no other reasonable candidate.

AN OD COMPARISON OF JFK'S DENTAL FILLINGS WITH THE 6.5 MM OBJECT

Next, I looked at JFK's teeth. These are not displayed in this book—but they were published by the HSCA.[46] They are trivial to see on the X-ray films at the Archives. JFK had extensive dental repairs; except for the incisors and canines, he had metal fillings almost everywhere. Most of these amalgams were probably inserted during his pre- and early adult years and typically would have been composed of nearly equal parts of mercury and silver. Both of these elements have high atomic numbers and therefore naturally appear transparent on an X-ray film. On the AP film, these amalgams mostly overlap one another—they are like a slab of mercury and silver many centimeters long. These dental amalgams can serve (in a relative sense) as a superb measuring ruler for other metal objects on the same film. In particular, the 6.5 mm object (on the AP X-ray film) had an OD of about 0.6, which suggested that it was very thick (from front to back).

But now, I wondered: how did the OD of the 6.5 mm object compare to the dental amalgams? As I expected, these amalgams were quite

---

46 Lowell J. Levine, "Report to the Select Committee on Assassination, US House of Representatives: Identification of the Skull X-ray Films Taken During the Autopsy of President John F. Kennedy," in *Appendix to Hearings Before the Select Committee on Assassination of the U.S. House of Representatives Ninety-Fifth Congress Second Session,* The Warren Commission, section 4, addendum B, vol. 7, op. cit., pp. 53-68.

transparent on the film. On the AP film, the ODs were about 0.78 on the right; on the left, they were about 0.74 (Table 2.1).

Object	OD	Apparent Length*	Actual Length**
6.5 mm	0.60	very long	3-4 mm
amalgams	0.74, 0.78	long	30-40 mm
7 x 2 mm	1.44	short	2 mm

*from front to back
**as seen on the lateral view

Table 2.1
ODs on the AP X-ray film.

These ODs all imply *less metal* (front to back) for the amalgams than for the 6.5 mm object! How could that be? How could the 6.5 mm object be longer (front to back) than all of those dental amalgams superimposed on one another? On the lateral film, I could see with my eyes that SOF (the supposed partner image of the 6.5 mm object) was only 3-4 mm thick (from front to back). That was clearly much, much thinner than all of those superimposed dental fillings—by almost a factor of ten! But this made no sense at all. On the other hand, of course, if someone had simply overexposed this 6.5 mm object, then that paradoxical result would not be surprising.

The remarkably low ODs (on the AP view) of the 6.5 mm object now remind us of that impossibly tall Chicago building. These low ODs imply that the 6.5 mm fake should be many centimeters long (from front to back). However, we can see with our eyes (from SOF on the lateral view) that it is actually *only a few millimeters long* (from front to back). In other words, we face a discrepancy of almost ten-fold—which is grossly impossible in our known physical universe.

There was one last question: on the lateral view, how did the ODs of the teeth compare to ODs of SOF? And here, again, there was nothing remarkable, which in itself, was convincing evidence that SOF had not been altered on the lateral X-ray. The ODs of the teeth are about 1.00 (Table 2.2). This implies less metal from right to left than from front to back. Of course, this is expected, since we see only one amalgam on the lateral, whereas on the AP film, we see four or more overlapping amalgams.

Object	OD	Apparent Width*	Actual Width**
6.5 mm	1.50	thin	2-3 mm
amalgams	1.00	wider	10 mm
7 x 2 mm	1.60	thin	2 mm

*from right to left
**as seen on the AP view

Table 2.2
ODs on the Lateral X-ray Film.

We have already seen that (on the lateral film) the ODs of SOF are about 1.5, so the amalgams must contain much more metal (from left to right) than SOF. But we can see with our eyes that SOF is not really 6.5 mm wide—it is really only 3 mm wide (or 4 mm at the very bottom). As seen with the naked eyes on the AP view, the dental amalgams are significantly wider (from left to right) than SOF, so the ODs of the amalgams and SOF are completely consistent with each other. After all, they should be—no one altered either SOF or the amalgams. We are dealing here with the known world—not fakes.

THE OD OF THE 7 X 2 MM FRAGMENT VS. THE 6.5 MM OBJECT

Next, recall that the pathologists actually removed two metal fragments from the skull. On the AP view, the larger of these (7 x 2 mm) has an OD of 1.44 (Table 2.1), a much higher OD than the 0.60 for the 6.5

mm object *on the same film.* These widely differing ODs suggest that the 6.5 mm object is, by far, the longer of the two (from front to back). But on the lateral X-ray, we can actually see that their true thicknesses (from front to back) are nearly identical! So, this makes no sense either.[47]

On the lateral view, the OD of the 7 x 2 mm fragment was 1.6 (Table 2.2). This is compelling evidence that the 7 x 2 mm fragment was real—after all, its ODs on the lateral and AP were consistent with one another. Furthermore, they were also consistent with what I saw with my naked eyes. So this real fragment behaved quite differently from the 6.5 mm fake. After all, authentic objects obey real-world physical laws. On the other hand, fake objects are completely lawless.

FORGERY: INDISPUTABLE PROOF

The evidence for X-ray film alteration is now overwhelming. But there is even more to come. All lines of evidence point in the same direction, and it is all self-consistent. To make this obvious, let's summarize:

1. On the lateral film, the supposed partner image of the 6.5 mm object (SOF) measures much thinner (left to right) by the OD data than a comparable slice from a real Mannlicher-Carcano bullet. This disagrees radically with the visible width of the 6.5 mm object on the AP film.

2. On the AP film, a superposition of images inside this 6.5 mm object is evident to the naked (and very myopic) eye: one image is the genuine bullet fragment (SOF) described by Sibert and O'Neill, while the second image is the 6.5 mm phantom added later in the darkroom.

---

47 I had to be sure, of course, that overlapping tissue within the skull (on the AP view) did not confound this conclusion. I was able to assure myself that this was not a problem by obtaining OD data just outside of these objects and also by correlating the lateral and AP views.

3. On the AP film, the OD scan across this 6.5 mm object is entirely consistent with the visual image seen by the myopic eye: the authentic metal fragment lies on the right side of the 6.5 mm object.

4. On the lateral film, the OD data over the supposed partner image of the 6.5 mm object (SOF), shows no less metal over the inferior pole than at the center or at the superior pole. But on the AP film, we can see with our eyes that a sizeable portion of the 6.5 mm object is missing at the four to six o'clock sector. In our known physical universe, this absent metal must be detectable via ODs on the lateral view. But this is not the case, so reality bites again.

5. On the AP film, the ODs of the 6.5 mm object confirm that it is longer (front to back) than all of the (four-plus) dental amalgams superimposed on one another. That is a pure farce.

6. On the lateral film, the ODs of the supposed partner image (SOF) of the 6.5 mm object imply that it is much thinner (front to back) than just one dental amalgam. This is, of course, to be expected since the fragment on the lateral film is authentic; this real metal was only 2-3 mm wide (right to left). But the length (back to front) of SOF is not supposed to be only 2-3 mm—if we believe the ODs of the 6.5 mm fake on the AP film.

7. On the lateral film, the ODs of the supposed partner image (SOF) of the 6.5 mm object are similar to the authentic 7 x 2 mm fragment—as they should be for authentic fragments of similar width (just several mm right to left)). This is consistent with the FBI report, but it is totally inconsistent with the visible 6.5 mm wide object on the AP film.

8. On the AP film, by the OD data, the 6.5 mm object is astonishingly longer (front to back) than the 7 x 2 mm fragment, even though the unaided eye can see (on the lateral film) that they are nearly the same length (front to back).

The OD evidence is completely self-consistent—besides, we know that the 6.5 mm object was absent from the original AP X-ray film. It was added later—and quite certainly not by the pathologists. We can be sure of that because each of the three pathologists was quite flummoxed when they first saw this 6.5 mm fake on the AP X-ray film. I would be captivated to view a video recording of the autopsy personnel meeting (in 1968) with the four doctors from the Clark Panel (if only it existed).[48] During that encounter, the Clark Panel demanded even more serious explanations from the autopsy doctors, but the panel[49] refused

48 Then-Attorney General Ramsey Clark headed the Clark Panel. The Justice Department chose four medical experts to review the JFK autopsy evidence in 1968. The four Clark Panel pathologists were William H. Carnes, MD, professor of pathology, University of Utah; Russell S. Fisher, MD, a Baltimore medical examiner; Russell H. Morgan, MD, the head of the radiology department at Johns Hopkins University, and Alan R. Moritz, MD, professor of pathology at Case Western Reserve University. The Clark Panel report elevated the entrance wound at the back of JFK's head by ten centimeters (approximately four inches) from the pathologists' entry site. The HSCA later agreed with the Clark Panel report. The 6.5 mm object first appeared in history with the Clark Panel. See: HSCA. "1968 Panel Review of Photographs, X-ray Files, Documents and Other Evidence Pertaining to the Fatal Wounding of President John F. Kennedy on November 22, 1963 in Dallas, Texas," MD 59: Clark Panel Report (2/26/68), ARRB Master Set of Medical Exhibits, Assassination Archives and Research Center, https://www.aarclibrary.org/publib/jfk/arrb/master_med_set/md59/html/Image00.htm.

49 The Clark Panel included four physicians, but just one radiologist, Russell Morgan. In the Clark Panel report, Morgan agreed with the *Warren Report*, i.e., just one headshot from the rear. However, immediately before JFK's X-ray films became public (September 1977—during the HSCA), Morgan, with impeccable timing, essentially *recanted* his earlier opinion, and implied that the fragment trail across the top of the skull was *not* consistent with a Mannlicher-Carcano bullet! Of course, his timing was ominous—he clearly knew that non-government radiologists would promptly recognize that these metal fragments could not derive from a Mannlicher-Carcano bullet. He was merely trying to save his own skin. For the newspaper article about Morgan's near confession, see my hardcover book: David W. Mantik, *The JFK Assassination Decoded: Criminal Forgery in the Autopsy Photographs and X-rays*, op. cit. See the last section of

to believe the autopsy doctors. Instead, the panel chose to believe the radiographs and photographs—even though these items had no chain of possession. Even more amazing, the Clark Panel did not know that the chain of possession for the photographs was missing.[50] That decisive information was only discovered by the HSCA in the 1970s.

In summary, the X-ray films were treated with a sacred reverence by the government agencies (the HSCA, especially)—as if they were as solid as the Rock of Gibraltar. (Quite bizarrely, that is exactly how former President Gerry Ford, my neighbor in Rancho Mirage, epically described the *Warren Report* itself.) The attitude of the Clark Panel and the HSCA was that witnesses could lie or could be mistaken, but that autopsy X-rays and photographs would never mislead. Therefore, if the X-ray films and photographs disagreed with the witnesses, wasn't it obvious that the witnesses must be wrong?

Before proceeding, we now embark on a brief historical detour. Although the first photographic forgery was produced in 1840, physicians (but especially lawyers) in the 1960s presumed that X-ray films could never be altered. But now we know better.

In 1840, Hippolyte Bayard, a largely unrecognized inventor of film photography, created a photograph (Figure 2.13) that depicted his body in a French morgue, supposedly after suicide by drowning. Bayard forged the photograph to make a political statement; he was protesting the official disregard of his photographic experiments. Even in these earliest days of photography, Bayard realized that a forged photograph could convey a powerful message, but he also recognized that a photograph could lie for effect.[51]

---

the reprinted eBook, *JFK's Head Wounds: A Final Synthesis—and a New Analysis of the Harper Fragment*; for Morgan, view page x.

50 Gary L. Aguilar, MD, and Kathy Cunningham, "How Five Investigations into JFK's Medical/Autopsy Evidence Got It Wrong," part 5, op. cit.

51 "The First Faked Photograph (1840)," *Open Culture*, October 22, 2019, https://www.openculture.com/2019/10/the-first-faked-photograph-1840.html.

Figure 2.13
The First Forged Photograph: Hippolyte Bayard in the Morgue. This depicts a staged suicide by drowning (1840). Source: Hippolyte Bayard, *Self Portrait as a Drowned Man*, 1840, public domain.

Six decades after Bayard, one of my favorite composites appeared: Nikola Tesla, surrounded by his high voltage arcs (Figure 2.14). The Tesla image, by photographer Dickenson V. Alley, appeared in the December 1899, *Century Magazine*. Alley had created a double exposure of Tesla calmly reading in his Colorado Springs laboratory (near NORAD's current location).

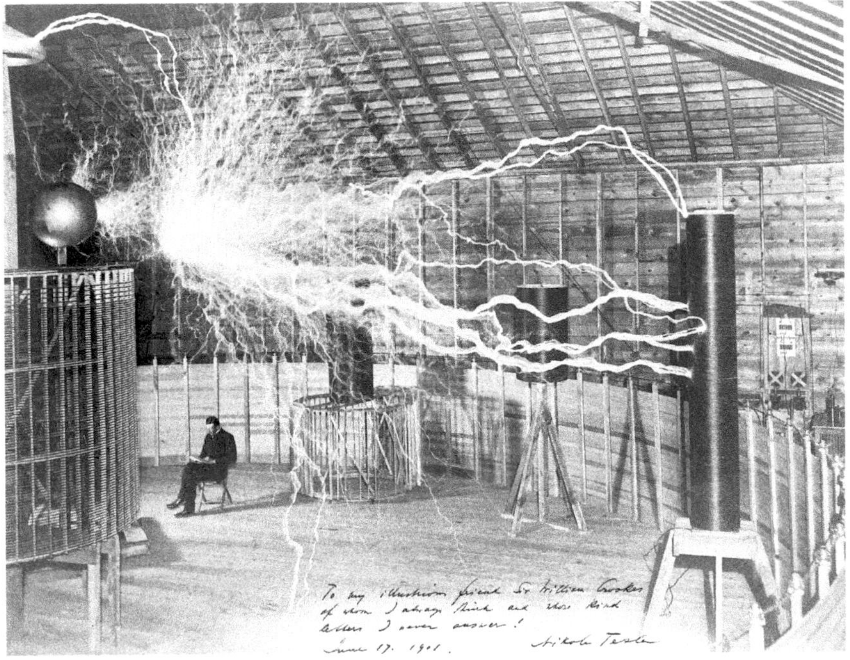

Figure 2.14

Double Exposure of Nikola Tesla, Colorado Springs Laboratory, December 1899. Source: Dickenson V. Alley, *Nikola Tesla, with his equipment for producing high-frequency alternating currents*, December 1899, Wellcome Collection, https://wellcomecollection.org/works/sq2828s9, licensed for reproduction under CC BY 4.0, https://creativecommons.org/licenses/by/4.0/.

So now, at last, we can explain how it was done. Sometime soon after the autopsy, the original X-ray films were taken into the darkroom. A 6.5 mm hole was cut into a simple piece of cardboard. Most likely, a perfect circle would have looked too suspicious, so a sector was not removed. Then the original film was exposed onto a duplicate X-ray film. But before this duplicate film was developed, it was exposed one more time. This time just the cardboard template was placed over the duplicate film so that light could only pass through this 6.5 mm hole. After development then, that specific site on the duplicate film looked very transparent, just like the 6.5 mm object.

So, the pathologists were right, after all. They really hadn't seen that

6.5 mm object at the autopsy. The forger had to be clever, however. If he had simply placed a counterfeit image onto the AP film haphazardly, most likely it would not have been spatially consistent on the two views, and the forgery would have been obvious even to an amateur. But by using an authentic, pre-existing metal fragment, Mother Nature solved the problem for him. He did not bother to alter the lateral—there was no need to (or so he thought). All he had to do was add the fake 6.5 mm image precisely over the preexisting shrapnel (SOF) that the FBI had reported. Mother Nature had already located this image on each film consistently with 3D reality, so the forger had no decisions to make. In fact, a small army of expert radiologists has noticed no paradox with the *locations* of SOF (on the lateral film) versus the location of the 6.5 mm object (on the AP film). But traditional radiologists are never asked to think about X-ray forgery.[52] Of course, in retrospect, it would be interesting now to ask the radiologists about the phantom image—i.e., being able to see the original shrapnel through the 6.5 mm object. Without high myopia, however, they would have to use a jeweler's loupe to see the authentic shrapnel, but they would then be quite stunned by the phantom image. However, even that might not be fair because traditional radiologists are not experts in special effects cinematography.

OPTICAL DENSITY ANALYSIS: THE SINGLE MOST IMPORTANT PIECE OF SCIENTIFIC EVIDENCE IN THE JFK ASSASSINATION

In volume 2 of his five-volume anthology, *Inside the Assassination Records Review Board*, Douglas Horne devoted a section to my work:

---

52 Of Rembrandt's six-hundred-plus officially listed paintings, about half may be forgeries. This was initially disclosed by X-ray analysis. Unfortunately, both forensic pathologists and forensic radiologists seem ignorant of this. They should take a Rembrandt tour in Amsterdam. More recent work has used AI along with the concept of entropy, see Margo Anderson "Amateurs' AI Tells Real Rembrandts From Fakes," IEEE Spectrum, April 25, 2019, https://spectrum.ieee.org/the-rembrandt-school-of-ai-an-algorithm-that-detects-art-forgery.

"The Crucial, Ground-Breaking Work of Dr. David Mantik with the Autopsy X-Rays in the National Archives Using Optical Density (OD) Measurements as an Analytic Tool."[53] Horne concluded that I had contributed "more to the study of the autopsy materials than any person to date." He explained (emphasis in original):

> I say this because he examined the original skull x-rays in the National Archives extensively (in 1993 and 1994), and he did so by taking an extremely large number of *empirical measurements* with an optical densitometer—empirical measurements represented by numbers, which can be checked by others who might wish to replicate his experiments and check on his findings.[54]

Horne understood that OD readings were determined by the laws of physics. He further expounded:

> The renowned British Physicist Sir Arthur Eddington once said that all true scientific evaluations are based upon numbers (i.e., empirical data acquired from precise measurement of the natural world), and. if you are not dealing with numbers, you are not doing science. Well, for those critics who may disparage the large extent to which the many controversies and conclusions in the JFK medical evidence depend upon eyewitness testimony and eyewitness recollections, I can emphatically say this: Dr. Mantik's work and conclusions are based 100 percent upon meticulously recorded numerical empirical data that are repeatable, and therefore subject to thoroughgoing outside peer review. It is true assassination science, in the very best sense of the word.[55]

---

53 Douglas Horne, *Inside the ARRB*, op. cit., vol. 2, pp. 541-553, at p. 541.

54 Ibid., p. 541.

55 Ibid.

Gregory Henkelmann, MD, a physics major and a current radiation oncologist in Baton Rouge and Covington, Louisiana, is a member of the Southeast Louisiana Radiation Oncology Group. Henkelmann has practiced radiation oncology for some thirty years. He has commented insightfully on my OD studies:

> Dr. Mantik's optical density analysis is the single most important piece of scientific evidence in the JFK assassination. Unlike other evidence, optical density data are as "theory free" as possible, as this data deals only with physical measurements. To reject alteration of the JFK skull X-rays is to reject basic physics and radiology. Dr. Mantik has a PhD in physics and has practiced radiation oncology for nearly 40 years; he is thus eminently qualified in both physics and radiology. His unusual background exposes the government-sponsored coverup that has deceived Americans into believing that Oswald was a "lone wolf." It is now past time to be crying wolf.[56]

William Keough, PhD, is a longtime medical physicist at the Edinburgh Cancer Centre in Scotland. Here is his Amazon review of my hardcover book, *JFK Assassination Paradoxes: Essays and Reviews & JFK's Head Wounds*:

> His [Mantik's] logical and scientific approach refutes the many inconsistencies that officials have promulgated as fact since the 22nd of November 1963. From the 6.5 mm metallic fragment in the AP autopsy X-ray to the "black rectangle" patch on the back of President Kennedy's skull identified in the copy of the Zapruder film, to name

56 Henkelmann's comments were reprinted in my hardcover book: David W. Mantik, *The JFK Assassination Decoded: Criminal Forgery in the Autopsy Photographs and X-rays*, op. cit., in the first three unnumbered pages of the book. An abbreviated version from Henkelmann appears on the back cover of that book.

> a few.... Although the majority of Americans still do not believe the Warren Commissions' fairy tale, only a limited number of people will be in a position to evaluate the overwhelming scientific and medical evidence that supports a different narrative.

Cyril H. Wecht, MD, JD, is one of the world's foremost forensic pathologists. Here is his Amazon review of my hardcover book:

> David Mantik's prodigious compilation volume...is a truly magnificent work of precision and expertise. His detailed analysis of JFK's head wounds is excellent. What he has accomplished in compiling this very special book is astounding.[57]

Michael Z. Chesser, MD, is a former primary care physician for the navy, who has subsequently been a neurologist for over thirty years in private practice and academics. He became interested in the JFK assassination in 2013, after reading *JFK and the Unspeakable* by James Douglass.[58] In 2015, and again in 2017, Chesser received permission to view the JFK autopsy X-ray films at the National Archives.[59] In 2017, he presented his findings. Regarding the 6.5 mm object, Chesser independently confirmed my findings:

---

57 Cyril H. Wecht, MD, JD, book review of *JFK Assassination Paradoxes: Essays and Reviews & JFK's Head Wounds*, by David W. Mantik, Amazon, October 30, 2022, https://www.amazon.com/JFK-Assassination-Paradoxes-Essays-Reviews/product-reviews/B0BCCVTM1T. This was the original title of what subsequently was published as David Mantik, *The JFK Assassination Decoded*, op. cit.

58 James W. Douglass, *JFK and the Unspeakable: Why He Died and Why It Matters* (Maryknoll, NY: Orbis Books, 2008). This is a foundational treatise on the JFK assassination. Douglass also cites my work.

59 Michael Chesser, "Reviewing the Autopsy X-Rays," The Future of Freedom Foundation (FFF), FFF.org, April 16, 2021, https://www.fff.org/freedom-in-motion/video/reviewing-the-autopsy-x-rays/.

> The bright object [in the AP JFK autopsy X-ray] measures 6.5 mm in diameter, and there is no counterpart found on the lateral image. There was no discussion of this in the Warren Commission report, and no official x-ray interpretation was included in the report. No bullet fragment of this size was removed at the time of the autopsy. Within the outline of this bright object are the shapes of two fragments. I agree with Dr. David Mantik that the film was copied, and this bright object was added to the image.[60]

Dr. Chesser has repeatedly acknowledged in print that his independent study of the JFK autopsy X-rays at the National Archives confirms my research methodology and conclusions. In 2015, after making his own OD readings of the X-rays, he wrote:

> I viewed the original autopsy skull X-rays at the archives this year [2015] and I confirmed [Mantik's] optical density readings of the lateral skull film, which support his conclusion that there was manipulation. Hopefully there will come a time when better copies of the autopsy x-rays and photographs will be made available for review by a wider audience and the evidence will speak for itself. I applaud Dr. David Mantik for his courage in reporting the truth.[61]

Douglas Horne gave the definitive synopsis of my work on the 6.5 mm object. First he commented upon the obvious brightness of the object (emphases in the original):

---

60 Michael Z. Chesser, "The Application of Forensic Principles for the Analysis of the Autopsy Skull X-Rays of President Kennedy and a Review of the Brain Photographs," Kennedys and King, November 27, 2017, https://www.kennedysandking.com/john-f-kennedy-articles/the-application-of-forensic-principles-for-the-analysis-of-the-autopsy-skull-x-rays-of-president-kennedy-and-a-review-of-the-brain-photographs.

61 Michael Chesser, "A Review of the JFK Cranial X-Rays and Photographs," Assassination of JFK, n.d., https://assassinationofjfk.net/a-review-of-the-jfk-cranial-x-rays-and-photographs/.

> To the human eye, the 6.5 mm wide object on the AP skull x-ray is the brightest object in the x-ray image, and is therefore presumably a very dense metal fragment. (It even seems brighter to the human eye than the President's dental amalgams, or fillings, when they are viewed *collectively* from front to back on the AP head x-ray.) However, it is not nearly as large or as bright on the *right lateral* skull x-ray as it appears to be on the AP skull x-ray, which presents a paradox.[62]

Horne described my journey into this paradox (emphases in the original):

> Dr. Mantik suspected, therefore, that the 6.5 mm "fragment" depicted on the A-P skull x-ray did not represent a real object present on the body at the autopsy. He set out to explore this hypothesis by taking OD measurements of the object on both the AP and right lateral skull x-rays, as well as the dental amalgams. The apparent bullet fragment is. *widest at the center when measured horizontally* on the AP skull x-ray, since there is a small bite taken out of the fragment in its lower right hand corner (from 4 to 6 o'clock), as seen by the viewer when examining the x-ray. Mantik therefore took very careful OD measurements of the same object on the right lateral x-ray; if the large 6.5 mm object depicted on the AP x-ray had been authentic, then OD measurements of the same object on the right lateral x-ray *should have shown it to be denser in the middle than at the bottom* of the fragment. This did not happen; the opposite happened. As Mantik said in November of 1993 in Dallas, this is "a gross violation of physical reality."[63]

Horne summarized my conclusions as follows (emphases in the original):

---

62 Douglas Horne, *Inside the ARRB*, op. cit., vol. 2, p. 549.

63 Ibid., pp. 549-550.

> His [Mantik's] conclusions: the extremely lucent AP fragment seen on the AP skull x-ray is an artifact, and the x-ray in evidence today is a forged copy film. The actual fragment is depicted on the right lateral skull x-ray, and is much smaller in dimensions, and less dense, than what is seen on the AP x-ray. In fact, the large 6.5 mm object on the AP skull x-ray is *so translucent* that the *actual fragment* over which it was superimposed can be seen inside the 6.5 mm image, and is only about 2-3 mm wide.[64]

But we are only beginning to explore the JFK X-ray films and photographs at the National Archives. Astonishingly, more Archives' nonsense (both radiographic and photographic)—all overlooked by official investigations—will be exposed in the following chapters. After all, nine full days at the National Archives was an advantage given to no one else, so surprises might well be expected.

CHAPTER 2: SUMMARY

The miraculous materialization of the 6.5 mm fake bullet cross section (on the AP X-ray film) is worthy of any magician's toolbox. Quite incomprehensibly, it has mostly been ignored, even by extremely vociferous WC critics. This includes Harold Weisberg, who claimed (in a personal letter to me) that no X-ray film alteration had occurred. Even David Lifton in his bestselling book, *Best Evidence* (1988), mostly ignored this fake. And Josiah Thompson, one of the most revered of all WC critics, completely omitted this mysterious image from his recent book, *Last Second in Dallas* (2021). The blighted vision of these three authorities clearly demonstrates the persistent complexity of this JFK case—due to fraud in the photographs and radiographs, and even fraud in the Oswald evidence (not discussed here). The alteration of

---

64 Ibid., pp. 551-552.

the Zapruder film provides an even more powerful demonstration of ongoing disagreement over the extent of this fraud, in which longtime (as opposed to more recent) WC critics are more likely to protect their pristine faith in the goodwill of the US government.

My many hundreds of OD measurements, taken from the extant JFK X-ray films at the Archives, demonstrate conclusively that the 6.5 mm object must be a fake, subsequently added in the darkroom. Based on its ODs on the AP X-ray film, it must be longer (front to back) than all of JFK's dental amalgams lined up in a row.

None of the three pathologists recalled seeing it that night, and the autopsy radiologist refused to discuss it with me. Furthermore, my experiments with an authentic bullet cross section placed on an authentic human skull reveal how vastly different a real object appears when compared to this 6.5 mm fake.

Larry Sturdivan served as the ballistics consultant for the HSCA. In his subsequent book, *The JFK Myths* (2005), he emphasized that he had never, in his entire career, seen a cross section of a bullet deposited in such an odd fashion on a skull. His conclusions were echoed by others with massive experience, e.g., Howard Donahue and Cyril Wecht.

Meanwhile, government radiologists saw nothing exceptional in this object—except for forensic radiologist, John Fitzpatrick, who, despite two successive days of trying (February 6-7, 1996), was unable to locate the partner image on the lateral X-ray film. But Fitzpatrick was too late; I had already reported this same paradox more than two years earlier at a Manhattan press conference (November 10, 1993).

3

THE WHITE PATCH AND THE BLACK HOLE, THE FRONTAL SHOT TO JFK'S RIGHT FOREHEAD, AND THE STRANGE "T-SHAPED" IMAGE

We have to face the unpleasant as well as the affirmative side of the human story, including our own story as a nation, our own stories of our peoples. We have got to have the ugly facts in order to protect us from the official view of reality.

—**BILL MOYERS**[1]

The stupidity of governments should never be underestimated.

—**HELMUT SCHMIDT**, West German chancellor (1974-1982)[2]

---

1 Of course, Bill did not practice what he preached. Ironically, Moyers, like Billy Graham, had been a Baptist preacher. He was ordained in 1954 and had served in Weir, near Austin. In 2004, on behalf of the Johnson (sic) Foundation, he and Gerald Ford, Jack Valenti, and Lady Bird Johnson succeeded in forever banning the final episode of *The Men Who Killed Kennedy* from the airwaves. So, obviously (per Bill) some things are far worse than merely "ugly facts." One of them was apparently my interview with Nigel Turner for this episode. See: Bill Moyers, AZQuotes.com, n.d., https://www.azquotes.com/quote/676889.

2 Reuters, "Remembering a giant of German politics…" Euronews, November 11, 2015, https://www.euronews.com/2015/11/11/remembering-a-giant-of-german-politics.

A reliable way to make people believe in falsehoods is frequent repetition, because familiarity is not easily distinguished from truth. Authoritarian institutions and marketers have always known this fact.

—**DANIEL KAHNEMAN**, *Thinking, Fast and Slow*, 2011[3]

(Recipient of the 2002 Nobel Memorial Prize in Economic Sciences)

David Mantik has devoted years of meticulous research to the autopsy of President Kennedy, and I highly recommend this book to anyone who wants to understand the various anomalies and issues surrounding the autopsy. There is a wealth of information in this book, based upon close examination of the autopsy materials. I know David to be an honest, careful and deliberate scientist/physician. I viewed the original autopsy skull x-rays at the archives this year [2015] and I confirmed his optical density readings of the lateral skull film, which support his conclusion that there was manipulation. Hopefully there will come a time when better copies of the autopsy x-rays and photographs will be made available for review by a wider audience, and the evidence will speak for itself. I applaud David Mantik for his courage in reporting the truth.

—**MICHAEL CHESSER**, MD[4]

---

3 Daniel Kahneman, *Thinking, Fast and Slow* (New York: Farrar, Straus and Giroux, 2011), p. 62.

4 Michael Chesser, Review of *John F. Kennedy's Head Wounds: A Final Synthesis—and a New Analysis of the Harper Fragment* by David W. Mantik, Amazon, August 11, 2015, https://www.amazon.com/John-Kennedys-Head-Wounds-Synthesis-ebook/product-reviews/B012HAOK2E/ref=cm_cr_arp_d_paging_btm_next_2?ie=UTF8&reviewerType=all_reviews&pageNumber=2.

I VISITED THE NATIONAL ARCHIVES on four separate days in 1993: October 21–22, and again on October 28–29. On the two lateral X-ray films of JFK's skull, I saw a conspicuous white area. Only one of these lateral X-ray films is in the public record. It was published by the HSCA and is shown in Figure 3.1. By contrast, the frontal areas of both lateral X-rays are improbably dark.

THE WHITE PATCH AND THE BLACK SPACE

When I first saw these two areas, I was struck by how extraordinarily white and extremely black they looked.

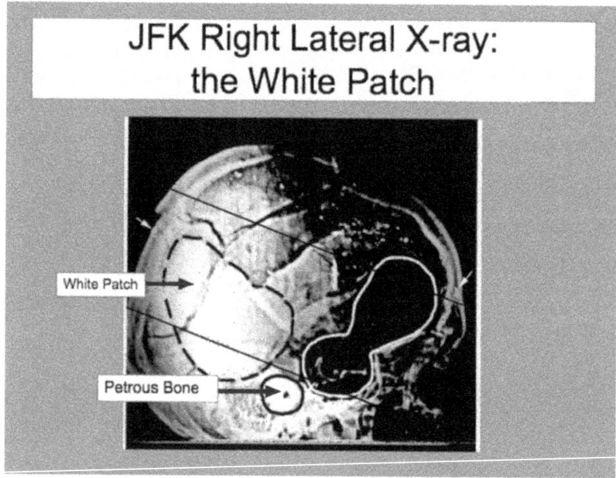

Figure 3.1

JFK Lateral X-ray Film. The White Patch at rear, Black Space at front (circled in white), and the petrous bone. The two black lines identify the angle at which the AP X-ray film was taken. The tiny black arrow at the back identifies the authentic metal fragment, reported by Sibert and O'Neill during the autopsy. The tiny black arrow at the front identifies the metal fragment removed at the autopsy.

The White Patch and the Black Space (Figure 3.1) were very different from my patients' X-ray films. Therefore, I was eager to measure the ODs of these areas at the Archives. What I found there was quite astonishing. The White Patch transmits an impossibly greater percentage of light than the Black Space. At the Archives, I measured many ODs of these two specific areas on both lateral X-ray films: the White Patch, sometimes labeled area "P" (for posterior), and the Black Space, sometimes labeled area "F" (for frontal). As shown in Table 3.1, these ODs imply that P transmitted about 1,100 times as much light as F.[5]

Area in Lateral X-ray Films	Range of ODs	Remarks
Area P The White Patch	0.5 to 0.7	These measurements imply implausibly dense bone.
Area F The Black Space	3.5 to 3.9	These measurements imply virtual absence of almost all brain and bone tissue.

Table 3.1
JFK Lateral Skull X-ray: ODs of White Patch vs. ODs of the Black Space.[6]

This ratio of over one thousand is quite remarkable, especially when compared to typical ratios found in patients. My ODs for patients showed only minor differences in optical densities between the front and the back. At most, the posterior skull was slightly whiter and transmitted up to twice as much light as the frontal portion. (See Appendix E for ODs on my patients.) So, I concluded that JFK's one-thousand-plus-fold differences were simply beyond belief—and likely beyond reality.

5

$$\frac{\text{mean transmission of area P}}{\text{mean transmission of area F}} = \frac{10^{-P}}{10^{-F}} = \frac{10^{-0.625}}{10^{-3.68}} = \frac{23.7\%}{0.0209\%} = 1130 \pm 110.$$

The stated uncertainty here is derived from the standard deviation of the actual measurements.

6 Table 3.1 is copied from Douglas Horne, *Inside the ARRB*, vol. 2, op. cit., p. 547.

A further comparison was obtained from nineteen forensic cases of fatal gunshot wounds to the skull. (See Appendix F for ODs on nine of these nineteen cases.) These X-rays, made on DuPont film, were obtained by Dr. Douglas DeSalles from a coroner's file dating to the 1960s and early 1970s. DeSalles reviewed these with me. Contrary to the JFK films, no large areas of whiteness or blackness were seen on any of these films. Three of these films showed small black areas at the anterior tip of the frontal lobe, consistent with brain loss from just this site. It is striking that four of the nine cases actually showed greater whiteness in the frontal area, i.e., the transmission ratios were *less than one!* The primary point, though, is this: none of these ratios was remotely like JFK's X-ray films, where the ratio was greater than one thousand.

In volume 2 of *Inside the ARRB*, Douglas Horne summarized my work (emphases in the original):

> As scientific "control," Mantik and his research partner Dr. Doug DeSalles took OD measurements of lateral skull X-rays from 9 coroner cases to obtain a *range* of numerical measurements *between the brightest and darkest areas* on these skull x-rays. In general, the brightest areas of the nine coroner's cases transmitted *about two or three times as much light* as the darkest areas. Furthermore, subjective visual examination of the lateral x-rays of these nine skulls did not reveal the extreme contrast between very bright and very dark areas that is seen in the JFK lateral skull x-rays. The subjective visual evidence was consistent with the OD measurements, and vice-versa.[7]

Even to the naked eye, the JFK X-ray films appear bizarre. This impression was reinforced by the HSCA's unusual request for computer enhancement of these X-ray films.[8] This is essentially never done in

---

7 Douglas Horne, *Inside the ARRB*, op. cit., vol. 2, p. 546.

8 For a technical discussion of such enhancements, see: Rafael C. Gonzalez and Paul Wintz, *Digital Image Processing* (Boston, MA: Addison-Wesley Publishing Company, 1992).

clinical practice. These enhanced images were published by the HSCA. For me, they added little to my direct viewing of the (unenhanced) X-ray films at the National Archives. JFK's X-ray films in this book are the enhanced images from the HSCA. (The unenhanced images are almost unusable in print format; the contrast range is even greater.)

The very lucent area (Area P) at the rear of the skull was almost as lucent as the densest bone in the body (the petrous bone). For comparison, I measured the petrous[9] ODs on the JFK X-ray films. This bone surrounds the ear canal. Not only is this bone very dense, but it is also very thick—it extends from one side of the skull to the other. For the ODs of Area P to match the petrous ODs, virtually all the brain in Area P must be replaced by very dense bone—and the bone would have to extend nearly from one side of the skull to the other. This points to a truly fantastic conclusion: this parietal portion of the skull, which should be mostly brain, is instead composed almost exclusively of bone. (For this reason, I whimsically described JFK as a bonehead.) No human parietal area with such dense osseous composition has been reported in clinical practice. As Horne notes, the petrous bone is "a region of almost solid bone running from right-to-left laterally through the human skull, and is the densest bone in the human body."[10]

But here is the ultimate paradox: given the extraordinary ODs of Area P, there is no correspondingly dense object anywhere on the AP X-ray film! If the skull is mostly bone, from left to right, then the AP film should surely show such a dense object as well. But it is nowhere to be found. Real-world objects don't just disappear because the X-ray

---

9 This petrous (rock-like) bone reminds us of St. Peter, the first pope (a Jew). Jesus had named him Peter because he was to be the rock on which the church would be built, although current popes (no Jews) have sometimes ignored this. See Paul L. Williams, *Operation Gladio: The Unholy Alliance between the Vatican, the CIA, and the Mafia* (Amherst, NY: Prometheus Books, 2018). Several sordid Vatican deals also appear in the movie, *Godfather III*. Also see "The Dangling Man: The Case of Robert Calvi, the Vatican Banker," in *Coroner at Large* by Thomas Noguchi, MD (Simon and Schuster, NY, NY, 1985). Paul's comments on the current pope (Francis) are particularly attention-grabbing.

10 Douglas Horne, *Inside the ARRB*, op. cit., vol. 2, p. 547.

machine is moved. I first reported this paradox in New York City on November 10, 1993. At that Manhattan press conference, I observed: "Such an extremely dense real-world object as the White Patch should have been as trivial to see on the AP X-ray film as a T-Rex in downtown Manhattan."[11] But T-Rex had already left town.

For further comparison, I viewed an eight-by-ten-inch black and white print, purchased from the National Archives, of JFK's premortem lateral X-ray film. No such extreme range of whiteness to blackness appears in this premortem print. In 2016, Dr. Michael Chesser traveled to the JFK Library in Boston to measure the ODs. They are radically inconsistent with JFK's postmortem films, but the premortem ODs are quite similar to all of my patients. They are also similar to the nineteen forensic cases that Dr. DeSalles and I examined (Appendix F).

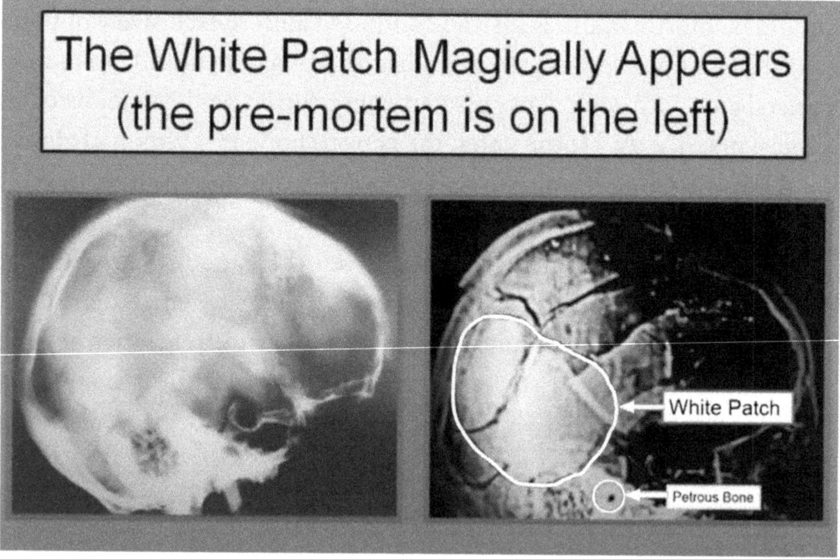

Figure 3.2
JFK's Premortem Lateral X-ray Film vs. JFK's Postmortem X-ray Film at the Archives.

---

11 David Mantik, "JFK Assassination Paradoxes: A Primer for Beginners," in David Mantik, *The JFK Assassination Decoded*, op. cit., pp. 1-18, at p. 9.

For several patient cases, I calculated a ratio: the typical OD of the petrous bone divided by the typical OD of the White Patch (Table 3.2). A ratio of 1.00 means that the White Patch is as dense as the petrous bone, i.e., a true bonehead. But a ratio of more than 0.6 approaches abnormal, i.e., the White Patch appears too transparent (or white in prints). This would imply too much bone in this parietal area.

I also compared JFK's premortem ODs with the postmortem ODs. At the Archives, the OD ratio was 0.89, which means that the real-world object represented by the White Patch is almost as dense as the petrous bone. In contrast, on the premortem film, the OD ratio was only 0.43. For my patients, this ratio of 0.46 was typical of my forty-plus years of clinical experience.

We don't have the petrous bone ODs for the nine forensic cases, but we can calculate a surrogate: the OD of Area P divided by the OD of Area F. The mean ratio for the forensic cases was 1.37, but this mean becomes 1.05 if victim number six—a large outlier—is ignored. Most patient ratios hover around 1.00. Recall that this ratio for JFK's postmortem was 1130, which is a truly stunning difference.

All of this implies that the White Patch does not exist for normal human beings—or even for dead victims. No patient (or dead victim) is nearly solid bone from left to right in the parietal skull, and JFK was (originally) decidedly not either. He only converted after death.

JFK Postmortem	0.89
JFK Premortem	0.43
Typical Patients	0.46

Table 3.2
OD of Petrous Bone ÷ OD of White Patch.

In his deposition before the ARRB on February 13, 1996, Humes's eerie reaction to seeing the Black Space on JFK's lateral X-ray film strongly suggests that it was not present originally. ARRB attorney

Jeremy Gunn showed Humes the X-ray as a prelude to his questions. My comments are in brackets.

> GUNN: [presents Humes with the right lateral skull x-ray] Dr. Humes can you identify this as being an autopsy x-ray taken on November 22, 1963?
>
> HUMES: I guess so. That's really—it's got some very—it's a peculiar exposure ... I don't know why this is so radio-opaque, this whole area. [Humes pointed at the extremely dark area toward the front of the skull. He misspoke—a radiolucent object would have produced a dark image.]
>
> GUNN: You're referring to the right frontal area.
>
> HUMES: What seems to be the frontal portion of it. I don't understand why that is. You'd have to have some radiologist tell me about that. I can't make that out ... I don't understand this great big void there. I don't know what that's all about [Humes seemed genuinely mystified by the dark 'void' in the frontal region.][12]

Gunn finally asked Humes what Horne called the "big question."[13]

> GUNN: Does that raise any question in your mind about the authenticity of the x-ray that you're looking at now in terms of being an x-ray of President Kennedy?

---

12 Douglas Horne, *Inside the ARRB*, op. cit., Volume I, p. 53.

13 Ibid.

HUMES: Well, there's aspects of it I don't understand. I don't understand this big void up—maybe a radiologist could explain it. I don't know what this big—

GUNN: You're referring to—

HUMES: —non-opaque area that takes up half of the skull here, I don't understand that.

GUNN: Do you remember seeing that on the night of the autopsy?

HUMES: No, I don't. That doesn't mean it wasn't there, but I don't remember it.[14]

Horne summed up Humes's reaction: "The obvious question at the time was whether Dr. Humes was genuinely reacting to a forged composite copy film whose contrast looked markedly different than the original x-ray examined by him in the morgue, during President Kennedy's autopsy."[15]

Steve Tilley permitted OD measurements of JFK's sequestered lateral X-ray film. But because the National Archives has not made this X-ray film public, I cannot show it here. While the White Patch also exists on this X-ray film, it does not exactly match the White Patch on the public X-ray film (which is suspicious in itself). Table 3.3 shows my White Patch ODs for each one of the lateral X-ray films.

---

14 Ibid., pp. 53-54.

15 Ibid., p. 54.

	White Patch ODs Area P	Petrous Bone ODs	White Patch OD - Petrous OD	OD Ratios (Petrous OD ÷ White Patch OD)
Left Lateral Skull X-ray Film (unpublished image)	.99	.73	.26	.74
Right Lateral Skull X-ray Film (public image)	.625	.53	.095	.85

Table 3.3
ODs of the White Patch on JFK's Left Lateral vs. the Right Lateral.

Horne emphasized the significance of these measurements (emphases in the original):

> Since there should be no difference at all between these ***ratios*** when comparing the right to the left lateral x-ray, the discrepancies noted above are therefore "problematic" in terms of what they say about authenticity. In other words, how can two different lateral X-rays of the same human skull show a different transmission ratio between area P (or any other area) and the bone around the ear canal? *The answer is that in real life, they could not.*[16]

He concluded (emphases in the original):

---

16 Ibid., pp. 547-548.

> The transmission ratios between area P and the ear canal [petrous bone] are different on the [two] JFK lateral skull x-rays because the forged composite copy films created after the autopsy were *imperfectly created*—that is, the right lateral was "light blasted" *more* than the left lateral was during the copying process, when the occipital-parietal blowout was obliterated by exposing the copy film to extra light in that region. The human eye cannot detect the difference, but the optical densitometer can, and the numerical readings it provided cannot be denied.[17]

There is one more problem when comparing the two lateral X-ray films: the White Patch is visibly different in size and in shape. On the unpublished lateral, a small, but sharply defined peninsula protrudes upward at one end of the superior border. No similar peninsula is seen on the other lateral film. Differing elevations of the X-ray tube might explain quite small changes in shape, but surely not the magnitude of those seen here. In addition, the location of the skull on the two films clearly implies only minimal changes in X-ray tube elevation. There is no obvious explanation for this protruding peninsula; no standard explanations in conventional radiography can account for this. This feature, along with those already noted, raise deeply disturbing questions about these X-ray films.

This suggests that each one is a separate and unique forgery. The White Patch on the public lateral is somewhat larger than its supposed twin on the unpublished lateral. This unequal size should imply that the real-world object lies closer to one side of the skull. However, the AP skull X-ray shows no such asymmetry. Well actually, it is worse than that—there is no corresponding object anywhere—on either lateral film! Moreover, the OD of the White Patch is distinctly different on

17 Ibid., p. 548.

the two lateral X-ray films, *in a manner not explicable by two different X-ray exposures.* (More precisely, the ratio of the White Patch OD to petrous bone OD is different.) This is not expected of a real-world object. Douglas Horne concluded: "Therefore, both laterals are also revealed to be forgeries by simply comparing them to the AP x-ray, and noting the absence of any 'hyperdense' area in the skull."[18]

These, along with other observations, suggest that, although most portions of these X-ray films are authentically JFK, certain critical areas, which lack uniquely identifiable anatomic features, have been altered. This was accomplished via composites (i.e., with a second darkroom exposure). Conventional explanations are sorely lacking.

THE BLACK SPACE AT THE RIGHT FRONT OF JFK'S LATERAL X-RAY FILMS

The Black Space on the two lateral X-ray films does not imply forgery. Instead, this dark area reflects an almost total absence of brain tissue—from the right to left side. Most likely, the anterior brain had settled to the rear, where an empty space had existed because much posterior brain had been blasted out. That empty space then permitted the rest of the brain to settle to the rear.

To show how absent brain would appear on an X-ray film, I performed control exposures with authentic cadaver skulls filled with various volumes of biologically equivalent material. My control experiments confirmed that the JFK ODs implied almost no brain tissue in this dark (bilateral) frontal area.[19] Neither the ODs from the nineteen coroner cases nor my ten patient cases ever showed such a black space; their frontal brains were mostly intact.

---

18 Ibid.

19 These experimental images are displayed here: David W. Mantik and Cyril H. Wecht, "Paradoxes of the JFK Assassination: The Brain Enigma," in *The Assassinations: Probe Magazine on JFK, MLK, RFK and Malcolm X*, eds. James DiEugenio and Lisa Pease (Los Angeles, CA: Feral House, 2003), pp. 250-271.

The ODs from the AP skull X-ray film clearly showed more brain tissue missing on the right than the left.[20] I was able to measure ODs directly above the cerebellum. These showed significantly less tissue directly above the right cerebellum than above the left cerebellum. Using my control data, along with ODs from JFK's AP X-ray film, I could closely estimate about five cm less brain tissue directly above JFK's right cerebellum (as measured from front to back) than above his left cerebellum. These results imply significant right brain loss in JFK—as confirmed by witnesses at both Parkland and Bethesda—i.e., due to a blowout at the right rear.[21] According to chief pathologist James Humes, "Two thirds of [JFK's] right cerebrum had been blown away."[22] Many witnesses confirmed such a major loss of brain tissue—at Parkland and at Bethesda. Furthermore, my ODs confirmed that only about 30 percent of the right brain remained. Furthermore, this missing right brain is entirely *inconsistent* with JFK's brain photographs.[23] It is also totally inconsistent with the official brain weight of 1500 grams.[24] (The average male brain weighs about 1300–1400 grams; it shrinks with age.)

---

20 Ibid.

21 Ibid., pp. 549.

22 Dennis L. Breo, "JFK: The Autopsy," *Chicago Tribune*, May 24, 1992, https://www.chicagotribune.com/news/ct-xpm-1992-05-24-9202160436-story.html.

23 Douglas Horne, "HSCA artist's rendering of autopsy photographs showing the superior view of a brain represented to be that of President Kennedy," in *Inside the AARB*, vol. 1, op. cit., figure 35 (ARRB MI 4), p. 130.

24 "Supplementary Report of Autopsy Number A63-272, President John F. Kennedy," *Hearings before the President's Commission on the Assassination of President Kennedy,* CE 391, vol. 16, op. cit., p. 987.

Also archived at: "MI 4 – Supplementary Autopsy Report (12/6/63?)," ARRB Master Set of Medical Exhibits, , History Matters, https://history-matters.com/archive/jfk/arrb/master_med_set/md4/html/Image1.htm.

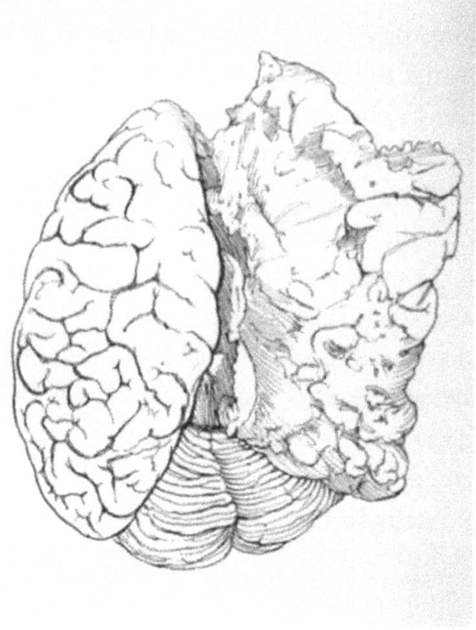

Figure 3.3
Ida Dox's drawing of *someone's* brain (superior view) for the HSCA, based on autopsy photograph numbers 20, 23, 24, 25, 50, 51, and 52.

The left brain in Figure 3.3 is fully intact, but the right brain is also mostly present.[25] This drawing means to imply that a bullet furrowed through the right side, exiting via the right front. As Horne pointed out: "The brain photographs in the Archives depict a brain that is severely disrupted in the right cerebral hemisphere, but which apparently retains most of its mass."[26]

When compared to the X-ray films, which show a huge frontal area of absent brain—on both sides—this drawing of the brain, which shows

25 Humes agreed with this: "They both [sides] look pretty good from above…" from "Deposition of Dr. James Joseph Humes," corrected transcript, op. cit., at p. 210.

26 Douglas Horne, *Inside the ARRB*, op. cit., vol. 1, footnote 13, p. 45.

no absent left brain at all, is a gross paradox, one of the most absurd in the entire JFK case. But that is no surprise; after all, when different, and obviously compartmentalized groups of forgers go their own ways, what else can be expected?

Of course, the total absence of trauma to the left brain makes no sense. The X-ray films and Boswell's drawing clearly show a major loss of skull bone at the vertex, immediately above the left brain. So how did the left brain remain so intact if the skull just above it had disappeared? Even worse, according to the pathologists, the skull had been severed from the falx, which lies at the superior midline; it tethers the brain to the skull. So, if the falx was totally severed, how could the immediately adjacent left brain not display at least a little trauma?[27] In other words, this simply cannot be JFK's brain.

John Stringer was the official autopsy photographer who attended the first brain examination several days after the assassination. FBI Special Agent Frank O'Neill attended the autopsy, and he had seen the removed brain. Before the ARRB, both men disavowed the photographs of JFK's brain. Stringer testified: "No, I couldn't say that they were

27 Dr. Chesser, a neurologist, originally noted this paradox in his contribution to *At The Cold Shoulder of History* (2018) by James Jenkins and William Matson Law. Jenkins recalled multiple sequences of X-ray films; he was particularly puzzled that useless duplicate X-ray films were being taken (presumably because no useful forensic metal could be located). He also noted that photographs were taken before any "...washing of the body or any manipulation of the head or scalp had occurred." He added that the body was not cleaned until the morticians took over after the autopsy. Most importantly, he described a right temporal entry, inside the hairline, just forward of the right ear. At this site, he recalled a gray perimeter around the wound. He stated, "Dr. Finck speculated that the gray material might have come from a bullet.... Dr. Humes returned to the table and immediately directed Dr. Finck away from the small wound in the temple—to the large posterior head wound. The temple wound was abandoned and ever returned to that night." It is also noteworthy that Humes denied that the hair had been cleaned or combed prior to the autopsy photographs. See also: "Deposition of Dr. James Joseph Humes," corrected transcript, op. cit., pp. 156 and 162.

President Kennedy's."[28] O'Neill testified that when JFK's brain was removed during the Bethesda autopsy "...more than half of the brain was missing."[29] When O'Neill was shown the brain photographs, he reacted with surprise, saying, "... this looks like a complete brain. Or am I wrong in saying that? I don't know."[30] So, O'Neill joined Stringer in impugning the official photographs. "In all honesty, I can't say that it looks like the brain I saw, quite frankly," O'Neill attested.[31]

One of the ARRB's more startling findings (apparently unknown to the ARRB board members) was its discovery of two distinctly separate examinations of two different brains. For the first brain event, Horne established a compelling case that only a *residual* brain was examined.[32] He stressed the importance of Stringer's testimony: "Stringer's testimony to Jeremy Gunn confirming that he saw *damage to the cerebellum* at the first brain exam is the clincher: the recollection is consistent with the Dallas (Parkland Hospital) observations of a hole—an apparent exit wound—in the right rear of the President's head, and of a macerated, severely damaged cerebellum."[33] The ARRB documented that a second brain exam was conducted sometime between November 29

---

28 Douglas Horne, "The Official Autopsy Photographer and an FBI Agent Impugn the Brain Photographs in the National Archives," from *Inside the ARRB*, vol. 1, op. cit., pp. 38-44, at p. 41. O'Neill's testimony was verified through John Stringer's deposition to the ARRB on July 16, 1996, as noted by Horne on pp. 43-44.

29 Douglas Horne, "Former FBI Frank O'Neill Weighs in on the Authenticity of the Brain Photographs," *Inside the ARRB*, op. cit., vol. 1, pp. 44-46, at p. 45.

30 Ibid.

31 Ibid., p. 46.

32 Douglas Horne, "JFK's Post Autopsy Brain Exam: A Major Deception," in *Inside the ARRB*, op. cit., vol. 1, pp. 35-38, at p. 36.

33 Douglas Horne, "The Meaning of John Stringer's Testimony (and that of Frank O'Neill)," in *Inside the ARRB*, op. cit., vol. 1, pp. 46-48, at p. 46. Emphasis in the original.

and December 2, 1963.[34] But, for the second exam, Horne concluded that the brain was a "fraudulent organ—the fixed brain of a deceased person who was *not* John F. Kennedy."[35]

In Oliver Stone's 2021 documentary *JFK Revisited: Through the Looking Glass,* Horne explained that the ARRB had relied on Dr. Robert H. Kirschner, a renowned forensic pathologist. According to Horne, Kirshner had examined the photographs of someone's brain. Horne quoted Kirshner's conclusions from the report Horne wrote after Dr. Kirschner's examination of autopsy photographs and X-rays: "When asked how well the brain in the photograph was fixed, Dr. Kirschner said that it was very well fixed, and initially estimated that it had been fixed two weeks or more, based on its appearance (very firm, and very pale—no pink color at all)."[36] Horne therefore inferred that the brain photographs were not of JFK's brain. The first brain examination probably occurred on November 25, 1963, just three days after the assassination.[37] He stressed the importance of this different time interval (emphases in the original):

> The brain photographs in the National Archives today *cannot be, and are not,* photographs of President Kennedy's brain. This we know beyond any reasonable doubt. The purpose for creating this false

---

34 The date of November 29 was chiefly based on Finck's report (on this date) when he was called to assist with a JFK brain examination.

35 Ibid., p. 36. Emphasis in the original.

36 See also: Douglas Horne, "Two Brain Examinations—Coverup Confirmed," in *Inside the ARRB,* op. cit., vol. 3, pp. 777-844, at p. 820. Also view Horne's lecture for The JFK Assassination at 60: The Cyril H. Wecht Institute of Forensic Science and Law, 22nd Annual Symposium, November 15-17, 2023, www.duq.edu/documents/academics/colleges-and-schools/science/wecht-jfk60-symposium-program-2023.pdf.

37 This timing would have permitted JFK's brain to be placed into his casket before burial, as RFK wanted to do. However, it is quite certain that the brain was not introduced into the casket at the *subsequent* reinterment, several years later.

> record was to suppress evidence that President Kennedy was killed by a shot or shots from the front, and to insert into the record false 'evidence' consistent with the official story that he was shot only from behind. This discovery is the single most significant "smoking gun" indicating a government coverup within the medical evidence surrounding President Kennedy's assassination, and is a direct result of the JFK Records Act, which in turn was fathered by [Oliver Stone's] movie JFK [1991].[38]

In Stone's documentary, *JFK Revisited: Through the Looking Glass*, Dr. Michael Chesser also supported Horne's conclusions. "At a teaching hospital [like Bethesda], there's no shortage of brains," Chesser said. "Autopsies were very frequent. Frequently, the brain was saved for teaching medical students, so, it would not have been difficult to find a brain for replacement. This is just one more reason why this cannot be President Kennedy's brain in the photographs that we have stored at the archives."[39]

Horne explained the need for a second brain examination (emphases in the original):

> John Stringer's testimony to the ARRB on July 16, 1996, provided proof of a medical coverup in the assassination of John F. Kennedy since the brain photographs disavowed by Stringer and O'Neill appear *compatible* with the damage that would conceivably occur when a shot transits a human skull *from the rear to the front*, this has major implications for the nature of the evidence <u>suppressed</u> by 'burying' the first brain exam, the one attended by Humes, Boswell, and Stringer

---

38 Ibid., p. 778.

39 James DiEugenio, *JFK Revisited*, op. cit., p. 54. For the education of the resident pathologists, Humes conducted the (usually) weekly brain cutting sessions at Bethesda. This means that he was no fool. But it also means that he had ready access to many brain specimens.

on Monday, November 25, 1963. (The pattern of the damage to the brain examined from the first examination must have been different from the damage seen in the photographs now in evidence, or that first exam *would not have been suppressed*). In other words, the evidence from the first brain examination must have been inconsistent with being shot from behind.[40]

He concluded (emphases in the original):

> The lesson here is that subsequent to the burial of the President, the 'best evidence' in his death has been the written autopsy report *and the autopsy photographs and X-rays*, the official visual record of the autopsy. By substituting inauthentic photographs of a brain from someone other than John F. Kennedy (which display a fraudulent pattern of damage), those responsible for the medical coverup found a simple way to fool two official investigations—the Clark Panel and the HSCA—and at the same time discredit the testimony of the treatment staff at Parkland hospital, should that ever become an issue of major concern.[41]

The fraudulent medical evidence convinced the Clark Panel and the HSCA that JFK was shot only once in the head. The only change from the WC was this: they elevated the (supposed single) rear entry wound by 10 cm into the cowlick area. This was a displacement from the WC site by nearly half the height of the head! The pathologists were not pleased.

So, why did the forgers add the White Patch (which it clearly is) to both lateral X-ray films? Most likely, the forgers merely wanted to

---

40 Douglas Horne, "The Meaning of John Stringer's Testimony (and that of Frank O'Neill)," in *Inside the ARRB*, op. cit., vol. 1, pp. 46-48, at p. 46.

41 Ibid., pp. 47-48.

distract attention from the rear of the skull, so that viewers would instead focus on the anterior skull, where much brain is missing (on both lateral X-ray films). The resulting visual impression would then imply that a bullet had exited from the front, but not from the rear; such a frontal exit would, of course, implicate Oswald.[42]

Had I altered the skull X-rays, I would have omitted the White Patch—it just seems like overkill. The 6.5 mm fake was quite sufficient. Why add more fake images? After all, the more fakes, the greater the risk of discovery. But when someone who likes to write crime fiction (e.g.,

---

42 But why did the brain settle to the rear of the skull? According to my now-deceased friend, Robert Livingston, MD (who founded the neuroscience department at the University of California, San Diego), gunshots alone cannot sever the brain from its very strong tethering to the skull (via the falx). On the other hand, Humes reported that the brain essentially fell out into his hands without any special effort. Finck's summary letter to Brigadier General Joseph M. Blumberg confirmed this: "Commander Humes told me that he had only to prolong the lacerations of the scalp before removing the brain. No sawing of the skull was necessary." (This is from "Other autopsy considerations," *Appendix to Hearings Before the Select Committee on Assassination of the U.S. House of Representatives Ninety-Fifth Congress Second Session*, vol. 7, op. cit., p. 135.) Humes also confirmed that the falx was loose. (See "Deposition of Dr. James Joseph Humes," corrected transcript, op. cit., p. 86.) Of course, this raises the vexing question of whether the brain had been surgically removed from the skull before the autopsy officially began. If so, then the brain, without any of its natural moorings, would indeed have felt free to migrate to the rear of the skull, as it responded to gravity. In fact, this may well be another clue to (illicit) pre-autopsy surgery. However, when skull trauma occurs from *multiple* gunshots, then indeed the brain may settle to the rear. When there were about six wound tracks per skull, this settling to the rear occurred in eight of ten cases (See: Angela D. Levy, et.al., "Virtual autopsy: preliminary experience in high-velocity gunshot wound victims," *Radiology*, vol. 240, no. 2, (August 2006), pp. 522-528). So, the argument may be reversed: because JFK's brain had settled to the rear, multiple bullets must have hit his skull! The HSCA never considered this.

James Jenkins adds one more argument to the possible (illicit) pre-autopsy extraction of the brain. In his autobiography, he emphasized that the cerebral blood vessels appeared "shriveled" and "had constricted," which suggested that they had been transected for quite some time before the autopsy. James Curtis Jenkins and William Matson Law, *At The Cold Shoulder of History: The Chilling Story of a 21-year-old Navy Hospital Corpsman Who Stood at the Shoulder of JFK during the Bethesda Autopsy* (Walterville, OR: Trine Day, 2018), p. 18. He also emphasized that the brain stem had been cut, an event he had not observed during the official autopsy, even though he never left JFK's right shoulder (as he told me). He was also puzzled that the cuts in the brain stem were at different levels on the two sides, which was not standard practice.

Dr. John Ebersole—as he told me) gets a clever idea, such as altering X-ray films in the darkroom, it can be difficult to stop.

THE SHOT TO JFK'S RIGHT FOREHEAD

In 2015, when Dr. Chesser visited the National Archives, he paid particular attention to the fragment trail near the forehead on the two lateral skull films. I had previously noted the presence of metallic debris at that site in my survey of all metal on the extant films at the Archives. (See Figure 3.9, or Figure 7.2 in a later chapter.)

As seen in Figure 3.4, Chesser identified a fragment trail that entered the upper right forehead near the hairline. The trail appears to widen from front to back, consistent with a frontal entry but not with a rear entry. The largest fragment lies at the rear, precisely where it would be expected. There is no obvious exit at the end of the fragment trail—as confirmed by both my OD data and multiple radiologists.

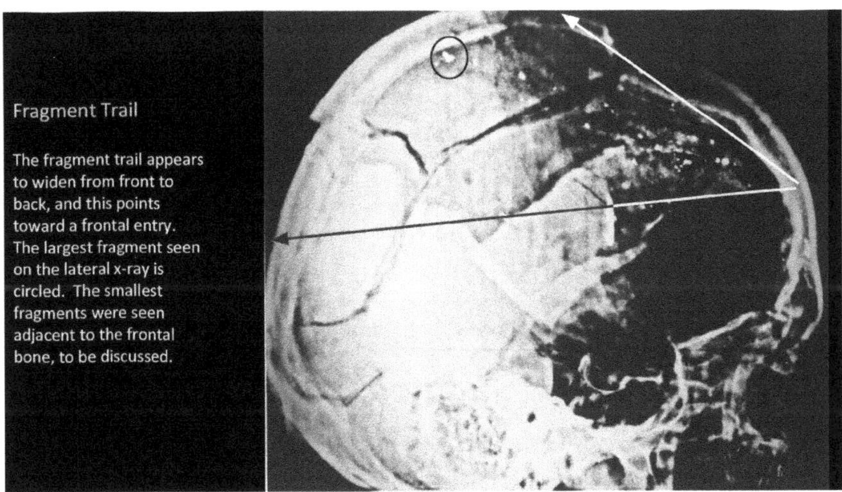

Figure 3.4
Metal Fragment Trail from a Frontal Bullet—Shown Between the Two Blue Diverging Lines, with an Apex at the Forehead. This bullet entered the right forehead near the hairline; the fragment trail widens to the rear. The largest metal fragment is circled.

Note: Figures 3.4 through 3.8 are excerpted from his lecture: Michael Z. Chesser, "The Application of Forensic Principles for the Analysis of the Autopsy Skull X-Rays of President Kennedy and a Review of Brain Photographs," Kennedys and King (formerly CTKA), November 27, 2017, https://www.kennedysandking.com/john-f-kennedy-articles/the-application-of-forensic-principles-for-the-analysis-of-the-autopsy-skull-x-rays-of-president-kennedy-and-a-review-of-the-brain-photographs.

Chesser presented this visual essay for the mock trial of Lee Harvey Oswald at the South Texas College of Law in Houston, November 16-17, 2017.

Chesser identified the point of entry of this frontal shot as two "white knobby" objects on the inside of the right forehead (Figure 3.5). He determined that these two "white knobby" objects were metallic, and not bone. I had previously noted this as well.

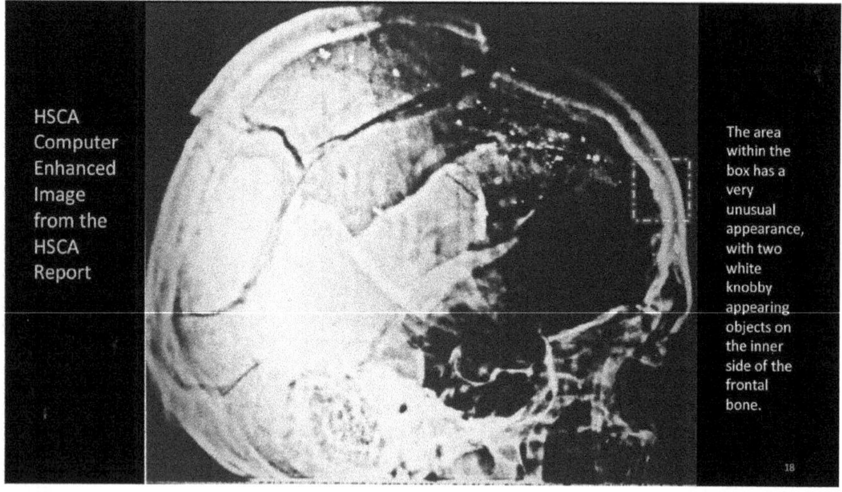

Figure 3.5

Entry Site (Within the Dotted Rectangle) into the Right Forehead. Notice the two "white knobby" objects just inside the frontal (forehead) bone, near the center of the box.

Figure 3.6 is a close-up of the two "white knobby" objects just inside of the right forehead.

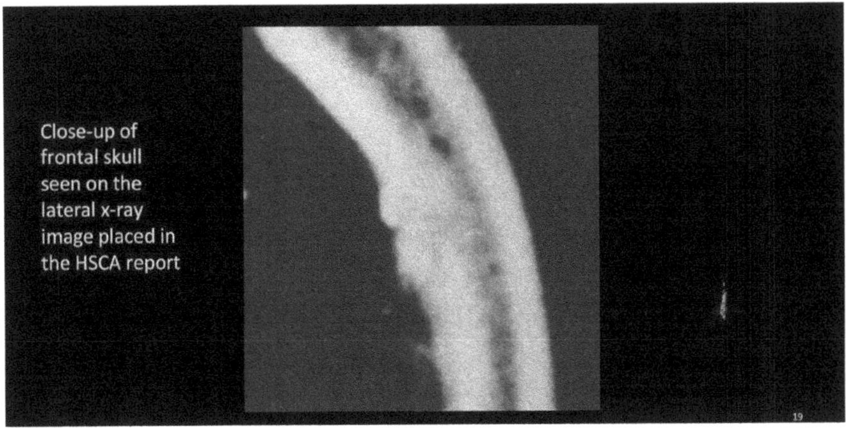

Figure 3.6
Close-up: The "Two "White Knobby" Objects Just Inside the Frontal (Forehead) Bone.

At the entry site (Figure 3.7), Chesser simulated the tiny, almost dust-like, particles. This was high in the right forehead near the hairline.

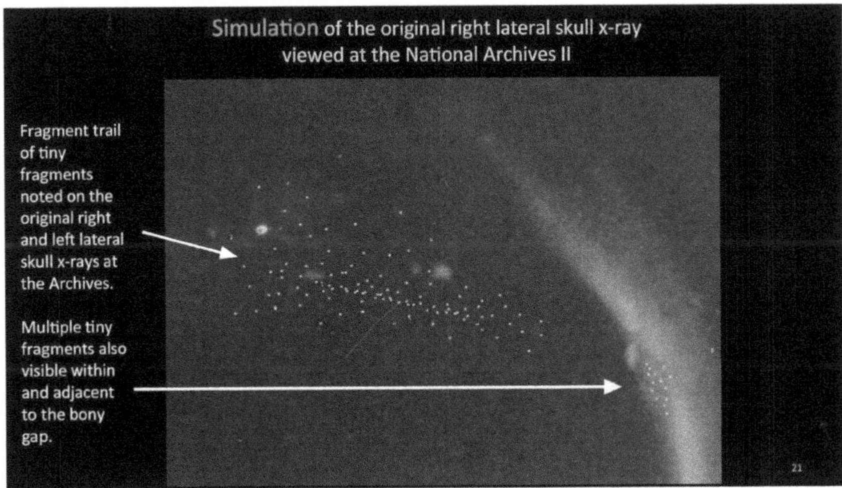

Figure 3.7
Chesser's Simulated Fragment Trail Near the Right Forehead. Fragments are also present at the entry site (to the right of the tiny white arrowhead and inferior to the two "knobby" objects).

Figure 3.8 identifies the entry of this forehead shot. Chesser clarified: "The fragment trail supports a right frontal entry site at approximately this location [referring to the dot placed on Kennedy's forehead as shown on the photograph]. An entry wound at this location would have been covered by hair, and easily missed by the Parkland personnel, who focused on resuscitation and the profusely bleeding right occipital wound."[43]

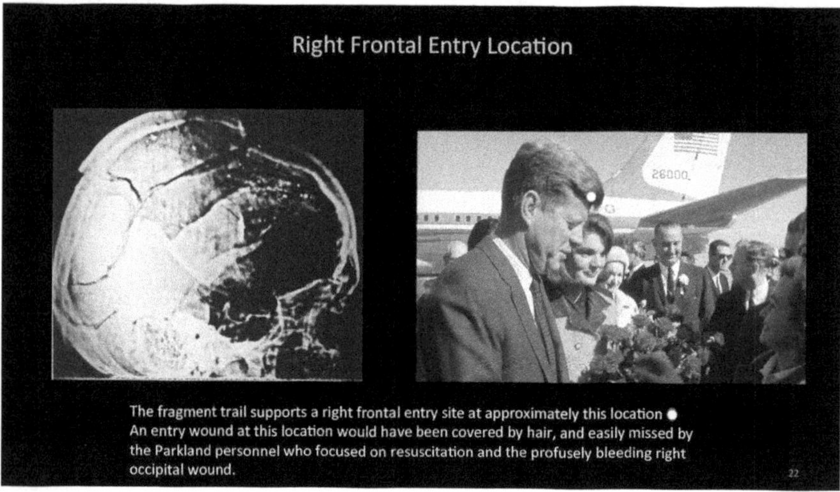

Figure 3.8
Right Frontal Entry (Solid white dot on JFK's forehead in the photograph). The photograph is from Love Field on November 22, 1963.

Chesser's independent observations of the lateral X-ray film precisely mirrored my observations and analysis. In Figure 3.9, I have highlighted (via the long blue line with the arrowhead) the fragment trail from the frontal entry at JFK's right forehead.[44]

---

43 Michael Z. Chesser, MD, "The Application of Forensic Principles for the Analysis of the Autopsy Skull X-Rays of President Kennedy and a Review of Brain Photographs," op. cit.

44 My tedious, but precise, identification (performed while at the Archives) of all apparent metallic debris on both the lateral and AP X-ray films is also shown in color in my hardcover book, p. 379.

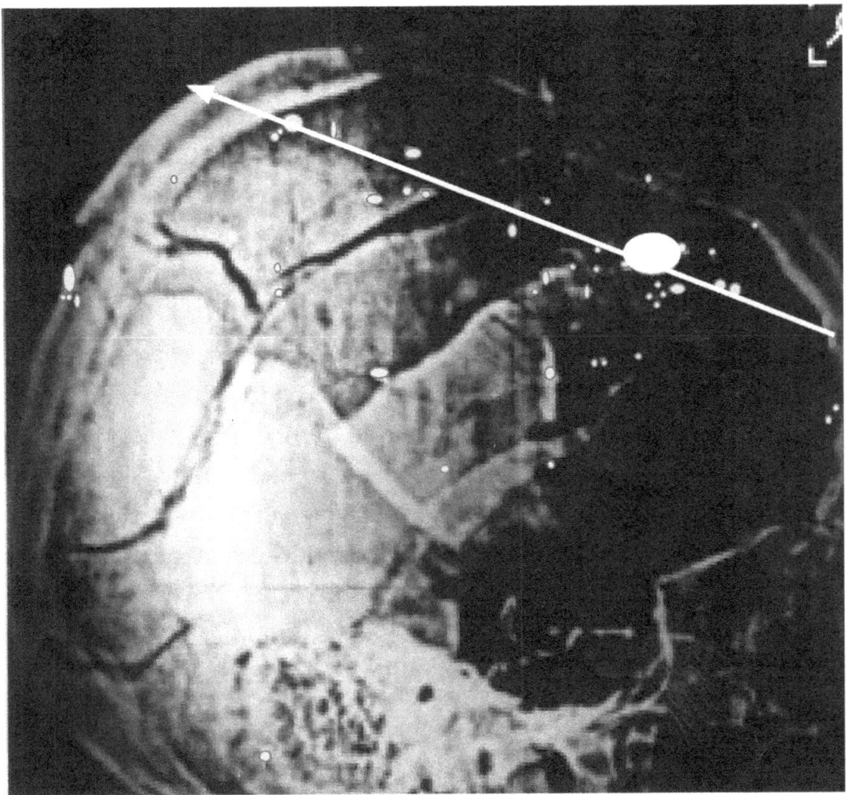

Figure 3.9
Bullet Fragment Trail from the Frontal Shot (Thin Oblique Arrow). This is my reproduction (done at the Archives) of all metallic debris. The bullet entered the right forehead near the hairline. The largest ellipse represents an amorphous metallic opacity, possibly mercury. This is not a single piece of solid metal.

The vertical arrow (at the rear) identifies the authentic fragment described by Sibert and O'Neill (labeled in this book as SOF). This was not removed at the autopsy. It served as an anchor in 3D space for the 6.5 mm fake on the AP X-ray film. The fragments in the trail must lie within soft tissue in the right hemisphere. Note that SOF lies too far from the trail to be part of it. Most likely, it represents shrapnel (from the rear).

Copper residue was identified at the holes on the back of the coat and shirt; the holes were likely caused by shrapnel. SOF most likely represents metallic shrapnel from a bullet that struck Elm Street. There are at least three arguments for shrapnel, as follows: (1) at least five witnesses (including several in the WC volumes) reported such a bullet (or even bullets) glancing off Elm Street; (2) on the skull X-rays at the Archives, I have observed tiny metal fragments to be widely scattered on both sides of the skull—all government investigations have ignored these; and (3) low energy X-ray scattering[45] showed metal at the holes on the rear of the shirt and coat; spectroscopic data[46] confirmed that this metal was copper, consistent with a (partially) copper-jacketed fragment. On the other hand, no metal was found on the front of the shirt. This negative result for the shirt implies either (1) a non-metallic projectile or (2) an entry superior to the shirt collar.[47] Furthermore, as would be expected for shrapnel, the pathologists reported that the back wound was very shallow. For additional evidence that shrapnel caused the back wound, note that the abrasion collar was located at the *inferior* edge of this wound;[48] this implies a *rising* projectile. In other words, the back wound was *not* caused by a descending bullet, e.g., a sabot from the County Records Building.[49]

---

45 Jerry McKnight, "Bugliosi Fails to Resuscitate the Single-Bullet Theory," Mary Ferrell Foundation, n.d., https://www.maryferrell.org/pages/Essay_-_Bugliosi_Fails_to_Resuscitate_the_Single-Bullet_Theory.html.

46 "Description of President Kennedy's wounds," *Appendix to Hearings Before the Select Committee on Assassination of the U.S. House of Representatives Ninety-Fifth Congress Second Session*, vol. 7, op. cit., p. 83.

47 Among other witnesses (e.g., Diana Bowron), Charles Carrico clearly implied that the throat wound lay above the collar ("Testimony of Dr. Charles James Carrico and Dr. Malcom Oliver Perry, "*Hearings before the President's Commission on the Assassination of President Kennedy*, vol. 3, op. cit., at pp. 361-362). For further discussion of its location, see my hardcover book, pp. 10-12.

48 "Summary of the forensic pathologists' perspective of wound ballistics," Appendix to Hearings Before the Select Committee on Assassination of the U.S. House of Representatives Ninety-Fifth Congress Second Session, vol. 7, op. cit., p. 175. The trajectory was slightly upward.

49 This, however, cannot totally rule out a sabot. After all, more bullets than CE 399 litter this farcical case.

Stavis "Steve" Ellis, a Dallas Police Department solo motorcycle officer, was in charge of the motorcycle escort. He offered firsthand testimony:

> About the time I started on a curve on Elm, I had turned to my right to give signals to open up the intervals since we were fixing to get on the freeway a short distance away. That's all I had on my mind. Just as I turned around, then the first shot went off. It hit back there.[50]

He saw the shot hit the south side of the curb on Elm Street:

> It looked like it hit the concrete or grass there in just a flash, and a bunch of junk flew up like a white or gray color dust or smoke coming out of the concrete.[51]

Ellis explained the concrete impact was from the first shot. After that, he heard two more shots (three shots altogether):

> The sounds were all clear and loud and sounded about the same. From where I was, they sounded like they were coming from around where the tall tree was in front of that building [the TSBD]. Of course, I'm forming an opinion based on where I saw that stuff hit the street, so I knew that it had to come from up that way, and I assumed the others came from the same place.[52]

---

50 Larry A. Sneed, "Stavis Ellis," in *No More Silence: An Oral History of the Assassination of President Kennedy* (Dallas, TX: Three Forks Books, 1998), pp. 142-153, at p. 145.

51 Ibid.

52 Ibid.

See also: Bonar Menninger, *Mortal Error: The Shot That Killed JFK*, op. cit., pp. 68-78. Howard Donahue was the protagonist in this book. In a simulation, he was the one rare marksman who succeeded in hitting a JFK-like target within the allotted time. I had the pleasure of meeting Howard Donahue and his wife at their home in Maryland.

Royce Skelton, a mail clerk at the Texas-Louisiana Freight Bureau, witnessed the assassination from the Triple Overpass. He testified to the WC:

> After those two shots, and the car came on down closer to the triple underpass, well, there was another shot—two more shots I heard, but one of them—I saw a bullet, or I guess it was a bullet—I take it for granted it was—hit in front of the President's car on the cement, and when it did, the smoke carried with it—away from the building [the TSBD].[53]

Skelton testified that when the shot hit the pavement, it "scattered" into a "spray." He saw spray go westward (in the downhill direction that the limousine was moving).[54]

Harry Holmes was an inspector for the US Post Office Department. He observed the scene via binoculars from his office window on the fifth floor of the terminal annex building at the corner of Houston and Commerce Streets. He testified to the WC about three firecracker-like sounds, one of which caused "dust fly up" that flew "off of President Kennedy."[55] Mrs. Donald Baker, a bookkeeper in the TSBD, watched the motorcade from the front of the TSBD. She testified to the WC that she saw "sparks" from an apparent firecracker that hit the street behind the limousine as it passed her on Elm Street.[56] Ira David Wood III noted in his extensive *JFK Assassination Chronology*: "On hearing the first burst of

---

53 "Testimony of Royce G. Skelton," *Hearings before the President's Commission on the Assassination of President Kennedy*, vol. 7, op. cit., pp. 236-239, at p. 238.

54 Ibid.

55 "Testimony of Harry D. Holmes," *Hearings before the President's Commission on the Assassination of President Kennedy*, vol. 7, op. cit., pp. 289-308, at p. 291.

56 "Testimony of Mrs. Donald Baker," *Hearings before the President's Commission on the Assassination of President Kennedy*, vol. 7, op. cit., pp. 507-515.

firing, [Dallas County] Sheriff [Bill] Decker glances back and thinks sees a bullet bouncing off the street pavement." Wood added: "Motorcycle officer James Chaney will also tell newsmen this day [November 22, 1963] that the first shot missed. It is suggested that JFK is hit by small pieces of the street pavement and stops waving for a moment."[57]

However, since copper residue was found on the coat and shirt (only on the back), it is unlikely that the clothing holes were caused by bits of street pavement, unless the street was paved with copper.

Chesser summed up his conclusions about the frontal shot to JFK's right forehead as follows:

> This is what I saw on the original right lateral skull x-ray at the archives. There is a gap in the bone—not very big, maybe 3 mm, but remember that this is a composite of all the material between the x-ray machine and the film—when viewed from the side, a hole in the frontal bone may not be seen at all, and if it is, it won't appear as wide as its actual width. I think that this defect is probably due to a combination of an entry wound and associated radial fracture line(s).[58]

He explained his findings:

> The most important finding here is the proximity of these tiny metallic fragments to this bone defect. This location, on the intracranial side of the bony defect, is highly suggestive of an entry wound.

---

57 Ira David Wood III, "22 November 1963: A Chronology," in *Murder in Dealey Plaza*, ed. James H. Fetzer, op. cit., pp. 17-118, at p. 36.

Wood's *JFK Assassination Chronicle* is also available as a Kindle e-book, https://amzn.to/3NK5Moz.

58 Michael Chesser, MD, "A Review of the JFK Cranial x-Rays and Photographs," Assassination of JFK, n.d., https://assassinationofjfk.net/a-review-of-the-jfk-cranial-x-rays-and-photographs/. This is from Chesser's lecture for the 2015 JFK Lancer Conference in Dallas, Texas.

> One of the principles of skull ballistics is that the largest fragments travel the furthest from the entry site, with the smallest fragments traveling the least distance, and that is exactly what is seen on this right lateral skull x-ray. Tiny fragments were seen on the inner side of this right front skull defect, and the largest fragments were noted in the back of the skull.[59]

Chesser concluded that the fragment trail was due to a bullet entry at the right forehead near the hairline. He added that on the AP X-ray film, the fragment trail is located superiorly, trailing upward and backward on the right side.[60]

In James DiEugenio's and Oliver Stone's documentary *JFK: Destiny Betrayed* (the four-hour version of Stone's 2021 *JFK Revisited: Through the Looking Glass*), there is a segment in which Drs. Chesser, Aguilar, and I discuss the frontal shot to JFK's right forehead.

> NARRATOR [WHOOPI GOLDBERG]: After the film *JFK* was released, several doctors went to the National Archives to view the X-rays of Kennedy's skull. They saw details in these X-rays which presented yet another problem for the Warren Report's claim that Kennedy was only shot from the rear.

> DR. DAVID MANTIK: Well, the government investigators did claim that there was no evidence of a shot from the front. But they didn't tell us a few things that were very important, which we have learned only in recent years. We have seen tiny metal fragments right at the forehead.

> DR. MICHAEL CHESSER: When you look at the X-rays that are stored at the archives now, on the lateral X-ray there is a fragment trail. It

59 Ibid.

60 Ibid.

actually expands from front to back, and there are dozens of very tiny dustlike fragment particles up in this location.

DR. DAVID MANTIK: Now why is that important? Well, what we know is that the larger bullet fragments travel farther, whereas the smaller ones tend to stay near the entry site. That's what we see on these X-rays. In other words, we can reasonably interpret these as being consistent with a frontal bullet, but being radically inconsistent with a posterior bullet.

DR. GARY AGUILAR: And that's not evidence you can erase. You can't make that disappear, but that's incontrovertible evidence of a shot from the right front by a non-jacketed bullet.[61]

In my interview with DiEugenio for the 2021 Stone documentary is another sequence about the frontal shot to the right forehead:

JAMES DIEUGENIO: Now, did the House Select Committee say that one of the reasons that they thought that all of the autopsy materials [were] genuine was because there was no evidence of a shot from the front?

DR. DAVID MANTIK: On the lateral X-rays in particular, the findings of Dr. Chesser and myself are quite remarkable. We have seen tiny metal fragments right at the forehead on these lateral X-rays and Chesser in particular has seen a small hole in the skull consistent with the passage of a bullet through the forehead. None of the government investigations have ever told us about these things.

61 James DiEugenio, "*JFK: Destiny Betrayed* (Annotated Transcript of Four-Hour Film)" in *JFK Revisited: Through the Looking Glass* (New York: Skyhorse Publishing, 2022), pp. 155-190, at p. 169.

> Further, most of the bullet fragments that we see on the lateral skull X-rays are in the anterior half of the skull. These are for the most part very, very tiny. Many of them are only one millimeter or so in size. In other words, we can reasonably interpret these as being consistent with a frontal bullet, but being radically inconsistent with a posterior bullet.[62]

Kinetic energy explains why larger fragments travel farther than smaller fragments. Kinetic energy = 1/2 mv^2, where m = mass and v = velocity. Thus, a particle with more mass has more kinetic energy. Besides that, though, smaller fragments decelerate faster—the drag forces on them are relatively greater. Hence, the tiny particles near the forehead suggest an entry near that site. The larger fragment at the right rear provides additional evidence for a frontal entry. As expected, larger fragments travel farther.

WC Exhibit 387 is the official autopsy report (see Appendix J), signed by Humes, Boswell, and Finck. The pathologists noted: "*Roentgenograms of the skull reveal multiple minute metallic fragments along a line corresponding with a line joining the above-described small occipital wound and the right supra-orbital ridge.*"[63] In his 2021 presentation to the Future of Freedom Foundation,[64] Chesser called this a "bald-faced lie." He is correct; there is no such trail—no metallic fragments are visible along that low-lying path. This lie by the pathologists suggests that they felt they had to acknowledge the metallic trail, so they simply displaced it downward (by 10 cm) in order to avoid a second headshot.

In September 1977, *immediately before* the HSCA made the JFK

---

62 Ibid., "Interview Excerpts: Dr. David Mantik," pp. 264-272, at p. 269.

63 "Clinical record of autopsy protocol prepared by the Naval Medical School, Bethesda, Md., on the autopsy performed on President Kennedy," in *Hearings before the President's Commission on the Assassination of President Kennedy,* vol. 16, CE 387, op. cit., pp. 978-983. at p. 981. See Appendix J.

64 Michael Chesser, "Reviewing the Autopsy X-Rays," op. cit.

X-ray films public for the first time, Russell Morgan, MD (the sole radiologist for the Clark Panel), almost surely to avert professional humiliation, essentially recanted his earlier opinion. In a statement reported in the newspapers[65] at the time, Morgan said he was no longer so certain that the single bullet that hit JFK's head from the rear was a Mannlicher-Carcano round. Instead, he suggested that the fragmentation of the bullet (i.e., the fragment trail) was so severe that the bullet might have been a so-called "dum-dum" (hollow point) round. With this statement, Morgan had essentially exonerated Oswald. He had also thereby left the 6.5 mm object free-floating in fantasy land; he simply ignored it! After all, this 6.5 mm fake does *not* lie on the fragment trail. Nonetheless, it had been the keystone for the Clark Panel's daft cowlick entry wound—which they had elevated by 10 cm above the WC's entry site. Morgan also admitted, for the first time, that he now favored exhuming JFK's body to answer questions about the bullet fragments.[66] Unfortunately, for the truth, he had withheld all of his new-found insights from the Clark Panel report, so that (in 1977) he was nine years too late. In any case, the HSCA ignored his new perceptions.

In his interview with DiEugenio for the 2021 Stone documentary, Chesser also commented on this sleight-of-hand elevation of the (proposed) rear entry site:

---

65 *Lansing State Journal* (Lansing, Michigan), September 16, 1977, p. 9. Curiously, Voyager I was launched on September 5, 1977, just eleven days before Humes publicly viewed the JFK X-ray films with the HSCA. Despite his alarming comments, Morgan was not further interrogated by the HSCA, and no one asked about Voyager either. The article was titled "Expert Backs Warren Report," when it more accurately should have been titled "Expert Questions Warren Report."

66 For the complete newspaper article about Morgan's near confession, see my hardcover book: *The JFK Assassination Decoded: Criminal Forgery in the Autopsy Photographs and X-rays*. The excerpted newspaper article appears immediately after the dedication to the e-book, *JFK's Head Wounds: A Final Synthesis—and a New Analysis of the Harper Fragment.*

DR. MICHAEL CHESSER: The [Warren] Commission placed the entry of a bullet fired from the sixth floor of the Texas School Book Depository low in the back of the head, right next to the external occipital protuberance. The Clark Panel and the HSCA moved u[this wound four inches, into the parietal bone. Four inches is quite a distance from the original location of the entrance wound. They did this for several reasons. They knew that an entry in the lower location would cause enormous damage to the cerebellum—and to their story. In the fake brain photograph the cerebellum is untouched. In the autopsy report, Commander Humes described a fragment trail beginning near the external occipital protuberance. The extant X-ray films disprove this.

JAMES DIEUGENIO: So there is no diagonal that leads upward in the present X-rays?

DR. MICHAEL CHESSER: The X-rays at the archives do not show a fragment trail extending from low up to here. They show a fragment trail from the back of the parietal bone to the frontal bone. But the fragment trail doesn't fit the conclusions of the Clark Panel or the House Select Committee. For several reasons. I think the most important reason is that the tiniest fragments on that trail, and there are dozens of them, are very thin or just inside the frontal bone. And the largest fragments are at the back of the skull. This goes against all forensic evidence that the tiniest fragments are not going to travel that far. So it's impossible for a shot here, in the back of the skull, to result in all of the tiniest bullet fragments in the frontal region.

JAMES DIEUGENIO: You're saying that the fact that there's all these dustlike particles in the front of the skull would indicate a point of entry from the front.

DR. MICHAEL CHESSER: Yes it does. It's very strong evidence.

JAMES DIEUGENIO: And you're also saying that because the larger fragments were in the back, that would also indicate a shot from the front.

DR. MICHAEL CHESSER: Yes.[67] [End of colloquy.]

However, even after this unwarranted elevation by the HSCA, the debris trail is still too high—the trail actually lies noticeably *above* the HSCA's entry site. Chesser concurred. During the 2015 JFK Lancer Conference, he stated: "I think that one of the reasons that they [the HSCA] moved the entry wound up was due to the fragment particle trail shown in the right lateral skull x-ray. If a line is drawn from the Warren Commission entry site to the proposed exit site, you'll notice that the particle trail doesn't correspond with these sites. The prominent particle trail is located in the upper portion of the skull."[68]

The HSCA illustrated their hypothetical trajectory for the sole headshot (Figure 3.10).

---

67 James DiEugenio, "Interview Excerpts: Dr. Michael Chesser," in *JFK Revisited: Through the Looking Glass*, op. cit., pp. 292-298, at pp. 293-294.

68 Michael Chesser, MD, "A Review of the JFK Cranial x-Rays and Photographs," op. cit.

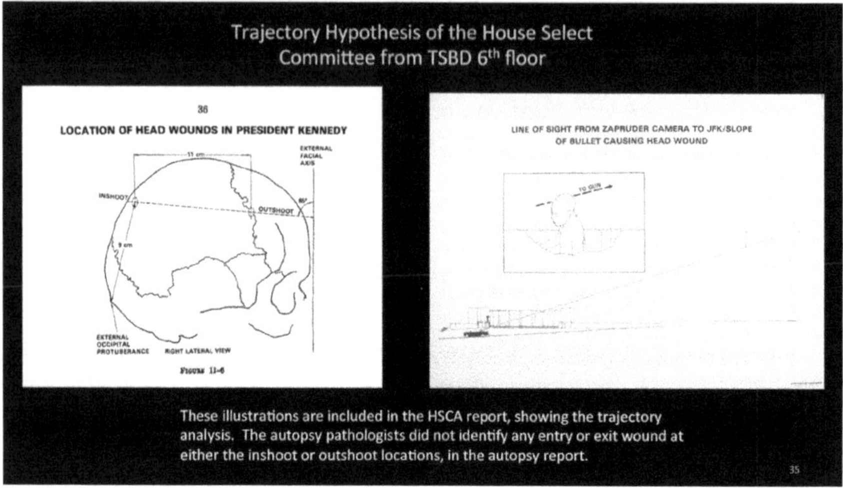

Figure 3.10

The HSCA's Imaginary Trajectory: From the TSBD to the Parietal Skull.

Figure 3.10 is from Michael Z. Chesser, MD, "The Application of Forensic Principles for the Analysis of the Autopsy Skull X-Rays of President Kennedy and a Review of Brain Photographs," Kennedys and King, November 27, 2017, op. cit.

A NEW WITNESS—AND A SINGULAR AUTOPSY PHOTOGRAPH[69]

At the Rochester Institute of Technology,[70] several years after the sunset

69 This section was previously published in David W. Mantik, *The JFK Assassination Decoded,* op. cit., specifically *John F. Kennedy's Head Wounds: A Final Synthesis—and a New Analysis of the Harper Fragment,* op. cit., from Appendix L, "A New Witness—and a Singular Autopsy Photograph," located at the back of my hardcover book, at p. 401, renumbered as 1-92, at pp. 86-87.

70 Rochester, New York, of course, was (and still is) the headquarters of the Eastman Kodak Company, whose film was used at the JFK autopsy—for the photographs and for the radiographs. It is also the likely site (Hawkeyeworks) for alteration of the Zapruder film. For "The Case for Alteration," view my recent lecture at The JFK Assassination at 60:

of the HSCA, a senior photography major, Quentin Schwinn, was invited by his teacher (a former consultant for the HSCA) to meet a visitor. Schwinn did not recognize the stranger, who was dressed in a trench coat or a London Fog–type coat. The visitor was not anyone Schwinn had seen before, and he did not seem to be from one of the other colleges on campus. He didn't seem like a professor. Among other images (that appeared to be classified), this visitor showed him a four-by-five-inch color transparency of JFK,[71] presumably from the autopsy; it was a nearly frontal shot of the face. No one said anything as Schwinn bent forward to study the image. On the right side of the face, Schwinn observed that the hair stuck out, as though the bone underneath had been displaced outward, but no entry hole was visible.

Here is his recollection:

> It looked like a trap door was hinged at the top and it was pushing a line of hair out above the right ear. There was an edge of hair separated from the hair underneath that formed a gap of maybe 1/8 – ¼ of an inch. I could see this because the photo was taken so close to the center line of the right side of the head.... It was nearly a straight line with rounded corners.[72]

The tracheotomy incision was both horizontal and vertical, i.e., four flaps of tissue had been produced by two separate incisions. The horizontal incision was not nearly so wide (or as ragged) as in the extant photographs. Schwinn continued:

The Cyril H. Wecht Institute of Forensic Science and Law, 22nd Annual Symposium, November 15-17, 2023, https://www.youtube.com/watch?v=_78XIQ6BRtQ.

71 The extant autopsy photographs are all color transparencies, as I confirmed at the Archives.

72 David W. Mantik, *The JFK Assassination Decoded,* op. cit., specifically *John F. Kennedy's Head Wounds: A Final Synthesis—and a New Analysis of the Harper Fragment,* op.cit. The quotation is from Quentin Schwinn, p. 86.

> The horizontal one was about an inch long and the vertical one was about 1½ inches. The resulting four corners of skin looked thick and were curled back at the tips. There were two clean cuts at right angles to each other. There was no tearing or ripping or missing skin, just curled back corners from the two cuts and a small hole in the middle.[73]

The most striking feature, however, was an obvious bullet hole in the right forehead, very near the hairline. This was located just where the forehead turns into the top of the head, and at the side, just where it turns into the temple. In 2013, at the urging of Douglas Horne (who had previously met him), Schwinn asked a medical illustrator to sketch this image (Figure 3.11). Schwinn said that, although this image is not a perfect representation, it accurately portrays the forehead entry. Here is how he described what he saw:

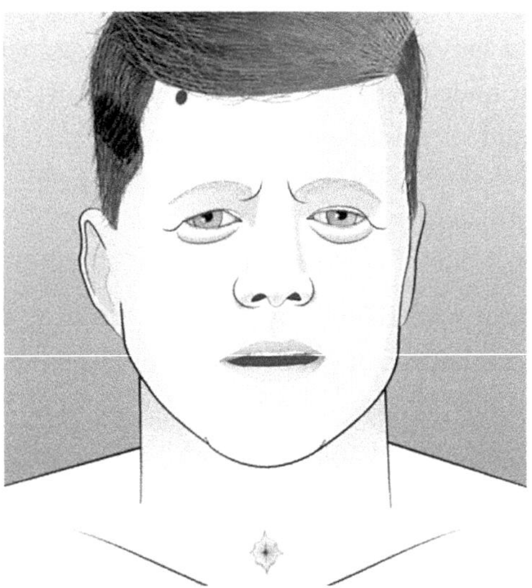

Figure 3.11

A Reproduction of an Autopsy Photograph Seen by Schwinn. A medical illustrator prepared this. The face was distinctly JFK's.

---

73 Ibid.

> The hole in the forehead was filled with a pink plug. It looked like bubble gum with the powdery sugar licked off. It looked dry. It was slightly rippled. It was depressed from the skin a little bit. I could not see the bone along the edge of the hole. I could see the top of his head, but really you could see the bangs brushed back and that there was hair on the top of the head. It was about the size of a dime, maybe smaller but no bigger.[74]

Schwinn still does not know why the photograph was shown to him. However, at the same encounter, he "…was also shown overhead photographs that I consider to have been classified. I was also questioned as if being interviewed." On graduation day Schwinn was offered a position at an American intelligence installation overseas.

The four-by-five-inch color transparency appeared to be an original:

> I looked at the transparency edges and concluded that the film was not a dupe or copy. The edges looked like it would if it was a camera original. The plane of focus was at the throat and ear. In other words, the eyes were a bit out of focus, but not by much.

I asked him if he could assess the age of the photograph:

> I do remember examining the 4"x5" Ektachrome and concluding that it looked as if it was old enough to be an original …. Ektachrome had a tendency to be slightly green. A professional photographer would test his batch of film and get a filter pack (a set of Wratten gelatin filters[75] of differing color and density) to correct the color balance.

74 Ibid. Quotation from Quentin Schwinn, p. 87.

75 Wratten gelatin filters are different colored lens filters used to filter out various wave lengths of light. They are named after British inventor Frederick Wratten. See "Wratten number," Wikipedia, last edited September 28, 2023, https://en.wikipedia.org/wiki/Wratten_number.

> If you didn't do that, it would look a bit green. This tendency for Ektachrome to look a bit green if not filtered on the camera to correct this bias is why Fuji film became so popular. Fuji film had a more natural color balance right out of the box. This transparency that I looked at was a bit green and it looked a bit faded as well, which indicated its age, and it told me at that time that I was looking at an original, from about 20 years earlier. The film notches were consistent with Kodak film designation for Ektachrome. It also looked a bit over-exposed. Exposure is tricky in these [autopsy] conditions and so I am not at all surprised that the exposure was not dead on. The difference between fading and over-exposure is in the saturation of color. You can have a high saturation of color that is bright, and you can have a low saturation of color that is bright. They can be easily confused, but I was a photography student and was expected to know the difference. It is the difference between chroma, hue and value. Even though the color was off and towards the green side and even though the exposure was off and toward the over exposed side, the combination indicated to me that the film was old and had faded, which is common to Ektachrome. It is not something that Kodachrome does, but Ektachrome does fade in density and color saturation.[76]

Since the extant autopsy photographs show no entry at this forehead site, but rather show an incision (precisely there), I asked Schwinn if he had seen any sign of an incision. He replied that he had not. This is, of course, consistent with the Parkland witnesses, who also denied seeing an incision there. The initial absence of an incision at the autopsy is also consistent with two autopsy paraprofessionals,[77] who had watched

76 Ibid. Quotation from Quentin Schwinn.

77 (Emphases in Horne's original) "Tom Robinson, who in 1963 was a twenty-year-old Gawler's embalming assistant (whose specialty was applying restorative art to cadavers to prepare them for open-casket funerals), said he was present all night long inside the morgue and had a '50-yardline

as Humes performed (illicit) surgery before the official autopsy began. The implication is obvious: Humes was forced to hide this forehead entry site, and he did so by incising precisely at that spot. Had he not done so, the game would have been up—and a conspiracy would have been inescapable. Curiously, Boswell almost did give the game away; in his testimony before the ARRB, he described this site as "an incised wound."[78] "Wound" means a bullet, while "incised" implies a scalpel.

THE STRANGE "T-SHAPED" IMAGE

On JFK's sequestered lateral X-ray film, during my ninth visit, I spotted a curious "T-shaped" image just below JFK's jaw at the top of his neck (Figure 3.12).

---

seat' in the gallery. He witnessed things that were NOT WITNESSED by the large audience to the official autopsy that began at 8:00 PM. [Two examples were: (1) his witnessing JFK's skull sawed open to remove the brain—something Humes did not have to do before his large audience at 8:00 PM; and (2) he saw about ten metal fragments removed from JFK's cranium and placed in a vial—this contradicts the official account that there were only two small metal fragments removed from the cranium.] In order to see these events, Robinson must have arrived early, with the body." Anthony DeFiore, "Tom Robinson, from Gawler's Funeral Home, actually watched the JFK autopsy in the Bethesda hospital morgue!" Deep Politics Forum, November 26, 2013, https://deeppoliticsforum.com/fora/thread-11770.html.

Dennis David typed a report that evening describing four bullet fragments (likely from more than one bullet). Oddly enough, four metal fragments said to be from JFK are shown in *High Treason: The Assassination of JFK & the Case for Conspiracy* (1980, 1989, 1998) by Harrison Edward Livingstone and Robert J. Groden, p. 562. I know nothing more about these, and Livingstone is now deceased. Perhaps we should ask the second author, Robert Groden, who still lives.

78 "Deposition of Dr. J. Thornton Boswell," corrected transcript, op. cit., p. 65, https://www.aarclibrary.org/publib/jfk/arrb/medical_testimony/pdf/Boswell_2-26-96.pdf.

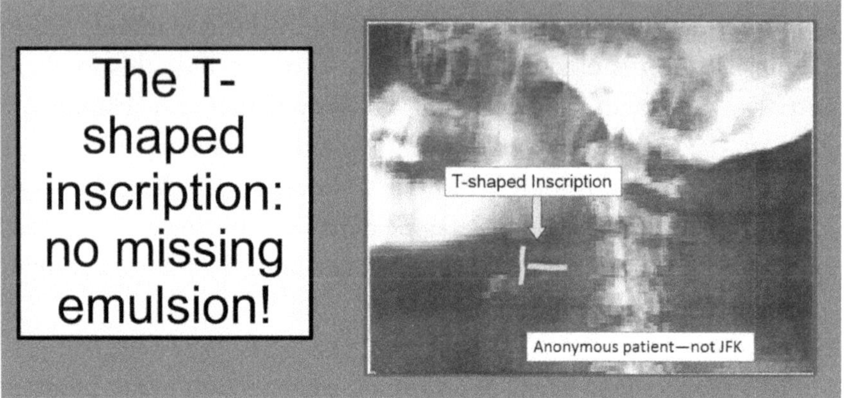

Figure 3.12
"T-shaped" Inscription on a Lateral X-ray Film. The Archives have never released this X-ray film of JFK, so I re-created the "T-shaped" image on an anonymous patient.

The T-shaped inscription must have been etched into the emulsion on the original (never-released) lateral X-ray film. Such etching is easy to do, e.g., by using a fingernail, metal file, or nail. The missing emulsion would have been easy to detect, especially while viewing the surface at an angle to a light source. Inspection of the other side would clearly have shown *no* missing emulsion (because the etching was only done on *one side* of the double emulsion film). Realizing this, during my final visit to the Archives (April 12, 2001), I scrutinized these emulsions very carefully.

I first asked Steve Tilley, the JFK archivist, to remove the X-ray film from its transparent plastic sheath so that I could view the surfaces directly. He did so. And then, after viewing at multiple angles, I recognized that no emulsion was missing from *either side* of the film! The implication was inescapable: this could only be a copy film—not an original. That is because the copy film would preserve the image of the T-shaped inscription, but it would also retain its own emulsion (on both sides)—since no one had scraped emulsion off either side of this copy film.

So, why does it matter if this is a copy? Here is the answer: if an X-ray film can be copied, it can also be altered during the same process—via a double exposure in the darkroom. And that is almost certainly how the 6.5 mm fake materialized on the AP X-ray film. Furthermore, this same process most likely yielded the two White Patches. Once I recognized that this lateral X-ray film was a forgery, I had a shocking insight. *None* of the three extant JFK skull X-ray films is an original—all three must be copies. In this case, it means that all three are altered images.[79] Most likely, all of the original skull X-ray films (of five to six total) had to be destroyed because they contained forensic proof that Oswald was not the sole assassin.

In Chesser's review (at the 2015 JFK Lancer Conference), he confirmed my observations of the T-shaped inscription:

> Dr. Mantik described emulsion over the T-shaped wax mark, which was attributed to Ed Reed marking the film. I agree with him that the surface of the film appeared smooth, when viewed at eye level.[80]

In other words, like me, Dr. Chesser saw that emulsion was fully present on both sides of this lateral X-ray film, thus leaving no doubt that the film is a duplicate.[81] At the original autopsy, X-ray technicians Jerrol Custer and Edward Reed, both navy corpsmen, operated the portable X-ray machine. Custer was the instructor for the twenty-four navy corpsmen enrolled in a one-year training program in X-ray

---

79 The oblique skull X-ray films are also missing. Jerrol Custer, in particular, told me about them. When I spoke to Ebersole, even he seemed to recall them. James Jenkins has also reported them.

80 Michael Chesser, MD, "A Review of the JFK Cranial X-Rays and Photographs," op. cit.

81 The media have routinely clamored that the ARRB produced no "smoking gun." My response has been that the medical evidence (ignored by every ARRB board member, none of whom had any medical background) constitutes precisely such a smoking gun (actually multiple guns). But my further retort is that the T-shaped inscription is even worse—in honor of my Jewish colleagues in this JFK escapade, it is (à la Moses) a "burning bush."

technology. Reed was one of his students.[82] In his testimony before the ARRB, Custer admitted to inserting various "markers" for subsequent identification into the X-ray films.[83] However, these were metal; they were separate and distinct from the T-shaped inscription, and they are not relevant to this analysis.

WHY WOULD ANYONE BOTHER FORGING JFK'S AUTOPSY X-RAYS?

Having scientifically proven that all three extant JFK skull X-ray films are forgeries—duplicate copies altered by double-exposure techniques in a darkroom—the next question is obvious: Why would anyone bother to alter JFK's autopsy X-rays?

At Parkland Hospital, the medical team observed a gaping exit hole at the right rear. The White Patch is clearly well *anterior* to the missing occipital bone, which is located at the far rear of the skull. Unfortunately, many researchers have wrongly concluded that the White Patch was designed to cover this missing bone, but that is not true. So, why was the White Patch added?

We can only guess, but most likely the forgers wanted to draw attention away from the rear of the skull (where brain was clearly missing), so that viewers would instead focus on the anterior skull, where brain was almost totally absent (in the X-ray film). The resulting visual impression would, of course, suggest that a bullet had exited from the front but not from the rear—thus further implicating Oswald. So, while the White Patch does not cover the missing occipital bone, its presence makes it difficult to assess how much brain is missing (on the lateral X-ray films). It merely distracts us—and thereby emphasizes the huge amount of missing brain at the front—on both left and right sides (despite the opposite impression of the brain photographs).

---

82 Douglas Horne, "Navy Enlisted X-Ray Technologists Jerrol Custer and Edward Reed," in *Inside the ARRB*, op. cit., vol. 2, pp. 419-478, at p. 420.

83 Ibid., pp. 444-446.

If I were to alter a lateral X-ray film with a White Patch, I would first have made certain that the left side mirrored the right side. This would have been simple: just flip the cut-out hole (left for right) when double exposing the second side. And then use a stopwatch to time the two exposures so that they were the same duration.[84] But, as the lateral films now stand, it appears that our forger was either rushed or careless. Or, just maybe, there is a third option: perhaps he really wanted to be exposed as a forger. If this latter had been Ebersole's goal, then conceivably he was caught off guard when I asked him my final question (about the 6.5 mm fake). In any case, he refused to respond.

When finally, I made this discovery, my then-fifteen-year-old (non-radiologist) son promptly understood the ominous significance of the T-shaped inscription, even before I had fully described it. I remain astounded that many JFK researchers still fail to appreciate its portent. Inserting a T-shaped image into an original X-ray film required scraping emulsion off the original X-ray (but only from one side). When copied, that T-shaped image would appear transparent (white in prints) but on the copied film both emulsions would still be intact. After all, neither side had been scraped off. So, the presence of two totally intact emulsions constitutes unimpeachable—and independent—proof that this particular lateral film must be a duplicate and cannot be an original. In spite of this, the Archives has claimed (via Steve Tilley) to have the original film. Of course, I have no idea whether Tilley ever read a single word I wrote. I suspect that he did not.

The fragment trail across the top of the skull is irrefutable evidence of a shot to the top of the head. The innumerable tiny fragments near the forehead (as well as the apparent hole in the forehead) are decisive proof that this shot came from the front.

At this point in our narrative, the JFK assassination is a closed case via at least two points: (1) a shot from the front means that Oswald was

---

84 The ODs imply that the forger used a shorter exposure for White Patch on the unpublished lateral X-ray film.

not the sole gunman and (2) the three extant JFK skull X-ray films are altered copies, which means that the US government was complicit in the destruction of the originals. After all, at no time did Cuba, Russia, or any other foreign power possess these items.

Anyone who understands the physics of OD measurements and the technique of X-ray duplication in a 1963 darkroom can now know with nearly 100 percent certainty that this was a conspiracy. Because the radiographs and photographs were always under the control of the SS, the highest levels of the US government are automatically implicated. The SS was under the direct aegis of the Secretary of the Treasury, C. Douglas Dillon.[85] And Dillon reported directly to LBJ.

So, in short, here is life at its most rudimentary level: a simple student X-ray corpsman innocently etches a routine identification mark onto a single X-ray film. But then, after copying, this inscription metamorphoses into something never intended: an undeniable proof of illegal evidence alteration—and overt evidence of a treasonous domestic coup d'état.

CHAPTER 3: SUMMARY[86]

The White Patch and the Black Space are quite extraordinary for lateral X-ray films. The Black Space does not mean forgery—it merely implies

---

85 Dillon had worked for John Foster Dulles in Thomas E. Dewey's 1948 presidential campaign. Earl Warren was on the ticket as the VP. In spite of persistent media disbelief, Truman won that election. Unless the negative verdict on the WC counts, this was the only election that Warren ever lost. Clarence Dillon (born Clarence Lapowski, son of an immigrant Polish Jew) was the father of C. Douglas Dillon. James Forrestal (who regularly golfed with Joe Kennedy) was once a partner in Clarence's firm—Dillon, Read, and Company. According to *Fortune*, Clarence was one of the richest men in America. Douglas served on ExComm during the Cuban Missile Crisis (see *Wikipedia*).

86 In an extraordinary exhibition of research, Vince Palamara cites 202 supporting witnesses for at least one frontal shot. See *Honest Answers about the Murder of President John F. Kennedy: A New Look at the JFK Assassination* (Walterville, OR: Triune Day, 2021). In Chapter Nine, read his "Master List of Witnesses Who Indicated That JFK Was Shot from the Front, Plus the Wounds to JFK," pp. 293-365. Quite bizarrely, 202 is the number of votes that LBJ "borrowed" during his Ballot Box 13 primary election recount for the Texas Senate seat in 1948, after which he became "Landslide Lyndon" (to his own amusement). See chapter 2 in *A Texan Looks at Lyndon: A Study in Illegitimate Power* by J. Evetts Haley (Canyon, Texas: The Palo Duro Press, 1964), p. 27.

a near total absence of brain on both the left and right sides, which stands in radical disagreement with the official brain photographs. The White Patch, on both lateral X-ray films, was an unnecessary forgery in the darkroom, via a second exposure. Paradoxically, the White Patch is absent from JFK's premortem lateral X-ray film. It was also absent from all nineteen forensic cases we reviewed. Furthermore, after forty-plus years in radiation oncology, I have never seen a White Patch on any patient.

Chesser's emphasis on the tiny metallic particles near the forehead clearly implies an entry there. This is consistent with the recollections of Crenshaw, and even some Bethesda witnesses, who saw an entry there. The mere existence of the two "knobby" objects in the publicly available lateral X-ray film is proof of alteration. These knobby objects are absent from the extant X-ray film at the Archives. They must have been deliberately added to the public image, surely to obscure the tiny metal fragments. This was not a random act. Someone performed this forgery at the behest of the HSCA.

In September 1977, *immediately before* the HSCA publicly displayed the JFK X-ray films for the first time, Russell Morgan, MD (the sole radiologist for the Clark Panel), essentially recanted. He instead suggested that the trail of metallic debris might be more consistent with a "dum-dum" bullet, rather than with a metal-jacketed bullet (like the Mannlicher-Carcano). By doing so, he essentially absolved Oswald, but the HSCA never displayed any interest in his unexpected revelation. After all, if accepted, it would have excised Oswald from their scenario.

At the Rochester Institute of Technology, Quentin Schwinn was shown a likely missing autopsy photograph, which was clearly an image of JFK. He saw an obvious bullet hole in the right forehead, very near the hairline, quite consistent with Crenshaw's observation and also consistent with Chesser's tiny forehead fragments. Contrary to the extant autopsy photograph, he did not see an incision there. This location is also completely consistent with the trail of metallic debris.

The T-shaped inscription was overlooked by all prior radiologists. Most likely, due to simple naivety, they simply lacked the imagination to explore it. After all, none of them were medical physicists. In fact, I only focused on it during my ninth, and final, visit to the Archives. But the presence of emulsion on both sides of this film is truly a smoking gun. Any original film, with such a T-shaped inscription, would surely show missing emulsion on one side (and only on one side) of the X-ray film. So, despite the official opinion of the Archives, that original lateral X-ray film has vanished. The Archives still does not understand the evidence.

4

THE OBLIQUE SHOT NEAR JFK'S RIGHT EAR (A SECOND FRONTAL HEADSHOT), THE HARPER BONE FRAGMENT, AND THE MYSTERY AUTOPSY PHOTOGRAPH (F8)

To be ignorant of what occurred before you were born is to remain always a child. For what is the worth of human life, unless it is woven into the life of our ancestors by the records of history?

—**MARCUS TULLIUS CICERO**[1]

There are some things the general public does not need to know and shouldn't....I believe democracy flourishes when the government can take legitimate steps to keep its secrets and when the press can decide whether to print what it knows.

—**KATHARINE GRAHAM**, ex-publisher of the *Washington Post*[2]

---

1 Marcus Tullius Cicero, *Orator*, chapter 34, section 120.

2 Katharine Graham, "Secrecy and the Press" (speech to CIA), November 16, 1988, CIA FOIA Reading Room, transcript, https://web.archive.org/web/20170123101736/https://www.cia.gov/library/readingroom/docs/CIA-RDP99-00777R000302440003-9.pdf.

See also: Alexander Cockburn and Jeffrey St. Clair, *Whiteout: The CIA, Drugs, and the Press* (New York, NY: Verso, 1998), p. 31.

The very word "secrecy" is repugnant in a free and open society; and we are as a people inherently and historically opposed to secret societies, to secret oaths and to secret proceedings.

—**JOHN F. KENNEDY**, Address before the American Newspaper Publishers Association, April 27, 1961 (seven days after the Bay of Pigs)[3]

What can we now conclude, in this year 2009, about the actual wounds inflicted on President Kennedy's body in Dealey Plaza? An analysis of the impact debris at the time of the fatal shot strongly supports the likelihood of a fatal shot from the front, and proves that Blakey and the HSCA were incorrect when they claimed the grassy knoll shot missed.

—**DOUGLAS HORNE**, *Inside the ARRB*, 2009[4]

The main thrust of the impact debris was directed over the rear of the car onto the two motorcyclists riding in the convoy to the left.

—**JOSIAH THOMPSON**, *Six Seconds in Dallas*, 1967[5]

---

3 John F. Kennedy, "Address: 'The President and the Press' Before the American Newspaper Publishers Association, New York City," April 27, 1961, American Presidency Project, University of California at Santa Barbara, https://www.presidency.ucsb.edu/documents/address-the-president-and-the-press-before-the-american-newspaper-publishers-association.

4 Douglas Horne, *Inside the ARRB*, op. cit., vol. 4, p. 1138. The capitalization and bold type in the original was eliminated to make reading easier. In the original, the first sentence is all capital letters in bold type. The second sentence is bold type with the first letter of every key word capitalized. This passage is a subsection heading of *Inside the ARRB*, chapter 13, "What Really Happened at the Bethesda Morgue (And in Dealey Plaza)?" pp. 987-1184.

5 Josiah Thompson, *Six Seconds in Dallas*, op. cit., p. 100.

IN HIS WC TESTIMONY ON MARCH 25, 1964, Dr. William Kemp Clark repeated his conclusion, first made at the Parkland press conference, at about 2:30 p.m. CST, on November 22, 1963. Clark told the WC that he still believed that the gaping wound at the right rear of the head was an exit wound—from an oblique shot.[6] The entry was at the right side of the head.

Clark continued:

> I then examined the wound in the back of the President's head. This was a large, gaping wound in the right posterior part, with cerebral and cerebellar tissue being damaged and exposed. There was considerable blood loss evident on the carriage, the floor, and the clothing of some of the people present. I would estimate 1,500 cc of blood being present.[7]

Under questioning, Clark held his ground:

> ARLEN SPECTER: What, if anything, did you say then in the course of that press conference?
>
> DR. CLARK: I described the President's wound in his head in very much the same way as I have described it here. I was asked if this wound was an entrance wound, an exit wound, or what, and I said it could be an exit wound, but I felt it was a tangential wound.[8]

---

6 "Testimony of Dr. William Kemp Clark," *Hearings before the President's Commission on the Assassination of President Kennedy*, vol. 6, op. cit., pp. 18-27, at p. 20.

7 Ibid., p. 21.

8 Ibid.

Clark explained a "tangential" wound as "striking an object obliquely, not squarely or head on."[9] He elaborated:

> DR. CLARK: The effects of any missile striking an organ or (sic) [are] a function of the energy which is shed by the missile in passing through this organ when a bullet strikes the head, if it is able to pass through rapidly without shedding any energy into the brain, little damage results, other than that part of the brain which is directly penetrated by the missile. However, if it strikes the skull at an angle, it must then penetrate much more bone than normal, therefore, is likely to shed more energy, striking the brain a more powerful blow.
>
> Secondly, in striking the bone in this manner, it may cause pieces of the bone to be blown into the brain and thus act as secondary missiles. Finally, the bullet itself may be deformed and deflected so that it would go through or penetrate parts of the brain, not in the usual direct line it was proceeding.[10]

Dr. Clark stressed that the wound to the back of the president's head "was obviously a massive one and was insurvivable [sic]."[11]

He was correct. His conclusion disagreed with the WC, which claimed that the (sole) headshot came from the rear. Another headshot struck JFK distinctly after Z-313 (the traditional headshot frame). This additional bullet entered just forward of the right ear and exited at the right rear. This oblique shot opened a massive avulsive wound that blew out brain and bone tissue onto the Dallas police motorcycle escort at the left rear of the limousine. SS Agent Clint Hill was also hit by debris.

---

9 Ibid., p. 21.

10 Ibid.

11 Ibid., p. 22.

Before Z-343, Hill was still running desperately from the follow-up car, aiming to grab the limousine handle at the left rear.

DR. MICHAEL CHESSER: X-RAY FILM EVIDENCE OF AN OBLIQUE SHOT

In JFK's lateral X-ray film, Dr. Michael Chesser spotted a keyhole fracture in the temporal bone, near JFK's right ear. Such a fracture was described in "Keyhole Fracture of the Skull," in the December 2008 issue of the *Military Medicine Radiology Corner*:

> A keyhole fracture has a characteristic pattern…of both gunshot entrance and exit trauma. Keyhole fractures can be created by bullets penetrating the skull at an angle, by a bullet yawing off path, or by grazing the skull at a tangential trajectory without penetrating into the intracranium. These fractures exhibit a circular entrance defect and a triangular exit deficit created by bone or bullet fragments propagating from the initial point of impact on external examination or CT imaging.[12]

To illustrate a keyhole fracture, Chesser referenced the 2000 *Journal of Forensic Sciences* (Figure 4.1).

12 CT = Computed Tomography. The reference is to Second Lt. Aaron M. Jackson, USA, et. al., "Keyhole Fracture of the Skull," *Military Medicine Radiology Corner*, vol. 173 (December 2008): 1, https://apps.dtic.mil/sti/pdfs/ADA528579.pdf.

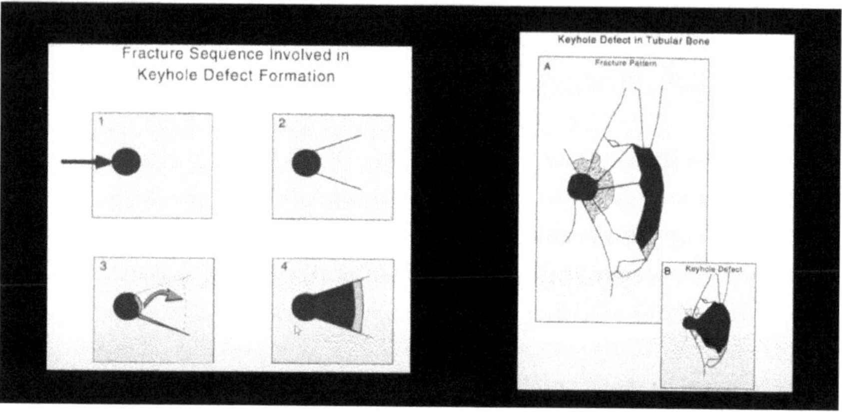

Figure 4.1

Keyhole Fracture Resulting from an Oblique Shot. The source for Figure 4.1 is H.E. Berryman and W.M. Gunther, "Keyhole defect production in tubular bone," *Journal of Forensic Sciences* 45, no. 2 (March 1, 2000): 483-487, https://europepmc.org/article/med/10782979. Figures 4.1–4.4 are from Michael Chesser's presentation: "Reviewing the Autopsy X-Rays," op. cit.

Chesser also cited a second peer-reviewed article (from the same journal in 1984):

> Keyhole lesions of the skull at the site of a gunshot entrance wound have been previously described: common to the lesions are a circular or ovoid component with internal beveling and a triangular portion with external beveling. The circular portion is, in fact, the point of initial impact or entrance, and the triangular portion is the exit. The lesion usually indicates a tangential shot, often with a portion of projectile being shaved off and exiting.[13]

13 D.S. Dixon, "Exit keyhole lesion and direction of fire in a gunshot wound of the skull," *Journal of Forensic Sciences* 29, no. 1, (January 1, 1984): 336-339, https://europepmc.org/article/med/6699601.

Chesser identified a triangular wound in JFK's right temporal bone, near the right ear, as seen in these slides from his 2021 presentation to the Future of Freedom Foundation (Figures 4.2 and 4.3).

The keyhole is indeed a crucial discovery—because the trail of metallic particles across the top of the X-ray films cannot explain the keyhole trauma that lies well *inferior* to this trail. In other words, the keyhole requires a quite different trajectory (from the trail) and that clearly implies a quite different bullet—and therefore conspiracy. Most likely, it was caused by the bullet that entered near the right ear. After causing the keyhole trauma, the bullet then triggered the large occipital hole associated with the expulsion of the Harper Fragment. To close the case, Chesser confirmed that the premortem X-ray film does not show this keyhole trauma. For the goals of prior investigations then, the appointed radiologists were wise to ignore it. We can only imagine the groans of government lawyers if such a keyhole had been cited by these official radiologists.

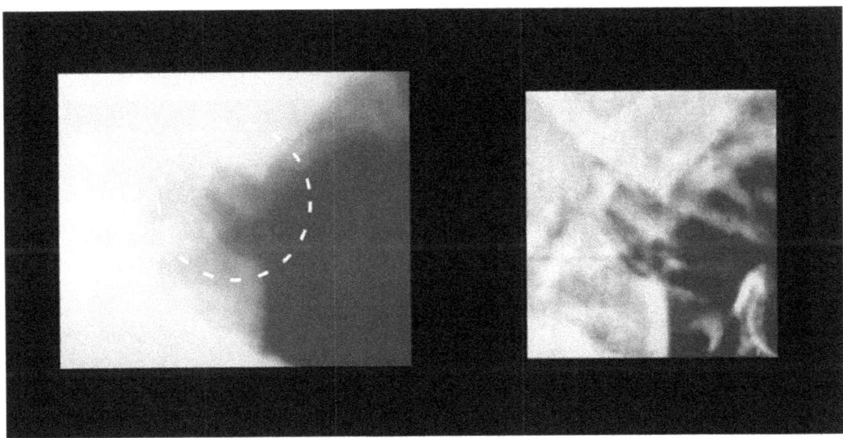

Figure 4.2
Keyhole Bullet Entry Wound. Temporal Bone: JFK Lateral X-ray Film.

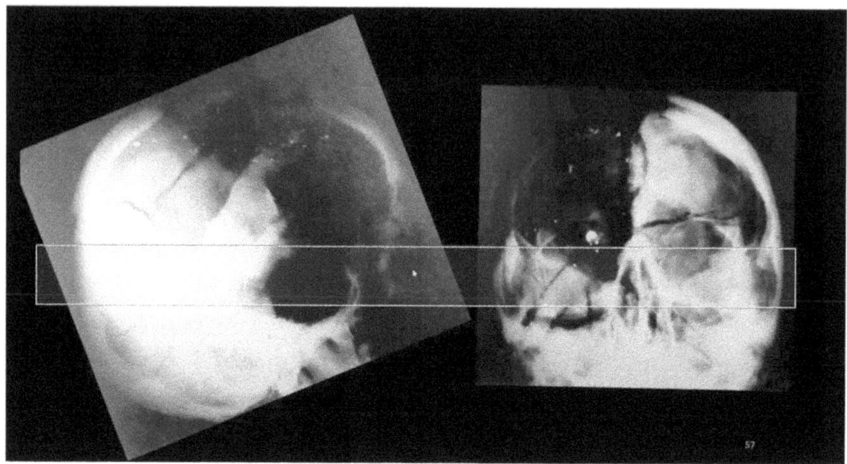

Figure 4.3
Temporal Bone: Bullet Entry Produces Keyhole Trauma. JFK Autopsy X-Ray Films.

In the AP X-ray film, just compare the right temporal region to the left temporal region (Figure 4.4). We see many fractured bones as well as bone fragments in the right temporal region; these are absent on the left.

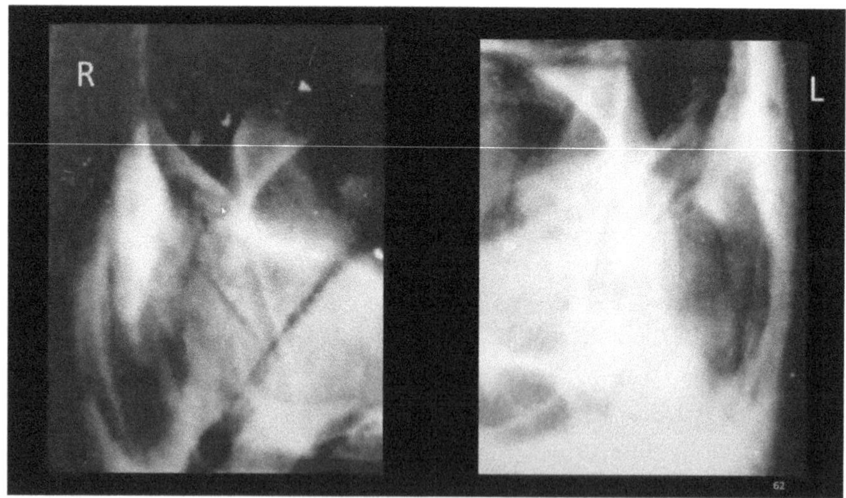

Figure 4.4
Right (R) Temporal Bone and Left (L) Temporal Bone, from JFK's AP Skull X-ray Film.

Dr. Don Curtis, DDS, was a first-year resident at Parkland Hospital in November 1963. Curtis told Chesser about his conversation with his supervisor, Dr. Robert Walker, DDS, a Parkland oral surgeon. Walker was in Trauma Room One. Curtis told Chesser:

> I [Curtis] was standing at the other side of the gurney on the left side and Dr. [Kemp] Clark, on the right side, raised [JFK's] head to describe the wound. I did hear him [Dr. Clark] say cerebellum, which places the wound posterior and inferior. After they [the other physicians] left, I went around to the head of the table, and what I saw, with the head back down on the pillow, was the right wound margin and cranial contents on the pillow. I did not see the right temporal wound, however, my chief, Dr. Robert Walker, told me the following morning that he did see what appeared to be a bullet hole in the right temple. He well knew a bullet hole.[14]

In 1985, Joseph McBride found a critical FBI memo buried among 98,755 pages of FBI documents released to the public during 1977–1978. Alan Belmont, the assistant director of the FBI, wrote the memo at the FBI's Washington headquarters after 8:00 p.m. EST on November 22, 1963. Belmont was responsible for directing the FBI investigation of the assassination. He addressed the memo to FBI Associate Director Clyde Tolson, J. Edgar Hoover's personal assistant, with copies to other top FBI bureaucrats.[15]

The memo reported Belmont's telephone conversation with Dallas Special Agent in Charge (SAC) J. Gordon Shanklin, which occurred at 9:18 p.m. EST, i.e., during the autopsy. Here is the first paragraph:

---

14 Email from Don Curtis to Mike Chesser, May 19, 2019.

15 Joseph McBride, *Into the Nightmare: My Search for the Killers of President John F. Kennedy and Officer J. D. Tippit* (Berkeley, CA: Hightower Press, 2013), pp. 556-568, at p. 556.

> I talked to SAC Shanklin in Dallas. He said arrangements have been made with Carswell Air Force Base to fly one of our Agents up to Washington with the rifle that was recovered by the police together with the fragments of bullet taken from Governor Connally and the cartridge cases. I told SAC Shanklin that Secret Service had one of the bullets that struck President Kennedy and the other is lodged behind the President's ear and we are arranging to get both of these.[16]

McBride immediately recognized the significance of this memo. In his detailed 2013 book, *Into the Nightmare*, he commented that the Belmont memo "indicates that a bullet was secretly removed from President Kennedy's head and never placed into evidence."[17] According to Belmont, the bullet was "lodged behind the president's ear," a fact never disclosed by the Warren Commission or the HSCA."[18] McBride stressed the importance of this document:

> This crucial document invalidates the official version of the assassination that only three bullets were fired, all from behind, and that none was recovered during the autopsy at Bethesda Naval Hospital in Maryland. Other evidence about the fatal crossfire, including a gunshot wound to the president's right temple, as well as the abundant evidence the president's body was secretly altered to disguise his wounds and their sources, supports the information in this memo.[19]

---

16 A. H. Belmont to Mr. Tolson, FBI memorandum, November 22, 1963, in *Inside the ARRB,* ed. Douglas Horne, Mary Ferrell Foundation, "Appendix 14: Two controversial FBI documents from November 22, 1963, pertaining to bullets," https://www.maryferrell.org/showDoc.html?docId=145280#relPageId=75.

17 Joseph McBride, *Into the Nightmare*, op. cit., p. 556.

18 Ibid. A subsequent chapter will introduce multiple, mostly intact, bullets into this case, so it is problematic for normal human beings to identify an authentic Magic Bullet. On the contrary, Specter found this to be trivial—he simply ignored all the other bullets. Life is painless when evidence can be disregarded without penalty.

19 Ibid.

EYEWITNESSES: A GRASSY KNOLL SHOT CAUSED THE TEMPLE WOUND

In volume 2 of *Inside the ARRB*, Douglas Horne listed witnesses who saw JFK's head struck from the right front. This shot blew out the right rear of JFK's head and sent tissue debris to the left rear.

The family of Phillip Willis, including his wife Marilyn and daughters Rosemary and Linda, were on the south side of Elm Street (left of the limousine). Willis took one of the famous color photographs as the limousine approached the Stemmons Freeway sign: "As I was about to squeeze my shutter, that is when the first shot rang out and my reflex just took that picture at that moment."[20]

In his 1967 book *Six Seconds in Dallas*, Josiah Thompson reported his interview with Marilyn Sitzman, the receptionist for Abraham Zapruder's clothing company. She stood with Zapruder on the concrete pedestal of the John Neely Bryan pergola on Elm Street while he filmed. Zapruder and Sitzman were within seventy-five feet of the limousine when the bullet shattered JFK's head.

> MISS SITZMAN: And the next thing that I remembered clearly was the shot that hit directly in front of us, or almost directly in front of us, that hit him on the side of his face.
>
> THOMPSON: Where on the side of the head did that shot appear to hit?
>
> MISS SITZMAN: I would say it'd be above the ear and to the front.
>
> THOMPSON: In other words, if one drew a line vertically upward from the tip of the ear, it would be forward of that line?

---

20 Richard B. Trask, *Pictures of the Pain: Photography and the Assassination of President Kennedy* (Danvers, MA: Yeoman Press, 1994), pp. 167-182, at p. 171. Trask commented: "Later government research placed this photograph as being taken at about the same time as Zapruder frame #Z202."

MISS SITZMAN: Yes.

THOMPSON: It would then be back of the temple, but on the side of the head?

MISS SITZMAN: Between the eye and the ear. And we could see his brains come out, you know, his head opening; it must have been a terrible shot because it exploded his head.[21]

Nigel Turner, in his 1988 television documentary, *The Men Who Killed Kennedy,* aired an interview with Marilyn Willis. In episode one, she recalled:

> The head shot seemed to come from the right front. It seemed to strike him here [gesturing to her upper right forehead, up high at the hairline], and his head went back, and all of the brain matter went out the back of the head. It was like a red halo, a red circle, with bright matter in the middle of it—it just went like that.[22]

She was asked to recall her most indelible memory. She responded: "[It was] the head shot; seeing his head blow up. I can see it just as plain [today as I could then] … it's red, it's very brilliant, it's cone-shaped, going back—that's my impression."[23]

Thompson also interviewed William Newman (Figure 1.3), who stood on the north curb of Elm Street (right of the limousine), about fifteen feet from JFK, with his wife Gayle Newman and their two small sons:

---

21 Josiah Thompson, *Six Seconds in Dallas*, op. cit., p. 102. Thompson taped this interview with Sitzman on November 19, 1966.

22 Douglas Horne, *Inside the ARRB*, vol. 4, op. cit., pp. 1138-1139.

23 Ibid., p. 1139.

THOMPSON: Now could you tell me about the impact on the President's head, what you saw? There's a diagram you drew for me where you put it right at the ear.

WILLIAM NEWMAN: That's what I saw. The way he was hit, it looked like he had just been hit with a baseball pitch; just like a block of wood fell over his ....

THOMPSON: You just bobbed your head backwards and over towards the left. The location that you drew is right about the ear.

WILLIAM NEWMAN: In my opinion the ear went.[24]

Newman was confident that the shot that detonated JFK's head came from the Grassy Knoll behind him.

THOMPSON: Now could I ask you a little more about this, try to get your immediate response? I take it, it was your immediate response—in your affidavit of the 22nd—that the shots were somehow right back of you?

WILLIAM NEWMAN: That's right. Well, of course the President's being shot in the side of the head, by the third shot—I thought the shot was fired from directly above and behind where we were standing. And that's what scared us, because I thought we were right in the direct path of gunfire.[25]

Newman never thought the gunfire came from the TSBD.

---

24 Josiah Thompson, *Six Seconds in Dallas*, op. cit., p. 103-104, at p. 103.

25 Ibid.

THOMPSON: But it's your feeling that the shots were coming from over your…right behind you, based on (1) the sound of the shots, (2) the impact on the President's head, and (3) the movement of the President's head after impact. Would that be a fair statement?

WILLIAM NEWMAN: Right. Well, I think everybody thought the shots were from where I'm saying—behind us—because everybody went in that direction. Must have.

THOMPSON: Everyone *did* run in that direction; I've seen the films. This is probably pushing your own recollections too far, but I'll try it anyway. When you say in back of you, do you have any feeling…say, if I stand here, and I say "in back of me," do you have any feeling if it was back of me in this direction or back of me in this direction? Did it appear to be back of you towards the Texas School Book Depository or towards the general area of the stockade fence and railroad? Do you have any recollection at all?

WILLIAM NEWMAN: Well, this is going to sound peculiar, but I was thinking more just the opposite of the building…actually the thought never entered my mind that the shots were coming from the building.[26]

In his 1966 book *Rush to Judgment*, Mark Lane interviewed Charles Brehm, who stood with his son near the south curb of Elm Street (left of the limousine). Brehm was within about twenty feet when the bullet "shattered the President's head."[27] He saw a piece of JFK's skull explode

---

26 Ibid., p. 104. Emphasis in original.

27 Mark Lane, *Rush to Judgment: A Critique of the Warren Commission's Inquiry into the Murders of President John F. Kennedy, Officer J. D. Tippit and Lee Harvey Oswald* (New York: Holt, Rinehart & Winston, 1996), p. 56.

out of the head. "That which appeared to be a portion of the President's skull went flying slightly to the rear of the President's car and directly to its left," Brehm said. "It flew over toward the curb to the left and to the rear."[28]

Lane pointed out that Deputy Constable Seymour Weitzman found skull fragments on the south side of Elm Street (left of the limousine), approximately "8 to 12 inches from the curb." Lane emphasized that this location "was consistent with the bullet having been fired from the north, where the grassy knoll is located, since bone matter tends to follow the trajectory of the bullet."[29]

"The Dallas Motorcycle Policemen to the Left Rear of the Limousine Were Covered by Bloody Debris"[30]

When a headshot struck Kennedy, Dallas police officer B. J. Martin was on the left outside motorcycle, about five feet to the left and six to eight feet to the rear.[31] Martin testified that he and his motorcycle were splattered with skull and brain debris. "I noticed that there were blood stains on the windshield on my motor[cycle], and then I pulled off my helmet and I noticed there were blood stains on the left side of my helmet."[32] He also noticed "other matter that looked like pieces of flesh."[33]

Martin's partner that day was police officer Bobby W. Hargis, who rode the inside rear motorcycle. Hargis testified to the WC that he was hit by debris from the fatal shot:

---

28 Ibid., p. 56.

29 Ibid.

30 Douglas Horne, *Inside the ARRB*, op. cit., vol. 4, p. 1142.

31 "Testimony of B. J. Martin," *Hearings before the President's Commission on the Assassination of President Kennedy*, vol. 4, op. cit., pp. 289-293, at p. 290.

32 Ibid., p. 292.

33 Ibid.

> Yes; when President Kennedy straightened back up in the car [after the first shot] the bullet hit him in the head, the one that killed him and it seemed like his head exploded, and I was splattered with blood and brain, and kind of a bloody water.[34]

The debris hit Hargis with such force that he told reporters the next day, "I thought at first I must have been hit."[35]

Horne commented:

> Hargis was so certain, based upon the impact debris, that the shot that caused it [JFK's head wound] had come from the right front that he parked his motorcycle at the curb on the south side of Elm and went running across the street to see if he could spot anyone in the grassy knoll area.[36]

In his testimony to the WC, Hargis made clear that his impression was that shots were coming from the grassy knoll. Hargis explained:

> Well, at the time it sounded like the shots were right next to me. There wasn't any way in the world I could tell where they were coming from, but at the time there was something in my head that said they probably could have been coming from the railroad overpass, because I thought since I had got splattered, with blood—I was just a little back and left of—just a little bit back and left of Mrs. Kennedy, but I don't know."[37]

---

34 "Testimony of Bobby W. Hargis," *Hearings before the President's Commission on the Assassination of President Kennedy*, vol. 6, op. cit., pp. 293-296. at p. 294.

35 Douglas Horne, *Inside the ARRB*, op. cit., vol. 4, pp. 1142.

36 Ibid.

37 Testimony of Bobby W. Hargis," op. cit., pp. 294-295.

Hargis testified that after being splattered with Kennedy's brain matter, he parked his motorcycle on the left side of the motorcade, i.e., the south side of Elm Street. He ran across Elm Street toward the railroad pass, running up the incline on the grassy knoll to see if he could find the shooter. In Richard Trask's 1994 book *Pictures of the Pain*, Wilma Bond's photograph shows Hargis returning to his motorcycle.[38]

In *Six Seconds in Dallas*, Thompson discusses police officer James Chaney, who rode the right inside motorcycle and police officer Marrion Baker, who rode the right outside motorcycle. After the shooting, Baker parked his motorcycle on the north curb in front of the TSBD and ran into the building. Baker told the WC that Chaney had said this: "... two shots hit Kennedy first and then the other one hit the Governor [Connally]."[39] Thompson wanted to know if Chaney had been struck by debris, but the police department blocked Thompson's efforts to locate Chaney. Thompson commented: "If it turns out that Chaney was not splattered with impact debris, then the [WC] had a double reason for not calling him to testify."[40]

In his WC testimony, Baker clarified that the police officers on the left (Martin and Hargis) were hit by impact debris, but he did not cite himself or Chaney (on the right) as hit. Baker described a conversation among the Dallas motorcycle men:

> Well, we were just discussing, each one of us had a theory, you know where, how it happened, and really none of us knew how it happened. It just happened, and where they was at in place, you know, in reference to the car, would be about the only thing they could say, and at

---

38 Richard B. Trask, *Pictures of the Pain*, op. cit., pp. 207-209, at p. 208.

39 "Testimony of Marrion L. Baker," *Hearings before the President's Commission on the Assassination of President Kennedy*, vol. 3, op. cit., pp. 242-270, at p. 266.

40 Josiah Thompson, *Six Seconds in Dallas*, op. cit., footnote 7, pp. 112-113.

> the time, the first shot they didn't know where the shot came from. The second shot they still didn't know, and then the third shot some of them over to the left hand side [of the limousine], the blood, and everything hit their helmets and their windshields and then they knew it had to come from behind.[41]

WC assistant counsel David Belin pressed Baker regarding officer B. J. Martin:

> MR. BELIN: What did he [officer B. J. Martin] say to you about blood or something?
>
> MR. BAKER: Like I say, we were talking about where the shot came from, and he said the first shot he couldn't figure it out where it came from. He [Officer B. J. Martin] turned his head backward, reflex, you know, and then he turned back and the second shot came off, and then the third shot is when the blood and everything hit his helmet and his windshield.
>
> MR. BELIN: Did it hit the inside or the outside of his windshield, did he say?
>
> MR. BAKER: It hit all this inside. Now, as far as the inside or outside of the windshield. I don't know about that. But it was all on the right-hand side of his helmet.
>
> MR. BELIN: Of his helmet?
>
> MR. BAKER: On his uniform also.
>
> MR. BELIN: On his uniform[?]

---

41 "Testimony of Marrion L. Baker," op. cit., pp. 264-265.

MR. BAKER: That is right.

MR. BELIN: And he was riding to the left of the President and you say ahead of the President?

MR. BAKER: On the left-hand side.

MR. BELIN: But a little ahead of him?

MR. BAKER: Yes, sir. They were immediately in front of the car.[42]

Multiple photographs clearly show four motorcycle escorts beside the limousine; each one was to the rear of the limousine during the fusillade. The Dallas police soon agreed that the lone assassin was Oswald, so every police officer was forced to toe the line: no frontal shots were allowed. Baker's statement clearly implies that Martin and Hargis (on the left rear) had been hit by debris, despite Baker's obvious attempts to claim that the motorcycle escort had been in front of the limousine. Clearly, Belin wanted Baker to testify that blood and brain matter would have hit the inside of the windshield, so as to position the fatal shot from the rear. This explains Baker's contorted answer: "It hit all this inside. Now, as far as the inside or outside of the windshield. I don't know about that. But it was all on the right-hand side of his helmet."[43]

TWO FRONTAL HEADSHOTS

Douglas Horne (*Inside the ARRB*) was the first to propose two separate frontal headshots. Before that, no one had seriously considered this option, so Horne had thereby decisively advanced the case. Before Horne, everyone saw an X-ray fragment trail that disintegrated before

---

42 Ibid., p. 265.

43 Ibid.

exiting and a large hole at the right rear of the head (without any associated bullet fragments). These two items did not truly correlate, but no one seriously objected until Horne had his epiphany. Now, over ten years later, the evidence for two separate frontal head shots is formidable. One bullet entered in front of the right ear and exited at the right rear, causing a large hole. The second frontal bullet entered the right forehead at the hairline, consistent with the fragment trail on the X-ray films, but it did not exit. Instead, it merely fragmented. Sadly, most researchers today still cannot distinguish between these two headshots. I have published supporting images in my hardcover book to discriminate between them. Some are shown here in Figure 4.5. For more, see Appendix G. To date, no one has even tried to refute these two different scenarios.

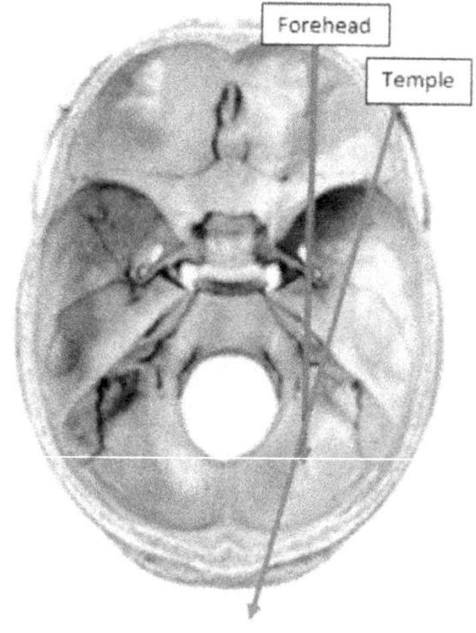

Figure 4.5

JFK: Two Frontal Headshots. The Vertical Arrow Represents the Forehead Shot. The Oblique Arrow Represents the Temple Shot. The source for Figure 4.5 is David W. Mantik, *The JFK Assassination Decoded,* op. cit., p. 300.

Figure 4.5 clearly distinguishes the two frontal shots. The vertical (AP) arrow represents the forehead shot, while the oblique arrow represents the temple shot. The forehead bullet does not exit the skull; instead it disintegrated into the particle trail on the X-ray films. The temple bullet is not represented by particles anywhere in the X-ray films, but it is consistent with the large right occipital blowout.[44] It is also consistent with many eyewitnesses (in Dealey Plaza, at Parkland Hospital, and at the Bethesda autopsy) who reported an entry site above and slightly in front of the right ear. The tissue debris from the temple bullet exited the skull, as suggested by the large occipital defect. It is also consistent with Dealey Plaza witnesses (especially those to the left of the limousine) who were struck by flying debris from the occipital blowout.

These two shots are also located at two quite different vertical levels (Figure G.2). It is time to stop conflating these two frontal shots, which is precisely what most researchers blindly do. (After all, these two assassins might prefer separate credit.)

THE HARPER FRAGMENT (HF)

At approximately 5:30 p.m., on the day after, William (Billy) Allen Harper, a premedical student at Texas Christian University in Fort Worth, was taking photographs in Dealey Plaza. He spotted a bone fragment in the infield grass (Figure 4.8A). According to the report by FBI Agent James W. Anderton (November 25, 1963), Dr. Jack Harper, Billy's uncle, told the FBI that his nephew "immediately brought the bone to him, and he and the chief pathologist at Methodist Hospital, Dr. C. E. Kerns, had examined the piece of bone and both definitely felt that it is a piece of human skull."[45]

---

44 However, this temple bullet may well have produced fragments that were visible on the original X-ray films. Several autopsy witnesses support this possibility. It is also striking that the pathologists reported precisely such a trail in their official autopsy report. Their mysterious lower trail is often overlooked, but perhaps it was originally authentic. It is obviously not there now.

45 James W. Anderton, FD-302 (Rev. 3-5-59), November 25, 1963, Warren Commission Document 5, Mary Ferrell Foundation, p. 150, https://maryferrell.org/showDoc.html?docId=10406#relPageId=155&search=Harper. Names in FBI field reports tend to be entirely capitalized. The capitalization is omitted here for ease of reading.

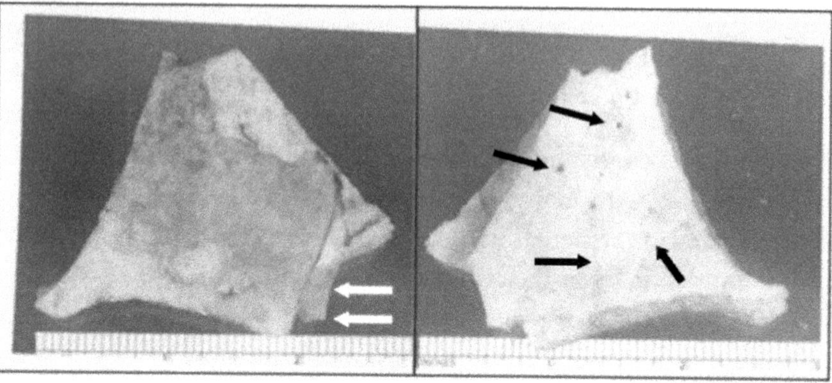

Figure 4.6

The Harper Fragment as Photographed in Dallas. In the left panel (exterior surface), note the faint metallic smear (two white arrows). In the right panel (interior surface), note several foramina (large black dots identified by two upper black arrows). Another groove (horizontal black arrow) has been cited by some as an ordinary vascular groove. On the contrary, most likely it is the sulcus for the superior sagittal sinus. The black oblique arrow (lower right) identifies a common vascular groove. The source for Figure 4.6 is David W. Mantik, *The JFK Assassination Decoded,* op. cit., specifically *John F. Kennedy's Head Wounds: A Final Synthesis—and a New Analysis of the Harper Fragment* located at the back of my hardcover book, at p. 401, renumbered as pp. 1-92. at p. 1.

In a second report, dated November 26, 1963, FBI Agent Anderton added that Dr. Harper said, "In view of the proximity of the place where the piece of bone was located it might possibly be part of President Kennedy's skull."[46] Anderton reported that Billy Harper volunteered this bone fragment to him "for whatever disposition the FBI desired."[47]

An addendum on November 27, 1963 noted that the FBI Laboratory "advised that a piece of bone located near where President Kennedy was shot had been x-rayed and examined microscopically for bullet metals but none were found."[48] It specified that a "small amount of blood on

46 Ibid.

47 Ibid.

48 Ibid. On the contrary, low X-ray exposures showed metallic debris on one edge (Figure 4.22). This site of metallic debris precisely matched the smear in the photograph (Figure 4.23).

the surface of the bone was determined to have been of human origin but was too limited in amount for grouping purposes." Finally, it noted that the bone fragment "was delivered to Admiral George Burkley, Physician to the President at the White House, according to the FBI Laboratory."

Another FBI memorandum (July 14, 1964) offered more detail.[49] Dr. A. B. Cairns, the chief pathologist at Methodist Hospital of Dallas, told the FBI that on November 25, 1963, he received a telephone call from Dr. Jack C. Harper, who asked if Cairns would look at the bone fragment. So that same afternoon Cairns and Jack Harper examined the bone and concluded that it "...looked like it came from the occipital region of the skull." Per the FBI memorandum, after Cairns and Harper had examined the bone, they asked M. Wayne Bolleter, the chief medical photographer at Methodist Hospital, to photograph it. Bolleter made two 35-mm color slides, one of each side. Harper gave the two slides to the FBI but asked that they return them.[50]

In an unaddressed November 27, 1963,[51] memorandum, Admiral George Burkley documented that at 5:15 p.m. that day, he received a

---

49 FBI memorandum, July 14, 1964, Warren Commission Document 1296, Mary Ferrell Foundation, https://maryferrell.org/showDoc.html?docId=11664#relPageId=2&search=Harper.

50 It later turned out that copies of the photograph had been retained in Dallas. Jack White, a photographer and former advertising executive who amassed a collection of JFK photographs and slides (JFK—Jack White Slides Collection, Baylor University, https://digitalcollections-baylor.quartexcollections.com/poage-collections/jfk-jack-white-slides-collection) informed me of this in a personal letter. He helped to present these images to the HSCA. There appears to be a discrepancy in the record cited here regarding the correct name of the chief pathologist at Methodist Hospital of Dallas. The FBI report cited in footnote 417 has his name as Dr. C. E. Kerns; footnote 421 has his name listed as Dr. A. B. Cairns. The correct name is Dr. A. B. Cairns. See: Marilyn Miller Baker, "The History of Pathology in Texas," published by the Texas School of Pathology, 1996, pp. 132, 215, and 261, https://www.texpath.org/amsimis/TSPI/Assets/Files/Publications/The_History_of_Pathology_in_Texas.pdf.

51 "2. Physical specimens retained during the autopsy or discovered at the scene of the assassination," in Appendix to Hearings Before the Select Committee on Assassination of the U.S. House of Representatives Ninety-Fifth Congress Second Session, op. cit., vol. 7, sec. 3, part 2, pp. 24-25, at paragraphs 105-107.

small Neiman Marcus box measuring about 2 by 3 inches with material that had been "discussed previously" with the FBI.[52] The HSCA determined that Burkley had received the HF; they inferred that the dimensions of the box matched the size of the HF (2 by 2 inches). Furthermore, the time interval between the two transfers (first to the FBI and then to Burkley) was just two days. Moreover, William Harper gave the fragment to the FBI—and Burkley said the box came from the FBI. Finally, Burkley had identified the contents as a specimen. Thus, the HSCA concluded: "Consequently, it is logical that the Neiman-Marcus box contained the Harper bone fragment."[53]

In his unaddressed memorandum, Burkley also stated that he would deposit the bone fragment with the commanding officer of the Bethesda Naval Hospital.[54] After this, the HF vanished. Burkley was the last known person to see it. So, the HF became just one more critical piece of evidence to disappear after reaching the black hole of Washington, DC. Nonetheless, the following HF items still exist: the Dallas photographs, the FBI photographs (Figure 4.7), and the FBI X-ray films. Douglas Horne commented that we "should all be thankful for the professionalism" of Wayne Bolleter.[55] Horne explained: "The two slides of the Harper fragment are everything that good medical macro-photography should be, unlike the autopsy photographs of the 35th President: they are in perfect focus, are perfectly illuminated, and the ruler placed in the images for scale is in focus also, and can be read."[56]

---

52 Ibid., p. 24, paragraph 106.

53 Ibid., p. 24, paragraph 107.

54 Ibid., p. 24, paragraph 106.

55 Douglas Horne, *Inside the ARRB*, op. cit., vol. 4, p. 1145.

56 Ibid.

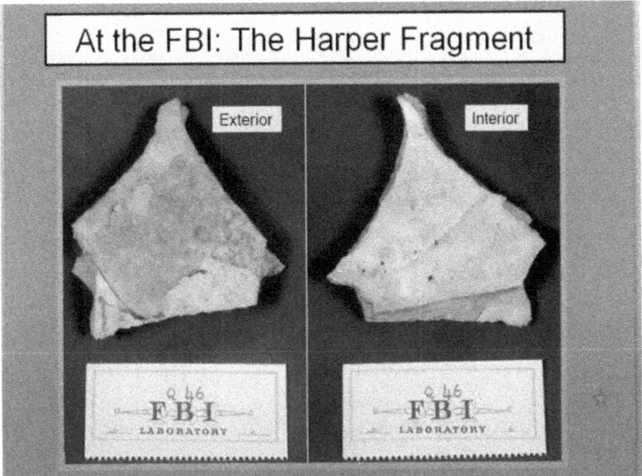

Figure 4.7
The Harper Fragment as Photographed by the FBI.

The HF clearly threatened the WC narrative. If occipital bone had been blown out, then a frontal shot was unavoidable—and so was conspiracy. But the HF was not at the autopsy, so it is not in the official autopsy report (Appendix J). In fact, every government investigation has tried mostly just to ignore it, with good reason.

WHERE EXACTLY WAS THE HF FOUND?

Harper's discovery site should have been the best clue to the exit trajectory—unless the bone had been moved. Unfortunately, as is typical for most critical data in this JFK case, this issue is also perplexing. In 1997, Milicent Cranor located Billy Harper, who agreed to mark a map to show where he found it. He marked the map with a large black dot (horizontal arrow in Figure 4.8A).

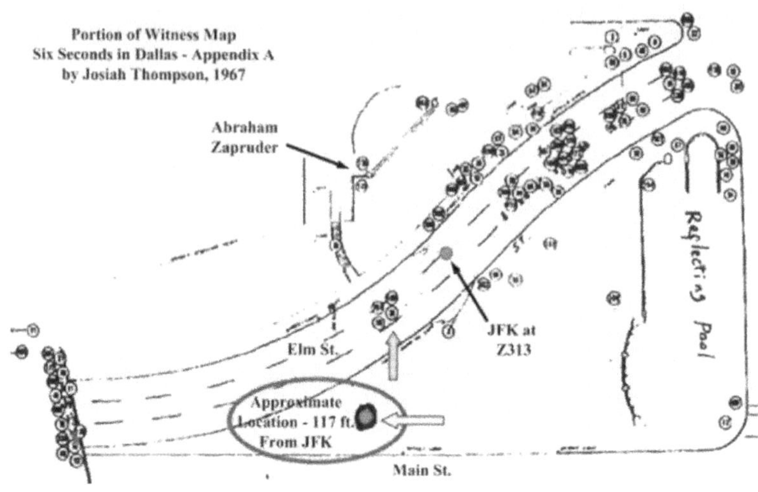

Figure 4.8A

Milicent Cranor's Map of Elm Street, Dealey Plaza, Dallas, Texas. In 1997, Billy Harper placed a black dot (inside the large ellipse) as his discovery site. The source for Figure 4.8A is Josiah Thompson, *Six Seconds in Dallas*, op. cit., Appendix A, pp. 252-271, at pp. 252-253. Also see: David W. Mantik, *The JFK Assassination Decoded*, op. cit., specifically *John F. Kennedy's Head Wounds: A Final Synthesis—and a New Analysis of the Harper Fragment* or located at the back of my hardcover book, at p. 401, renumbered as 1-92, at p. 31.

So, the precise site where HF alighted is not known. In Figure 4.8A, the vertical arrow is close to the final shot in the WC data, but this location was ignored by the WC—and it has been largely ignored by nearly everyone ever since, including most contemporary JFK researchers!

The official FBI report (citing Billy Harper) placed it "approximately 25 feet south [the Grassy Knoll is north] of the spot where President Kennedy was shot."[57] But where exactly was that "spot"? Unfortunately, no contemporaneous physical reference or map clarifies this "spot." Tim Nicholson, a Stanford-trained engineer who has developed mathematical models of the shots, has estimated that if the HF was ejected

57 James W. Anderton, FD-302 (Rev. 3-5-59), November 25, 1963, Warren Commission Document 5, op. cit.

from JFK's skull at Z-313, the distance to the HF discovery site was about 117 feet plus or minus 17 feet.

According to JFK assassination researcher Pat Speer, Milicent Cranor was not the first to get Harper to mark the spot. Speer noted that Harper had identified his site in 1969 on a map for Howard Roffman[58] (Figure 4.8B).[59]

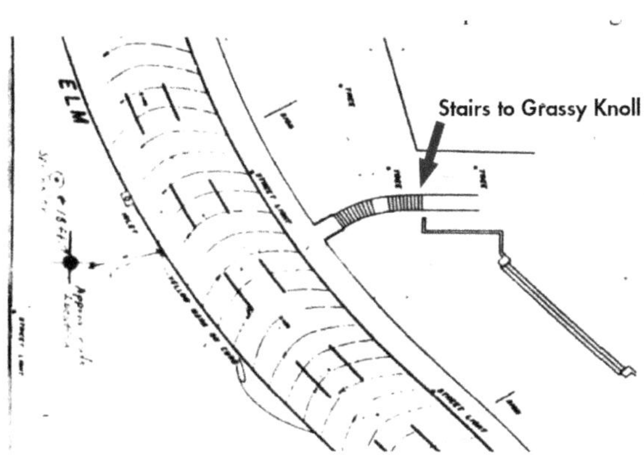

Figure 4.8B

Howard Roffman's Map of Elm Street in Dealey Plaza. In 1997, Billy Harper marked his discovery site with the crosshairs (inside the left rectangle). The view is downhill toward the railroad overpass. The source for Figure 4.8B is Larry Rivera, *The JFK Horsemen: Framing Lee, Altering the Altgens6 and Resolving Other Mysteries* (Crestview, FL: Moon Rock Books, 2018), p. 403.

58 In 1976, at the age of twenty-two, Howard Roffman wrote a book on the JFK assassination entitled *Presumed Guilty: How and Why the Warren Commission framed Lee Harvey Oswald.* After receiving a JD degree from the University of Florida College of Law, Hoffman became general counsel for George Lucas of Lucasfilm. See: Howard Roffman, Wikipedia, n.d., https://en.wikipedia.org/wiki/Howard_Roffman.

59 Pat Speer, "Chapter 16b: Digging in the Dirt," PatSpeer.com, n.d., https://www.patspeer.com/chapter16bigginginthedirt.

The Roffman map places the discovery site closer to the stairs (that ascend the Grassy Knoll) than shown in the Cranor map.

In 1997, when Harper marked the Cranor map, his site moved farther west (downhill) than his 1969 site. Either site is about twenty-five feet south of Elm Street.[60] However, as we now know, there were multiple headshots, with the final headshot coming distinctly *after* the traditional headshot at Z-313. If the temple bullet blew out HF, then that bullet probably came after the posterior headshot. This would place the last shot closer to the bottom of the stairs (that ascend the Grassy Knoll)—intriguingly only about sixty-five feet from the HF site on the Cranor map. Even so, this would still place the site ahead of the limousine at the time of a late headshot.

Paradoxically, careful analysis of the original WC data tables casts grave doubt on Z-313 as the sole headshot. In his splendid, but often ignored, 1998 essay "The JFK Assassination Reenactment: Questioning the Warren Commission's Evidence," Chuck Marler pointed out that the WC survey on May 24, 1964 "...was orchestrated by Arlen Specter to insure his single-bullet theory would not be contradicted."[61] In radical disagreement with Specter, an overhead image of Dealey Plaza in *Newsweek*[62] (Figure 4.9) showed a final shot about thirty to forty feet farther down Elm Street, near the steps that ascend the Grassy Knoll. This is distinctly closer to Harper's discovery site, on both the Cranor and Roffman maps (Figures 4.8A and 4.8B, respectively).

---

60 Is it just possible that the FBI meant "street" where it wrote "spot"? That is, perhaps the FBI quotation should read "just south of the street where President Kennedy was assassinated." If so, that curiously agrees with the distance of Harper's site from the street. Unfortunately, the FBI report does not tell us where *along* the street it was found.

61 Chuck Marler, "The JFK Assassination Reenactment: Questioning the Warren Commission's Evidence," in *Assassination Science,* op. cit., pp. 249-262, at p. 250.

62 "What Happened at Dealey Plaza?" *Newsweek*, November 22, 1993, p. 74.

Figure 4.9

Newsweek: "What Happened at Dealey Plaza?" This astonishing photograph shows the final headshot at thirty to forty feet farther down Elm Street than Z-313 (the traditional final headshot frame). This downhill location is strongly supported by early reenactments, data tables, and documents. All were ignored by the WC—and are still mostly ignored today by JFK researchers. The source for this figure is *Newsweek*, November 22, 1993, p. 74.

This location was not invented by the *Newsweek* staff; it was based on early WC reenactments, data tables, and documents. Particularly striking are visible *alterations* in those data tables, whose sole apparent purpose was to confirm the WC scenario!

So where did the FBI think this "spot" was? If they spoke to the SS, they may well have picked a site well past Z-313. The SS engaged Dallas County Surveyor Robert West to establish the exact locations of shots. The SS photographs taken shortly after the event (Figure 4.10) clearly show a second shot (left arrow in the second photograph) and a third shot (right arrow in the second photograph) much farther down Elm Street, well past the flowers, which are supposedly close to the site of Z-313.

Secret Service reconstruction of positions of Presidential car at first (above) and second and third shots (road markers), like FBI's, says Governor Connelly was hit by a separate bullet. This denies the basic conclusion of the Report.

Figure 4.10

SS Photographs Taken Several Days after the Assassination. The left black arrow marks the SS location of the second shot; the right white arrow marks the location of the third shot (of three official shots). Even today, most JFK researchers totally ignore these official photographs. The Source for Figure 4.10 is Harold Weisberg, *Whitewash II: The FBI-Secret Service Coverup* (New York: Skyhorse Publishing, 2013), p. 248.

As Chuck Marler explained (emphasis in the original):

> This survey plat, again made by Dallas Surveyor Robert West [a second time for the WC reenactment on May 24, 1964] came wrapped and sealed in a container—one which was *never* opened[63] and to date has never been released to the public. It was Commission Counsel Arlen Specter who asked Chairman Earl Warren that the seal not be broken and the plat not taken out of its container.[64]

However, the flowers are not a reliable indicator. After all, were the future flower donors on site during the motorcade, just standing by in order to identify the final shot? Furthermore, the flowers on the north side (nearer the Grassy Knoll) were widely scattered, so it is difficult to identify the exact "spot" just based on the flowers. Moreover, the SS, like the FBI, had concluded that two shots had struck JFK, and a *separate* shot had hit Connally. Neither invoked the SBT. As expected, Specter never showed the SS reenactment photos (Figure 4.10) to the WC. It is easy to understand why.

SS Agent Forrest Sorrels rode in the lead car. In his February 14, 1964 memorandum, he reported his examination of a manhole cover that showed signs of a bullet ricochet. But there is a problem for the WC: this manhole cover is over seventy feet past Z-313![65]

---

63 The authors of this book wonder if November 22, 2023, the sixtieth anniversary, might be the appropriate time to unseal this never-before-seen document. Unfortunately, we can no longer ask for permission from either Specter or Warren. Perhaps we should ask John Tunheim (of the ARRB) for permission.

64 Chuck Marler, "The JFK Assassination Reenactment: Questioning the Warren Commission's Evidence," in *Assassination Science*, op. cit., pp. 249-262, at p. 251.

See also: Harold Weisberg, *Whitewash II: The FBI Secret Service Cover-Up* (New York: Skyhorse Publishing, 1966), pp. 167, 243, and 248.

65 SAIC Sorrels, Dallas to Chief, attn. Inspector Kelly, Secret Service memorandum, February 13, 1964, in *Hearings before the President's Commission on the Assassination of President Kennedy*, CE 2111, op. cit., vol. 24, p. 540.

Also note this: Emmett Hudson, an employee of the Dallas Parks Department, was the groundskeeper for Dealey Plaza. He told the WC that he was sure that the second shot hit JFK in the head. Then after this shot, a young man told him to "lay down, Mister, somebody is shooting the President." After this warning, Hudson noted that he was still close to the ground when he heard a third shot. This occurred when the limousine was "about even with these steps." He testified that he had been standing on those steps (that ascend the Grassy Knoll) when the shooting started.[66]

CLINT HILL AND THE OBLIQUE SHOT THAT DETONATED JFK'S HEAD

SS Agent Clint Hill was assigned to Jacqueline Kennedy on November 22, 1963. He jumped from the follow-up car and ran to the rear hand-hold on the limousine after the first shots. Horne noted that Hill was "the closest reliable witness" to JFK's head wounds.[67]

In November 30, 1963, Hill recalled:

> As I lay over the top of the back seat I noticed a portion of the President's head on the right rear side was missing and he was bleeding profusely. Part of his brain was gone. I saw a part of his skull with hair on it lying in the seat.[68]

Hill described the first lady's reaction:

---

66 "Testimony of Emmett J. Hudson," *Hearings before the President's Commission on the Assassination of President Kennedy*, op. cit., vol. 7, pp. 558-565, at 560-561.

67 Douglas Horne, *Inside the ARRB*, op. cit., vol. 4, p. 1140.

68 "Statement of Special Agent Clinton J. Hill, dated Nov. 30, 1963," in *Hearings before the President's Commission on the Assassination of President Kennedy*, CE 1024, op. cit., vol. 18, pp. 740-745, at p. 742.

> Mrs. Kennedy shouted, "They've shot his head off;" then turned and raised out of her seat as if she were reaching to her right rear toward the back of the car for something that had blown out.[69]

In his WC testimony, he also offered a graphic description of the scene at Parkland:

> The right rear portion of his head was missing. It was lying in the rear seat of the car. His brain was exposed. There was blood and bits of brain all over the entire rear portion of the car. Mrs. Kennedy was completely covered with blood. There was so much blood you could not tell if there had been any other wound or not, except for the one large gaping wound in the right rear portion of the head.[70]

Hill testified that Jackie climbed onto the trunk to retrieve skull or brain tissue:

> MR. SPECTER: You say that it appeared that she [Jacqueline Kennedy] was reaching as if something was coming over to the rear portion of the car, back in the area where you were coming to?
>
> MR. HILL: Yes, sir.
>
> MR. SPECTER: Was there anything back there that you observed, that she might have been reaching for?
>
> MR. HILL: I thought I saw something come off the back, too, but I cannot say that there was. I do know that the next day we found the portion of the President's head.

---

69 Ibid.

70 "Testimony of Clinton J. Hill, Special Agent, Secret Service," *Hearings before the President's Commission on the Assassination of President Kennedy*, op. cit., vol. 2, pp. 132-144, at p. 141.

> MR. SPECTER: Where did you find that portion of the President's head?
>
> MR. HILL: It was found in the street. It was turned in, I believe, by a medical student or somebody in Dallas.[71]

Most likely then, Hill saw the HF blown out of the back of JFK's head.

At a book signing (available on YouTube.com), Hill described his run from the follow-up car to the limousine:

> As I approached the vehicle [JFK's limousine] there was a third shot. It hit the President in the head, upper right rear of the right ear, causing a gaping hole in his head, which caused brain matter, blood, and bone fragments to spew forth out over the car, over myself. At that point Mrs. Kennedy came up out of the back seat onto the trunk of the car. She was trying to retrieve something that had gone off to the right rear. She did not know I was there. At that point I grabbed Mrs. Kennedy, put her in the back seat. The President fell over into her lap, to his left.

He continued:

> The right side of his head was exposed. I could see his eyes were fixed. There was a hole in the upper right rear portion of his head about the size of my palm. Most of the grey matter in that area had been removed, and was scattered throughout the entire car, including on Mrs. Kennedy. I turned and gave the follow-up car crew the thumbs-down, indicating that we were in a very dire situation. The driver

71 Ibid., p. 140.

accelerated; he got up to the lead car, which was driven by Chief Curry, the Dallas Chief of Police....[72]

On the right side of JFK's head is a massive bloody wound in Z-331 (Figure 4.11).

Figure 4.11
Z-331. The right side of JFK's head explodes.

[72] James H. Fetzer, "Who's telling the truth: Clint Hill or the Zapruder film?" The Education Forum, January 12, 2011, https://educationforum.ipbhost.com/topic/17242-whos-telling-the-truth-clint-hill-or-the-zapruder-film/.

Also see: Warwick's Books, "Warwick's Books Presents The Kennedy Detail: JFK's Secret Service Agents," December 14, 2010, https://www.youtube.com/watch?v=lYpY8zI_wwA&t=1482s.

Z-343 is where the FBI said that Hill first placed his hand on the limousine—thirty frames (nearly two seconds) after Z-313 (Figure 4.12).

Figure 4.12
Z-343. Hill reaches the limousine nearly two seconds after Z-313.

By Z-346, JFK has collapsed to his left, sinking into the back seat (Figure 4.13).

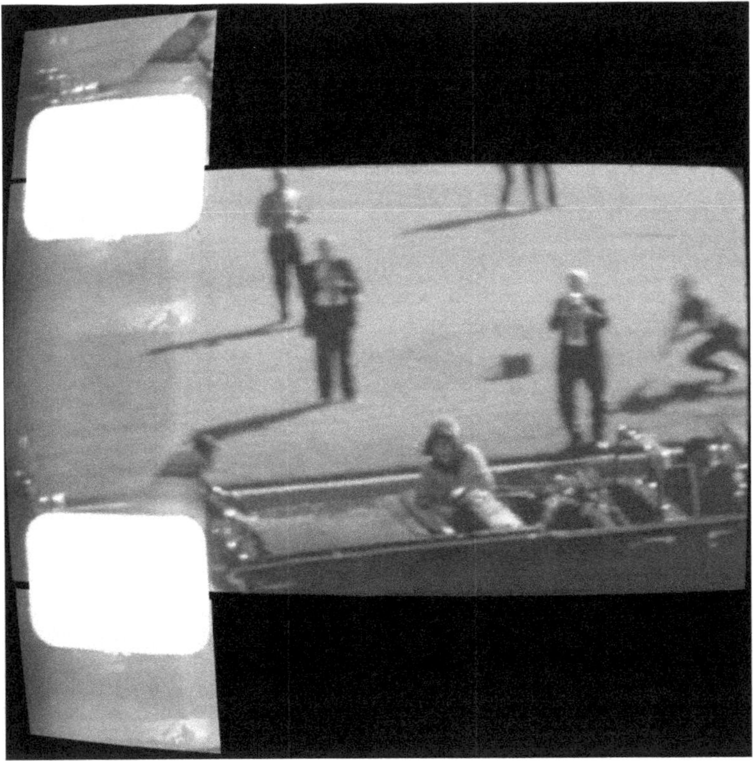

Figure 4.13
Z-346. JFK collapses to his left, sinking into the back seat.

By Z-348, Jackie approaches the trunk (Figure 4.14).

Figure 4.14
Z- 348. Jackie climbs onto the trunk.

According to the FBI, Hill's foot did not reach the bumper until Z-368; both feet reached at Z-381 (Figure 4.15).

Figure 4.15
Z-381. Both of Hill's feet reach the bumper.

By Z-388, Clint Hill appears to be assisting Jackie back into her seat (Figure 4.16).

Figure 4.16
Z-388. Clint Hill tries to assist Jackie.

In his 2012 book *Mrs. Kennedy and Me*, Hill offered a similar description. He described running toward the limousine (emphasis in the original):

> *I'm almost there. Mrs. Kennedy is leaning toward the president. I am almost there.* I was almost there. And then I heard the shot. The third shot. The impact was like the sound of something hard hitting something hollow—like the sound of a melon shattering onto cement. In the same instant, blood, brain matter, and bone fragments exploded from the back of the president's head. The president's blood, parts of his skull, bits of his brain were splattered all over me—on my face, my clothes, in my hair.[73]

73 Clint Hill with Lisa McCubbin, *Mrs. Kennedy and Me* (New York: Gallery Books, 2012), p. 290.

In his 2010 book, *The Kennedy Detail*, former SS agent Gerald Blaine confirmed Hill's memory: "Clint Hill was just feet from his goal, his eyes focused on Mrs. Kennedy, when he heard the third shot and the gruesome thump of President Kennedy's head exploding."[74]

Hill leaves little doubt that the oblique headshot occurred well after Z-313. Most likely, this shot struck just before Hill's hand reached the limousine. Drs. A. B. Cairns and Jack C. Harper were correct: HF was occipital bone.

JACKIE'S REACTION

At the end of the Zapruder film, just before the Triple Overpass, a frantic Jackie is propping JFK up into a full sitting position, as if he were alive. JFK researcher Gerda Dunckel has produced a remarkable YouTube video using a rarely watched sequence in the Zapruder film, from Z-452 to Z-457.[75]

In her YouTube video, Dunckel identified the occupants of the limousine as the car approached the triple underpass (Figures 4.17).

---

74 Gerald Blaine and Lisa McCubbin, *The Kennedy Detail: JFK's Secret Service* Agents ***Break Their Silence*** (New York: Gallery Books, 2010), p. 216.

75 GerdaDunckel, "Dead JFK rising from his seat ...(?)" January 9, 2012, https://www.youtube.com/watch?v=lDCJ3Ndvz9M.

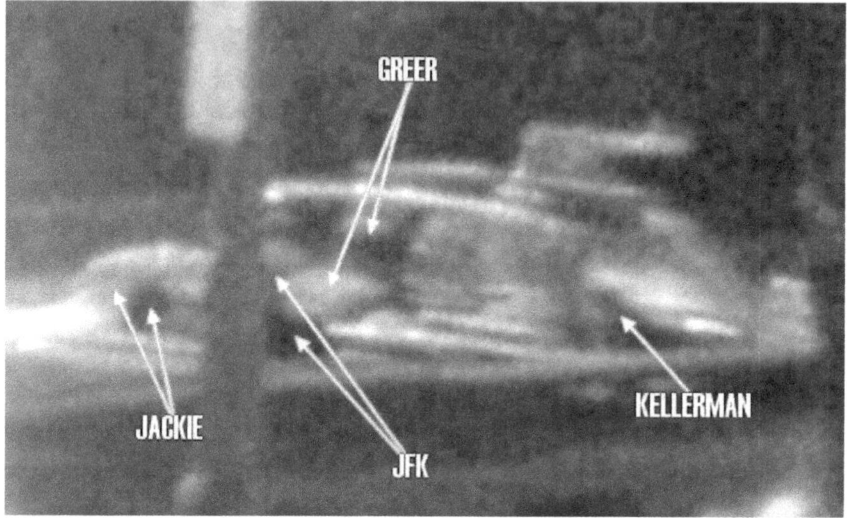

Figure 4.17
Gerda Dunckel YouTube Video. Z-458, Enhanced and Enlarged: Limousine Occupants, Just Before the Triple Overpass.

A few frames later, Dunckel enhanced and enlarged Z-456 to show the gaping wound at the right rear of JFK's head (Figure 4.18).

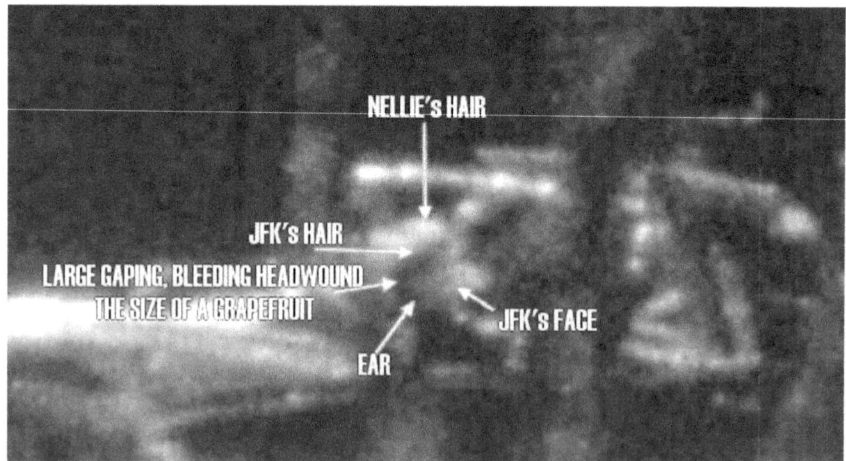

Figure 4.18
Gerda Dunckel YouTube Video. Z-456, Enhanced and Enlarged: Exit Wound at Right Rear of JFK's Head, Just Before the Triple Overpass.

MARY MOORMAN'S POLAROID

Mary Moorman's famous Polaroid photograph (Figure 4.19) is widely believed to have been taken an instant after a headshot.

Figure 4.19
Just After a Headshot, Mary Moorman's Polaroid Photograph. Bobby Hargis is closest to the camera, with James Chaney on the far right. Bill Newman appears behind Chaney's helmet. Abraham Zapruder and Marilyn Sitzman stand on the pedestal above Newman.

On the evening of November 20, 2013, at a downtown Dallas hotel, Mary recalled the events of fifty years earlier. After she took her famous photograph, she brought the camera down and then, after a short pause, she heard more shots. Only with these last shots did she see the hair rise on JFK's head.

This is fully consistent with her WC testimony. Immediately after the shooting, Moorman made a statement to the Dallas County Sheriff's Department:

> As President Kennedy was opposite me, I took a picture of him. As I snapped the picture of President Kennedy, I heard a shot ring out. President Kennedy kind of slumped over. Then I heard another shot ring out and Mrs. Kennedy jumped up in the car and said, "My God, he has been shot." When I heard these shots ring out, I fell to the ground to keep from being hit myself. I heard these three or four shots in all. [76]

Moorman's photograph has been interpreted as nearly coincident with the final headshot. In the WC view, this was the only headshot. Oddly, she said nothing about impact debris reaching her, even though she stood near Hargis, who was hit.

WAS THE HF MOVED BEFORE BILLY HARPER FOUND IT?

A second bone fragment was found in Dealey Plaza that day; it was picked up—and then put back down again:

> As we [Jack Faulkner, deputy sheriff, and A. D. McCurley, deputy sheriff, Dallas County Sheriff's office] were crossing Elm Street, McCurley picked up a white piece of bone near the north curb. He asked me, "Do you suppose that could be part of his skull?" I said, "There's no blood on it," and he put it down. Later, we got to thinking, and somebody said your skull doesn't necessarily have to be touching something that's bloody. We went back and looked for it later but never found it. To this day, I believe it was a piece of Kennedy's skull.[77]

---

76 Mary Ann Moorman, "Voluntary Statement, Sheriff's Department Country of Dallas, Texas," November 22, 1963, *Hearings before the President's Commission on the Assassination of President Kennedy*, op. cit., vol. 19, p. 487.

77 Larry A. Sneed, "The Police: Initial Reactions, Jack Faulkner," in *No More Silence*, op. cit., pp. 215-223, at p. 216.

Likewise, someone might have picked up the HF, and then later dropped it, perhaps even some distance from its original site, leaving it for Billy to discover. Possible reasons for dropping it are easy to understand: (1) a reluctance to get involved, (2) a distaste for the macabre, or (3) simple embarrassment. It should also be emphasized that twenty-nine hours had passed before Harper arrived—but this very plaza was the focus of worldwide attention for that entire weekend. So, is it truly credible that no one had spied this bone until Billy saw it?

I strongly suspect that we cannot now know where this bone initially landed—that information is forever lost to history. After all, Billy could only tell us where he found it, but that may well be useless information.

Now suppose this: HF was ejected at Z-313 and landed just where Harper found it. Also assume this: HF was from the parietal area (as the HSCA would wish). We then have this problem: Not only did HF travel surprisingly far, but how did it journey from the right side of the head and land twenty-five feet to the left of the street against a brisk wind? Tim Nicholson has estimated the wind speed as fourteen mph. (Note the orientation of the limousine flag in the Zapruder film.)

But so far we have avoided a direct question: Could a posterior shot have ejected HF? The WC would have said so (had they focused on HF, which they never did)—while the HSCA assumed that a posterior shot had ejected parietal bone. Each investigation permitted only one headshot, another distinct difference from reality. But the long flight distance from Z-313 to Harper's site (about 117 feet), especially against the wind, is formidable.

In his 1980 book, *Kennedy and Lincoln: Medical and Ballistic Comparisons of their Assassinations*, John Lattimer, MD, a strong apologist for the WC, replicated the shooting studies conducted by Dr. Luis Alvarez. Alvarez had introduced the "jet effect" to explain how JFK's head snapped backward after a posterior shot.[78] Lattimore, then

78 As a Michigan medical student, I attended his 1975 lecture on this subject at Los Alamos, New Mexico.

chairman of the Department of Urology at the College of Physicians and Surgeons at Columbia University, suggested that the upward-flying fragments at Z-313 were characteristic of his own tests. He suggested that, in his tests, a bone fragment could have flown as much as forty feet upward and forward from the rear entry at Z-313.[79] The problem is that forty feet still falls well short of the 117 feet that Nicholson calculated for Harper's site.

Someone will have to explain how HF was ejected from the right parietal area at Z-313 (from either a frontal or a posterior shot—take your pick) and then flew 117 feet (in violation of Lattimer's experimental evidence) against the wind to eventually land to the left of the limousine. I leave that to others to explain. That is not my scenario.

So, what do I really think? My conclusion, after reviewing all of this evidence (regarding the HF discovery site) is that we cannot now know where HF initially landed. Most likely it did not land where Harper found it. In my opinion, therefore, Harper's discovery site is useless for deciding where HF originated (in the skull). Based on his discovery site alone, we simply cannot decide between occipital and parietal. Also consider this: even if Harper had (accurately) labeled a map when he found the bone, already by then too much time (twenty-nine hours) had passed to be sure that HF had not been moved before he got there. So instead, the issue of occipital versus parietal must be decided by other criteria. Next, we will explore the ample medical evidence that HF was occipital, not parietal. That additional evidence will decide the case.

THE MYSTERY AUTOPSY PHOTOGRAPH (F8)[80]

In November 1966, two pathologists, Humes and Boswell, along with John Ebersole, the radiologist, and John Stringer, the photographer,

---

79 John K. Lattimer, MD, ScD, FACS, *Kennedy and Lincoln: Medical and Ballistic Comparisons of their Assassinations* (New York: Harcourt Brace Jovanovich, 1980), pp. 250-251, at p. 250.

80 See Figure 4.20.

came to the Archives at the request of the Department of Justice (DOJ) to review the autopsy materials. The next year, on January 20, 1967, they met at the DOJ in Washington, DC. They spent five hours examining the photographs and radiographs. Quite bewilderingly, and despite its explicit image on the AP X-ray film, their report denied the existence of the 6.5 mm object! This (false) claim is in the penultimate subsection of the ARRB's Medical Exhibit 14 (MD 14), "NO OTHER WOUNDS":

> The x-ray films established that there were small metallic fragments in the head. However, careful examination at the autopsy, and the photographs and x-rays taken during the autopsy, revealed *no evidence of a bullet or of a major portion of a bullet* [emphasis added] in the body of the President and revealed no evidence of any missile wounds other than those described above.[81]

This was, of course, a flagrant lie. After all, during *five hours* they could not have missed the 6.5 mm (fake) object on the AP skull X-ray film. So, we can justly conclude this: Humes, Boswell, and Finck had now unambiguously proven that they were quite capable of lying.[82]

Finck, in his subsequent trip report, specified that DOJ had prepared this statement for them to sign—it was not prepared by the

81 "Review of Autopsy Materials by Humes, Boswell and Finck," MD 14, ARRB Master Set of Medical Exhibits, January 26, 1967, p. 4, https://history-matters.com/archive/jfk/arrb/master_med_set/md14/html/Image3.htm.

82 Of course, by using two brain examinations (another deception—but Finck is excused this time), we already knew that Humes and Boswell were capable of misrepresenting in this case. Furthermore, moving the trail of debris downward by ten centimeters (in their official autopsy report) hardly characterizes a search for truth. Ignoring the forehead and right temple entries are not marks of good character, either. Likewise, pretending to see no throat entry wound is merely the final straw. And Boswell's much-delayed elevation of the back wound (in the 1970s) was merely over the top. Of course, Humes had also lied about the two FBI notetakers—he claimed they had not been at the autopsy at all (see William Matson Law, *In the Eye of History*, op. cit., p. 290).

participants.[83] During his ARRB deposition, Jeremy Gunn showed Humes their four-page report—and Humes responded, "I don't know who wrote this, and reading it, it doesn't seem like I wrote it, just because of the phraseology and some of the comments. I don't know who wrote it."[84] Douglas Horne, who witnessed this humiliation, wrote that "Humes's face turned bright pink when he said this, and when he spoke those words, his head was buried in his hands, and he was looking down at the table because he would not look us in the eye."[85]

Gunn next asked Humes, "Do you recall what the purpose was for your going to the Archives in November of 1966 to prepare the inventory? What circumstances led to that?" Humes answered: "Well, the photographs were there. Nobody knew exactly what they depicted,[86] so they asked us to attempt to resolve that problem, and that's what we tried to do."[87] On November 10, 1966, Humes, Boswell, Ebersole, and Stringer had signed a "military inventory" of the autopsy. Finck, in his trip report, commented: "I had seen the x-rays, not the photos."[88] The military inventory listed photo numbers 17 and 18, as "depicting missile wound of entrance in posterior skull, following reflection of the scalp," and numbers 44 and 45 as the color versions of 17 and 18,

---

83 "Finck Privileged Communication Dated 10 FEB 67," MD 32, ARRB Master Set of Medical Exhibits, February 10, 1967, https://www.history-matters.com/archive/jfk/arrb/master_med_set/md32/html/Image1.htm.

84 "Deposition of Dr. James Joseph Humes," op. cit., p. 197.

85 Douglas Horne, email to the authors, May 4, 2023.

86 If the photographs were that useless, why even bother taking them? Of course, the *original* photographs were not useless. They had been taken by John Stringer, an award-winning photographer. They were likely far too good keep.

87 "Deposition of Dr. James Joseph Humes, op. cit., p. 197.

88 "Finck Privileged Communication Dated 10 FEB 67," op. cit.

showing "the missile wound in posterior skull with scalp reflected."[89]

The DOJ's reason for calling the autopsy personnel was clear: they had described these four photographs (F8[90]) in their signed report as depicting the *posterior skull*, which was embarrassing to the official dogma. Moreover, if autopsy photographs numbered 17, 18, 44, and 45 (often called F8) show the posterior skull, then JFK was shot from the front!

By themselves, these photographs are difficult to orient. Multiple lines of evidence imply that F8 is mostly a posterior view. A compelling visual clue unexpectedly confronted me at the Archives as I viewed the color transparencies in stereo. In the upper left corner of F8 (as oriented in Figure 4.21 below), I was surprised to see fat tissue (in the far distance), and even a nipple extending outward from the skin of the chest.[91] (This area is not visible in public images.) Rather strangely, until the ARRB, no one else had reported such fatty tissue. However, the ARRB's forensic pathologist, Robert H. Kirschner, described this

---

89 "Report of Inspection by Naval Medical Staff on November 1, 1966, at National Archives of X-Rays and Photographs of Autopsy of President John F. Kennedy," MD 13: Signed Military Inventory of Autopsy Photos and X-rays, ARRB Master Set of Medical Exhibits, November 10, 1966, https://www.aarclibrary.org/publib/jfk/arrb/master_med_set/md13/html/Image00.htm. Referred to in the ARRB depositions of Humes and Finck (cited above) as "Exhibit 13."

90 The designation of the four photographs numbered 17, 18, 44, and 45 as F8 derives from James Fox's list of autopsy photographs. Fox was the SS agent who oversaw Petty Officer Saundra Kay Spencer's development of JFK autopsy photographs at the Naval Photographic Center in Anacostia, Washington, DC, a day or two after the assassination. See: "Saundra K. Spencer" in William Matson Law, *In the Eye of History*, second edition, 2015, op. cit., pp. 429-433, at pp. 429-430, and 467. We use F8 as the label because 44 and 45 are color versions of the black-and-white 17 and 18 in the Fox photographic set. These latter two constitute a pair; they are nearly identical. The color versions, 44 and 45, constitute another pair. The fact that each member of a pair is slightly different is what makes stereo viewing possible for each pair.

91 Dr. Michael Chesser has made the same observations, even including his identification of a JFK nipple. Read his description in the autobiography by James Jenkins.

fat.[92] Kirschner had thus corroborated my critical observation. So also has Chesser now. These fat pads probably resulted from retracting the abdominal skin after the Y-incision. (Kirschner made the same point.) Seeing such fatty tissue (in that location) is possible only if F8 is a view from the back of the head. Once that is granted, a large occipital defect can readily be appreciated in F8. Writers who deny this have not had the privilege of viewing these color transparencies in stereo.[93]

Horne commented that "DOJ's challenge was to reorient these photos (black and white #17 and 18 as well as color #44 and 45) from photos the military inventory described as the posterior skull and an entrance wound into one that showed the right front of the head and an exit wound." [94] He characterized these four photos as depicting "mystery wounds."[95]

The DOJ was desperate that these four autopsy photographs should depict the exit wound at the front right of JFK's head.[96] Per the WC, no large exit wound should appear in the occiput. But if autopsy photos 17, 18, 44, and 45 show the posterior skull, then JFK was shot from the front. Figure 4.20 (Fox photograph F8) is the ARRB's Figure 66.

---

92 "[Point] (7)" in *Inside the ARRB*, ed. Douglas Horne, Mary Ferrell Foundation, "Appendix 45: "ARRB staff report of observations and opinions of forensic pathologist, Dr. Robert H. Kirschner, after viewing JFK autopsy photographs," April 11, 1996, p. 230, https://www.maryferrell.org/showDoc.html?docId=145280#relPageId=229.

93 The required pair of F8 images for stereo viewing is not in the public domain. However, two large color images of the back of JFK's head appear in my hardcover book. They are on the page opposite the preface to *JFK's Head Wounds*. So, there is no longer any excuse for delaying one's own viewing. More explicitly, there is no need to defer to experts.

94 Douglas Horne, email to the authors, May 4, 2023.

See also: "Report of Inspection by Naval Medical Staff on November 1, 1966, at National Archives of X-Rays and Photographs of Autopsy of President John F. Kennedy," MD 13, op. cit.

95 Ibid.

96 James Jenkins (autopsy diener) recalled that a photograph was explicitly taken to show the empty cranium—specifically to show the large right rear hole. William Matson Law, *In the Eye of History*, op. cit., p. 607.

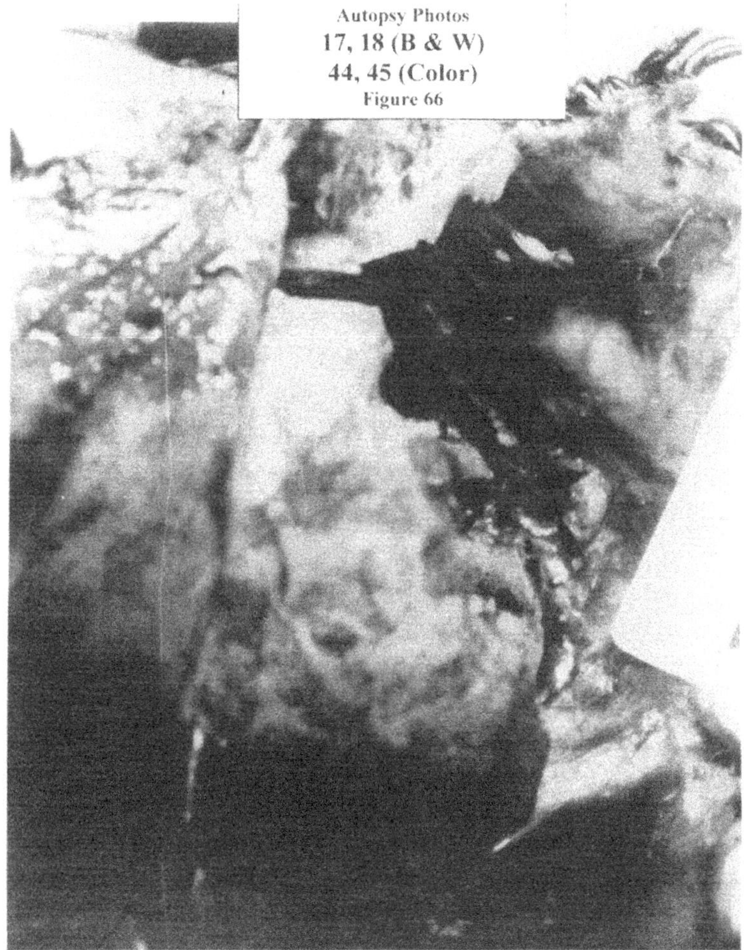

Figure 4.20

Autopsy Photographs 17 and 18 (B&W) or 44 and 45 (color). This enlargement shows external beveling (ARRB Figure 66).

The Military Inventory identifies autopsy photographs 17 and 18 as nearly identical posterior skull views, following reflection of the scalp (two contact and two eight-by-ten-inch prints). For number 18, the military inventory specifies: "(18) 4 x 5" negative similar to number 17 (above) with three contact and two 8 x 10" prints."

When Finck was shown photographs 17 and 18 during his 1996 ARRB deposition, he had little to say because "I have difficulties to orient [sic] this." His hesitation was likely due to the semi-circular beveled notch, which he perceived as a posterior exit wound.[97] Humes, in his 1996 ARRB deposition, was also elusive. Horne inferred that the report (January 26, 1967) "was radioactive to Humes, which is why he deflected with the ARRB and said, 'I don't know who wrote this.'" Finck also tried to dissociate himself from the changed description of these photos; he also emphasized that he had not written the report. In his ARRB testimony on February 13, 1996, Humes identified the entry wound near the external occipital protuberance (EOP) in photograph F8 (see Figure 4.21—with my annotations). This clearly implies that Humes interpreted F8 as a posterior view.[98]

---

97 "Deposition of Pierre A. Finck, MD," corrected copy (College Park, Maryland: Miller Reporting Company, Inc., 1996), pp. 125-126, https://www.maryferrell.org/showDoc.html?docId=787.

98 "Deposition of Dr. James Joseph Humes," op. cit., pp. 190-191.

See also: Douglas Horne, "Testimony About the Entry Location of the Entry Wound in the One Existing Close-Up View of the Skull," in *Inside the ARRB*, op. cit., vol. 2, photos no. 17, 18, 44, and 45, pp. 335-341, at p. 338.

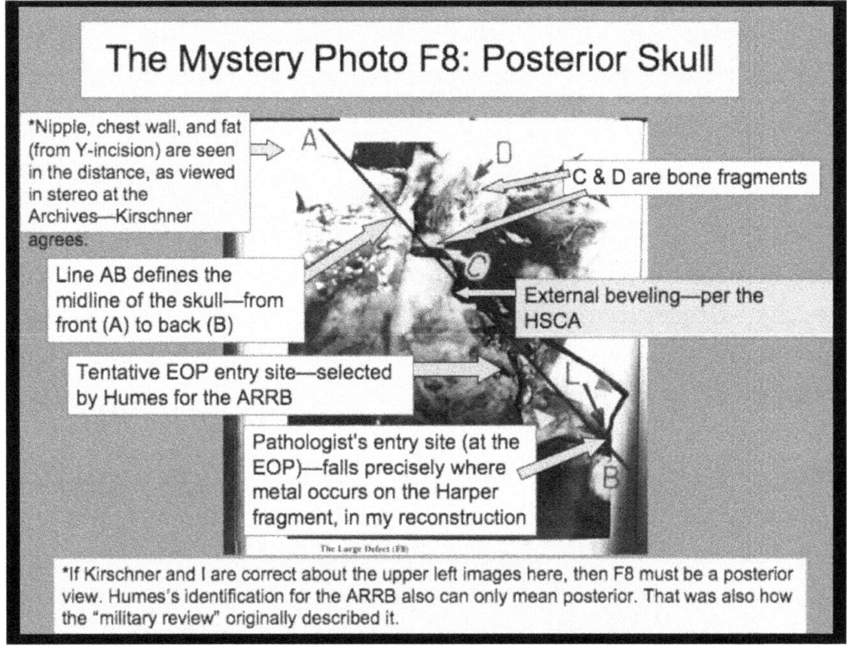

Figure 4.21

The Mystery Photo F8: Posterior Skull. The black oblique line (AB) identifies the skull midline. The large hole extends somewhat to the left of midline. This leftward extension of the large occipital hole (which includes the HF defect) is obvious on the AP skull X-ray film. The source for Figure 4.21 is slide twenty-two from my 2009 lecture, "The JFK Skull X-rays: Evidence for Forgery," from the JFK Lancer conference in Dallas, Texas, on November 21, 2009: http://www.assassinationscience.com/JFK_Skull_X-rays.htm.

In January 1967, their report was finally ready to be signed. As expected, they affirmed the official narrative that framed Oswald:

> The photographs and x-rays corroborate our visual observations during the autopsy and conclusively support our medical opinion as set forth in the summary of our autopsy report.
>
> It was then and is now our opinion that the two missiles which struck the President causing the neck [sic] wound and the head wound were fired from a point behind and somewhat above the level of the deceased.[99]

---

99 "Review of Autopsy Materials by Humes, Boswell and Finck," MD 14, op. cit., p. 5.

This DOJ episode reinforces a sorry conclusion: Humes, Boswell, and Finck were willing to sign any autopsy document prepared by the government, so long as they were allowed to retain their positions and pensions.

The conclusion is obvious: by January 1967, Humes, Boswell, and Finck finally understood—they had been hoodwinked! Despite this, they desperately wanted to avoid trouble, so they *overtly*—and unnecessarily—denied seeing this 6.5 mm (fake) object. They clearly hoped that no one would notice. Yet they could not have known that the Clark Panel would soon expose their deliberate lie. Ironically, just over a year later, these same pathologists spent one half day with the Clark Panel doctors while reviewing the autopsy materials. This surely included the 6.5 mm object on the AP X-ray film, which the Clark Panel later publicly described for the first time. This is the *same* object that the autopsy personnel had clearly stated was *not* present! What the pathologists told the four Clark Panel doctors about this fake object will never be known, and the Clark Panel never said a word either. But then that same panel accused the pathologists of making a four-inch mistake in locating the posterior bullet entry. Based on the altered autopsy images (both photographic and radiographic), the panel self-righteously deemed that it was their privilege to accuse the pathologists of gross errors. But what the panel did not know (and did not ask) was paralyzing for them—the autopsy photographs had no chain of custody![100] Nor did the panel know about Ebersole's adventures in the X-ray darkroom. After all, the panel had *no experts* on the alteration of photographs or radiographs. So, the autopsy personnel had been fatally co-opted into a multi-level cover-up, but they were in no position to protest.

---

100 This was not discovered until the HSCA located the camera and lens combination used at the autopsy. See Gary L. Aguilar, MD, and Kathy Cunningham, "How Five Investigations into JFK's Medical/Autopsy Evidence Got It Wrong," part 5, op. cit.

WHERE DOES HF FIT INTO THE SKULL?

The HF has great importance for one reason: if it derives from the occiput, a frontal shot is strongly implied—and that means conspiracy. The Forensic Pathology Panel (FFP) of the HSCA (1977–1979) and their consultant J. Lawrence Angel disagreed with one another on the precise origin (in the skull) of this fragment, but they agreed that it was not occipital. Two subsequent researchers, Joseph N. Riley, PhD, an expert in neuroanatomy, and Randy Robertson, a diagnostic radiologist, also disagreed with an occipital origin.

The HSCA placed HF into the right parietal area (top of the head) where they claimed a bullet exited. But, in order to avoid a conspiracy, only one entry was allowed. So, they were required to regard the metallic smear on HF as an exit. But this requires that the smear be on the inside. Unfortunately for them, the metallic smear is on the *outside*. The HSCA merely (and wisely) evaded this conundrum. So also did Riley and Robertson. On the contrary, the smear is on the outside because it represents an entry (near the EOP), which is consistent with the pathologists' report. This is one conclusion that they got right. My reconstruction accepts their entry site.

Riley's brief article[101] had concluded that HF was right parietal, thereby agreeing with Angel and with the HSCA. Riley emphasized two generic features of skull bones: (1) vascular grooves and (2) parietal foramina. The foramina are tiny holes in the bone that transmit blood vessels perpendicular to the skull surface (Figure 4.6). The grooves are shallow, linear indentations that carry blood vessels parallel to the surface. Riley claimed that these two features are characteristic of parietal bone, but that "occipital bone does not show a pattern of vascular grooving." He also asserted that foramina occurred "only in parietal bone."

---

101 Joseph N. Riley, PhD, "Anatomy of the 'Harper Fragment,'" February 23, 1997, https://kenrahn.com/Marsh/Jfk-conspiracy/harperfrag.html.

Based on a survey of many anatomy textbooks, and on my authentic (purchased) human skull, both of Riley's two arguments are wrong.[102] Riley noted an additional feature that, in his opinion, excluded an occipital site: the absence of deep grooves on HF for two specific, large blood vessels (the transverse sinus and superior sagittal sinus). However, since the transverse sinus is from the lower occiput, that identification is quite irrelevant. That is because, in my reconstruction, HF is from the upper occiput, not the lower occiput.

Independent researcher John Hunt (RIP) offered me the FBI X-ray images of HF (Figure 4.22). He had obtained these directly from the Archives. As I have observed, the originals contain a wide range of X-ray exposures; most do not reveal the metallic debris. However, at the lowest exposures, this can be seen, as in Figure 4.22.

Most importantly, the location of the metallic deposit in the X-ray image precisely matches the smear in the photographs (Figure 4.23). So, we know that the smear is relevant. The Dallas pathologists were also quite struck by it.

---

102 For further details about Riley's misadventures, consult my hardcover book. My original e-book appears at the end of-*JFK's Head Wounds: A Final Synthesis—and a New Analysis of the Harper Fragment*, op. cit. This e-book is also reprinted in my hardcover book, *The JFK Assassination Decoded*, "Section 4: Vascular Grooves and Foramina in Occipital Bone: A Refutation of Riley's Arguments," op. cit., pp. 23-30.

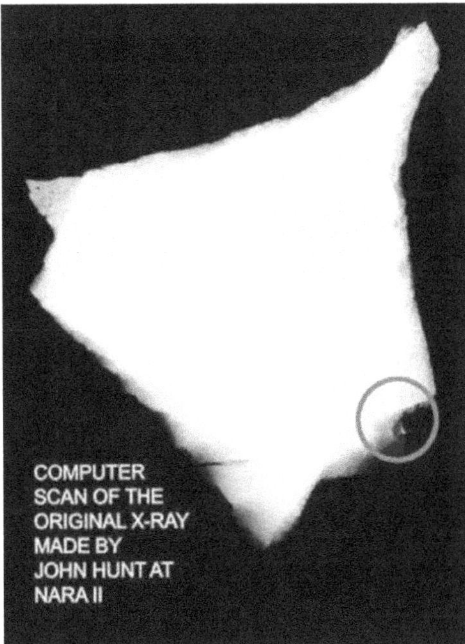

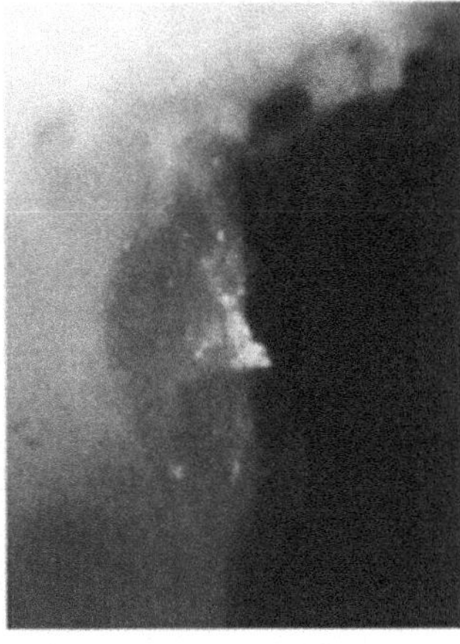

Figure 4.22

X-ray of HF (courtesy of John Hunt). The metallic smear is circled on the left image, then shown magnified on the right. The source for Figure 4.22 is David W. Mantik, *The JFK Assassination Decoded,* op. cit., specifically *John F. Kennedy's Head Wounds: A Final Synthesis—and a New Analysis of the Harper Fragment* located at the back of my hardcover book, at p. 401, renumbered as 1-92, at p. 10.

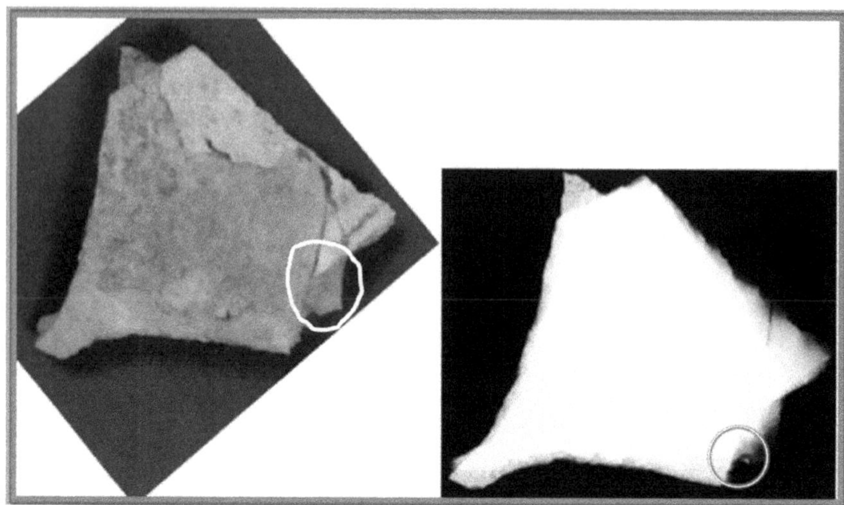

Figure 4.23
The location of the metal debris on the HF X-ray film precisely matches the site of the visible smear on the HF photograph.

My reconstruction of where the HF fits into the skull (Figures 4.24) first appeared in 2000.[103] In Figure 4.27, the 6.5 mm object (a circle with a bite taken out) lies within JFK's right orbit on the AP X- ray film. This is the critical object on which the HSCA founded its case for a posterior shot—one that entered about 10 cm above the EOP. However, this object first appeared in history only with the Clark Panel report (1968). This 6.5 mm object is not cited in the official autopsy report—nor do any autopsy attendees describe it, nor was it discussed at the autopsy, nor has it ever been seen at the National Archives. Even more preposterous (for the HSCA) is the fact that their own ballistics

103 David Mantik, "Paradoxes of the JFK Assassination: The Medical Evidence Decoded," in *Murder in Dealey Plaza*, ed. James H. Fetzer, op. cit., pp 219-298, at pp. 229 and 292.

See also: David Mantik, "The JFK Autopsy Materials: Twenty Conclusions after Nine Visits," *Assassination Research*, 2003, http://assassinationresearch.com/v2n2/pittsburgh.pdf.

expert, Larry Sturdivan, later (correctly) claimed that this 6.5 mm object could not possibly represent a real metal fragment.

In my reconstruction (Figure 4.24), the occipital hole was formed by the bone flap labeled "McC" (after this flap had swung outward) and by the immediately adjacent HF defect. Together, these two defects formed the single hole that was observed at Parkland Hospital and at Bethesda.

In his WC testimony, McClelland explained that he had observed the damage from the oblique shot near the right ear:

> As I took the position at the head of the table that I have already described, to help out with the tracheotomy, I was in such a position that I could very closely examine the head wound, and I noticed that the right posterior portion of the skull had been extremely blasted. It had been shattered, apparently, by the force of the shot so that the parietal bone was protruded up through the scalp and seemed to be fractured almost along its right posterior half, as well as some of the occipital bone being fractured in its lateral half, and this sprung open the bones that I mentioned in such a way that you could actually look down into the skull cavity itself and see that probably a third or so, at least, of the brain tissue, posterior cerebral tissue, and some of the cerebellar tissue had been blasted out. There was a large amount of bleeding which was occurring mainly from the large venous channels in the skull which had been blasted open.[104]

---

104 "Testimony of Dr. Robert M. McClelland," *Hearings before the President's Commission on the Assassination of President Kennedy*, op. cit., vol. 6, March 21, 1964, pp. 30-36, at p. 33.

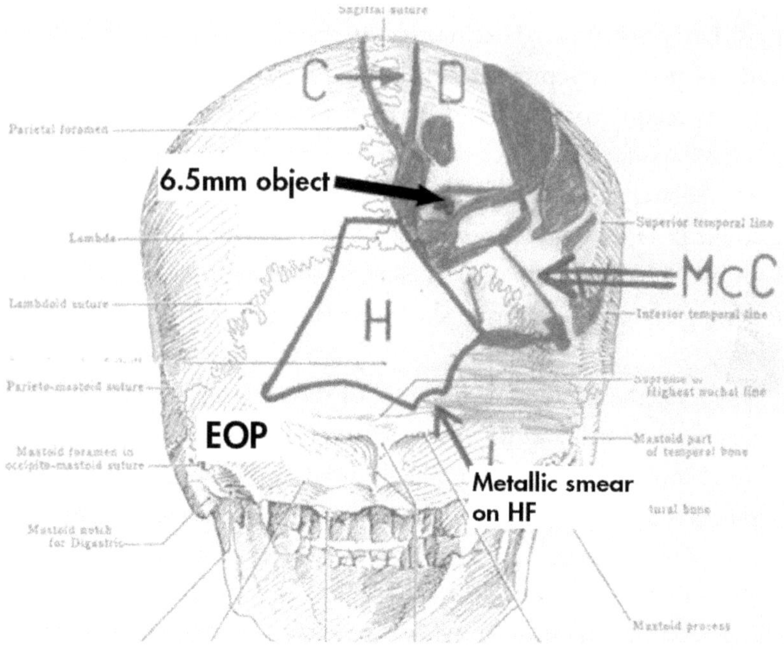

Figure 4.24

HF (labeled as H here) as Situated in the High Occiput. C and D are bone fragments visible on the AP X-ray film; they are also sketched on the autopsy face sheet. The metallic smear on HF matches the pathologists' entry site. McC identifies the fracture line, which acted like a hinge for McClelland's flap.

Boswell's sketch at the autopsy (Figure 4.25) is consistent with my location of the bone fragments C and D. Figure 4.26 shows my placement of HF within the mystery photograph F8. The missing frontal bone in Boswell's autopsy sketch is in close agreement with the missing frontal bone in the AP X-ray film (Figure 4.27).

The lambdoid suture[105] is a fibrous connective tissue joint on the

105 Sutures, sometimes called synarthroses, firmly fasten the adult skull bones together. They once functioned as slightly moveable joints in the developing skull. The lambdoid sutures are the fibrous tissue that connects the back of the head (the occipital bone) with the parietal bones, the two bones that form the sides and top of the head.

posterior skull that joins the occipital bone to the parietal bone. In the debate over the placement of HF on JFK's skull, many WC supporters have argued for decades that HF is parietal bone.

In Figure 4.27, I note precisely where the lambdoid sutures cannot be seen on the AP X-ray film. My observations at the Archives about the missing lambdoid sutures were recorded in my written notes while there. Quite pertinently, these observations were made before I became fully aware of their relevance to missing occipital bone. Consistent with this, also note the missing lambdoid sutures on Boswell's sketch on a skull (for the ARRB), as now located at the Archives (Figure 4.29). In particular, Boswell agrees with me that these medial lambdoid sutures (i.e., the lambdoid sutures that lie closer to midline) were no longer on the skull. They were probably lying in Elm Street.

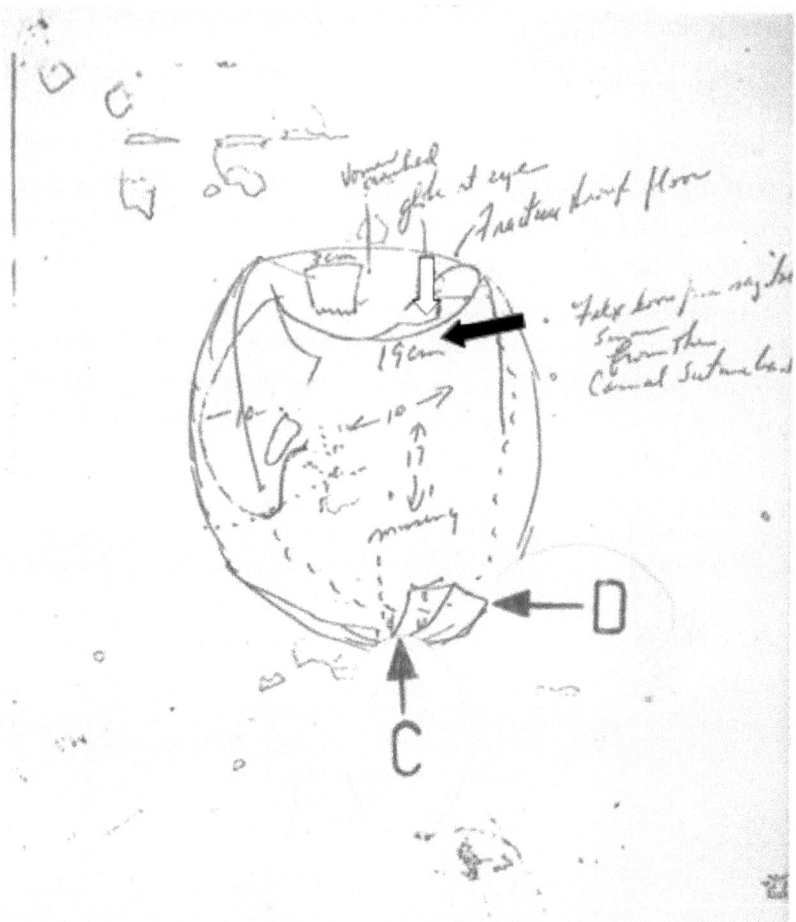

Figure 4.25

Boswell's Sketch on the Autopsy Descriptive Sheet (aka Face Sheet). Frontal bone is absent (arrow near "19 cm") anterior to the coronal suture. Also notice the notch (vertical arrow), where a frontal shot likely entered. C and D are bone fragments, also labeled C and D in Figure 4.24. The source for Figure 4.25 is David W. Mantik, *The JFK Assassination Decoded*, op. cit., specifically *John F. Kennedy's Head Wounds: A Final Synthesis—and a New Analysis of the Harper Fragment* located at the back of my hardcover book, at p. 401, renumbered as pp. 1-92. Listed as Figure 13, at p. 18.

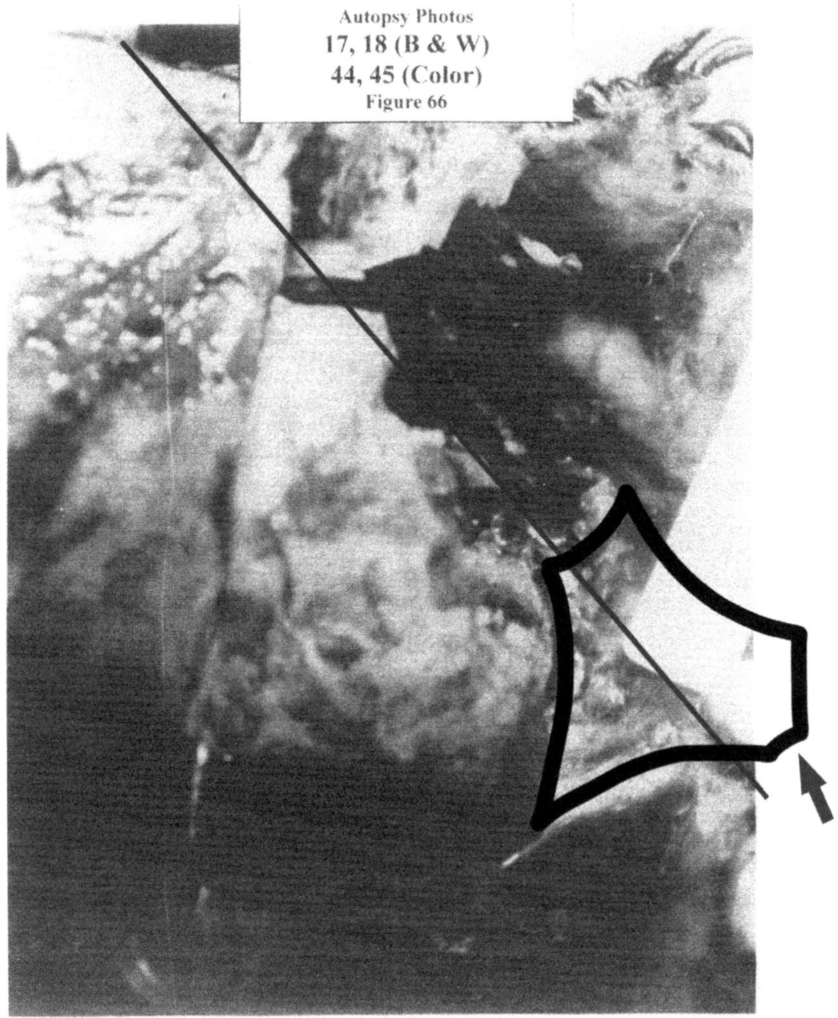

Figure 4.26
HF (solid black perimeter) as Situated in Photograph F8 (aka B&W #17–18, or color #44–45). My sketch is only approximate. The long oblique line defines the skull midline. The black arrow identifies the smear site, which closely matches the pathologists' entry site. The lambdoid sutures are not clearly visible here.

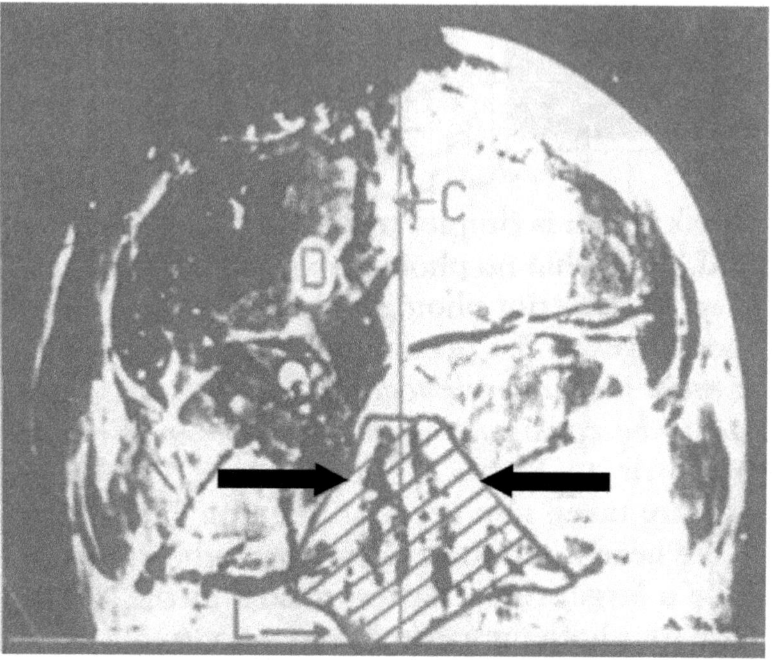

Figure 4.27

HF Defect (cross-hatched) on the AP X-ray Film. Based on my observations at the Archives, the bilateral lambdoid sutures (superior to the black arrows) are absent on the AP X-ray film. (They were probably lying on Elm Street.) The lambda point lies close to the upper edge of HF. The dark areas represent either missing brain or bone (or both). The slender, dark arrow at the very bottom left identifies the metallic smear on HF. The 6.5 mm object lies within the right orbit, just below the letter D. C and D are bone fragments noted on the autopsy face sheet. The source for Figure 4.27 is David W. Mantik, *The JFK Assassination Decoded*, op. cit., specifically *John F. Kennedy's Head Wounds: A Final Synthesis—and a New Analysis of the Harper Fragment* located at the back of my hardcover book, at p. 401, renumbered as pp. 1-92. Listed as Figure 7C, at p. 12.

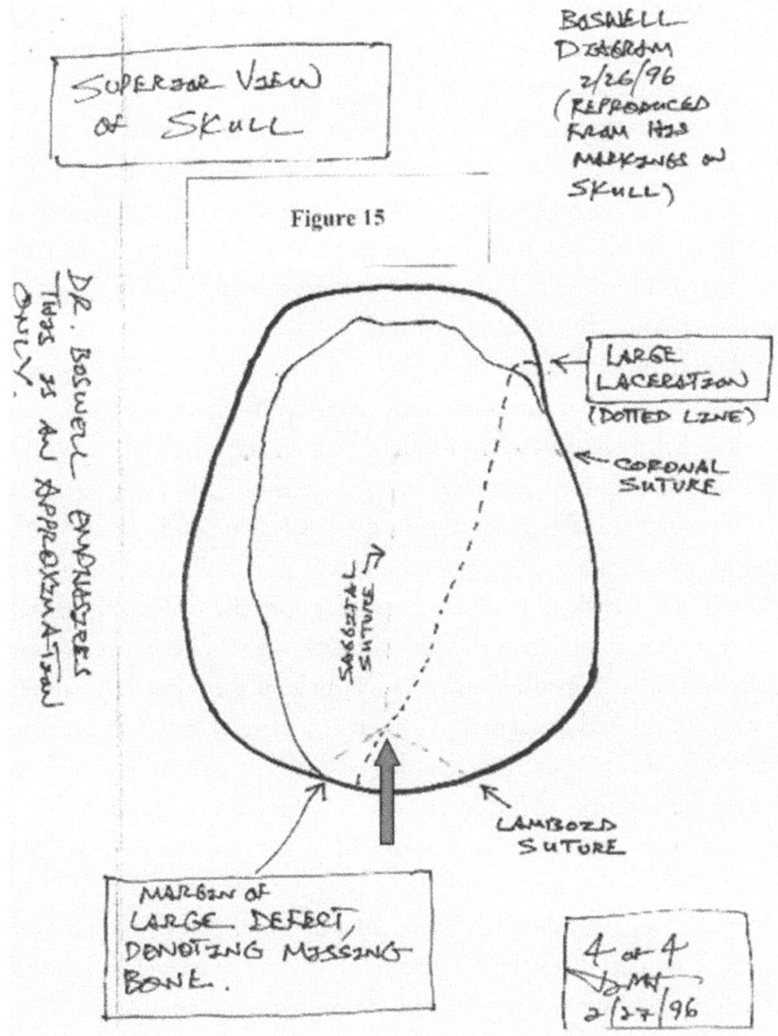

Figure 4.28

Boswell's Overhead View of the Skull for the ARRB. Compare the location of the lambdoid sutures here to my very similar location for them in Figure 4.27. My placement for HF in Figure 4.27 lies within Boswell's area of missing bone, as it should. The lambda point is just above the tip of the arrow. The source for Figure 4.28 is David W. Mantik, *The JFK Assassination Decoded,* op. cit., specifically *John F. Kennedy's Head Wounds: A Final Synthesis—and a New Analysis of the Harper Fragment* located at the back of my hardcover book, at p. 401, renumbered as pp. 1-92. Listed as Figure 8A, at p. 13. Figure 4.28 can also be found in Douglas Horne, *Inside the ARRB,* op. cit., vol. 1, Figure 15, among the unnumbered pages following p. 130.

The bilateral lambdoid sutures are mostly easy to see on the AP X-ray film, except near the midline.[106] Their location on the lateral X-ray film can also be compared to JFK's premortem lateral X-ray. All of this evidence is self-consistent. The medial lambdoid sutures are missing on the autopsy X-ray films because that bone was gone—perhaps lying in small pieces in Dealey Plaza. In that case, the entire occipital hole was larger than HF (or perhaps even larger than HF plus McClelland's flap). This is consistent with the loss of bone (on the AP X-ray film) immediately inferior to these sutures.

Although often ignored, the metallic smear is a critical clue. *This smear lies on the outside.* That can only mean an entry. In my reconstruction, the smear lies slightly to the right and slightly above the EOP. This is virtually a verbatim description from the Bethesda pathologists' own report. On the other hand, if HF had been from the parietal area, the exterior smear would require a bullet entry into the top of the skull. No one has even suggested this—parietal partisans merely ignore the smear. Nonetheless, the HSCA placed HF into the parietal area—but they never explained why the smear was on the outside. Of course, if the smear was an entry, then the HSCA had two entries: one in the parietal area and one in the cowlick area. Obviously, that would have meant conspiracy. It was far easier for them simply to ignore the smear, which is exactly what they did. They really had no choice. At all costs, they had to avoid two skull entry sites, which automatically would have meant conspiracy.

When I began taking ODs, I had not quite grasped their power. Initially, I had innocently measured ODs over the back of the skull (Figure 4.29). Only much later did I recognize that they identified the hole left behind by the missing HF.

---

106 Although JFK's premortem AP X-ray film (it does not exist) would have been even more useful, the premortem lateral X-ray film is still useful for locating the lambdoid sutures on the autopsy X-ray films.

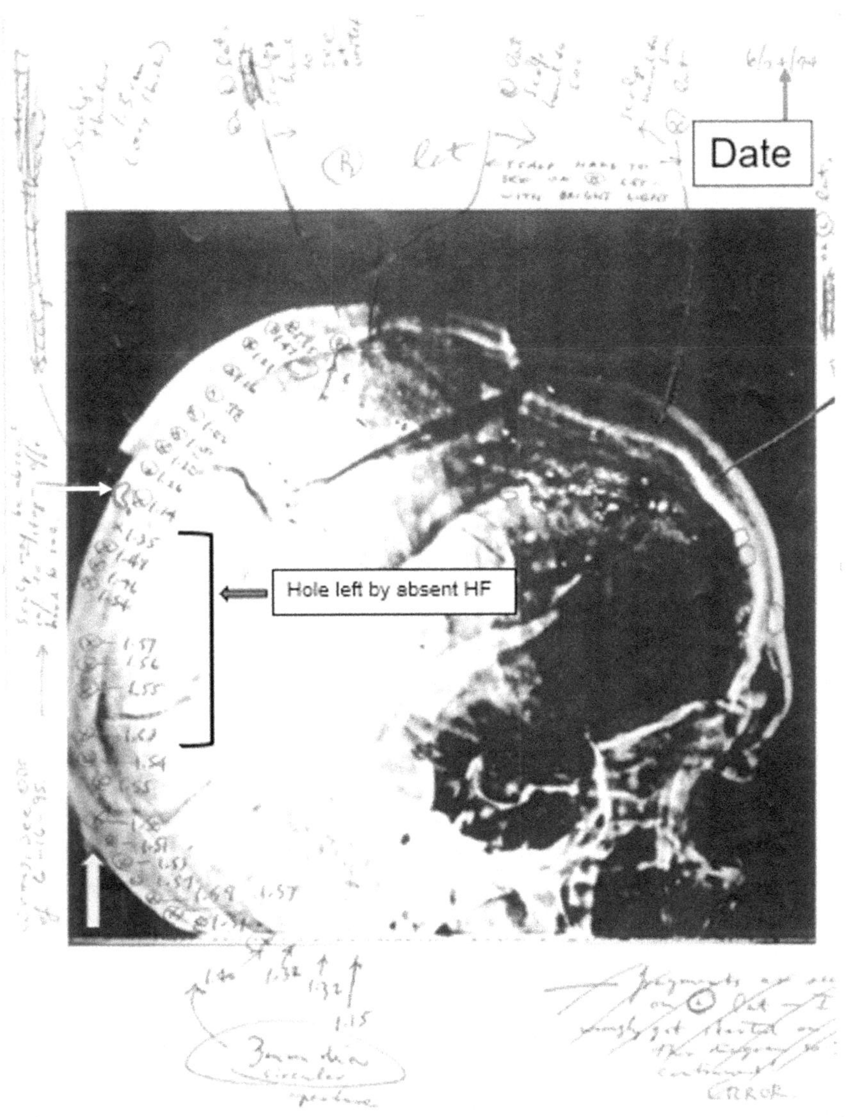

Figure 4.29

ODs on the lateral X-ray film demonstrate quantitatively where HF lay in the upper occiput. These ODs were measured on June 24, 1994 at the National Archives. This image was copied directly from my notebook. The left upper white arrow (outside the skull) identifies SOF, the Sibert-O'Neill Fragment. The lower left white vertical arrow identifies the EOP. The marginal notes also were made while at the Archives.

Although the human eye cannot distinguish the HF defect on the lateral X-ray film, as I examined the OD data, a discontinuity in OD numbers appeared close to the missing lambdoid sutures.[107] These ODs indicate two distinctly different numerical plateaus, i.e., the ODs are nearly constant (at about 1.10), just superior to the HF defect (where bone is present), and then again nearly constant (at about 1.46) in the area of the HF defect itself (Figure 4.30). The difference between these two ODs is consistent with missing bone. The total area of the defect may well be somewhat larger than HF itself; recall that small bone fragments were found in Dealey Plaza. Some of these probably contained the missing lambdoid sutures.

A similar discontinuity might have been expected inferior to the HF defect (because bone was present there), but the ODs do not show such a discontinuity. There is a good explanation for this apparent paradox though. At this lower level, the skull width continuously decreases—and the skull surface has much greater curvature. Therefore, the X-ray beam would traverse much less bone at this lower level. This would, of course, cause the ODs to change in the direction of less bone, which is what I observed.

It is also noteworthy that this OD data is consistent with the missing lambdoid sutures (Figure 4.27). This origin for HF also is consistent with the Parkland physicians' report of seeing cerebellum (Figure 4.30). Uncannily, the HF defect in the OD data also matches the specific site for HF as described by Dallas pathologist, A. B. Cairns. Since he had held HF in his hand, he should have known (Figures 4.31 A and B).

On November 21, 1992, on a Palm Springs radio talk show (KPSI), my colleagues and I interviewed one of the Dallas pathologists, Dr. Gerard Noteboom, who confirmed the occipital origin of HF. He recalled that he had held the bone; he also recalled a trace of metal (like

---

107 I actually took additional ODs of this area on other days. The data were all consistent with those shown here.

a lead smudge from a bullet) on one edge of HF, which Cairns had also noted. Cairns interpreted this smudge as due to a bullet entry. He said he had had experience with lead-caused damage, which looked similar to this discoloration.

On August 17, 1977, Andy Purdy (for the HSCA) interviewed Dr. A. B. Cairns, who recalled[108] that the "fragment came from an area approximately 2 1/2 to 3 inches above the spine area." (See Figures 4.32A and B.) He said it had the markings of a "skull fragment from the lower[109] occipital area, specifically: suture and inner markings where blood vessels run around the base of the skull." He also recalled, by virtue of the way the "tables" had been broken, that HF derived from an area close to an entry site. My reconstruction is consistent with Cairns.[110]

---

108 Andy Purdy to File, memorandum, August 17, 1977, MD 19: HSCA Interviews by Purdy with Harper (8/8/77), Cairns (8/9/77), Burkley (n.d.), Humes (8/10/77), Stringer (8/12/77 and 8/15/77), in AARB Master Set of Medical Exhibits, p.2, https://www.maryferrell.org/showDoc.html?docId=600#relPageId=1.

109 Ibid. Of course, we don't really know if Cairns had actually said "lower occipital." This is, after all, a quote prepared by the FBI. Cairns may well have said "lower skull, occipital," which the FBI then mangled in their report.

110 Ibid. For a 3D image of HF, as developed by Larry Rivera, see: Larry Rivera, *The JFK Horsemen*, op. cit., p. 403. For readers who like details, I have listed fifteen clues to the (high) occipital origin of HF in my e-book. See *JFK's Head Wounds: A Final Synthesis—and a New Analysis of the Harper Fragment*, "Section 6. Fifteen Indicators of an Occipital Origin for HF," op. cit. The e-book is also reprinted in my hardcover book. *The JFK Assassination Decoded*, op. cit.

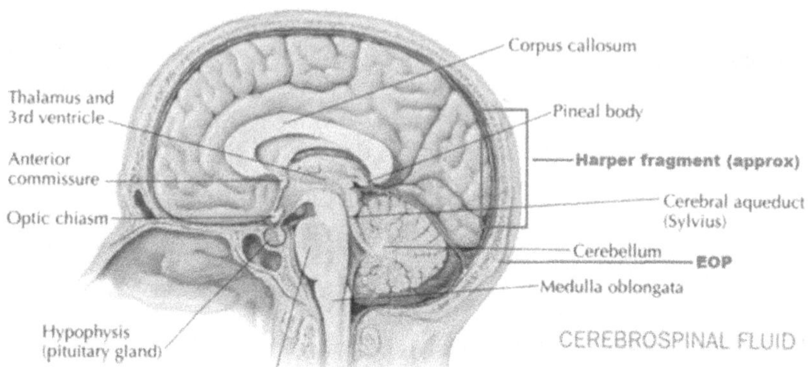

Figure 4.30

This sagittal view shows HF in relation to the cerebellum, which was easily visible as severely damaged at Parkland. When JFK's body reached Bethesda, however, the cerebellum had miraculously regenerated, just in time for the brain examination.

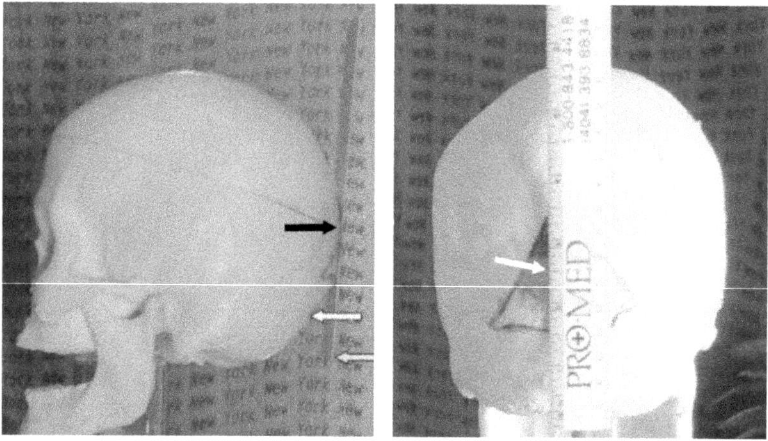

Figures 4.31A and 4.31B

This is my reconstruction of HF on the skull, as described by A. B. Cairns in Dallas. The remarkable agreement with the OD data (Figure 4.29) is obvious. On the left, the upper arrow identifies the center of HF, while the middle arrow identifies the EOP. The lowest arrow identifies the inferior border of the skull, a landmark that Cairns used. Note the ruler, which confirms the 2½–3 inches above "the spine area" cited by Cairns.

Of course, none of the above analysis was actually required. Virtually every one of the witnesses—in Dealey Plaza, at Parkland, and at Bethesda—knew exactly where the large hole was located in the back of head. Indeed, these witnesses closely agree with the above analysis (Figure 4.32).

Robert Groden, *The Killing of a President* (1994), Expanded

Figure 4.32

Parkland Hospital medical staff illustrate JFK's exit wound. Each person uses his/her right hand to locate the wound. Source: Robert J. Groden, *The Killing of a President: The Complete Photographic Record of the JFK Assassination* (Viking Studio Books, expanded paperback edition, January 1, 1994).

The only dissonant "evidence" in this case is the photograph of the back of JFK's head—the one that appears freshly washed[111] and shows the Red Spot that no one saw in Dallas. (Nor did the pathologists see it.) But now we know that stereo viewing fails in that critical photographic pair—even though every other photographic pair (of many pairs) at the Archives does show a 3D effect (as I ascertained after many viewings). A 3D image fails to appear because the forgers were careless—they inserted the exactly identical hairpiece image into each member of the pair, instead of using slightly different hairpiece images. There is no longer any reason to doubt the countless—and consistent—eyewitnesses. The *authentic evidence* is all completely coherent:

1. Even though every other autopsy photographic pair exhibits a stereo image, this pair (of the back of the head) does not. I have personally—and repeatedly—performed all of these observations at the National Archives. Robert Groden concurs.

2. Virtually scores of witnesses—in Dallas and at Bethesda—recalled a large baseball-sized hole—incongruously at this very site.

3. The autopsy photographs have no chain of possession (i.e., provenance), as determined by the Department of Defense.

---

111 The following comment is from James C. Jenkins and William Matson Law, *At the Cold Shoulder of History*, op. cit., p. 16. "Floyde Riebe, who was the assistant to the civilian photographer John Stringer, had taken the first photographs of the president's head immediately after the head was unwrapped. This was before any washing of the body or any manipulation of the head or scalp had occurred. At some point in the process of taking pictures, I was vaguely aware of some kind of commotion near the back of the gallery. I was later told that Riebe had his camera taken and the film exposed by the Secret Service. After the x-rays were finished, I don't remember much about Stringer taking photographs. I have seen the so-called 'Fox' set of photographs, and I do remember that the body was not clean, nor was the back of the president's head intact when Stringer was taking pictures. There were additional pictures taken throughout the autopsy, but the body was not cleaned until it was turned over to the morticians after the autopsy had ended." Humes also agreed with this (lack of cleaning).

4. The Black Spot on JFK's *left* back (Figure A.4) is proof that photographic manipulation has occurred in at least this image. See the detailed discussion of this site in the penultimate page of my hardcover book.

5. The "Red Spot" is most likely just another photographic manipulation. None of the autopsy pathologists saw it. Nor did anyone at Parkland.

6. The mismatch of the telephone location between the autopsy photograph (Figure H.1) versus Rydberg's sketch (Figure 6.2) strongly implies manipulation of the photograph.

7. If darkroom alteration of the skull X-ray films has occurred, as we now know with virtual certainty, why would the conspirators leave the autopsy photographs so virginally sacrosanct? After all, an untouched hole at the back of JFK's head (Figure 1.8) would indisputably have proclaimed a frontal shot. That image—by itself— would have shattered the entire conspiracy. To echo Allan Nevins, this specific step was the most mandatory manipulation in "...behalf of a cause...and intended to bring about a permanent falsification of history."

8. The occipital exit hole, as originally seen in the Zapruder film, necessarily also required a cover-up. Of those 70+ film professionals who viewed the Black Patch in Wilkinson's 6k scans of the film (purchased directly from the National Archives), nearly all agreed that it had to be a fake—and a rather poor one at that. Furthermore, Wilkinson and I have seen the pathetic Black Patch on *first generation* images in the MPI collection at the Sixth Floor Museum. The conspirators were so desperate—and probably so short on time—that they were forced to accept a slapdash fake. On first viewing this bogus image in the 6k scan, Ned Price, Head of Warner Brothers Restoration, exclaimed,

> "Oh my God, I can't believe they made such a bad fake." Those were precisely my own sentiments when I first saw this Black Patch in the first generation MPI images. My gifted 7 year old daughter would not have allowed such a juvenile effort to stand. But only such a forbidden forgery could scrub out JFK's flagrant occipital blow-out. Anything less than that would have endangered the entire scheme. After all, without that, lives and careers were seriously in jeopardy.

CHAPTER 4: SUMMARY

Two frontal headshots struck JFK. One of these entered just in front of the right ear. This temple wound was witnessed by many in Dealey Plaza, but even James Jenkins at the autopsy recalled it; he claims that Finck also saw it. The keyhole injury to JFK's temporal bone can only have been due to such a temple shot. After all, the trail of metallic debris (from the forehead shot) lies far too high to produce the keyhole trauma.

The forehead shot led to the metallic trail in the X-ray films, but it cannot explain the large hole at the back of the head; the metal fragments died out well before that. However, a temple shot, at an oblique angle, explains the large hole. It would also explain the tissue debris that fell on the witnesses behind the limousine. Of course, it also explains the cerebellar damage seen at Parkland, although it cannot explain the intact cerebellum in the brain photographs (which are of someone else's brain).

Billy Harper found his bone fragment in Dealey Plaza the next day. It measured about 7 x 5.5 cm and was trapezoidal in shape. (A baseball is 7.5 cm in diameter.) Based on at least fifteen clues (as detailed in my hardcover book), HF originated in the high occiput. This location is consistent with the large hole recalled by virtually all of the witnesses. On one edge, HF contains a metallic smear, which is consistent with the posterior headshot identified by the pathologists. Because HF was blown out of the back of the head, a frontal headshot must have triggered its exit. Most likely, this was the oblique shot to the temple, which also caused the keyhole injury.

As James Jenkins recalled, an autopsy photograph was taken after the brain had been removed; its purpose was to demonstrate the large exit hole. Paul O'Connor also specifically recalled such a photograph.[112] That is precisely what autopsy photograph F8 reveals. The best clue to its orientation is via stereoscopic viewing, where abdominal fat pads are visible in the distant background, along with a glimpse of a nipple. Dr. Chesser, Robert H. Kirschner (the ARRB expert), and I have all reported this. The only possible interpretation is that F8 shows the large hole at the back of the head. Even the bone fragments in the AP skull film match those seen in F8—they also match those same bone fragments on the autopsy face sheet. Any other interpretation totally destroys this correlation and leads to chaos.

Although the HF provides decisive evidence, it is often ignored. The metallic smear identifies an entry in the occiput near the EOP. This matches the entry site in the official autopsy report. So, via the smear, the HF provides direct evidence of a rear headshot—the smear (lead from a bullet) was deposited on the outside. But because HF was blown out of the back of the head, we must conclude that a frontal shot triggered its exit. So, merely based on HF, we arrive directly at two headshots and unavoidable conspiracy. Unfortunately, the WC did not evaluate HF, while the HSCA totally bungled it—when they were not simply ignoring it. Even today, most researchers seem unaware of the portent of the external smear. Our foremost example is the venerable Josiah Thompson, whose entire shot sequence depends on ignoring the smear.[113]

This chapter concludes our discussion of the medical evidence. Next, we turn to a totally different subject, but one which also involves misdirection. Fitzkee would most likely enjoy this, too, although he probably had never had to make a windshield disappear.

---

112 William Matson Law, op. cit., p. 215. See photo number 5 in the book.

113 My critique of Thompson's many calamities occupies an entire chapter in my hardcover book. See my review called, "*Last Second in Dallas* (LSID) by Josiah Thompson—a Mantik Review," in *The JFK Assassination Decoded,* op. cit., pp. 262-315.

5

THE FRONTAL SHOT THROUGH THE LIMOUSINE WINDSHIELD

Always be looking through the front windshield. Reflect on what's behind you, but always be looking ahead or you can trap yourself in a bubble that is destructive.

—**COLIN POWELL**[1]

People come in two varieties: those who look out the windshield and those who stare in the rearview mirror.

—**NICHOLAS SPARKS**[2]

It is my belief that the Secret Service could have sent the car anywhere they chose without issue after the 23rd. They had managed to prove that the car was not relevant to the assassination.

—**PAMELA MCELWAIN-BROWN**, *Kennedy Assassination Chronicles*[3]

---

1 Belinda Luscombe, "Colin Powell Reflects on His Mistakes in This Unpublished *Time* Interview," *Time*, October 19, 2021, https://time.com/6107966/colin-powell-time-interview/.

2 Nicholas Sparks, *The Guardian* (New York: Warner Books, 2003), p. 210.

3 Pamela McElwain-Brown, "An Examination of the Presidential Limousine in the White House Garage," *Kennedy Assassination Chronicles*, vol. 5, issue 4 (Winter 1999): pp. 18-23, at p. 22, https://www.maryferrell.org/showDoc.html?docId=4886#relPageId=21&search=vaughn_ferguson.

AT THE TIME OF HIS AUTOPSY, JFK had a throat wound. Multiple lines of evidence confirm that this was an entry wound—and that the pathologists understood this while at the autopsy. As previously cited, we now have quite recent corroborative (and contemporaneous) evidence discovered by author Rob Couteau. On the evening of December 2, 1963, Dallas reporter Martin Steadman and two other journalists joined Dr. Malcolm Perry at his home. Perry confessed to these journalists that he genuinely believed that the throat wound was an entry. Furthermore, besides the overwhelming evidence from telephone calls (between Bethesda and Parkland)[4] during the autopsy, the Bethesda pathologists recognized that the five-centimeter contusion at the right lung apex could not have been caused by Perry's tracheotomy. Rather, the throat wound (and the associated lung contusion)—as well as the pathologists' reasonable consternation about it—was due to a frontal projectile that struck on Elm Street. However, the pathologists never understood exactly what had caused this throat wound.

This projectile entered near the midline of the throat, at about the third tracheal ring, and traveled obliquely to the right lung apex, where it stopped. As further confirmation of this limited (i.e., non-exiting) trajectory, the pathologists found no deep penetration at the upper back wound. They ignored this, however, and instead invented the single-bullet theory (SBT). As a consequence, Arlen Specter magically converted the throat wound into an exit—from an entry in the back.

Such a throat trajectory (ending at the lung apex) can only be consistent with a shot from the left front, e.g., from the South Knoll. This scenario is explored and illustrated extensively by Anthony Edward

4 The autopsy radiologist, John Ebersole, MD, confirmed this to me personally. Our conversation is transcribed here: "A Conversation with John Ebersole M.D, 2nd December 1992," ed. David W. Mantik, https://themantikview.org/pdf/Conversation_with_John_Ebersole.pdf. Note: Much of chapter 5 is drawn directly from my essay "The JFK Limousine Redux: November 21, 2021," published in my hardcover book, *The JFK Assassination Decoded*, pp. 316-400.

DeFiore at his website.[5] DeFiore pictured a trajectory between the throat wound and the windshield hole; then he projected this outward from the limousine to its origin at the South Knoll (Figure 5.1). He argued that this wound occurred at about Z-225 when JFK emerged from behind the Stemmons Freeway sign.

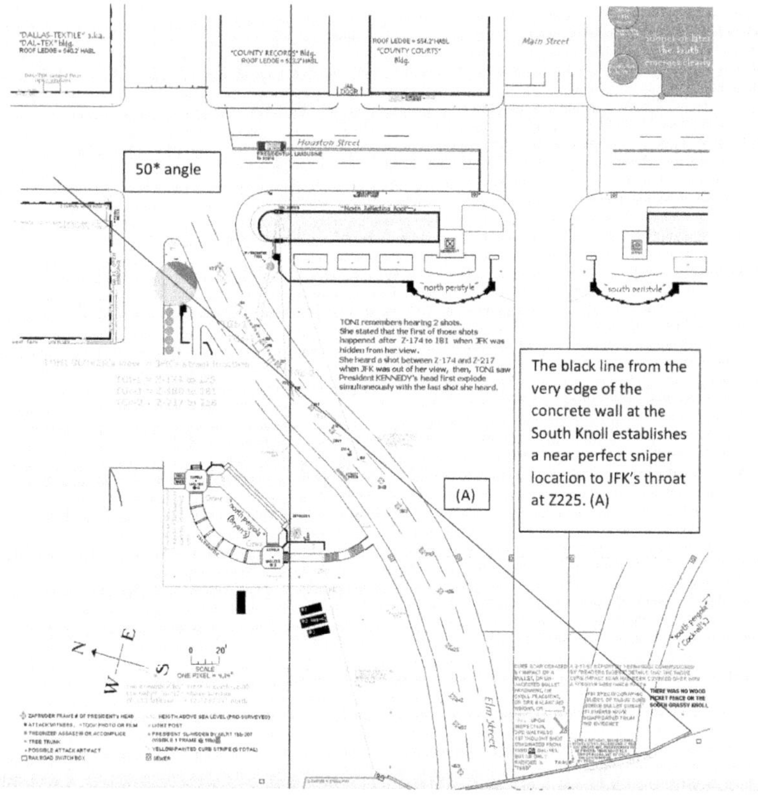

Figure 5.1

Trajectory: From the South Knoll Overpass to the Limousine at Z-255. Source: Anthony Edward DeFiore, "Z225: A Research Analysis of the frontal shot at President John F. Kennedy on November 22, 1963," op. cit.

---

5 Anthony Edward DeFiore, "Z225: A Research Analysis of the front shot at President John F. Kennedy on November 22, 1963," https://nebula.wsimg.com/9392bbdc7543ebb26015be8fe6dc1ebb?AccessKeyId=E4C9234584F3D40DC23C&disposition=0&alloworigin=1.

Roy Schaeffer of Dayton, Ohio, claims first discovery of the windshield damage seen in the Altgens 6 photographs.[6] No one has disputed this. Schaeffer was at the *Dayton Daily News* when he received the Mary Moorman and the Altgens 6 photographs and removed them from the Thermofax machine at 7:15 a.m., on Saturday, November 23, 1963. He is considered "an expert of the highest order, with intricate knowledge of the newspaper business of the late '50s and early '60s and beyond."[7] Schaeffer, in his unpublished article, "A Matter of a Reasonable Doubt," claimed that Z-222 shows the windshield hole.[8]

When the limousine emerges from behind the Simmons Freeway sign at Z-225, JFK is reaching for his throat (Figure 5.2).

---

6 "Part II: The Press Conference That Never Was," in *Assassination Science*, ed. James H. Fetzer, op. cit., 141-144, at p. 145.

I asked Roy Schaeffer when he had first noticed the windshield damage. Here is his reply in an email to me on October 30, 2021:

Dr. Mantik,

It was near Christmas of 1963, after learning at Willard's garage of bullet damage to the Presidential Limousine. I then noticed the bullet hole in the Presidential Limousine from looking at the Saturday Evening Post near New Years that year. I told two editors from the Dayton Daily News that I remember, one Carl Byers, staff writer, and then Lou Rotterman, Washington Bureau Chief. You have to remember Ralph McGill was Pres. of the Atlanta Constitution. I also told later Jim Nickols, writer and friend at the Dayton Daily News. That was as far as it went. At that time, I was an Apprentice. I didn't notice the bullet hole on 11/23/1963. My father had been a friend of Humphrey since 1930. Sadly, when my father died in 1968 my mother got rid of all their correspondence. After that, from time to time, I would mention it at the newspaper. As far as going to the outside media, I didn't until 1991, Channel 22, ABC news, Dayton.

Roy Schaeffer

7 Larry Rivera, *The JFK Horsemen*, op. cit., pp. 14-15, at p. 14.

8 Roy Schaeffer, "A Matter of Reasonable Doubt," unpublished manuscript, from a copy provided to me by the author.

Figure 5.2
Z-225. JFK reacts to a throat wound.

At Z-230, a white dot of reflected light is visible on the limousine windshield. As viewed from the front, this appears just above and to the right of the rearview mirror (Figure 5.3).

Figure 5.3
Z-230. The circle identifies damage to the windshield. Z-230 is a fair representation of the windshield damage I saw on the first generation MPI images at the Sixth Floor Museum in Dallas.

On Friday, November 20, 2009, I viewed the first generation, large format MPI transparencies[9] of the Zapruder film at the Sixth Floor Museum in Dallas with Sydney Wilkinson, a Zapruder film expert.[10] The MPI transparencies had incredible clarity. The first sign

9 The Sixth Floor Museum in Dallas has four-by-five color transparencies of the Zapruder film; they were made in March 1997 for the MPI Media video project titled *Image of an Assassination: A New Look at the Zapruder Film*. The project prepared a DVD and a VHS tape, which have been available to the public since 1998. The Zapruder family donated the MPI transparencies to the museum between late December 1999 and early January 2000. See the letter from Megan P. Bryant, the director of collections and intellectual property at The Sixth Floor Museum at Dealey Plaza, Dallas, Texas: https://educationforum.ipbhost.com/topic/17719-zapruder-4x5-inch-transparencies/. The letter is also included in my hardcover book: David W. Mantik, *The JFK Assassination Decoded: Criminal Forgery in the Autopsy Photographs and X-rays,* op. cit., p. 31.

In 1997, with Douglas Horne of the ARRB staff serving as a neutral observer, MPI's designated film contractor (McCrone Associates) photographed each frame of the extant Zapruder film at the Archives, using large format (four-by-five inch) Kodak 6121 color positive transparency duplicating films. Those MPI transparencies constituted the first generation copies of each frame in the extant film. The extant film is considered generation zero.

10 According to Horne (emphases in the original): "Sydney Wilkinson purchased a 35 mm dupe negative of the Zapruder film from the National Archives in 2008—a third generation rendition, according to the Archives—and with the assistance of her husband, who is a video editor at a major post-production film house in Hollywood, commissioned both "HD" scans (1920 x 1080 pixels per scan) of each frame of the dupe negative, as well as "6K" scans of each

of windshield damage appears at Z-193. This is uncannily consistent with the National Photographic Interpretation Center (NPIC) conclusion that JFK was hit in the throat at Z-190.[11] Quite naïvely, as I examined the MPI images, I had forgotten this NPIC conclusion, so my observations were quite unbiased. In these MPI images, this windshield site is obscured during Z-203 to Z-214, but the damage is visible (consistently at the same site) in Z-215 to Z-232. It is especially obvious in Z-229 and Z-230, but it is more difficult to see after Z-232. The windshield damage in the Zapruder frames appears at the same site as seen in Altgens 6 and Altgens 7. Roy's description is also consistent with this. I would emphasize that if the shot had occurred earlier than Z-222 (i.e., that was Roy's selected frame), then a windshield transit would have been more likely—because the windshield elevation would have been higher.

---

frame. Because the Zapruder film's image, from edge to edge, only partially fills each 35 mm film frame obtained from the Archives, the so-called "6K" scan of each frame is therefore 'only' the equivalent of a "4K" image, i.e., 4096 x 3112 pixels, *for each Zapruder frame imaged.* Each frame scan constitutes an enormous amount of information: 72.9 MB, or 12.7 million pixels per frame. These "4K equivalent" scans of the Zapruder film used by this couple to conduct their forensic, scientific study of the assassination images are 10-bit *log color* DPX scans, otherwise known in common parlance as "flat scans." These *logarithmic color* scans bring out much more information in the shadows than would the *linear color* normally viewed on our television screens and computers. Therefore, much more information in each Zapruder film frame is revealed by these *logarithmic scans,* than would be revealed in a *linear color scan* of the same frame." Source: Douglas Horne, "The Two NPIC Zapruder Film Events: Signposts Pointing to the Film's Alteration," Assassination of JFK, https://assassinationofjfk.net/the-two-npic-zapruder-film-events-signposts-pointing-to-the-films-alteration/.

See also: David W. Mantik and Sydney Wilkerson, "Masquerade at the Museum," April 15, 2013, revised November 2021. It is reprinted in my hardcover book: David W. Mantik, *The JFK Assassination Decoded: Criminal Forgery in the Autopsy Photographs and X-rays,* op. cit., pp. 31-41.

11 "NPIC Analysis of Zapruder Filming of John F. Kennedy Assassination," HSCA Request Dated 3 Nov 1977; OLC 77-5058 – 13 May 15-18 Nov 77—MU, HSCA Segregate CIA Collection, Box 49, May 13, 1975, Mary Ferrell Foundation, https://www.maryferrell.org/showDoc.html?docId=105096#relPageId=2. The National Photographic and Interpretation Center (NPIC) is part of the National Geospatial-Intelligence Agency (NGA).

The Altgens 6 photograph (Figure 5.4) was taken at about Z-255, just thirty frames after Z-225 (i.e., less than two seconds later); it shows windshield damage consistent with a South Knoll shot. Shaeffer was the first to notice this windshield damage that lay very near JFK's left ear (in the Altgens 6—see Figure 5.4). He observed that "the small spiral nebula has a dark spot at the center, strongly suggesting a through-and-through bullet hole."[12] Of note, the official view is that the windshield damage was caused by a fragment from the headshot; that is nonsense, of course—because the headshots occurred after Z-300, far too late to affect the windshield at Z-255.

Figure 5.4
Altgens 6. The circle highlights damage to the windshield.

---

12 James H. Fetzer, *Assassination Science*, op. cit., pp. 141-144, at p. 144.

The damage to the windshield can also be seen in Altgens 7 (Figures 5.5 and 5.6), taken as the limousine sped toward the Triple Overpass.

Figure 5.5
Altgens 7. The circle highlights the windshield damage.

Figure 5.6
Altgens 7 Close-up. Windshield damage is visible inside the white box that overlies the antenna. Source: Pamela Brown, *Midnight Blue to Black: The Vanishing Act of the JFK Presidential Assassination Limousine SS100X in Broad Daylight* (Kindle Edition e-book, 2018).

EYEWITNESSES WHO SAW THE HOLE IN THE LIMOUSINE WINDSHIELD

The following witnesses saw a perforation (i.e., a through-and-through hole) in the windshield.[13]

STAVIS ELLIS AND H.R. FREEMAN

DALLAS POLICE OFFICERS WHO RODE IN THE JFK MOTORCADE

Douglas Weldon, an attorney for the county of Kalamazoo's circuit court and an adjunct professor for Western Michigan University's Department of Justice, became an expert on the bullet hole in the windshield. He noted that Officer Stavis Ellis, who was in charge of the motorcycle escort through Dallas, recalled actually putting a pencil into the hole. Ellis claimed there were numerous people and police officers at Parkland Hospital who viewed the hole. Weldon wrote:

> He [Stavis Ellis] vividly remembers that while he was observing the hole a Secret Service agent came up to him and tried to persuade him that he was seeing a "fragment" and not a hole. Mr. Ellis noted: "It wasn't a damn fragment. It was a hole." Mr. Ellis has been totally consistent with this statement over the years and has not wavered in his insistence that he saw a hole in the windshield immediately after the assassination. Ellis, moreover, had a distinguished career with the United States Army and the Dallas Police.[14]

Dallas Police Officer H. R. Freeman also rode in the motorcade. He observed the limousine at Parkland Hospital immediately after the shooting. "I was right beside it," he said. "I could have touched it. It was a bullet hole. You could tell what it was."[15]

---

13 Douglas Horne, "Photographic Evidence of Bullet Hole in JFK Limousine Windshield 'Hiding in Plain Sight,'" LewRockwell.com, June 4, 2012, https://www.lewrockwell.com/2012/06/douglas-p-horne/photographic-evidence-of-bullet-hole-in-jfk-limousine-windshield-hiding-in-plain-sight/.

14 Douglas Weldon, JD, "The Kennedy Limousine: Dallas 1963," in *Murder in Dealey Plaza,* ed. James Fetzer, op. cit., pp. 129-158, at pp. 139-140.

15 Ibid., p. 139.

EVALEA GLANGES, MD

A MEDICAL STUDENT AT PARKLAND HOSPITAL IN 1963

Glanges appeared in the seventh episode of Nigel Turner's *The Men Who Killed Kennedy*. In "The Smoking Guns," she is seen with a shotgun on a skeet shooting range. Glanges explained that on November 22, 1963, she was a second-year medical student at Southwestern Medical University in Dallas:

> I've been handling guns since I've been a child. We ran around the side of the building [Parkland Hospital] to the emergency room exit, and the presidential limousine was there. I had been standing there just watching the back of the emergency room when I realized there that was a bullet hole in the windshield. I talked to my friends next to me and said, "Look, there's a bullet hole in the windshield", and pointed it out to them. At the time, I did not know any of the details of the shooting. I was quite shocked when I looked up and saw the bullet hole. But was very clear it was a through-and-through bullet hole through the windshield of the car, from the front to the back. I don't believe there was even any cracks associated with that bullet hole. It seemed like a high-velocity bullet that had penetrated from front-to-back in that glass pane. At which point, a security officer of some type raced forward and jumped in the limousine and drove it off, even as I was leaning against it, to an area back of us somewhere. And that was the last time I saw the limousine.[16]

Weldon reported that when he interviewed Glanges, she was the chairperson of the Department of Surgery at John Peter Smith Hospital in Fort Worth, Texas. She told him that she felt she "needed to keep her mouth shut." Weldon summarized:

---

16 Douglas Horne, "The Bullet Hole in the Windshield is Proof of a Shot Fired from the Front," in *Inside the ARRB*, op. cit., vol. 5, pp. 1439-1445, at p. 1441. Transcribed from Nigel Turner's *The Men Who Killed Kennedy*, episode 7, "The Smoking Guns."

She was insistent that the official story was "phony." When I interviewed her, she was anticipating retirement in the near future. She confirmed that she was 100% certain that there was a hole in the windshield in the limousine at Parkland hospital. I am sorry to report that Dr. Glanges was unable to enjoy her retirement. A most credible witness, she died on 27 February 1999, one month after our interview.[17]

In this same episode of *The Men Who Killed Kennedy*, an interview with Weldon followed the interview with Glanges:

NARRATOR: The Secret Service made certain no authority in Dallas had the opportunity to examine the bullet damage to Kennedy's car.

DOUGLAS WELDON: The Secret Service also usurped Dallas authority in removing the Kennedy limousine from Parkland Hospital, and flew that limousine back to Washington, D.C. Just as an autopsy on the president's body could have given us many answers, a thorough study of that limousine at that time, without evidence being tampered with, could also have given us many important answers as to what really happened.[18]

Douglas Horne, in his *Inside the ARRB*, explained why he believes this and other episodes of *The Men Who Killed Kennedy* were suppressed:

Most researchers assume that the reason the three episodes that aired in 2003 were suppressed was because the final episode, about LBJ's culpability, was objectionable to Lady Bird Johnson, LBJ's aging

17 Douglas Weldon, JD, "The Kennedy Limousine: Dallas 1963," in *Murder in Dealey Plaza*, ed. James Fetzer, op. cit., p. 140.

18 Transcribed from Nigel Turner's *The Men Who Killed Kennedy*, episode 7, "The Smoking Guns."

widow. I believe that another more likely reason for the suppression was the clear and convincing examination of the bullet hole evidence, and the accompanying discussion of the Secret Service's malfeasance in arranging inadequate security for the Dallas motorcade, and in covering up the true damage to the windshield. Once you become aware of the way the Secret Service actively covered up the evidence of a bullet hole in the windshield, you can never view the history of this country in the same way as you did before you became aware of that information.[19]

SS AGENT CHARLES TAYLOR, JR.

ONE OF TWO SS AGENTS WHO DROVE THE LIMOUSINE FROM ANDREWS AIR FORCE BASE TO THE WHITE HOUSE GARAGE THE NIGHT OF THE ASSASSINATION.

The SS placed the limousine (SS-100-x, the SS code name for the limousine) in an Air Force C-130 cargo plane to be flown back to Washington. The C-130 arrived at approximately 8:00 p.m. at Andrews Air Force Base. SS Special Agent Samuel Kinney, accompanied by SS Special Agent Charles Taylor, Jr., drove the limousine under police escort to the White House garage.[20] On November 27, 1963, Taylor wrote an official report documenting the security of the X-100 (the SS abbreviation) in the White House garage after its return from Dallas. He noted that a team of four FBI agents, led by Robert A. Frazier, removed "bullet fragments" from the windshield, starting at 1:00 a.m. on November 23, 1963 (the night of the assassination). Taylor wrote: "In addition, of particular note was the small hole just left of center in the windshield from which *what appeared to be bullet fragments* [emphasis added] were

---

19 Douglas Horne, "The Bullet Hole in the Windshield is Proof of a Shot Fired from the Front" from *Inside the ARRB*, op. cit., vol. 5, pp. 1439-1445, at p. 1441.

20 Douglas Weldon, JD, "The Kennedy Limousine: Dallas 1963," in *Murder in Dealey Plaza*, ed. James Fetzer, op. cit., pp. 135-136.

removed."[21] CE 841 is a photograph of a container marked: "Scraping from inside windshield in area of crack."[22]

SS AGENT JOE PAOLELLA

SS Agent Joe Paolella was assigned the task of guarding the X-100 in the White House garage; this meant overseeing staff members from Bethesda Naval Hospital, who were expected "to search the presidential limousine and collect scalp, brain tissue, and bone matter."[23] Some forty years after the assassination, Paolella broke his silence in a radio interview with his friend Dr. John DeSalvo. Paolella clearly recalled the windshield bullet hole:

---

21 Charles Taylor, Jr., "FBI Protective Research Report of 27 November 1963" in *Murder in Dealey Plaza*, ed. James Fetzer, op. cit., pp. 428-430, at p. 430.

The HSCA staff interviewed SS Agent Taylor on December 10, 1975. On that occasion, Taylor was positive that there had (originally) been a hole *through* the windshield. *He stated that a pin could definitely have been inserted through this hole from one side of the windshield to the other.* However, the HSCA staff was not convinced that Taylor had had the opportunity to examine the supposed hole. With HSCA staff present, Taylor then (for the first time) examined the Archives' windshield. He stated that this windshield was the same one he had seen in 1963; i.e., contrary to his initial report, there was now no internal defect and no penetration. The staff subsequently prepared an affidavit and forwarded it to the SS for Mr. Taylor's review and signature. See: Charles E. Taylor, affidavit, House Select Committee to Study Governmental Operations with Respect to Intelligence Operations, JFK Collection: HSCA (RG 233), March 12, 1976, http://www.scribd.com/doc/16573650/TaylorAff.

My response to this is simple: the windshield that Taylor examined later (for the HSCA) was not the motorcade windshield. After all, that original windshield had been trashed in Dearborn by George Whitaker, Sr.—and no one had told Taylor about this. See more discussion about Whitaker below.

22 "Commission Exhibit 841 (CE 841)," *Hearings before the President's Commission on the Assassination of President Kennedy*, op. cit., vol. 17, p. 840.

23 Gerald Blaine and Lisa McCubbin, *The Kennedy Detail: JFK's Secret Service Agents Break Their Silence*, op. cit., p. 268.

> Walking around the car, I didn't want to sit back there—it was pretty horrible. I noticed that there appeared to be a bullet hole in the windshield on the driver's side, several inches over the hood of the car (i.e., elevated up on the windshield) but I, in turn, was in a state of shock myself, and I had heard that he got shot from the back, from the Dealey Plaza. So I didn't really look to see if the glass particles from the windshield were in the driver's side or on the hood. That would have given me some indication where the bullet came from.[24]

RICHARD DUDMAN

REPORTER, *ST. LOUIS POST-DISPATCH*

Richard Dudman was an eyewitness that day. On December 12, 1963, he published an article in *The New Republic*, entitled, "Commentary of an Eyewitness."[25] Here is an excerpt:

> A few of us noticed the hole in the windshield when the limousine was standing at the emergency entrance [to Parkland Hospital] after the President had been carried inside. I could not approach close enough to see on which side was the cup-shaped spot that indicates a bullet had pierced the glass from the opposite side.[26]

---

24 Vince Palamara, "JFK Secret Service Agent: hole in windshield of limo! INTERVIEW BY DR. JOHN DESALVO," August 2, 2018, https://www.youtube.com/watch?v=Wg_x4sx_m-w&t=164s. The quotation begins at 0:53 seconds from the start of the video.

On the radio show, Paolella emphasized that he had told Gerald Blaine that he had seen a bullet hole in the windshield, "but it never really made it into the publication for whatever reason" (i.e., into *The Kennedy Detail*). In posting the video, Palamara commented (emphases in the original): "***INTERVIEW BY DR. JOHN DESALVO.***JFK Secret Service Agent Joe Paolella, who passed away in 2017, admits that he saw a bullet hole in the windshield of President Kennedy's bloody limousine the night of the assassination AND that Gerald Blaine omitted this from his book *The Kennedy Detail*!!!"

25 Richard Dudman, "Commentary of an Eyewitness," *The New Republic,* December 21, 1963, https://newrepublic.com/article/115638/eyewitness-account-jfk-assassination-and-lee-harvey-oswald-murder.

26 Ibid.

Weldon commented that Dudman told interviewers that a SS agent shoved him and the other reporters away when he tried to examine the hole to determine the direction from which it had been fired.[27]

Dudman also noted that five bullets were found that day, which was far too many for Oswald to deliver:

> As for the number of bullets, although all who heard them agreed there were three shots, authorities repeatedly mentioned four bullets found afterward—one found in the floor of the car, a second found in the President's stretcher, a third removed from Governor Connally's left thigh, and a fourth said to have been removed from President Kennedy's body at the Naval Hospital in Bethesda. On the day the President was shot, I happened to learn of a possible fifth. A group of police officers were examining the area at the side of the street where the President was hit, and a police inspector told me they had just found another bullet in the grass. He said he did not know whether it had anything to do with the assassination.[28]

NICK PRENCIPE

US PARK POLICE MOTORCYCLE OFFICER

Nick Prencipe, a US Park Police motorcycle officer, drove to the White House garage on the evening of the assassination, after having a conversation with the JFK limousine driver, SS Agent Bill Greer. Greer told Prencipe that there were "shots coming from every direction," adding that "one of them came right through the windshield."[29]

---

27 Douglas Weldon, JD, "The Kennedy Limousine: Dallas 1963," in *Murder in Dealey Plaza*, ed. James Fetzer, op. cit., pp. 135-136.

28 Richard Dudman, "Commentary of an Eyewitness," op. cit.
Horne and Weldon both attribute the comment to a speech by Mark Lane at Amherst in 1964. See: Douglas Horne, "The Bullet Hole in the Windshield is Proof of a Shot Fired from the Front" from *Inside the ARRB*, op. cit., vol. 5, p. 1440.

29 "Nick Principe in 'SS-100-X' chapter of CAR CRASH CULTURE," posted by pjfk on alt.assassination.jfk.narkive.com, https://alt.assassination.jfk.narkive.com/ozeXanIn/nick-prencipe-in-ss-100-x-chapter-of-car-crash-culture.

DR. ROBERT LIVINGSTON TELEPHONES DR. JAMES HUMES BEFORE THE AUTOPSY BEGINS

My friend Robert B. Livingston, MD, shed critically important light on Dudman's claims.[30] (Livingston was also Dudman's friend.) Livingston

---

In a discussion string posted at The Education Forum on July 4, 2009, titled "Barb Junkkarinen's article: A HOLE THROUGH THE WINDSHIELD," she wrote:

Barb Junkkarinen: "Principe's [sic] claim has little probative significance not only because it was first made thirty-five years after the event but also because his claimed conversation with Greer could not have occurred. Principe [sic] could not have talked to Greer that night since Greer accompanied the body to Bethesda Hospital and stayed at Bethesda throughout the autopsy and morticians' preparation, driving JFK's body home to the White House for the last time after 3:30 AM on Saturday, November 23, 1963. Bests, Barb :-)"

See: https://educationforum.ipbhost.com/topic/14532-barb-junkkarinens-articlea-hole-through-the-windshield/.

My complete disagreement with her statement appears in my hardcover book; it relies on the recollections of Greg Burnham, who frequently interacted with Prencipe over many years. Greg Burnham is the publisher of the AssassinationOfJFK.net blog, referenced at https://assassinationofjfk.net/about-me/.

Greg Burnham: "I do not recall the exact time Nick said, but often we use 'night' even when it is really during the wee hours of the next morning. Nick was not one to insert himself into history nor did he seek attention. He was quite modest and unassuming."

In a follow-up to his comment, I asked Greg whether Prencipe had this discussion with Greer within twenty-four hours of the assassination, and Greg replied, "*Absolutely!*"

In an online interview with Len Osanic, Doug Weldon also responded to Barb's bogus issue by quoting Prencipe, who insisted that he did meet with Greer that night.

According to the Cornell Law School: Under the Federal Rules of Evidence, an excited utterance (like Greer's) "is defined as a statement that concerns a startling event, made by the declarant when the declarant is still under stress from the startling event." Since an excited utterance "does not constitute hearsay under the logic that people after a startling event will most likely be reacting to the event and will not have had the time to consider making false statements," excited utterance "*is an exception to the hearsay rule* [emphasis added]." See: "Excited Utterance," Cornell Law School, Legal Information Institute (LII), last updated November 2022, https://www.law.cornell.edu/wex/excited_utterance.

30 As I wrote the initial draft of the windshield article for my hardcover book, I was just a few blocks from my last breakfast site with Bob Livingston in Pacific Beach, California. James Fetzer published this photograph of me with Dr. Livingston in Rancho Mirage, California, on June 12, 1997.

was a distinguished physician. In World War II, he earned a Bronze Star by establishing and directing the only hospital for wounded Okinawans and Japanese prisoners during the bloody battle of Okinawa. While there, he personally cared for hundreds of bullet and shrapnel wounds during his service with the navy medical corps. Livingston explained:

> Dick Dudman is a classmate of mine from Stanford. He telephoned me about this [the bullet hole in the windshield of JFK's limousine] from Dallas shortly after the assassination; and our families had a dinner discussion on this subject in Washington, D.C., within a week or so of the assassination. Dick Dudman told me about the windshield then, although to the present he does not know whether the hole he saw penetrated the windshield. He was prevented by the Secret Service from testing the hole's presumed patency by probing it with a pen or pencil.[31]

Robert B. Livingston, MD, at my home in Rancho Mirage, California, on June 12, 1997

Dr. Livingston passed away on April 26, 2002, aged eighty-three. See: "The JFK Limousine Redux," in my hardcover book, *The JFK Assassination Decoded: Criminal Forgery in the Autopsy Photographs and X-rays,* op. cit., p. 321.

31 Robert B. Livingston, "Statement of 18 November 1993," in *Assassination Science*, ed. James Fetzer, op. cit., pp. 161-166, at p. 165. Livingston repeated these recollections, under oath, during Dr. Crenshaw's lawsuit against *JAMA*.

In the Eisenhower and Kennedy administrations, Dr. Livingston held high positions in two of the National Institutes of Health (NIH). He was the scientific director of the National Institute of Mental Health and the National Institute of Neurological Diseases and Blindness. On the day of the assassination, he watched the press conference that was conducted with Drs. Malcolm Perry and William Kemp Clark. Livingston recalled his conversation with Dr. Humes, which had occurred before the autopsy began. Because he was the scientific director of two NIH institutes (both relevant to brain injuries), he had called the Bethesda Naval Hospital. The officer on duty put Livingston through to Humes, who was preparing for the autopsy. Livingston had called before JFK's body had arrived. He described their conversation:

> Dr. Humes said he had not heard much reporting from Dallas and Parkland Hospital because he had been occupied preparing to conduct the autopsy. I told him about reports describing the small wound in the President's neck. I stressed that, in my experience, that would have to be a wound of entrance. I emphasized the importance of carefully tracing the path of this projectile and of establishing the location of the bullet or any fragments. I said carefully, that if that wound were confirmed as a wound of entrance, that would prove beyond peradventure of doubt that a bullet had been fired in front of the President—hence that if there were shots from behind, there had to have been more than one gunman. At just that moment, there was an interruption in our conversation. Dr. Humes returned after a pause to say, "Dr. Livingston, I'm sorry, but I can't talk with you any longer. The FBI won't let me." I wished him good luck, and the conversation ended. I wondered aloud to my wife, who had overheard my side of the conversation, why the FBI would want to interfere with a discussion between physicians relating to the important problem of how best to investigate and interpret the President's wounds. Now, with knowledge of the apparently prompt and massive control of information that was imposed in order to fix the responsibility for

> the assassination of President Kennedy on a single assassin—working alone—I can appreciate that the FBI interruption of our conversation may have been far more meaningful than I presumed at the time.[32]

This interrupted phone call made a powerful impact on Livingston:

> I conclude, therefore—on the basis of direct, personal experiences—that Dr. Humes did have his attention drawn: (a) to the small neck wound of projectile entry, (b) to its significance for the autopsy as well as (c) for its potential forensic significance. Dr. Humes's testimony to the Warren Commission that he only learned about the neck wound on the day after completion of the autopsy, after he had talked with Dr. Perry in Dallas by telephone, means that the autopsy (and Dr. Humes) were already under explicit non-medical control prior to the start of the autopsy.[33]

Livingston added one more curious recollection before he drew the obvious conclusion:

> There is evidence that the Ford Motor Company had an order for a dozen windshields for the Lincoln limousine similar to that which bore President Kennedy on the day of his assassination. These were for "target practice," presumably to see how much or how little security the windshield provides. But that "target practice" on a dozen windshields leaves in some doubt whether the windshield in the National Archives is the same one that was in the Kennedy limousine at the time of the assassination.[34]

In a letter to David Lifton (dated May 2, 1992), Livingston drew a major conclusion (emphases in the original):

32 Ibid., p. 162.

33 Ibid., p. 163.

34 Ibid., p. 165.

> I conclude, therefore, on the basis of personal experience, that Dr. Humes did have his attention drawn to the specifics and significance of President Kennedy's neck wound prior to his beginning the autopsy. His testimony that he only learned about the neck wound on the day after completion of the autopsy, after he had communicated with Doctor Perry in Dallas by telephone, means that he either forgot what I told him (although he appeared to be interested and attentive at the time) or that the autopsy was already under explicit non-medical control.[35]

Livingston continued:

> That event, coupled with Dick Dudman's report to me around the same time, of what appeared to him to be a penetrating hole through the Lincoln windshield, seems to me to add two grains of confirming evidence to the conspiracy interpretation. Incidentally, sometime later, I learned that the Secret Service had ordered from the Ford Motor Company a number of identical Lincoln limousine windshields—"for target practice." It seems to me that they might have wanted to learn how much protection could be expected from such a windshield. Alternatively, they might have wanted to produce an inside nick in a windshield, without through-and-through penetration, so they could substitute that nicked windshield for the other one, if it were needed for corroborative evidence relating to the Warren Commission's investigative interpretation and thesis.[36]

Livingston's personal experiences, with both Dudman and Humes, leaves little doubt that—from the very first moment—the US government had already determined to quash any frontal shots.

---

35 Robert B. Livingston, "Letter to David Lifton of 2 May 1992," in *Assassination Science*, ed. James Fetzer, op. cit., pp. 168-171, at p. 171.

36 Ibid.

NOVEMBER 25, 1963: THE FIRST DEARBORN WITNESS

George Whitaker, Sr., a Ford Motor Company (FMC) supervisor when interviewed in August of 1993, told Douglas Weldon that he had replaced the limousine windshield on Monday, November 25, at the River Rouge Assembly Plant, Building B. He recalled a hole in the windshield, four to six inches to the (driver's) side of the rearview mirror, and he claimed the shot came from the front. In other words, the major damage was on the inside, as would be expected for standard contemporaneous safety glass. Weldon confirmed that Whitaker's description matched the damage seen in Altgens 6, as initially discovered by Roy Schaeffer.

Weldon first cited this witness in "The Kennedy Limousine: Dallas 1963," published in *Murder in Dealey Plaza* (2000).[37] At Whitaker's request, Weldon kept Whitaker's name confidential. After Whitaker's death in 2001, his family released Whitaker's written testament to Nigel Turner who, with their permission, revealed Mr. Whitaker's name, as well as the text of his "memo for history," in episode seven of *The Men Who Killed Kennedy* (2003), "The Smoking Guns." Whitaker's name does not appear in Weldon's article—although he is cited anonymously. Weldon noted that Whitaker had worked for the Ford Motor Company for forty years, starting in 1934. Here is his statement:

> This is November 22, 1993, 30 years after the assassination of John F. Kennedy, and as I will be 80 years old in about two months I think it is about time I put this bit of history in writing or on tape, so when I am gone the record will still be here. This is what I know about this part of the records. I know they are incomplete. JFK was shot and killed on November 22, 1963. This was a Friday afternoon. On Monday morning (November 25th) the Lincoln was in the Rouge Plant of the Ford Motor Co. When it [sic] around there I do not know

37 Douglas Weldon, JD, "The Kennedy Limousine: Dallas 1963," in *Murder in Dealey Plaza*, James Fetzer, op. cit., pp. 129-158.

> at about 9:00 I was called to report to [the] glass laboratory, which I did. When [I] arrived at the lab the door was locked. I was let in. There were two glass engineers there. They had a car windshield that had a bullet hole in it. The hole about 4 or 6 inches to the right of the rear view mirror [as viewed from the front]. The impact had come from the front of the windshield. (If you have spent 40 years in the glass [illegible] you know which way the impack [sic] was from.) [38]

In his 2000 article, Weldon published several excerpts from his 1993 interview with Whitaker (who was unnamed in the earlier article). Interspersing his own comments with Whitaker's quotations, Weldon described Whitaker's experience at the Ford Motor Company's River Rouge Assembly Plant, Building B, in Dearborn, Michigan on Monday, November 25, 1963. (This was also the day of JFK's funeral.) Weldon cited Whitaker's recollection:

> Around noon, we got it around 2:00 that he had been killed. So, right away they called meetings to find out what we were going to do. Are we gonna run Monday morning with the President being killed? We didn't decide on anything at that meeting, and being that I had charge of all power service, I was in charge of getting that plant ready to run or to shut it down and everything. So, they decided that they would let everything ride and they would call me on Sunday. So, on Sunday, around noon-I had just finished dinner-they called me up and told me to go in and make arrangements to start the plant up. Cause we would have to start that plant up around midnight to get it going for the day shift and number two shift. So, that I did, but then I arrived my normal time on Monday and they had me on a two-way radio

38 Douglas Horne, *Inside the ARRB*, op. cit., vol. 5, p. 1447. This is also reprinted in my hardcover book. See: David W. Mantik, "Appendix F: George Whitaker's Written Statement," in *The JFK Assassination Decoded: Criminal Forgery in the Autopsy Photographs and X-rays,* op. cit., p. 370.

> and they had me on a Cushman scooter because I was covering a large plant. So I got a call from the Vice President of the division, and he told me on the radio that I was wanted in the glass plant lab, now! So I went down to the lab and the door was locked....[39]

Weldon continued:

> I knocked on the door and they let me in. There were two of the lab men in there and they had the windshield there. And they told me that we were to use that to—see now the car was a special built car. We were to use that windshield as a template to make a new windshield. And the windshield had a bullet hole in it, coming from the outside through. You could see it, from the way it was broken....
>
> But the car was in the B building, where we had a repair garage. And they had taken the windshield out, it was back in the glass plant, we were using it as a template. And to make a windshield, and we were told to follow it right straight through until it was a finished product and get it back to the B building. We were told if anybody asked us what we were doing, we were running a template for a prototype....[40]

Weldon described Whitaker's surprise to see the limousine already stripped down:

> After describing the process for making a new windshield he [Whitaker] noted, "We laminated it, when we took it out of there, it was a finished windshield. We took it to the B building; it was put in that limousine. Now that limousine had the entire interior completely stripped out....The carpeting and everything was gone...."

---

39 Douglas Weldon, JD, "The Kennedy Limousine: Dallas 1963," in *Murder in Dealey Plaza*, ed. James Fetzer, op. cit., pp. 142-143.

40 Ibid., p. 143.

> "It was gone, it was nothing, it was down to metal, and they restored the whole interior." When asked if the limousine had been "stripped" at the plant, he [Whitaker] replied, "…I assumed it was there, that's what they did…."[41]

Curiously, the vice president of that Ford Motor Company division did not want to touch Whitaker's story. Whitaker recalled:

> Later on that day, I met the Vice President of the division and I said to him, "Bob," I said, "Do you know what they were doing down there in that lab this morning?" He said, "I don't know what was happening." He evidently knew, but he didn't want me to know he knew. That's the whole story….[42]

Whitaker was certain JFK's limousine was hit by a bullet from the front:

> It was a good clean bullet hole, right straight through, from the front. And you can tell, when the bullet hits the windshield, like when you hit a rock or anything, what happens? The back chips out and the front may just have a pinhole in it….This had a clean round hole in the front and fragmented in the back….
>
> I went on from there and I became superintendent of the division and I had the whole five plant divisions.[43]

---

41 Ibid. Laminated safety glass consists of two panes of glass separated by a plastic layer. Source: Letter from J. Edgar Hoover to James J. Howley, dated March 26, 1964, reproduced in my hardcover book: "The JFK Limousine Redux," in *The JFK Assassination Decoded: Criminal Forgery in the Autopsy Photographs and X-rays,* op. cit., Appendix H, pp. 371-373.

42 Ibid.

43 Ibid.

Weldon then noted his follow-up exchange with Whitaker [who was still unidentified]:

QUESTION: "Do you know what ever happened to the window [windshield]?"

ANSWER: "As far as I know it's sitting out in Dearborn, in Greenfield Village."

QUESTION: "The original windshield, with the bullet [hole]?"

ANSWER: "No, no, [the windshield with the] bullet, we scrapped it. We broke it up and scrapped it."

QUESTION: "Were you told to scrap it?"

ANSWER: "That's right!"

QUESTION: "Who told you to scrap it?"

ANSWER: "That was the orders the two lab man [sic] had. They got the initial instructions and I was called in after they had got their instructions."

QUESTION: "Do you have any idea who gave them those orders?"

ANSWER: "I assume that it came from the Vice President of the division, I would assume....All I know is that somebody told me is that we want you down there now! "[44]

---

44 Ibid., p. 144.

Weldon persisted in his 1993 interview with Whitaker by asking him a vitally important question: How certain was he that the bullet hole in the windshield came from the front?

> ANSWER: I worked in the industry for forty years and I've seen all kinds of testing on glass and I know it came from the front.
>
> QUESTION: So you're 100% certain.
>
> ANSWER: I'm 100% positive that it came from the front![45]

Weldon concluded by noting that November 25, 1963, was "the only date in the White House garage log that doesn't show anyone checking in to see the limousine." His obvious conclusion: nobody came to the White House garage the day of JFK's funeral because the limousine was not there.

Weldon confirmed that Whitaker's description matched the damage seen in Altgens 6, as initially discovered by Roy Schaeffer. In his 1999 lecture, Weldon established that Whitaker had correctly described the limousine hole as clearly from a frontal shot. He noted that when safety glass is struck by a bullet, the entry site remains relatively smooth, with noticeable fragmentation only on the exit side (Figure 5.7).

---

45 Ibid., pp. 144-145.

Figure 5.7
Doug Weldon: The Response of Standard Safety Glass to a Bullet; the FBI Concurred. Source: Kevin Clancey, "Doug Weldon 1999 Assassination of John F. Kennedy Research Windshield coverup," YouTube.com, December 13, 2014, https://www.youtube.com/watch?v=OACTLn75I30.

Weldon promised Whitaker that he would not use Whitaker's story during Whitaker's lifetime, but Whitaker was hardly a well-rehearsed provocateur. Weldon detailed Whitaker's naïvety about the assassination as well as his ignorance of the SS-100-x:

- He thought the SS-100-x had been flown to Dearborn from Houston.
- He thought it was leased for $1 per year.
- He had neither researched nor read any assassination books.

- He was unaware of any other windshields.
- He was unaware of any WC testimony about windshields.
- He was very reluctant to talk, and only later gave permission (over the protests of his wife).
- He did not want to name the vice president at the FMC, whom he had encountered later on that fateful Monday, November 25.
- He had never been to Dealey Plaza.
- He was very troubled by his experience.
- He never sought any publicity.
- Shortly before he died, he wrote a detailed memo of his experience.
- His son confirmed that his father had often spoken of his encounter with the limousine.
- Altogether, he had spent 40 years at the FMC.[46]

In *Inside the ARRB*, Doug Horne agreed with Weldon that the JFK limousine was flown on the evening of November 24, 1963 (or during the day on November 25, 1963) to Dearborn, Michigan, most likely aboard a C-130 Air Force cargo airplane.[47] But, Horne also concluded: "Both the official and unofficial record of what happened to the

46 I first published this list in my essay, "The JFK Limousine Redux," published in my hardcover book, *The JFK Assassination Decoded*, op. cit., at p. 324.

47 Douglas Horne, *Inside the ARRB*, op. cit., vol. 5, p. 1447.

windshield is incomplete, and is replete with false leads, red hearings, and subterfuge meant to confuse researchers and investigators—as well as evidence of a botched, inept coverup."[48]

THE FERGUSON MEMO (DECEMBER 18, 1963)

Doug Weldon noted that the JFK limousine was always the property of the Ford Motor Company, which leased the vehicle to the SS for $500.00 per year. "The Ford Motor Company leased the vehicle for such a token amount because of the positive publicity that would be generated by the President using the vehicle in parades and other ceremonial events," Weldon explained, "It is also very important to observe that this leasing arrangement established a close relationship between the Ford Motor Company and the Secret Service."[49]

In 1963, the Ford Motor Company assigned Vice President F. Vaughn Ferguson to the White House as liaison with the SS for X-100. On December 18, 1963, Ferguson wrote an intracompany memo discussing "Changes in the White House 'Bubbletop.'"[50] Ferguson did not report the purpose for this memo, nor did he justify the rather late date.

Ferguson made several assertions about the timeline. The direct quotes about the timeline are excerpted directly from his memo.

NOVEMBER 23, 1963

When Ferguson initially visited the White House garage, a canvas covered the unit (i.e., the X-100). Nonetheless, he was allowed to ascertain that there was no hole in the windshield (why this was specifically

48 Ibid., p. 1448. As an indicator of the importance that Horne gave to this statement, consider this: in the original, the sentence is in bold type, beginning in capital letters.

49 Douglas Weldon, JD, "The Kennedy Limousine: Dallas 1963," in *Murder in Dealey Plaza*, ed. James Fetzer, op. cit., pp. 131-132.

50 F. Vaughn Ferguson, "Ford Motor Company Intra-Company Communication of 18 December 1963," in *Murder in Dealey Plaza*, ed. James Fetzer, op. cit., pp. 431-432.

emphasized was left unsaid), but he saw "substantial cracks radiating a couple of inches from the center of the windshield at a point directly *beneath* [emphasis added] the mirror." No one today who views CE 350 (i.e., the windshield in the White House garage—Figure 5.8) would describe the windshield damage as "beneath" the rearview mirror. It is obviously on the driver's side and slightly *above* the mirror. "I was at the garage only about one hour that day, but while I was there [SS Agent] Morgan Geis [of the White House garage detail] contacted the Secret Service and told them to have me make arrangements to replace the windshield."[51]

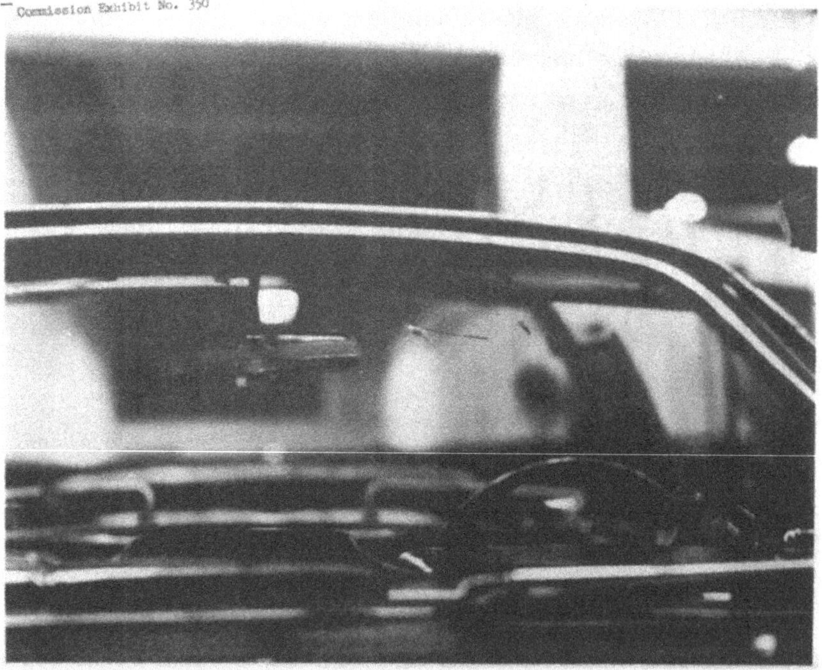

Figure 5.8
Warren Commission Exhibit CE 350. The windshield in the White House garage, as seen from the front. Source: *Hearings before the President's Commission on the Assassination of President Kennedy*, op. cit., vol. 16, p. 946.

---

51 Ibid.

NOVEMBER 24, 1963

Ferguson claimed that in the garage, he "pulled up these upholstery buttons and with a knife removed the caked blood around them."

NOVEMBER 25, 1963

Ferguson then reported that Arlington Glass came to the White House garage to repair the windshield the next day.

> In response to my call of November 25, personnel from Arlington Glass came to the White House garage *that same day* [emphasis added] to replace the windshield. The Arlington Glass personnel advised Morgan Geis and me that removal would cause additional damage to the windshield but Geis told them to go ahead and remove it anyway. The Arlington Glass personnel did remove it by putting their feet against the inside of the windshield and pushing it out. In doing so, additional cracks formed (downward to the bottom of the windshield). A Mr. Davis of the Secret Service then took the windshield and put it in the stockroom under lock and key and I have not seen it since.[52]

In direct contradiction to this, the log for the White House garage shows only two visitors that day. One was a "heat check," and the other was an elevator inspection.[53] Despite this, Ferguson's memo claimed that Arlington Glass had removed the windshield on Monday, November 25, 1963. (More likely, Arlington replaced the windshield on Wednesday, November 27. By citing Monday for the Arlington visit, was Ferguson merely trying to distract us from his Monday trip to Dearborn?)

---

52 Ibid.

53 Kevin Clancey, "Doug Weldon 1999 Assassination of John F. Kennedy Research Windshield coverup," op. cit.

QUESTIONS ABOUT THE FERGUSON MEMO

The Ferguson memo raises numerous—and quite serious—unanswered questions.

1. It was written curiously late (three weeks later)—as if in a cover-up mode, probably after some internal questions had arisen behind the scenes.

2. The memo cites what is not seen, which is a bizarre perspective. For example, would you report on a visit to the house of an old friend and then stress that his hallway mirror was not cracked? It appears as if Ferguson, especially with this offbeat observation, had merely executed an assigned mission.

3. It is not likely that the windshield showed significant cracks on the date of his initial inspection (November 23, 1963). On that date, he would have seen the motorcade windshield. Recall that his memo is dated December 18, so we cannot be certain what image he is recalling at this late date—was he recalling the motorcade windshield or the Dearborn replacement windshield (with its bogus damage)? More likely, Ferguson was commenting on the latter, which did show large cracks.

4. Ferguson sees a windshield crack directly *beneath* the mirror, which is clearly the wrong location. If he cannot recall the location correctly, why should we trust him about not seeing a perforation?

5. Ferguson reported that the windshield was replaced by the Arlington Glass Company on Monday, November 25, which is surely the wrong date. Writing merely several weeks later, could his memory really be that defective? In view of his personal involvement, that seems totally far-fetched.

6. Ironically, Ferguson's date of November 25 is precisely the same date when Whitaker saw the X-100 in Dearborn. Did Ferguson deliberately make this mistake—to further cover-up the Dearborn visit on that same date? Also recall that—according to the logbook—no one except two service technicians visited the White House garage to see the X-100 on November 25. Was that because it was not there? Was everyone distracted by JFK's funeral that day? Furthermore, didn't Ferguson attend JFK's funeral?

7. Ferguson claimed that Morgan Geis was present during the windshield removal. But Geis signed in on the next day, Tuesday, November 26, not on Monday, November 25. So, was Ferguson merely careless, or was there a method to his audacity?

What is more likely is that after dark on Sunday, November 24, 1963, the X-100 was flown to Dearborn from Andrews Air Force Base, likely with Ferguson on board. On November 25, at the Dearborn River Rouge Assembly Plant in Building B, Whitaker supervised the removal of the X-100 windshield and its replacement by an undamaged windshield (using the original windshield as a template). Later that day, November 25 (possibly that same evening), the X-100 was flown back to Andrews Air Force Base—with its *new windshield*, again accompanied by Ferguson. In his December 18 memo, Ferguson insisted that he called the Arlington Glass Company on that day (November 25). More likely, he waited until at least the next day (Tuesday, November 26) to make this call. What was he waiting for? Why was he so busy on Monday?

The correct date for the Arlington Glass Company windshield replacement seems to be Wednesday, November 27, 1963. Although Ferguson received the SS order to replace the windshield on Sunday, he likely waited until Tuesday to call Arlington Glass (despite his claims to the contrary). Perhaps he was simply too busy in Dearborn on that Monday. Furthermore, Ferguson could not invite the Arlington

Glass Company to visit until the fake damage inflicted to the (initially immaculate) Dearborn windshield was credible.

In Dearborn, Ferguson deep-sixed the motorcade windshield with the obvious bullet hole. Now Ferguson had a new, unblemished windshield. But witnesses in Dallas had seen the original windshield; Altgens 6 and 7, as well as the Zapruder film, showed the windshield damage. So now, Ferguson had to damage the unblemished Dearborn windshield so that it looked like a shot from the rear. But no perforation could be allowed.

Another mystery surrounds the location of the X-100 after the assassination. On January 6, 1964, James Rowley, head of the SS, wrote to J. Lee Rankin, the WC general counsel, in which he claimed that, on December 20, 1963, the limousine was driven to Dearborn, Michigan—approximately five hundred miles away—to design a new bubble-top. Rowley claimed that the X-100 was subsequently driven from Dearborn to Cincinnati, Ohio on December 20, for the manufacture and installation of a new bullet-resistant bubble-top.[54] Weldon noted that "not one newspaper article or radio or television report mentioned the limousine being driven hundreds of miles in the harsh winters of Michigan and Ohio."[55] He elaborated:

> Common sense dictates that the Secret Service would not have wanted to chance a breakdown, a flat tire, or even the obvious necessity of refueling it by driving the bloody limousine. An examination of the weather reports reveals that the road conditions were quite treacherous during that period of time. The Chief of the Secret Service, James Rowley, apparently was not telling the truth.[56]

---

54 Douglas Weldon, JD, "The Kennedy Limousine: Dallas 1963," in *Murder in Dealey Plaza*, ed. James Fetzer, PhD op. cit., p. 132.

55 Ibid., p. 133.

56 Ibid.

The HSCA reported that the limousine had been delivered to the Hess & Eisenhardt Company in Cincinnati on December 13, 1964. Ferguson claimed he drove the X-100 to Dearborn, Michigan, on December 20, 1964, but Willard Hess stated authoritatively that Ferguson's trip on December 20 to Cincinnati "could not have happened and did not happen."[57] In response to this astonishing claim of arriving at Hess & Eisenhardt on December 20, Willard Hess exclaimed, *"Heck no!"*[58] So, obviously, Hess disagreed with Vaughn Ferguson and so also do the official records at Hess & Eisenhardt. Contrary to the HSCA record (and contrary to Ferguson), George Whitaker, Sr., a Ford Motor Company employee, saw the limousine in Dearborn, Michigan on Monday, November 25, the same day (and the first weekday after the assassination) that no investigator logged into the White House garage to see the limousine. Quite beguilingly, that Monday also happened to be the day of JFK's funeral, when no one was concerned about the limousine.

Dr. Charles Crenshaw advanced another (likely incorrect) version in his 1992 book, *JFK: Conspiracy of Silence*:

> Three days after the assassination, Carl Renas, head of security for the Dearborn Division of the Ford Motor Company, drives the limousine, helicopters hovering overhead, from Washington to Cincinnati. In doing so, he noted several bullet holes, the most notable being the one on the windshield's chrome molding strip, which he said was clearly "a primary strike" and not a fragment." The limousine was driven by Renas to Hess and Eisenhardt in Cincinnati, where the chrome molding was replaced. The Secret Service told Renas to "Keep your mouth shut." Renas recalls thinking at the time, "Something is wrong."[59]

---

57 Ibid., p. 134.

58 David Mantik, *The JFK Assassination Decoded*, op. cit., p. 327.

59 Charles Crenshaw, *Conspiracy of Silence*, op. cit., p. 106.

Weldon commented:

> There is no record in any form of media that would support this story. Carl Renas, in this interesting account, should certainly be given credit for being perceptive enough to recognize that something was wrong.[60]

Most likely, an Air Force C-130 flew the limousine to Wright-Patterson Air Force Base in Dayton, Ohio in December, from where it was driven to Cincinnati (probably by Ferguson).

J. Gary Shaw stated in his 1976 book *Cover-Up: The Governmental Conspiracy to Conceal the Facts About the Public Execution of John Kennedy*:

> Within 48 hours of the shots in Dealey Plaza the Kennedy death car was shipped to the Ford Motor Company in Detroit and completely destroyed, as far as evidence was concerned."[61]

After being flown to Hess & Eisenhardt on December 13, 1964, the car was completely rebuilt, destroying any possibility that the JFK limousine X-100 could produce valuable evidence of the crossfire that killed the president. In making this statement, Shaw referenced Penn Jones, Jr., one of the earliest JFK assassination researchers, in his 1969 book, *Forgive My Grief III.*

One of the most blatant acts of destruction points directly to Lyndon Johnson. The X-100, the actual murder scene, was pirated to Dearborn where the forensic legal evidence was vaporized. In our

---

60 Douglas Weldon, JD, "The Kennedy Limousine: Dallas 1963," in *Murder in Dealey Plaza*, ed. James Fetzer, op. cit., p. 133.

61 J. Gary Shaw with Larry R. Harris, *Cover-Up: The Governmental Conspiracy to Conceal the Facts About the Public Execution of John Kennedy* (Austin, TX: Collector's Editions, an imprint of Thomas Publications, Inc., 1976), p. 77, https://archive.org/details/CoverUp_201510/page/n93/mode/2up?q=car.

judicial system, this is a clear case of destruction of material evidence; simple justice required an accounting from LBJ, but he was too busy planning for a war in Vietnam.[62]

WINDSHIELD IMAGES COMPARED

We turn next to a series of windshield images. These images contrast typical windshield damage (images are from an online physics website[63]) to the damage depicted in CE 350, the photograph purportedly taken in the White House garage. This online website shows typical spiderweb-like damage in safety glass (i.e., not the X-100). [For further comparison, I have displayed the damage caused at the Capitol on January 6, 2021. See my hardcover book, p. 331.] Figure 5.9 is a close-up of CE 351, supposedly taken in the White House garage.

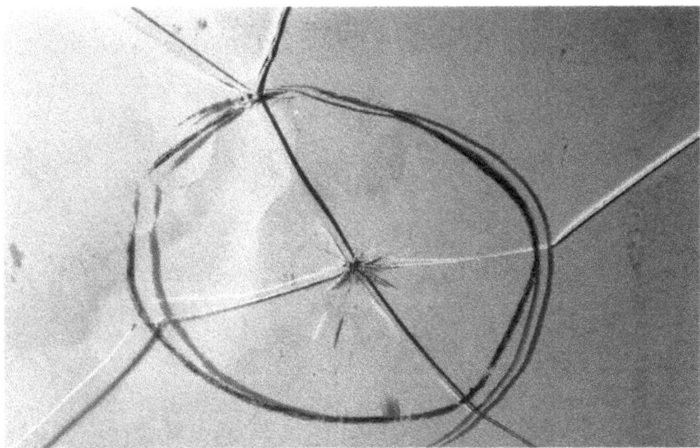

Figure 5.9

Warren Commission Exhibit CE 351. Windshield Damage in White House Garage. Source: *Hearings before the President's Commission on the Assassination of President Kennedy*, op. cit., vol. 16, p. 947.

62 Penn Jones Jr., *Forgive My Grief III* (Midlothian, TX: The Midlothian Mirror, Inc., 1969), p. 2, https://archive.org/details/ForgiveMyGriefPennJonesJr/Forgive_My_Grief_03/mode/2up.

63 "Crack pattern of safety glass—what gives rise to spider web-like shape," Physics.StackExchange.com [forum], June 23, 2016, https://physics.stackexchange.com/questions/264264/crack-pattern-of-safety-glass-what-gives-rise-to-spider-web-like-shape.

In my opinion, CE 350 (Figures 5.8 and 5.9) shows the Dearborn replacement windshield, after its intervening (deliberately—and illegally—created) damage and before its replacement by the Arlington windshield (probably performed on Wednesday, November 27, 1963). Although the strike site in that Dearborn windshield seems consistent with the damage site in the Altgens photographs, the shape may not accurately replicate the damage in Altgens 6 and 7. In my opinion, the windshield seen in CE 350 was installed in Dearborn and is currently at the NARA. In CE 350, most likely, we see the damage inflicted upon it under Ferguson's direction. Then on Wednesday, November 27, the Dearborn windshield was replaced by the Arlington windshield. The third replacement occurred in late December (or early January), when the Arlington windshield was replaced by a more bulletproof version (with five layers of glass) from the Pittsburgh Plate Glass Company—while it was at Hess & Eisenhardt in Cincinnati. The current location of the Arlington replacement windshield is not very relevant, as it was undamaged (as would be expected)—per Willard Hess.

The X-100 windshield was laminated (i.e., security or shatterproof) glass that fractures into cracks resembling a spider web, with radial and concentric cracks spreading out from the point of impact (Figure 5.10).

Figure 5.10

Typical *Spiderweb-like* [my emphasis] Damage in Safety Glass. Laminated Safety Glass Spiderweb Fracture with Radial and Concentric Cracks Extending from the Point of Impact. Source: "Crack pattern of safety glass—what gives rise to spider web-like shape," Physics StackExchange [forum], op. cit. The photograph is a stock photograph found at https://previews.123rf.com/images/smithore/smithore0911/smithore091100032/5902118-broken-window-glass-like-a-spider-web-Stock-Photo.jpg.

The professional literature makes clear that the greater the impact, the larger the number of radial cracks and the more impressive are the concentric fractures. Richard Bradt, of the University of Alabama in Tuscaloosa, Alabama, published a 2011 article entitled "The Fractography and Crack Patterns of Broken Glass" in the *Journal of Failure Analysis and Prevention*.[64] In this professional article, Professor Bradt explained the nature of the damage:

> Highly energetic impact crack patterns are readily identified from the multiple radiating star-like cracks that emanate from the point of impact and also the numerous circular or circumferential cracks which are generated. They lend a "spider's web" type of appearance to the crack pattern.... If the impact is from a sharply pointed object, then the radial cracks appear to emanate from a point. When the impact is by a blunt object, then there is an impact crush zone from which the radial cracks emanate. Severe spalling[65] also frequently occurs on the back side of glass panels subjected to high-energy impacts. For high-velocity projectiles, the numbers of radial cracks have been found to be proportional to the kinetic energy of the projectile, once again illustrating the importance of energy contributions to the development of crack patterns.[66]

If we apply these insights to the limousine windshield cracks, the following conclusions result:

1. Bullets produce star-like and circumferential cracks. They look like a spider web. CE 350 does not display a spider web, but the Altgens 6 and 7 images do suggest one.

---

64 Richard Bradt, "The Fractography and Crack Patterns of Broken Glass, *Journal of Failure Analysis and Prevention*, volume 11, (2011): 79–96, https://link.springer.com/article/10.1007/s11668-011-9432-5.

65 Spall are fragments of material that are broken off from a larger solid body.

66 Ibid.

2. If a sharp object impacts, then radial cracks emanate from the impact point. The greater the energy, the more radial cracks appear.

3. If a blunt object impacts (such as a ball-peen hammer), then radial cracks emanate from a crush zone. CE 350 appears to show such a crush zone.

4. The number of radial cracks is usually few for low energy impacts; CE 350 shows a small number of radial cracks. In other words, whoever used a blunt object on the X-100 windshield was far too timid. He (or she) should have been much more forceful—but they had little time to practice; furthermore, this was not a routine part of their job. If they had been more vigorous, some circumferential cracks might have ensued, thus producing a more convincing spiderweb pattern. But their greatest nightmare, of course, was causing an obvious hole in the windshield. That would have been game over—so they were cautious instead of vigorous. The larger the damaged area (presumably reflecting greater deposited energy), the more impressive are the concentric fractures. If the damaged area is small (due to little deposited energy), no concentric fractures appear—very much like the X-100 images from the White House garage. So, a light touch with a ball-peen hammer seems consistent with the radial-only X-100 fractures seen in the White House garage.

5. When the impact energy is high, glass shards may be produced on the opposite side of the initial strike. Even without a hole, this tenet suggests the production of glass shards (from the inside) due to a frontal shot. Such shards may have struck JFK's throat and cheek. Notice that there has never been an explanation for JFK's cheek wounds (that the embalmer plugged)—other than glass shards. Furthermore, what other autopsy report describes such mysterious cheek wounds?

After viewing Figures 5.8 and 5.9, the reader should ask him/herself: Do these photographs of the windshield currently in the National Archives show spiderweb-like damage? For my part, I see only radial fractures, but not a single spider web. Now view again the above image (Figure 5.10) labeled, "Typical *spiderweb-like* [my emphasis] damage in safety glass." Next think about this comment—from James Rowley himself:

> SA Hickey, who drove the car from Parkland Hospital to Love Field said that he noticed some slight damage to the windshield on the drive to the airport, but that the damage was not extensive enough to affect his vision. The windshield, in the area around the damage, was spattered with debris. However, SA Hickey noticed upon the arrival in Washington and at the White House garage the '***spidering***' [emphasis added] had increased and the damage to the windshield was more noticeable.[67]

So, if Hickey saw "spidering," why can't we see it?

In the immediate aftermath of the assassination, two major—and related—problems faced the new elite: They had to cancel the frontal throat shot (by gagging Dr. Malcolm Perry), which they did, and then they had to destroy the original windshield—with its obvious and incriminating through-and-through frontal entry hole. Trashing the windshield in DC posed serious risks. After all, too many individuals would then either have seen that hole—or they would later have asked about the windshield's whereabouts. From the history of the Arlington replacement, we already know that the removed windshield in DC was closely guarded and not easily lost. So, I conclude that the new Dearborn windshield was deliberately damaged by blunt trauma; most likely this

---

67 Letter from James Rowley, head of the SS, to J. Lee Rankin, the WC general counsel, January 6, 1964. A copy of the letter is in the authors' files.

occurred during the early morning of November 26, 1963, before the Arlington employees arrived.

Evidence for this conclusion comes from a letter (March 26, 1964) from J. Edgar Hoover to James Rowley. Hoover began by explaining that the FBI had requested the X-100 windshield from the White House garage because the WC had requested the FBI laboratory "to determine whether cracks in the windshield were caused by an object striking the glass in front of the vehicle or behind the vehicle."[68] Hoover's letter concluded that the windshield damage resulted from a bullet (or a bullet fragment) from the rear that did not perforate. His letter appears to describe Figures 5.8 (CE 350) and 5.9 (CE 351), i.e., the windshield in the National Archives today. The cracks radiate out from an impact point, but there is no evidence of spiderweb fracturing. Hoover's letter to Rowley strained to emphasize that the windshield that Arlington Glass removed was struck from the inside. But what Hoover ignored was this: when laminated safety glass is struck, it is the side opposite the strike that is rough (Figure 5.7).

After the motorcade windshield was destroyed in Dearborn on November 25, the Ford Motor Company and the SS were ready to welcome Arlington Glass on November 26. That day, the Arlington Glass employees may merely have inspected the windshield; then the next day (November 27), they returned to remove it. The key point is that the Arlington Glass employees would naturally expect that they had removed the motorcade windshield, without realizing that they had been duped into this false belief.

The round (peen) head of a ball-peen hammer (shown below) seems a reasonable choice for the illegal task of inflicting new damage onto the Dearborn windshield (Figure 5.11). A brief trip to an automobile

---

68 Letter from J. Edgar Hoover to James J. Howley, March 26, 1964, reproduced in "The JFK Limousine Redux," in my hardcover book, *The JFK Assassination Decoded: Criminal Forgery in the Autopsy Photographs and X-rays,* op. cit., Appendix H, pp. 371-373.

junkyard would have yielded many windshields for practice. Permission (from the junkyard owners) for such an adventure should have been easy to obtain via SS credentials. The perpetrators could even have tried striking both front and back surfaces (in separate events) so as to compare results. But the final smashing event required only seconds.

Figure 5.11
A Ball-Peen Hammer

If Ferguson had assisted in the destruction of critical evidence in a murder case, he was criminally liable. Furthermore, if he had assisted in creating bogus evidence in the Dearborn windshield, he would then have been doubly liable. Roy Kellerman was in charge of the trip to Dallas and, according to Douglas Horne, he was also the stage manager at the JFK autopsy. If Ferguson had alerted anyone to the (inexplicable) pristine state of the Dearborn windshield on the morning of Tuesday, November 26 (and the need for prompt action to mutilate that flawless windshield so as to match the government scenario), then Roy Kellerman was the man for the job.

In volume 5 of *Inside the ARRB*, Doug Horne pointed out that "Secret Service agent Roy Kellerman testified[69] that he examined the windshield on November 27, 1963, shortly before it was removed from

69 "Testimony of Roy H. Kellerman, Special Agent, Secret Service," *Hearings before the President's Commission on the Assassination of President Kennedy*, vol. 2, pp. 61-112, at p. 86.

the limousine, and that its surface was "smooth on the outside, and *damaged on the inside.*"[70] Horne noted that Jim Bishop, in his 1968 book *The Day Kennedy Was Shot,* quoted a similar statement from the two SS agents who drove X-100 to the White House garage the night of the assassination (emphases added):

> [SS Agent] Morgan Gies looked across the hood of the car. "Whatever it is," he said, "the crack isn't on the outside. This side is smooth."[71]
>
> Horne wrote (emphases in the original):
>
> The problem with these observations [by Kellerman and Gies/Hickey] is that safety glass windshield exhibits damage *on the opposite side from which it is hit*—meaning that if a safety glass windshield exhibited damage on the inside as claimed by Kellerman and Gies, it was actually an indication of impact from the front. It looks like someone "screwed up" royally, and whatever false damage had been inflicted upon the new windshield installed in Detroit [i.e., Dearborn, Michigan] on November 25th ***had been placed on the wrong side!*** So, not only had there been a windshield switch on November 25th, but that fraudulent windshield had to be swapped out again so that the damage recorded 'for history' would match the expected damage that should be found on safety glass, if inflicted by a shot from behind.[72]

Horne stressed that the FBI Laboratory had provided the ARRB testimony "that asserted safety glass exhibits damage on the opposite side from which it is struck, *implying that those in charge of the coverup damaged the new windshield on the wrong surface initially* (as witnessed

70 Douglas Horne, *Inside the ARRB*, op. cit., vol. 5, p. 1449. Emphases, bold type, and underlining added by Horne in the original.

71 Jim Bishop, *The Day Kennedy Was Shot* (New York: Funk & Wagnalls, 1968), pp. 395-396, at p. 396.

72 Douglas Horne, *Inside the ARRB*, op. cit., vol. 5, p. 1449.

by Kellerman and Geis (aka Gies), and then must have realized their error and corrected it after the improperly damaged windshield was removed on November 27th in the White House garage."[73]

David Lifton in *Best Evidence* (footnote on p. 371) said that "assassination researcher Robert P. Smith interviewed Bill Ashby, the crew leader of the Arlington Glass. Lifton reported:

> In February 1972, assassination researcher Robert P. Smith interviewed Bill Ashby, crew leader of the Arlington Glass Company team that removed the windshield on November 27, 1963. It was Ashby's recollection that the inside surface of the windshield was damaged.[74]

Horne noted that "Secret Service agent Roy Kellerman testified that he had examined the windshield on November 27th, 1963, shortly before it was removed from the limousine, and that its surface was smooth on the outside and *damaged on the inside* [original emphases]."[75] Lifton noted that Kellerman had failed to understand that safety glass is smooth on the entry side and damaged on the exit side.[76] The reality is that this statement by Kellerman, under oath, actually supported a frontal shot. Horne explained how massively the government coverup had gone wrong:

> It looks like someone 'screwed up' royally, and whatever false damage had been inflicted upon the new windshield installed in Detroit on November 25th ***had been placed on the wrong side!*** So, not only had there been a windshield switch on November 25th, but that

---

73 Ibid., p. 1450. Emphases in the original.

74 David Lifton, *Best Evidence*, op. cit., footnote, p. 371.

75 Douglas Horne, *Inside the ARRB*, op. cit., vol. 5, p. 1450. Emphasis in original.

76 David Lifton, *Best Evidence*, op. cit., footnote, p. 371.

fraudulent windshield had to be swapped out again so that the damage recorded 'for history' would match the expected damage that should be found on safety glass, if inflicted by a shot from behind.[77]

Horne continued:

During Roy Kellerman's Warren Commission testimony in March of 1964, he was asked to run his hand over the inside surface (which he had testified was damaged when he inspected it on November 27th), and he said, "... it feels rather smooth today." The FBI laboratory provided testimony that asserted safety glass exhibits damage on the opposite side from which struck, implying that those in charge of the coverup damaged the new windshield on the wrong surface initially (as observed by Kellerman and Geis), and then must have realized their error and corrected it after the *improperly damaged* windshield was removed on November 27th in the White House garage.[78]

Horne concluded:

Ashby told Smith in 1972 that the inside surface of the windshield was damaged, confirming Kellerman's initial recollection under oath—and indirectly confirming, in light of what we know today, that Kellerman himself was dealing with a windshield that had already been switched (because there was no hole in it), but which clearly had been damaged by incompetent actors in a coverup, who did not yet understand the characteristics of safety glass! Since the windshield in the Archives today is damaged on the outside, and not on the inside as recalled by Kellerman, Geis, and Ashby, it cannot be the

---

77 Douglas Horne, *Inside the ARRB*, op. cit., vol. 5, p. 1450. Emphasis in original.

78 Ibid., pp. 1450-1451. Emphasis in original.

windshield removed on November 27th in the White House garage. It is fraudulent evidence, just like the photographs of 'President Kennedy's brain' introduced into the Archives—both were placed there initially to backstop the official story that a lone gun assassin, firing from behind, killed President Kennedy.[79]

If words mean anything, Kellerman actually testified that he did not see this windshield damage right after the assassination!

MR. SPECTER. My next question is: Did you observe any crack in the windshield after the shooting on November 22?

MR. KELLERMAN. No.

MR. SPECTER. Did you have any occasion to look for or examine for any crack in the windshield after the shooting?

MR. KELLERMAN. I had no occasion whatsoever.

MR. SPECTER. If the crack in the windshield had been as prominent as it was on or about November 27, 1963, would you have observed it after the shooting on November 22?

MR. KELLERMAN. No, sir; I don't think I would have.

SENATOR COOPER. Is it correct then to say that you didn't find any occasion to examine the windshield after you heard the shots?

MR. KELLERMAN. That is right, I did not have the opportunity.

---

79 Ibid., p. 1451. Emphasis in original.

MR. SPECTER. And after the President was removed from the automobile, did you ever go back and examine the car, including the windshield?

MR. KELLERMAN. Not in Dallas; no, sir.

MR. SPECTER. To be absolutely certain our record is straight on this point, when you observed this windshield on or about November 27, 1963, was the windshield in or out of the car?

MR. KELLERMAN. It was in the car. This was the same day they were going to remove it.

MR. SPECTER. Did they remove it later that day, to your knowledge?

MR. KELLERMAN. Yes; they did, and the mechanics were there.

MR. SPECTER. Were you there at the time this was removed?

MR. KELLERMAN. No, sir.

MR. SPECTER. But the mechanics had arrived preparatory to removing it?

MR. KELLERMAN. That is right.[80]

This is an astonishing interchange. Roy Kellerman, a passenger in the X-100 *during* the motorcade, denied seeing any windshield crack(s) right after the assassination. But then he added that, while inside the

80 Ibid.

X-100 on November 22, he would not even have noticed the obvious cracks depicted in CE 351 (see Figure 5.9). And the physical windshield, with its obvious cracks, sat there right in front of him as he testified! I can only observe that, given his unmistakable visual disability, this man should never again have been allowed to drive.

A SECOND DEARBORN WITNESS

We now have a second Dearborn witness to the windshield—Robert D. Harrison, automotive engineer. During medical school at the University of Michigan, I shared a Phi Chi apartment at 2260 Fuller Road, Ann Arbor[81] with two fellow medical students. One of them, Duane Harrison, was our wedding organist and has been a lifelong friend. In 1963, Duane's family lived at 13954 Archdale in Detroit. Duane recalled that his father worked at the Ford Motor Company's Experimental Vehicles Building at the northeast corner of Village Road and Oakwood—across the street from the Henry Ford Museum (which now displays the X-100). This building adjoins the FMC River Rouge plant where George Whitaker worked. I had previously discussed Duane's father's recollections of the X-100 in one of my articles. Duane had specifically recalled that his father's encounter with the X-100 had been a contemporaneous topic of conversation within the family. In particular, I had learned that his father had seen the X-100 in Dearborn after the assassination. But Duane had not previously consulted with his brother. Staying at arm's length, I prompted Duane to contact his brother, so his brother's response was voluntary and not influenced by

---

81 Phi Chi Medical Fraternity Incorporated in Ann Arbor, Michigan, NonProfit Locator, n.d., https://nonprofitlocator.org/organizations/mi/ann-arbor/386068502-phi-chi-medical-fraternity-incorporated.

My future wife, Patricia L. James, and I worked together as official Phi Chi scribes for the radiology lectures. Since, as a Phi Chi member, I was ineligible for an award, Patricia won DeGowin and DeGowin's *Diagnostic Examination* for her skillful transcription.

me. Duane's brother independently recalled[82] that his father had seen the *perforated* windshield—and that his father had been "very upset" about this. Duane also recalled his father telling the family that there were several bullet holes in the JFK limousine.

THE WINDSHIELD SHOT: TRAJECTORY DETAILS

Roy Schaeffer[83] measured the height of the bullet hole as fifty-four inches above the pavement and the throat wound as fifty inches above the pavement—a difference of four inches. A scale model of the X-100 suggests a horizontal separation from the windshield to JFK as six and a half feet. I calculated that the bullet's impact with the windshield created a conical scattering of particles into the limousine at a total angle of 2.95°. Such narrow angle scattering (typical of a bullet striking a windshield) would explain why no one else in the X-100 was hit with debris from the windshield shot. Furthermore, a car window does not fracture like window glass. Instead, "glass in car windows…breaks up into very tiny, granular pieces, whereas a house window will break up in larger fractured pieces."[84] Shooting from the outside of the windshield to the inside, Schaeffer expected the bullet would be deflected downward by a small amount (Figure 5.12).

---

82 Duane Harrison, email to author, August 4, 2021.

83 Roy Schaeffer, email to author, October 22, 2021.

84 Dr. Tindall, "Fundamentals of Shooting Through Glass," Survival Training School, September 8, 2020, https://www.survivaltrainingschool.com/2020/09/08/fundamentals-of-shooting-through-glass/.

Figure 5.12
Shooting through the car windshield from the outside: deflection is generally small—two to three inches downward (as seen in this image). Source: Dr. Tindall, "Fundamentals of Shooting Through Glass," Survival Training School, SurvivalTraining.com, September 8, 2020, op. cit.

Since JFK was more than twice as far from the windshield (based on a scale model of the limousine) as depicted in Figure 5.12, the downward deflection of the windshield bullet at JFK's throat (assuming the cited 2.5 inches) would be about 2.5 x 2 = 5 inches (reference Figure 5.2). That conclusion matches Schaeffer's 4 inches fairly well.

This downward trajectory might well explain the two tiny puncture holes in JFK's cheek. Robinson reported these holes in JFK's cheek, which he plugged to prevent fluid leakage.[85] Why else were these holes there? How many other autopsies have reported such holes? These holes were cited to Horne by Robinson. Here are Robinson's notes, prepared for the ARRB.

85 Ira David Wood, III, "November 1963: A Chronology," in *Murder in Dealey Plaza*, ed. James Fetzer, pp. 17-119, at p. 117.

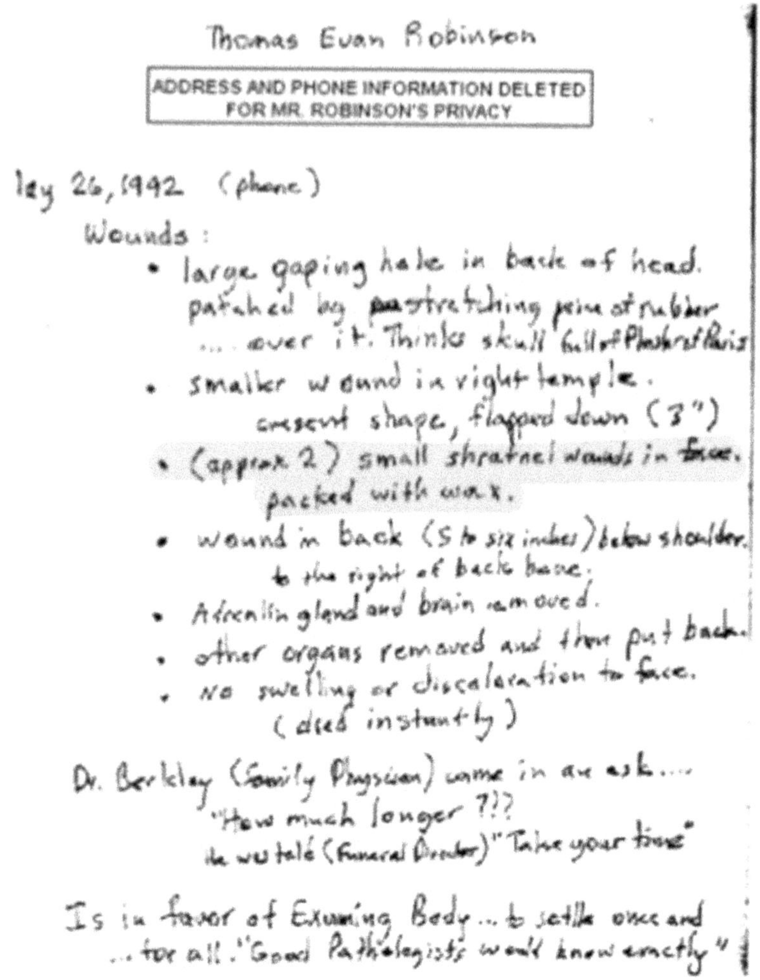

Thomas Evan Robinson

ADDRESS AND PHONE INFORMATION DELETED
FOR MR. ROBINSON'S PRIVACY

ley 26, 1992 (phone)

Wounds:

- large gaping hole in back of head. patched by stretching piece of rubber ... over it. Thinks skull full of Plaster of Paris
- smaller wound in right temple. cresent shape, flapped down (3")
- (approx 2) small shrapnel wounds in face. packed with wax.
- wound in back (5 to six inches) below shoulder. to the right of back bone.
- Adrenalin gland and brain removed.
- other organs removed and then put back.
- No swelling or discoloration to face. (died instantly)

Dr. Berklay (family Physician) came in an ask.... "How much longer ???" He was told (Funeral Director) "Take your time"

Is in favor of Exuming Body ... to settle once and ... for all. "Good Pathologists would know exactly"

Figure 5.13

Tom Robinson's Notes as Presented to the ARRB. Source: "ARRB Meeting Report Summarizing 6/21/96 In-Person Interview of Tom Robinson," MD 180, ARRB Master Set of Medical Exhibits, June 21, 1996, https://aarclibrary.org/publib/jfk/arrb/master_med_set/md180/html/md180_0005a.htm Copy of handwritten notes in authors' files.

In 1985, Roy Schaeffer first imagined that a glass shard had struck Kennedy's throat.[86] I only (independently) thought of that option years later; before that time, I was busy with my career and with raising my children. I did not focus on the JFK case until the movie *JFK* (1991) arrived. Today, I agree with Schaeffer that the windshield bullet probably produced a shower of small glass shards, confined to a small scattering angle. Several-millimeter-sized glass shard could easily have caused the throat wound. This shard would have been invisible to the pathologists, and it would also have been invisible on X-ray films. Furthermore, its range would have been strictly limited (to the right lung apex)—just as the autopsy showed (Appendix J). Additional smaller shards probably caused JFK's tiny cheek wounds, where embalming fluid oozed out. No one has proposed any other explanation for these cheek wounds—and they are surely atypical autopsy findings.

WHAT ABOUT THE MEDICAL EVIDENCE?

For the windshield, the medical evidence assumes center stage. The anatomic evidence of a left frontal projectile to the throat (terminating at the right lung apex) is overwhelming. And DeFiore's work (Figure 5.1) makes it clear that, for any shot from the South Knoll, the bullet absolutely must traverse[87] the windshield. DiFiore's detailed website

---

86 Roy Schaeffer, email to author, October 30, 2021.

87 Several witnesses recalled that the first shot had a different sound from the rest. They may have heard the bullet piercing the windshield. For example, Bill Newman recalled that this unusual sound came from the X-100 itself. James Altgens heard a loud noise at about the same time as his photograph near Z-255. And Merriman Smith reported: "Suddenly we heard three loud, almost painfully loud cracks. The first sounded as if it might have been a large firecracker. But the second and third blasts were unmistakable. Gunfire." Merriman Smith, "UPI Archives: Merriman Smith's account of JFK's assassination," UPI, originally published November 22, 1963, https://www.upi.com/Top_News/Special/2011/11/22/UPI-Archives-Merriman-Smiths-account-of-JFKs-assassination/9391321983592/?ur3=1.

makes a powerful case for a shot from the South Knoll.[88]

Figure 5.14

The Railroad Overpass on the South Side of Elm Street. The thin black arrow identifies the ideal firing site from the South Knoll (between Z-207 and Z-225, per DeFiore). The large rectangle outlines a less desirable firing site. The throat shooter must have lurked nearby, according to Anthony E. DeFiore. Source: Magnified photo taken by JFK assassination Frank Cancellare, an experienced United Press International (UPI) photographer, on November 22, 1963, about twenty seconds after the shooting, https://www.jfkassassinationgallery.com/displayimage.php?album=33&pos=1.

James Jenkins, one of two Bethesda navy corpsmen who assisted at the JFK autopsy, had reported damage to the middle lobe of the lung, which is inconsistent with the right lung apex. However, I have examined JFK's shirt and coat at the Archives. The bullet holes in the clothing (which can be seen in Appendix A) are not consistent with the middle lobe of the lung. See: James Curtis Jenkins and William Matson Law, *At The Cold Shoulder of History*, op. cit.

88 Jones Harris, well-known for his extensive research into the JFK assassination, objected that no professional shooter would have taken a shot through the windshield, knowing that the windshield would redirect the shot with the possibility of missing JFK altogether, but instead hitting one of the two SS agents in the front seat, or even worse, Jacqueline Kennedy. Jones Harris believes an intelligence-trained operative standing along Elm Street inflicted the throat wound, having been trained to use a clandestine weapon unnoticed. One of us (Dr. Corsi), a long-time friend of Jones Harris in New York City, has greatly respected Mr. Harris's investigations, though on this point, we disagree. Dr. Corsi dedicated his first book on the JFK assassination to Jones Harris. See: Jerome R. Corsi, *Who Really Killed Kennedy: 50 Years Later, Stunning New Revelations about the JFK Assassination* (Washington, DC: WND Books, Inc., 2013).

Figure 5.15
DeFiore: This is the viewpoint from the preferred South Knoll site (seen in Figure 5.13). The vertical black line identifies the approximate windshield damage seen in Altgens 6 and 7. This car closely mimics the X-100 location when the throat shot arrived from the South Knoll. The photo in Figure 5.15 is taken from the following source: Anthony Edward DeFiore, "Z225: A Research Analysis of the front shot at President John F. Kennedy," op. cit.

WHERE DID THAT WINDSHIELD BULLET GO?[89]

One of the 1963 White House physicians, James Morningstar Young, MD, may hold the key. He reported that an intact bullet (with a bent tip—perhaps bent from striking the windshield) was found inside the X-100 that night. But this was not overtly acknowledged by James Humes, even though it was handed directly to him. Here is that report from Young [with my emphases added]:

---

89 Surely, this bullet did not enter JFK's forehead. We now know that this windshield shot must have been fired before Z-255, well before any head shots. Furthermore, the forehead shot (especially as documented by Michael Chesser) deposited the trail of debris across the top of the skull. In the extant X-ray films, these particles look more like liquid mercury than like solid metal. Furthermore, the entry site for this trail contains many tiny particles; the small sizes are also consistent with mercury. If a mercury bullet had struck the windshield, then much of its energy would promptly have dissipated and mercury would have sprayed widely, but there is no evidence for this. Furthermore, it is unlikely that the long trail of debris would have resulted from such an energy-depleted shot. Finally, only lead residue was found on the inside of the windshield—but no mercury. The bottom line is this: The windshield bullet likely missed JFK, but the resulting glass shards did not.

> In December of 2001 and January of 2002 during an interview with US Navy Bureau of Medicine and Surgery historians, Dr. James Young, a physician who had worked with White House Physician Admiral George Burkley during the Kennedy administration, related that during the autopsy he had been given *a bullet in an envelope* [sic—one bullet, not two] by White House Medical Corpsman Chief Petty Officer Thomas Mills after his [Mill's] return from the White House garage to retrieve skull fragments from the rear of the limousine. Young described this bullet as jacketed, straight but with a bent tip and visually close in diameter to CE 399, which he estimated to be ½ centimeter. Dr. Young voiced his concerns to the interviewers that he had never seen any reference to it in the Warren Commission investigation. The last thing he remembers is that he gave the *envelope containing the bullet* with the bent tip to Dr. Humes, the head autopsy pathologist, and that the bullet was never seen or documented after that. [90]

Dr. Young also did an oral history interview on December 4, 10, and 17, 2001.[91] He recalled that he and Dr. Burkley were present during essentially the entire autopsy. Like most witnesses, Young recalled JFK's right occipital defect, but he also added that it included the "middle cerebral areas" and that no skull covered either of these sites. (This agrees precisely with my reconstruction.) More pertinent to the present discussion, however, he recalled that hospital corpsmen William Martinell and

---

90 Dr. Randy Robertson, "White House Physician, Autopsy Eyewitness, questions President Ford about Missing Bullet," Assassination Archives and Research Center, n.d., https://aarclibrary.org/white-house-physician-autopsy-eyewitness-questions-president-ford-about-missing-bullet/.

91 James Young, "Navy Medicine and President Kennedy's Autopsy: Recollections from a former White House Physician," 2001, Archive.org, https://archive.org/details/NMAndTheKennedyAssassination. See also: See: Milicent Cranor, "Bending the Story on a Bent Bullet," Kennedys and King, April 23, 2021, https://www.kennedysandking.com/john-f-kennedy-articles/bending-the-story-on-a-bent-bullet.

Thomas Mills brought *an envelope into the morgue* that contained three bone fragments *and one "brass slug"* (sic—not two slugs). The latter had been *found on the floor* "in the *back* of the car."[92]

Young was so concerned about his memory's accuracy of this bullet that he telephoned Mills in Johnson City, Texas:

> He [Mills] confirmed exactly what I had put down in my notes, that there was *a bent brass slug* that they had brought out that they had picked up off the floor of the Queen Mary [he meant the X-100].[93]

Now consider this (my emphases are italicized): In 1963, Captain David P. Osborne was chief of surgery at Bethesda. In 1978, the then-Admiral Osborne recalled, for the HSCA, that he had seen a slug that was *"copper-clad"* and *"fully intact"* roll out of JFK's clothing onto the table when his shoulders were raised to remove his clothing. Lifton contacted Osborne the next year, and Osborne described a "reasonably clean, *unmarred*"[94] bullet. He even recalled holding this bullet *in his hand* and noting that it had no blood on it.[95] "Upon further inquiry [by the HSCA], Osborne emphasized that the slug [sic] was a fully intact missile and *not a fragment* [my emphasis]."[96]

But the HSCA discounted his testimony, thus implying that an

---

92 Ibid. My emphases were added.

93 Ibid. My emphases have been added.

94 "Medical Evidence and Related Issues Pertaining to the Assassination of President John F. Kennedy," *HSCA*, vol. 7, March 1979, p. 15. See also the reference to "Outside Contact Report, Capt. David Osborne, June 20, 1978, HSCA (JFK Document No. 013624," footnote 41 in HSCA, vol. 7, p. 19.

95 HSCA outside contact report of interview of Admiral David Osborne, MD 66, ARRB Master Set of Medical Exhibits, June 20, 1978, p.3, https://aarclibrary.org/publib/jfk/arrb/master_med_set/md66/html/md66_0003a.htm.

96 See: Milicent Cranor, "Bending the Story on a Bent Bullet," op. cit.

American admiral could not be trusted.[97] Also note that Osborne did not describe two metal fragments like CE 567 and CE 569. Nor did the autopsy report describe two metal fragments like CE 567 or CE 569.[98] Finally, we have Captain John H. Stover's persistently mysterious receipt for "*a* [i.e., single] missle [sic]."[99] This has usually been described as "removed" by Humes (and as referring to *two small* metal fragments—not an entire bullet), but Denise Hazelwood has (reasonably) proposed that this misconceived typewritten word may actually be "*received*."[100] Or perhaps, in view of the misspelled "missle," this misshapen word was meant to be "received." Since Stover did recall a bullet, "missle" may actually have described the intact bullet that White House physician James Morningstar Young, MD, reported as found inside the presidential limousine that night. Young reported that White House Medical Corpsman, Chief Petty Officer Thomas Mills, gave him the bullet in an envelope after he returned from the White House garage to retrieve skull fragments from the rear of the limousine. In April 1980, David

---

97 Admiral David P. Osborne reported that a bullet rolled out from the "clothing" that was wrapped around JFK's body, and that he actually handled the missile. The HSCA asserted that Osborne "thought" he saw a bullet roll out, but that he later said he wasn't sure when told no one else at the autopsy recalled such an event. Admiral Osborne told David Lifton that he and the HSCA had disagreed over the matter (See: David Lifton, *Best Evidence*, op. cit., pp. 645–646).

Said Osborne (emphases added; brackets in original):

"I told them [HSCA investigators] that this was the way I remembered it, and they said, "Well, it must be wrong, because the Secret Service testified that the bullet was found in the hospital in at Parkland, and brought back to Washington." And so I said, "Well, if that's true, then they brought it back to the morgue because *I had that bullet in my hand*, and looked at it." This is from "JFK Assassination (The Facts)," Mysterious Worlds, n.d., https://mysteriousworlds.bravesites.com/entries/conspiracy-theories/jfk-assassination-the-facts-.

98 Osborne had survived the Normandy landings and later became the commander of the National Naval Medical Center in Bethesda (1967) and then Deputy Surgeon General of the Navy (1976).

99 Denise Hazelwood, "A Benign Conspiracy Part 8: 'The Five Shots,'" documentary series, November 20, 2021, starting at timestamp 49:03, https://youtu.be/nTTEIRFAwgM.

100 Ibid.

Lifton contacted Stover, who had been the commanding officer (i.e., Humes's immediate superior) of the US Naval Medical School and, like Osborne, had been present during the autopsy. Lifton said that Stover confirmed Osborne's assertion that *there was a bullet* in the autopsy room, saying (my emphases): "It seems to me that the one they found in Dallas they brought up....I think it was in *a brown paper envelope*."[101]

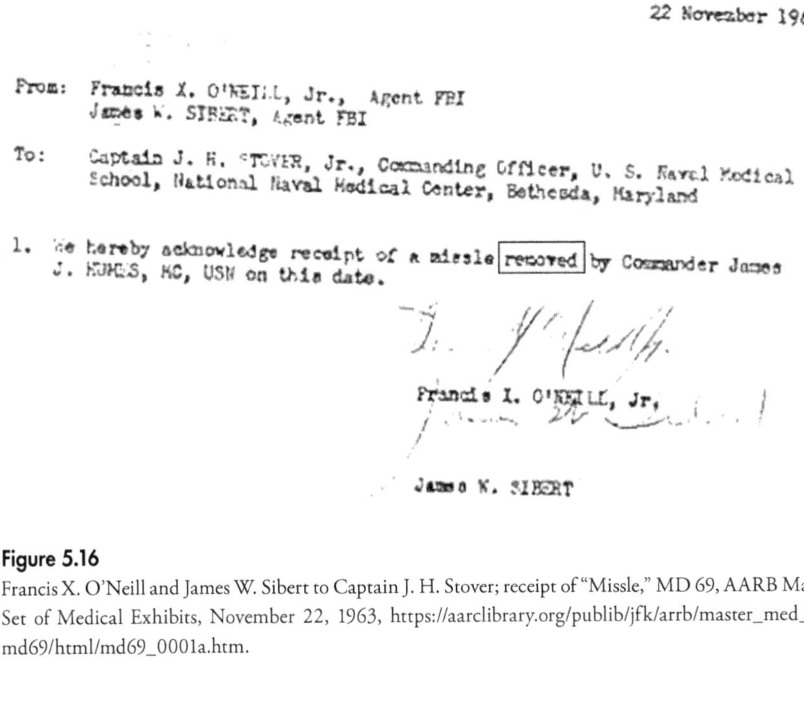

22 November 1963

From: Francis X. O'NEILL, Jr., Agent FBI
James W. SIBERT, Agent FBI

To: Captain J. H. STOVER, Jr., Commanding Officer, U. S. Naval Medical School, National Naval Medical Center, Bethesda, Maryland

1. We hereby acknowledge receipt of a missle removed by Commander James J. HUMES, MC, USN on this date.

Francis X. O'NEILL, Jr.

James W. SIBERT

Figure 5.16

Francis X. O'Neill and James W. Sibert to Captain J. H. Stover; receipt of "Missle," MD 69, AARB Master Set of Medical Exhibits, November 22, 1963, https://aarclibrary.org/publib/jfk/arrb/master_med_set/md69/html/md69_0001a.htm.

So, we now have a scenario where the following individuals may all have seen *the same bullet*: Young, Mills, Martinell, Osborne, and Stover. (Curiously, Jerrol Custer described a "king-sized" metal fragment from

101 David Lifton, *Best Evidence*, op. cit., p. 651. Emphasis added.

JFK's back.[102]) But Osborne and Stover did not know the origin of this bullet, whereas the first three individuals (Young, Mills, and Martinell) did. Humes also must have known, but he remained eternally—and

102 Zach Jendro, "An analysis of the ARRB testimony of Jerrol Custer," debunked.wordpress.com [blog], December 13, 2015, https://debunked.wordpress.com/2015/12/13/an-analysis-of-the-arrb-testimony-of-jerrol-custer/.

In his 2005 interview with William Matson Law and Vince Palamara, Custer gave a graphic description of this "king-sized" bullet fragment:

Palamara: Were you aware of the allegations of—I don't know if it was Admiral or Captain David Osborne—about the bullet falling out of the body? During the autopsy? Did you see a whole bullet or. a fragment fall out of President Kennedy.

Custer: Well, I wouldn't call it a fragment, I'd say it was a pretty good sized bullet. Because it created such a fuss. They ran over with a set of forceps—and they grabbed it, picked it up and put it in a little basin of water.

Law: Now is this the bullet—when you were doing the X-rays, and you had him on the table and moving him around, didn't you tell me at some point in an earlier conversation that a bullet fragment had fallen out of the president?

Custer: That was the time that they found that.

Law: Okay. And what happened? What was their demeanor? What happened when that bullet fragment fell out?

Custer: I called one of the pathologists over and said, "Hey, we have a bullet here." Soon as they heard that, they came down off the raised platform and they ran over and picked it up. Then Sibert and O'Neill also came over and said, "Well, we want that, that's—"

Palamara: Yes, they wrote out a receipt for a missile so people think it's semantics—was it a fragment? So you're saying it wasn't a whole bullet? It was a sizable fragment of a bullet?

Custer: It was about—see, you're getting into semantics here about the size. It was distinguishable enough to know it was a bullet. It wasn't complete because there was some fragmentation. Some area of destruction on the bullet.

Law: Just for clarification, what area of the body did it fall out of?

Custer: That was the upper thorax. The upper back.

Law: It literally fell out of the back wound.

Custer: Right.

Source: William Matson Law, "Interview with Jerrol F. Custer," in *In the Eye of History*, first edition, 2005, op. cit., pp. 109-142, at p. 132. Also printed in the second edition, 2015, op. cit., pp. 253-280, at p. 272.

disingenuously—silent. Even worse, he was never asked, not even by the ARRB.

Young's bullet must not be confused with either CE 567 or with CE 569, which were only bullet fragments. Furthermore, CE 567 was discovered between the front seats, while CE 569 was discovered on the front floor. On the other hand, Young found his bullet on the floor near the back seat of the JFK limousine.[103] In addition, Young reported that his bullet had a tip. Do you see a tip in either CE 567 or in CE 569? Young not only reported a bullet tip, but he also described this bullet as a "bent brass slug."[104] Neither of these two fragments (CE 567 or CE 569) match Young's intact bullet.

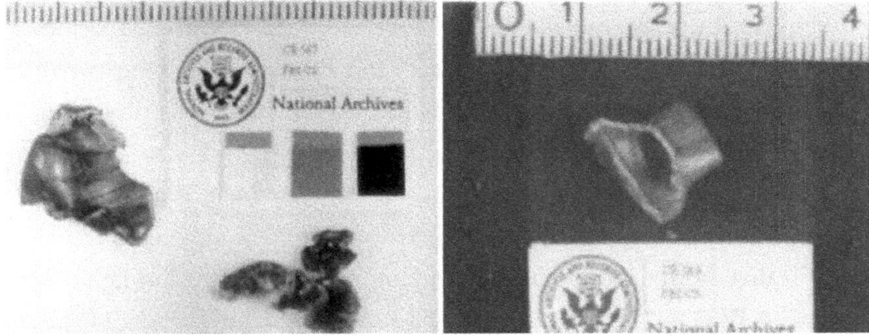

Figure 5.17

The Supposed Nose (CE 567, left) and Tail (CE 569, right) of the Bullet from the WC's (fantasized) Single Head Shot.

103 Milicent Cranor, "Navy Doctor: Bullet Found in JFK's Limousine, and Never Reported.," WhoWhatWhy, October 6, 2017, https://whowhatwhy.org/politics/government-integrity/navy-doctor-bullet-found-jfks-limousine-never-reported/.

104 James Young, "Navy Medicine and President Kennedy's Autopsy: Recollections from a former White House Physician," op. cit.

Then there is Osborne, who held in his hand a slug that was "copper-clad" and "fully intact."[105] Does that description appear to fit either CE 567 or CE 569? Finally, think about this: Young had been directly involved with the retrieved items from the limousine, but he had desperately wanted to avoid any personal publicity. ("I do not choose to be identified in this matter at all.")[106] So, does it seem likely that he would write a letter to Gerald Ford (in my hometown of Rancho Mirage) to explicitly emphasize a missing bullet if he had already assisted in transferring two metal fragments (from the limousine) to the autopsy personnel?[107]

Finally, in his oral history, Young reported this:

> And I came across this issue of the bullet [sic] that we had asked the two corpsmen to go down to the White House and pick up what was in the back of the car. They picked up the bullet [sic] off of the floor in the back of the car. Well, I decided that this is something, you know, the third bullet [sic] has never been decided about ever, apparently. So, what I did was I decided there was only one person still alive from the original Warren Commission. I went through the entire Warren Commission book. I've got the whole report of the Warren Commission as a matter of fact. I went through the whole thing and there was nothing in it. Now, at that particular time nobody said anything about this. And I know what we did. We brought that in, I mean Chief Martinell and Chief Mills went to the White House,

---

105 HSCA outside contact report of interview of Admiral David Osborne, MD 66, ARRB Master Set of Medical Exhibits, op. cit.

106 "White House Physician, Autopsy Eyewitness, questions President Ford about Missing Bullet," Courtesy of AARC Board member, Dr. Randy Robertson, Assassination Archives and Research Center, AARCLibrary.org, n.d., https://aarclibrary.org/white-house-physician-autopsy-eyewitness-questions-president-ford-about-missing-bullet/.

107 Milicent Cranor, "Navy Doctor: Bullet Found in JFK's Limousine, and Never Reported," op. cit.

> went to the Queen Mary [sic], got the stuff off of the floor in the back seat, brought it back out to us and we gave that to Commander Humes at the time.[108]

I would only add this question: After his self-described thorough review of the *Warren Report*, why would the reluctant Young expose himself if he had already identified either CE 567 or CE 569 as his "bent bullet"?

It was only after I wrote the above paragraphs that I was reminded of this (already cited) comment by Dudman:

> Authorities repeatedly mentioned four bullets found afterward—one found in the floor of the car, a second found in the President's stretcher, a third removed from Governor Connally's left thigh, and a fourth said to have been removed from President Kennedy's body at the Naval Hospital in Bethesda.[109]

So, now we can make more sense of Dudman's summary; he may have been correct about four bullets. A bullet materialized (possibly with Humes's assistance) from JFK's back, after which Osborne handled it. According to Dr. Young, a bullet was found in the limousine—and therefore it should not be counted twice. But Young's bullet was discovered well after Osborne's encounter with a bullet, so it cannot be the same bullet. Sam Kinney claims to have transferred another bullet from the limousine to someone's stretcher (but not JFK's stretcher), so that one should not be cited twice. So, that leaves three bullets (Osborne, Young, and Kinney), but when Connally's bullet is added, we get back to four.

As this chapter was being finalized, former SS agent Paul Landis recalled that he had collected a bullet from the rear seat of the limousine

---

108 James Young, "Navy Medicine and President Kennedy's Autopsy: Recollections from a former White House Physician," op. cit.

109 Douglas Weldon, JD, "The Kennedy Limousine: Dallas 1963," in *Murder in Dealey Plaza*, ed. James Fetzer, op. cit., p. 139.

and then placed it onto JFK's stretcher inside of Trauma Room One.[110] Although Landis soon wrote two reports, neither cites this bullet![111] Nor does the *Vanity Fair* review by James Robenalt (see prior footnote) cite Sam Kinney's similar experience of transferring a bullet from the limousine to someone's stretcher. (Robenalt's review also ignores Young's bullet—and Connally's bullet. Was Landis, or maybe just Robenalt, truly this naively ignorant of other bullets?) In any case, if Landis is correct, we have not just four, but rather five, wayward bullets. But since Landis's bullet was not found near Connally, it cannot become a magic bullet. On the contrary, if authentic, it destroys the SBT. Adding

---

110 See: *The Final Witness* (2023) by Paul Landis. The comments here are based solely on a review by James Robenalt in *Vanity Fair* called "A New JFK Assassination Revelation Could Upend the Long-Held 'Lone Gunman Theory.'" The review suggested that Landis believes that he had found CE 399. This is highly unlikely because Darrell Tomlinson (at Parkland) refused to identify CE 399 as the bullet he found. Although Robenalt cited Tomlinson, Robenalt dared not mention Tomlinson's refusal to identify this bullet. Nor did he disclose that the FBI advised Tomlinson to keep his mouth shut about this bullet (see *Best Evidence*, p. 591). Landis also recalled seeing two bullet fragments on the *back seat*, "next to where Jackie had been sitting." Of course, this disagrees with the WC's discovery site for CE 567 and CE 569; these two bullet fragments were found in the *front* of the limousine. Finally, regarding a possible fragment exit from the headshot through the throat, Robenalt had obviously not read the devastating anatomic critique of this trajectory in my hardcover book (pp. 297-299). Not even the pathologists were so foolhardy as to confirm that myth in their final report—although Josiah Thompson tried to revive it. Also see the testimony of Landis to the WC: https://www.maryferrell.org/showDoc.html?docId=1135#relPageId=773.This is from *Hearings before the President's Commission on the Assassination of President Kennedy*, vol. 18, pp. 751-758, especially at p. 758.

111 This is what he reported in his written statement dated November 30, 1963: "My immediate thought was that the President could not possibly be alive after being hit like he was. I still was not certain from what direction the second shot came, but my reaction at this time was that the shot came from somewhere towards the front, right-hand side of the road. I did not notice anyone on the overpass, and I scanned the area to the right of and below the overpass where the terrain sloped towards the road on which we were traveling. The only person I recall seeing was a Negro male in light green slacks and a beige colored shirt running from my left to right, up the slope, across a grassy section, along a sidewalk, towards some steps and what appeared to be a lone stone wall. He was bent over while running and I started to point towards him, but I didn't notice anything in his hands and by this time we were going under the overpass at a very high rate of speed." Statement of Special Agent Paul E. Landis, Jr., dated Nov. 30, 1963, *WCH*, vol. XVIII, CE 1024, pp. 751-757, at p. 755.

credibility to Landis's account, Parkland nurses, Sharon Lee Tuohy and Phyllis J. Hall[112], also observed a bullet on JFK's stretcher.[113]

FINAL THOUGHTS

We finally have a resolution to the ostensibly conflicting, but nonetheless highly credible, eyewitnesses—from both Dearborn and DC. The key to the puzzle is a previously secret round-trip flight with the X-100 from DC to Dearborn, beginning on Sunday night, November 24, with a return about twenty-four hours later to Andrews Air Force Base. Once this is granted—and we now have *two independent witnesses* to this Dearborn appearance—the pieces fall into place with surprising ease. Although, at first, such a flight seems preposterous, in retrospect virtually nothing in this entire JFK case fits a normal pattern. Furthermore, we now know about the alteration of the autopsy X-ray films and photographs, as well as the alteration of the Zapruder film. Moreover, it was categorically imperative for this windshield to disappear—and do so with all possible speed. The persistent—and *multiple* "no hole"—memos merely mark the original windshield as a target for annihilation. Lives and futures were at stake—and perhaps even prison sentences. The guilty men (women were innocent, as usual) did whatever was required to assist the state coup—and to save their carcasses and careers. No one should be surprised—especially after reading Herodotus.[114]

---

112 The recollections of Phyllis J. Hall are here: "Nurse claims JFK had another bullet lodged in body after assassination," NY Daily News, updated January 10, 2019, https://www.nydailynews.com/news/national/jfk-mystery-bullet-lodged-body-nurse-article-1.1512283. She saw an undamaged bullet "On the [JFK] cart, halfway between the earlobe and the shoulder...."

113 Denis Morisette, "HSCA Interview with Parkland Intern Sharon Thuoy [sic]," August 8 2018, https://www.youtube.com/watch?v=nPLgFuQS7Y4.

114 Or you might instead enjoy *Reading Herodotus: A Guided Tour through Wild Boars, Dancing Suitors, and Crazy Tyrants of The History* (2012), by Debra Hamel. Better yet, consider China's first emperor and contemplate his 2,200-year-old terra-cotta army of more than eight thousand *life-size* soldiers, six hundred horses, and one hundred chariots, which (successfully—at least until 1974) guarded the burial site of this ancient Chinese tyrant, Qin Shi Huang Di: https://www.nationalgeographic.com/history/article/emperor-qin. Compared to an American tyrant, who may

Ferguson had unrestricted access to the White House garage. Moreover, it was judiciously stripped of guards that Sunday night (November 24), when he most likely left for Dearborn with the X-100; the garage remained unguarded after that as well. Although he did not make the trip to Dallas (which may be suspicious in itself), he had often accompanied the X-100 on its trips and frequently drove the X-100. Finally, Ferguson had connections everywhere—from top executives in Dearborn to leading White House officials, including James Rowley.

So, which vice president did Whitaker speak to on Monday, November 25? Was it someone named Miller?[115] The most likely candidate seems to be Arjay Miller (a Whiz Kid), although Rodney Markley and Ben Mills (another Whiz Kid) cannot certainly be ruled out.[116] Also

---

have ordered a top-secret, round-trip flight to Dearborn, the Chinese emperor wins easily for indulgence and audacity. Twentieth-century America had nothing over ancient China.

115 Douglas Weldon, "The Kennedy Limousine: Dallas 1963," in *Murder in Dealey Plaza* (2000), ed. James Fetzer, pp. 145-146. Weldon wrote:

"The information was, until now, never shared outside his [Whitaker's] immediate family. He wants nothing tangible or intangible for this information. He did not want to name his superior, the Vice President of the division at that time. He was continuing to protect that name during his interview in 1993. I have subsequently discovered the name through another source. The name of the Vice President that he would not reveal to me was 'Bob Miller.' Mr. Miller has reportedly retired in Colorado. I do not know if he is still alive."

In Weldon's recording (played during his 1999 lecture—which was still accessible online as I wrote), the *unnamed* witness (Whitaker) clearly stated the name "Bob," but he never stated the name "Miller." Was Whitaker merely misdirecting Doug by saying Bob—or was he thinking of Bob McNamara? Or maybe he meant Rodney Markley, who came from Denver, *Colorado*? And then there is Ben Mills, who in 1955 was elected a *vice president* of the Ford Motor Company and appointed general manager of the *Lincoln* Division. When the Lincoln and Mercury Divisions were consolidated in 1957, Mr. Mills became general manager of both divisions. In any case, I have not been able to identify a suspect named Bob Miller—nor any other reasonable Bob (except for McNamara—who by then had left the FMC to become JFK's secretary of defense).

116 "The year was 1946. The Ford Motor Company had not turned a profit in fifteen years and was losing money at the rate of one million dollars per day. Henry Ford II, not yet thirty years of age, was now firmly at the helm of [the] Ford Motor Company, and he needed help. "I am green," he said, "and searching for answers." The answer came in the form of a telegram from 32-year-old Charles B. "Tex" Thornton, an ambitious and charismatic colonel of the Army Air Force. The telegram read: "Dear Mr. Ford. I represent a group of associates who have served under me at

recall that Markley and Miller were clearly friends of LBJ. I do not know about Mills, but he also seems to be of that ilk.

Here is another issue to ponder: even without a perforation, the windshield must at least have cracked on the inside from the impact of any frontal bullet (or fragment)—and this encounter could easily have yielded a few glass shards. After all, we know that inside damage was

---

the office of statistical control, Army Air Force. We would like to discuss with you personally a matter of management importance and request an early meeting." It was an all or nothing proposal. Either the young Mr. Ford hired all ten members of the group, or he would get none. A day after the telegram was sent, the group was invited to Dearborn. In addition to Thornton, the group included Wilbur Andreson, Charles Bosworth, Robert McNamara, J. Edward Lundy, Ben Mills, George Moore, Jack Reith, James Wright and Arjay Miller. This group of ten, soon to be known as "The Whiz Kids," ultimately would provide the Ford Motor Company with two presidents and six vice presidents. Not only did they aid the Ford Motor Company, [but] they [also] became one of the most celebrated success stories in all of American business. The son of a Nebraska farmer, Arjay Miller's unique name came from combining his father's first and middle initials, R and J (for Rawley John)." Source: "Arjay Miller: Inducted 2006," Automotive Hall of Fame, n.d., https://www.automotivehalloffame.org/honoree/arjay-miller/.

Rodney Markley (the *recipient* of Vaughn Ferguson's memo) was not one of the Whiz Kids. However, "he was a friend of Gerald R. Ford and Lyndon B. Johnson and a close associate of Henry Ford." Source: "Rodney Markley, 75, Ex-Lobbyist for Ford," *The New York Times*, October 15, 1988.

"In 1951, Mr. Markley, a native of Denver, joined Ford in Washington, where for the next 27 years he represented the company's interests." Source: "Rodney Markley, 75, Ex-Lobbyist for Ford," op. cit.

"Rodney W. Markley Jr., former vice president for governmental relations at the Ford Motor Company, died of bladder cancer Wednesday at the Sunny Bank Anglo-American Hospital, Cannes, France. He was 75 years old and lived in Theoule sur Mer, France." Source: "Rodney Markley, 75, Ex-Lobbyist for Ford," op. cit.

NOTE: Vaughn Ferguson's December memo was addressed to R. W. Markley, Jr. Is it possible that Markley was called "Bob"?

"[Arjay] Miller was named vice president in charge of Ford's staff group in February 1962 and became Ford's seventh president in May 1963, succeeding John Dykstra." Source: "Remembering Arjay Miller," Automotive Hall of Fame, November 15, 2017.

"[President] Johnson tapped [Arjay Miller] to become the first president of the Urban Institute, a think tank launched to address the nation's growing urban problems." (Source: "Remembering Arjay Miller," op. cit.) So LBJ clearly knew who Arjay was.

seen, i.e., scrapings were taken from the inside, *but no scrapings were ever taken from the outside.* In any case, a non-perforating bullet seems very unlikely, given the long distance (over two hundred yards) required for this shot. It must have been a high-velocity bullet—and that would inevitably have perforated the windshield.

Although JFK author Pamela Brown must have known about it, her 2018 update of her initial 1999 exploration of the JFK limousine windshield[117] does not cite Rowley's letter to Rankin. Even more surprising though, she also ignored Dr. James Young's memo about the lost bullet, which became public knowledge in October 2017—*well before her 2018 update!*[118] Furthermore, in her 2018 update, she totally ignored George Whitaker, Sr., whose name became public in 2003 in Nigel Turner's *The Men Who Killed Kennedy.* We are also entitled to wonder why she never interviewed Ferguson. After all, the Archives sent her that Ferguson memo in 1988, and he did not die until 2003—an interval of fifteen years. What if she had asked Ferguson this: Did you meet George Whitaker, Sr. at the FMC? But since Ferguson had died the same year that Whitaker's name went public, Ferguson may not have known his name. So, instead, she could have tried this question: Did you hear about an anonymous FMC witness to the windshield hole? At the very least, she could have asked: Did you attend JFK's funeral? And if not, why not? Unfortunately, these opportunities are now lost to history. I do not know if Ferguson's wife (Catherine) still lives, but if she does, will Brown now ask her whether Ferguson attended JFK's funeral? As a memorabilia collector, surely he would have brought something home from the funeral. But if he did not attend, that would fuel further

---

117 Pamela McElwain-Brown, "An Examination of the Presidential Limousine in the White House Garage," *Kennedy Assassination Chronicles*, vol. 5, issue 4 (Winter 1999), op. cit. Her 2018 update is her Kindle eBook: Pamela Brown, *Midnight Blue to Black: The Vanishing Act of the JFK Presidential Assassination Limousine SS100X in Broad Daylight,* 2018, op. cit.

118 Milicent Cranor, "Navy Doctor: Bullet Found in JFK's Limousine, and Never Reported," op. cit.

suspicions about his presence in Dearborn on Monday, November 25.

Although Brown tried (but failed) to get the National Archives to date the FBI windshield photographs, she did not ask the most fundamental question: *Why were these undated in the first place?* To be explicit, what competent FBI agent would omit a date from such a central piece of forensic evidence? It was, after all, the most important case in American history. Quite strikingly, there is a possible answer: It is highly likely that these photographs were obtained on *at least two different dates*, i.e., on the early morning of Saturday, November 23 (taken of the motorcade windshield) and then again on Wednesday, November 27 (taken of the *Dearborn* windshield with the *bogus* damage). In particular, if the FBI had taken true close-ups of the original windshield, these might well have shown the spiderweb-like damage that several individuals (including Rowley himself) had reported. And those images would then have been deadly (for the cover-up) because images of the Dearborn windshield (placed under lock and key by the SS on Wednesday, November 27, and now at the Archives) *would not have matched the close-up images* of the motorcade windshield; although the location seemed correct, their shapes would have differed. Given the circumstances, omitting close-ups of the original windshield, as well as omitting the different dates, was the safest course of action for Robert Frazier of the FBI. Finally, the fact that Robert Frazier did not volunteer to help the Archives to date these photographs (even after Brown requested such help) speaks for itself—i.e., *res ipsa loquitur.*

It is now time to let Vaughn Ferguson rest in peace. Besides, if you had played golf with him (which he loved), he would have seemed quite unthreatening.[119] Moreover (according to Pamela Brown), his wife and

---

119 "The Banality of Evil" is a phrase coined by the philosopher Hannah Arendt while she covered the trial of the Nazi war criminal, Adolf Eichmann. She meant that atrocities aren't necessarily committed by monsters but by fairly ordinary human beings out of a mixture of motives—careerism, conformism, fear, greed, and bureaucratic convenience. "Monsters exist, but they are too few in number to be truly dangerous. More dangerous are the common men, the

his granddaughter would have agreed with this. Perhaps, were he still alive, even our second Dearborn witness to the perforated windshield would have understood why Ferguson was required to play his special role.

So finally, we have reached a two-way conclusion:

1. We know that the X-100 was in Dearborn on Monday, November 25, 1963, because we now have two independent eyewitnesses, as well as overwhelming circumstantial evidence.

2. We also know that there was a through-and-through (perforated) hole in the windshield—*because the X-100 was in Dearborn* on Monday, November 25, 1963. After all, there is no other reason for its presence there—except to remove the incriminating windshield. Furthermore, if its Dearborn visit had been appropriate, it would not have been so surreptitious.

As Pamela Brown has written so eloquently, "Unfortunately, as a result, most research of the Presidential Limousine has been destined to suffer from well-intended misconception and even unproven myth."[120] Allow me to acknowledge Pamela Brown, who inspired much of my thinking about the X-100. I only wish I could listen to her accomplished flute playing. I would remind her that, once upon a time, I played the French horn for the University of Wisconsin-Madison concert band.

---

functionaries ready to believe and to act without asking any questions," said Primo Levi (an Auschwitz survivor). See: "Remembering the Holocaust," *The Behavioral Insights Team,* January 20, 2020, https://www.bi.team/blogs/remembering-the-holocaust/. Also see Primo Levi, with Stuart Woolf as translator, *If this is a man/The Truce* (New York: The Orion Press, 1959). To close the case, see Philip Zimbardo, *The Lucifer Effect: Understanding How Good People Turn Evil* (New York: Random House, p. 2007).

120 Pamela McElwain-Brown, "The Presidential Lincoln Continental SS-100-X," *Dealey Plaza Echo,* vol. 3, issue 2, (July 1999) pp. 22-29, https://www.maryferrell.org/showDoc.html?docId=16241#relPageId=32.

Meanwhile, I can say it no better than St. Paul: "When I was a child, my speech, feelings, and thinking were all those of a child; now that I am an adult, I have no more use for childish ways."[121]

CHAPTER 5: SUMMARY

For the new elite, JFK's limousine (the X-100) was a landmine, just waiting to explode. Too many witnesses had seen the perforated hole in the windshield. Even if a posterior shot had caused it, that would still have meant too many bullets for the three-shot Oswald scenario. So, the conspirators had no choice—at all costs, the windshield had to vanish. Evidence of such a hole, especially if from a frontal bullet, would have shattered lives and careers. Too many powerful men were at risk. Surely James Rowley understood this all too well, as he must have quite promptly explained to Vaughan Ferguson. Only one safe site existed for the secure disposal of the windshield—the Ford plant in Dearborn, where Ferguson was a well-known employee. And only one tight window of time existed for its final rendezvous—Monday, November 25, the day of JFK's funeral, when the entire world was distracted. So on Sunday, the White House garage security detail was lifted (probably by Rowley), and Ferguson easily escaped with the limousine that day, probably via a C-130 from Andrews Air Force Base. Most likely, after landing near Dearborn, he personally drove the limousine to the Ford plant late that Sunday night, and then flew back the next day, with an immaculate new windshield.

Early on Monday, November 25, the first Dearborn witness was called at home; he was ordered to report to work on the windshield. When interviewed in August 1993, George Whitaker, Sr., then a FMC supervisor, recalled these events for Douglas Weldon. His name first became public in 2003 in *The Men Who Killed Kennedy*. As he had promised, Weldon revealed it only after the witness had died.

Only recently did I become aware of the second eyewitness, Robert D. Harrison, automotive engineer, who worked at the same plant, and

121 1 Cor. 13:11, from the Good News Translation.

who was the father of my medical school roommate. Both men recalled a perforation in the windshield, which they found highly disconcerting—especially in view of the official story. Whitaker was firmly convinced, by the pattern of damage, that the hole resulted from a frontal shot. We do not have Harrison's opinion on the direction of the windshield bullet, but he did recall multiple bullet holes in the limousine (which I had previously reported).

So, the windshield removal that shortly followed in the White House garage was purely for show—it was no longer the motorcade windshield, so it was quite irrelevant.

The overwhelming number of cover stories, about limousine visits to Dearborn and to Cincinnati, only demonstrate the depth of this cover-up. The stories are provably and ridiculously wrong—the dates and locations are disorganized, almost certainly on purpose. They were meant only as smoke screens.

Although the Archives has a windshield today, it is not the motorcade windshield. It is the Dearborn windshield, appropriately damaged to match the site of original trauma. So, it is totally irrelevant to the case. And Whitaker's (and especially his family's) reluctance to release his name during his lifetime only speaks to the conniving power of our clandestine elite. And the confession by Whitaker's boss—that he did not even want to know what was happening in the glass shop that day—is even more powerful evidence of this stealthy assignation.

Next to muzzling Dr. Malcolm Perry (about the frontal throat shot), the windshield was the most critical element of the post-assassination whitewash. In fact, it has been so successful that even many WC critics have been seduced by it, as is evident in Pamela Brown's work. In summary, this cover-up has now lasted sixty years, which is a permanent testimony to its deviousness and cleverness. But finally now, it is over.

POSTSCRIPT: TIMELINE MATTERS

During the final minutes of writing this book, Horne focused my attention even further on the limousine timeline.

Horne had previously written that the C-130 aircraft, carrying the Queen Mary and SS-100X, arrived at Andrews Air Force Base at 8:00 p.m. local time, and that the limousine arrived at the White House garage at "about 9:00 PM, local time."

He added that Floyd Boring, the #2 Assistant Special Agent in Charge (ASAIC) of the White House detail, and Special Agent Paul J. Paterni had inspected JFK's limousine and the Secret Service follow-up car from 10:10 p.m. on the night of November 22, 1963 until 12:01 a.m., on November 23, 1963.[122] This search included William Martinell and Thomas Mills from Admiral Burkley's office.[123]

This timeline tells us exactly when Chief Mills began his search, in which he found the bullet that he gave to Dr. James Young. *It was at 10:10 p.m.*

On the other hand, Dr. David Osborne almost certainly saw his bullet in the morgue shortly after the Dallas casket arrived at 8 p.m. Therefore, Osborne's bullet cannot be the bullet described by Dr. James Young. Young's limousine discovery was simply too late for Osborne.

This was quite a revelation to me. I had missed this timeline issue before. So, we have no idea where Osborne's bullet originated, but we know that many individuals saw such a bullet in the morgue.

Osborne's bullet could also not be identical with CE 399. That bullet had gone to the FBI laboratory and was never in the morgue.

Likewise, we know that two Parkland nurses described a bullet on JFK's stretcher in Trauma Room One, where SS Agent Paul Landis said he placed it. The bullet that Connally heard strike the floor in Trauma Room Two (the Parkland Hospital emergency room where he was taken for treatment) remains a mystery. So also, is the bullet that SS agent Sam Kinney claimed he transferred from the limousine to *someone's* stretcher. This interminable French farce just never ends.

---

122 Vince Palamara, "Boring's interesting ARRB interview," JFK-Assassination.net, n.d., https://www.jfk-assassination.net/parnell/vp5.htm.

123 Douglas Horne, *Inside the ARRB,* vol. 5, op. cit., p. 1442.

6

THE MEDICAL COVERUP: ILLICIT BETHESDA SURGERY BEFORE THE OFFICIAL AUTOPSY

Dr. Pierre A. Finck and Dr. Humes started examining the head wounds. They found a small wound on the right side of the head in the temporal area just forward and slightly above the right ear. The small hole (wound) was rounded and about the size of the tip of one's little finger. There appeared to be graying around the margins of the wound, but it was difficult to see because the wound was in the hair line. Dr. Finck speculated that the gray material might have come from a bullet.... Dr. Humes returned to the table and immediately directed Dr. Finck away from the small wound in the temple to the large posterior head wound. The temple wound was abandoned and never returned to that night.

—**JAMES C. JENKINS,** *At the Cold Shoulder of History*, 2018[1]

Well, after about 20 minutes, Dr. Humes took out a saw, and began to cut [JFK's] forehead with...the saw. Mechanical saw, circular, small, mechanical—almost like a cast saw, but it's made—specifically for bone.

—**EDWARD REED,** Enlisted navy X-ray technologist, describing pre-autopsy surgery by Dr. Humes at the Bethesda morgue, between 6:35 p.m. and 7:55 p.m., November 22, 1963[2]

---

1 James C. Jenkins and William Matson Law, *At The Cold Shoulder of History*, op. cit., p. 16.

2 Douglas Horne, *Inside the ARRB*, vol. 2, p. 437.

If there is only one thing that you know about the medical evidence, it should be this—two government sponsored medical panels overruled the military pathologists who performed the autopsy at Bethesda, and they moved the location of the skull entry wound from the lower occipital area over 4 inches up to the posterior parietal area. Let that sink in—the military pathologists who saw the skull and brain, and explored the wounds during the autopsy, were told that they were wrong. They were told that they could not possibly have recorded the correct entry location in the back of the skull, and the entry location was moved up four and a half inches, to the top of the back of the skull. The two government-sponsored panels were the Clark Panel, in 1967, and the medical panel for the House Select Committee on Assassinations, which followed suit a decade later. There is no way that the importance of this can be overstated. How can a group of physicians overrule the pathologists who examined the body? What this tells us is that there was something seriously wrong with the medical evidence.

—**MICHAEL CHESSER, MD,** 2018[3]

ALTHOUGH SOME MEN BELIEVE that women age like fine wine, in this case it is Douglas Horne himself who has aged well—he waited over one decade after his experiences with the ARRB before publishing his five-volume masterpiece, *Inside the ARRB*.[4] In volume 4, chapter 13, "What Really Happened at the Bethesda Morgue (And in Dealey Plaza)?", he

3 Michael Chesser, "The Cranial Autopsy X-Rays and Photographs," in *At The Cold Shoulder of History*, James C. Jenkins and William Matson Law, op. cit., pp. 146-185, at p. 147.

4 My full critique of Horne is at my website: "The Mantik View: Articles and Research on the JFK Assassination" at https://themantikview.org/.

focused on the illicit surgery performed just after 6:35 p.m. by pathologist James J. Humes and witnessed by his colleague, J. Thornton Boswell. On the other hand, the official autopsy did not begin until shortly after 8:00 p.m. that evening. So, the medical cover-up began with this covert, illicit surgery. Its purpose was to leave no trace of frontal shots. Only shots from the rear were to be reported in the autopsy conclusions. These could then be attributed to Oswald.

A JFK CASKET ARRIVES THREE SEPARATE TIMES AT THE BETHESDA NAVAL HOSPITAL:

EVENING, NOVEMBER 22, 1963

In order to paint Humes and Boswell as the morbid co-conspirators, Horne needed first to clarify the timeline for JFK's body in transit from Parkland to Bethesda. After a painstaking search to locate key eyewitnesses, Horne brilliantly completed this daunting task. He identified participants who transferred the body from Parkland to Love Field in Dallas, and then from Andrews Air Force Base to Bethesda. Horne uncovered casket switches that would have astounded even master magician Dariel Fitzkee. In short, a casket arrived at the Bethesda Naval Hospital, not once, but at three distinct times.

TRAUMA ROOM ONE, PARKLAND HOSPITAL:

NOVEMBER 22, 1963, SHORTLY AFTER 1:00 P.M., CST.

According to William Manchester in *The Death of a President*, after JFK was pronounced dead, SS Agent Clint Hill telephoned from Parkland to the Oneal Funeral Home (Figure 6.1) in Oak Lawn, Texas to order their premier casket. Oneal chose "his most expensive coffin, the Elgin Casket Company's 'Britannia' model, eight hundred pounds of double-walled, hermetically sealed solid bronze."[5]

---

5 William Manchester, *The Death of a President*, op. cit., p. 292.

Figure 6.1
The Oneal Funeral Home. Newspaper Advertisement, Dallas, Texas, 1963.

In his 1993 book *Killing the Truth*, Harrison Edward Livingstone described tracking nurse Diana Bowron to the United Kingdom. She was one of several nurses who prepared JFK for the casket. In a written statement to Livingston, Bowron explained:

> When the body was placed in the coffin, the wound at the back of the head was packed with gauze squares and wrapped in a small white sheet. There was no terry cloth or other type of towel used.[6]

---

6 Harrison Edward Livingstone, *Killing the Truth: Deceit and Deception in the JFK Case* (New York: Carroll & Graf Publishers, Inc., 1993), p. 183.

She continued:

> A clear plastic sheet was placed in the bottom of the coffin, which may have been a mattress cover. The body was wrapped in—at the most—two sheets plus the one around the head. All the sheets were white and none had zips. There was no "body bag."[7]

Ambulance driver Aubrey Rike, who then worked for the Oneal Funeral Home, helped transfer the body to the casket inside Trauma Room One. In the first volume of *Inside the ARRB*, Horne explained how he met Rike, despite being denied permission to interview him formally on behalf of the ARRB:

> I met Aubrey Rike on the grassy knoll in Dealey Plaza in 1993, on the 30th anniversary of the assassination, and asked him if there was any way he could be certain that President Kennedy's head wound was in the rear of the head, as opposed to the top of the head (as shown in the autopsy photographs). He told me in 1993 that there was no doubt in his mind that President Kennedy had a large defect in the *rear* of his head, because when he helped lift the President's body into the bronze casket in Trauma Room One at Parkland hospital, he could feel the sharp edges of broken bone at the edges of the wound in the occipital area *through the sheet wrapped around President Kennedy's head* as he lifted up the *bottom* of the skull; he said that the edges of the bone were so sharp that they almost cut into his fingers, even though the material of the bed sheet.[8]

But that was not how JFK's body appeared when first delivered to the Bethesda morgue.

---

7 Ibid.

8 Douglas Horne, *Inside the ARRB*, vol. 1, pp. 65-66. Italics in original.

THE FIRST CASKET ENTRY AT BETHESDA:

6:35 P.M., WASHINGTON, D.C., NOVEMBER 22, 1963

Navy Corpsman Dennis David reiterated to the ARRB what he had consistently told author David Lifton in 1979 and 1980: JFK's body initially arrived at the morgue in a hearse, a black Cadillac mortuary conveyance designed to carry caskets. He told the ARRB staff, during his 1977 telephone interview, that the hearse arrived at the morgue loading dock about twenty minutes *before* he saw the Andrews Air Force Base motorcade arrive in front of the hospital. For the first time, the ARRB was able to definitively identify (from a contemporaneous document) that the arrival time of the hearse was at exactly 6:35 p.m. EST. This precise arrival time derives from an after-action report (written on November 26, 1963) by Marine Sergeant Roger Boyajian, who was in charge of the US Marine Corps (USMC) security detail at Bethesda that night.[9] Quite astonishingly, Boyajian had retained an onionskin carbon copy of his report; he subsequently presented an authenticated photocopy of this onionskin to the ARRB. This arrival time is consistent with the independent recollections of Dennis David, the E-6 navy corpsman who was "Chief of the Day" at the Bethesda Naval Medical School Command. David had consistently recalled that the casket (carrying JFK's body) had arrived at about 6:40 or 6:45 p.m., well before the Andrews Air Force Base motorcade arrived at the front of Bethesda Naval Hospital.[10] The Boyajian report agrees so well with Dennis David that this clearly verifies his credibility as a witness.

---

9 Ibid., Figure 68 and p. xxxiii. See the appendices from *Inside the ARRB,* especially "Appendix 38: After-action report prepared by USMC Sergeant Roger E. Boyajian about the activities of his Marine Corps barracks security detail": https://www.maryferrell.org/showDoc.html?docId=145280#relPageId=189.

Douglas Horne, "The JFK Medical Coverup," The Future of Freedom Foundation, April 9, 2021, *https://www.fff.org/freedom-in-motion/video/the-jfk-medical-coverup/.*

For the narrated presentation, see: The Future of Freedom Foundation, "The JFK Medical Coverup," YouTube, op. cit., slide 14.

10 David Lifton, *Best Evidence*, op. cit., pp. 569-588.

In the chapter "Summary of Shipping Casket and Body Bag Witnesses," in volume 4 of *Inside the ARRB*,[11] Horne listed those who saw the cheap, unadorned aluminum shipping casket when it arrived. At the request of the SS, Dennis David had assembled a working party of navy sailors to offload JFK's casket when his body arrived. The navy sailors who carried the shipping casket from the morgue loading dock into the anteroom (adjacent to the morgue) did not open it. Other Bethesda personnel, who opened it a few minutes later inside the morgue proper, reported that JFK's nude body was encased in a zippered body bag. It is critical to recognize that this first casket was a plain shipping container, not the dark bronze, ornate viewing coffin (with fancy side rails and a viewing lid) provided by the Oneal Funeral Home. After the casket was offloaded by Dennis David's working party, it was opened and the body was removed from a body bag—which had *not* been used at Parkland. Horne rightfully credited Lifton with much of this groundbreaking work. Dennis David and others recalled civilians (men in suits) emerging from a "black, Cadillac ambulance" (a hearse), which delivered a cheap, lightweight, "pinkish gray" aluminum shipping casket, with turnbuckles and no side rails, to the morgue loading dock. David stated that the two ambulance attendants in the front of the hearse were wearing "white operating room smocks." The DC mortuary (Joseph Gawler's Sons) provided the black Cadillac hearse. The two ambulance attendants were Joe Hagan and Tom Robinson, employees of that funeral home. David had also observed several federal agents in suits (presumably SS) exit the hearse.[12]

David recalled many individuals at the morgue dock when the shipping casket arrived.[13] These included Humes, Boswell, General

---

11 Douglas Horne, *Inside the ARRB*, vol. 4, op. cit., pp. 989-992.

12 Douglas Horne, *Inside the ARRB*, vol. 4, pp. 1002-1003.

13 Ibid., p. 989.

Philip C. Wehle (commanding general of the Military District of Washington), Captain John Stover (commanding officer of the National Naval Medical School), Captain Robert Canada (commanding officer, US Naval Hospital, Bethesda), Commander Ebersole (radiologist), and Paul O'Connor (a student at the Medical Technology School at Bethesda Naval Hospital). Paul O'Connor and James Jenkins (both navy corpsmen who were students at the Bethesda Medical School) assisted Humes and Boswell with the autopsy that night.[14] David's party of sailors off-loaded the cheap shipping casket from the black hearse, placed it on the floor of the anteroom outside the Bethesda morgue, and then walked away.[15]

Horne concluded that Boyajian's arrival time of 1835 hours (6:35 p.m.) must now be accepted as a foundation stone in this case—because it appears in a contemporaneous document from November 1963, which has been authenticated by its author. As further corroboration for this time, he emphasized that even Humes agreed with it; before the ARRB, Humes cited the initial arrival as possibly as early as 6:45 p.m.[16] Horne summarized Dennis David's conversation with Dr. Boswell as follows:

> There is something very important to me that I didn't mention earlier, which is that Dennis David has consistently told the same story over and over. And part of the story that he has consistently told is that he asked Dr. Boswell, way after midnight, after the autopsy was over, something to the effect, "When did the President arrive?" or "What casket was the body in?" or something to that effect and Boswell replied, "You should know, you were there." Boswell thereby

14 William Matson Law, "Interview with Douglas Horne," in *In the Eye of History: Disclosures in the JFK Assassination Medical Evidence*, second edition, op. cit., pp. 83-118, at p. 99.

15 Ibid. at p. 96.

16 Douglas Horne, *Inside the ARRB*, vol. 4, p. 1002.

> confirmed that the casket offloaded by Dennis David's working party of sailors contained the President's body, and that is critical information. This is also additional corroboration that the bronze casket ferried from Andrews AFB in the light-gray navy ambulance, which arrived at Bethesda 20 minutes later, had to be empty.[17]

Horne also emphasized a contemporaneous confirmation of the shipping casket. It is the "First Call Sheet," a proprietary Gawler's business document prepared that night and later authenticated for the ARRB by Joe Hagan, the supervisor of Gawler's crew. In volume 4, Horne noted the pertinent entry: "Body removed from metal shipping casket at USNH [US Naval Hospital] at Bethesda."[18] He added:

> Supervisor Joe Hagan confirmed to me in a follow-up interview, via telephone in 1996, that the term "shipping casket" had an undeniable and unique meaning within the funeral trade. It is most unlikely that anyone from Gawler's funeral home would have used the term "shipping casket" to describe the 400-plus pound ceremonial bronze viewing coffin provided by the Oneal Funeral Home in Dallas. And that entry on the Gawler's "First Call Sheet" was not made by "just anyone"—it was made by Joe Hagan himself, in his own hand, as he attested in his ARRB interview.[19]

In my [Mantik] opinion, therefore, it is very difficult to disagree with this early arrival time. If this is accepted, though, the repercussions are colossal—it means that the bronze casket (the one publicly

---

17 William Matson Law, "Interview with Douglas Horne," in *In the Eye of History*, second edition, op. cit., p. 100.

18 Douglas Horne, *Inside the ARRB*, vol. 4, p. 998.

19 Ibid.

off-loaded at Andrews Air Force Base) was empty. Therefore, the chain of custody for JFK's body had been broken.

Paul O'Connor also recalled that JFK's body had arrived in a shipping casket and in a body bag. He first related this to the HSCA staff in a 1977 interview; he repeated it later to both David Lifton and William Matson Law. Here is an excerpt from O'Connor's interview with Law:

> PAUL O'CONNOR: ...the back of the morgue opened up and a crew of hospital corpsmen and a higher ranking corpsman [Dennis David] brought in a plain pinkish-gray, what I call a shipping casket. It was not ornate. It was not damaged. It was just a pinkish-gray casket. They brought it up into the morgue and set it—we had two tables in the morgue—autopsy tables—and they were back to front. They weren't side by side. They were back to front. They brought it up front where we were. At that time we opened up the coffin. Inside was a body bag.
>
> WILLIAM MATSON LAW: Now you're sure there was a body bag.
>
> PAUL O'CONNOR: Absolutely sure there was a body bag. We unzipped it quickly. Inside was a nude body with a bloody sheet wrapped around the head of the body. We lifted the body onto the table.[20]

Clearly, someone had handled JFK's body. At Parkland, JFK's body had been wrapped in sheets, with a separate sheet wrapped around his head. But inside the body bag, JFK's body was naked, with only a bloody sheet wrapped around his head.

To picture the scenario, see Paul O'Connor's sketch of the Bethesda morgue in Figure 6.2. Also see Harold Rydberg's sketch in Figure 6.3.

---

20 William Matson Law, *In the Eye of History* second edition, op. cit., pp. 191-218, at p. 195.

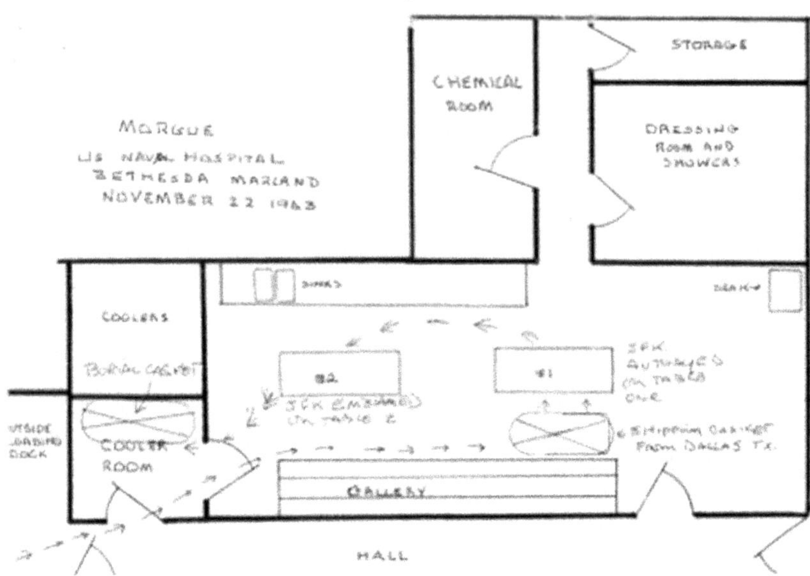

Figure 6.2
Bethesda Hospital Morgue, as drawn by Paul K. O'Connor in 2003. Source: William Matson Law, *In the Eye of History*, op. cit., p. 470, photograph #11.

Figure 6.3
Bethesda Hospital Morgue as drawn by Harold A. Rydberg in 2003. Note the location of the telephone. It is grossly inconsistent with the autopsy photograph (Figure H.1). Either Rydberg was stoned or the autopsy photograph was manipulated.

THE SECOND CASKET ENTRY AT BETHESDA:
7:17 P.M., WASHINGTON, DC, NOVEMBER 22, 1963

About twenty minutes after the 6:35 p.m. arrival of the black hearse, Dennis David observed a light gray navy ambulance (with the bronze casket from Dallas inside) arrive at the front of the hospital, where he also saw Jacqueline exit from the ambulance. The time was either 6:53 p.m. or 6:55 p.m. (the sources vary).[21] David watched Jacqueline enter the main lobby (the Bethesda rotunda), from where she ascended to the seventeenth floor.[22] The gray navy ambulance had been driven from Andrews Air Force Base to Bethesda by William Greer (who had driven the limousine in the Dallas motorcade). Just as in Dallas, Roy Kellerman rode with Greer, but this time they delivered the (empty) bronze casket to the morgue.[23] However, Jacqueline Kennedy did not know that JFK's body was missing from the Dallas casket when it was offloaded from Air Force One at Andrews Air Force Base. Nor did she know that it had been secretly transported to Bethesda by helicopter as soon as the television coverage at Andrews ended. The gray navy ambulance was delayed in front of hospital for about twelve minutes because Greer did not know where the morgue was located. Kellerman had already left the ambulance to walk into the hospital and proceed to the morgue. The ambulance occupants, including Admiral Burkley (JFK's military physician) had accompanied Jacqueline Kennedy into the hospital, leaving Greer alone in the ambulance.

Finally, FBI agents Sibert and O'Neill directed Greer to the morgue (at the rear of the hospital). They told him, "Well, we know where it [the

---

21 SS Agent Hill stated: "The motorcade arrived Bethesda Naval Hospital at 6:55 p.m." This is from "Statement of Special Agent Clinton J. Hill, dated November 30, 1963," Commission Exhibit 1024 (CE 1024), *Hearings before the President's Commission on the Assassination of President Kennedy*, op. cit., vol. 18, pp. 740-745, at p. 744.

22 William Matson Law, *In the Eye of History*, second edition, op. cit., pp. 165-190, at p. 174.

23 Douglas Horne, *Inside the ARRB*, vol. 4, p. 1006.

morgue] is, we get our physical done over here every year."[24] Kellerman was already there in time to meet the Dallas casket. Kellerman, Greer, Sibert, and O'Neill then transferred the empty, but still very heavy, Dallas casket from the navy ambulance into the morgue anteroom, via a wheeled dolly. We now know that this second casket entry occurred at approximately 7:17 p.m. (This precise time is inferred from a statement that Sibert and O'Neill gave to FBI inspector A. Rosen in a 1964 interview [more on this below]. It is consistent with our knowledge that the light gray navy ambulance sat out in front of the hospital, unmoving, for twelve minutes before Greer drove it around to the loading dock.)

During their interviews with Sibert and O'Neill, the HSCA staff learned that the two FBI agents, in concert with Kellerman and Greer, had offloaded the Dallas casket from the navy ambulance without any assistance from the Joint Service Casket Team (or "honor guard"). Sibert and O'Neill, under oath, later confirmed this second casket entry—conducted by these four Federal agents—to the ARRB during their 1997 depositions.[25]

---

24 "Interview with Douglas Horne," in William Matson Law, *In the Eye of History*, second edition, op. cit., pp. 83-117, at p. 97.

25 In the first two pages of their HSCA interviews, both Sibert (1977) and O'Neill (1978) said they carried the Dallas casket into the Bethesda morgue with two assistants. Sibert said the two men were "some Secret Service agents." In an email to the authors dated September 15, 2023, Douglas Horne explained: "O'Neill specifically states that he, Sibert, Kellerman, and Greer carried the Dallas casket into the Bethesda morgue. This is the earliest (and therefore the best) evidence that the Dallas casket entry into the Bethesda morgue was totally separate from the 1835 hours (6:35 p.m.) entry in the Boyajian report, and the 2000 hours (8:00 p.m.) entry mentioned in the report of the Joint Service Casket Team. It is totally separate from any other casket entry—because the actors are so different! Only 4 federal agents participated: no navy sailors and no Honor Guard." See: "HSCA Interview Report of August 25, 1977, Interview of James W. Sibert," MD 85, ARRB Master Set of Medical Exhibits, Assassinations Archives Research Center, pp. 1-2, https://aarclibrary.org/publib/jfk/arrb/master_med_set/md85/html/md85_0002a.htm.

See also: Donald A. [Andy] Purdy, Jr., HSCA Interview Report of Francis X. O'Neill, MD 86, ARRB Master Set of Medical Exhibits, Assassinations Archives Research Center, January 10, 1978, pp. 2-3, https://aarclibrary.org/publib/jfk/arrb/master_med_set/md86/html/md86_0001a.htm

So how can we assign the time of 7:17 p.m. to the second casket entry? In 1964, FBI Agent Rosen interviewed FBI Agents Sibert and O'Neill after they had been interviewed by Arlen Specter of the WC staff. Rosen recorded Specter's question to them: "What was the time of preparation for the autopsy?" Their answer was "Approximately 7:17 p.m."[26] Horne has (correctly) inferred this to be the approximate time the Dallas casket was placed into the anteroom. At the same time Sibert and O'Neill were (temporarily) barred from the morgue. (Presumably, the excuse given to them by the SS was: "You can't go in now because they are preparing for the autopsy." Otherwise, the quote makes no sense whatsoever; subterfuge by the SS is the most reasonable explanation for the meaning of this quote.) Sibert confirmed to the ARRB in his 1997 deposition that the Dallas casket was delivered by them to the morgue anteroom and was not taken directly into the morgue proper.[27] After Kellerman and Greer deposited the empty Dallas casket into the morgue anteroom, Kellerman barred Sibert and O'Neill from entering the morgue. A vehement argument ensued in which Sibert and O'Neill insisted to Kellerman that the FBI had a right to be present at JFK's autopsy. Shortly after the 8:00 p.m. entry into the morgue of the Dallas casket containing JFK's body brought in by the joint service casket team,

---

See also: (1) "Deposition of Francis X. O'Neill," (Washington, DC: Miller Reporting Company, Inc., September 17, 1997), p. 54-57, http://www.aarclibrary.org/publib/jfk/arrb/medical_testimony/pdf/Oneill_9-12-97.pdf;

(2) "Deposition of James W. Sibert," (Washington, DC: Miller Reporting Company, Inc., September 11, 1997), pp. 44-45, http://www.aarclibrary.org/publib/jfk/arrb/medical_testimony/pdf/Sibert_9-11-97.pdf.

26 "FBI Internal Memorandum To: Mr. Belmont From: A. Rosen (dated 3/12/64) Summarizing, in Q and A Format, An Interview that Same Date of BUAGENTS Sibert and O'Neill by Commission Staff Member Arlen Specter," ARRB Master Set of Medical Exhibits, History-Matters.com, p. 2," MD 153, ARRB Master Set of Medical Exhibits, March 12, 1964, https://www.history-matters.com/archive/jfk/arrb/master_med_set/md153/html/md153_0002a.htm.

27 "Deposition of James W. Sibert," op. cit., p. 45.

Kellerman relented, allowing Sibert and O'Neill to enter the morgue. Horne explained:

> These two guys [Sibert and O'Neill]—who knew nothing about the covert operation underway (the clandestine surgery to expand wounds and obliterate or remove evidence)—could not be allowed inside the morgue while that illicit activity was underway. They would have seen the president's body lying there on a table with his skull being X-rayed. These guys would have "lost it," they would have gone berserk, and the whole cover-up would have been blown.[28]

We know for a fact that the two FBI agents were thereafter (temporarily) barred from entering the morgue, because they wrote about this "interference" in their FD-302 (FBI) report, as documented by David Lifton in *Best Evidence.*[29] Sibert and O'Neill wrote: "Bureau agents [i.e., Sibert and O'Neill] assisted in the moving of the casket to the autopsy room. A tight security was immediately placed around the autopsy room by the naval facility [i.e., Boyajian's Marines] and the US Secret Service [i.e., Kellerman]. Bureau agents [i.e., Sibert and O'Neill] made contact with Mr. Roy Kellerman, the Assistant Secret Service Agent in Charge of the White House Detail, and advised him of the Bureau's interest in this matter."[30]

In a conversation with one of his neighbors (Jim Snyder), Humes confirmed that the two FBI agents were initially barred from the morgue. This was documented in an internal CBS memo (dated January 10, 1967). In the memo, CBS line producer Bob Richter, Snyder's neighbor,

---

28 "Interview with Douglas Horne," in William Matson Law, *In the Eye of History*, second edition, op. cit., pp. 83-117, at p. 103.

29 David Lifton, *Best Evidence*, op. cit., pp. 475-476.

30 Francis X. O'Neill, Jr. and James W. Sibert, "Autopsy of Body of President John Fitzgerald Kennedy," op. cit., p. 2.

(mis)reported to CBS senior producer Leslie Midgley: "Humes said [to Snyder] the FBI agents were not in the autopsy room during the autopsy; they were kept in an anteroom, and their report [FD-302] is simply wrong."[31] Humes told the truth about their initial exclusion from the morgue, but then he lied and said that they were not present during the entire autopsy! We know this is not true, for Sibert and O'Neill witnessed the "autopsy of record" from 8:15 until 11:00 p.m. and wrote about it in considerable detail in their FD-302 report (Appendix I). Thus, when O'Neill later testified to the ARRB that he and Sibert were never kept out of the morgue at any time, he committed perjury. In an email to the authors, Horne explained: "After Lifton's *Best Evidence* came out, the FBI agents were mortified that they had been hoodwinked by the SS and had forfeited the body's chain-of-custody and therefore had failed in their mission. (Their responsibility had been to safeguard the chain-of-custody and receive bullet fragments from the body.) On the other hand, O'Neill's response was to lie about this under oath before the ARRB."[32]

The real reason that Sibert and O'Neill were kept out of the morgue at approximately 7:17 p.m. is because the SS (i.e., Roy Kellerman) did not want them to know that illicit surgery had already occurred. Barring the FBI agents from the morgue proper at 7:17 p.m. prevented them from discovering that skull X-ray films and photographs were already being taken. *They could never be allowed to see the body lying on the morgue table; after all, they thought it was inside the Dallas casket—the one they had just wheeled in from the loading dock!* Obviously, Sibert

---

31 "CBS Memorandum from Bob Richter to Less Midgley," MD 16, ARRB Master Set of Medical Exhibits, January, 10, 1967, https://aarclibrary.org/publib/jfk/arrb/master_med_set/md16/html/Image0.htm.

32 Douglas Horne, email to the authors, September 18, 2023. In his 1997 interview with the ARRB, O'Neill insisted that he "only left [the autopsy] once" to obtain a sandwich. See: "Deposition of James W. Sibert," op. cit., p. 5.

and O'Neill had a strong motivation for lying, when they denied years later that they had been barred from the morgue when they first set the Dallas casket down in the morgue anteroom.

The second casket entry, at 7:17 p.m., is easily distinguished from the first casket entry by (1) a different casket and (2) by a different set of actors. The second entry employed four federal agents instead of Dennis David's working party of navy sailors.

THE THIRD CASKET ENTRY:

8:00 P.M., WASHINGTON, DC, NOVEMBER 22, 1963

In summary then, here was the situation at about thirty minutes before the third and final casket entry. JFK's body lay on the morgue table. The skull X-ray films had been exposed, and an initial round of photographs had been taken. The two prior caskets were probably in the anteroom (see "BURIAL CASKET" in Figure 6.2), adjacent to the main morgue.

But now the honor guard comes into focus. This team had been assembled at Andrews Air Force Base before Air Force One landed at 6:00 p.m. It included members of the US Navy, US Army, US Air Force, US Marine Corps, and US Coast Guard. The officer in charge was First Lt. Samuel Bird. All members wore dress uniforms with white gloves. They had already assisted several SS personnel with the confused and uncoordinated unloading of the Dallas casket from Air Force One into the light gray navy ambulance at Andrews Air Force Base.[33] The Joint

---

33 From Douglas Horne, email to both authors, October 8, 2023 (emphases in the original): "It is imperative that the reader understand JFK's body did not arrive at Andrews AFB on Air Force Two (AF2), as Phil Nelson claimed [Phillip F. Nelson, *LBJ: The Mastermind of JFK's Assassination* (Bloomington, IN: Xlibris, 2010)]." Douglas Horne further clarified that "Air Force Two could *not* have carried JFK's body to Washington, D.C. because AF2 landed at 6:30 p.m. local time, per an Andrews AFB logbook obtained by the ARRB. That is a 'wheels down' time and does not include taxi time to the ops terminal. Since we know with certainty that USMC Sergeant Boyajian recorded an arrival time for JFK's casket of 6:35 p.m., the body could not have arrived in Washington on AF2. *Period.* There was insufficient time to transport *any* AF2 passengers to Bethesda National Naval Medical Center (NNMC) by 6:35 p.m., *by any means.*"

Service Casket Team then flew in a helicopter to the helipad in front of the hospital. They landed at about 6:45 p.m., about ten minutes before the light gray navy ambulance arrived.[34]

Once at Bethesda, the six-man Joint Service Casket Team boarded a pickup truck and trailed a gray navy ambulance (there were two in use that night!), which they (mistakenly) believed contained the Dallas casket. Thus, they began a high speed, "wild goose chase" for ten to fifteen minutes around the grounds of the medical center. They followed a "decoy ambulance," a *second* light gray navy ambulance driven by Rear Admiral Galloway, commander of the Bethesda National Naval Medical Center (NNMC). In *Best Evidence*, David Lifton noted the eccentric episode involving the NNMC commanding officer, Rear Admiral Galloway, whose role as chauffeur was first reported in a *Washington Post* article the very next day.[35] The use of a "decoy ambulance" was documented by Army Lt. Richard Lipsey during his 1978 HSCA staff interview.[36] The explanation for this decoy ambulance was given to the confused and demoralized Joint Service Casket Team after their "wild goose chase." Lt. Bird (officer in charge of the honor guard) had been advised that this was "for security purposes" by Major General Philip Wehle (in charge of the Military District of Washington) and by Lt. Richard Lipsey (aide to General Wehle).[37] Horne described what this means (emphases in the original):

---

34 The Future of Freedom Foundation, "The JFK Medical Coverup," op. cit., slide 18.

35 David Lifton, *Best Evidence*, op. cit., p. 416. See: "Officials to View Body Today at White House," *Washington Post*, November 23, 1963, p. A-11.

36 "HSCA Interview Report of January 18, 1978, Interview of Richard A. Lipsey," MD 87, ARRB Master Set of Medical Exhibits, January 18, 1978, p. 3, https://aarclibrary.org/publib/jfk/arrb/master_med_set/md87/html/md87_0003a.htm.

37 Douglas Horne, "The AF1 Tapes and Subsequent Events at Andrews AFB on November 22, 1963," The Future of Freedom Foundation, July 8, 2013, https://www.fff.org/explore-freedom/article/the-af1-tapes-and-subsequent-events-at-andrews-afb-on-november-22-1963-what-was-supposed-to-happen-vs-what-did-happen/.

> Clearly, it was Admiral Galloway's role to mislead the Casket Team and get them to follow him. This delay provided time for the manipulations on JFK's body. Seeing a flag officer get into an ambulance and drive it away was so unusual—admirals and generals *never* drive vehicles—that it was clearly designed to attract the attention of the casket team, and it succeeded. This had to occur after 6:55 p.m., when the Andrews motorcade arrived, and before 7:07 p.m., when the ambulance Greer was driving with the Dallas casket inside, was driven around to the back of the hospital to the morgue loading dock. The timing here means Admiral Galloway was involved in the cover-up, and the casket shell game, up to his eyebrows! Galloway clearly knew what the casket team did not know…they would be allowed to "find it" outside the front of the hospital in a gray ambulance, and (in their minds) preserve the chain-of-custody and perform their intended ceremonial function as pallbearers.[38]

The Casket Team finally did locate a light-gray ambulance (with the Dallas bronze casket inside). Of all possible places, it had now returned to the front of the hospital (shortly before 8 p.m.), and so the team was finally able to perform its duties as pallbearers. They then transferred the bronze casket from the gray ambulance into the morgue at 2000 hours (8:00 p.m.), per their after-action report. Horne emphasized "the precise time given for the third casket entry [was] in the after-action report written by Lt. Bird."[39] As a result, 8 p.m. has traditionally been accepted as the official casket entry. Most of the large audience (of about thirty-five persons, plus FBI agents Sibert and O'Neill) sat in the three-tiered bleachers inside the morgue; the two FBI agents stood while taking notes in their little interview notebooks.

---

38 The Future of Freedom Foundation, "The JFK Medical Coverup," op. cit., slides 23-26.

39 Ibid.

In 1979, David Lifton interviewed two key witnesses to this third casket entry: the Chief of Surgery, David P. Osborne, and Navy Corpsman James Metzler.[40] Metzler said that as soon as the Casket Team deposited the Dallas casket onto the floor of the morgue, they left. Osborne reported that when he arrived, the casket was still closed. "It was a very elaborate casket, as one might expect." He recalled that Humes insisted that it remain closed until everyone had arrived. "We were all standing there…there was quite a delay." He recalled that "everyone" included Pierre Finck (who arrived at 8:30 p.m.—by his report). Osborne told Lifton that the delay lasted "at least fifteen, twenty, thirty minutes." After the casket was finally opened, Osborne saw a "reasonably clean," "unmarred" bullet fall from JFK's clothing onto the autopsy table.[41] "The bullet was not deformed in any way," he told Lifton. He recalled that clothing had been around JFK's body. To observers who had witnessed neither the shipping casket arrival at 6:35 p.m. (as recorded by Sergeant Roger Boyajian), nor the first arrival of the empty Dallas casket at 7:17 p.m. (as delivered by four federal agents), "nothing would appear amiss."[42]

James Jenkins told me (Mantik) emphatically that he never left the body that night. If so, especially after observing the first casket entry, how could he possibly overlook this bizarre transfer? Unhappily for his memory, however, he had previously told Lifton that he was indeed absent for one brief period.[43] He recalled that he had been sent on an errand with a SS escort—perhaps precisely so that he could not observe this eerie transfer maneuver. Regarding Jenkins's memory, recall this:

---

40 David Lifton, *Best Evidence*, op. cit., pp. 630-634 (Metzler) and 645-652 (Osborne).

41 David Lifton, *Best Evidence*, op. cit., pp. 645-646. See also: "Investigation of the Assassination of President John F. Kennedy," *House Select Committee on Assassinations (HCSA)*, U.S. House of Representatives, Ninety Fifth Congress, Second Session, March 1979, Appendix, volume 7, p. 15.

42 Douglas Horne, email to the authors, September 10, 2023.

43 Lifton, *Best Evidence,* op. cit., p. 643.

he saw a transparent plastic bag of metal and bone fragments lying next to JFK's head that night, but he had never seen these items removed from the body. He did recall that these items had been brought into the morgue by "a man in a suit and tie."[44] Clearly, these items were introduced only because they had been previously removed from JFK—surely they did not derive from some other body. So where was Jenkins when these items were extracted? Obviously not with the body.

Paul O'Connor's memory is yet another conundrum. He kept insisting that the shipping casket arrived precisely at 8 p.m. However, if he had attended the 8 p.m. entry (with the Dallas casket) and had seen the body then, he would surely have been perplexed—after all, he had seen the *first* entry, and so had promptly seen JFK's body inside the shipping casket, in a body bag, at 6:35 p.m. (But James Jenkins recalled that the head was kept wrapped at this entry, and he was told not to remove the wrapping.) Most likely, however, O'Connor (like Jenkins) was not allowed to observe this 8 p.m. entry. In fact, he tells us that in plain English: "The largest fragment in his body…that I never got to see, which was possibly retrieved by somebody standing around the table at the time the X-rays were taken, and was taken away *before I got back into the room.*" So, O'Connor (like Jenkins) was probably absent at *the exact moment* of the 8 p.m. casket entry.[45]

There is even further confirmation for his timely exclusion. In his 1977 HSCA staff interview.[46] O'Connor recalled being told to leave the morgue, after which he was placed under guard by a Marine in the hallway for possibly as long as forty minutes. He told the HSCA staff that when he returned to the morgue, one of his colleagues informed him that a bullet fragment had been removed from the intercostal

---

44 William Matson Law, *In the Eye of History*, second edition, op. cit., p. 229.

45 Ibid, p. 218. Emphasis added.

46 "O'Connor-Purdy HSCA Interview," MD 64, ARRB Master Set of Medical Exhibits, August 29, 1977, https://www.history-matters.com/archive/jfk/arrb/master_med_set/md64/html/Image0.htm.

tissue (i.e., from the thorax between the ribs). Of course, no one at the autopsy proper after 8 p.m. recalled such an event. This proves that he was ejected from the morgue at some time after 6:35 p.m. (when the body first arrived), but this ejection surely occurred before 8 p.m. O'Connor's HSCA interview summarizes a highly reliable recollection of the shipping casket and also of the body bag—reliable because others corroborated these two items. But why he initially recalled the time as 8 p.m. seems less reliable as well as less clear. Douglas Horne has concluded (and we agree) that O'Connor never saw JFK's head unwrapped at Bethesda *until shortly after 8 p.m.*, after the Joint Service Casket Team deposited the Dallas casket and quickly left the morgue.

Horne postulates that if O'Connor was not allowed to reenter the morgue until *immediately after the Casket Team departed*, he then looked at the clock and remembered the time of "approximately eight o'clock" quite vividly, for the following reason: what was graphically revealed to him at that moment, when he helped unwrap JFK's head before a large morgue audience, were the shocking results of post mortem surgery by Humes. O'Connor was stunned by a "gaping" wound in the throat (a "big old gash" that was a crudely enlarged tracheotomy), i.e., exploratory surgery that tried to locate an entering bullet or metal fragment.[47] He was also astonished by a huge, superior cranial defect devoid of most right parietal bone, as well as much absent anterior brain tissue. (O'Connor subjectively *misinterpreted* and *exaggerated* this in his statements that "nothing was left in the cranium but splattered brain matter" and "there were no brains.")[48] As Horne has explained to us (i.e., the authors), O'Connor was most likely a victim of "memory merge"; by 1977 he was *conflating* the entry of the shipping casket (at 6:35 p.m.) with his very first viewing of JFK's head (after 8 p.m.), which

47 Douglas Horne, *Inside the ARRB*, vol. 4, pp. 1014-1015.

48 Ibid.

was when he first unwrapped the bloody sheet around the cranium. That was when he first saw the macabre results of the postmortem surgery, performed by Humes to sanitize the crime scene. By then, Humes had removed bullet fragments; quite possibly he had also extracted anterior brain tissue that displayed the two frontal bullet tracks. O'Connor had ample reason to be stunned.

Here are several short excerpts from O'Connor's 1977 HSCA staff interview, which documents that he was ejected from the morgue sometime after 6:35 p.m. and prior to 8 p.m.:

> O'Connor said it was "… a funny autopsy." He said one reason was because when they started viscerating [sic] the body O'Connor was asked to leave. He noted that Jenkins remained. He said Dr. Boswell or Humes told him to go outside the room (he was guarded by a Marine while there); he remained outside for approximately thirty or forty minutes. He said that while he was outside the X-Rays of the "… entire body …" were taken, according to what an X-Ray technician told him.
>
> O'Connor returned to the room after the suturing was done and found out later he had missed the probing by the doctors. When he had returned he said the doctors had the back up and appeared to be "…very interested in it…to see what the spine looked like."
>
> O'Connor said he later asked Jenkins about what he missed and noted that they both were very afraid to talk about it. O'Connor recalls that Jenkins or someone else told him that the doctors had "… found a fragment of a bullet lodged in the intercostal muscle on the right rear side…" of the President's body. O'Connor was also told that "…a lot of blood infiltrated the intercostal muscle." O'Connor believes he was told this information by "…one of the corpsman [sic], possibly the photographer."[49]

---

49 "O'Connor-Purdy HSCA Interview," op. cit., pp. 6-7. The intercostal muscle is the muscle between the ribs that is responsible for expanding and contracting the chest during breathing.

The disappearance of most morgue personnel is also attested to by James Sibert: "That's about the time when they said, 'Well, we're going to clear everybody out of here now, and you have to go out into the hall.'"[50]

Here is yet one more clue that the third entry was distinctly separate from the first entry. Sibert (at the 8 p.m. entry) recalled seeing JFK's face when the casket was opened: "...that head was just blood soaked and it wasn't all covered up, his face wasn't all covered up because I remember you could definitely see his face."[51] No one had said this about the face at the first casket entry; it had been securely wrapped—and Jenkins had been commanded not to unwrap it. Obviously, given the tight time constraints, this *second* facial wrapping had been done rather carelessly. But what Sibert never clarified was this: When was this Dallas casket opened? Was it before—or after—everyone was evicted from the morgue? Law tried heroically to squeeze this answer out of Sibert, but he failed.

LAW: But you don't remember the sequence of—

SIBERT: I don't remember anything.[52]

On the other hand, James Jenkins does recall some things. After noting that he was instructed not to unwrap the head (after the 6:35 p.m. entry), he reports that everyone (except for O'Connor and him) was instructed to leave the room. And then, Boswell left, too! "After about 15-20 minutes, Dr. Boswell returned, he and I unwrapped the body and covered it with a sheet from the waist down." During this

---

50 William Matson Law, *In the Eye of History*, second edition, 2015, op. cit., p. 373.

51 Ibid., p. 374.

52 Ibid., p. 371.

time, Humes returned to the autopsy table. Only then was the sheet and blood-soaked towel removed from JFK's head, as Humes threw that sheet to the floor![53]

Now, taking into account O'Connor's memory merge, this event must have occurred after 8 p.m.—because, at the 6:35 p.m. event, Jenkins had been advised *not* to unwrap the sheet around the head. Jenkins, quite specifically, recalls this event; he was upset because he knew that he would later have to clean up this mess. He remembers that Humes should have just used the waste bucket instead of the floor.

Jenkins then notes that several military officers came into the morgue at this time, and "other individuals began to filter in." This description does not fit with the 6:35 p.m. casket entry, but it fits quite well with the 8 p.m. event, when the honor guard entered the morgue.

O'Connor's HSCA interview cites his absence from the morgue for thirty to forty minutes. Jenkins was also clearly absent for some time, although he seems oddly reluctant to admit this—or perhaps his memory has failed him. So, when exactly were O'Connor and Jenkins absent from the morgue? Surely, they could not be allowed to observe the body transfer from the Dallas casket to the morgue table after 8 p.m. By watching such a transfer, *for the second time,* each one would have been visibly flabbergasted. But neither one has ever commented on this outlandish sequence of events. That can only mean that they did not observe this second transfer of the body to the morgue table. As stage manager that night, SS agent Roy Kellerman shrewdly understood that these two autopsy assistants (dieners) were the critical pieces of the cover-up. At all costs, they could not be allowed to witness this second transfer. So Jenkins was sent on an errand by a SS man, while O'Connor (per his HSCA interview) remained in the hallway for thirty to forty minutes, while under Marine guard!

---

53 James Curtis Jenkins and William Matson Law, *At The Cold Shoulder of History*, op. cit., Kindle edition, about 10 percent into the book.

Only after the body had safely completed its second and final transfer to the morgue table could O'Connor and Jenkins be permitted to reenter to the morgue (probably at the same time), where they now observed that the head was still wrapped. Furthermore, by then, the Dallas casket must also have been safely returned to the anteroom, where it had been stored after its 7:17 p.m. entry. Therefore, its location after 8 p.m. now matched its earlier location, so neither O'Connor nor Jenkins, even if they had seen the Dallas casket in the anteroom, would have taken any notice. Their eternal silence, on all of these dizzying events, is fully consistent with this eccentric scenario.

In his 1977 HSCA testimony, mortician Tom Robinson recalled that the autopsy was "being moved" to a different location temporarily.[54] Robinson was asked if there was something about the autopsy that struck him as incorrect. He responded: "The time the people moved (autopsy). The body was taken…and the body never came…lots of little things like that."[55]

This sequence of three casket entries looks to me (Mantik) like a classic French farce, i.e., an affair concocted by a half-mad scriptwriter. Unfortunately, all of the evidence points strongly in the direction of three separate casket entries. Perhaps this would have been unnecessary, as Horne points out, if only Jacqueline Kennedy had not insisted on staying with the bronze casket en route to the morgue. The trouble began when she had declined a helicopter ride to the White House, which would have separated her from the Dallas casket. Most likely, the plan had been to surreptitiously transfer the body back into the empty Dallas casket at the Walter Reed Army Medical Center. In northwest Washington, DC, Walter Reed Army Medical Center is approximately

---

54 Douglas Horne, *Inside the ARRB*, op. cit., vol. 4, p. 1007.

55 Andy Purdy and Jim Conzelman, Interview of Thomas Evan Robinson, HSCA Medical Testimony and Interviews, ARRB Master Set of Medical Exhibits, January 12, 1977, p. 10, https://history-matters.com/archive/jfk/arrb/master_med_set/md63/html/Image09.htm.

one mile south of Bethesda Naval Hospital. But her unexpected decision to remain with the bronze Dallas casket waylaid those plans. This meant that Kellerman (who Horne nominates as the morgue manager) had to improvise on the spot. It was a highly risky business, during which this escapade was nearly uncovered, according to Horne.

Horne explained in more detail what the original plan had likely been:[56]

> The original intent of the conspirators seems to have been to reunite the President's body with the empty Dallas casket at Walter Reed hospital (which is co-located with the AFIP [Armed Forces Institute of Pathology]), and then take the Dallas casket, with the body inside it once again, to Bethesda. This plan was foiled by the President's widow, who refused a helicopter ride back to the White House, and instead insisted on remaining with the Dallas casket all the way to Bethesda Naval Hospital. In her loyalty, she wanted to remain with her husband's body until it reached the White House. This decision of hers, which no one could countermand, created major problems for those in charge of the cover-up who had been planning to quietly reintroduce the body back into the Dallas casket at Walter Reed. It not only created unwanted witnesses to multiple casket entries at Bethesda, and to the broken chain-of-custody for the body, but there are still indicators in the documentary record today of this original plan to go to Walter Reed—of the original intent of those managing the cover-up. LBJ's secretary onboard Air Force One took notes that indicated "body to Walter Reed," and an official USAF command history of Andrews AFB states that President Kennedy's body was transported to Walter Reed after Air Force One landed; but that doesn't mean that these things happened. Rather, these entries are a

56 Douglas Horne, *Inside the ARRB*, op. cit., vol. 4, pp. 1004-1005.

reflection of the original plans that were in place and known by others that night, up until the time that Jackie Kennedy 'upset the apple cart' of those in charge of the cover-up by deciding to remain with the Dallas casket. My 1997 ARRB interview with Dr. Dick Davis, the acting Head of Neuropathology at the AFIP (see Appendix 50), documents the fact that even though he was set up and prepared to conduct a craniotomy at the AFIP, the body never arrived at the Walter Reed compound.

Tables 6.1–6.3 summarize the three casket entries.

Table 6.1
Casket Entry #1. Morgue Loading Dock and Anteroom

Time (p.m.)	Casket Type	Witnesses	Remarks
6:35	Shipping casket	Roger Boyajian Dennis David Paul O'Connor Donald Rebentisch Floyd Riebe	Black hearse. Body was inside a black body bag. (O'Connor, Van Hoesen)

Note: The first entry was documented by Boyajian and corroborated by Dennis David, Paul O'Connor, Donald Rebentisch (navy corpsman from Dennis David's working party), Floyd Riebe (E-5 navy corpsman, medical photography student with John Stringer), Gawler's Funeral Home (first call sheet entry), and by Dr. Boswell. Source: Douglas Horne, *Inside the ARRB*, op. cit., vol. 4, pp. 1002-1013 (modified above).

Table 6.2

Casket Entry #2. Morgue Loading Dock and Anteroom

Time (p.m.)	Casket Type	Witnesses	Remarks
7:17	Bronze casket (from Dallas)	Jim Sibert Frank O'Neill Roy Kellerman William Greer	Light gray navy ambulance. Empty casket.

Note: This second entry is documented in the HSCA staff interviews of FBI Agents Sibert and O'Neill in 1977 and 1978, and by their ARRB depositions in 1997. Source: Francis X. O'Neill, Jr. and James V. Sibert, "Autopsy of Body of President John Fitzgerald Kennedy," op. cit. See also: David Lifton, *Best Evidence*, op. cit., pp. 484-485. See also: HSCA staff interview reports with O'Neill and Sibert in 1977 and 1978, and ARRB transcripts of O'Neill and Sibert depositions in 1997. Also see Appendix I in this present book.

Table 6.3

Casket Entry #3. Bethesda Morgue

Time (p.m.)	Casket Type	Witnesses	Remarks
8:00	Bronze casket (from Dallas)	Joint Service Casket Team HM3 James Metzler Admiral David Osborne	Light gray navy ambulance The body was wrapped in sheets or clothing—but no body bag.

Note: This entry was supervised by Lt. Samuel Bird from Fort Myers. Source: Douglas Horne, *Inside the ARRB*, op. cit., vol. 4, p. 1008 and vol. 1, Figure 70 (modified above). See also: Military District of Washington After-Action Report, "The Joint Casket Bearer Team," the "Bird Report" authored by First Lt. Samuel Bird, December 10, 1963, History-Matters.com, https://www.history-matters.com/archive/jfk/arrb/master_med_set/md163/html/md163_0001a.htm. See also: David Lifton, *Best Evidence*, op. cit., at 399, 406-407. See also: Jacob G. Hornberger, "The Story of Sam Bird," The Future of Freedom Foundation, FFF.org, October 31, 2023, https://www.fff.org/explore-freedom/article/the-story-of-sam-bird/.

HOW DID JFK'S BODY ORIGINALLY DISAPPEAR?

If the body arrived at 6:35 p.m. in a cheap shipping casket, when did it exit the Dallas casket? We know that the casket went onboard Air Force One at 2:14 p.m., while Jackie boarded at 2:18 p.m., and Judge

Hughes did not arrive until 2:30 p.m.[57] (Lifton again blazed this trail.) In his 2015 interview with William Matson Law, Horne disclosed that after he published his five-volume magnum opus, he studied the work of Jamie Sawa, a researcher who became a self-educated expert on Air Force One. Initially, the bronze Dallas casket with the body was loaded into the aft passenger compartment—after some seats had been removed. Sawa said the bronze casket "was placed on the left-hand side of the aft compartment in the fuselage, with the hinge alongside the left-wall of the airplane, which would have allowed the lid of the casket to be opened."[58] Horne and Sawa came to the joint conclusion that if the Dallas casket was empty when Air Force One arrived at Andrews, the body must have been removed from the bronze casket prior to the swearing in of Lyndon Johnson.[59] When Jacqueline Kennedy got settled into Air Force One (after this casket was aboard), she entered her stateroom to compose herself. Horne summed up:

> He [Sawa] and I came to the joint conclusion that the body of JFK was probably removed from the bronze Britannia casket prior to, or during, the swearing in of Lyndon Johnson. I would imagine this probably occurred prior to the swearing in, and that the body was probably then taken out of the starboard aft galley door by Secret Service agents and then placed in either the forward or aft luggage compartment prior to takeoff.[60]

---

57 Neither Manchester nor Bishop addresses every moment of the timeline from boarding until the swearing in.

58 William Matson Law, "Interview with Douglas Horne," in *In the Eye of History: Disclosures in the JFK Assassination Medical Evidence,* second edition, op. cit., pp. 83-118, at pp. 92-93.

59 Ibid.

60 Ibid., p. 93.

"So the body almost certainly was removed from that casket either before or during the swearing in, and was taken out of the aft passenger compartment [by the SS] via the starboard aft galley door."[61] Horne concluded that if Air Force Aide Godfrey McHugh stood guard over the Dallas casket during the swearing in of LBJ, as he says he did, then JFK's body must have been removed from the Dallas casket sometime between 2:20 and 2:30 p.m. prior to Judge Sarah Hughes administering the oath of office to LBJ. Intriguingly, William Manchester opens the door to another option. He documented that Godfrey McHugh left the tail section of Air Force One to go forward in order to yell at the pilots (to begin the flight)—not once, but at least three times—before the plane finally took off at 2:47 p.m. If this is true, then McHugh could not even have been continuously present with the casket before the swearing in began.

Horne indicated that transferring JFK's body from the aft galley compartment in the tail of Air Force One to the aft luggage compartment required moving the body "down a few feet, and a few feet forward," while placing it in the forward luggage compartment would have involved "moving the body the length of the airplane in broad daylight."[62] A forklift would have been required to move the body from the starboard aft galley door to one of these luggage compartments. Curiously, forklift activity was noted on the ground at Love Field, ostensibly related to the "luggage transfer" from Air Force Two to Air Force One.

In summary, Horne has concluded that the body was transferred to one of the two luggage compartments (in the hold of Air Force One), during the concurrent transfer of LBJ's luggage from Air Force Two to Air Force One, when a forklift was available. Horne has opined that the

61 Ibid., p. 94.

62 Ibid.

"casket shenanigans" began on Air Force One prior to takeoff because the SS feared that County Coroner Earl Rose and the Dallas police might appear and ask for JFK's body, demanding a Texas autopsy. Horne stressed, "It is now obvious that the principal job of the Secret Service once JFK was dead was to prevent an honest autopsy in Texas—to get JFK's body to Washington, where the autopsy results could be manipulated." After takeoff, the Kennedy loyalists held an Irish wake around the Dallas casket, but the empty casket was not opened during the flight, nor was it ever opened in the gray navy ambulance enroute to Bethesda from Andrews Air Force Base.[63]

Douglas Horne also reviewed the audiotapes of the conversations between Air Force One and Washington (made while en route to Andrews Air Force Base). The audiotapes indicated that Army General Ted Clifton (the army aide to JFK) was desperate to have Jacqueline Kennedy separated from the body upon landing.[64] The initial plan was for three helicopters to transfer the entire Kennedy entourage, including Jacqueline Kennedy, to the south grounds of the White House. Two more helicopters would go from Andrews Air Force Base to Bethesda. Roy Kellerman was told by Gerald Behn, special agent in charge (SAIC) of the White House detail: "You accompany the body aboard the helicopter."[65]

What actually happened was that Captain Canada (the commanding officer at Bethesda) sent a navy ambulance to Andrews Air Force Base because of rumors that LBJ had experienced a heart attack. When Jacqueline Kennedy saw the navy ambulance, she said, "We'll go in that." Horne noted that she had thereby "destroyed a cleverly crafted covert operation."[66] The public, watching on television, naturally assumed

63 The Future of Freedom Foundation, "The JFK Medical Coverup," op. cit., slide 14.

64 Douglas Horne, *Inside the ARRB*, op. cit., vol. 4, pp. 1099–1102.

65 The Future of Freedom Foundation, "The JFK Medical Coverup," op. cit., slides 22-23.

66 Ibid.

that the body was in the bronze casket from Dallas; after all, they saw that it had been unloaded from Air Force One and transferred to the gray navy ambulance. This ambulance quickly departed Andrews Air Force Base with Jacqueline and Robert Kennedy aboard, along with Dr. Burkley. After President Johnson deplaned, he made a brief speech before the TV cameras, then boarded the "Army One" helicopter and took off for the White House. The bright television lights were switched off only after LBJ departed Andrews Air Force Base.

Navy corpsman Paul O'Connor told author William Matson Law that he believed JFK's body arrived by helicopter at the officer's club parking lot near the rear of Bethesda Naval Hospital, about five minutes before the shipping casket was brought into the morgue. This helicopter was very loud, he said, and sounded different from helicopters that landed at the front of the hospital complex (at the usual helipad). Using O'Connor's time estimates for the helicopter, its arrival at Bethesda NNMC would have been about 6:30 p.m.[67] Horne concluded that the officer's club parking lot is where the black Cadillac hearse met the helicopter. JFK's body was then placed inside a black, zippered body bag and encased in a shipping casket provided by the funeral home, and immediately transported to the morgue via the hearse. The black Cadillac delivered the metal shipping casket to the morgue at 6:35 p.m.

Before Horne's work, I (Mantik) had become convinced that someone had messed with the throat wound, most likely to try to extract bullet fragments (which were probably not there). The evidence for this was straightforward: the two sets of witnesses—those at Parkland vs. those at Bethesda—had disagreed profoundly about the appearance of the tracheotomy. Furthermore, Malcolm Perry, who had performed the tracheotomy, claimed that he had left the throat wound "inviolate," meaning that it was easily visible after the tube was pulled. In addition, Parkland

---

67 William Matson Law, "Paul K. O'Connor," in *In the Eye of History*, second edition, op. cit., pp. 191-218, at p. 195.

resident Charles Crenshaw insisted that the tracheotomy at Parkland was nothing like the incision in the autopsy photographs. Furthermore, I had also had my own (telephone) encounter with the autopsy radiologist, John Ebersole.[68] I still sense the horror in his voice as he recalled the tracheotomy and declared that he would never do one like that. Horne's witnesses (there are more) only validate my prior conclusion about throat tampering. Horne has now finally concluded that the throat wound was not tampered with while en route to the morgue; rather it was Humes himself who did this. I have no evidence to the contrary.

Horne does not believe that JFK's head wounds were tampered with prior to the arrival of the body at Bethesda; David Lifton was just plain wrong about that, he has concluded. The head wound descriptions (and diagrams) provided by mortician Tom Robinson to the ARRB[69] and the head wound descriptions provided to JFK researchers Henry Hurt[70] and Michael Kurtz[71] by Admiral Burkley and Captain Canada prove conclusively to Horne that JFK arrived at Bethesda with the same head wounds *as seen in Dallas*. Horne now believes that the throat wound was expanded *at Bethesda*, just as the head wound was. Unless the intervention occurred onboard Air Force One (for which we have no evidence), the timeline leaves no option for surgery elsewhere. Furthermore, no witness reports such early tampering, so this remains an unsupported Lifton speculation. So, I am on Horne's side here, too.

---

68 David W. Mantik, trans. "Conversation with John Ebersole, MD of 2 December 1992," in *Murder in Dealey Plaza*, op. cit., pp. 433 and 436. Actually, Ebersole practiced my own specialty of radiation oncology.

69 "ARRB Meeting Report Summarizing 6/21/96 In-Person Interview of Tom Robinson," MD 180, ARRB Master Set of Medical Exhibits, op. cit.

70 Henry Hurt, *Reasonable Doubt: An Investigation into the Assassination of John F. Kennedy* (New York: Holt, Rinehart and Winston, 1985), p. 49. See also: William Matson Law, "Interview with Douglas Horne," in *In the Eye of History*, op. cit., p. 105.

71 Michael Kurtz, *The JFK Assassination Debates: Lone Gunman versus Conspiracy* (Lawrence, KS: University Press of Kansas, 2006). For Dr. Burkley's description of JFK's wounds, see pp. 39-40.

While the autopsy photographs depict a radically enlarged tracheotomy,[72] that does not prove tampering before Bethesda; it just had to occur before the photographs were taken. The (illicit) surgeon was looking for a bullet (or metal fragments), but perhaps there never was any such bullet, as I have suggested in describing the glass fragments that struck JFK's neck from the frontal shot through the windshield.[73] At Bethesda, the skull (upon arrival of JFK's body at 6:35 p.m.) had the same (right occipital) exit wound as at Parkland and the brain had not yet been removed. (Lifton was wrong about that, too.) So, the initial Bethesda brain looked like the Parkland brain. When the body arrived at Bethesda, the brain still contained all of the bullet fragments from Dealey Plaza. Of course, most of these metal fragments are absent from the official record today.

WHY PERFORM ILLICIT SURGERY?

Horne stressed that the throng of high-level military commanders and military physicians who met the body at the landing dock at 6:35 p.m. were there to conduct "an immediate cursory inspection of [JFK's] wounds," so as to give Humes and Boswell "instructions from their military superiors."[74] Horne explained:

> I think that the first cursory examination of JFK's body must have quickly confirmed what they already knew: "The President has been killed by a crossfire in Dallas, and it was an ambush. We can't tell that to the American people, can't admit JFK was killed by an international communist conspiracy, because if we do, the people will demand that

72 Douglas Horne, *Inside the ARRB*, op. cit., vol. 1, at Figure 60.

73 David W. Mantik, "Paradoxes of the JFK Assassination: The Medical Evidence Decoded," in *Murder in Dealey Plaza*, op. cit., pp. 258-259.

74 William Matson Law, "Interview with Douglas Horne," in *In the Eye of History*, op. cit., pp. 103-104.

his death be avenged and we will have World War III on our hands, and millions will be killed in a nuclear exchange." I think they were given a very nice, simple national security cover story, very similar to the one above. I think it was the "WW III cover story," because it's the same one Lyndon Johnson used on Chief Justice Earl Warren, to get him to chair the Warren Commission.[75]

He continued:

I think that from the moment the body arrived, and perhaps prior to that, Drs. Humes and Boswell already had their marching orders, and those marching orders were: "You are going to inspect the damage and remove any evidence of shots from the front, and you are only going to put in the record the evidence you find of shots from behind."[76]

Horne explained that after a brief, initial examination of JFK's wounds, the military brass had determined upon their strategy; Humes and Boswell were then coached to execute the plan. Horne explained:

Their decision: the entrance wound above the right eye had to be surgically obliterated, removed. (It was, but the evidence of its removal—a bright red, bloody "V" shaped incision, remained as evidence of postmortem surgery.) The exit wound in the rear of the skull had to be grossly expanded, for two reasons: (1) to gain access to the brain and remove all noteworthy bullet fragments from the cranium, so as to remove all gross evidence of crossfire; and (2) this modified craniotomy, or radical expansion of the Dallas exit wound to five times its original size, to include the top and right side of the head,

75 Ibid., p. 104.

76 Ibid.

created a truly massive cranial defect that could then be represented as an "exit wound" in the top and right side of the skull, as if it had resulted from a shot from behind. [This is what Lifton referred to as "changing the geometry of the shooting."][77]

Horne continued:

Any brain tissue that showed a clear bullet track consistent with a shot from the front would have been removed also. I am convinced that when we look at the [extant] autopsy photographs… two thirds of those photos that are in the record today, were taken immediately after this postmortem cranial surgery. So instead of the entry wound high above the right eye (which was obscured by the President's bangs in Dallas, an entry that was recalled by Dennis David (in the Pitzer photos), seen by Tom Robinson in the morgue, and recalled by USIA photographer Joe O'Donnell from a postmortem photo shown to him by Robert Knudsen, what we see now (instead of an entry wound high above the right eye) is a rather dramatic, bright red V-shaped incision, that to me is evidence of postmortem surgery and removal of an entrance wound high above the right eye. Behind the "V" shaped incision are two pieces of white bone that appear to have been split apart and pushed aside by the force of the frontal bullet as it entered. The "V" shaped incision is startlingly clear in the color positive transparencies in the National Archives.[78]

Dennis David claimed that his friend Lieutenant Commander William Pitzer (head of the audiovisual department at Bethesda) had a 16 mm movie film as well as both black-and-white and color stills, and

---

77 Ibid., pp. 106-107.

78 Ibid., p. 107.

35 mm slides (all presumably made from the 16 mm film) of JFK's body, which was taken prior to the illicit surgery. David claimed that Pitzer's films and photographs clearly showed the exit wound in the right occiput, an entry wound near the right ear, and an entry wound in the right forehead at the hairline. David's recollection is complicated by Pitzer's untimely death (ruled a suicide, but fiercely disputed by his family[79]) and by the (unsurprising) disappearance of Pitzer's films.[80]

White House photographer Robert Knudsen claimed that he took photographs of JFK in the Bethesda morgue. He showed these to USIA photographer Joe O'Donnell, who was frequently detailed to the White House during the Kennedy era. O'Donnell claimed that, within a month of the assassination, he saw autopsy photographs from Knudsen on two occasions. On the first occasion, O'Donnell "remember[ed] a photograph of a gaping wound in the back of the head, which was big enough to put a fist through, in which the image clearly showed a total absence of hair and bone, and a cavity which was the result of a lot of interior matter missing from inside the cranium."[81] O'Donnell also

---

79 According to Harold A. Rydberg, Finck not only participated in JFK's autopsy, but also in the autopsy of William Pitzer. Finck was also involved in the case of the My Lai massacre (March 16, 1968) and Second Lt. William Calley (Law, second edition, op. cit., p. 418). Finck seems to have been yet another "man for all seasons."

80 Douglas Horne, *Inside the ARRB*, op. cit., vol. 2, pp. 380-385.

See also: "Dennis D. David," in *In the Eye of History*, William Matson Law, op. cit., pp. 183-190. See also: David W. Mantik, foreword to *In the Eye of History*, by William Matson Law, op. cit., pp. 147-156, at pp. 148-149.

81 ARRB interview with Joe O'Donnell, February 28, 1997, ARRB Medical Interviews, Phone Interview Report, MaryFerrell.org, https://www.maryferrell.org/pages/ARRB_Medical_Interviews.html.

See also: Gary L. Aguilar, MD, "The Converging Medical Case for Conspiracy in the Death of JFK," in *Murder in Dealey Plaza*, op. cit., pp. 175-218, at p. 209.

See also: "ARRB Call Reports of Telephone Interviews of Mr. Joe O'Donnell," MD 231, ARRB Master Set of Medical Exhibits, January 29 and February 28, 1997, https://www.history-matters.com/archive/jfk/arrb/master_med_set/md231/html/md231_0002a.htm.

recalled the entrance wound in the right forehead at the hairline. On the second viewing, Knudsen showed him a photograph "in which the back of the head now looked completely intact...the hair...was wet, clean, and freshly combed."[82] On this second viewing, the wound over the right eye had disappeared. Knudsen insisted that he had developed negatives from the autopsy (even though no one saw him there—or in the darkroom); he claimed that at least one image (now missing from the HSCA inventory) showed a metal probe (or probes) through JFK's body. One entered the back at a lower level than the throat wound. As Gary Aguilar, MD, noted: "If the back wound was indeed lower than its supposed exit mate in the throat, Oswald simply didn't do it."[83]

I (Mantik) agree with Horne: when the body arrived at Bethesda at 6:35 p.m., it showed the same avulsed exit wound (in the right occiput) as at Parkland. Furthermore, the brain had not yet been removed from the skull. The illicit surgery by Humes and Boswell expanded wounds in order to access metal debris in the brain and to obfuscate the obvious forehead entry wound. After this illicit surgery was completed, the plan was to reintroduce the body into the Dallas casket and reunite the military casket team with the Dallas casket before the official autopsy, thus forging the appearance of an unbroken chain-of-custody.[84]

Horne noted that Harrison Livingstone had interviewed James Jenkins for his 1992 book *High Treason 2*.[85] One detail made a huge impact on Horne (emphases in the original):

See also: David W. Mantik, "Paradoxes of the JFK Assassination: The Medical Evidence Decoded," in *Murder in Dealey Plaza,* op. cit., p. 242-243.

See also: Douglas Horne, *Inside the ARRB*, op. cit., vol. 2, pp. 287-291.

82 Ibid.

83 Gary L. Aguilar, MD, "The Converging Medical Case for Conspiracy in the Death of JFK," in *Murder in Dealey Plaza*, op. cit., pp. 175-218, at p. 208.

84 Douglas Horne, "The JFK Medical Coverup," op. cit.

For Horne's narrated slide show see: The Future of Freedom Foundation, "The JFK Medical Coverup," op. cit., slide 24.

85 Harrison Edward Livingstone, *High Treason 2*, op. cit.

> At one point during the interview, Jenkins told Livingstone that early in the evening, after the President's body had arrived, "The head remained wrapped in sheets and towels...we were specifically told not to remove the sheets and towels." Eureka! This statement of Jenkins has great significance to me. I believe he is recalling instructions given to "audience one" that had just witnessed the President's arrival in a shipping casket at 6:35 p.m., and removed the body from the body bag and placed it on the examining table. It would make sense that they were told *not to remove the wrappings around the head* prior to being cleared from the morgue. Those controlling the coverup would not have wanted audience one to see the way the exit wound looked in Dallas or to see Dr. Humes performing his clandestine postmortem surgery to the brain.[86]

Horne noted that, without mortician Tom Robinson and X-ray technologists Jerrol Custer and Edward Reed, we might not know about this illicit surgery. Horne continued (emphases in the original):

> The two mistakes made by whoever was in charge of the coverup before Kellerman arrived, were: (1) that Gawler's mortician Tom Robinson was allowed to remain in the morgue; and (2) that likewise, navy x-ray technicians Custer and Reed were also allowed to remain. Once the surgery began, Reed and Custer were summarily dismissed, and then recalled about 15 minutes later; but Robinson (fortunately for us) was unaccountably allowed to remain throughout the entire procedure. If not for these crucial mistakes in regard to who was dismissed, we would still not be able to figure out today *when and where* the head wound was altered. The Jenkins recollection that "audience one" was initially told *not to unwrap the President's head* is strong corroboration for my hypothesis that the head wound was altered

86 Douglas Horne, *Inside the ARRB*, op. cit., vol. 4, p. 1035.

at the Bethesda morgue, and not at Walter Reed or Love Field; the conspirators did not want witnesses who were not "read in" on the cover-up (like Ebersole and Canada) to see the original, "Dallas" exit wound in the back of the head.[87]

Horne concluded that Robinson arrived with the Cadillac hearse (with the body) at 6:35 p.m. After that, he simply observed events from the gallery. Contrary to Reed, he was not asked to leave. Just before 7 p.m., Robinson saw Humes and Boswell use a saw to remove large portions from the rear and top of the skull, in order to access the brain.[88] (Robinson was not aware that this activity was off the record.) He also observed ten or more bullet fragments extracted from the brain; these were placed into a glass vial and were never officially entered as evidence in the case. Furthermore, although these do not appear in the official record either, Dennis David also recalled[89] preparing a receipt for at least four additional fragments. Dennis David's four fragments were noticeably larger (in total mass) than the ten tiny fragments Robinson recalled. Dennis David consistently stated (to Lifton and to the ARRB) that his four fragments totaled more mass than one bullet, but less mass than two complete bullets.[90]

So why does Horne conclude that Humes and Boswell illicitly removed (and altered) the brain shortly after 6:35 p.m., before the official autopsy began? I (Mantik) agree with Horne on the importance of the two *R*'s, namely Reed and Robinson. Rather consistently with one

---

87 Ibid.

88 Douglas Horne, *Inside the ARRB*, op. cit. vol. 4, p. 1005.

89 David Lifton, *Best Evidence*, op. cit., p. 579.

90 "ARRB Call Report Summarizing 2/14/97 Telephonic Interview of Dennis David, "MD 177, ARRB Master Set of Medical Exhibits, Assassinations Archives Research Center, February 14, 1997, aarclibrary.org/publib/jfk/arrb/master_med_set/pdf/md177.pdf.

another, but quite independently, both describe critical steps by Humes and Boswell that no one else reported seeing after 8:00 p.m. Horne documented why no one else reported these events—almost everyone else had been deliberately evicted from the morgue. After the body was placed on the morgue table (and before X-ray films were taken), Reed had briefly sat in the gallery (Figure 6.2). Reed stated that Humes first used a scalpel across the top of the forehead, so that he could then reflect, and pull the scalp back.[91] Then he used a saw to cut the frontal bone above the forehead (just above the hairline) from left to right, after which Reed (and Custer, too) were asked to leave the morgue. (Reed was not aware that this intervention by Humes was unofficial.) This activity was augmented by Humes when he made a separate incision high in the forehead to obliterate and remove the small entrance wound in the forehead above the right eye. The autopsy photographs show a blatant red incision at this site. This red incision was very different in character from the entry wound seen in postmortem photographs by Dennis David and Joe O'Donnell. No Parkland witness ever saw this incision, but Quentin Schwinn saw an apparent original autopsy photograph (in the early 1980s) that showed the original entrance wound—prior to its removal by surgical incision. The implication is obvious: this specific entry wound was purposefully obliterated (Figure 6.4).

---

91 Douglas Horne, *Inside the ARRB*, op. cit. vol. 4, pp. 1163-1171, and vol. 2, pp. 426 and 437.

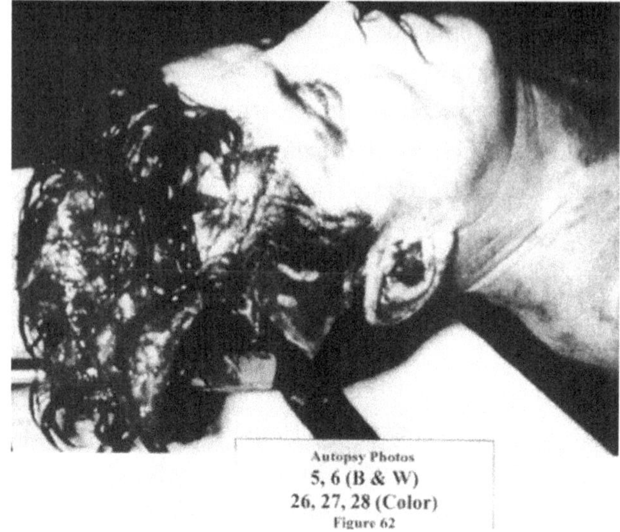

Figure 6.4
JFK Autopsy Photo with Likely Pre-Autopsy Incision by Humes, Source: Douglas Horne, *Inside the ARRB*, op. cit., vol. 1, Figure 62

Horne described how Reed watched Humes and Boswell remove JFK's brain from the skull (capital letters and brackets in the original):

> In his deposition before us in 1997, navy x-ray tech Ed Reed described how Dr. Humes had taken a scalpel and cut open JFK's scalp from left to right, high in the frontal bone above what the layman would call the forehead, just inside the hairline. After making this incision, Reed testified that Humes then took a circular bone saw to the same area and began cutting the bone. At this point, Reed says, he and Custer were summarily dismissed. [They were recalled to the morgue a short time later, to take the skull x-rays—which like the surviving autopsy photos were taken AFTER the cranial surgery was completed.][92]

92 William Matson Law, "Interview with Douglas Horne," *In the Eye of History*, op. cit., p. 109.

Horne commented that Reed's testimony was "extremely significant" since Humes "testified before the Warren Commission in 1964 that he never had to perform a craniotomy, since the skull wound was so large." Horne noted that Humes also "repeated this incredible fish story before the HSCA and the ARRB."[93]

Horne clarified that Robinson had also witnessed the modified craniotomy:

> Gawler's mortician Tom Robinson is the other witness to postmortem cranial surgery, and he told both the HSCA staff in 1977 and the ARRB staff in 1996, that he witnessed the doctors saw open the skull to get to the brain, and that he then saw the brain removed.[94]

Horne described how Robinson made a sketch for the ARRB of what he had witnessed, using an anatomical template. He sketched a circular wound about the size of an orange squarely on the back of the head. Above and below the wound, Robinson drew dotted lines (Figure 6.5).

---

93 Ibid.

94 Ibid.

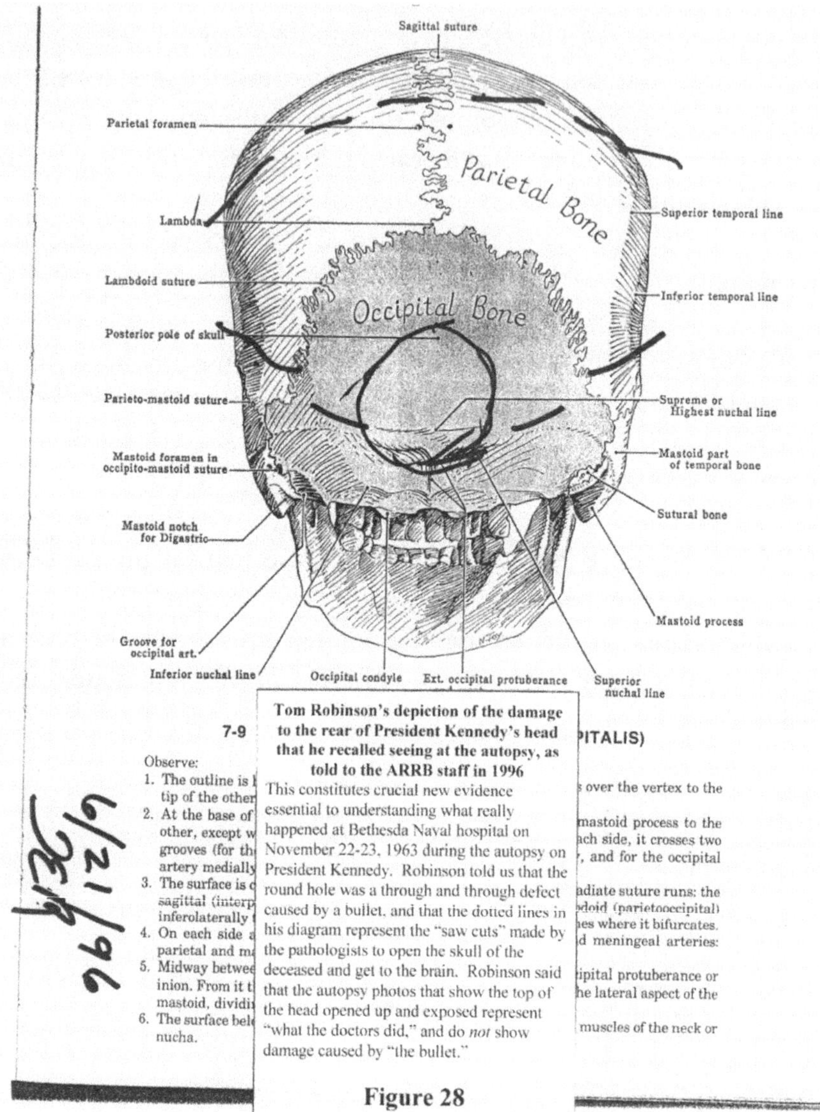

Figure 6.5

Mortician Tom Robinson sketched the exit wound, using dotted horizontal lines above and below the wound to show where Humes sawed the skull open in order to access the brain. Source: "Drawings of President Kennedy's Head Wounds prepared for ARRB by Thomas E. Robinson on 6/21/96," MD 88, ARRB Master Set of Medical Exhibits, https://history-matters.com/archive/jfk/arrb/master_med_set/md88/html/md88_0004a.htm.

Horne continued his narrative:

> Jeremy Gunn asked Tom Robinson what the dotted lines represented, and he immediately answered, "That's where the doctors sawed the skull open to get to the brain." This was an electrifying moment, I can tell you, for it confirmed that the postmortem surgery took place at Bethesda Naval Hospital. [One year later, in 1997, Ed Reed provided independent corroboration of this.][95]

He expressed their (his and Gunn's) reaction to this:

> Jeremy Gunn and I exchanged significant glances when Robinson made that statement about the doctors having to saw open the skull to get to the brain; we knew we had achieved a significant breakthrough in the case. Postmortem surgery had been confirmed, and its location had been confirmed: Bethesda Naval Hospital.[96]

Next, Gunn and Horne showed Robinson an autopsy photograph from the bootlegged Fox set. This showed "almost the entire top of JFK's head removed, with the rear of his skull resting in the U-shaped metal brace [that was not typically used in the Bethesda morgue], and a good two-thirds of the cranial skull cap removed [Figure 6.5], with nothing but lacerated scalp and brain tissue visible."[97]

---

95 Ibid., p. 109.

96 Ibid., p. 110.

97 Ibid. Brackets added to the original.

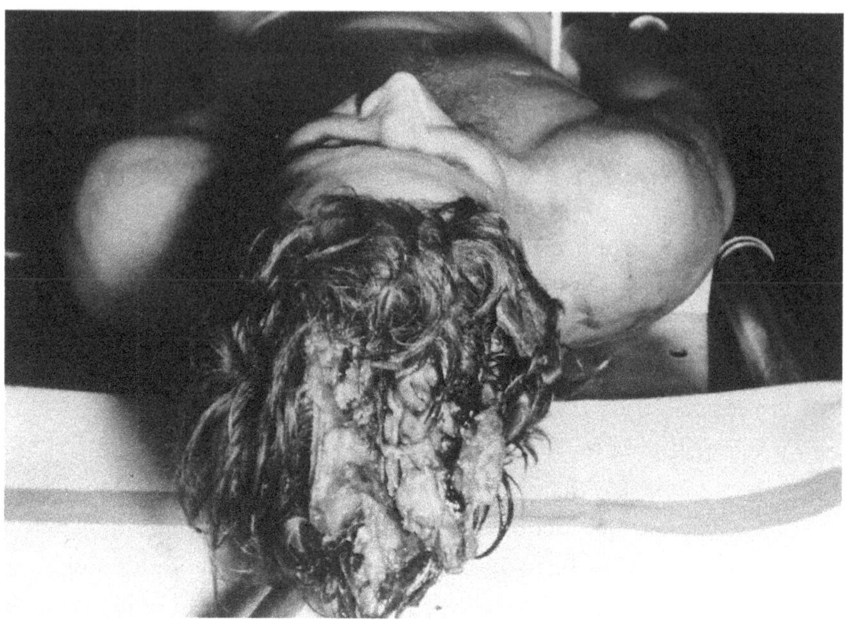

Figure 6.6
Autopsy Photograph the ARRB Showed to Mortician Tom Robinson. Source: The Future of Freedom Foundation, "The JFK Medical Coverup," op. cit., slide 34.

What was Robinson's reaction? Horne continued (emphases in the original):

> He [Robinson] immediately frowned with disapproval and said, "This makes it look like the bullet did that. But all this [damage] was what the doctors did." Now THAT was an electrifying moment. The hair stood up on the back of my neck—it was one of only three or four times when that happened while I was on the staff of the ARRB. This was the moment I knew that there had been a cover-up of the medical evidence by the US government, for Humes denied until his death that he had ever performed a craniotomy to gain access to the brain. These denials were the lies of a guilty man who was carrying out the orders of his superiors to sanitize a crime scene.[98]

98 Ibid. Brackets added to the original.

Contrary to Reed and Robinson, Humes declared that a saw was not essential:

> We had to do virtually no work with a saw to remove these portions of the skull, they came apart in our hands very easily, and we attempted to further examine the brain.[99]

Although James Jenkins does not explicitly describe a saw, he recalled that damage to the brain (as viewed inside the skull) was less than the corresponding damage to the skull; this indirectly implies surgical removal of some of the skull—before the official autopsy.[100] Horne stressed that Boswell's autopsy sketch (Figure 6.7) clearly depicted almost all of the skull vertex as absent.

99 "Testimony of Commander James J. Humes," Hearings before the President's Commission on the Assassination of President Kennedy, op. cit., vol. 2, p. 354.

100 Douglas Horne, *Inside the ARRB*, op. cit., vol. 4, pp. 1042-1043.

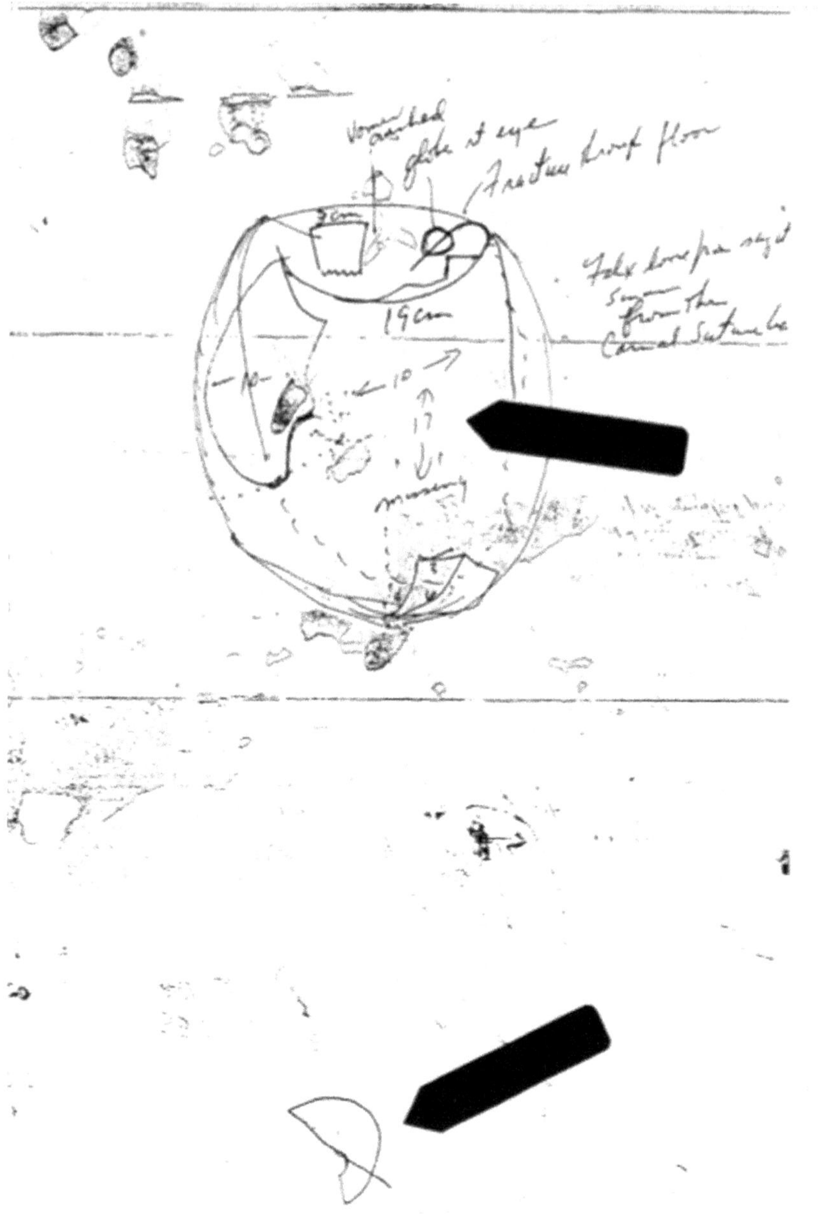

Figure 6.7

Boswell's Sketch on the Autopsy Descriptive Sheet (aka Face Sheet) Note: 10 x 17 cm area of bone was missing from the top of the skull. Source: The Future of Freedom Foundation, "The JFK Medical Coverup," op. cit., slide 46.

Horne, in volume 4 of *Inside the ARRB*, summarized Robinson's observation of Humes and Boswell's illicit premortem surgery; it occurred at approximately 6:56–7:00 p.m. in the Bethesda morgue (emphases in the original):

> Tom Robinson witnesses "the doctors" removing significant portions of the rear and top of the President's skull with a saw, to gain access to the brain. [He recalls this vividly, but matter-of-factly, to the ARRB in 1996.] He also witnesses numerous bullet fragments removed from the brain (which he recalls for both the HSCA and the ARRB). I have concluded that Humes surgically removed evidence of a bullet's entry from very high up in the right forehead above the right eye, leaving evidence of this illicit, post mortem surgery in the form of an ugly, bright red incision high in the right forehead which *no one recalls seeing in Dallas at Parkland Hospital.* Humes also removed significant portions of brain tissue from the forebrain, to eliminate any evidence of a bullet track which would prove there was a shot from the front. He removed at least 10 bullet fragments from the brain (per Tom Robinson), and at least 4 of them were large enough to warrant a receipt being prepared (per Dennis David). A bullet may also have been removed from behind the right ear (per the FBI headquarters memo written the night of the autopsy from Alan Belmont to Clyde Tolson).[101]

Horne concluded that Humes and Boswell had (disingenuously) depicted the results of their own postmortem surgery as if it were due to a bullet. Horne commented that Humes burned all of his other autopsy notes, but not Boswell's diagram (Figure 6.7). When asked under oath by the ARRB, Humes could not explain why only this one page remained. Horne suspected that this diagram was a "con job" just

---

101 Douglas Horne, *Inside the ARRB*, op. cit., vol. 4, p. 1005.

like "all of the autopsy photographs of the head with the metal head brace [Figures 6.4 and 6.6]." So, this diagram seemed to represent the extensive damage from a bullet, but not from a "modified craniotomy, which is what it really was." Humes concluded that Boswell's autopsy diagram depicted the true extent of the "surgery to the head area" admitted during the official autopsy by a panicked Dr. Humes and recorded by FBI agents Sibert and O'Neill in their FD-302 report.[102]

In their report, Sibert and O'Neill had quoted what Dr. Humes had said in front of a large morgue audience after 8:00 p.m. Horne made it clear that, in 1966, Sibert and O'Neill had confirmed internally to the FBI that they had recorded Humes's exact words: there had been "surgery of the head area, namely, in the top of the skull."[103] Horne noted that "Humes panicked, and to combat the astonishment and no-doubt skeptical comments from the gallery about the enormous head wound supposedly caused by one bullet, he blurted out a cover for himself, declaring that 'someone' (clearly not him!) had performed surgery on the top of the skull."[104] Paul O'Connor recalled (in the documentary, *The Men Who Killed Kennedy*) that, when he first saw the head wound unwrapped from the white sheet, he was shocked. "What I saw was the whole side of his head blown off," O'Connor said. "It was gone."[105] When Humes was greeted by open astonishment at the moment the audience first saw the head wounds, his terrified response had been to claim prior surgery to the head, although not performed by him.

At this point, James Jenkins has recalled that Boswell played along

---

102 The Future of Freedom Foundation, "The JFK Medical Coverup," op. cit., slide 46.

103 William Matson Law, "Interview with Douglas Horne," in *In the Eye of History*, op. cit., p. 110.

104 Ibid., pp. 110-111.

105 Paul O'Connor, in Nigel Turner's *The Men Who Killed Kennedy*, episode one, "The Coup d'État," at 30:10 into the video. See also: Richard Bradley, "*The Men Who Killed Kennedy Full Series,*" September 26, 2019, https://www.youtube.com/watch?v=G0XNiu-yutk.

by asking senior officers in the gallery, "Was there surgery in Dallas?" Of course, there had not been any surgery to the skull in Dallas; Boswell knew this because he had just watched Humes perform this precise surgery. Humes was merely play acting with the audience when he made his surgery statement; he was engaged in *dissociation.* In other words, "I see what you see, but because I'm admitting to that, of course I didn't do it."[106] When queried by the FBI circa 1966, after Lifton began asking questions of the FBI, Sibert and O'Neill both insisted that they only recorded direct quotes from the pathologists. They did not paraphrase anything. When asked at his ARRB deposition if he saw any evidence of surgery to JFK's skull, Humes perjured himself and answered "No."[107]

We should go on to ask: What other evidence exists for this illicit surgery? Lifton initially introduced this issue by citing the FBI report (by Sibert and O'Neill), which quoted Humes as describing head surgery.[108] Sibert, in the 2000s, still insisted that they had quoted Humes correctly about such surgery.[109] (I also heard Sibert say this in Fort Myers, Florida, during one of Law's taping sessions.) Furthermore, the FBI had no reason to fabricate such a statement. On Lifton's tape (which I have heard), he queried Humes about this; to me, Humes did sound remarkably suspicious and evasive. But the FBI men are not the only witnesses to this statement (of surgery to the head). Another is James Jenkins, who said Boswell asked if they did surgery at Parkland.[110] Furthermore,

106 William Matson Law, "Interview with Douglas Horne," in *In the Eye of History,* op. cit., p. 111.

107 "Deposition of Dr. James Joseph Humes," corrected transcript, op. cit. p. 73.

108 David Lifton, *Best Evidence,* op. cit., pp. 295-307.

109 William Matson Law, "James W. Sibert & Francis X. O'Neil," parts one, two, and three, in *In the Eye of History,* op. cit., pp. 281-412.

110 Douglas Horne, "The James Curtis Jenkins Revelations at JFK Lancer Confirm a Massive Medical Cover-up in 1963," InsideTheARRB.livejournal.com [blog], November 26, 2013, https://insidethearrb.livejournal.com/10811.html.

Humes was later told, when some skull fragments arrived at the morgue, that these had been "removed" during surgery at Parkland. We know that did not happen during the official autopsy, so where did these bone fragments come from? Horne implied that Humes himself had removed them during the illicit surgery, before the official autopsy.

In his volume 4, Horne expanded on Humes's comments about prior surgery. He clarified that Sibert and O'Neill had confirmed internally to the FBI in 1966 that they had recorded Humes's exact words: there had been "surgery of the head area, namely, in the top of the skull."[111] Horne explained Humes's excited utterance:

> In front of the large morgue audience following the second Dallas casket entry at 8:00 p.m.—remember, this is audience #2, who knew nothing about the clandestine surgery that Humes had performed earlier that evening—it is clear to me that Humes panicked, and to combat the astonishment and no-doubt skeptical comments from the gallery about the enormous head wound supposedly caused by one bullet, he blurted out a cover for himself, declaring that "someone" (clearly not him!) had performed surgery on the top of the skull. At least one other witness in the morgue recalls him asking if surgery had been performed in Dallas (Humes clearly knew that was not the case, since he had performed it himself at Bethesda).[112]

Douglas Horne distinguished between two audiences. Audience one observed events at 6:35 p.m., when the black hearse delivered the body in a shipping casket and a body bag. They witnessed the illicit pre-autopsy surgery. Audience two witnessed the official autopsy shortly after 8:00 p.m., when the Casket Team wheeled the bronze Dallas casket into the morgue.

---

111 William Matson Law, "Interview with Douglas Horne," in *In the Eye of History,* op. cit., p. 110.

112 Ibid., pp. 110-111.

Another supporting argument is the remarkable ease of removing the brain from the skull (during the official autopsy phase), but this is not so surprising if it had previously been removed during the unofficial phase. James Jenkins[113] observed that the brainstem had been cut, as if by a scalpel (i.e., it was not severed by a bullet), which also suggests its earlier removal. In any case, such an early removal was likely required for any attempt to extract bullet debris. Even Finck[114] bore witness to a transected spinal cord: to the defense team at the Shaw trial in 1969, Finck stated that the autopsy report (presumably an earlier one, as the extant one [Appendix J] does not say this) described the spinal cord as severed when the body arrived at Bethesda. Finck had not yet arrived at the morgue when the brain was removed during the official autopsy, so someone must have told him about this; most likely it was Humes. (Per his notes to General Blumberg in 1965, Finck stated that when he arrived at the morgue at 8:30 p.m., the brain, heart, and lungs had already been removed.)[115]

The reader might well ask why Reed and Robinson (and Custer, too) were permitted to observe (at least briefly) this illegal surgery by Humes and Boswell. Horne emphasized that the morgue manager that night (Roy Kellerman) was not present for the first casket entry at 6:35

---

113 Douglas Horne, *Inside the ARRB*, op. cit., vol. 4, p. 1037.

114 Ibid., pp. 1036-1037.

115 "Commander Humes, MC, USN, Director of Laboratories, Naval Medical School, National Naval Medical Center, Bethesda, Maryland, called me at home by telephone on 22 Nov 1963, 2000 hours. He told me to go immediately to the Naval Hospital....The brain, the heart and the lungs had been removed before my arrival. X ray films of the head and chest had been taken.... The autopsy had been in progress for thirty minutes when I arrived....Cdr. Humes told me that he only had to prolong the lacerations of the scalp before removing the brain. No sawing of the skull was necessary....The CONVOLUTIONS of the brain are flat and the SULCI are narrow, but this is interpreted as a fixation artifact because the change was not observed at the time of autopsy." [Upper case, as in the original.] Source: "Personal notes on the Assassination of President Kennedy, " Pierre Finck memorandums, jfk-assassination.net, February 1, 1965, https://www.jfk-assassination.net/weberman/finck1.htm.

p.m.—that was because he was riding with Jacqueline Kennedy and the bronze casket in the gray navy ambulance. Therefore, before he arrived at the morgue (most likely shortly after 7:00 p.m.), there was no hands-on stage manager in the morgue. It is even possible that Kellerman himself ejected Reed and Custer as soon as he arrived. Robinson, on the other hand, dressed in civilian clothing and a rather young funeral home employee, may have seemed to Kellerman to be merely an insignificant person, so he was simply ignored.

Several conclusions follow from this. First, the official skull X-ray films[116] cannot reliably show the condition of the skull or the brain as seen at Parkland. Instead, they were taken after tampering by Humes and Boswell, perhaps even after significant tampering, especially if Robinson and Reed are correct. Furthermore, the massive damage seen in the photographs and X-ray films was not caused just by a bullet or even by multiple bullets, but instead by the hands of the pathologists. In particular, for a single, full metal-jacketed bullet (the WC's inevitable scenario) to generate such an enormous defect has always defied belief.[117] Likewise, Boswell's sketch (for the ARRB) of this enormous defect on a skull model only shows the condition of the skull after tampering by Humes and Boswell—and cannot reflect the skull as seen at Parkland.[118] The wound descriptions of the Parkland witnesses fully concur with this.

---

116 Douglas Horne, *Inside the ARRB*, op. cit., vol. 1, Figures 37-38.

117 See: Boswell's sketch from the autopsy, in Douglas Horne, *Inside the ARRB,* op. cit., vol. 1, Figure 11.

118 Douglas Horne, *Inside the ARRB*, op. cit., vol. 1, Figures 12-15.

What Was the Goal of the Covert Operation at Bethesda Naval Hospital?

1. **Remove All Evidence of Frontal Shots from JFK's Body Before the "Autopsy of Record" Began:**
   - Expand wounds (postmortem surgery) to obtain access to bullets.
   - Remove all metal from the body: "sanitize the crime scene."
   - To the extent possible, obliterate frontal entry wounds.
   - Report only shots from behind during the autopsy of record, in front of audience witnesses; do not report shots from the front.
   - Ensure that the official autopsy report is consistent with the official cover story: one lone shooter, from above and behind.
2. **Reintroduce JFK's Body into the Dallas Casket and reunite the Military Casket Team (from Andrews [Air Force Base]) with the Dallas Casket before the autopsy of record, creating the appearance of an unbroken chain-of-custody.**

Figure 6.8
What Was the Purpose of Illicit Surgery? Source: The Future of Freedom Foundation, "The JFK Medical Coverup," op. cit., slide 24.

BULLET FRAGMENTS WERE REMOVED

JFK was struck by three headshots, probably more than one after Z-313. The precise sequence of the three headshots can be debated. Most likely, the EOP shot deposited bullet fragments in the brain.[119] Of the two frontal headshots (possibly included in the final "flurry" that so many witnesses recall), one struck high in the right forehead, leaving behind the metallic trail now seen on the X-ray films. The other (an oblique shot) struck near the right ear, exited via the occiput, and simultaneously

119 Curiously enough, although the X-ray films do not exhibit such a trail, the autopsy report describes precisely such a trail of metallic debris (on the lateral X-ray films), ascending from the EOP. Maybe, after all, Humes did not lie about seeing such a trail—perhaps he had merely removed these fragments before the extant X-ray films were taken.

ejected the Harper fragment. This one also likely deposited bullet fragments within the brain (recall the Belmont memo about the bullet near the ear). In his early, illicit foray into the skull, Humes likely extracted these solid metal fragments, except for two tiny particles superior to JFK's orbit; these latter two were officially collected during the autopsy. However, the location of these two particles cannot be matched to either the oblique shot or to the forehead shot—so they must derive from the EOP shot. However, the metallic trail on the X-ray films (from the forehead shot) may derive from a mercury bullet.[120] So why didn't Humes extract more of these? I have previously proposed, based on their actual appearance—as viewed in detail on multiple occasions at the Archives—that they look more like mercury than like lead. If so, then Humes would not have been able to palpate them (mercury is liquid at room temperature) and would therefore have been unable to remove them during his illicit surgery phase.

In particular, if Humes could have removed these (probably mercury) particles, he would then have left untouched the (officially reported) fragment trail that ascended from the EOP. After all, such a trail would have confirmed an EOP entry, which would have meant a gunman behind JFK. And that, of course, was precisely what Humes was trying to prove. It was just Humes's bad luck that one gunman fired a (likely) mercury bullet—whose remnants Humes could not remove. Those remnants obviously implied a second headshot; worse yet, though, those fragments were more consistent with a frontal shot. Humes (and Boswell and Finck, too) have always insisted on the EOP entry, except when Humes was almost exposed as a (supposed) hapless bumbler by

---

120 An attempt to kill Charles de Gaulle with a mercury bullet occurs in the thriller novel by Frederick Forsyth, *The Day of the Jackal* (New York: Viking Press, 1971). Amazingly enough, this plot occurs in the summer of 1963. On JFK's skull X-ray films, except for the two tiny metal fragments that Humes officially removed (which do have sharply defined borders), the borders of the other metallic fragments in the trail are strangely ill-defined. Likewise, on JFK's pelvic X-ray film, the residual radio-opaque myelogram dye (which I have viewed) may also have similar fuzzy borders. This dye, like mercury, is also a liquid at body temperatures.

the HSCA. At that moment (I have watched him on videotape), under heavy duress, he finally caved in and agreed to an entry 10 cm above the EOP. (For a vivid description of these stressful events read Gary Cornwell's account.[121]) However, Humes's conversion did not stick; many years later, with the *JAMA* article, Humes backslid to the much lower EOP site. Under oath for the ARRB, on a public stage for his final bow, when shown the (far superior) metallic trail on the X-ray films, which disagreed with his own autopsy report by 10 cm, Humes became so nonplussed that he almost walked out (according to Douglas Horne, who witnessed this deposition). Humes had painted himself into a dead end, from which no escape was possible (without an incredible loss of face). Of course, Humes was not that incompetent; after all, he had conducted the weekly brain cutting sessions at Bethesda. But on that ominous night, he had no options—he was forced to follow military orders. In particular, he had been told that the sole gunman was behind JFK—so he knew what to do.

Tom Robinson had watched the pathologists remove about ten small metal fragments from the brain.[122] Dennis David typed a report describing four much larger bullet fragments (likely from more than one bullet).[123] More recently, James Jenkins (at the JFK Lancer conference in November 2013) corroborated this: he saw a transparent plastic bag (on the autopsy table, placed near JFK's right ear)[124] containing bullet

---

121 Gary Cornwell, *Real Answers* (Spicewood, TX: Paleface Press, 1998), pp. 71-74.

122 "ARRB Meeting Report Summarizing 6/21/96 In-Person Interview of Tom Robinson," MD 180, ARRB Master Set of Medical Exhibits, p. 3.

123 "They were not separate bullets but had jagged edges like shrapnel. There was more material than would come from one bullet, but maybe not enough for two....To my knowledge that memo was never made part of the commission report or any other report." This is a quote from Dennis David, cited by David Lifton in *Best Evidence*, op. cit., p. 492, also discussed on p. 579.

124 Jenkins made this comment publicly at JFK Lancer; privately, I (Mantik) asked him if these were the same fragments that Dennis David had seen, but he did not know. See *The JFK Assassination Decoded: Criminal Forgery in the Autopsy Photographs and X-rays* (2023), op. cit., footnote 919.

and bone fragments—which he had never seen being removed from JFK. For this medical cover-up to succeed, it was mandatory that Humes (illicitly) remove the fragments of these two (non-mercury) bullets, i.e., from the EOP shot and from the oblique shot. Had he left this evidence in situ, sixty years of controversy would never have followed. But that night, Humes's entire career—including pension and promotion—hung in the balance. At that precise moment, he was just then completing his twenty-year navy career. So, he really had no choice. In fact, he was promoted shortly afterward, and then later retired to Florida, where he spent his final years on the golf course.

FINALE: THE JFK AUTOPSY AS A FRENCH FARCE

In his 2015 interview with William Matson Law, Douglas Horne agreed with my (Mantik) assessment of the disarray[125] in the medical evidence. Horne concluded that interview with the following observation:

> The medical cover-up's goal was to suppress all medico-legal evidence of shots from the front, and to only record evidence of shots from behind. It has failed miserably, and as David Mantik has said, the cover-up was so abysmal, and so poorly coordinated, that if it were not such a serious subject, the cover-up could be likened to a French farce—high comedy.[126]

---

125 Jones Harris has long maintained that the JFK assassination is a comedy (or is it a tragedy?) of errors. His point was that despite the advanced planning, the coup d'état was a covert operation replete with errors, miscalculations, and just plain things gone wrong. Jones insists that focusing on the things that went wrong are perhaps the most important insight needed to unravel the JFK assassination mystery. The conspirators' missteps (i.e., not contemplating that Jackie Kennedy would insist upon remaining with her husband's casket at Bethesda) complicated the cover-up by requiring a lot of improvising that later demanded a proliferation of government backtracking with disinformation manufactured on the spot. That the most famous autopsy in the history of the United States was such a chaotic travesty of well-established medical procedures affirms Mr. Harris's point.

126 William Matson Law, "Interview with Douglas Horne," in *In the Eye of History,* op. cit., p. 116.

Horne continued, detailing just how botched the medical evidence cover-up truly was:

> Many autopsy photos were destroyed, and at least two skull X-ray films are missing. The three remaining skull x-ray films are altered copy films (forged composites). Many of the surviving photographs do not resemble anything that autopsy witnesses recall. The brain is missing; actually two brains are missing! So are skull fragments, including the Harper fragment, and the Burros fragment. The extant brain photos are a fraud and are demonstrably photos of a substitute brain, not JFK's brain. The substitute brain which was photographed is missing also—and it has to remain missing—otherwise DNA tests would prove that it bears no relation to the Kennedy family. Three separate casket entries at Bethesda Naval Hospital (when there should only have been one) should serve as the final proof that this was a coordinated, inept cover-up, arranged on the fly.[127]

He ended the interview forcefully:

> The longer the stonewalling and evasion continues, the less faith we will have in our own government. The lies perpetuated by the media and the government about the JFK assassination constitute a cancer on the soul of America, and that cancer must be excised.[128]

We concur. Especially as a radiation oncologist, I strongly favor cancer surgery.

CHAPTER 6: SUMMARY

Roy Kellerman was having an interesting day. Jacqueline Kennedy had just vetoed his plans for transferring JFK's body from Andrews to

---

127 Ibid., pp. 116-117. The "Burros" fragment was found on Elm Street. It was turned over to the SS by Davis Burris (Burros was a typo). Both fragments were then handed to Dr. Burkley, and then they vanished. See Douglas Horne, *Inside the ARRB*, op. cit., vol. 2, pp. 392-394.

128 Ibid., p. 117.

Bethesda by helicopter. He had planned to reintroduce it into the Dallas casket (perhaps at the Armed Forces Institute of Pathology) before that casket reached the Bethesda morgue, but Jacqueline torpedoed that plan when she decided to stay with the casket, which was carried to Bethesda by the gray Navy cardiac ambulance, at her specific request. Unbeknownst to her, though, the Dallas casket was then empty. Nor did she know that a helicopter would transport the body directly from Andrews Air Force Base to the morgue shortly after she left Andrews in the navy ambulance, at 6:10 p.m. After she entered the front of the Bethesda Naval Medical Center, the (empty) Dallas casket was promptly driven to the rear of the hospital, where the morgue was located. But the body had already been delivered (in a plain shipping casket) many minutes earlier, and X-ray films were soon being taken.

So, Kellerman had no choice—the empty Dallas casket was delivered from the navy ambulance into the morgue anteroom (not the main room), via a wheeled dolly. Unfortunately, the Casket Team was still waiting to unload the casket, so Roy had to misdirect them. The only other option was to tell them that they were too late—but that came with serious consequences! So, once the team later found a gray navy ambulance in front of the hospital with the Dallas casket inside, they were ready to complete their task; they finally brought the casket into the morgue at about 8 p.m.

Deniers of the three-casket entries ignore the credibility of the testimony about (1) how different the caskets were, and they fail to note (2) the three different sets of actors, one for each separate casket entry. This is all well documented not only from verbal recollections, but also from written records. In particular, no one has ever explained why three quite distinct sets of actors made three separate casket entries. You can look for it, but you will not find it.

CONCLUSION

FORENSIC ANALYSIS OF THE JFK X-RAY FILMS PROVES TWO HEADSHOTS FROM THE FRONT[1] AND ONE HEADSHOT FROM THE REAR

Where I come from we believe all sorts of things that aren't true. We call it history.

—The wizard of Oz in the musical *Wicked*.[2]

---

1 Douglas Horne e-mail to the authors (December 3, 2023, emphases in the original): "Reasonable people can disagree about what some facts mean. My personal inclination now, in 2023, regarding the forehead bullet, is that it was fired ***from the left front of the limousine*** by an overpass shooter above Commerce Street, as postulated by retired policeman and noted firearms expert (and tactician) Brian Edwards. If JFK's head was then in a position approximating the position of his head in frame 312 of the extant (altered) Zapruder film, this makes the most sense, since his head is turned slightly to the left in that frame. I do not believe that the forehead bullet was fired from the South Knoll (i.e. on the south side of Elm Street, to the left front of the limousine), because Jackie Kennedy was leaning very far forward at the time of the frontal headshots, and she would have blocked a headshot from the South Knoll. I do, however, believe that the windshield bullet almost certainly came from the South Knoll, as postulated in ***Z-225*** by Anthony DeFiore. The blowout seen at Parkland Hospital in the right rear of the head was certainly caused by a bullet that entered the right temple, just in front of the ear (in the hair); it was an oblique shot fired from the grassy knoll [which was located] to the right front of the limousine. The shot to JFK's head from behind did not come from the Book Depository; it came from a low floor of the DALTEX building."

2 Stephen Schwartz, *Wicked*, music and lyrics, libretto by Winnie Holzman. See: https://www.allmusicals.com/lyrics/wicked/script.htm.

See also: Gregory Maguire, *Wicked: The Life and Times of the Wicked Witch of the West* (New York: Harper, an imprint of HarperCollins Publishers Inc., 1995).

The whole aim of practical politics is to keep the populace alarmed (and hence clamorous to be led to safety) by an endless series of hobgoblins, most of them imaginary.

—H. L. MENCKEN[3]

You've just got to trust us. We are honorable men.

—RICHARD HELMS, Director of Central Intelligence[4]

IN RETROSPECT, the JFK autopsy is more breathtaking than a French farce. For example, the pathologists never did discover the cause of JFK's back and throat wounds.[5] In this state of profound ignorance, they were

---

3 H. L. Mencken, *In Defense of Women* (New York: Alfred A. Knopf, Inc, 1918), p. 53.

4 This comment was reported in the *New York Review of Books* on December 30, 1971; Helms had just given a rare address to the National Press Club. To the contrary, late in life, David Phillips told former HSCA investigator Kevin Walsh that he thought JFK was killed by unnamed "rogue" CIA officers. See: Jefferson Morley, "JFK Most Wanted: Dave Phillips' CIA operations files," JFKfacts.org [blog], n.d., https://jfkfacts.org/jfk-most-wanted-dave-phillips-cia-files/.

Phillips is the most prominent spook featured in John Patrick Quirk, *The Central Intelligence Agency: A Photographic History* (Guilford, CT: Foreign Intelligence Press, 1986). See also: David Atlee Phillips, *The Night Watch: 25 Years of Peculiar Service* (New York: Atheneum, 1977).

Thomas Powers (a devotee of Curtis LeMay) wrote Helms's hagiographic biography: *The Man Who Kept the Secrets: Richard Helms and the CIA* (New York: Alfred A. Knopf, 1979).

Helms was likely subliminally recalling *Julius Caesar*, act 3, scene 2, where Antony speaks: "Here, under leave of Brutus and the rest—For *Brutus* [an assassin] *is an honorable man*; So are they all [all assassins], all honorable men—Come I to speak in Caesar's funeral." Emphasis added.

5 As noted earlier, I (Mantik) suspect that the back wound was caused by shrapnel that ricocheted from the street. Traces of copper were detected on the back of the shirt and coat (but not on the front), and the abrasion collar of the back wound lay at the inferior border (which implies an *ascending* projectile). A glass shard from the windshield most likely caused the throat wound; additional minuscule glass shards likely caused the two tiny wounds in the cheek that the embalmer had to plug.

also crushed in the vise of the top military brass—they were not allowed to report any frontal shots. Then, after all of that, they were duped. X-ray films were altered so that they barely recognized them. While before the ARRB, Humes specifically protested that he needed help in interpreting these films, even though he had had a radiologist (Dr. John Ebersole) at the autopsy—and he drafted the official report as if he understood the X-ray films.[6] All three pathologists denied seeing the flagrantly obvious 6.5 mm object on the AP X-ray film. Moreover, none of them recognized the Red Spot in the photograph of the back of the head. (Nor did any of the Parkland physicians.) To finally confuse them, the brain photographs were not of JFK. So, the pathologists were quite bewildered when the official reviewers (from both the Clark Panel and the HSCA) totally ignored their consistent and concordant testimony and instead adopted these two faked images as the foundation for their preposterous scenario.

THOSE MULTIPLE AUTOPSY REPORTS

Douglas Horne is the reigning expert on the sequence of JFK autopsy reports.[7] At the autopsy, the pathologists were promptly in trouble: (1) they did not know what had caused either the back or throat wound (they initially [during the autopsy] even publicly ignored the tiny throat entry wound), (2) they were not allowed to report any frontal shots, (3) they had not seen the Zapruder film, (4) they did not know that a deflected fragment had hit a bystander, and (5) they were told that only three shots had been fired. Given these Procrustean constraints, it is hardly surprising that they got things wrong. In fact, they finally quit

---

6 Jerrol Custer, the X-ray technologist, was also perplexed by the X-ray films: "This area was gone, not this [black on the right] area." Like Humes, he did not recall the extreme contrast on the extant X-ray films, which had almost certainly been exacerbated by Ebersole's antics in the darkroom. See William Matson Law, *In the Eye of History*, second edition, op. cit., p. 279.

7 Douglas Horne, *Inside the ARRB*, vol. 3, op. cit., chapter 11.

only after their fourth and final version (of three total written versions). Unfortunately, even that one is still wrong. Of course, today we do not have written versions of these earlier mistakes. We have only the single, official version. So instead, we must reconstruct events to interpolate what preceded their final folly (Appendix J).

Their first version did not include the throat wound. Although they certainly recognized it, they had promptly understood that life would be easier if they simply ignored it. So initially, they recognized only two successful shots, both from the rear. One hit the back and one hit the head, near the EOP. They concluded that this head bullet (or major fragments from it) had exited from the top of the skull, just right of the vertex.

But after 11 p.m. they were forced to recognize the throat wound. By this time, however, Sibert and O'Neill had already exited, so their FBI report did not recognize the throat wound (Appendix I). So, what caused this admission after 11 p.m.? The obvious answer, of course, is a telephone call with Parkland. The FBI report does not cite any such phone calls,[8] so these calls must have occurred after the FBI men had

---

8 Perry originally recalled that such phone calls had occurred on November 22 (*during the autopsy*). Parkland nurse Audrey Bell reported that Perry had told her that he had been kept awake by such calls during the night. Dr. John Ebersole, the autopsy radiologist, told me (now on a recorded interview at NARA) that the first phone call had occurred at 10:30 p.m., and that a second one followed during the autopsy. Pathologist Dr. Robert Karnei (who would have performed the autopsy on anyone but JFK—and who retired in July 1991 as director of the Armed Forces Institute of Pathology) recalled hearing of such calls before the body left the morgue. And William Manchester, in his 1967 book *The Death of a President*, wrote: "Commander James J. Humes, Bethesda's chief of pathology, telephoned Perry in Dallas shortly after midnight" (see p. 433). Finally, the commanding officer of the Bethesda Naval Hospital (Capt. Robert Canada, MD) told Michael Kurtz that "we were aware from telephone calls to Dallas and from news reports that the president had an entrance wound in the throat, but we could not write that in the official protocol because it would have proven the existence of a gunman firing from the front" (See: Michael L. Kurtz, *The JFK Assassination Debates*, op. cit., p. 87). Also see my acerbic review called "*Last Second in Dallas* (LSID) by Josiah Thompson—A Mantik Review," in *The JFK Assassination Decoded*, op. cit., pp. 262, at pp. 281-282. See also: "Clinical Record, Autopsy Protocol, John F. Kennedy, Naval Medical School, November 22, 1963," CE 387, *Hearings before the President's Commission on the Assassination of President Kennedy*, vol. 16, p. 978-983.

exited the morgue. In fact, that is precisely what John Ebersole, the radiologist, told me; shortly after the FBI agents exited, the pathologists spoke on the telephone to a Parkland doctor, who confirmed the throat wound. So now they could no longer ignore it. And only such a telephone call could have forced them to alter their scenario so dramatically. This rather vivid turnabout is therefore independent—and enormously powerful—evidence that at least one telephone call occurred *during* the autopsy.

That the pathologists did, in fact, change their minds—during the autopsy—is proven by the testimony of an autopsy witness, Army Lt. Richard Lipsey, who first revealed this changed scenario. Lipsey even documented this new trajectory via his anatomic diagram for the HSCA (Figure 7.1). In his HSCA drawing, Lipsey noted that after FBI agents Sibert and O'Neill left the morgue, Humes retracted his first opinion: now instead he concluded that JFK had been shot *three times* from behind, not just twice as the FBI had reported.

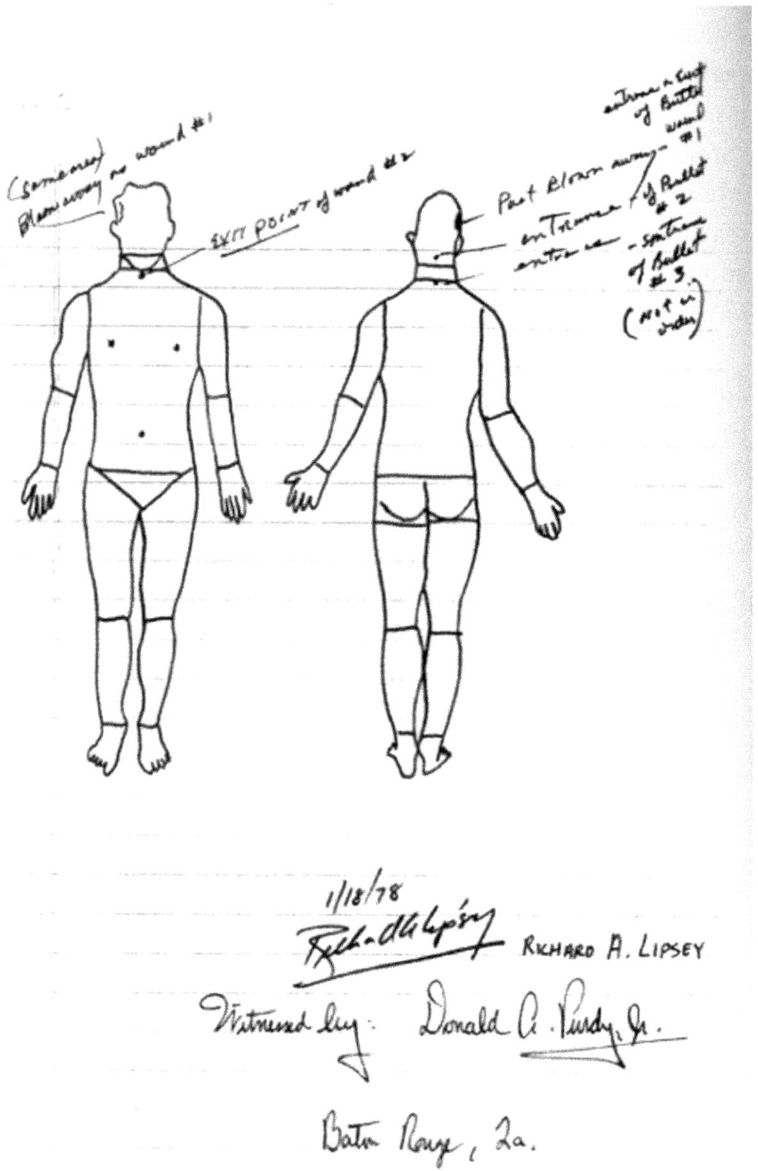

Figure 7.1
Lipsey's Three-Hit Scenario: This Is His Autopsy Diagram. Source: Douglas Horne, *Inside the ARRB*, op. cit., vol. 1, Figure 83.

Figure 7.1 shows a bullet exiting the front of the throat from a rear shot. In other words, Humes now speculated that a third bullet—*not a fragment*—had transited the skull from a low, rear skull entry. This was likely contained in the first written draft of the autopsy report, prepared by Humes on Saturday, November 23 and signed on Sunday, November 24, 1963.

But when this autopsy report was reviewed on Sunday with Admiral Galloway, he [Galloway] was displeased.[9] So Humes was required to start over. Now, he was forced to invent the "fragment from the head shot out the front of the throat." This is the infamous version that was leaked to the media.[10] It is also the version that was reviewed by the WC in a special session.[11] Josiah Thompson also adopted it in *Last*

9 Rear Admiral Calvin Galloway, the commanding officer of the National Medical Center, personally ordered changes in the autopsy report after it was drafted. See Harold Weisberg, *Post Mortem* (New York: Skyhorse Publishing, Inc., 2013), p. 236. This is from the "Testimony of Pierre Finck" during his second day at the Clay Shaw trial in New Orleans, pp. 4-6.

10 It was cited in *Newsweek* (December 30, 1963) and in *JAMA* (January 4, 1964).

11 Mr. Rankin. "Then there is the great range of material in regard to the wounds, and the autopsy and this point of exit or entrance of the bullet in the front of neck and that all has to be developed much more than we have at the present time. We have an explanation there in the autopsy that probably a fragment came out the front of the neck, but with the elevation the shot must have come from, and the angle, it seems quite apparent now, since we have the picture of where the bullet entered in the back, that the bullet entered below the shoulder blade to the right of the backbone, which is below the place where the picture shows the bullet came out in the neckband of the shirt in front, and the bullet, according to the autopsy didn't strike any bone at all, that particular bullet, and go through. So that how it could turn and—" Quote from a "top secret" document that Horne reported (*Inside the ARRB*, op. cit., vol. 3, p. 864) was "carelessly declassified just a few years later, in time to be published with Harold Weisberg's 1969 *Post Mortem*." See: Report of Proceedings, pages 127–212, President's Commission on the Assassination of President Kennedy [Warren Commission], January 27, 1964, p. 20, aarclibrary.org/publib/jfk/wc/wcexec/pdf/WcEx0127.pdf. Rankin was staff director for all the WC attorneys. He clearly had doubts about Humes's story that a fragment of a back bullet had exited the throat. Horne noted: "This transcript (WC Executive Session, January 17, 1964) is one of the evidentiary smoking guns in the Kennedy assassination that proves a coverup of the medical evidence was instituted shortly after that assassination, for Rankin, in his reference to the throat wound being caused by a 'fragment,' is referring to an explanation that is *not in the autopsy report in the*

Second in Dallas.[12] The theory that a fragment from the head shot exited through the throat has subsequently been wholly discredited by 3D anatomic considerations.[13]

As noted earlier, Horne explained what had happened:

> The "bullet #2" conclusions overheard by Lipsey, and depicted here, were abandoned within 24 hours because Humes learned that a bullet had missed the limousine and struck a curb in Dealey Plaza, wounding James Tague—necessitating a return to a 2-hit scenario. But the troublesome photos of this purported "bullet wound" remained in the official collection, creating many problems for the autopsy pathologists in future years.[14]

At this juncture, the Zapruder film begins to matter—after all, the obvious headshot occurs well *after* JFK reacts to a throat shot! So, the throat wound must have occurred *before* the head shot. Therefore, the prior written version had to be scrapped.

The final version could have no fragment (either bone or bullet) exiting from the throat before the headshot. Quite astonishingly, this

---

Archives today. The autopsy report in the Archives today (CE 387) states that a bullet entered the President's back and transited the body without striking bone, exiting from his throat; *it contains no mention of a 'fragment' causing the throat wound.*" (Source: Douglas Horne, *Inside the ARRB*, op. cit., vol. 3, p. 865. Emphases in the original.)

12 Josiah Thompson, *Last Second in Dallas* (Lawrence, KS: University Press of Kansas, 2021). The critical image in Thompson's book is found at p. 98: Figure 7-1, showing what he considered "a possible path of a bone or bullet from the head impact out the throat."

13 See Appendix B in my review of *Last Second in Dallas* in my hardcover book *The JFK Assassination Decoded*, op. cit., pp. 297-299. Also note that this trajectory is likely to damage the cerebellum, but the official brain photographs show no cerebellar damage. Thompson likewise seems insensible to this dilemma, as he displayed the official brain photographs as if they were of JFK's brain. They were surely not. Thompson also committed many other mishaps in his recent book.

14 Douglas Horne, *Inside the ARRB*, op. cit., vol. 1, Figure 83.

is exactly what Thompson (in an anachronistic mode) forgot to confront in his latest book, *Last Second in Dallas*. So, for Humes, whatever exited the throat must now derive from the back shot—not the head shot. And so, lo and behold, now an entire bullet exits the throat from the back shot—and at last we have the single-bullet theory (SBT)! So, officially then, a bullet (still nearly intact) entered the back and exited the throat (still nearly intact), without striking any JFK bone. (The previously fantasized fragment just vanished from history.) This (unlikely) conclusion still resides in the Archives today.

Clearly, the ricochet from the missed shot (that hit Tague in the cheek) was the undeniable evidence that forced the adoption of the SBT. Cyril Wecht has often described this desperate invention by Arlen Specter as the sine qua non for the lone gun assassin. Aside from all the evidence in this book, the final word is clear: the SBT has been shattered, thereby committing the WC report to the dustbin of history.

HORNE'S THREE-SHOT SCENARIO

In volume 4 of his magnum opus *Inside the ARRB*, Horne presented his 2009 conclusions that three headshots had killed JFK, two from the front and one from behind (most likely from the Dallas Textile, or Dal-Tex, building).[15] Because each additional headshot had seemed, a priori, less and less likely, I suspect that I had subconsciously suppressed such a complex sequence. However, the usual rules never seem to fit this JFK case. In particular, if the assassination was a professional contract, then the extraordinary may merely reduce to the almost ordinary. The real challenge to the single headshot scenario, though, is the evidence itself, which is far from simple—and extremely difficult to fit into just one shot.

The three successful headshots are shown in Figure 7.2—as first proposed by Douglas Horne.

15 Douglas Horne, *Inside the ARRB*, op. cit., vol. 4, pp. 1147-1154.

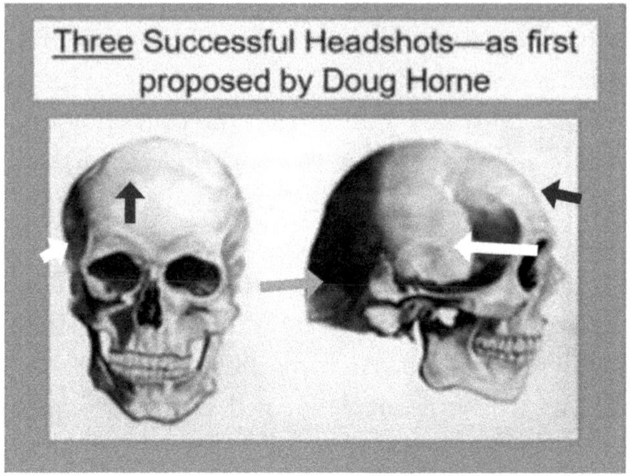

Figure 7.2
Schematic of the Three Successful JFK Headshots. Entry sites are only approximate. The temple shot (white arrow) likely derived from the Grassy Knoll, and therefore is better appreciated in the left image. Source: *JFK's Head Wounds: A Final Synthesis—and a New Analysis of the Harper Fragment* [reprinted e-book] in *The JFK Assassination Decoded,* David W. Mantik, op. cit., starting at p. 401, renumbered as pp. 1-92, at p. 82.

Let us begin with a simple question: What is the strongest evidence for a headshot at all? Aside from the thorough destruction of JFK's skull, the answer lies in the skull X-rays: metallic debris is clearly visible across the top of the skull. The HSCA interpreted this trail as a shot from the rear, entering at their so-called red spot on the autopsy photographs.[16] Furthermore, they also relied on the 6.5 mm fake on the AP skull X-ray film for their scenario. (In order to match that Red Spot, they mistakenly claimed that this 6.5 mm fake object lay at the back of the skull.) They

16 All three pathologists disavowed the Red Spot as a bullet entry. For example, Humes said, "I don't know what that [red spot] is.... I don't, I just don't know what it is, but it certainly was not a wound of entrance" (Source: "Interview of Drs. James J. Humes and J. Thornton Boswell by the Forensic Pathology Panel, Subpanel of Doctors Had Not Reviewed the Autopsy Materials Previously," in *Appendix to Hearings Before the Select Committee on Assassination of the U.S. House of Representatives Ninety-Fifth Congress Second Session,* vol. 7, addendum I, op. cit., p. 254). In fact, no one at Parkland had reported such a Red Spot either.

utilized these two fundamental pieces of (mis)information—despite the pathologists' uniform disavowal of the Red Spot and even though Larry Sturdivan, their ballistics expert, later claimed that the 6.5 mm object could not represent an authentic piece of metal. Furthermore, the metallic fragments in the X-ray trail are clustered near the front of the skull, which obviously suggests a shot from the front. To further cripple their case (of a posterior shot as the cause of the fragment trail), the largest fragment (aside from the fictitious 6.5 mm fake) lies at the posterior end of the trail. Because the largest fragments should travel the farthest, these two observations clearly imply a shot from the front, but no government investigation ever acknowledged this elementary maxim.

The HSCA refused to consider a second headshot; after all, that would have meant conspiracy. Their refusal to admit conspiracy was the main reason they disagreed so radically with the autopsy pathologists, who reported an entry 10 cm inferior to the Red Spot. Another entry there (i.e., at the EOP) would clearly have meant a second headshot—and therefore conspiracy. If the HSCA had been even mildly open-minded, they might have agreed to (1) an entry near the Red Spot (that almost explained the trail of metallic debris) and (2) a second entry near the pathologists' EOP entry site. But in that case, of course, conspiracy would have been inescapable.

But the situation is even more complex than that. The X-ray trail does not fit with several other fundamental facts:

1. The X-ray trail cannot explain the large posterior hole that was widely reported, both at Parkland and Bethesda. The debris trail is far too superior to explain that hole. (Likewise, the EOP shot is an unlikely cause of this hole.)

2. The X-ray trail cannot explain the location of the 7 x 2 mm metal fragment above JFK's right orbit (the fragment that Humes removed). This 7 x 2 mm fragment also lies well off the debris trail. However, this fragment might derive from the EOP shot.

3. The X-ray trail cannot explain the solitary metal fragment in the left scalp (easily visible on the actual X-rays and even visible on most prints in the public domain—see the vertical violet arrow in the left scalp in Figure 7.3). That fragment also lies well off the debris trail. The EOP shot cannot explain this either.

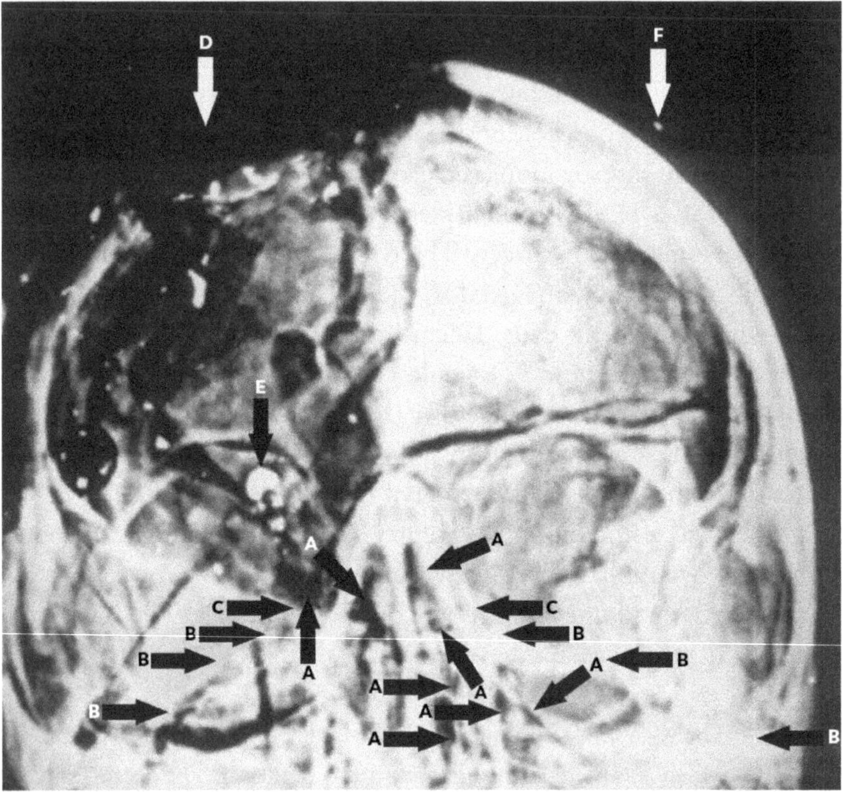

Figure 7.3

AP Skull X-ray of JFK. Note the sites of missing occipital bone based on OD data, at the points of darkness (A arrows—near the center). Lambdoid sutures (B arrows—lateral and inferior) are seen bilaterally, except superior to the tips of the two C arrows (on either side of the nose). The missing sutures may have been on small bone fragments that were ejected. Missing right frontal bone is identified by the D arrow (top right skull). The mysterious 6.5 mm object is identified by the E arrow (inside the right orbit). The vertical F arrow (top of left skull) identifies a metal fragment in the left scalp, which is also visible on the lateral X-ray. It was not described by any government investigation.

A third headshot could resolve this impasse (see Figure 7.2). What follows next is a discussion of these three headshots.[17]

> *Headshot #1.* (At the rear of the head in Figure 7.2.)[18] That someone fired a weapon from the rear is nearly universally accepted—after all, something hit James Tague. A shot from the rear (e.g., from a lower story of the Dal-Tex building) may have entered at the pathologists' EOP site. My reconstruction of the Harper fragment, with the lead deposit precisely at the pathologists' site, may be considered objective proof of their honesty and accuracy on this issue. If additional metal fragments had been deposited inside the skull with this shot, they must have been removed before the official autopsy began (except for the two small particles above JFK's right orbit).[19]

The autopsy report describes a fragment trail from the EOP to the right parietal bone, near the top of the skull. Such a trail is not seen in the extant X-ray films, but perhaps such a trail once did exist—before these fragments were removed, i.e., perhaps Humes even told the truth in his autopsy report. It is even possible, if not likely, that the 7 x 2 mm metal fragment (and its very tiny companion) above the right orbit was part of that trail. There is also eyewitness evidence for a successful posterior headshot: early viewers of the Zapruder film described a brief and

---

17 The other side of the coin should also be emphasized: shot number three, by itself, likewise cannot encompass all the data. Shots one and two are also needed to explain the entire data set.

18 Milicent Cranor has advanced compelling arguments that one headshot occurred about seven frames before Z-313 (See: Milicent Cranor, "The Magic Skull," *The Fourth Decade*, vol. 2, no. 5, (July 1995), https://archive.org/stream/nsia-CranorMillicent/nsia-CranorMillicent/Cranor%20Millicent%2008_djvu.txt.) She also reminds us that when JFK was hit, he went "downward and leftward," according to both Bill and Gayle Newman. This does not suggest a head snap.

19 Douglas Horne, *Inside the ARRB*, op. cit., vol. 4, pp. 1000-1013.

abrupt leftward "jerk" of JFK's head (no longer seen in the film).[20] Such a rotation could have been induced by a shot striking the right rear of the skull (the torque would have been appropriately counterclockwise).[21] That fits with the EOP shot.

It is even possible, if not likely, that early viewers of the Zapruder film took this jerking motion as evidence for a successful shot.[22] On the other hand, a shot from the South Knoll (i.e., opposite the Grassy Knoll) could not have caused such a rotation unless it struck the left skull, e.g., behind the left ear, but no evidence supports such a shot.

An unsuccessful posterior shot (one that first struck the street) is strongly implied—by four clues: (a) the metallic fragment in the left scalp (in JFK's AP skull X-ray film), (b) the metallic fragment in the posterior scalp (visible on JFK's lateral skull X-ray film), (c) an unknown projectile that caused the superficial back wound, and (d) five witnesses (including three cited by the WC) who recalled a shot that struck the street (an event that may have produced these ricochet fragments that hit JFK).[23] Another argument for a successful posterior shot is the presence of debris on the inside of the windshield and on the hood ornament.[24] The chrome strip that surrounded the windshield was also

---

20 Milicent Cranor cited the HSCA: "Rotational movement of the head...may also occur." See: "Effect of a missile on the body," paragraph 446, *Appendix to Hearings Before the Select Committee on Assassination of the U.S. House of Representatives Ninety-Fifth Congress Second Session*, vol. 7, p. 171. See also: Milicent Cranor, "The Magic Skull," op. cit.

21 David W. Mantik, M.D., Ph.D, "Special Effects in the Zapruder Film: How the Film of the Century Was Edited," in *Assassination Science*, op. cit., pp. 263-344, at pp. 298-299.

22 See: Douglas Horne, "Interviews with former NPIC [National Photographic Interpretation Center] Employees: The Zapruder Film in 1963," in *Murder in Dealey Plaza*, op. cit., pp. 311-324.

23 Bonar Menninger, *Mortal Error*, op. cit., pp. 67-78.

24 "There were blood and particles of flesh scattered all over the hood, the windshield, in the front seat and all over the rear floor rugs, the jump seats, and over the rear floor rugs, the jump seats, and over the rear seat, and down both sides of the side rails or tops of the doors of the car." Source: "Testimony of Robert A. Frazier," *Hearings before the President's Commission on the Assassination of President Kennedy*, op. cit., vol. 5, pp. 58-74, at p. 66.

dented. Forward spatter from a posterior shot might explain this debris, but a frontal shot almost certainly cannot. In other words, a posterior shot is required to explain this debris.

According to Sherry Fiester,[25] a JFK assassination researcher with expertise in crime scene investigations, debris from a frontal shot cannot travel more than three to four feet; the hood ornament is well beyond that distance.[26] In short, the evidence for a posterior shot does not rely only on the word of the pathologists. On the contrary, several lines of evidence support such a shot—but the strongest and most objective evidence is the debris on the hood ornament. Also recall that the limousine was traveling into a head wind of fifteen to twenty mph, which would have further decreased the probability that a frontal shot could have deposited debris that far forward (from back spatter).

> *Headshot #2.* (At the forehead in Figure 7.2.) A frontal (forehead) shot most likely produced the particle trail now seen in the X-rays. (The debris trail is far too high to derive from a posterior EOP shot.) This bullet entered high on the right forehead, near the hairline (where

---

See also: "We found blood and tissue all over the outside areas of the vehicle from the hood ornament, over the complete area of the hood, on the outside of the windshield, also on the inside surface of the windshield …." Source: Testimony of Robert A. Frazier at the Clay Shaw Trail, HSCA (RG 233), February 22, 1969, https://www.maryferrell.org/showDoc.html?docId=1297#relPageId=11.

25 Fiester (who was a professional forensic analyst) reported that back spatter only travels four feet (p. 101) or perhaps just three feet (p. 181). See: Sherry P. Fiester, *Enemy of the Truth: Myths, Forensics, and the Kennedy Assassination* (Southlake, TX: JFK Lancer Productions & Publications, Inc., 2012).

26 Dr. Robert Grossman executed a wound diagram for the ARRB in 1997 (See: Douglas Horne, *Inside the ARRB*, op. cit., vol. 1, Figure 23) that depicted a "trap door" (that could open and close) due to a right parietal bone flap. Although no one at Parkland except Grossman recalled this, it would explain the (1) vertical head explosion described by Dino Brugioni from the NPIC and (2) the debris on both sides of the windshield and all over the occupants of the limousine. Such an explosion through the top of the skull might well be expected due to cavitation from any headshot. Milicent Cranor has emphasized this point.

the incision is seen in the autopsy photographs—an incision that was not seen at Parkland). The metallic trail on the AP X-ray goes nearly straight back; therefore, this shot should not be called "tangential," as some writers have mistakenly done.[27]

For a shot from anywhere on the Triple Overpass, the observed particle trail is truly only possible when JFK's head is nearly erect, i.e., it cannot occur with the forward head orientation seen in Z-312 (or in Z-313).[28] If JFK's head had been rotated far enough to the left, then this particle trail might derive from a left frontal shot, although not too close in time to Z-312. On the other hand, since the moment of this shot is not precisely known, so also is JFK's head orientation unknown at this moment. (The Zapruder film is an unreliable clock.)

Brian Edwards has meticulously compared the photograph taken on November 22, 1963, by veteran UPI photographer Frank Cancellare to the photograph taken that same day by *The Dallas Morning News* photographer Thomas C. Dillard.[29] Both show the Triple Overpass above Commerce St. after shots were fired. The Cancellare was taken about 20 seconds after shots were heard. But the Dillard photograph was taken a just few seconds after shots were heard—well *before* the Cancellare photograph. While the Dillard photograph shows a fuzzy figure (between the vertical pillars) on the Overpass, in the Cancellare

---

27 Albert Rossi added that shot number three (see below) is not actually tangential either. More correctly (if you accept geometry), it should be called "secantial," i.e., following a secant. Actually though, the simplest word to describe shot three is *"oblique."*

28 This is a critical point (i.e., that JFK's head must have been nearly erect during headshot number two), an argument I first made decades ago. All by itself, this argument destroys the standard scenario of a single headshot at (about) Z-313. See: David W. Mantik, PhD "Special Effects in the Zapruder Film: How the Film of the Century Was Edited," in *Assassination Science*, op. cit., p. 286.

29 For the Cancellare photograph, see: Richard B. Trask, *Pictures of the Pain*, op. cit., p. 399. For the Dillard photograph, see Trask, *Pictures of the Pain*, at p. 453.

photograph this figure has vanished—just a few seconds after the Dillard photograph.[30] (See: "A Special Supplement: Brian Edwards Targets the Triple Overpass—A Possible Origin for JFK's Forehead Wound" following the Epilogue.)

> *Headshot #3.* (Near the ear in Figure 7.2) The second frontal shot fired from the Grassy Knoll, entered obliquely, anterior to the right ear, and then exited to produce the large hole at the right rear. This shot blew the Harper Fragment out of the high occiput. Since the Harper Fragment bears metallic traces from the posterior bullet, the oblique shot to the temporal bone must have followed the rear bullet.

Witnesses to a wound near the right ear have already been cited: Zapruder, Kellerman, Robinson, Jenkins, and both Newmans. The Belmont report (discussed below) may also be an echo of this wound. There is, in fact, a very old tradition for such a wound near the right ear; Josiah Thompson listed several important witnesses.[31] These include Herchel Jacks, the Texas state trooper who drove Vice President Johnson's car in the motorcade. Jacks noted in his deposition that "it appeared that the bullet had struck him above the right ear or near the temple."[32] Reporter Seth Kantor's handwritten notes at Parkland Hospital that recorded a bullet had "intered [sic] right temple."[33] An early NBC broadcast reported "the President was struck in the right

---

30 Brian Edwards e-mail to the authors (December 3, 2023): "The analysis/examination of the Dillard photo was part of a PowerPoint presentation I gave to the Dealey Plaza UK group earlier this year. The title was 'A Tactical Analysis of the Dealey Plaza Ambush.'" (1390) JFK Assassination - Dealey Plaza UK-Canterbury Conference -Brian Edwards - YouTube. Also see brian Edwards website jfk - Search (bing.com).

31 Josiah Thompson, *Six Seconds in Dallas*, op. cit., pp. 105-106.

32 Ibid., p. 105.

33 Ibid.

temple by the bullet."[34] An NBC broadcast thirty minutes later amplified the initial report: "The President was wounded in the back of the head and on the right side of the head: there was a loss of blood and brain tissue."[35] The *New York Times* reported the next day that "Mr. Kennedy also had a massive gaping wound in the back and one on the right side of the head."[36]

This oblique shot could not have deposited the metallic trail seen on the X-rays; the fragments are too far forward and also too superior. In addition, though, it is quite unlikely that such an oblique headshot could have deposited the 7 x 2 mm fragment (above the right orbit). Such an oblique shot would have entered too far posterior (as well as too far inferior) to leave that fragment behind. On the other hand, this shot (number three) could well have produced the spatter that Hargis encountered. However, shot number 2 (i.e., the one that deposited the metallic trail) is an unlikely candidate for the Hargis spatter (because those bullet remnants mostly—or completely—stopped inside the skull). But if shot number two had come from the rear and deposited the metallic trail (not my belief), then it is even less likely that it could account for the Hargis spatter. (That would require a remarkably energetic back spatter.) Another key point is Clint Hill's recollection, which implies that the shot (that produced the large posterior hole, i.e., number three) was the last shot.

Table 7.4 summarizes the three headshots and at least one ricochet shot.

---

34 Ibid.

35 Ibid.

36 Ibid., pp. 105-106.

Evidence	#1 (EOP)	#2 (forehead)	#3 (oblique)	#4 (ricochet)
Debris on hood ornament	√			
7x2 mm fragment	√			
Leftward head jerk	√			
HF in occiput: smear near EOP	√			
Metallic trail on X-rays		√		
Witnesses to forehead wound		√		
Forehead incision		√		
Pre-autopsy surgery	√		√	
Debris flying forward	√		√	
Debris to left rear			√	
HF ejection			√	
Occipital hole			√	
Witnesses to wound near right ear			√	
Belmont memo			√	
James Tague wound				√
Metal fragment in left scalp				√
Back wound				√
Metal fragment at back of head				√
Small metallic particles in Figure 9				√
Witnesses to bullet hitting street (cf. Z-144)				√

Table 7.4

Summary of Three Headshots and At Least One Ricochet. Forward flying debris could have arisen due to forward spatter from shot number one as well as due to back spatter from both shot number one and shot number three. Humes may have removed bullet fragments from both number one and number three. Source: *JFK's Head Wounds: A Final Synthesis—and a New Analysis of the Harper Fragment* [reprinted e-book] in *The JFK Assassination Decoded*, David W. Mantik, op. cit., starting at p. 401, renumbered as pp. 1-92, at Table 1, p. 85.

OD MEASUREMENTS: IRREFUTABLE SCIENTIFIC PROOF OF FRONTAL SHOTS

Figure 7.5 shows the survey I made at the National Archives of all the metallic fragments on the JFK AP and lateral skull X-ray films.

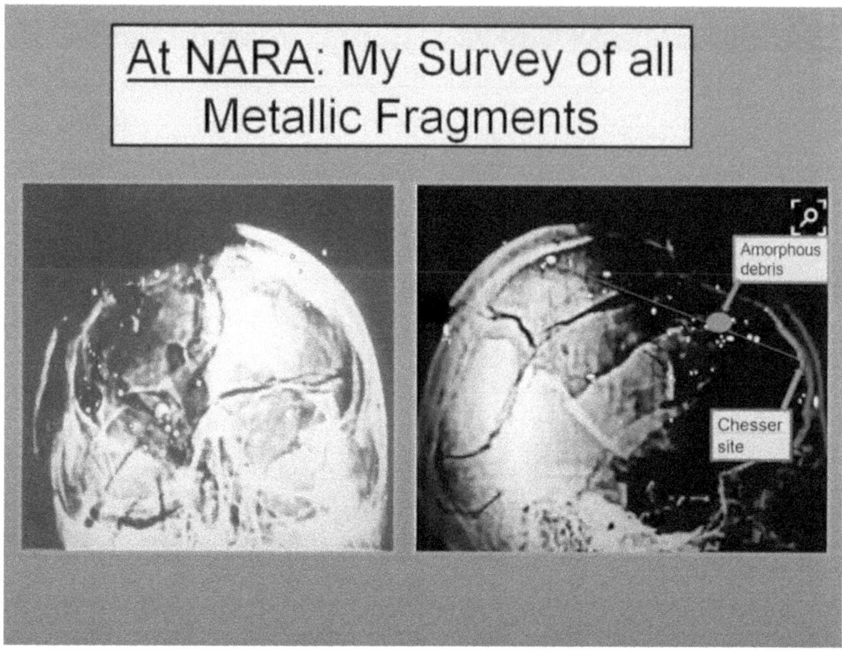

Figure 7.5

My Survey of All Metallic Fragments in the Extant JFK AP and Lateral X-Ray Films, as Traced at the Archives. Source: David Mantik, "JFK's Head Wounds," The Future of Freedom Foundation, op. cit. For this presentation with color slides see: The Future of Freedom Foundation, "JFK's Head Wounds," op. cit. Or see the color images in my hardcover book.

On the lateral X-ray film, note that the largest fragment stops well short of the posterior skull. Because the fragment trail does not leave the skull, it cannot explain the occipital hole—but the temporal shot can explain the hole. Also note that this trail begins in the forehead—not in the temporal area. While eyewitness reports may not be accurate, these OD measurements depend only on the laws of physics. Furthermore, they can be verified by others, as Chesser has already done. Moreover, the metallic fragment trail can only be explained by the frontal shot to the right forehead, entering at the site that Chesser identified. With the largest metallic fragment coming to rest in the posterior skull, we have further evidence for a frontal shot.

The ODs of the 6.5 mm fake and the ODs of the White Patch are indisputable scientific proof of the medical cover-up. The T-shaped inscription and the ghost image inside the 6.5 mm fake on the AP X-ray film merely add to the massif of evidence. That JFK's body made three separate morgue entrances and that Drs. Humes and Boswell performed preliminary illicit surgery on JFK's head means that the cover-up occurred with the full knowledge of—or perhaps even under the direction of—the highest US government officials. This year, on the sixtieth anniversary, the truth is now naked: the JFK assassination was a US government coup d'état. Did you vote for this?

ON TRUE BELIEVERS AND FALSE MYTHS

John Gotti, the boss of the NYC Gambino family, apocryphally claimed, "I never lie because I don't fear anyone. You only lie when you're afraid."[37] Applying Gotti's logic, the CIA's memo (January 4, 1997), proves that the CIA does indeed fear that the public will learn the truth.[38] Former CIA director William Colby, in his 1978 biography *Honorable Men: My Life in the CIA*, acknowledged the reality: "The public can no longer be expected to follow [Richard] Helm's 1971 admonition that it 'must take it on faith that we too are honorable men devoted to the nation's service.'"[39]

---

37 "John Gotti," Biography.com, updated April 15, 2021, https://www.biography.com/crime/john-gotti.

38 For regular (usually weekly) updates on the JFK assassination (often related to the CIA), join Jeff Morley's site for a modest fee at jfkfacts@substack.com. Morley follows the Mary Ferrell Foundation in its lawsuit for records release. Here is a recent sample from his site:

> A recently declassified CIA memo identifies for the first time a clandestine operative who read the mail of accused assassin Lee Harvey Oswald for 20 months before the assassination of President John F. Kennedy in 1963.
>
> His name, reports the *New York Times*, was Reuben Efron, a career employee who staffed the Agency's illicit "mail intercept" program in the early 1960s. His photo is published here for the first time.

39 William Colby with Peter Forbath, *Honorable Men: My Life in the CIA* (New York: Simon & Schuster, 1978), p. 459. Helms was CIA director from 1966 to 1973. Colby was CIA director from 1973 to 1976.

During the Cold War, our intelligence community was obsessed with the belief that the USSR would soon launch a land war against western Europe. These "experts" also advanced the myth of a missile gap.[40] Both were lies. This myth of a land attack was exploded when eavesdropping from the Berlin tunnel (Figure 7.6) uncovered no evidence for such a planned attack.[41] Furthermore, "The rise and fall of the missile gap myth is a cautionary tale, which should continue to inform efforts to achieve more realistic and sober appraisals of the threats faced today," reported former US Foreign Service officer Greg Thielmann.[42]

40 The missile gap was a (mis)perception, during the late 1950s and early 1960s, that the Soviet Union was developing a greater ICBM capability than the United States. Kennedy learned the truth during his 1960 campaign. Shortly later, Eisenhower confirmed this to him. The Soviets had only ten to twenty-five launchers at the time, while the Americans had more than one hundred.

41 David Corn, *Blond Ghost: Ted Shackley and the CIA's Crusades* (New York: Simon and Schuster, 1994), p. 64. This is the definitive biography of Ted Shackley, former chief of the largest CIA station in the world—in Miami during the JFK assassination. Corn emphasized that the Berlin tunnel (1954–1958) shaped Shackley's career. Shackley had served in Berlin under William King Harvey, a principal suspect in the JFK murder. While in Miami, Ted's underling was David Morales, another principal suspect in the JFK murder. Morales also later served under Shackley as chief of Pakse base in Laos. Even more improbably, Ted had apparently been trained (in assassinations) by that unsurpassed connoisseur of assassinations, Otto Skorzeny (Hitler's top commando). See: Daniel Sheehan, *The People's Advocate: The Life and Legal History of America's Most Fearless Public Interest Lawyer* (Berkeley, CA: Counterpoint, 2013), p. 473.

42 Greg Thielmann, "The Missile Gap Myth and Its Progeny," Arms Control Association, 2011, https://www.armscontrol.org/act/2011-05/missile-gap-myth-its-progeny#bio.

Figure 7.6
The Berlin Tunnel, 1954-1955. Source: James Wilkinson, "How the CIA and MI6 built a 1,500-foot tunnel under Berlin and spied on Soviet communications for a year—until the word of a double-agent led to the plot being uncovered," *Daily Mail*, January 19, 2017, https://www.dailymail.co.uk/news/article-4137980/How-CIA-MI6-built-1476ft-spy-tunnel-BERLIN.html.

In the name of national security, the CIA has compiled a litany of covert actions due to its resolute belief that the assassination of foreign leaders is justifiable. In that case, democracy bids farewell, as even former CIA director William Colby agreed:

> Considering the importance and all-consuming nature of the work I was doing at the Agency; considering the missionary zeal, sense of elitism and marvelous camaraderie among my colleagues there...one can see how easy it would have been for me to drop out of [the outside] world and immerse myself exclusively in the cloak-and-dagger life. And some of my colleagues at the Agency did just that. Socially as well as professionally they cliqued together, forming a sealed fraternity. They ate together at their own special favorite restaurants, they partied almost only among themselves; their families drifted to each other, so their defenses did not always have to be up. In this way they increasingly separated themselves from the ordinary world and developed

a rather skewed view of that world. Their own dedicated double life became the proper norm, and they looked down on the life of the rest of the citizenry. And out of this grew...an inbred, distorted, elitist view of intelligence that held it to be above the normal processes of society, with its own rationale and justification, beyond the restraints of the Constitution, which applied to everything and everyone else.[43]

Just one month after the JFK assassination, former President Harry Truman wrote a letter to the *Washington Post*, "to take another look at the purpose and operations of our Central Intelligence Agency"—an organization whose existence he had authorized while in office (under the National Security Act of 1947). "For some time I have been disturbed by the way [the] CIA has been diverted from its original assignment," Truman wrote. "It has become an operational and at times a policy-making arm of the Government. This has led to trouble and may

---

43 David Corn, *Blond Ghost: Ted Shackley and the CIA's Crusades*, op. cit., p. 36.

In spring 1996, on a stormy night, Colby abandoned his half-eaten supper of clams and white wine at his weekend home in Maryland. He had apparently been gripped by a mad and sudden passion for fishing, but he skipped his usual life jacket. His canoe was found the next day on a sandbar of a Potomac tributary, about a quarter mile from his home. On May 6, 1996, his body was found in a marshy riverbank lying face down not far from his canoe. An autopsy ruled his death to be accidental, probably due to a stroke or heart attack. Oddly, just days before his death, James Gordon Meek had interviewed him about his knowledge of the JFK assassination.

Colby (with Shackley's assistance) had supervised the Phoenix program in Vietnam that killed over two hundred thousand Asians. To quote David Corn in *Blind Ghost* (p. 136), "they [Shackley and William Sullivan, the US ambassador] juiced up the Hmong to fight in the more conventional manner, and it would be a total f***ing disaster for the Hmong." Colby, using his insider status as a devout Catholic, is also infamous for planting microphones throughout the papal apartments. This listening did not stop until 1984. See: Paul L. Williams, *Operation Gladio,* op. cit., p. 52. As for Shackley, for all of his "heroic work," he received the Distinguished Intelligence Medal from the CIA. On the other hand, when Corn interviewed him, Ted answered fewer than 1/5th of Corn's written questions (Corn, pp. 77, 407). Eventually, in a fit of justice delayed, Mother Nature caught up with Ted—and repaid him with cancer. Soon after this (2002) he died at his home in *Bethesda, MD.*

have compounded our difficulties in several explosive areas."[44] Truman concluded by suggesting the CIA should be stripped of its covert operational authority and return solely to its original purpose of gathering foreign intelligence.

With the 1998 declassification of a CIA memorandum (January 4, 1997), "Countering Criticism of the *Warren Report*," we now know the CIA engaged in a psychological operation (a "psyop") to discredit anyone who dared criticize the official version of Oswald as the sole gunman.[45] Donald E. Wilkes, Jr., a professor emeritus at the University of Georgia Law School, published (November 23, 2016) "The Single-Assassin Theory, the Media Establishment and the CIA." Wilkes clarified that the government conspiracy behind the JFK coup d'état has never stopped:

> What investigative reporters Russ Baker and Milicent Cranor call "the mystery of the constant flow of JFK disinformation"—the mainstream media's remarkable, persisting commitment to defending the *Warren Report's* conclusion that Lee Harvey Oswald, acting alone, assassinated President John F. Kennedy—is now fully comprehensible. We have long known that, criminally, outrageously and repeatedly, the Central Intelligence Agency stonewalled official government investigations of the JFK assassination. But we also now know that for the last half-century, using its numerous and influential assets and supporters in the mainstream media, the CIA has engaged in a clandestine crusade to preserve, protect, and defend the *Warren Report's* sole-assassin claim from criticism, even when the criticism is warranted. We also know now that many of the defenses of the lone-assassin claim, as well as

44 Harry S. Truman: "Limit CIA Role to Intelligence," *Washington Post*, December 22, 1963. For the complete text, see: "Harry Truman's December 1963 Letter to the *Washington Post* on the CIA," January 21, 2021, GaryNorth.com, https://www.garynorth.com/public/21814.cfm.

45 "Countering Criticism of the Warren Report (Clayton P. Nurnad and Ned Bennett), CIA File Number 201-289248 (Psyop Against 'Conspiracy Theorists.') (1967)," https://ia800705.us.archive.org/30/items/COUNTERINGCRITICISMOFTHEWARRENREPORT/COUNTERING%20CRITICISM%20OF%20THE%20WARREN%20REPORT.pdf.

> many of the attacks on Report critics, may be traced to persons with known or suspected CIA connections or pro-CIA sympathies.[46]

Wilkes also emphasized that we can establish a conspiracy "even if the identity of the individual conspirators is unknown and regardless of whether Oswald was one of the conspirators."[47] The OD measurements do just that. Although there are now strong suspects, we cannot finally expect to prove their guilt (the paper trail never existed or has been destroyed), but we can conclude beyond any doubt that the conspirators must include the top ranks of the US government.

It is ironic that I was able to establish two frontal headshots merely by taking a tedious series of ODs (at intervals of 0.10 millimeter) across the three extant JFK skull X-ray films. In a rather glorious simile, shining light through the X-ray films likewise shined an intense light on the cover-up. That these ODs are dangerous was clearly made manifest by my (and Chesser's) eternal banishment from the National Archives.

Leave aside for a moment the question of "Who killed JFK?" Instead ask, "Why was JFK killed?" For this, we cite James Douglas, based on his foundational book, *JFK and the Unspeakable: Why He Died and Why It Matters* (2008):

> Dr. Mantik's optical density tests confirmed a radical hypothesis. The autopsy's skull X-rays, in which the Harper fragment had so wondrously rejoined a dead president's skull in spite of the fragment's simultaneous existence elsewhere, had indeed been cleverly altered. Precisely where the government had rested its case for a lone assassin on a claim of scientific evidence—in its autopsy X-rays—the public could now see for itself was evidence of fakery. The scientific evidence claimed by Warren Commission apologists had been forged in the

---

46 Donald E. Wilkes, Jr., "The Single-Assassin Theory, the Media Establishment and the CIA," originally appeared on Flagpole.com, November 23, 2016, https://digitalcommons.law.uga.edu/fac_pm/271/.

47 Ibid.

X-ray darkroom. Thanks to Dr. Mantik's experiments conducted during his visits to the National Archives (now available to anyone who Google's "Twenty Conclusions After Nine Visits"), the unspeakable has been proved verified, and documented.[48]

Douglas continued:

> In the case of the government's X-rays, their exact duplication of the Harper fragment, as if that bullet-blasted bone were still in the slain president's skull, has turned out to be a revelation of the cover-up. When the government's "best evidence" was finally examined independently, the tests showed the X-rays were a hoax. The bottom line of the *Warren Report* was a forgery. A fragment of the head that Jacqueline Kennedy had tried unsuccessfully to put together again has come back decades later to haunt the government's cover-up.[49]

The Republic thrives in those rare historical moments when truth flourishes. The OD measurements—and the T-shaped inscription—are smoking guns. They defy common sense and the laws of physics. So does the White Patch and the ghost image inside the 6.5 mm fake. Treason in the JFK assassination by US intelligence agencies is no longer safe from scrutiny. And the more the CIA persistently releases rather benign documents that they had withheld for decades, the more the public understands that their behavior announces only reckless self-centeredness.

Robert Kennedy, Jr., now claims that the CIA "killed" his uncle and his father. Therefore, the CIA memorandum "Countering Criticism of the *Warren Report*" should be seen as prima facie evidence that he has been on target.

---

48 James W. Douglas, *JFK and the Unspeakable: Why He Died and Why It Matters* (Maryknoll, NY: Orbis Books, 2008), p. 283.

49 Ibid.

EPILOGUE

BY DAVID W. MANTIK, M.D., PH.D.

To become aware of an obsolete bias is to prove your wisdom. The door to this discovery may be the next book you read. It may even be this book!

—DAVID W. MANTIK[1]

DR. THOMAS YOUNG,[2] a physician-physicist (like me) has long been one of my heroes. Not only did he decipher the Rosetta Stone, but he also proved that light is a wave (1801–1803). That partial truth was not updated until 1905 by Albert Einstein, who proved that light is also a particle. Just as Young helped Jean-Francois Champollion decipher the Rosetta Stone, perhaps I have helped to decipher Oliver *Stone's* movie, *JFK*.

---

1 *The Assassination of John F. Kennedy: THE FINAL ANALYSIS*

2 For an excellent biography of Dr. Thomas Young, see: Andrew Robinson, *The Last Man Who Knew Everything: The Anonymous Polymath Who Proved Newton Wrong, Explained How We See, Cured the Sick, and Deciphered the Rosetta Stone, Among Other Feats of Genius* (Oxford, England: Oneworld Publications, 2006). In 1799, he began practicing as a physician at 48 Welbeck Street, London (now identified with a blue plaque). Later, he was attached to St. George's Hospital, near Hyde Park. Young published many of his first academic articles anonymously to protect his reputation as a physician. Just so, even today, physicians who publish on the JFK assassination do not necessarily win popularity among their colleagues. In 1801, Young, at age twenty-eight, was appointed professor of natural philosophy (mainly in physics) at the Royal Institution. In two years, he delivered ninety-one lectures. As for me, I was appointed assistant professor of physics at the University of Michigan at age twenty-eight and delivered multiple lectures per week over three years (before medical school arrived). Young was the eldest child in a large Quaker family, while I am the eldest child (of four children) in a Pentecostal family. William Gilbert was another physician-physicist; he described the earth as a giant dipole magnet and he was also private physician (1601–1603) to Queen Elizabeth I.

As we now finally know, the WC[3] was designed to protect the assassins. As a WC member, Allen Dulles, the longest-serving director of the CIA (1953–1961), played the most active role in its cover-up. In particular, he never revealed to the other members the assassination plots against Fidel Castro.[4] As director, he had overseen the 1953 Iranian coup d'état, the 1954 Guatemalan coup d'état, the Lockheed U-2 aircraft program, the Project MK-Ultra mind control program, and the Bay of Pigs invasion. For his incompetence in the latter, he was fired by John F. Kennedy. Another WC member, Gerald Ford[5] (my future neighbor in Rancho Mirage), played the role of WC liaison with J. Edgar Hoover's FBI. A third member, John J. McCloy, was a reliable representative of the reigning elite. He had served as assistant secretary of war, World Bank president, US high commissioner for Germany, and chairman of Chase Manhattan Bank (for David Rockefeller[6]).

The final three members were not reliable; each of them refused

---

3 The WC met formally for the first time on December 5, 1963, on the second floor of the National Archives I in Washington, DC. Ironically, almost exactly thirty years later, I entered the same building to examine the JFK autopsy materials.

4 Dulles is infamous for his supposed cynical remark: "That little Kennedy...he thought he was a god." For the definitive biography of Dulles, see: David Talbot, *The Devil's Chessboard: Allen Dulles, the CIA, and the Rise of America's Secret Government* (New York: Harper, 2015), prologue, p. 1.

5 As he autographed (with his left hand) his Oswald biography (Gerald Ford and John R. Stiles, *Portrait of the Assassin* (New York: Simon and Schuster, 1965)), Gerry turned to me and stated, "I am the last surviving member of the Warren Commission."

6 Jonathan Kwitny notes that, from 1953 to 1977, the elite who determined US foreign policy were all on the Rockefeller payroll. For example, Dean Rusk and Henry Kissinger were kept solvent by Rockefeller funds. See *Endless Enemies*, by Jonathan Kwitny (New York: Congdon and Weed, 1984), p. 178. In *The Federalist #10*, James Madison had worried about rule by oligarchs; unfortunately, he failed to prevent this outcome, as is all too obvious today. See: James W. Loewen, *Lies My Teacher Told Me: Everything Your American History Textbook Got Wrong* (New York: Simon and Schuster, 1995), p. 209.

to accept the single-bullet theory,[7] but J. Lee Rankin, general counsel for the WC, took great care to scrub their disagreement from the final report, which infuriated Senator Richard Russell. One WC member, Representative Hale Boggs (House majority leader) vanished on October 16, 1972, rather mysteriously in an Alaskan plane crash. Jim Garrison told Joan Mellen (known for chronicling the Jim Garrison investigation)[8] that Hale Boggs[9] had prompted him to reopen his investigation into JFK's death.

JFK's autopsy was not merely a fraud. After sixty years, we can now see the entire episode as a French farce. The three pathologists, under orders to avoid multiple headshots and conspiracy, deliberately lowered their description of the location of the trail of metallic debris (obvious in the X-ray films) by four inches (over half the height of the head). They purposefully incised the forehead wound in order to obscure a frontal bullet entry high above the right eye, which witnesses had observed shortly after the autopsy in unofficial postmortem photographs (that never made it into the official collection).

They ignored another bullet entry that many Dealey Plaza witnesses recalled; it lay in the hair, just in front of the right ear, and both Army pathologist Pierre Finck and Navy Corpsman James Jenkins briefly inspected this wound during the autopsy, before they were told not to

---

7 Excluding Warren himself, half (three of six) of the WC commissioners, Senator Richard B. Russell (D-GA), Senator John Cooper (R-KY), and Congressman Hale Boggs (D-LA), did not accept the WC's single-bullet theory. See: Gerald D. McKnight, *Breach of Trust: How the Warren Commission Failed the Nation and Why*, op. cit., p. 283.

8 Joan Mellen, *A Farewell to Justice: Jim Garrison, JFK's Assassination, and the Case That Should Have Changed History* (Dulles, VA: Potomac Books, Inc., 2005).

9 Hale's daughter was Cokie Roberts, the TV and public radio journalist.

examine it by high-ranking spectators in the morgue gallery.[10] Their official report obfuscated the exact size and location of the large posterior skull exit hole, which was seen by virtually all observers in Dealey Plaza, at Parkland Hospital, and at the Bethesda Naval Medical Center. Pathologists James J. Humes and J. Thornton Boswell promptly examined the authentic brain on Monday, November 25 (in the absence of their colleague Finck), but then about a week later, all three (now including Finck) examined a substitute brain. My optical density data from the extant skull X-ray films (data taken at the National Archives) are consistent with the authentic brain—but they are inconsistent with the substitute/fake brain.

We now know, with certainty, that the pathologists lied; they were forced into this impossible impasse in order to save their careers. After they acknowledged reviewing all the extant autopsy photographs and X-ray films in their "Report of Inspection," they summarized their findings in their January 26, 1967, Justice Department–prompted written report.[11] This report related their 1963 autopsy protocol (Appendix J)

10 Among the countless top-brass officers in the gallery, Paul O'Connor spotted Air Force Chief of Staff Curtis LeMay (William Matson Law, *In the Eye of History*, 2015, op. cit., p. 195). O'Connor had seen him before and, of course, promptly recognized his perpetual cigar. To the eternal anguish of his opponents, Celtic coach Red Auerbach displayed his arrogance by smoking a cigar when victory was certain. By smoking in the morgue, LeMay was merely mimicking Red, and by doing so, he personified widespread Pentagon sentiments. It was well known that JFK and LeMay were mortal enemies. Humes had smelled the smoke and loudly ordered, "Put the damn thing out!" O'Connor, obeying orders, walked over to the gallery, where LeMay blew smoke into his face. When Humes recognized LeMay, he [Humes] turned quite pale (Horne, *ARRB*, volume 2, p. 487). LeMay, a former Olympian, was hardly a political naïf, as he would run for vice president in 1968 on an independent ticket with George Wallace. Oddly, LeMay was not a segregationist, and he was an early "green" candidate. He died at March Air Force Base in Riverside County, California, at age 83 on October 1, 1990. Decades later, when I visited March Air Force Base with one of my patients (a colonel), the main lobby wall was nearly covered with a full color portrait of Curtis LeMay. Incidentally, LeMay persistently chomped on a cigar to control his Bell's palsy.

11 "Report of Inspection by Naval Medical Staff on November 1, 1966, at National Archives of X-Rays and Photographs of Autopsy of President John F. Kennedy," MD 13, op. cit.

to the autopsy photographs and X-ray films that they had just viewed. Amazingly, however, despite just spotting the 6.5 mm object (ostensibly a large bullet cross-section) on the AP X-ray film—it was as plain as day—they specifically denied seeing "any major portion of a bullet." See the highlighted excerpt just below.

NO OTHER WOUNDS

The x-ray films established that there were small metallic fragments in the head. However, careful examination at the autopsy, and the photographs and x-rays taken during the autopsy, revealed no evidence of a bullet or of a major portion of a bullet in the body of the President and revealed no evidence of any missile wounds other than those described above.

Figure 8.1

Signed Military Inventory. Source: "Report of Inspection by Naval Medical Staff on November 1, 1966, at National Archives of X-Rays and Photographs of Autopsy of President John F. Kennedy," MD 13, op. cit.

This is irrefutable evidence of their eagerness to oblige their masters. Of course, substituting a stranger's brain for JFK's brain in the photographic record of the autopsy was not exactly a mark of good character, either.

And the extreme pressure exerted on Parkland's Trauma Room One physician, Dr. Malcolm Perry, was quite beyond the pale. Via repeated telephone calls from Bethesda Naval Hospital, *both during* and after the autopsy, he had been commanded to change his description of the frontal throat wound from one of entry to one of exit—or else suffer a major medical inquisition.[12]

Humes also managed to disguise the presence of an intact bullet at the autopsy (*not* the Magic Bullet), which had been found in the limousine and then handed to him via White House physician, Dr. James Young. Not until 2017 did we learn that Young had transferred

12 History Conspiracy Podcast, "JFK Assassination—Witness to History—Nurse Bell/History conspiracy podcast," June 23, 2020, https://www.youtube.com/watch?v=LLrEaTkMwmc.

this bullet to Humes *during* the autopsy. This had been found during a search of the limousine in the White House garage that night.[13] Young recalled that he gave that envelope containing the bullet with the bent tip to Dr. Humes, the head autopsy pathologist.[14] Humes understood all too well that just one more bullet would have shattered the lone gunman scenario. In addition, though, a bullet had already materialized on the autopsy table when (even before Young's bullet), JFK's body was transferred from the casket. But, providentially for the WC, this bullet also managed to dodge the official autopsy report.

The following six individuals all recall an intact bullet at the autopsy (not a fragment): Young, Mills, Martinell, Stover, Osborne and Custer. Chief of Surgery (later Rear Admiral) David P. Osborne had held the bullet in his hand that night; he later served as deputy surgeon general of the navy and as the commander of the Bethesda National Naval Medical Center.[15]

Soon after the autopsy, however, these same pathologists were later themselves unexpectedly bamboozled by (illegal—but federally authorized) alterations to the autopsy photographs and skull X-ray films. Before the HSCA Forensic Pathology Panel, all three denied that the high Red Spot in the altered/fake back-of-the-head photographs marked a bullet entry; and two of the three pathologists denied seeing the 6.5 mm fake bullet cross section on the AP X-ray film. This was all while under oath before the ARRB. (All three of them testified to the ARRB

---

13 Milicent Cranor, "Navy Doctor: Bullet Found in JFK's Limousine, and Never Reported," op. cit. I do not know if James Young and Thomas Young, both deceased physicians, were related, but nothing in this case surprises me anymore.

14 Michael T. Griffith, *A Comforting Lie: The Myth That a Lone Gunman Killed President Kennedy* (Kindle Direct Publishing, 2023), pp. 81-84. See also: Navy Bureau of Medicine and Surgery, "Navy Medicine and President Kennedy's Autopsy: Recollections from a Former White House Physician," Washington, DC, Navy Bureau of Medicine and Surgery, 2013.

15 "David Osborne, 81; Led Navy Doctors," obituary, *New York Times*, December 9, 1996, https://www.nytimes.com/1996/12/09/us/david-osborne-81-led-navy-doctors.html. Osborne had previously survived the Normandy landings.

that no bullet fragment that large had been removed from JFK's body.) On the other hand, subsequent forensic "experts" ingenuously accepted these two falsified images (i.e., the fraudulent intact back-of-the-head photograph and deceitful 6.5 mm fake on the AP skull X-ray film) and so displayed no faith in the pathologists (or in the radiologist—to whom I have twice spoken). These experts reached this incorrect conclusion even though the autopsy photographs had no legal provenance and even though these official committees had scores of lawyers but absolutely no experts on X-ray film alteration.[16] Furthermore, they had failed to ask Ebersole about his clever darkroom chicaneries with the X-ray films.

The HSCA staff proved the lack of legal provenance for the autopsy photographs (no chain of possession); they wrote that the extant autopsy photographs were inconsistent with the camera and lens combination provided by the Department of Defense. The DOD was very confident that the camera and lens provided to the HSCA were the ones used during the JFK autopsy; in particular, the DOD had no other combination to offer. Because the camera and lens provided to them could not have produced the extant autopsy photographs, the HSCA, in its circular logic, chose to disbelieve the DOD. Of course, if they had accepted the verdict of the DOD, their entire case would have exploded, so they made (in their eyes) the politically correct decision.

And so today an entirely new era has dawned—even though the CIA still pretends to slumber in the pre-dawn darkness of the night. Of course, both the FBI and the Secret Service still refuse to accept the single-bullet theory, although every November, the media persistently forget to ask them about this. Officially then, the murder of JFK is still an open case. Sixty years later, it is now flagrantly obvious that the public knew almost nothing in 1963. Almost more amazing is this: we now know a good deal more than we knew just ten years ago. I can only hope to be alive for ten more years to learn what else has been concealed.

---

16 Even today, no such experts officially exist—just search the internet.

SPECIAL SUPPLEMENT

BRIAN EDWARDS TARGETS THE TRIPLE OVERPASS—A POSSIBLE ORIGIN FOR JFK'S FOREHEAD WOUND[1]

#1 TITLE OF PRESENTATION

Was there a shooter on top of the triple underpass?

1 A presentation Brian Edwards gave to the Dealey Plaza UK group in 2023. The title was "A Tactical Analysis of the Dealey Plaza Ambush." (1390) JFK Assassination - Dealey Plaza UK-Canterbury Conference - Brian Edwards - YouTube. Also see Brian Edwards website jfk - Search (bing.com).

#2 OVERHEAD VIEW OF DEALEY PLAZA

#3 VIEW FROM THE TRIPLE OVERPASS

#4 OVERHEAD VIEW OF COMMERCE ST.

#5 STRAIGHT PATH OF LIMOUSINE ON ELM STREET

#6 VIEW FROM A SHOOTER'S PERSPECTIVE

#7 DILLARD PHOTOGRAPH—CROPPED

#8 DILLARD PHOTOGRAPH—UNCROPPED

Dillard photo -- uncropped

#9 UNKNOWN, ILL-DEFINED OBJECT AT UPPER LEFT BETWEEN THE VERTICAL PILLARS

#10 JAMES TAGUE, IN RELATION TO THE UNKNOWN OBJECT

#11 CLOSE-UP FROM THE DILLARD PHOTOGRAPH

#12 CLEAR IMAGE OF A POSSIBLE SHOOTER SITE

#13 A COMPARISON OF IMAGES AT A POSSIBLE SHOOTER SITE

#14 CAMELOT REDUX: A KNIGHT (DAVID) MIMICS A SHOT AT LANCER (JFK), DIRECTLY ABOVE COMMERCE STREET

#15 CANCELLARE PHOTOGRAPH, TAKEN JUST AFTER THE DILLARD PHOTOGRAPH

#16 SOMETHING (OR SOMEBODY) WAS THERE.

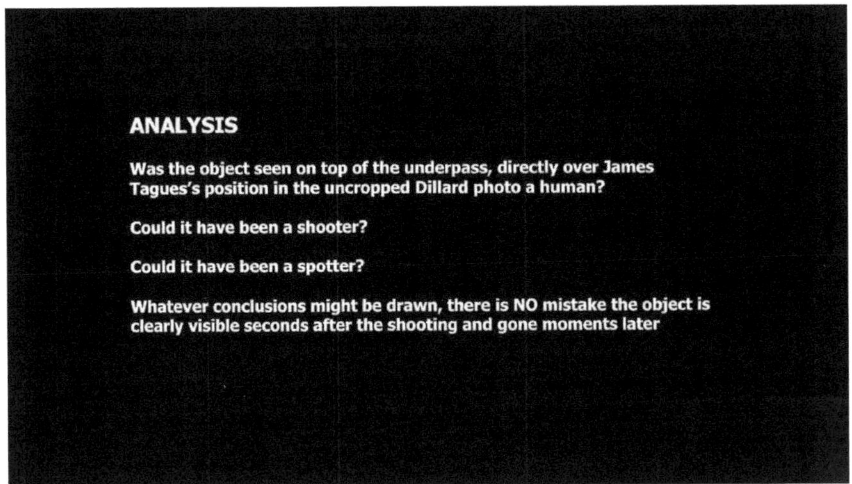

#17 NOTE THE AREA WITHIN THE BLACK RECTANGLE—A SHOOTER'S SITE?

BRIAN K. EDWARDS has researched the JFK assassination since 1969. He has accumulated and read over 600 books. He has interviewed the majority of the Dealey Plaza eyewitnesses, including the entangled Dallas police officers and detectives. He has interviewed many of the doctors and medical personnel from Trauma Room One, as well as several of the navy corpsmen from the Bethesda Naval Medical Center.

Brian has given hundreds of presentations. Since 2001, he has been a regular presenter at the JFK Lancer Conference in Dallas. He has been a frequent contributor to many JFK publications, including *Dealey Plaza Echo, The Third Decade, The Fourth Decade, Deep Politics Quarterly and the JFK Assassination Chronicles.*

He holds a master's degree in criminal justice from Washburn University. During 1994-2001, he served as an adjunct instructor with the criminal justice department at this university.

He has been a police officer in Lawrence, Kansas, and was assigned to their crime scene search team as a photographer. He has served as an instructor and as a field training officer in the police academy, and as one of their self-defense instructors. During 1983-1990, he served on the counter-assault team.

His research on the Zapruder film has been cited in several books: *Assassination Science* (1998)[2]; *Murder in Dealey Plaza* (2000)[3]; *The Zapruder Film* (2003)[4] and *The Hoax of the Century* (2004)[5].

---

2 James H. Fetzer, Ph.D., ed, *Assassination Science*, op. cit.

3 James H. Fetzer, Ph.D., ed., *Murder in Dealey Plaza*, op. cit.

4 David R. Wrone, *The Zapruder Film: Reframing the Assassination* (Lawrence, KS: University of Kansas Press, 2003).

5 Harrison Livingstone, *The Hoax of the Century: Decoding the Forgery of the Zapruder Film* (Victoria, BC: Trafford Publishing, 2004).

He is the co-author of *Beyond the Fence Line*[6] and is now at work on *Lancer is Down: A Tactical Analysis of the Ambush in Dealey Plaza.*

On November 17, 2017, he testified as an expert witness for the defense in the mock trial of Lee Harvey Oswald at the North Texas School of Law in Houston.[7]

6 Casey J. Quinlan and Brian K. Edwards, *Beyond the Fence Line: The Eyewitness Account of Ed Hoffman and the Murder of President Kennedy* (Southlake, TX: JFK Lancer Productions and Publications, 2008).

7 Robert K. Tanenbaum, "Watch Mock Trial Video Series: State of Texas v Lee Harvey Oswald," Number 11, "Witness Testimony: Brian Edwards," RobertKTanenbaumBooks.com, November 17, 2017, South Texas College of Law, Houston, https://robertktanenbaumbooks.com/mock-trial-video-series.

APPENDIX A

SPECTER'S ESCAPADES

Figure A.1
Specter Models the SBT. Warren Commission Photograph, 1964. Source: "Commission Exhibit 903 (CE 903)," *Hearings before the President's Commission on the Assassination of President Kennedy*, op. cit., vol. 18, p. 96.

THIS PHOTOGRAPH (one of two, see also Figure A.3) is Arlen Specter's reenactment of the SBT for the WC. The witnesses recalled seeing JFK's throat wound *above* the knot in the tie. (The stick here lies well below the tie knot.) The shirt has only slits (as if from a scalpel); it does not show typical bullet holes—as even FBI Special Agent Robert Frazier agreed. Frazier was assigned to the firearms identification unit of the

FBI Laboratory in Washington. In his testimony to the WC, Frazier affirmed that he saw the coat, shirt, tie, bandages, and support belt that JFK wore that day. "The hole in the front of the shirt does not have the round characteristic shape caused by a round bullet entering cloth," Frazier told the WC.[1] Even the slits lie noticeably superior to the exit site shown in this photograph. JFK's shirt is shown in Figure A.2. Note the slits in the shirt lie superior to the exit site shown in the above photograph (Figure A.1). Harold Weisberg obtained the photograph of JFK's shirt from FBI Exhibit 60. The photograph was first published in Weisberg's 1969 book *Post Mortem*.[2]

Figure A.2

JFK's shirt shows two slits (probably from a scalpel). This image is from FBI Exhibit 60. It was excluded (for good reason) from all twenty-six volumes of the Warren Commission. Source: Harold Weisberg, *Post Mortem*, op. cit., p. 598.

1 "Testimony of Robert A. Frazier," *Hearings before the President's Commission on the Assassination of President Kennedy*, op. cit., vol. 5, pp. 58-74, at p. 61.

2 Harold Weisberg, *Post Mortem*, op. cit., pp. 328-329. This book was originally published in 1969. Figure 4.2 appears on p. 598 of the 2007 edition.

In *Post Mortem*, Weisberg explained the importance of the photograph seen in Figure A.2. He wrote:

> In itself, this picture, presented here for the first time anywhere, destroys the entire Warren Report and means the falsity could not have been accidental. It shows not bullet holes, but slits. It also shows that when the shirt is buttoned they do not coincide and on this added basis could not have been made by a bullet. Note that the slit on the button side is entirely below the neckband while that on the buttonhole side extends well up onto it. The FBI and the Commission both knew their representations were false. The Commission blundered into the truth separately when Dulles asked Dr. Carrico where the President's front neck wound was and Carrico told him it was above the shirt. Carrico confirmed this to me when he confirmed the obvious, that this damage to the shirt was done when the necktie was cut off by nurses under his supervision during emergency treatment.[3]

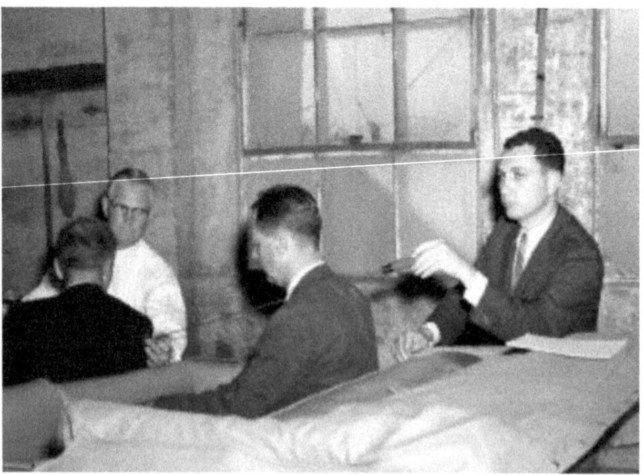

Figure A.3
Specter sells the SBT. (Compare to Figure A.8.) Warren Commission Photograph, 1964.

3 Ibid., p. 598. Underlining in the original.

Figure A.3 is another photograph from Specter's reenactment for the WC. Examine the hole in the back of JFK's shirt (Figure A.4), which seems lower than Specter's entry site in this photograph. Also note that the holes in the back of the coat and shirt are not slits; after all, these holes were not caused by a scalpel. Even the back wound on the face sheet (Figures 1.7A and B) seems lower than Specter's entry in the above photograph. So does the wound in the autopsy photograph (Figure A.4), which may have been surreptitiously elevated.[4]

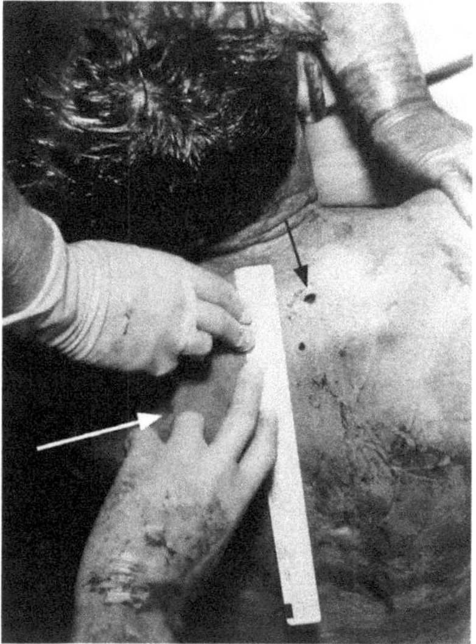

Figure A.4

This is the back wound (vertical black arrow) in an autopsy photograph. The mysterious Black (Dark) Spot is barely visible, but it is identified by the white arrow on the left back. No one else has ever noted its bizarre photographic properties. It took me nine visits even to recognize this. Source: Douglas Horne, *Inside the ARRB*, op. cit., vol. 1, Figure 43, autopsy photos 11, 12 (B & W), and 38, 39 (color).

---

4 Although he tried to minimalize the discrepancy, even James Jenkins told William Matson Law that the back wound in the autopsy photograph seemed higher than he recalled it (See: William Matson Law, *In the Eye of History*, second edition, op. cit., p. 244). Also note the dark spot (horizontal arrow in Figure A.4) on JFK's *left* back. This image is totally inconsistent for a stereo pair, as discussed in the penultimate page of my hardcover book (or see Figure A.4 here). Unfortunately for the public, this wildly inconsistent image is not in the public record. I only noticed it during my ninth visit!

Also compare Specter's back entry in the above photographs versus Boswell's transformation of the back wound into a neck wound (Figure 1.7A)—Boswell's new site overlay the shirt collar! Specter also ignored the abrasion collar, which lay at the inferior border of the back wound. To any pathologist, that clearly should have implied an *upward* trajectory—just the opposite of what Specter demonstrated here. The back wound and the clothing holes most likely resulted from a piece of shrapnel that ricocheted from the street and deposited copper residue onto the back of the shirt and coat. No residue was found on the front of the shirt. Of course, the pathologists had no access to JFK's clothing during the autopsy.

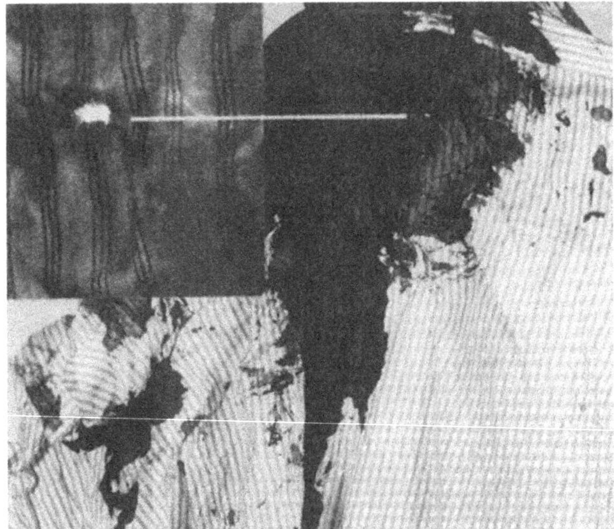

Figure A.5

JFK's Shirt. Notice the absence of a slit (which was seen on the front of the shirt). Source: Warren Commission Document 107, exhibit 60, NARA. Reprinted in: Stewart Galanor, *Cover-Up* (New York: Kestrel Books, 1998), Document 7.

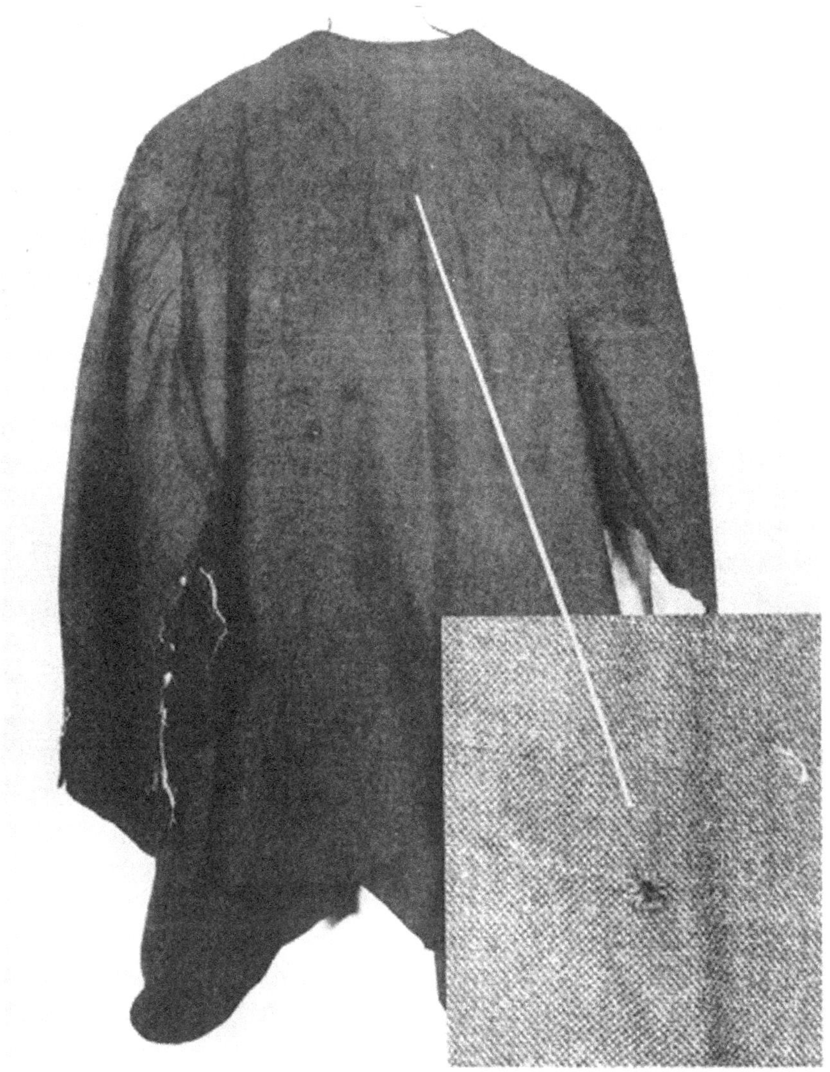

Bullet hole is about 6 inches below the top of the collar and 2 inches to the right of the midline seam of the jacket. (2H365)

Figure A.6

JFK's Coat. Again, notice the absence of a slit. Source: Warren Commission Document 107, exhibit 59, NARA. Reprinted in: Stewart Galanor, *Cover-Up*, op. cit., Document 6.

For further demolition of the SBT, examine the trajectory on the CT scan just below. This trajectory utilizes the two wound locations described by the pathologists. However, this trajectory must inescapably traverse either the spine or the lung. But, according to the pathologists, neither event occurred.[5] Of course, we should be kind—the autopsy occurred years before CT scans became available; that revolution would require almost another decade.

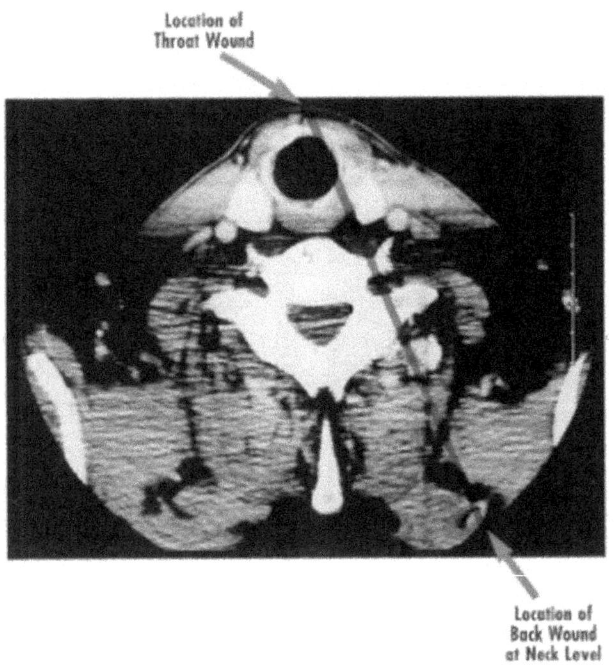

Figure A.7
CT Scan of a Patient at Eisenhower Memorial Hospital. The patient had similar upper chest and neck dimensions as JFK. By itself, this cross section demolishes the SBT. Source: Stewart Galanor, *Cover-Up*, op. cit., Document 45.

5 *The Warren Commission Report: Report of the President's Commission on the Assassination of President Kennedy*, (New York, NY: St. Martin's Press, 1964), p. 88: "No bone was struck by the bullet which passed through the President's body."

Galanor commented: "Clearly, any bullet along this path would have shattered the spine. But the autopsy pathologists observed and the X-rays confirmed no major trauma to the President's spine had occurred. Thus, a bullet entering the President's back could not have exited his throat. With one simple stroke Dr. Mantik had scientifically disproved the lone assassin theory." (Ibid., p. 111)

On the other hand, for Oswald's autopsy, which was performed by an authentic forensic pathologist (Earl Rose), a chart was titled, "Cross Section Through Upper Abdomen," in which the bullet trajectory was traced through the internal organs. Such a comparable JFK cross section would have endlessly frustrated Humes.

Just below is JFK's death certificate. Note that the back wound was at T3.

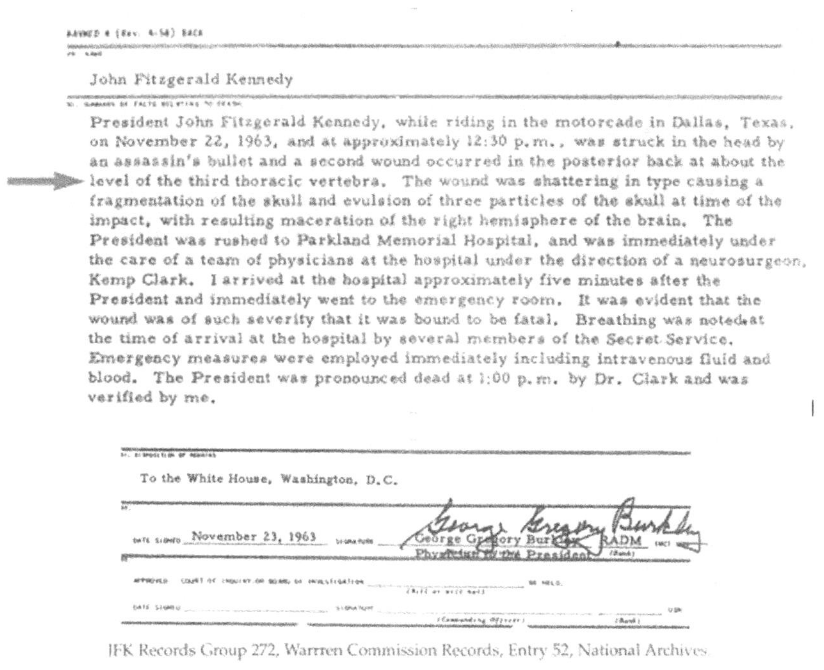

John Fitzgerald Kennedy

President John Fitzgerald Kennedy, while riding in the motorcade in Dallas, Texas, on November 22, 1963, and at approximately 12:30 p.m., was struck in the head by an assassin's bullet and a second wound occurred in the posterior back at about the level of the third thoracic vertebra. The wound was shattering in type causing a fragmentation of the skull and evulsion of three particles of the skull at time of the impact, with resulting maceration of the right hemisphere of the brain. The President was rushed to Parkland Memorial Hospital, and was immediately under the care of a team of physicians at the hospital under the direction of a neurosurgeon, Kemp Clark. I arrived at the hospital approximately five minutes after the President and immediately went to the emergency room. It was evident that the wound was of such severity that it was bound to be fatal. Breathing was noted at the time of arrival at the hospital by several members of the Secret Service. Emergency measures were employed immediately including intravenous fluid and blood. The President was pronounced dead at 1:00 p.m. by Dr. Clark and was verified by me.

To the White House, Washington, D.C.

November 23, 1963 — George Gregory Burkley, RADM — Physician to the President

JFK Records Group 272, Warren Commission Records, Entry 52, National Archives

The President's physician Dr. Burkley placed the back wound at the level of the third thoracic vertebra.

Figure A.8

JFK's Death Certificate, as signed by Admiral George Burkley. Source: JFK Records Group 272, entry 52, NARA.

John Ebersole, the radiologist, told me that the level of the back wound was at T4. James Jenkins has also cited T4.[6] In assessing Ebersole's credibility, it should be emphasized that his specialty (like mine) was radiation oncology, where correlation of exterior anatomy with internal anatomy actually matters. In no other specialty is this very critical; but for us, the X-ray beam may miss the cancer if we ignore external landmarks. So, the next figure here shows this correlation for T3.

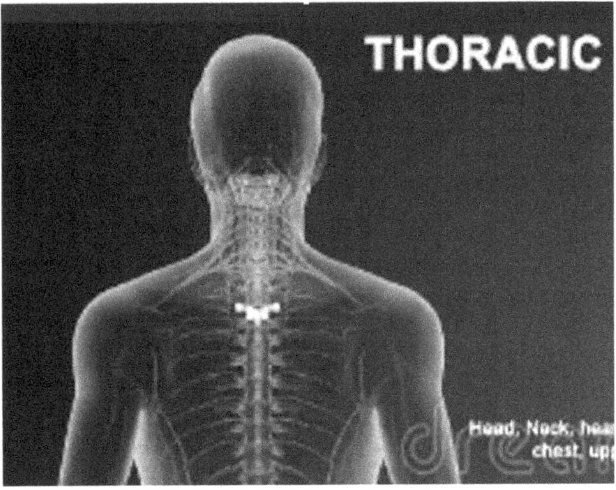

Figure A.9

T3 Correlated with External Anatomy. This is clearly not the neck. And T4 is hopelessly too low for the SBT. Source: 7active Studio, "Thoracic vertebrae or thoracic spine bone T3 [ID 231458391]," Dreamstime, n.d., https://www.dreamstime.com/thoracic-vertebrae-thoracic-spine-bone-t-thoracic-spine-serves-many-functions-protects-spinal-cord-bundle-image231458391.

The final figure here (Figure A.9) was prepared by Paul O'Connor for Law's book.[7] It displays a rather superior location for the back wound. So perhaps Jenkins was right about the autopsy photograph—the back

6 William Matson Law, *In the Eye of History*, second edition, op. cit., p. 226.

7 Law, *In the Eye of History*, op. cit., p. 480.

wound seems too high. Since we now know (from my observations) that the Dark Spot (on JFK's *left* back) is photographically inconsistent on the two stereo views, we know that some manipulation was done on these back photographs. That leaves the door quite open to deliberate photographic elevation of the back wound in the autopsy photograph.

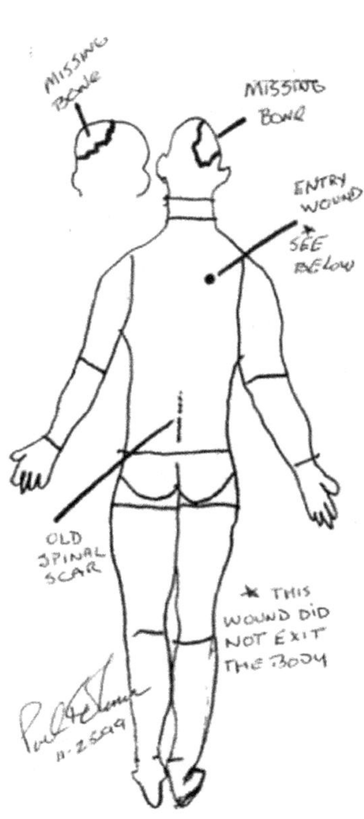

Figure A.10
Paul O'Connor's Sketch of the Back Wound. Source: William Matson Law, *In the Eye of History*, op. cit., photo 22.

JUST THE GURNEY—OR WAS JFK ON THE METAL EXAMINATION TABLE?

Since it is not discussed elsewhere in this book (or perhaps anywhere else at all), here is a final question for this appendix: While treated in Trauma Room One, was JFK always on the rolling gurney (aka stretcher or cart) or had he been transferred to the fixed metal examination table? A meticulous survey of the evidence strongly implies that JFK was treated on the gurney—and was never transferred to the metal table.

This work was primarily by Douglas Mizzer,[8] a longtime researcher in the JFK case. I first met him during the 1990s, when I spent time with him at Harry Livingstone's house and at a local Baltimore bar.

After his research through the WC volumes, Mizzer found at least nine Parkland physicians who recalled that, during treatment, JFK was lying on a cart, carriage, or stretcher: Drs. Carrico, Perry, Clark, (Pepper) Jenkins, Jones, Bashour, Peters, Giesecke and White. Furthermore, here is one comment from Dr. Robert McClelland:

> When I came into the trauma room, I was immediately confronted with a horrid sight—the president lying on his back *on the gurney* [emphasis added] with a light shining down on his bloody head. That was the first thing I saw.[9]

Dr. Kemp Clark added this:

> I then examined the wound in the back of the President's head. This was a large, gaping wound in the right posterior part, with cerebral and cerebellar tissue being damaged and exposed. There was considerable blood loss evident on the *carriage* [emphasis added], the floor, and

8 An anonymous scholar, who has researched this independently (apparently including more recent interviews with surviving Parkland doctors), has confirmed Mizzer's conclusion.

9 ABC News, "9 People Who Witnessed JFK's Assassination," ABCNews.go.com, November 20, 2013, https://abcnews.go.com/US/people-witnessed-jfks-assassination/story?id=20531350.

> the clothing of some of the people present. I would estimate 1,500 cc of blood being present.[10]

Quite recently, Doug Mizzer located the following news item from the UPI Archives (November 30,1963) by Bryce Miller:

> One week ago the assassin's bullets [note no accomplices] struck President Kennedy. It is now possible to reveal the step-by-step struggle of a team of 15 doctors to save his life though they knew from the start it was hopeless. The first call came to Parkland Hospital from the Dallas Police Department. "The President has been shot. He is on the way to Parkland." Surgical teams sprang into action.
>
> Dr. Charles James Carrico, a resident in surgery, was in the emergency room when a SS man burst through the swinging doors. A second one, with a submachine gun cradled in his arms, was right on his heels. The first agent asked for two portable hospital carts (he called them "stretchers"), one for Gov. John Connally, the other for the President. In moments the portable carts were wheeled into Emergency Operating Room No. 1. Connally was first. Then the President, with Mrs. Jacqueline Kennedy walking beside the cart, holding his head, her pink suit bloody. Connally was wheeled into Room No. 2, an identical 15-by-10-foot room directly across the hall.
>
> Vice-President Lyndon Johnson walked in, hand on chest. Sen. Ralph Yarborough, who had been riding in the motorcade with him, was in tears. At first, some feared Johnson might have suffered a heart attack.
>
> *The operating table in Room No. 1 had been shoved out of the way* [emphasis added]. The doctors were moving so swiftly they did not want to take time to lift the President off [of] the cart....Jones began

10 "Testimony of Dr. William Kemp Clark," *Hearings before the President's Commission on the Assassination of President Kennedy*, op. cit., vol. 6, pp. 18-27, at p. 21.

> a "cut-down" on Kennedy's left arm to insert a catheter—a device to force more blood into a vein and keep the passage open. Curtis completed the same procedure on the left leg....By now, the *cart* [emphasis added] had been elevated at the foot to help the blood get back to the heart.

So now, when we picture the scene in Trauma Room One, we need only focus on the gurney—the fixed metal examination table was not used. And if Secret Service SA Paul Landis deposited a bullet on JFK's stretcher in Trauma Room One, as he claims in his 2023 book, *The Final Witness*,[11] that could only be the rolling gurney, where JFK himself lay. And for the two nurses (Sharon Lee Tuohy and Phyllis J. Hall),[12] each of whom saw a bullet on JFK's stretcher, their report means that this naughty bullet lay adjacent to JFK. This bullet could not have been the Magic Bullet—to qualify for that misnomer it had to lie on Connally's stretcher.[13] Meanwhile, in his own emergency room,

---

11 Paul Landis, *The Final Witness*, op. cit.

12 Two Parkland nurses, Sharon Lee Tuohy and Phyllis J. Hall, each observed a bullet on JFK's stretcher. See: Denis Morissette, "HSCA Interview with Parkland Intern Sharon Thuoy [sic]," op. cit.

The recollections of Phyllis J. Hall are here: "Nurse claims JFK had another bullet lodged in body after assassination," *NY Daily News*, updated January 10, 2019, https://www.nydailynews.com/news/national/jfk-mystery-bullet-lodged-body-nurse-article-1.1512283. She saw an undamaged bullet "On the [JFK] cart, halfway between the earlobe and the shoulder...." Did both Sharon and Phyllis see the Landis bullet? And was this later called the Belmont bullet?

13 Landis claimed to have found the Magic Bullet CE 399 on the limo seat behind Jackie Kennedy after she left the limo at Parkland Hospital. He wrote:

"When Mrs. Kennedy finally stood up, I looked again at the seat and saw a bullet on top of the tufted black leather cushioning behind where she had been sitting. It was resting in a seam where the tufted leather padding ended against the car's metal body. It was a completely intact bullet. It had been hidden behind Mrs. Kennedy all the time she was seated. No wonder I hadn't seen it sooner." (Source: Paul Landis, *The Final Witness*, op. cit., p. 166.)

Connally heard a bullet fall to the floor. But, for many reasons, this could not have been the bullet that Darrell Tomlinson found in the hallway, which later transformed into CE 399, the Magic Bullet.[14] We can only wonder today: how much of this did Specter know?

According to Specter's SBT, CE 399 glided from JFK's neck to Connally's thigh. The bullet that Landis allegedly found at the top of the rear limousine seat behind Mrs. Kennedy must have been gifted with magical properties that would have astonished even master magician Dariel Fitzkee. Bizarrely, upon leaving Connally's thigh, this bullet then had to soar (like a guided missile) *backwards* to Jackie's seat! The magic never ends.

14 Josiah Thompson, *Six Seconds in Dallas*, op. cit., pp. 156-158.

APPENDIX B

THE SCIENCE AND MATHEMATICS OF OPTICAL DENSITY

OD = $\log_{10}(I_o/I)$ = $\log_{10}(1/T)$, where I_o is the incident light, and I is the transmitted light (I). The transmission T is I/I_o; notice that in this equation, it is *inverted*. In other words, large transmissions become small optical densities—but recall that T must be $\leq$100%. An OD of zero means that all light is transmitted. A really thick piece of lead could produce such a result: it would yield a very transparent image so that $I_o/I = 1$. In that case, $\log_{10}(I_o/I) = \log_{10}(1) = \log_{10}(10^0) = 0$. In summary, an OD of zero means a 100% transmission. A transmission of 10% would then correspond to OD = $\log_{10}(1 \div 0.1) = \log_{10}(10) = \log_{10}(10^1) =$ 1. Table B.1 displays how logarithms work in this setting.

Table B.1
OD as Logarithm of (inverse) Transmission (T) to Base 10

Logarithm of (1/T)	1/T	OD
10^0 $\log_{10}(1) = 0$	$10^0 = 1$ (by definition, i.e., no 10)	0.0
10^1 $\log_{10}(10) = 1.0$	10^1 =just one 10	1.0
10^2 $\log_{10}(100) = 2.0$	10^2 $= 10 \times 10 = 100$	2.0
10^3 $\log_{10}(1{,}000) = 3.0$	10^3 $= 10 \times 10 \times 10 = 1{,}000$	3.0
10^4 $\log_{10}(10{,}000) = 4.0$	10^4 $= 10 \times 10 \times 10 \times 10 = 10{,}000$	4.0

The inverse relationship, which gives the transmission T through the film as a function of OD, is:

$$T = I / I_O = 10^{-OD}$$

An OD of zero represents 100% transmission. This is the setting in which the densitometer is zeroed. For example,

- An OD of 1.00 represents $T = 10^{-OD} = 10^{-1} = 1/10$ or 10%.
- An OD of 2.00 represents $T = 10^{-OD} = 10^{-2} = 1/100$ or 1%.
- An OD of three yields 0.1%; an OD of four, 0.01%, etc.

This definition makes optical density proportional to the amount of silver halide reduced to black metallic silver. It also allows ODs to be additive. For example, if light passes through two films, each with a uniform OD of 1, then the effective OD (for the two-film combination) is 1 + 1 = 2. To be specific, each film transmits 10%, so together the two films will transmit 10% x 10% = 1%. That is precisely a combined OD of 1 + 1 = 2. As already noted, an optical density of 2 implies a transmission of 1%.

An X-ray film functions like a negative in print film photography. Objects appear black on X-rays because most of the X-rays pass through the real-world object (e.g., air) and strike the film. So, after development, the radiation-sensitive emulsion on the X-ray film (typically 95% silver bromide and 5% silver iodide) turns black—because the bromide (or iodide) salt has been converted to metallic silver, and so the metal silver remains on the film. Images with low ODs (e.g., 0.0–1.0) represent dense real-world objects, like bone or metal. Images with high ODs (e.g., 2.0–4.0) represent real world objects that are transparent to X-rays (like air). Table B.2 summarizes this relationship.

In daily radiological practice, most ODs for X-ray films are centered about 1.0. This choice is automatically made by the human eye for convenience in discrimination among human tissues. The usual working range is from about 0.5 to 2.0. It is unusual for the OD of observed tissues to exceed 3.0, except as a byproduct of exposure requirements at other sites on the film. An OD of 2.0 will appear quite dark, while an OD of 0.5 will appear transparent on the film (white in prints).

Table B.2
OD vs. Light Transmission[1]

OD	Transmission	Remarks
0.0	100%	All of the light passes through the X-ray film.
1.0	10%	Only 10% of the light passes through the X-ray film.
2.0	1%	Only 1% of the light passes through the X-ray film.
3.0	0.1%	Only 0.1% of the light passes through the X-ray film.
4.0	0.01%	Only 0.01% of the light passes through the X-ray film.

The semi-logarithmic graph below (Graph B.1) demonstrates the relationship between OD and transmission.

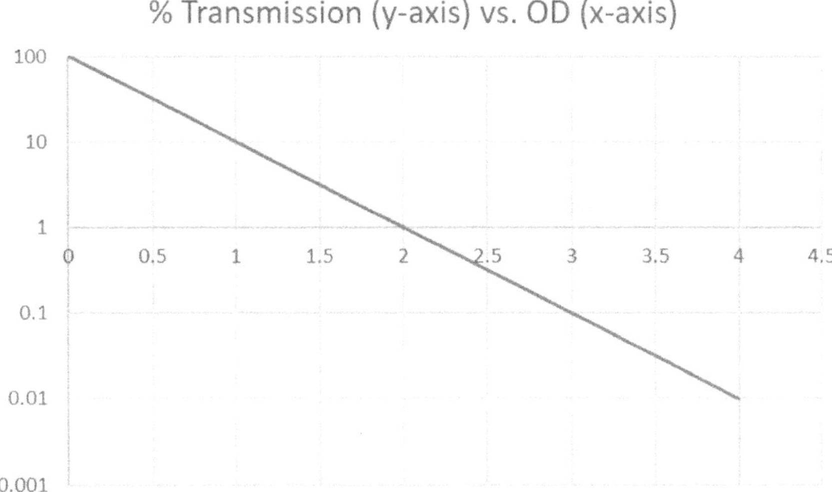

Graph B.1
Percent Transmission (y-axis) vs. OD (x-axis)

1 Douglas Horne, *Inside the ARRB*, op. cit., vol. 2, p. 543.

Table B.3 illustrates that dense objects, like bone or metal, appear transparent in X-ray films, and have low ODs. Conversely, less dense objects, like air cavities, appear black in X-ray films, and have higher ODs.

Table B.3
How Real-World Objects Translate into ODs

Real-World Object	Real-World Density	X-Ray Quality	Appearance on X-ray film	ODs
Bone or Metal	Dense Blocks X-Rays	Radio-opaque	Transparent (white)	0.0 to 1.5
Air Cavity	Not Dense Transparent to X-rays	Radiolucent	Black	2.0 to 4.0

CHARACTERISTIC X-RAY CURVES

Each type of X-ray film is characterized by a graph of OD vs. logarithm of exposure. The graphs are also sensitive to the development process, which must be specified for each curve. The X-ray films at the JFK autopsy were produced by Kodak; they are clearly labeled as such. The current Kodak technical staff was unable to locate the unique characteristic curve for these films, but they did supply one from the 1970s which they believe is quite similar to the 1960s. It shows excellent linearity between an OD of about 0.6 and 3.0.

The characteristic curve for a generic X-ray film is shown in Figure B.1.[2] The general shape for DuPont Cronex film, as used in my work,

2 "Characteristic Curve," National Film and Sound Archive of Australia," NFSA.gov.au, n.d., https://www.nfsa.gov.au/preservation/preservation-glossary/characteristic-curve.

is very similar to the Kodak film.[3] Like the Kodak film, it is also quite linear in the OD range of 0.6 to 3.0. Furthermore, this linearity between 0.6 and 3.0 occurs over more than one logarithm of exposure, very much like the Kodak film. This similarity between these two characteristic curves provides a reliable basis for comparing images produced on the two different films.

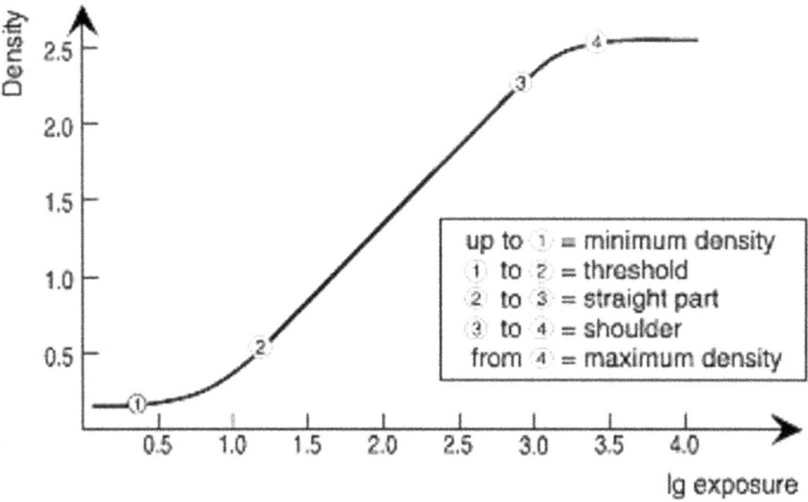

Figure B.1
A Characteristic Curve for a Generic X-ray Film. The ordinate is OD, while the abscissa is the logarithm of exposure. The "toe" (threshold—on the left) implies very low exposures. The center region is the linear response range, where OD is proportional to the log of the exposure. The "shoulder" region represents higher exposures, where the curve begins to flatten. The slope of the "straight line" region indicates the contrast of the film.

3 The remarkable similarity of slopes for many different films is displayed in this article: Adam Kouvelis, John R. Prince, and Joe C. Leonard, "Determining Characteristic Curves for Films Used in Analog Nuclear Medicine," *Journal of Nuclear Medicine Technology*, vol. 15, no. 3, (September 1987): 115-118, https://tech.snmjournals.org/content/jnmt/15/3/115.full.pdf.

The typical dimensions of human anatomy and the physiology of the human eye place fairly tight constraints on these characteristic curves. In order for the eye to discriminate effectively among human tissues, an OD range of 0.6 to 3.0 is optimal. Occasionally ODs as high as 4.0 are encountered, usually as an indirect and unavoidable result of choosing an exposure for a different site. In high OD areas, some detail can often be visualized by holding a bright light directly behind the film, but this should be avoided if possible.[4] For typical X-ray tube voltages of 80–120 kV, the attenuation of the X-ray beam by human tissues is well known. Examples are shown in Table B.4.The range of transmissions shown in Table B.4 extends over a factor of about ten.

Table B.4
X-ray Attenuation in Human Tissues

Tissue	View	Thickness (cm)	Transmission (%)
Brain	AP	15 cm	8.5%
Brain	Lateral	12 cm	14.0%
Upper Chest	AP	20 cm	2.6%
Lower Chest	AP	24 cm	1.2%
Maxillary Sinus	Lateral	7 cm	28%

The transmitted X-rays (via the intensifying screen) produce the exposures in the X-ray film.[5] The attenuation (decreased transmission)

4 Harold Elford Johns and John Robert Cunningham, *The Physics of Radiology* (London, UK: Charles C. Thomas Publishers Ltd., fourth edition, 1983), pp. 579-585.

5 This line of reasoning assumes that the number of visible and UV photons, which are produced by the X-ray screen and which go on to strike the film, is proportional to the number of X-rays

range of about ten in Table B.4 implies a range of about one in the logarithm of the exposure, just as was described for the above characteristic curves. If the X-ray film were instead designed to accommodate 2–3 logarithms of exposure, then a large portion of the film potential would be unusable—since human tissues generally span only about one logarithm of attenuation. If the film were designed to accommodate much less than one logarithm of exposure, then the extremes of human tissue attenuation would cause some ODs to lie either on the lower nonlinear portion of the curve (the toe) or on the upper nonlinear portion of the curve (the shoulder). In either case, because the curve is flatter at the toe and at the shoulder, OD differences would be very small even for large exposure differences at these two extremes. This means that the discrimination of the film for tissues of widely different densities would be lost, just the opposite of what is desired in general radiology.

In summary, in general radiology, characteristic curves should encompass only about 1–2 logarithms of exposure, with an OD range up to about 3.0. That is, of course, exactly the case for both the Kodak film (at the autopsy) and also for the DuPont film used in my experiments. Specialized films (e.g., mammography, angiography) have differing requirements and therefore may differ from films of general radiology.

The precise shape of the characteristic curve depends on the variables of the development process (temperature, time, and chemical

---

that first strike the X-ray screen. This assumption is well documented in radiology and is widely used. In radiation oncology, such film measurements can be used to assess doses to human tissues. By analogy, the Hounsfield numbers obtained in CT scans also utilize this assumption of proportionality between the X-ray beam and the exposure seen by the detection equipment. The Hounsfield number is defined as:

$$\frac{\mathbf{u}\,(\text{tissue}) - \mathbf{u}\,(\text{water}) \times 1000,}{\mathbf{u}\,(\text{water})}$$

where **u** is the linear attenuation coefficient. These numbers are used in radiation oncology departments when it is desired to take into account the differences among tissues within the radiation beam.

concentration) and also on the X-ray tube parameters (voltage, current, and time). However, the general shape of the characteristic curve over a fairly wide range of these values looks quite similar; all curves have a toe and a shoulder as well as a central linear portion. The exposure ranges and OD ranges are also fairly similar. The OD range may be compressed or expanded modestly, and the curve may be shifted somewhat to the left or to the right. In the usual case, the slope of the linear portion does not change by much.[6] Specifically, changing the current does little to alter the slope. The main effect of a temperature change is to alter the speed of the film, i.e., to shift it laterally.[7] In my articles, the only quantitative use made of the characteristic curve was the value of the slope. I used this to calculate how much brain was missing (about 5 cm) low in JFK's right hemisphere.

To illustrate this point, the slope of the curve for the Kodak film was measured in this work as 3.09. For the DuPont film, it was measured to be 3.44. For my estimates of missing brain, the differences in slope between these two brands of film is relatively unimportant. For all of the above reasons, even though the original curve for these JFK X-rays was not available, it is not likely that it would differ by much, especially in slope, from the one supplied by Kodak. In fact, of course, that is just what Kodak stated.

The presence of the toe and shoulder of the curve is readily explained and would be expected to be common to all such characteristic curves. The toe results from an exposure too low to consistently photoconvert a silver granule. Such a conversion requires more than one photon acting almost simultaneously. When the exposure is too low, the probability of such simultaneous photons is greatly decreased, until a threshold photon intensity is reached. At the shoulder of the curve, on the other

---

6 Harold Elford Johns and John Robert Cunningham, *The Physics of Radiology*, op. cit., p. 583.

7 Ibid., p. 582.

hand, the number of unconverted silver granules is quite small, so the probability of simultaneous photons striking such a rare unconverted grain is again low. The shoulder region is sometimes called the saturation region because the film is nearly fully exposed here.

To measure the ODs of the JFK autopsy X-ray films at the National Archives, I used a Model TBX optical densitometer from Tobias Associates of Ivyland, Pennsylvania. I began by taking ODs, point by point, manually via 1 mm diameter circles. For my graphs, I later employed a 0.1 mm aperture. This device measures the transmission of ordinary light through X-ray film. Many of these sites were measured repeatedly on successive days in order to assess reproducibility. This was found to be within 1 or 2% and sometimes even less, with the main uncertainty due to manual positioning within the required 1 mm. The densitometer was repeatedly zeroed by a built-in control knob. Calibration against external reference film strips of known optical density was quickly and easily achieved across the observed OD range. These reference strips were supplied by the Small Systems Group, Incorporated of Chico, California. The densitometer was found to be very stable and consistent with respect to these external reference calibrations.

APPENDIX C

HOW WERE X-RAYS COPIED IN 1963?

AS PHOTOGRAPHIC EXPERT T. Thorne Baker explained in his classic 1941 book *Photographic Emulsion Technique*, "the image formed by the lens of a camera is recorded on a light-responsive surface which in present-day photography takes the form of sensitive silver salts in a film of gelatin."[1] Exposed to light or X-rays (via a screen), the silver salts in the emulsion turn black (i.e., into metallic silver). Thus, a negative is the reverse of the real world, i.e., objects that are a light color in the real world are black on the negative.

When copying X-ray films, however, the situation is exactly reversed. Now, we want the transparent areas of the film (which represent opaque real-world objects) to *remain transparent* on the copied film. If we simply insert an (unexposed) *standard X-ray film* (Figure 3.5) into the film copier we will get a *negative* X-ray copy (Figure 3.6). As expected then, the dark area in the original X-ray (e.g., the dark frontal area in Figure 3.3) will become white in the copy (Figure 3.6)—because the dark area in the original X-ray film blocked the light from striking

1 T. Thorne Baker, *Photographic Emulsion Technique*, op. cit., p. 1.

that area on the (unexposed) copy film. So, the copy film interprets dark areas (on the original film) as representing transparent real-world objects. Today, we use specially designed X-ray copy film to make copies of original X-rays—these are typically single emulsion films, officially called *duplicating film*. Today's duplicating film creates a direct positive image from a positive image. But in 1963, X-ray duplicating film was not commercially available; I checked the historical inventories at Kodak for this purpose.

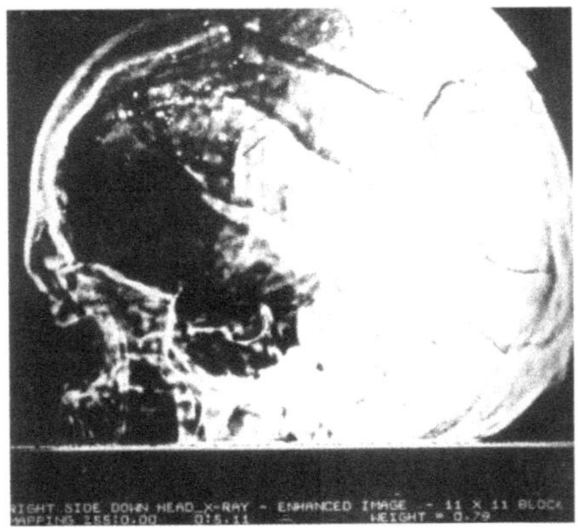

Figure C.1
The Original X-ray Film

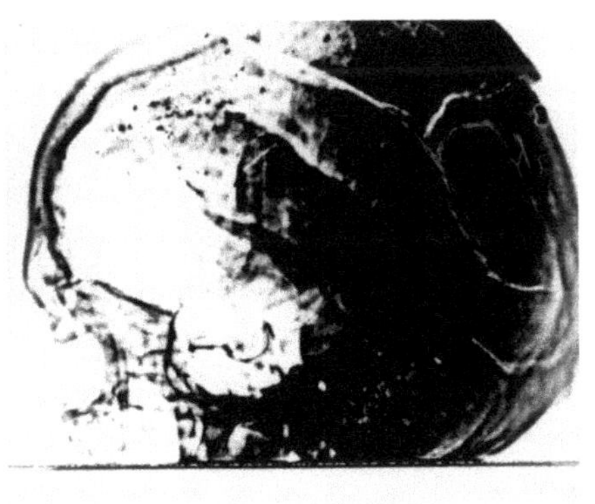

Figure C.2
A Copy of the Original X-Ray Film, using Standard (not Duplicate) X-ray Film

In a 1948 article (in *Public Health Reports)*, surgeon David M. Gould, physicist Willard W. Van Allen, and Photographer Charles Bailey demonstrated that X-rays could be duplicated in that era through three different methods.[2] The authors were interested in producing duplicate X-rays for patients with TB. Gould, Allen, and Bailey explained that copy X-rays had to be exact copies of the original X-ray in every respect. They wrote:

> Any method for reproducing radiographs [i.e., X-rays], to be fully satisfactory, must meet certain standards. The reproduction must be a faithful copy, preserving all the detail and clarity of the original [X-ray] film. In chest films especially, where pathologic lesions are often recorded by very slight variations in density, it is imperative that the copy, to be of any value at all, must have the same tonal scale. Furthermore, to be practical, it is desirable that the whole process be as nearly automatic as possible, involving a minimum of judgment and special skill on the part of the operator.[3]

Their recommended method (based on photographic prints) is known as "contact printing." Using a light box, the original X-ray is first placed over a sheet of 70 mm photographic film; both are then exposed to light. The X-ray image is then printed on 70 mm photographic film as an "intermediate positive" transparency image of the X-ray. They then suggest using Eastman Negative Material #5203, prepared in a DK 76 developer. In the final step, the "intermediate positive" transparency is inserted into a photographic enlarger, which projects the image onto an unexposed sheet of photographic film. The end result is an exact

---

2 David M. Gould, Willard W. Van Allen, and Charles M. Bailey, "Copying X-Ray Films," *Public Health Reports*, vol. 63, no. 23, Tuberculosis Control Issue No. 28 (June 4, 1948): 763-765, https://www.jstor.org/stable/4586580?read-now=1&seq=1.

3 Ibid., p. 763.

duplicate of the original X-ray. Both the "intermediary positive" and the duplicate X-rays are both technically negative images.[4] "The method described gives very faithful reproductions of [X-ray] films," the authors commented. "It has been used successfully for both transparencies and paper prints."

During my career (since the mid-1970s), I had never learned how X-ray films were copied before the era of commercially available duplicate films. On my journey (in the 1990s), the further assistance of a close colleague (diagnostic radiologist, Dr. John Szabo) helped to solve the riddle of copying X-ray films in the 1960s and earlier. In particular, I soon discovered a technologist's textbook[5] that contained detailed recipes for converting standard (double-sided) X-ray films into effective duplicate films.

In the 1961 fifth edition of his classic textbook *Formulating X-Ray Techniques*,[6] John B. Cahoon, JR, RT, FASRT, a professor of radiologic technology, explained how the process of solarization could be used to duplicate X-ray films. In 1890, F. Hunter and V.C. Driffield, two employees of United Alkali Company, published an early mathematical formula that explained solarization.[7] In a 1942 textbook *The Theory of the Photographic Process*, C.E. Kenneth Mees, then a vice president in charge of research and development at the Eastman Kodak Company, described solarization as follows:

4 Most likely, the 1963 forger did not have this option. He probably did not even know about this.

5 John B. Cahoon, *Formulating X-ray Techniques* (Durham, NC: Duke University Press, Fifth Edition, 1961). Recall that the Gould, Allen, Bailey article was published in 1948. In my work, I have often cited the much later work of Cahoon, who claimed this: "By variations of the copying time [with solarization], one may even improve on the original." This technique should have been readily available in 1963.

6 John B. Cahoon, *Formulating X-ray Techniques*, op. cit., p. 56.

7 F. Hurter and V.C. Driffield, "Photochemical Investigations and a New Method of Determination of the Sensitiveness of Photographic Plates," *Journal of the Society of Chemical Industry*, vol. 9, (1890): 455.

If areas of a photographic emulsion layer are exposed to increasing amounts of light, the densities produced after development will not increase indefinitely but will reach a limit and then, with continued exposure, will diminish somewhat. This is known as reversal or solarization.[8]

Figure C.3
Cahoon's Contemporaneous Textbook

In Figure 29 on page 55 of his (fifth edition) textbook, Cahoon published a graph to guide copying an X-ray film (Figure C.4A). In Figure C.4A, the right portion (B to C) of the curve is called the solarization region. The left part (A to B) is used during standard X-ray exposures.

8 C.E. Kenneth Mees, *The Theory of the Photographic Process* (New York: The Macmillan Company, 1942), p. 261.

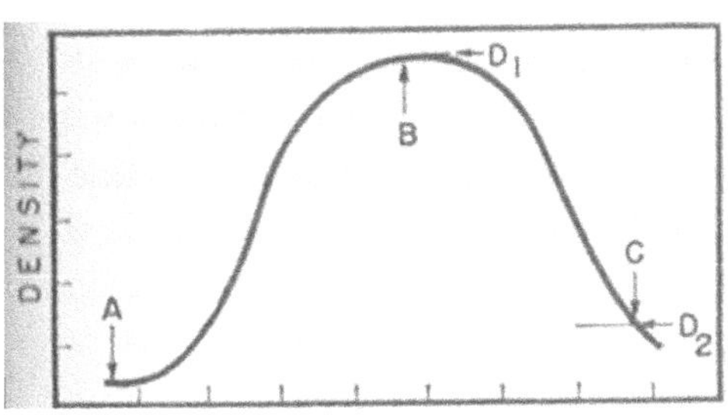

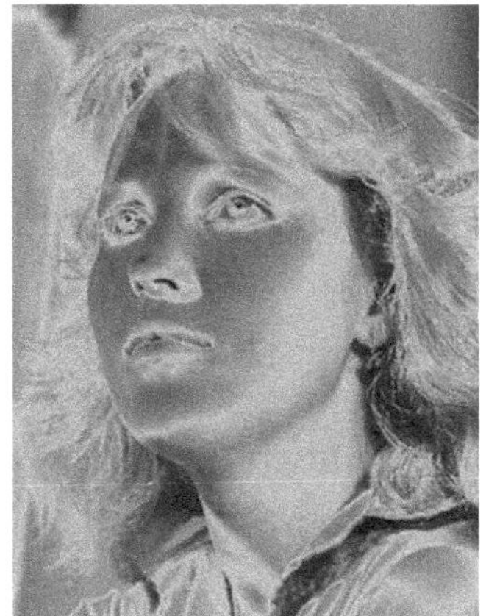

Figure C.4A (Left) and Figure C.4B (Right)

Figure C.4A

The solarization region lies in the right portion of the graph.

Figure C.4B

Girl's face: the solarization region was exploited to create this artistic image.

Left of the peak, the increasing exposure creates greater density on the copy. But, to the right of the peak, this is reversed on the downward slope. Cahoon explained that merely shining light on standard photographic film (but not developing it) causes a latent tone reversal when the X-ray film is contact printed onto the photographic film. He added that, in the range A to B on Figure C.4A, increased exposure produces higher density (D_1) on the photographic film. But increasing exposure (beyond ordinary limits), from B to C in Figure C.4A, reverses the situation, thus causing a decrease in density (D_2) or *solarization of the emulsion*. Cahoon elucidated:

> The clear portions of the original radiograph transmit the most light, producing lower density on the copy; the darker portions transmit less light, producing higher density. Thus, a copy is obtained, the tones of which directly follow the original. By variations of the copying time, one may even improve on the original.[9]

9 John B. Cahoon, *Formulating X-ray Techniques*, p. 55.

When I followed the recipes in Cahoon's book (for converting standard, double-sided X-ray films into duplicate films) and then performed double exposures with these, every film showed a strange greenish hue. I soon learned that, sometime soon after 1963, Kodak added a color dye to its standard, double-sided films. Presumably that was done specifically so that copies would never be confused with originals—quite possibly so that altered X-ray images could easily be detected! But that was definitely not the case in 1963.

APPENDIX D

HOW COULD X-RAYS BE ALTERED IN 1963?

ONCE I KNEW that X-ray films could be copied (rather easily) in 1963, I still had to explain how X-ray films could be *altered* in 1963. Here is how to do it.[1]

- STEP ONE: In the darkroom, place the original film directly over the light box. Then place the (unexposed) duplicate film on top of the original film. Now expose the duplicate film (i.e., turn the light on)—but do not develop it yet!

- STEP TWO: Remove the original film.

- STEP THREE: Replace that original film with a mask. For example, this mask may be a large piece of cardboard with a 6.5 mm hole that has been cut out. Place the mask directly over the light box, under the duplicate film.

---

1 My 2009 Dallas lecture demonstrated how the JFK X-rays were altered. This is highly recommended as it provides the critical details, as well as visual images: David Mantik, "JFK Skull X-Rays: Evidence of Forgery," Assassination of JFK, 2009, https://assassinationofjfk.net/jfk-skull-x-rays-evidence-of-forgery-david-mantik/.

- STEP FOUR: Expose the duplicate film again via the lightbox.
- STEP FIVE: Develop this doubly exposed film—and observe the image of a 6.5 mm (apparently) metallic object superimposed over the original image.

In Figure D.1, the mask consisted of a pteranodon from my then-young daughter's plastic tracing kit. In the second exposure, the pteranodon mask transmitted light to the duplicating film. The result was a dinosaur hovering in the brain. I have therefore labeled this image as a "birdbrain." The many dark opacities in the skull bone suggest a diagnosis of multiple myeloma, for which this patient (long-ago deceased) was then receiving radiation therapy to the spine.

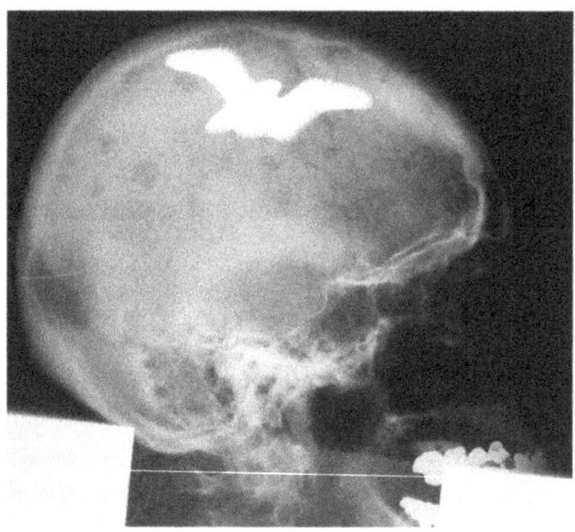

Figure D.1
A superimposed pteranodon (i.e., a birdbrain) from my daughter's plastic tracing kit.

In Figure D.2, instead of using a mask (i.e., Step Three above), I merely placed a pair of scissors directly over the light box and performed step four. By blocking the light, the scissors became a dark image on the duplicate film—so it became an "air" scissors. Just like the dark area outside the skull, the scissors also blocked light from striking the duplicate film.

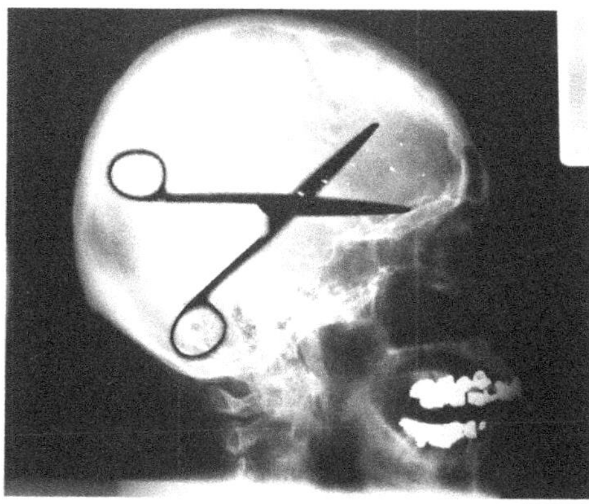

Figure D.2
A superimposed scissors: its dark appearance implies that it is merely composed of air, not of metal. No lawyers need apply.

Since the 6.5 mm object was so strangely transparent, the forgery was obvious. This 1963 secretive, darkroom worker had simply over-done the second exposure. If so, I reasoned, it should be feasible to prove this conjecture—by means of optical densitometry.[2] I was able to confirm this at the National Archives via hundreds of OD data points.

Anyone in the pre-digital era understood how double exposures worked. Like me, they had probably produced their own accidental double exposures when the film in their camera failed to advance. Figure D.3 is an example of such a double exposure. In Figure D.3, a building appears inside someone's head.[3]

---

2 As noted in the text, areas on the X-ray film that appear *transparent* (to light) are called radio-*opaque*, which can seem paradoxical. These areas are transparent (to light) because the real-world object (e.g., lead, or in JFK's case, mercury-silver amalgams) was *opaque* to X-rays. In these transparent areas on the film, the original silver salt is washed off during development. On the other hand, in areas where mostly unimpeded X-rays have struck the film (such as for the air around JFK's head), the X-rays convert the silver salt to black metallic silver, which is *not* washed off during development. So naturally these areas (e.g., air pockets) on the film are visibly dark.

3 Some wags would call this a "head's up."

Figure D.3.
An Intentional Double-Exposure: One Photograph Superimposed on Another

APPENDIX E

PATIENTS' SKULL ODS

OPTICAL DENSITY DATA FOR "NORMAL" PATIENTS

Patient	Posterior-Parietal	Petrous Bone	Ratio*
KR	.64 .65 .67	.39 .42 .41	.58
	.71 .73 .75	.38 .41 .41	
JB	1.07 .95 .92	.54 .49 .55	.54
	1.00 .89 .95	.48 .50 .57	
JH	.52 .72 .54	.36 .36 .31	.57
	.67 .55 .58	.35 .35 .29	
RS	.72 .87 .83	.38 .40 .38	.48
	.75 .99 .82	.40 .40 .42	
RC	.69 .72 .63	.27 .29 .27	.41
	.73 .61 .63	.27 .30 .26	
GH	1.10 1.13	.62 .61 .65	.54
	1.16 1.20	.62 .62 .63	
	1.15 1.23		
IU	1.07 1.05	.32 .28 .30	.28**
	1.01 .95	.35 .27 .28	
	1.17 1.29		
RD	.62 .65 .67	.31 .36 .34	.51
	.59 .65 .69	.32 .33 .32	
GJ	1.06 .88	.40 .43 .43	.41
	1.02 .96	.42 .42 .43	
JI	1.09 1.02	.34 .33 .37	.32+ → .46
	1.29 .88	.36 .37 .32	
	1.10 1.18		

* petrous ÷ P-P

** oligodendroglioma of frontal ~~bone~~ lobe

+ neck cancer patient (actually my expert furniture finisher)

APPENDIX F

FORENSIC SKULL ODS

CORONER'S CASES: DEATH VIA HEADSHOTS

SKULL X-RAYS IN NINE (OF 19) CORONER'S CASES

	ODs		Transmissions		Transmission Ratios
Case	Area P	Area F	Area P	Area F	P / F
1	0.71	0.93	19.5	11.7	1.67
2	1.29	1.36	5.1	4.4	1.16
3	1.15	1.11	7.1	7.8	.91
4	.34	0.44	45.7	36.3	1.26
5	.80	0.72	15.8	19.1	.83
6	1.20	1.62	6.3	1.62	3.89
7	1.00	1.11	10.0	7.8	1.29
8	1.08	0.82	8.4	15.2	0.55
9	0.43	0.32	37.3	47.9	0.78

Mean = 1.37 Mean without #6 = 1.05

These data represent nine cases (of nineteen total inspected cases) of fatal gunshot wounds to the skull, usually via a single headshot. These images, made on DuPont X-ray film, were collected by Dr. Douglas DeSalles from a coroner's file dating to the 1960s and early 1970s. DeSalles and I together measured these ODs. Contrary to the JFK

X-ray films, no large areas of whiteness or blackness were seen on any of these films. Three showed small black areas at the anterior tip of the frontal lobe—consistent with brain loss from this site. Measurements were made on nine of these skulls; the other ten did not appear visibly different in any way and were not specifically measured. For the nine cases above, five sites were randomly selected in each frontal area and five in each posterior area. Means (averages) were obtained and ratios calculated. Case number six, with the highest ratio of 3.89, did have numerous tiny metal fragments in the frontal area; this somewhat higher ratio may have resulted from some missing frontal lobe.

The very low ODs in cases four and nine resulted from quite improper exposure times; despite this, however, the transmission ratios of 1.26 and 0.78 fell within the range of the other seven cases. It is striking that four of the nine cases actually showed greater whiteness (transparency) in the anterior area, i.e., the transmission ratios were less than one! The primary point, though, is that none of these ratios was remotely like the JFK lateral autopsy films, where the ratio (P/F) was greater than one thousand. Also recall that JFK had two lateral autopsy X-ray films; both were quite anomalous. By contrast, JFK's premortem transmission ratios were not remarkable.

APPENDIX G

AN ANATOMY LESSON ON THE FRONTAL HEAD SHOTS

IN HIS 2021 BOOK *Last Second in Dallas*,[1] Josiah Thompson (like most researchers) conflated the right temple shot with the right forehead shot. The next figure demonstrates the great dissimilarity between these two trajectories. The AP arrow represents the forehead shot, while the oblique arrow represents the temple shot. The AP bullet does not exit the skull, which is consistent with the particle trail in the superior portion of JFK's skull X-ray films. The oblique arrow is not represented by particles anywhere on JFK's skull X-ray films, but it is consistent with the large right occipital blowout. The entry is also consistent with many eyewitnesses (in Dealey Plaza and at the autopsy, e.g., James Jenkins). They reported an entry site above and slightly in front of the right ear. The oblique trajectory exits the skull, as suggested by the large occipital defect. It is also consistent with Dealey Plaza witnesses who were struck by flying debris from the occipital blowout.

---

1 Josiah Thompson, *Last Second in Dallas*, op. cit.

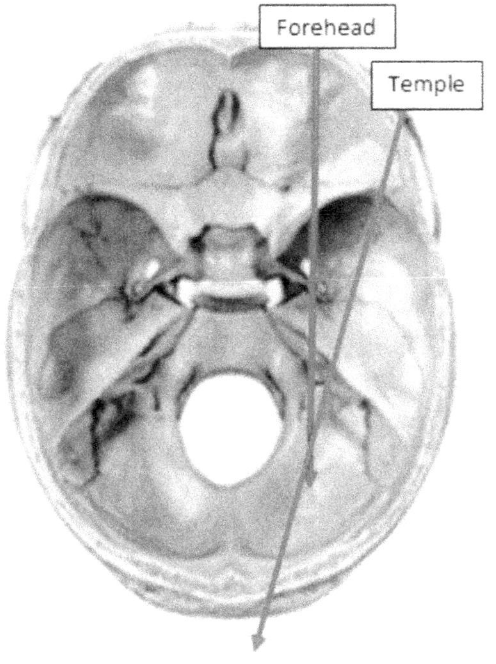

Figure G.1
Note that the oblique trajectory transects the right temporal bone (and caused the keyhole fracture). The AP trajectory is far too superior to do that.

Another major difference between these two trajectories is their *vertical* level. The next figure (JFK's AP X-ray film—missing from Thompson's book) displays the far superior location (i.e., the AP arrow) of the trail of metallic particles—as compared to the much lower, cross-hatched site of the large occipital hole (mostly due to the missing Harper fragment). This inferior location is also consistent with some missing *temporal* bone—as observed by both Michael Chesser, MD, and G. M. McDonnel, MD (the latter for the HSCA). The AP arrow is far too superior to damage temporal bone, while the oblique arrow likely struck temporal bone. The oblique arrow therefore has a significant *downward* trajectory, while the AP arrow does not. The projectile (probably fired from the Grassy Knoll) on this downward (oblique) trajectory expelled the Harper fragment (HF). The AP arrow cannot possibly account for the ejection of an occipital bone fragment like HF; after all, it is far too superior, and the fragments in that trail stop way before exiting the skull.

Immediately below is JFK's AP X-ray film. Compare the inferior level of the HF defect (cross-hatched area) versus the fragment trail near the very top of the skull. Thompson ignored all of these decisive factors—and even omitted this AP X-ray film altogether from his book. The left upper ellipse identifies the metallic fragment in JFK's left scalp. The circle on JFK's right identifies the bogus 6.5 mm object. The cross-hatched area locates HF. The fragment trail is identified by the thin upper arrow. The lambdoid sutures are missing bilaterally superior to the bilateral, lower grey arrows. This latter issue is not discussed in this review—or by Thompson. It is, however, discussed in my e-book, *JFK's Head Wounds*.

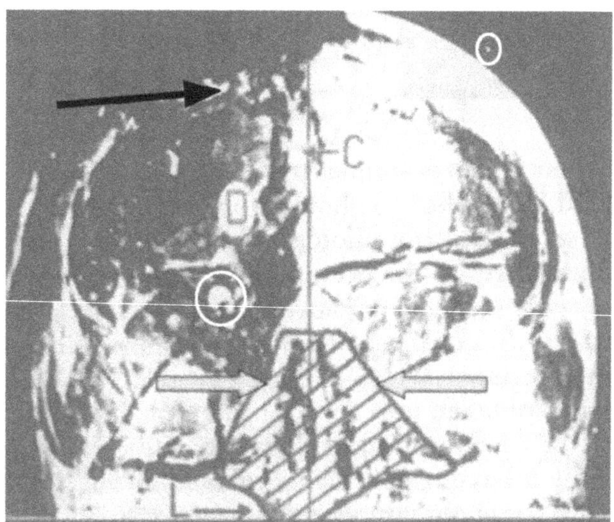

Figure G.2

JFK's AP X-ray Film (never displayed in Thompson's book). The white ellipse (at the top) identifies the authentic metal fragment in the left scalp. The white circle (inside JFK's orbit) identifies the 6.5 mm fake. The white arrow (at the top) identifies the trail of metallic debris. Superior to the two grey arrows (either side of the nose), no lambdoid sutures are visible. (They probably lay on Elm St.) The oblique shot entered near the top of the right ear, which lies well below this visible fragment trail (arrow at the top of the right skull)—thus again confirming two *separate* frontal shots.

APPENDIX H

FUTURE RESEARCH TO BE DONE AT THE NATIONAL ARCHIVES

MANTIK NOTE: I have left this time capsule for any ambitious and diligent researcher who wants to do something useful at the Archives. As I (and Michael Chesser, too) have now been outlawed by the Archives, this is beyond my scope.

BRING THESE ITEMS TO USE AT NARA

1. Loupe
2. Stereo viewer
3. Bright flashlight
4. Notebook and pen
5. Ruler
6. Recorder
7. Printed copies of the autopsy skull X-rays and the premortem
8. Optical densitometer—you should be able to borrow theirs!

NOTE: To request access to these JFK materials, contact:

Kevin T. Baine
Williams & Connolly LLP
680 Maine Avenue SW
Washington, DC
Telephone: 202-434-5010
Facsimile: 202-434-5018
kbaine@wc.com
(Note: WC ≠ Warren Commission)

AUTOPSY X-RAYS

1. LATERAL X-RAY: THAT T-SHAPED INSCRIPTION.

- *Purpose:* Confirm the absence of emulsion on both sides of the lateral skull X-ray film with the T-shaped inscription.

- My observation of intact emulsion *over both sides* (where it *must* be absent on one side) of the T-shaped inscription on the left lateral skull X-ray provided prima facie proof that this X-ray must be a copy. That clearly means that (1) the *original* lateral X-ray is missing and (2) the door is thrown wide open to alteration (i.e., via a second exposure during copying). Surprisingly, *no one* (except for Chesser) has attempted to confirm my observation of intact emulsion (on both sides). Chad Zimmerman[1] and Larry Sturdivan had that opportunity *after* my observation became

1 Chad Zimmerman is a chiropractor who received approval from the Kennedy family representative to view the JFK autopsy X-rays at the National Archives. In his book *The JFK Myths*, Larry Sturdivan commented: "On September 23, 2004, I made the approved visit [to NARA] in the company of Dr. Chad Zimmermann, who had received similar approval." See: Larry M. Sturdivan, *The JFK Myths: A Scientific Investigation of the Kennedy Assassination* (St. Paul, MN: Paragon House, 2005), p. 193.

public, but they ignored it. In my emails with Sturdivan, he seemed ignorant of that observation. Do take the film out of its protective envelope, so you can inspect the emulsion unobstructed by any intervening surface!

2. LATERAL X-RAY: FOREHEAD.

- *Purpose:* Confirm Chesser's report of numerous tiny, metallic fragments near the forehead. Although I noticed these in passing, Chesser is the only one who truly focused on them.

- Look for tiny metallic debris near the forehead. A loupe might be useful for this. Chesser also noticed a small hole in the forehead at this site, which suggests that a bullet had traversed the skull here. If necessary, review his presentation (cited below).

3. BONE FRAGMENT X-RAYS.

- *Purpose:* Determine whether these three X-ray films are identical. If so—or even if nearly so—we might conclude that such an unnecessary repetition was only done to maintain the total count of X-rays—after several skull films were destroyed.

- There are three X-ray films of the bone fragments. Dr. Aguilar and I viewed these together many years ago. Three such films seem excessive. Is it possible that these three extra films were taken to replace those skull X-ray films that had been (illegally) discarded—so that the total number of X-ray films remained fixed at fourteen? Is it even possible that these three films (of bone fragments) are *identical* (in image content as well as overall optical density) to one another? If so, that would be even more suspicious. To check on this (for the first time—no one has ever done this), the films should simply be overlaid on a view box to determine whether their images match *precisely*. A side-by-side inspection should suffice for optical densities, although actual OD measurements would be even more convincing.

4. THE METAL BRACE (in the X-rays).

- *Purpose:* Although the metal brace routinely appears in the photographs, it is not present in the skull X-ray films. Such a convincing absence from the X-ray films raises even more questions about the authenticity of the photographs—and adds further questions about where they were taken.

- I have never looked for the *metal* head brace (that's the one clearly seen in the photos) on the X-rays nor, apparently, has anyone else. Since the autopsy personnel never used such a metal brace, it would be useful to look for this on the X-ray films. Because it is metal, it really should show up. If it does not, that would also be powerful evidence of forgery—after all, we can clearly see it in the photos. In view of Horne's proposal that Knudsen took autopsy photographs with the metal head brace in position (apparently while *no* autopsy personnel were present), the presence of such a metal brace on the X-rays might shed further light on Horne's proposed timeline for Knudsen (*if* he was involved at all). This attempt might require a bright flashlight to illuminate darker areas of the X-ray film (behind JFK's head, as he lies supine).

5. OPTICAL DENSITY.

- *Purpose:* This would merely confirm, once again, that my ODs are valid.

- NARA has its own densitometers; perhaps they would loan you one for a few minutes. Alternately, you can purchase your own (for as low as forty-five dollars) and bring it to NARA.

Even an amateur can learn how to use a densitometer in a few minutes. Actually, the data need not be too extensive—even a few select data points inside the 6.5 mm object and inside the "white patches" could strongly confirm my data.

6. LATERAL SKULL X-RAYS: Are these mercury droplets?

- *Purpose:* To further assess whether the particle trail consists mostly of liquid mercury.

- Observe the fuzzy edges of metal particles within the fragment trail. Now scrutinize the two small particles (superior to the right orbit) that Humes removed (i.e., *solid* metal). I would expect these latter edges to be quite sharp—and not fuzzy. What do you see—is there a difference in the sharpness of their borders?

7. L-SPINE X-RAY.

- *Purpose:* Compare the edges of the droplet of the myelogram dye to the edges of the particles in the fragment trail. Are both fuzzy? If so, it would suggest that the particles are mercury droplets.

- Stare at the droplet of myelogram dye in the lumbar area—are its borders fuzzy? Are its edges similar to those on the fragment trail in the skull X-rays, or are the edges *sharp*—as in the tiny particles removed by Humes (superior to the right orbit)?

8. THAT 6.5 mm FRAGMENT.

- *Purpose:* Confirm my sketch of the metal particles near the 6.5 mm fake. At the same time, note your impression of whether the primary image itself is a superposition.

- Identify several metal particles *inside* the 6.5 mm object (*use a loupe*). Sketch them! Also, identify the cross-hatched fragment shown just below. Sketch it also. This fragment is the partner image of the fragment on the back of the lateral skull X-ray. Here is my sketch, as performed at NARA:

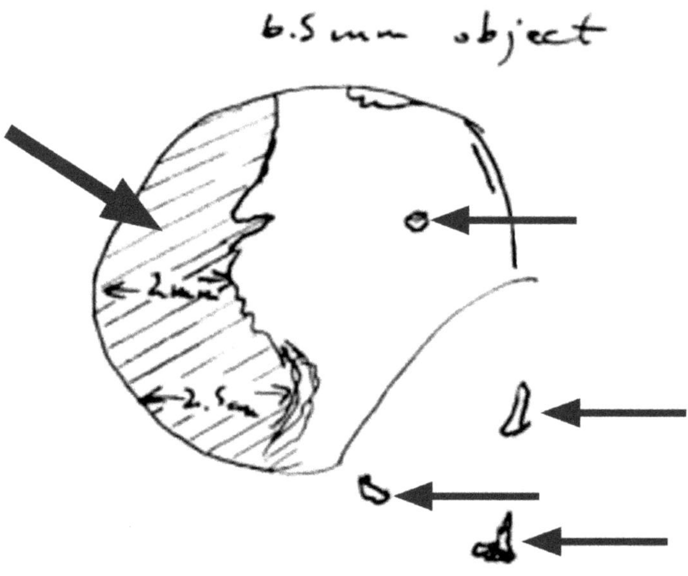

My sketch at the Archives of the 6.5 mm object, as seen with my very myopic (i.e., jeweler's) eyes. Notice the three fragments just outside of it, but especially another one (paradoxically) *inside* of it (highest right arrow). In addition, notice the original, authentic fragment (cross-hatched—left arrow), which correlates with the small authentic fragment on the posterior skull on the lateral skull X-ray. That this cross-hatched object is seen *separately* from the rest of the 6.5 mm object is also a paradox—that should not happen. These two paradoxes are examples of the "phantom image" effect, sometimes produced deliberately in Hollywood via a double exposure. In the dark room, using X-ray films, someone had deliberately superimposed the 6.5 mm object (e.g., by exposing a hole in a piece of cardboard) over the preexisting (authentic) cross-hatched fragment—thus causing the phantom effect.

AUTOPSY PHOTOGRAPHS

1. POSTERIOR SCALP: "wet" hair.

- *Purpose:* A perfect overlap of the "wet" hair in the posterior scalp photographs would strongly suggest image manipulation. After, photographs taken in immediate succession should not appear exactly alike.
- At NARA, two autopsy photographs of the posterior scalp (from a matched pair of the transparencies) should be overlaid on a view box. If the images of the suspect ("wet" hair) area *perfectly align*, that would constitute powerful evidence of photo alteration. After all, two similar (but *not identical*) photographs should *not* precisely overlap.

2. POSTERIOR SCALP: normal background.

- *Purpose:* Determine whether the background in the non-suspect photographs appears normal.
- Control areas in the photograph should also be extensively compared, just to see what non-identical (but stereo-matched) pairs look like. Surprisingly, no one has done this. In particular, because they are stereo pairs, the images in these other areas should *not* exactly overlap.

3. BACK PHOTOS.

- *Purpose:* This is a big deal. I am the only individual who has done this. Confirm that the images in a matched pair do not match at all. This would be incontrovertible proof that these films were altered.

- View the photos of JFK's left back and focus on the small "Dark Spot" (between the left fourth and fifth knuckles). Compare the companion photo (of the pair—the second member is not in the public domain) and note that this dark spot has disappeared. Instead, it is now a much lighter-colored spot—with a horizontal line through it! See my online JFK Lancer talk (slide 64) for further details,[2] or just view the penultimate page in my hardcover book—or the image below.

4. BACK PHOTOS.

- *Purpose:* Do stereo viewing of the back of the head in this pair of photographs. Is the image truly 3D—or is it merely 2D? If the latter, it is one more proof of image alteration.

5. JFK ON HIS BACK: LEFT SIDE VIEW.

- *Purpose:* Do stereo viewing for this pair of photographs. Is the image truly 3D—or is it merely 2D? If the latter, it is one more proof of image alteration. Also pay attention to the tiles in the wall and to the wall telephone. None of the eyewitnesses to the autopsy seem to recall seeing the telephone in that location.

---

2 David. W. Mantik, "The JFK Skull X-rays: Evidence for Forgery," slides from presentation to the JFK Lancer conference in Dallas, Texas, November 21, 2009, https://www.assassinationscience.com/JFK_Skull_X-rays.htm.

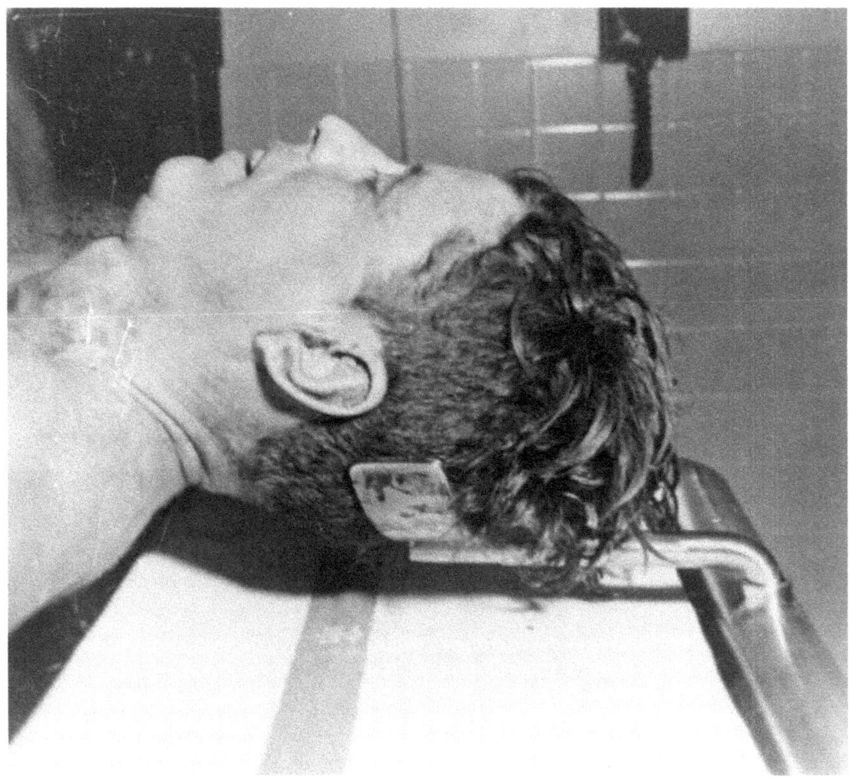

Figure H.1

JFK on His Back: Side View. Note that the telephone location is a total mismatch for Rydberg's sketch of the morgue (Figure 6.3). Also note the distinctively narrow tile directly above JFK's forehead. Source: Autopsy Photos 1, 2, 3, 3 (B&W); 29, 30, 21 (Color) in Douglas Horne, *Inside the ARRB*, op. cit., vol. 1, Figure 59.

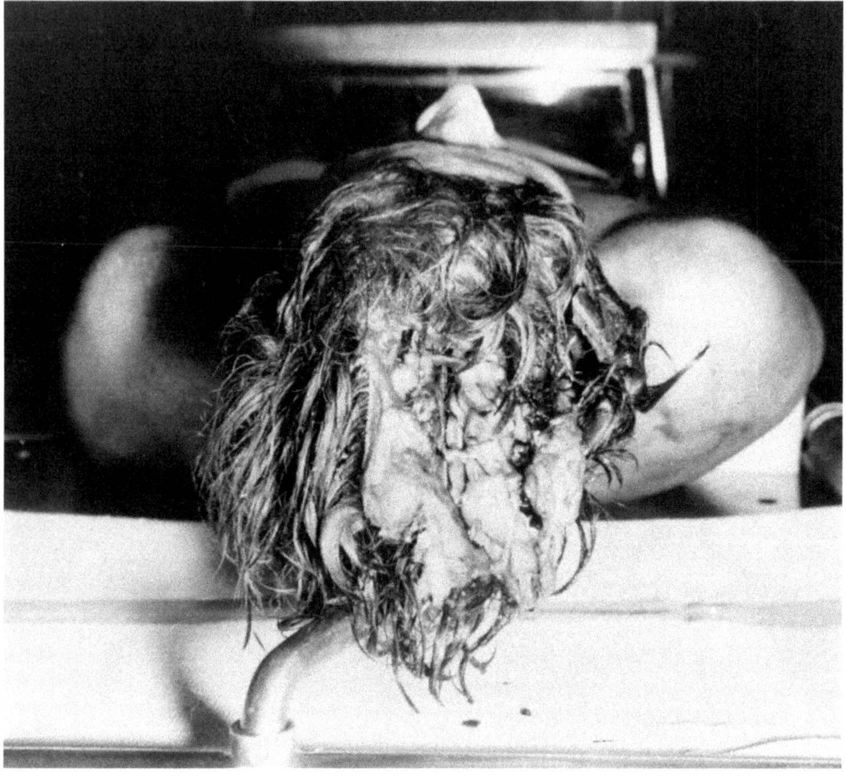

Figure H.2
JFK on his Back: Superior View. Source: Autopsy Photos 7, 8, 9, 10 (B&W); 32, 33, 34, 35, 36, 37 (Color) in Douglas Horne, *Inside the ARRB*, op. cit., vol. 1, Figure 61.

CLOTHING

1. JFK'S SHIRT AND COAT:

- *Purpose:* Disprove those early reports of a bullet into the front of the chest. This could also dispense with James Jenkins's claim of a contusion in the *middle* lobe.

- Look for bullet holes in the *front*. Early news reports (which I have reviewed—using original newspapers) suggest that a bullet had entered JFK's mediastinum. I don't specifically recall looking for such bullet holes in the front of the jacket or shirt—that issue simply was not on my radar at the time. I suspect that there are no such holes, but at least an inspection of the shirt and jacket would put to rest such ideas. Curiously, James Jenkins (at the 2013 JFK Lancer) recalled a contusion at the top of JFK's *middle* lobe—so there is yet another reason to look for such holes!

BALLISTICS

- *Purpose:* Once, and for all, does CE 399 contain the initials of Elmer Lee Todd? This answer would help to clarify its chain of possession.

    1. NIST image of CE 399. Does this bullet have the initials of Elmer Todd? You must examine the *physical* bullet at NARA—not images of it! Astronomer Steve Majewski and I missed seeing Todd's initials during our viewing in 1994 or 1995.[3]

- CC: Gary Aguilar, Cyril Wecht, Douglas DeSalles, Mike Chesser, Larry Schnapf, Jim DiEugenio, Laurie A. Loevner, and Bill Kelly

3 Steve Roe, "A Single Photograph Disproves Oliver Stone's Conspiracy Claim," Washington Decoded, June 11, 2022, https://www.washingtondecoded.com/site/2022/06/roe3.html.

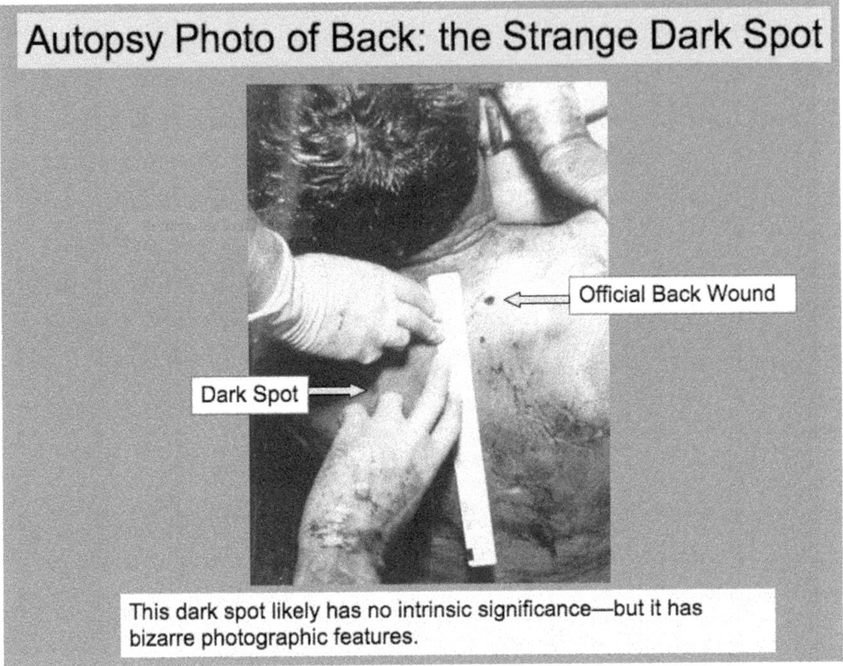

Figure H.3
Autopsy Photo of JFK's Back. The Strange Black (Dark) Spot. Source: Autopsy Photos 11, 12 (B&W); 38, 39 (Color) in Douglas Horne, *Inside the ARRB*, op. cit., vol. 1, Figure 63.

In preparing to visit NARA to review the medical evidence (if given permission), please review the work of Michael Z. Chesser, MD.[4]

4 Michael Chesser, MD, "A Review of the JFK Cranial x-Rays and Photographs," op. cit. See also: Michael Z. Chesser, MD, "The Application of Forensic Principles for the Analysis of the Autopsy Skull X-Rays of President Kennedy and a Review of the Brain Photographs," op. cit.

APPENDIX I

FBI SPECIAL AGENTS FRANCIS X. O'NEILL, JR. AND JAMES W. SIBERT, "AUTOPSY OF BODY OF PRESIDENT JOHN FITZGERALD KENNEDY," FBI 302 REPORT, GEMBERLING VERSION, ARRB MASTER SET OF MEDICAL EXHIBITS NOVEMBER 26, 1963

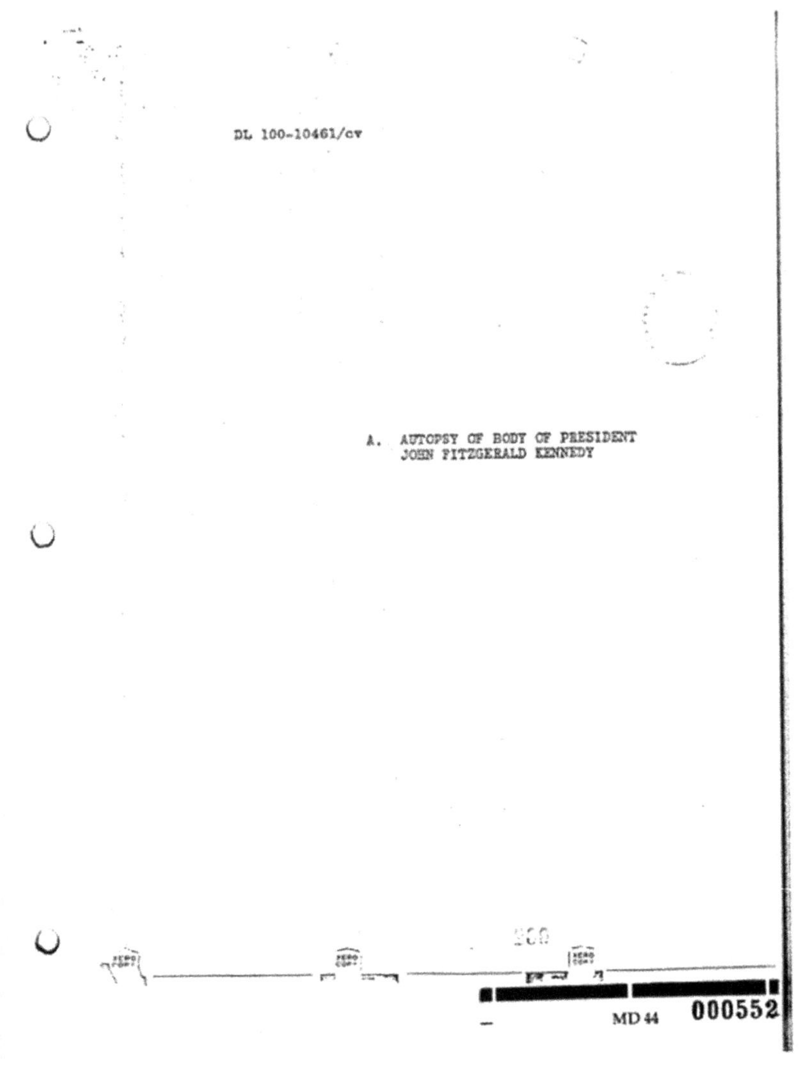
DL 100-10461/cv

A. AUTOPSY OF BODY OF PRESIDENT
JOHN FITZGERALD KENNEDY

MD 44 000552

BA 89-30
FXO/JWS:dfl
2

He advised that he had already received instructions from Director ROWLEY as to the presence of Bureau agents. It will be noted that aforementioned Bureau agents, Mr. ROY KELLERMAN, Mr. WILLIAM GREER and Mr. WILLIAM O'LEARY, Secret Service agents, were the only personnel other than medical personnel present during the autopsy.

The following individuals attended the autopsy:

Adm. C. B. HOLLOWAY, U. S. Navy, Commanding Officer of the U. S. Naval Medical Center, Bethesda;

Adm. BERKLEY, U. S. Navy, the President's personal physician;

Commander JAMES J. HUMES, Chief Pathologist, Bethesda Naval Hospital, who conducted autopsy;

Capt. JAMES H. STONER, JR., Commanding Officer, U. S. Naval Medical School, Bethesda;

Mr. JOHN T. STRINGER, JR., Medical photographer;

JAMES H. EBERSOLE;

LLOYD E. RAIHS;

J. T. BOZWELL;

J. G. RUDNICKI;

PAUL K. O'CONNOR;

J. C. JENKINS;

JERROL F. CRESTER;

EDWARD F. REED;

JAMES METZLER.

During the course of the autopsy, Lt. Col. P. FINCK, U. S. Army Armed Forces Institute of Pathology, arrived to assist Commander HUMES in the autopsy. In addition, Lt. Cmdr. GREGG CROSS and Captain DAVID OSBORNE, Chief of Surgery, entered the autopsy room.

Major General WEHLE, Commanding Officer of U. S. Military District, Washington, D.C., entered the autopsy room to ascertain from the Secret Service arrangements concerning the

000554

BA 89-30
FXO/JWS:dfl
3

transportation of the President's body back to the White House. AMC CHESTER H. BOYERS, U. S. Navy, visited the autopsy room during the final stages of such to type receipts given by FBI and Secret Service for items obtained.

At the termination of the autopsy, the following personnel from Gawler's Funeral Home entered the autopsy room to prepare the President's body for burial:

JOHN VAN HAESEN
EDWIN STROBLE
THOMAS ROBINSON
Mr. HAGEN

Brigidier General GODFREY McHUGH, Air Force Military Aide to the President, was also present, as was Dr. GEORGE BAKEMAN, U. S. Navy.

Arrangements were made for the performance of the autopsy by the U. S. Navy and Secret Service.

The President's body was removed from the casket in which it had been transported and was placed on the autopsy table, at which time the complete body was wrapped in a sheet and the head area contained an additional wrapping which was saturated with blood. Following the removal of the wrapping, it was ascertained that the President's clothing had been removed and it was also apparent that a tracheotomy had been performed, as well as surgery of the head area, namely, in the top of the skull. All personnel with the exception of medical officers needed in the taking of photographs and X-Rays were requested to leave the autopsy room and remain in an adjacent room.

Upon completion of X-Rays and photographs, the first incision was made at 8:15 p.m. X-Rays of the brain area which were developed and returned to the autopsy room disclosed a path of a missile which appeared to enter the back of the skull and the path of the disintegrated fragments could be observed along the right side of the skull. The largest section of this missile as portrayed by X-Ray appeared to be behind the right frontal sinus. The next largest fragment appeared to be at the rear of the skull at the juncture of the skull bone.

The Chief Pathologist advised approximately 40 particles of disintegrated bullet and smudges indicated that the projectile had fragmentized while passing through the skull region.

000555

BA 89-30
FXO/JWS:dfl
4

During the autopsy inspection of the area of the brain, two fragments of metal were removed by Dr. HUMES, namely, one fragment measuring 7 x 2 millimeters, which was removed from the right side of the brain. An additional fragment of metal measuring 1 x 3 millimeters was also removed from this area, both of which were placed in a glass jar containing a black metal top which were thereafter marked for identification and following the signing of a proper receipt were transported by Bureau agents to the FBI Laboratory.

During the latter stages of this autopsy, Dr. HUMES located an opening which appeared to be a bullet hole which was below the shoulders and two inches to the right of the middle line of the spinal column.

This opening was probed by Dr. HUMES with the finger, at which time it was determined that the trajectory of the missile entering at this point had entered at a downward position of 45 to 60 degrees. [Further probing determined that the distance travelled by this missile was a short distance inasmuch as the end of the opening could be felt with the finger.]

Inasmuch as no complete bullet of any size could be located in the brain area and likewise no bullet could be located in the back or any other area of the body as determined by total body X-Rays and inspection revealing there was no point of exit, the individuals performing the autopsy were at a loss to explain why they could find no bullets.

A call was made by Bureau agents to the Firearms Section of the FBI Laboratory, at which time SA CHARLES L. KILLION advised that the Laboratory had received through Secret Service Agent RICHARD JOHNSON a bullet which had reportedly been found on a stretcher in the emergency room of Parkland Hospital, Dallas, Texas. This stretcher had also contained a stethescope and pair of rubber gloves. Agent JOHNSON had advised the Laboratory that it had not been ascertained whether or not this was the stretcher which had been used to transport the body of President KENNEDY. Agent KILLION further described this bullet as pertaining to a 6.5 millimeter rifle which would be approximately a 25 caliber rifle and that this bullet consisted of a copper alloy full jacket.

[Immediately following receipt of this information, this was made available to Dr. HUMES who advised that in his opinion this accounted for no bullet being located which had entered

00055

BA 89-30
FCO/JWS:dfl
5

the back region and that since external cardiac massage had been performed at Parkland Hospital, it was entirely possible that through such movement the bullet had worked its way back out of the point of entry and had fallen on the stretcher.

Also during the latter stages of the autopsy, a piece of the skull measuring 10 x 6.5 centimeters was brought to Dr. HUMES who was instructed that this had been removed from the President's skull. Immediately this section of skull was X-Rayed, at which time it was determined by Dr. HUMES that one corner of this section revealed minute metal particles and inspection of this same area disclosed a chipping of the top portion of this piece, both of which indicated that this had been the point of exit of the bullet entering the skull region.

On the basis of the latter two developments, Dr. HUMES stated that the pattern was clear that the one bullet had entered the President's back and had worked its way out of the body during external cardiac massage and that a second high velocity bullet had entered the rear of the skull and had fragmentized prior to exit through the top of the skull. He further pointed out that X-Rays had disclosed numerous fractures in the cranial area which he attributed to the force generated by the impact of the bullet in its passage through the brain area. He attributed the death of the President to a gunshot wound in the head.

The following is a complete listing of photographs and X-Rays taken by the medical authorities of the President's body. They were turned over to Mr. ROY KELLERMAN of the Secret Service. X-Rays were developed by the hospital, however, the photographs were delivered to Secret Service undeveloped:

11 X-Rays
22 4 x 5 color photographs
18 4 x 5 black and white photographs
1 roll of 120 film containing five exposures

Mr. KELLERMAN stated these items could be made available to the FBI upon request. The portion of the skull measuring 10 x 6.5 centimeters was maintained in the custody of Dr. HUMES who stated that it also could be made available for further examination. The two metal fragments removed from the brain area were hand carried by SAs SIBERT and O'NEILL to the FBI Laboratory immediately following the autopsy and were turned over to SA KURT FRAZIER.

00055

APPENDIX J

CLINICAL RECORD, AUTOPSY PROTOCOL A63-272, DRS. J.J. HUMES, "J" THORNTON BOSWELL, AND PIERRE A. FINCK, CE 387

Standard Form 503
Revised August 1954
Promulgated
By Bureau of the Budget
Circular A—32 (Rev.)

CLINICAL RECORD	AUTOPSY PROTOCOL A63-272 (JJH: ec)			
DATE AND HOUR DIED A.M./P.M. 22 November 1963 1300(CST) P.M.	DATE AND HOUR AUTOPSY PERFORMED A.M./P.M. 22 November 1963 2000(EST) P.M.	CHECK ONE		
		FULL AUTOPSY	HEAD ONLY	TRUNK ONLY
PROSECTOR (497831) CDR J. J. HUMES, MC, USN	ASSISTANT (489878) CDR "J" THORNTON BOSWELL, MC, USN LCOL PIERRE A. FINCK, MC, USA (04 043 322)	X		

CLINICAL DIAGNOSES (Including operations)

Ht. - 72½ inches
Wt. - 170 pounds
Eyes - blue
Hair - Reddish brown

PATHOLOGICAL DIAGNOSES

CAUSE OF DEATH: Gunshot wound, head.

APPROVED—SIGNATURE

J. J. HUMES, CDR, MC, USN

MILITARY ORGANIZATION (When required)	AGE	SEX	RACE	IDENTIFICATION NO.	AUTOPSY NO.
PRESIDENT, UNITED STATES	46	Male	Cauc.		A63-272

PATIENT'S IDENTIFICATION (For typed or written entries give: Name—last, first, middle; grade; date; hospital or medical facility)

REGISTER NO.	WARD NO.

KENNEDY, JOHN F.
NAVAL MEDICAL SCHOOL

AUTOPSY PROTOCOL
Standard Form 503

MD 3

000078

PATHOLOGICAL EXAMINATION REPORT A63-272 Page 2

CLINICAL SUMMARY: According to available information the deceased, President John F. Kennedy, was riding in an open car in a motorcade during an official visit to Dallas, Texas on 22 November 1963. The President was sitting in the right rear seat with Mrs. Kennedy seated on the same seat to his left. Sitting directly in front of the President was Governor John B. Connolly of Texas and directly in front of Mrs. Kennedy sat Mrs. Connolly. The vehicle was moving at a slow rate of speed down an incline into an underpass that leads to a freeway route to the Dallas Trade Mart where the President was to deliver an address.

Three shots were heard and the President fell forward bleeding from the head. (Governor Connolly was seriously wounded by the same gunfire.) According to newspaper reports ("Washington Post" November 23, 1963) Bob Jackson, a Dallas "Times Herald" Photographer, said he looked around as he heard the shots and saw a rifle barrel disappearing into a window on an upper floor of the nearby Texas School Book Depository Building.

Shortly following the wounding of the two men the car was driven to Parkland Hospital in Dallas. In the emergency room of that hospital the President was attended by Dr. Malcolm Perry. Telephone communication with Dr. Perry on November 23, 1963 develops the following information relative to the observations made by Dr. Perry and procedures performed there prior to death.

Dr. Perry noted the massive wound of the head and a second much smaller wound of the low anterior neck in approximately the midline. A tracheostomy was performed by extending the latter wound. At this point bloody air was noted bubbling from the wound and an injury to the right lateral wall of the trachea was observed. Incisions were made in the upper anterior chest wall bilaterally to combat possible subcutaneous emphysema. Intravenous infusions of blood and saline were begun and oxygen was administered. Despite these measures cardiac arrest occurred and closed chest cardiac massage failed to re-establish cardiac action. The President was pronounced dead approximately thirty to forty minutes after receiving his wounds.

The remains were transported via the Presidential plane to Washington, D.C. and subsequently to the Naval Medical School, National Naval Medical Center, Bethesda, Maryland for postmortem examination.

GENERAL DESCRIPTION OF BODY: The body is that of a muscular, well-developed and well nourished adult Caucasian male measuring 72½ inches and weighing approximately 170 pounds. There is beginning rigor mortis, minimal dependent livor mortis of the dorsum, and early algor mortis. The hair is reddish brown and abundant, the eyes are blue, the right pupil measuring 8 mm. in diameter, the left 4 mm. There is edema and ecchymosis of the inner canthus region of the left eyelid measuring approximately 1.5 cm. in greatest diameter. There is edema and ecchymosis diffusely over the right supra-orbital ridge with abnormal mobility of the underlying bone. (The remainder of the scalp will be described with the skull.)

JJH

000079

PATHOLOGICAL EXAMINATION REPORT A63-272 Page 3

There is clotted blood on the external ears but otherwise the ears, nares, and mouth are essentially unremarkable. The teeth are in excellent repair and there is some pallor of the oral mucous membrane.

Situated on the upper right posterior thorax just above the upper border of the scapula there is a 7 x 4 millimeter oval wound. This wound is measured to be 14 cm. from the tip of the right acromion process and 14 cm. below the tip of the right mastoid process.

Situated in the low anterior neck at approximately the level of the third and fourth tracheal rings is a 6.5 cm. long transverse wound with widely gaping irregular edges. (The depth and character of these wounds will be further described below.)

Situated on the anterior chest wall in the nipple line are bilateral 2 cm. long recent transverse surgical incisions into the subcutaneous tissue. The one on the left is situated 11 cm. cephalad to the nipple and the one on the right 8 cm. cephalad to the nipple. There is no hemorrhage or ecchymosis associated with these wounds. A similar clean wound measuring 2 cm. in length is situated on the antero-lateral aspect of the left mid arm. Situated on the antero-lateral aspect of each ankle is a recent 2 cm. transverse incision into the subcutaneous tissue.

There is an old well healed 8 cm. McBurney abdominal incision. Over the lumbar spine in the midline is an old, well healed 15 cm. scar. Situated on the upper antero-lateral aspect of the right thigh is an old, well healed 8 cm. scar.

MISSILE WOUNDS: 1. There is a large irregular defect of the scalp and skull on the right involving chiefly the parietal bone but extending somewhat into the temporal and occipital regions. In this region there is an actual absence of scalp and bone producing a defect which measures approximately 13 cm. in greatest diameter.

From the irregular margins of the above scalp defect tears extend in stellate fashion into the more or less intact scalp as follows:

a. From the right inferior temporo-parietal margin anterior to the right ear to a point slightly above the tragus.

b. From the anterior parietal margin anteriorly on the forehead to approximately 4 cm. above the right orbital ridge.

c. From the left margin of the main defect across the midline antero-laterally for a distance of approximately 8 cm.

d. From the same starting point as c. 10 cm. postero-laterally.

000080

Situated in the posterior scalp approximately 2.5 cm. laterally to the right and slightly above the external occipital protuberance is a lacerated wound measuring 15 x 6 mm. In the underlying bone is a corresponding wound through the skull which exhibits beveling of the margins of the bone when viewed from the inner aspect of the skull.

Clearly visible in the above described large skull defect and exuding from it is lacerated brain tissue which on close inspection proves to represent the major portion of the right cerebral hemisphere. At this point it is noted that the falx cerebri is extensively lacerated with disruption of the superior saggital sinus.

Upon reflecting the scalp multiple complete fracture lines are seen to radiate from both the large defect at the vertex and the smaller wound at the occiput. These vary greatly in length and direction, the longest measuring approximately 19 cm. These result in the production of numerous fragments which vary in size from a few millimeters to 10 cm. in greatest diameter.

The complexity of these fractures and the fragments thus produced tax satisfactory verbal description and are better appreciated in photographs and roentgenograms which are prepared.

The brain is removed and preserved for further study following formalin fixation.

Received as separate specimens from Dallas, Texas are three fragments of skull bone which in aggregate roughly approximate the dimensions of the large defect described above. At one angle of the largest of these fragments is a portion of the perimeter of a roughly circular wound presumably of exit which exhibits beveling of the outer aspect of the bone and is estimated to measure approximately 2.5 to 3.0 cm. in diameter. Roentgenograms of this fragment reveal minute particles of metal in the bone at this margin. Roentgenograms of the skull reveal multiple minute metallic fragments along a line corresponding with a line joining the above described small occipital wound and the right supra-orbital ridge. From the surface of the disrupted right cerebral cortex two small irregularly shaped fragments of metal are recovered. These measure 7 x 2 mm. and 3 x 1 mm. These are placed in the custody of Agents Francis X. O'Neill, Jr. and James W. Sibert, of the Federal Bureau of Investigation, who executed a receipt therefor (attached).

2. The second wound presumably of entry is that described above in the upper right posterior thorax. Beneath the skin there is ecchymosis of subcutaneous tissue and musculature. The missle path through the fascia and musculature cannot be easily probed. The wound presumably of exit was that described by Dr. Malcolm Perry of Dallas in the low anterior cervical region. When observed by Dr. Perry the wound measured "a few millimeters in diameter", however it was extended as a tracheostomy incision and thus its character is distorted at the time of autopsy. However, there is considerable ecchymosis of the strap muscles of the right side of the neck and of the fascia about the trachea adjacent to the line of the tracheostomy wound. The third point of reference in connecting

000081

PATHOLOGICAL EXAMINATION REPORT A63-272 Page 5

these two wounds is in the apex (supra-clavicular portion) of the right pleural cavity. In this region there is contusion of the parietal pleura and of the extreme apical portion of the right upper lobe of the lung. In both instances the diameter of contusion and ecchymosis at the point of maximal involvement measures 5 cm. Both the visceral and parietal pleura are intact overlying these areas of trauma.

INCISIONS: The scalp wounds are extended in the coronal plane to examine the cranial content and the customary (Y) shaped incision is used to examine the body cavities.

THORACIC CAVITY: The bony cage is unremarkable. The thoracic organs are in their normal positions and relationships and there is no increase in free pleural fluid. The above described area of contusion in the apical portion of the right pleural cavity is noted.

LUNGS: The lungs are of essentially similar appearance the right weighing 320 Gm., the left 290 Gm. The lungs are well aerated with smooth glistening pleural surfaces and gray-pink color. A 5 cm. diameter area of purplish red discoloration and increased firmness to palpation is situated in the apical portion of the right upper lobe. This corresponds to the similar area described in the overlying parietal pleura. Incision in this region reveals recent hemorrhage into pulmonary parenchyma.

HEART: The pericardial cavity is smooth walled and contains approximately 10 cc. of straw-colored fluid. The heart is of essentially normal external contour and weighs 350 Gm. The pulmonary artery is opened in situ and no abnormalities are noted. The cardiac chambers contain moderate amounts of postmortem clotted blood. There are no gross abnormalities of the leaflets of any of the cardiac valves. The following are the circumferences of the cardiac valves: aortic 7.5 cm., pulmonic 7 cm., tricuspid 12 cm., mitral 11 cm. The myocardium is firm and reddish brown. The left ventricular myocardium averages 1.2 cm. in thickness, the right ventricular myocardium 0.4 cm. The coronary arteries are dissected and are of normal distribution and smooth walled and elastic throughout.

ABDOMINAL CAVITY: The abdominal organs are in their normal positions and relationships and there is no increase in free peritoneal fluid. The vermiform appendix is surgically absent and there are a few adhesions joining the region of the cecum to the ventral abdominal wall at the above described old abdominal incisional scar.

SKELETAL SYSTEM: Aside from the above described skull wounds there are no significant gross skeletal abnormalities.

PHOTOGRAPHY: Black and white and color photographs depicting significant findings are exposed but not developed. These photographs were placed in the custody of Agent Roy H. Kellerman of the U. S. Secret Service, who executed a receipt therefore (attached).

JJH

000082

PATHOLOGICAL EXAMINATION REPORT A63-272 Page 6

ROENTGENOGRAMS: Roentgenograms are made of the entire body and of the separately submitted three fragments of skull bone. These are developed and were placed in the custody of Agent Roy H. Kellerman of the U. S. Secret Service, who executed a receipt therefor (attached).

SUMMARY: Based on the above observations it is our opinion that the deceased died as a result of two perforating gunshot wounds inflicted by high velocity projectiles fired by a person or persons unknown. The projectiles were fired from a point behind and somewhat above the level of the deceased. The observations and available information do not permit a satisfactory estimate as to the sequence of the two wounds.

The fatal missile entered the skull above and to the right of the external occipital protuberance. A portion of the projectile traversed the cranial cavity in a posterior-anterior direction (see lateral skull roentgenograms) depositing minute particles along its path. A portion of the projectile made its exit through the parietal bone on the right carrying with it portions of cerebrum, skull and scalp. The two wounds of the skull combined with the force of the missile produced extensive fragmentation of the skull, laceration of the superior saggital sinus, and of the right cerebral hemisphere.

The other missile entered the right superior posterior thorax above the scapula and traversed the soft tissues of the supra-scapular and the supra-clavicular portions of the base of the right side of the neck. This missile produced contusions of the right apical parietal pleura and of the apical portion of the right upper lobe of the lung. The missile contused the strap muscles of the right side of the neck, damaged the trachea and made its exit through the anterior surface of the neck. As far as can be ascertained this missile struck no bony structures in its path through the body.

In addition, it is our opinion that the wound of the skull produced such extensive damage to the brain as to preclude the possibility of the deceased surviving this injury.

A supplementary report will be submitted following more detailed examination of the brain and of microscopic sections. However, it is not anticipated that these examinations will materially alter the findings.

J. J. HUMES CDR, MC, USN (497831)	J. THORNTON BOSWELL CDR, MC, USN (489878)	PIERRE A. FINCK LT COL, MC, USA (04-043-322)

000083

APPENDIX K

CIA DISPATCH MEMORANDUM

TO: CHIEFS CERTAIN STATIONS AND BASES

FROM: CHIEF, WOVIEW

SUBJECT: COUNTERING CRITICISM OF THE WARREN REPORT

APRIL 1, 1967

DISPATCH

CLASSIFICATION: ~~SECRET~~

PROCESSING ACTION

MARKED FOR INDEXING

X NO INDEXING REQUIRED

ONLY QUALIFIED DESK CAN JUDGE INDEXING

TO: Chiefs, Certain Stations and Bases

INFO.

Document Number 1035-960

FROM: Chief, WOVIEW

for FOIA Review on SEP 1976

CIA HISTORICAL REVIEW PROGRAM
Release in Full 1996

SUBJECT: Countering Criticism of the Warren Report

ACTION REQUIRED - REFERENCES

PAUL H. PSYCH

FOR OSWALD FILE 2 COPIES

THIS WAS PULLED TOGETHER BY NED BENNETT OF CA STAFF IN CLOSE CONJUNCTION WITH CI/R&A. ~~WE FURNISHED~~ MOST OF THE SOURCE MATERIAL, PROVIDED MANY OF THE THEMES, AND PROVIDED GENERAL "EXPERTISE" ON THE CASE. THE SPECTATOR ARTICLE WAS WRITTEN BY BENNETT.

1. Our Concern. From the day of President Kennedy's assassination on, there has been speculation about the responsibility for his murder. Although this was stemmed for a time by the Warren Commission report (which appeared at the end of September 1964), various writers have now had time to scan the Commission's published report and documents for new pretexts for questioning, and there has been a new wave of books and articles criticizing the Commission's findings. In most cases the critics have speculated as to the existence of some kind of conspiracy, and often they have implied that the Commission itself was involved. Presumably as a result of the increasing challenge to the Warren Commission's Report, a public opinion poll recently indicated that 46% of the American public did not think that Oswald acted alone, while more than half of those polled thought that the Commission had left some questions unresolved. Doubtless polls abroad would show similar, or possibly more adverse, results.

2. This trend of opinion is a matter of concern to the U.S. government, including our organization. The members of the Warren Commission were naturally chosen for their integrity, experience, and prominence. They represented both major parties, and they and their staff were deliberately drawn from all sections of the country. Just because of the standing of the Commissioners, efforts to impugn their rectitude and wisdom tend to cast doubt on the whole leadership of American society. Moreover, there seems to be an increasing tendency to hint that President Johnson himself, as the one person who might be said to have benefited, was in some way responsible for the assassination. Innuendo of such seriousness affects not only the individual concerned, but also the whole reputation of the American government. Our organization itself is directly involved: among other facts, we contributed information to the investigation. Conspiracy theories have frequently thrown suspicion on our organization, for example by falsely alleging that Lee Harvey Oswald worked for us. The aim of this dispatch is to provide material for countering and discrediting the claims of the conspiracy theorists, so as to inhibit the circulation of such claims in other countries. Background information is supplied in a classified section and in a number of unclassified attachments.

3. Action. We do not recommend that discussion of the assassination question be initiated where it is not already taking place. Where discussion is active, however, addressees are requested:

CS COPY

201-289248

ABSTRACT X INDEX	DISPATCH SYMBOL AND NUMBER	DATE
9 attachments h/w	BD 5847	4/1/67
1 - SECRET 8 att. 8 - Unclassified	CLASSIFICATION ~~SECRET~~	HQS FILE NUMBER DESTROY WHEN NO LONGER NEEDED

CONTINUATION OF DISPATCH	CLASSIFICATION SECRET	DISPATCH SYMBOL AND NUMBER BD 5847

a. To discuss the publicity problem with liaison and friendly elite contacts (especially politicians and editors), pointing out that the Warren Commission made as thorough an investigation as humanly possible, that the charges of the critics are without serious foundation, and that further speculative discussion only plays into the hands of the opposition. Point out also that parts of the conspiracy talk appear to be deliberately generated by Communist propagandists. Urge them to use their influence to discourage unfounded and irresponsible speculation.

b. To employ propaganda assets to answer and refute the attacks of the critics. Book reviews and feature articles are particularly appropriate for this purpose. The unclassified attachments to this guidance should provide useful background material for passage to assets. Our play should point out, as applicable, that the critics are (i) wedded to theories adopted before the evidence was in, (ii) politically interested, (iii) financially interested, (iv) hasty and inaccurate in their research, or (v) infatuated with their own theories. In the course of discussions of the whole phenomenon of criticism, a useful strategy may be to single out Epstein's theory for attack, using the attached Fletcher Knebel article and Spectator piece for background. (Although Mark Lane's book is much less convincing than Epstein's and comes off badly where contested by knowledgeable critics, it is also much more difficult to answer as a whole, as one becomes lost in a morass of unrelated details.)

4. In private or media discussion not directed at any particular writer, or in attacking publications which may be yet forthcoming, the following arguments should be useful:

a. No significant new evidence has emerged which the Commission did not consider. The assassination is sometimes compared (e.g., by Joachim Joesten and Bertrand Russell) with the Dreyfus case; however, unlike that case, the attacks on the Warren Commission have produced no new evidence, no new culprits have been convincingly identified, and there is no agreement among the critics. (A better parallel, though an imperfect one, might be with the Reichstag fire of 1933, which some competent historians (Fritz Tobias, A.J.P. Taylor, D.C. Watt) now believe was set by Van der Lubbe on his own initiative, without acting for either Nazis or Communists; the Nazis tried to pin the blame on the Communists, but the latter have been much more successful in convincing the world that the Nazis were to blame.)

b. Critics usually overvalue particular items and ignore others. They tend to place more emphasis on the recollections of individual eyewitnesses (which are less reliable and more divergent -- and hence offer more hand-holds for criticism) and less on ballistic, autopsy, and photographic evidence. A close examination of the Commission's records will usually show that the conflicting eyewitness accounts are quoted out of context, or were discarded by the Commission for good and sufficient reason.

c. Conspiracy on the large scale often suggested would be impossible to conceal in the United States, esp. since informants could expect to receive large royalties, etc. Note that Robert Kennedy, Attorney General at the time and John F. Kennedy's brother, would be the last man to overlook or conceal any conspiracy. And as one reviewer pointed out, Congressman Gerald R. Ford would hardly have held his tongue for the sake of the Democratic administration, and Senator Russell would have had every political interest in exposing any misdeeds on the part of Chief Justice Warren. A conspirator moreover would hardly choose a location for a shooting where so much depended on conditions beyond his control: the route, the speed of the cars, the moving target, the risk that the assassin would be discovered. A group of wealthy conspirators could have

CONTINUATION OF DISPATCH	CLASSIFICATION ~~SECRET~~	DISPATCH SYMBOL AND NUMBER BD 5847

e. Oswald would not have been any sensible person's choice for a co-conspirator. He was a "loner," mixed-up, of questionable reliability and an unknown quantity to any professional intelligence service.

f. As to charges that the Commission's report was a rush job, it emerged three months after the deadline originally set. But to the degree that the Commission tried to speed up its reporting, this was largely due to the pressure of irresponsible speculation already appearing, in some cases coming from the same critics who, refusing to admit their errors, are now putting out new criticisms.

g. Such vague accusations as that "more than ten people have died mysteriously" can always be explained in some more natural way: e.g., the individuals concerned have for the most part died of natural causes; the Commission staff questioned 418 witnesses (the FBI interviewed far more people, conducting 25,000 interviews and reinterviews), and in such a large group, a certain number of deaths are to be expected. (When Penn Jones, one of the originators of the "ten mysterious deaths" line, appeared on television, it emerged that two of the deaths on his list were from heart attacks, one from cancer, one was from a head-on collision on a bridge, and one occurred when a driver drifted into a bridge abutment.)

5. Where possible, counter speculation by encouraging reference to the Commission's Report itself. Open-minded foreign readers should still be impressed by the care, thoroughness, objectivity and speed with which the Commission worked. Reviewers of other books might be encouraged to add to their account the idea that, checking back with the Report itself, they found it far superior to the work of its critics.

CLAYTON P. NURNAD

APPENDIX L

AN UNCOMMON BIBLIOGRAPHY

BY DAVID W. MANTIK, M.D., PH.D.

You can learn interesting things from dubiously sourced information. Do not be afraid to read something, but be careful what you believe.

—**KRIS MILLEGAN,** Publisher of Triune Day[1]

In my whole life, I have known no wise people who didn't read all the time—none, zero.

–**CHARLIE MUNGER**[2]

Some books are to be tasted, others to be swallowed, and some few to be chewed and digested; that is, some books are to be read only in parts; others to be read, but not curiously; and some few are to be read wholly, and with diligence and attention.

–**FRANCIS BACON**[3]

---

1 Douglas Caddy, *Being There: Eyewitness to History* (Walterville, OR: Triune Day, 2018), Foreword.

2 *Forecasts and Strategies* (Salem Eagle, Washington, DC, 2024), January 2024, Vol. 45, No. 1, p. 3.

3 Sir Francis Bacon, *Essaies. Religious Meditations. Places of Perswasion and Disswasion* (London, by Iohn VVindet for Humfrey Hooper, 1598).

NOTE: Other authors rarely cite these books, but each one rests comfortably in my personal library—and each is relevant to the JFK case. After compiling this list, just for comparison, I reviewed the bibliographies of two other authors: David R. Wrone (*The Zapruder Film*) cites *none* of my uncommon books. Even James D. DiEugenio (*Reclaiming Parkland*) cites only Ian Griggs and John Newman. On the other hand, I have read the vast majority of the books that they cite.

For an exhaustive (if not exhausting) bibliography (through 2021), see the heroic 56-page compilation in Vince Palamara, *Honest Answers about the Murder of President John F. Kennedy: A New Look at the JFK Assassination* (Walterville, OR: Triune Day LLC, 2021), pp. 389-444.

I list my favorite authors (of books) at the end.

Albarelli, H.P., Jr., *A Terrible Mistake: The Murder of Frank Olson and the CIA's Secret War Experiments* (Walterville, OR: Trine Day, 2009).

———, *A Secret Order: Investigating the High Strangeness and Synchronicity in the JFK Assassination* (Walterville, OR: Triune Day, 2013).

———, *Coup in Dallas: The Decisive Investigation into Who Killed JFK* (New York: Skyhorse Publishing, 2021).

Agee, Philip, *Inside the Company: CIA Diary* (New York, New York: Stonehill Publishers, 1975).

Arrows, Four and Fetzer, James H., *American Assassination: The Strange Death of Senator Paul Wellstone* (Brooklyn, New York: United Graphics, Inc., 2004).

Bagley, Tennant H., *Spy Wars: Moles, Mysteries, and Deadly Games* (New Haven, CT: Yale University Press, 2007).

Belzer, Richard, *Dead Wrong* (New York, NY: Skyhorse Publishers, 2012).

———, *Hit List* (New York, NY: MJF Books, 2013)

Blair, Joan and Clay, Jr., *The Search for JFK* (New York, NY: Berkley Publishing Corp., 1976).

Bobo, William (aka Roy Schaeffer), *The CIA Killed Camelot, Didn't They?* (Dayton, Ohio: Crimson Crack, 1997).

Brown, Walt, *The Guns of August are Upon You* (Williamsport, PA: Last Hurrah Press, 2005).

Cahoon, John B., *Formulating X-ray Techniques* (Kingsport, TN: Duke University Press, 1965).

Curington, John, *H. L. Hunt: Motive and Opportunity* (no site, 23 House Publishing, 2018).

DeBrosse, Jim, *See No Evil: The JFK Assassination and the U.S. Media* (Walterville, OR: Triune Day, 2018).

Diamond, Jared, *Upheaval: Turning Points for Nations in Crisis* (New York, NY: Little, Brown and Company, 2019).

DiMaio, Vincent and Franscell, Ron, *Morgue: A Life in Death* (New York, NY: St. Martin's Press, 2016). [Ron purchased my sister's house!]

Evica, George Michael, *A Certain Arrogance* (Walterville, OR: Triune Day, 2006).

Fetzer, James and Palecek, Michael, *JFK—Who, How, and Why: Solving the World's Greatest Murder Mystery* (Crestview, FL: Moon Rock Books, 2017).

Furiati, Claudia and Shaw, Maxine, *ZR Rifle: The Plot To Kill Kennedy and Castro* (Melbourne, Australia: Ocean Press, 1994).

Ganis, Ralph and Russell, Dick, *The Skorzeny Papers: Evidence for the Plot to Kill JFK* (New York, NY: Skyhorse Press, 2018).

Goodwin, Richard N., *Remembering America: A Voice from the Sixties* (Canada: Blithdale Press, 1988).

Green, Joseph E., *Dissenting Views: Investigations into History, Culture, Cinema & Conspiracy* (Scotts Valley, CA: CreateSpace Independent Publishing Platform, 2014).

Griggs, Ian, *No Case to Answer* (Southgate, TX: JFK Lancer, 2011).

Haley, J. Evetts, *A Texan Looks at Lyndon* (Canyon, Texas: The Palo Duro Press, 1964).

Hancock, Larry, *Someone Would Have Talked* (Southgate, TX: JFK Lancer Productions & Publications, Inc., 2006).

———, *Nexus: The CIA and Political Assassinations* (Southlake, TX: JFK Lancer Productions and Publications, Inc., 2011).

Hazelwood, Denise, *The JFK Cut-N-Paste Assassination: Putting it Back Together* (Denise Hazelwood, self-published, 2015).

Hill, Gary, *The Other Oswald: A Wilderness of Mirrors* (Walterville, OR: Triune Day, 2020).

Hopsicker, Daniel, *Barry & 'the Boys': The CIA, the Mob and America's Secret History* (USA: Mad Cow Press, 2016).

Jackson, Gayle Nix, *Orville Nix: The Missing JFK Assassination Film* (Semper Ad Meliore Publishing, 2014).

Johnston, James P. and Roe, Jon, *Flight from Dallas: New Evidence of CIA Involvement in the Murder of President John F. Kennedy* (Bloomington, IN: Johnston & Row, 2003).

Kessler, Ronald, *Inside the CIA: Revealing the Secrets of the World's Most Powerful Spy Agency* (New York: Atria Publishing Group, 1992).

Kiel, R. Andrew, *J. Edgar Hoover: The Father of the Cold War* (Lanham, MD: University Press of America, 2000).

Livingstone, Harrison, *The Hoax of the Century: Decoding the Forgery of the Zapruder Film* (Victoria, BC: Trafford Publishing, 2004).

Mahoney, Richard D., JFK: *Ordeal in Africa* (Oxford, U.K.: Oxford University Press, Inc., 1983).

Mangold, Tom, *Cold Warrior: James Jesus Angleton: The CIA's Master Spy Hunter* (London: Simon & Schuster, 1991).

Martin, David C., *Wilderness of Mirrors: Intrigue, Deception, and the Secrets that Destroyed Two of the Cold War's Most Important Agents* (New York, NY: Harper & Row, 1980).

McCoy, Alfred, *The Politics of Heroin: CIA Complicity in the Global Drug Trade* (New York, NY: Harper & Row, 1991).

Milgram, Stanley, *Obedience to Authority: An Experimental View* (New York, NY: Harper & Row, 1974).

Miller, Nathan, *Stealing from America: A History of Corruption from Jamestown to Reagan* (New York, NY: Paragon House, 1992).

Moyers, Bill, *The Secret Government: Our Constitution in Crisis* (Saline, MI: McNaughton & Gunn, 1988).

Newman, John, *Oswald and the CIA: The Documented Truth About the Unknown Relationship Between the U.S. Government and the Alleged Killer of JFK* (New York, NY: Skyhorse Publishing, illustrated edition, 2008). Originally published as Newman, John, *Oswald and the CIA* (New York, NY: Carroll & Graf Publishers, Inc., 1995).

Noguchi, Tom, *Coroner* (New York, NY: Simon & Schuster, 1985).

Oliver, Beverly and Buchanan, Coke, *Nightmare in Dallas* (Duncanville, TX: Extreme Services, Inc., 2003).

Palamara, Vincent, *Honest Answers About the Murder of President John F. Kennedy* (Walterville, OR: Triune Day, 2021).

Parenti, Michael, *Dirty Truths* (Monroe, OR: City Lights Books, 1996).

Phillips, David Atlee, *Secret Wars Diary: My Adventures in Combat, Espionage Operations and Covert Action* (Bethesda, MD: Stone Bridge Press, 1989).

Popkin, Richard, *The Second Oswald: A Startling Alternative to the Single Assassin Theory of the Warren Commission* (New York, NY: Avon Books, 1966).

Prouty, L. Fletcher, *JFK: The CIA, Vietnam, and the Plot to Assassinate John F. Kennedy* (New York, NY: Birch Lane Press, 1992).

Ray, Pamela J. and Files, James, *Primary Target: JFK – How the CIA Used the Chicago Mob to Kill the President* (Bloomington, IN: Authorhouse, 2020).

Reed, Terry and Cummings, John, *Compromised: Clinton, Bush and the CIA* (New York, NY: S.P.I. Books, 1994).

Rivera, Larry, *The JFK Horsemen: Framing Lee and Altering the Altgens6* (Crestview, FL: Moon Rock Books, 2018).

Roberts, Craig, *Kill Zone: A Sniper Looks at Dealey Plaza* (Tulsa, OK: Typhoon Press, 1994).

Salyer, Kenneth, *A Life That Matters: Transforming Faces, Renewing Lives* (New York, NY: Center Street, 2013).

Salandria, Vincent, *False Mystery: Essays on the Assassination of JFK* (Louisville, CO: Square Deal Press, 2004).

Sample, Glen and Collum, Mark, *The Men on the Sixth Floor* (Garden Grove, CA: Sample Graphics, 1997).

Sauvage, Léo, *The Oswald Affair: an Examination of the Contradictions and Omissions of the Warren Report* (Cleveland, OH: World Publishing Company, 1966).

Savage, Gary, JFK: *First Day Evidence* (Monroe, LA: The Shoppe Press, 1993).

Schotz, E. Martin, *History Will Not Absolve Us* (Brooklyn, MA: Kurtz, Ulmer & DeLuca, 1996).

Schwimmer, George, *Doppelganger: The Legend of Lee Harvey Oswald* (Santa Fe: NM: Phoenix 11 Productions, 2016).

Sheehan, Daniel, *The People's Advocate: The Life and Legal History of America's Most Fearless Public Interest Lawyer* (Berkeley, CA: Counterpoint, 2013).[4]

Smith, Matthew, *JFK: The Second Plot* (Edinburgh: Mainstream Publishing Company, 1992).

Stich, Rodney, *Defrauding America: Encyclopedia of Secret Operations by the CIA, DEA, and Other Covert Agencies* (Edinburgh, Scotland: Mainstream Publishing Company LTD., 1992).

4 See the complex flowchart of characters in the JFK assassination: Daniel Sheehan, "JFK Assassination Flow Chart," DanielPSheean.com, n.d., https://www.danielpsheehan.com/wp-content/uploads/2018/11/JFK-flow-chart-02.jpg.

Stockton, Bayard, *Flawed Patriot: The Rise and Fall of CIA Legend Bill Harvey* (Dulles, VA: Potomac Books, 2006).

Storrs, James and Ramsland, Katherine, *A Voice for the Dead: A Forensic Investigator's Pursuit of Truth in the Grave* (New York, NY: G. P. Putnam, 2005).

Swanson, Michael and Wayne, Larry, et al., *The War State: The Cold War Origins of the Military-Industrial Complex and the Power Elite, 1945-1963* (North Charleston, SC: CreateSpace Independent Publishing Platform, 2013).

Theoharis, Athan G., *A Culture of Secrecy: The Government Versus the People's Right to Know* (Lawrence, Kansas: University Press of Kansas, 1998).

Thomas, Gordon, *Journey into Madness: The True Story of Secret CIA Mind Control and Medical Abuse* (New York, NY: Bantam Books, 1989).

Trento, Joseph John, *The Secret History of the CIA* (Rosedale, CA: Prima Publishing, 1991).

Turner, Stansfield, *Secrecy and Democracy: the CIA in Transition* (Boston, MA: Houghton Mifflin, 1985).

Ventura, Jesse and Russell, Dick, *American Conspiracies: Lies, Lies, and More Dirty Lies That the Government Tells* (New York, NY: Skyhorse Publishing, revised and expanded version, 2015).

West, John, *Fry the Brain: The Art of Urban Sniping and Its Role in Modern Guerrilla Warfare* (Countryside, VA: Independently Published, 2008).

Wilbur, Charles, *A Medicolegal Investigation of the JFK Murder* (Springfield, IL: Charles C. Thomas, 1978).

Williams, Paul L. and Prichard, Michael, et al., *Operation Gladio: The Unholy Alliance Between the Vatican, the CIA, and the Mafia* (Amherst, NY: Prometheus Books, 2018).

Wise, David, *Molehunt: The Secret Search for Traitors That Shattered the CIA* (Toronto: Random House, 1992).

Zepezauer, Mark and Naiman, Arthur, *The CIA's Greatest Hits* (Monroe, ME: Odonian Press, 1994).

MY FAVORITE (BOOK) AUTHORS

THE DEPARTED

John B. Cahoon
Mark Lane
David S. Lifton
Harrison E. Livingstone
Jim Marrs
Gerald D. McKnight
Sylvia Meagher
Stanley Milgram
Noel Twyman
Harold Weisberg

STILL INCARNATE

Gary Aguilar
Walt Brown
Jim DiEugenio
James Douglas
Brian Edwards
Stewart Galanor
Robert Groden
Larry Hancock
Douglas Horne
William Matson Law
Joseph McBride
Joan Mellen
Jefferson Morley
John Newman
Vince Palamara
Lisa Pease
Larry Rivera
Dick Russell
Roy Schaeffer
J. Gary Shaw
Larry Sneed
David Talbot
John West

APPENDIX M

DEALEY PLAZA MAPS

DALLAS, TEXAS

NOVEMBER 22, 1963

The assassination of John F. Kennedy

President Kennedy was killed Nov. 22, 1963, during a motorcade on a trip to Dallas. Lee Harvey Oswald was arrested for the shooting, but was shot before he could stand trial.

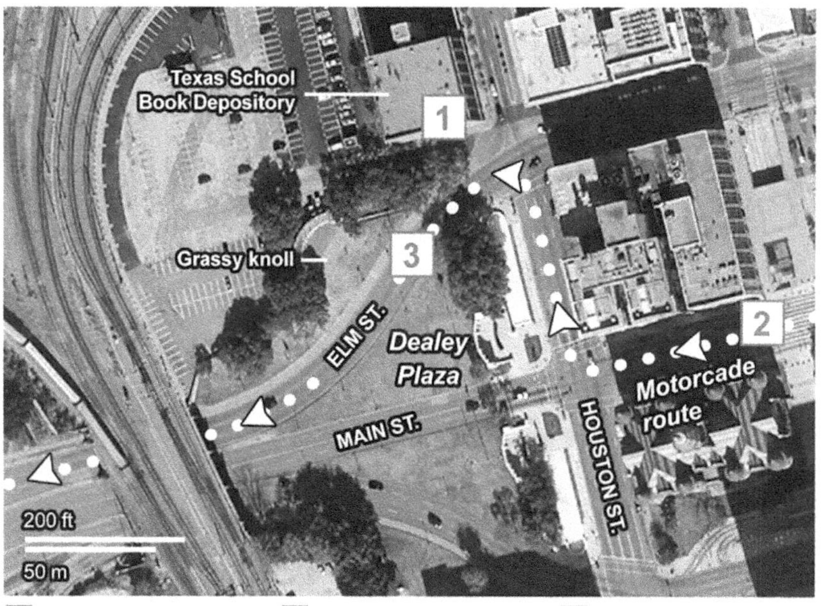

1 7:50 a.m.

Oswald enters the book depository with a package he tells everyone holds curtain rods. He assembles his rifle shortly before noon.

2 12:27 p.m.

Over 150,000 people assemble to greet Kennedy, Texas Gov. John Connally and their wives as they travel down Main St.

3 12:30 p.m.

Kennedy and Connally are hit by gunfire after the car enters Dealey Plaza. The limousine races toward Parkland Memorial Hospital.

SOURCES: Associated Press reports, Sixth Floor Museum at Dealey Plaza — AP

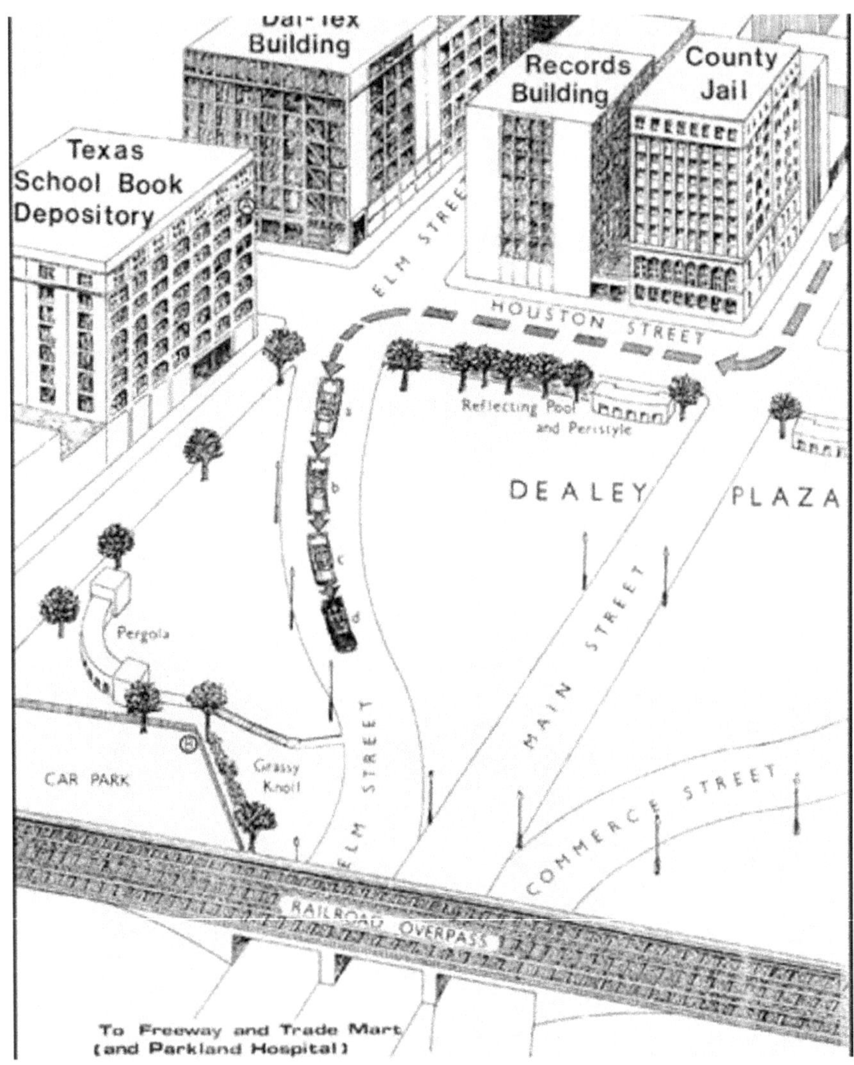

Building
Records
Building
County
Jail
Texas
School Book
Depository
ELM STREET
HOUSTON STREET
Reflecting Pool
and Peristyle
DEALEY
PLAZA
MAIN STREET
Pergola
ELM STREET
Grassy
Knoll
CAR PARK
COMMERCE STREET
RAILROAD OVERPASS
To Freeway and Trade Mart
(and Parkland Hospital)

APPENDIX N

ANATOMY OF THE HUMAN SKULL

A midsagittal view showing the inner boundaries of the lobes of the cerebral cortex
(Structures outside of the cerebrum are labeled in italics.)

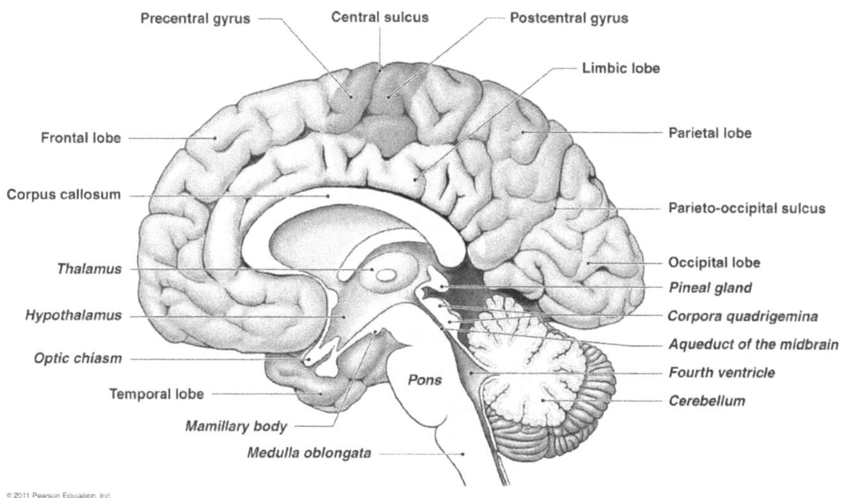

ABOUT THE AUTHORS

DAVID W. MANTIK, M.D., PH.D.

With numerous publications over the past three decades on the JFK medical evidence to his credit, Dr. David W. Mantik, M.D., Ph.D., is one of the most respected authors in the JFK assassination research community. Having appeared in both the noteworthy documentary *A Coup in Camelot* and in Oliver Stone's 2021 sister-documentaries *JFK Revisited: Through the Looking Glass* and the greatly expanded version titled *Destiny Betrayed*, Dr. Mantik is well known for his brilliant analysis of the JFK skull X-rays in the National Archives. A frequent panelist at JFK assassination research seminars, Dr. Mantik commands a comprehensive understanding of the various official government investigations of the JFK assassination and the vast scholarly literature on the subject. In addition to specializing in the medical evidence of the assassination, Dr. Mantik has conducted groundbreaking research into the falsification of the Zapruder film. Dr. Mantik received his Ph.D. in physics from the University of Wisconsin and served as an assistant professor in the university's physics faculty before attending medical school at the University of Michigan. He completed his internship and residency in radiation oncology at LAC/USC Medical Center in Los Angeles. Dr. Mantik is now in his fourth decade of active medical practice.

JEROME R. CORSI, PH.D.

Having received his Ph.D. from Harvard University's Department of Government in 1972, Jerome R. Corsi has published over thirty books on economics, history, and politics, including six *New York Times* bestsellers, two at number one. From 2004 to 2016, Dr. Corsi was a senior editor at WorldNetDaily.com, where he authored hundreds of articles. Dr. Corsi has decided to reengage in the political discussion by establishing a new website and podcast, TheTruthCentral.com. As founder and CEO of Corstet LLC, Dr. Corsi has ventured into telemedicine, developing HablaConUnMD.com, offering Spanish-speaking patients an affordable electronic consultation with a Spanish-speaking physician licensed in their state, and GetLongevityMeds.com, for those interested in medical consultations aimed at living longer and better.

In 1964, the Warren Commission dismissed the extensive testimony of numerous eyewitnesses to the JFK assassination who stated that shots were fired from the front.

Drawing upon Douglas Horne's masterful five-volume book *Inside the Assassination Records Review Board* (ARRB), plus six decades of revisionist investigative reporting conducted by a host of independent citizen-researchers, Dr. David W. Mantik and Jerome R. Corsi expose a government-created narrative constructed to shift attention away from the professional snipers who created the lethal crossfire that violently removed JFK from the presidency at the end of a successful motorcade through the streets of Dallas.

Mantik and Corsi document the testimonial and documentary evidence from the first moments after the assassination as well as the CIA disinformation campaign aimed at demonizing as a "conspiracy theorist" anyone who dares challenge the Warren Commission's official narrative. Even today, the CIA refuses to allow the American public to see thousands of pages of still-classified government documents related to the assassination of President Kennedy.

Are you curious to learn how the US government coerced the Parkland Hospital physicians to change their testimony? Prepare to be startled by a stunning casket switch after JFK's body was secretly helicoptered to Bethesda Naval Hospital, where Navy pathologists were ready to perform pre-autopsy surgery on JFK's skull. Are you prepared to understand how federal officials framed Lee Harvey Oswald as the assassin to cover up a government coup d'état? Mantik and Corsi present the final analysis that reveals the disturbing truth about the JFK assassination, exposing a sixty-year coverup executed by the CIA, the FBI, the Pentagon, and the Secret Service to frame Lee Harvey Oswald as the Warren Commission's "lone gun assassin."

www.ingramcontent.com/pod-product-compliance
Ingram Content Group UK Ltd.
Pitfield, Milton Keynes, MK11 3LW, UK
UKHW021710190726
13853UKWH00001B/482

9 798888 457160